HANDBOOKS

WISCONSIN

THOMAS HUHTI

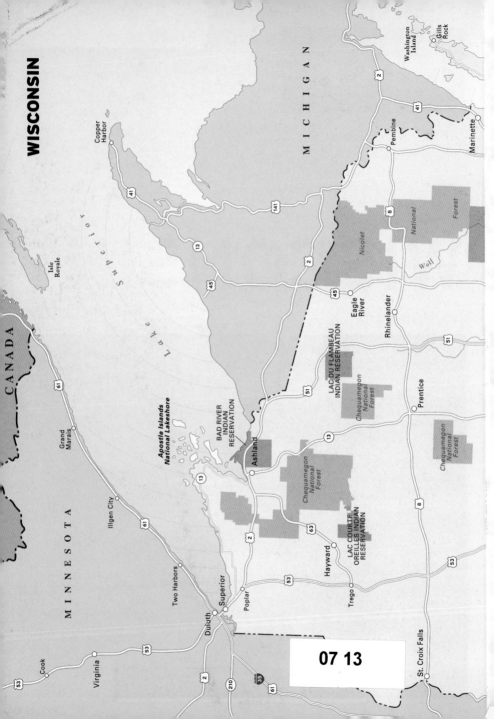

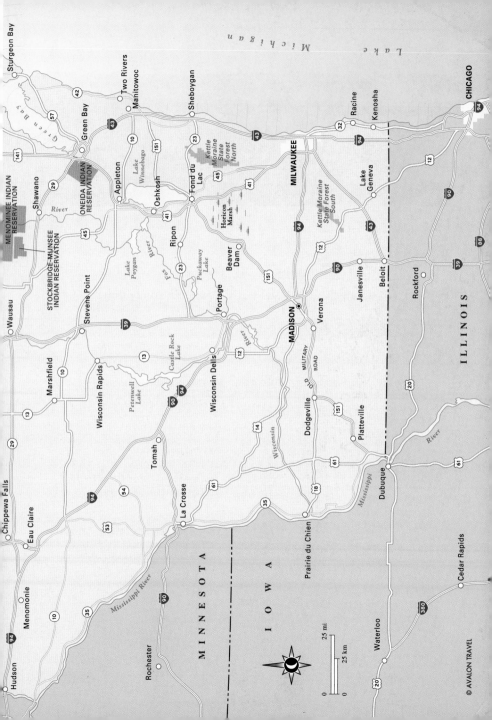

Contents

Discover Wisconsin

Wisconsin puts the lie to all those clichés about flyover land, cowflop redolence, hayseeds, corn-fed . . . you get the picture. Indeed, John Muir chose his words carefully when he wrote, "Oh, that glorious Wisconsin wilderness!"

Wisconsin is truly Midwestern. Incapable of braggadocio, it's generally content to remain in the middle on most things – except such important issues as livability quotients, at which it tends to excel. Superlatives about the place abound. It's one of the top five most livable states in the nation. It's the Midwest's overall most popular travel destination. It's one of the country's most ethnically rich regions. It boasts the planet's most diverse glacial topography, countless glacial pools and streams, the United States' middle section's most amazing cataracts, and an immense North Woods region so big the national forest has to have two names. Recreation is second to none – tops in bicycling (on and off road), cross-country skiing, snowmobiling, fishing, and scenic hiking trails. Some of the country's largest events take place here and ethnic heritage sites are unrivalled.

From the first permanent Native Americans, who marveled at the fecundity of nature, visitors have come and become enamored. Blackfly-weary explorers, buckskin-clad and thunderstick-booming voyageurs,

Jesuit Black Robes, lumberjacks, all saw opportunity but also magnificence. Muir, among those other immigrant Europeans, gaped awestruck at the mighty Great Lakes, the minor seas leading to a lush new home.

Fast forward a couple centuries and things haven't changed all that much. Folks come for a visit or to attend university and genuinely miss it when they leave. In fact, more than a few stay. I've met some who came for a visit decades ago and loved it so much they return, often to the same cabin on the same lake, every single year.

Oh, and tranquility and aesthetics notwithstanding, this has as much to do with the people of Wisconsin who, I'm happy to report, are in toto clearly and proudly the type who will chat you up and consider you a friend five minutes after they meet you. This as much as anything is what makes national media rank the state so highly in national polls.

And if this makes us rubes, then we'll happily plead guilty.

Planning Your Trip

Plan a road trip of a few days to "do" Wisconsin and you'll leave frustrated. If you had a month and a reliable car you could theoretically hit all the highlights of each region. Keeping in mind that one person's Road Warrior day is another's lazy roll, you can reasonably cover most regions in 4–7 days.

Travel media have consistently voted Wisconsin one of the greatest road-touring states in the country—the Department of Transportation has even highlighted more than 100 of the state's best back-roads trips in an effort to preserve the lightly traveled avenues into the real Wisconsin. A road trip through Wisconsin is a phenomenal way to view the countryside and the culture up close and personal.

▶ WHERE TO GO

Milwaukee

Dash the blue-collar images. This low-key citizenry is darned proud of cultural, educational, and architectural gems along its fabulous lakefront. The wonderfully preserved ethnic neighborhoods and Historic Third Ward offer the state's best urban trekking tours—just see what beer hath wrought at the sublime Pabst Mansion. Yet that lakefront beckons. Hop aboard a fishing charter? Meander along the spectacular bike paths? And don't forget the names that made Milwaukee famous: the gargantuan Miller Brewing and Harley-Davidson.

Madison

The Mad City, Madtown, the Island Surrounded by Reality, a vibrant and fetching city plopped among a quartet of jewel-like lakes—upon one of which sits eye-catching Monona Terrace.

IF YOU HAVE . . .

- **TWO DAYS:** Visit Milwaukee and Madison.

- **ONE WEEK:** From Milwaukee, head to Door County; return to Madison via Fox River Valley.

- **TWO WEEKS:** Circumnavigate the perimeter of the state, adding the Great River Road, Driftless Region, and the Apostle Islands and Indianhead Country (St. Croix River Region). Finish in Madison and relax with a jaunt to the Wisconsin Dells.

unique rock formations on the Wisconsin River

There's a push and pull between the state government—the grand State Capitol mustn't be missed—and the University of Wisconsin. But most denizens are nature lovers; you'll find no better chances to walk amid native state flora than at the UW's Arboretum and the Olbrich Botanical Gardens.

From the Windy City: Southeastern Wisconsin

This true gateway region welcomes many a traveler barreling in via the Windy City. Extraordinary museums and parks await in

the State Capitol in Madison

Kenosha and Racine, the latter also sporting Badger native Frank Lloyd Wright architecture. Hop onto the narrower ribbons and discover the Geneva Lake area. Holy Hill allows for sublime vistas of the topography. And a triumvirate of essential historical museums: Watertown's Octagon House, Eagle's Old World Wisconsin, and Fort Atkinson's Hoard Historical Museum and Dairy Shrine. A crucial North American migration flyways is Horicon Marsh.

Door County

Jutting into Lake Michigan, the "thumb" of Wisconsin geographically, merely offers, mile for mile, the most sublime collection of state parks in the Midwest and the highest concentration of lighthouses of any U.S. county. How about picturesque towns right out of 19th-century postcards? Off the northern tip lies Washington Island, an isolated community where time seems not to matter much at all. Beyond, another island—Rock Island State Park, the most superb camping spot in the state.

Gateway to Door County: East-Central Waters

These waters truly made the state, welcoming legions of immigrants and floating timber for

Madison's Lake Monona

paper mills of the Fox Cities, dominated by the enormous Lake Winnebago. To the west are such picturesque resort lands you'll run out of digital storage, as well as the wild and wonderful Wolf River. No visit to Wisconsin would be complete without a pilgrimage to one of the NFL's most, well, sacred institutions: Lambeau Field, home of the Green Bay Packers.

Woods and Waters: Northeastern Wisconsin

Here find one of the world's highest concentrations of lakes and two of the Midwest's grandest rivers, Peshtigo River and Wisconsin's own version of the Boundary Waters Canoe Area, the Turtle-Flambeau Flowage. Marinette and Iron County waterfalls offer the most scenic drive in the region. Sleds have always ruled in northern Wisconsin, and the mecca is Snowmobile Alley near the Eagle River Chain of Lakes. Waswagoning, a re-created Ojibwa village, nearby, is the best glimpse at native culture.

Indianhead Country: Northwestern Wisconsin

Hydrophiles adore the St. Croix National Scenic Riverway. Anglers battle lunker

muskies near Hayward. From preciously anachronistic Bayfield, head to the magnificent Apostle Islands National Lakeshore. Along WI 13 everyone should trace the Lake Superior coast along the most scenic drive in the state, bar none. Pattison State Park offers the best glimpse at the region's superb waterfalls, but don't forsake Superior's hardest-working harbor in the country. And we haven't even gotten to our lumber memorial or the highest point in Wisconsin yet!

Great River Road

For 200 miles find river towns that refuse to get sucked into tourist trapdom: Alma, funky Trempealeau, or Cassville, where eagles soar and one of the nation's last river ferries chugs you across the Ol' Miss. See the commanding view at Granddad's Bluff in La Crosse. At Wyalusing State Park a ridgetop hike offers lovely views of the confluence of the Wisconsin and Mississippi Rivers. No better example of what sprang from ambitious settler souls is Prairie du Chien's Villa Louis.

The Driftless Region: Southwestern Wisconsin

This, the largest unglaciated region in the

Door County caves

northern Midwest, is where the land gets ambitious. Spring Green, the heart and soul of the area's picturesque towns, was the home of Frank Lloyd Wright. Nearby, the opposite: House on the Rock. Roll through Mineral Point, damn near still a 19th-century Cornish village, and New Glarus, damn near a slice of Switzerland. Water lovers head for Lower Wisconsin State Riverway and,

particularly, the Kickapoo River through the twists and turns of the Kickapoo Valley Reserve. Rails-to-trails biking got its start in Wisconsin, and the Elroy-Sparta Trail is the granddaddy of 'em all.

Central Wisconsin Sands

Central Wisconsin sports the state's number one family attraction—water park–heavy

a boat tour in the Wisconsin Dells

Mt. Olympus water park in the Wisconsin Dells

Wisconsin Dells. But the preternaturally lovely sandstone rises are easily the nicest boat tour in the state. Stretch the legs at the outstanding Devil's Lake State Park, but don't overlook the park's eastern segment, home to Parfrey's Glen Natural Area. Both will explain how Central Wisconsin inspired two of the United States' greatest ecologists—John Muir and Aldo Leopold. Continue east on a scenic drive to Merrimac and its ferry across the Wisconsin River and do some birding at the Central Necedah Wildlife Reserve. Farther north, Wausau's Leigh Yawkey Woodson Museum houses one of the state's most fascinating collections—this one dedicated to ornithological art.

▶ WHEN TO GO

This is a four-season kind of place—there is something for everyone no matter if it is winter, spring, summer, or fall. That said, most visitors do come between Memorial Day and Labor Day. All accommodations, restaurants, and attractions will be open during this time; prices will also rise precipitously in more popular spots (and many lodgings will require a two- or three-night minimum stay). Another peak season is from late September through late October, when throngs arrive to witness fall's splendorous colors. (Between Labor Day and late September, you can often get great rates and, if cold weather comes early, great colors!) Winter in general sees fewer visitors except for snowmobilers and skiers, and areas popular with those types will not have lower rates. Other places may shut down entirely from November to April. Pretty much nobody comes here from March through early April—grim, gray, muddy, and windy, and this is a native Cheesehead speaking. Then again, it's dirt, dirt cheap!

Highway 42 near Northport in Door County

▶ BEFORE YOU GO

You can buy most anything you need in the state, even in the village outposts of the Great North Woods (though this does not include spare parts for your laptop), but one thing you don't want to be caught without is mosquito repellent. Trust me. A face net for black-flies and skeeters wouldn't be a bad idea if you plan on delving into the woods (or even camping).

Regarding clothing, Wisconsin is a place where most consider L. L. Bean dress-up clothing. Heels, ties, and fancy skirts are fine for clubbing in Milwaukee or Madison, but you'll be absolutely conspicuous in all but the most chichi restaurants anywhere else (hey, Badger sweatshirts are perfectly fine in even the most famous supper clubs).

Weather is often the deciding factor. Dress appropriately for the weather at all times—that includes wearing a hat. Do not come to Wisconsin in winter without a good pair of gloves or mittens. Inuit-worthy mittens are

something you'll be ever so grateful for on a sleigh ride or while you await a tow truck. A good pair of boots is also a necessity; some people carry a heavy-duty pair in the car at all times, in case of an emergency.

Given the state's somewhat iffy weather, it's paramount to prepare your car for any possibility by winterizing your vehicle. Carry an emergency kit with booster cables, sand or gravel (in a pinch, try sandpaper strips or kitty litter), flares, candles, matches, a shovel and scraper, flashlight and extra batteries, blankets (space blankets are excellent), extra heavy clothing, high-calorie nonperishable food, and anything else you might need if you have to spend the night in a snowbank. I cannot emphasize how important it is—more than once I've stumbled upon out-of-staters stuck in a snowy forest ditch and been amazed that, had someone not stumbled along, they were woefully unprepared to spend a winter night in the car.

Explore Wisconsin

▶ THE BEST OF WISCONSIN: WEEKEND TRIPS

One must, of course, balance the ideal with the realistic and remember that caveat about how everyone travels at different speeds. That said, this road warrior has done 'em all! And a note: Door County and the Wisconsin Dells are the most famous weekend getaways there are. The Great River Road is also perfectly laid out for two days (overnight in La Crosse); I dunno why more folks don't do it.

The Beer City and Beyond

All right, let's save this one for a *long* weekend! Assuming driving in from the Chicago area, choose Kenosha, Racine, *or* a boat tour of Lake Geneva along the way. As you roll, a drive through the Kettle Moraine State Forest-Southern Unit is a primer on glacial history right near a walk-through people's history at Old World Wisconsin.

Arrive and relax, planning for day two. The Milwaukee lakefront is a must. Tour Miller Brewing *or* the Harley-Davidson Museum and bop into the unduplicated Milwaukee Public Museum and with time, strike northward for postcard-perfect Cedarburg. You'll be eminently happy if you can coincide your visit to the Beer City with Summerfest.

A Capital Trip

One day is easy: Architectural gems are where to start—Frank Lloyd Wright's Monona Terrace and, a few steps away, the magnificent State Capitol. Stroll the pedestrian-friendly State Street area to the University

Olbrich Botanical Gardens in Madison

RUSTIC ROAD TRIPPING

Travel media have consistently voted Wisconsin one of the greatest road-touring states in the country. Much of this comes from natural beauty; a good deal also comes from the fact that many rural roads, originally known as farm-to-market roads, seem to have changed little (other than having pavement) in a century and a half.

You'll find more than 100 fantastic roads that cannot be rivaled. Naturally, it is beyond the scope of this guide to highlight them all (though I've got lots).

- Near **Milwaukee,** head for Cedarburg, a grand little place with its own lovely road-trip (#52).

- Near **Madison,** this author's favorites are south (#19 near Goodman Park) and east (#96, south of Cottage Grove).

- In **Southeastern Wisconsin,** those near Burlington (#42), Lake Geneva (#11 and #29), Horicon Marsh (#106), and Fort Atkinson (#84) are unrivalled.

- As for **Door County** – well, the entire thing is a rustic road!

- Heading for **East-Central Waters?** Go to Hartman Creek State Park, at which you'll find #23 and #24 together amidst amazing village scenery.

- In **Northeastern Wisconsin,** the parks and waterfalls of Peshtigo River Parkway (#32) are grand, as is #60 east of Boulder Junction.

- In the **Indianhead region,** history and gorgeous beauty are found along the old Flambeau trail voyageur route on #100 north of Mercer (in the Turtle-Flambeau Flowage) and #6, west of Brunet Island State Park.

- For the **Great River Road,** #51 east of Maiden Rock is preternaturally lovely, and history doesn't get any better than #99 out of Potosi.

- In **Southwest Wisconsin,** #66 east of Hazel Green has agriculture and mining history (or any road at all in Coulee Country).

- In **Central Wisconsin,** off Interstate 39/90/94 at WI 33, then north, you'll find #49, which rolls through Aldo Leopold's favorite lands.

Options for serpentine blue highways are infinite; thankfully, the Department of Transportation has highlighted more than 100 of the state's best back-roads trips in an effort to preserve the lightly traveled avenues into the real Wisconsin. A road trip on one of these roads is a phenomenal way to view the countryside and the culture. Every single Rustic Road of the state is guaranteed to offer an amazing palette of colors **mid-September–late October.** It's so popular they've run out of books, so print out yours early by visiting the website of the **Wisconsin Department of Transportation** (dot.wi.gov/travel/scenic/rusticroads.htm).

fall color in Marinette County, in Northeastern Wisconsin

Eagle Bluff Lighthouse in Door County

of Wisconsin campus for the lakeside Union Terrace. The University of Wisconsin Arboretum has the best urban trails anywhere and follow that natural-world beauty with a visit to the Olbrich Botanical Gardens.

On day two, choose a longish drive northeast to the extraordinary Horicon Marsh Wildlife Area; a historical tour southeast to the Hoard Historical Museum and Dairy Shrine and Old World Wisconsin; or a combination circus/sweat duo in Baraboo/Devil's Lake State Park.

Door County

Snoop out the sublime natural world, some grand food, lodging, and shopping (and the Packers on the way up/back). Spend night one in Sturgeon Bay, overnight the next night anywhere along the road; I use Fish Creek as a central base and explore from there! Must-sees are Potawatomi, Peninsula, Whitefish Dunes, Rock Island, and Newport State Parks; Ridges Sanctuary; and the nation's densest county concentration of lighthouses.

Wisconsin Dells

Pick a mega-resort and let the water slide fun commence! Then, on the second day, after you're all tuckered out, see the real Dells of the Wisconsin River on the obligatory Second World War–era "duck" boat tour. Then again, if you've had your fill of water, Devil's Lake State Park down the road offers superb hiking and, next door, fetching Baraboo is small-town quaint and has a grand circus museum, replete with outdoor shows.

The Northern Cap: Islands and Falls

Here's my many-times route: Drive like a madman to get to Bayfield Friday and eat whitefish. Early Saturday morning either kayak the sea caves, bike the rolling hills filled with apple orchards, or take a shuttle to an island and hike. Sunday is spent driving the extraordinary WI 13 along Lake Superior to Superior for

Apostle Islands on Lake Superior

big-boy lakers (freight ships) and waterfalls. There's no better trip for me in the state.

Great North Woods

Get a cabin/cottage/resort room in Hayward, the Minocqua area, Eagle River, or Boulder Junction (for me it's the latter)—pick one. Whichever you choose, one day should be spent with a rowboat (often comes with the cabin) or canoe on your lake fishing or, more likely, napping to the sound of lapping water. With Hayward as a base one day has to be spent at the National Freshwater Fishing Hall of Fame and a lumberjack show. In Minocqua, you must visit Waswagoning or

the Turtle-Flambeau Flowage. In Eagle River, well, it's all about snowmobiles!

Crooked Rivers and Buggies

This author's better half's favorite weekend is the following: camping at Wildcat Mountain State Park or, more likely, getting a cozy B&B room; either canoe the extraordinary Kickapoo River or bike the Elroy-Sparta Trail (or any county road) one day; and on the second, drive *very slowly* around the region, the Coulee Range, to wave at horse-drawn buggies of the Amish and visit one of their amazing bakeries for great sustenance.

▶ A PERFECT WEEK IN DOOR COUNTY

It seems such a tiny "thumb" on the map, and so, how could you possibly need a week? Trust me, you can *easily* do a week here. (Heck, lots of folks do the whole summer here!)

at its Maritime Museum and heading for Potawatomi State Park, and then visiting the town's better-than-you'd-think art center and museum.

Day 1

Start in Sturgeon Bay, learning about the history of shipping and shipbuilding

Day 2

On day two, forsake the sclerotic state highway for county byways (whip out that

beach chairs along the shoreline in Door County

FOLLOWING FRANK LLOYD WRIGHT

The famed architect Frank Lloyd Wright, a native Badger, was legendary for essentially melding the natural world into his architecture. In 1938, even *Time* magazine called him "the greatest architect of the twentieth century."

Highlights of Wright's work in Wisconsin include the following:

- In Wauwatosa, west of Milwaukee, check out Wright's "little jewel" – the **Annunciation Greek Orthodox Church.** If you're lucky, your tour will coincide with one of the infrequent open-house days of Wright's American-Built System homes in Milwaukee, homes designed to be affordable for those of average means.

- Wright's **SC Johnson Wax Building** and **Golden Rondelle Theater** in Racine helped *Time* make its grandiose claim.

- In southeastern Wisconsin, stop off in the **Delavan Lake** area (probably basing yourself in Lake Geneva), where more and more Wright-designed homes are occasionally opening to the public.

- Wright's Madison masterwork, the **Monona Terrace Community and Convention Center** has a view so sublime that even his haters will be in awe. (One of my favorite sunrises in Wisconsin is here!) After a tour, drive to Madison's west side to view his **First Unitarian Church,** recently named a National Landmark.

- In the Wisconsin Dells, you can lay your head in the only Frank Lloyd Wright-designed building available for rent – the **Seth Peterson Cottage** in Mirror Lake State Park.

- Along the Wisconsin River is the pilgrimage of pilgrimages for Wright aficionados – Spring Green, home to **Taliesin,** his home and studio. Lunch in the visitors center, again, the only Wright-designed eatery anywhere. Drive the area, looking at "Wright-inspired" everything.

You can add to this list and find more information about Wright's extraordinary work by checking out the numerous websites devoted to The Man, among them, wrightinwisconsin. org, taliesinpreservation.org, wrightplus.org, and franklloydwright.org.

Frank Lloyd Wright's Taliesin in Spring Green

Peninsula State Park at sunset

gazetteer!) northward to Egg Harbor. No "attractions" are cartographically apparent, yet you'll be surprised by how the short trip up the bay takes the entire morning, before unpacking at a historic inn in Fish Creek. Unwind with a stroll through the historic downtown.

Day 3

Save those legs, since the bulk of day three is spent exploring the worth-a-week-itself Peninsula State Park. The sunset here is not to be missed. Continue up the coast, appreciating the vistas around Ephraim—take in some ice cream at Olson's and visit the historic structures—before deciding where to lodge in Sister Bay.

Days 4-5

On day four, wow yourself with a drive up and over the bluffs in Ellison Bay and unpack that gazetteer again, for the road between here and Gills Rock offers some outstanding side-road pulloffs to explore. Drive aboard the ferry to Washington Island and decide between chichi gentrified or absolute rustic (or somewhere in the middle) for your abode that

night. Come morning, drive to the northeast side, and hop the ferry to this author's fave Door retreat, Rock Island State Park, easily explored as a half-day trip (but packing a backpack and tent for camping is never, ever a bad idea!).

footprints on the beach

Day 6

On day six, hop the earliest ferry back to the mainland, lunch on Swedish pancakes in Rowleys Bay, and delve into the wilderness of Newport State Park. Ever so slowly, continue south and prepare to stop and strike off into estuary preserves south of Rowleys Bay. Be careful of traffic, as most travelers will be barreling to the next stop—the must-see Moonlight Bay area, home to the most splendid of the county's lighthouse sentinels and one of the country's most precious ecological preserves. Baileys Harbor makes for an excellent, unassuming retreat.

Day 7

The final day's peregrinations begin with a casual drive down the lake side to another of this author's happy places—Whitefish Dunes State Park. The name says it all, really, those buttermilk dunes. Time left? Well, have you gone fishing yet?

► A BREATH OF FRESH AIR

Every car in the state is either towing a boat or lugging canoes, kayaks, or bikes. This tour allows you to experience the absolute musts that type-T personalities crave.

Day 1

Stretch your legs on a hike around Geneva Lake (that is, the lake, not Lake Geneva, the town).

Day 2

Stroll some trails and do some birding at Horicon Marsh before espying geological residual topography from a bike in the Kettle Moraine State Forest-Northern Unit.

Day 3

Hmm, that Lake Michigan, so full of fish. But where to get out onto the water and land

Strong Falls on the famous Peshtigo River in Marinette County's Goodman Park

fishing for trout and salmon at sunrise from a Sheboygan pier

one? Sheboygan, Manitowoc, and Two Rivers are all excellent choices!

Days 4-5

More splendid hiking in Door County and its spectacular state parks. Newport State Park is the top choice for hiking and biking. Whitefish Dunes State Park is the best for beachcombing!

Day 6

Raft the Peshtigo River, one of the Midwest's best.

Day 7

If it's winter, you simply must experience snowmobiling in Eagle River! If it's summer, head north to Boulder Junction to try your hand at landing a muskie.

Day 8

Spend your time either kayaking about the Apostle Islands National Lakeshore or hopping a water shuttle and hiking an isolated island.

Day 9

Using Hayward as a base, rent a mountain bike and strike off into the Chequamegon Area Mountain Bike Trails.

Days 10-11

Spend two days paddling the legendary St. Croix National Scenic Riverway.

Day 12

Bike a segment of the granddaddy of all rails-to-trails adventures, the Elroy-Sparta State Recreational Trail.

Day 13

Bike along classic southwestern hills, waving at Amish buggies as you pass.

Day 14

Drive to Wisconsin Dells for a sunny day scaling the ridges and bluffs of Devil's Lake State Park.

kayaking in the Squaw Bay sea caves, in the Apostle Islands National Lakeshore's mainland unit

MOO!

How could one come to America's Dairyland and *not* learn more about moo juice and all the rest? Check out wisdairy.com before you go for their eye-poppingly detailed map of 120 **cheese factories** and **dairy operations** open for visits as you drive along – or just look for the hand-lettered signs saying "fresh cheese curds today!" (You could also expand it by going to visitdairyland.com and viewing all agricultural tourism offerings!)

If I were to choose one place to really poke around the countryside, it'd be Green County, south of Madison (New Glarus and Monroe are mentioned here), home to a number of operations.

- Fort Atkinson in southeastern Wisconsin is home to the **Hoard Historical Museum and Dairy Shrine,** which traces the history of dairying in Wisconsin.

- Kids love to try their hand at churning butter and milking cows at **Old World Wisconsin,** in Eagle, not far from Fort Atkinson.

- Examine – and sample (natch!) – the synthesis of high-tech research in the dairy industry at the University of Wisconsin's **Babcock Hall Dairy Plant** in Madison.

- Most typical of newer operations (but it seems 100 years old in practice!) is tiny **Bleu Mont Dairy,** in Blue Mounds, west of Madison, where all the cheese is organic and made from all-chemical free raw milk, and where all power comes from the sun, wind, and cow!

- Bike the **Sugar River State Trail** from New Glarus. Mile for mile, there are more moo

Cheese is everywhere you go in Wisconsin.

cows than anywhere in the state. The glacier-fed minerals in these soils are credited with producing the richest milk anywhere.

- **Monroe** is the site of the only **limburger cheese factory** in the country.

- Northeast of Sheboygan in tiny Kiel is **Henning's Wisconsin Cheese,** notable for being possibly the last U.S. cheesemaker to create those ginormous (up to 12,000 pounds!) "wheels" of cheese!

▶ GEOLOGY ROCKS

Wisconsin's landscape is so unusual that the topography is, virtually in its entirety, federally recognized as part of the Ice Age National Scientific Reserve.

Day 1

Start in Door County, where you can explore the bluffs of the Niagara Escarpment on its rise toward Ontario at Potawatomi and Peninsula State Parks.

Day 2

Drive south along Lake Winnebago, with a stop-off at High Cliff State Park. From here, the afternoon is best spent on the Kettle Moraine State Forest-Northern Unit scenic drive, designed to take you past every type of glacial topography.

Day 3

Bend northwest to another node of the scientific reserve in Devil's Lake State Park, which has an interpretive center and the state's best hiking trails atop glacial land. Take in the vistas of the Wisconsin River on a Wisconsin Dells boat tour.

Day 4

A quick jaunt off the geological trail is in order. From Devil's Lake State Park, drive west on a loop trip following U.S. 14, U.S. 61, and the south side of I-90. Within is Wisconsin's Coulee Country, a landscape of undulating hills and crooked rivers—the largest unglaciated region in the world.

Day 5

Starting from Devil's Lake State Park, follow the Wisconsin River north through the Sands Country, filled with glacial detritus. In Wisconsin Rapids, head west to the Chippewa Moraine Unit of the National Scientific Reserve.

Peninsula State Park in Door County

Devil's Lake State Park in Central Wisconsin

Day 6

Head northwest to St. Croix Falls and Interstate State Park, site of the final interpretive center explaining the state's postglacial natural history: stunning views!

Day 7

Then, go east, weary traveler, into the lands of those 16,000 glacial lakes and relax; you've earned it!

▶ ARE WE THERE YET? A FAMILY ROAD TRIP

Got kids? Well, load 'em up—Wisconsin has plenty to offer kids of all ages.

Days 1-2

Boisterous and wet revelry is in Wisconsin Dells. Soak yourself in the country's most amazing lineup of gargantuan water parks or on a tour of the gorgeous river scenery.

Day 3

Drive east to Milwaukee and let the kids go wild at the Discovery World at Pier Wisconsin.

Day 4

In Oshkosh, let the kids ogle the unbelievable EAA Air Adventure Museum displays and let 'em try their escape skills at A.K.A. Houdini in Appleton.

Day 5

Door County has plenty for kids to do: petting zoos, trail rides, beach dune climbing, hay rides, fruit picking, swimming, boating, biking, and more.

Day 6

Adults adore Lambeau Field, home of the Green Bay Packers, and kids can emulate the Packer greats in its interactive zone. Downtown Green Bay also has one of the quaintest anachronisms in the state, the Bay Beach Amusement Park.

Day 7

Kids scream as you raft the Wolf River; later, let 'em frolic in one of Marinette County's numerous waterfalls as you rest!

MILWAUKEE

You need any proof that Milwaukee—a funky and utterly unpretentious amalgamation of hard (as hell) working blue and white collar—just doesn't get any respect (a la Cleveland or any other Great Lakes metropolis, for that matter)? For goodness sake, even Milwaukeeans' Badger siblings down I-94 in Madison can't escape ingrained imagery of belching smokestacks and tannery effluvia; yes, honest Madison denizens will admit they picture Milwaukeeans as beer-and-bowling knuckleheads (more on the reverse later).

Milwaukee *is* decidedly more lunch box than bento box, but that's only one piece of this wondrous mosaic of half a million with a low-key, rootsy feel. The lingua franca in the city's older neighborhoods is often a mother tongue peppered with accented English. In fact, you'll often hear people speak of *gemütlichkeit* (warmth, hospitality in German) in Milwaukee, and it's by no means hyperbole. Hang out here long enough and you'll appreciate it. Hey, the city even rates in the top 5 percent in the nation in arts, attractions, and recreation!

More proof? Well, the *Utne Reader* and its readers once chose it as "America's Top Underrated City!" So there!

Oh, and a climatic by-the-way: In every weather report, you'll hear the tagline "cooler near the lake." The Great Lakes establish their own microclimates and influence inland areas for miles. Temperatures along littoral stretches endure much less extreme fluctuations than you find in inland communities. A popular local forecasting method is to espy

© THOMAS HUHTI

HIGHLIGHTS

LOOK FOR ◖ TO FIND RECOMMENDED SIGHTS, ACTIVITIES, DINING, AND LODGING.

◖ **Historic Third Ward and Riverwalk:** Milwaukee's most historic commercial district is gentrified but not tacky, with shops, a farmers market, cafés, museums, grand architecture, and a cool riverwalk (page 35).

◖ **Milwaukee Art Museum:** Its stunning, sail-like addition by Santiago Calatrava is ever trumpeted in international media; don't forget the fantastic collections inside the building (page 36).

◖ **Discovery World at Pier Wisconsin:** Wow. This lakefront addition is architecturally and educationally a magnificent exclamation point (literally, from above, and figuratively) on the city's massive downtown works projects (page 36).

◖ **Pabst Mansion:** It drops most visitors' jaws – yes, this indeed was the Beer City, and the brewery families spared no expense showing off their riches (page 40).

◖ **Milwaukee Public Museum and IMAX:** This phenomenal museum – which pioneered the concept of walk-through exhibits – has the nation's largest number of exhibits, so many a day is needed to stroll through them all (page 40).

◖ **Villa Terrace:** Smashing terraced gardens and renowned art collections make this museum unparalleled in the Midwest (page 42).

◖ **Miller Brewing:** It soldiers on in the grand tradition of Milwaukee brewing. This megacomplex simply must be seen to be believed. Moreover, it's a definite point of pride for Milwaukeeans (page 44).

◖ **Harley-Davidson Museum:** Beer may have made Milwaukee famous, but its denizens are likely prouder of this true-blue heritage (page 45).

◖ **Summerfest:** Otherwise known as the Big Gig, it's the granddaddy of U.S. festivals – an 11-day blowout of music, food, and fun, with zillions of people partying heartily (page 51).

◖ **Cedarburg:** To Milwaukee's north is a gem of an anachronism, a preserved village with charm and lots of shops (page 64).

© AVALON TRAVEL

the tear-shaped light atop the Wisconsin Gas Company building downtown: Gold means cold, red means warm, blue means no change, and any color flashing means precipitation is predicted.

HISTORY

The Mascoutin and Fox Indians were the first to live in the tamarack swamps along the Milwaukee, Menomonee, and Kinnickinnic Rivers, though the Potawatomi were most likely to, around 1675, have welcomed the initial French voyageurs, Jesuit Black Robes, and renegade beaver-pelt traders. The city's name purportedly originates in an Algonquian language: *Mahn-a-waukee, Millioki,* and any number of other conjectures have all been translated as, roughly, "gathering place by the waters," a fitting appellation.

Wealth-copping fur traders built the first cabins in the malarial mucklands in the 18th century. Northwest Fur Company trader Jacques Vieau is generally credited with erecting the first shack along the Menomonee River in 1795. The United States duped the Potawatomi and Menominee into ceding all lands east and north of the Milwaukee River in 1831; a couple of years later, all Native American lands in southeastern Wisconsin were gone.

The Bridge War

The first of Milwaukee's famous native sons, Solomon Juneau—the city's first permanent European—arrived around 1820 and grabbed erstwhile Native lands. Juneau, George H. Walker, and Byron Kilbourn built rival communities in and around the rivers near Lake Michigan, and none of the three could deflate his ego enough to cooperate on creating one city. Internecine squabbles escalated into claim-jumping and sabotage in what became known as the Bridge War. Irate east-siders considered actually going to war with the west side and at one point even buried a cannon pointed across the waters at Kilbourntown. (Attentive visitors can still discern traces of the Bridge War on a walk of the downtown streets and bridges.)

Immigrants

The first of three massive waves of German immigrants occurred in 1836. By the 1880s, 35 percent of Milwaukee would be German-born, making up 70 percent of Milwaukee's total immigrant population and contributing to its status as the most ethnically rich area in the country. (It was even dubbed the German Athens.) The ethnic mosaic includes Poles, Serbs, Italians, Irish, African Americans, Dutch, Scandinavians, Bohemians, and Hispanics; in the 2000 census, more than 50 ethnic groups were represented. Milwaukee had the country's first Polish-language newspaper, and the German publishing industry there rivaled any in the homeland.

American Made

The Civil War provided Milwaukee's biggest economic boon. Milwaukee's deepwater harbor provided both an outlet for goods and an inlet for immigrant labor. More than 3,300 tanneries, meatpacking plants, and machine and ironworks became industrial stalwarts, and through the 1870s Milwaukee remained the wheat-milling and transport capital of the world. Nowadays, though Milwaukee has shed a bit of its rough exterior, nearly 20 percent of the population is still employed in manufacturing (the highest average of any city in the United States), and the city has retained the moniker "machine shop of America."

Socialist Central

Immigrant labor gave Milwaukee its trademark socialistic overtones. Workers—many of them enlightened freethinkers from Germany fleeing oppression—organized the first trade and labor unions and played a direct role in the establishment of the country's first unemployment compensation act. In 1888, Milwaukee elected the first socialist ever elected in a major city. Socialist mayor Dan Hoan once said, after refusing to invite the king of Belgium to the city, "I stand for the common man; to hell with kings." Socialists

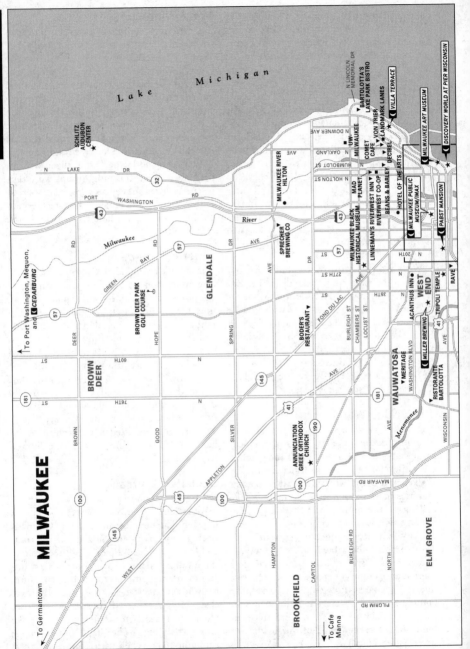

MILWAUKEE

To Germantown

To Cafe Manna

To Port Washington, Mequon, and CEDARBURG

BROOKFIELD

ELM GROVE

BROWN DEER

GLENDALE

WAUWATOSA

WEST END

Lake Michigan

L a k e   M i c h i g a n

SCHLITZ AUDUBON CENTER

Milwaukee River

River

SPRECHER BREWING CO

BODER'S RESTAURANT

ANNUNCIATION GREEK ORTHODOX CHURCH

BROWN DEER PARK GOLF COURSE

MERITAGE
RISTORANTE BARTOLOTTA
MILLER BREWING
ACANTHUS INN
TRIPOLI TEMPLE
RAVE

MILWAUKEE RIVER HILTON
MILWAUKEE BLACK HISTORICAL MUSEUM
LINNEMAN'S RIVERWEST INN
RIVERWEST CO-OP
MAD PLANET
BEANS & BARLEY
HOTEL OF THE ARTS
MILWAUKEE PUBLIC MUSEUM/IMAX
PABST MANSION

N LINCOLN MEMORIAL DR
BARTOLOTTA'S LAKE PARK BISTRO
LANDMARK LANES
VILLA TERRACE
MILWAUKEE ART MUSEUM
DISCOVERY WORLD AT PIER WISCONSIN

UW-MILWAUKEE
COMET CAFE
VON TRIER
DECIBEL

N DOWNER AVE
N OAKLAND AVE
HUMBOLT ST
N HOLTON ST

PORT WASHINGTON RD

LAKE DR

GREEN BAY RD

HOPE AVE
SPRING DR
FOND DU LAC AVE

BURLEIGH ST
CHAMBERS ST
LOCUST ST

WASHINGTON BLVD
WISCONSIN AVE

Menomonee

MAYFAIR RD

PILGRIM RD
BURLEIGH RD
CAPITOL
NORTH

HAMPTON

WEST

APPLETON

SILVER

GOOD

BROWN

DEER ST
60TH ST
76TH ST

27TH ST
35TH ST
20TH

32
43
57
57
43
100
145
45
41
190
100
100
181
181
145

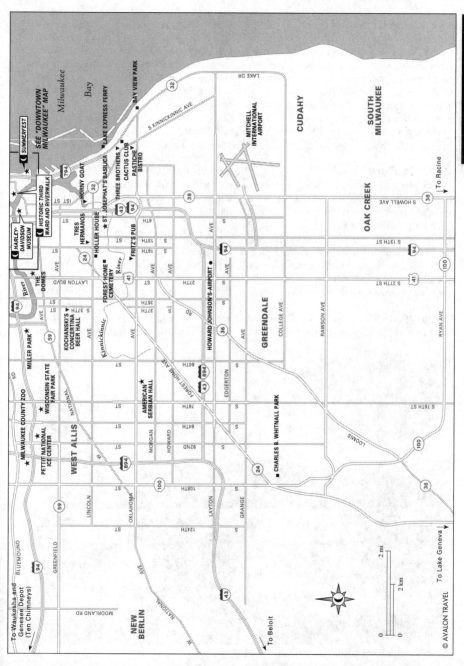

© AVALON TRAVEL

were later elected to a few county posts, and Milwaukee eventually sent the first socialist to the House of Representatives. Milwaukee labor unions were among the initial and definitely most vociferous proponents of workplace reform; by the mid-1880s, up to 15,000 workers at a time would stage demonstrations, and in 1886 militia groups fired on crowds in the eastern European enclave of Bay View, killing five immigrant laborers.

20th Century

World War I was not a particularly good time for German-heavy Milwaukee, but worse was the Prohibition that followed. The Beer City switched to root beer, the socialists organized quasi-WPA relief agencies that predated the Depression, and everybody held on tight. (Interestingly, at 12:01 A.M. on the day Prohibition was officially repealed, Milwaukee somehow managed to ship 15 million bottles of beer!)

After World War II, as African Americans migrated to factory jobs along the Great Lakes, Milwaukee's African American population reached 17 percent within three decades. Unfortunately, Milwaukee remained one of the nation's most segregated cities as riots and marches of the 1960s showed.

Lucrative factory days waned, and the central city declined. Exhaustive machinations to overhaul the downtown began in the mid-1980s, and a careful gentrification—no sickening ersatz tourist-shakedown sheen—has real history. Still, that's not to say Milwaukee isn't striving for a new image. And it works: In all, tourism in Milwaukee generates around $2 billion, accounting for more than 20 percent of the state economy.

PLANNING YOUR TIME

Milwaukee is great for a day, a weekend, or even a few days. Most folks find lovely—and not too pricey—accommodations downtown in historic, retro, or fashionably fun hotels, and from there much of everything is walkable (and use the skywalks downtown in winter!). Even better—traffic off the interstates at rush hour

Barges still work the Milwaukee River.

© THOMAS HUHTI

© THOMAS HUHTI

historic Milwaukee architecture

is rarely bad and you've almost always got a nice lake view.

If you're blowing through, make an effort to stop in and ogle the amazing Milwaukee Art Museum and check out the Harley-Davidson Museum. Any visit, if possible, should be planned around the huge music festival **Summerfest** in late June/early July—12 hours here aren't enough and you'll sleep for a day after, but it's a hell of a great time. (Plan ahead and book accommodations in advance.)

NEIGHBORHOODS AND HISTORIC DISTRICTS

"Indeed, it is not easy to recall any busy city which combines more comfort, evidences of wealth and taste and refinement, and a certain domestic character, than this town on the bluffs," an impressed easterner once observed more than a century ago.

The unusually high concentration of magnesium and calcium in Milwaukee clay created the yellowish tint that gives much of the city's original architecture a distinctive flair.

Factories produced top-quality bricks of such eye-catching light hues that the city became known as Cream City.

The Convention and Visitors Bureau offers detailed brochures covering all Milwaukee neighborhoods; it also has lists of tour companies, including **Historic Milwaukee Inc.** (828 N. Broadway, 414/277-7795, www.historicmilwaukee.org), which offers an astonishing number of strolling tours ($7).

Yankee Hill

Yankee Hill makes other grand Milwaukee neighborhoods appear raffish. This grande dame enclave arose north of East Mason Street to East Ogden Avenue and west off the lakefront to North Jackson Street. Originally owned by Milwaukee's first resident, Solomon Juneau, this became the city's center of government, finance, and business. Find oodles of churches as well as examples of Victorian Gothic, Italianate, and every other 19th-century architectural predilection.

Juneautown

Juneautown constituted the east side of the 19th-century internecine Milwaukee wars and developed into the effective heart of the city. Today, both Water Street and Wisconsin Avenue atavistically claim the title of most-happening area in the city. Original architectural gems such as the Milwaukee City Hall, Pabst Theater, Iron Block, and funky old Milwaukee Street are still chockablock with baroque Victorian buildings. **St. Mary's Church** (836 N. Broadway, at the corner of E. Kilbourn Ave. in Juneautown) is precisely the same age as Milwaukee. Made of Cream City brick in 1846, it is the oldest Catholic church in the city. The Annunciation painting above the altar was a gift from King Ludwig I of Bavaria.

Kilbourntown

Kilbourntown went up as a direct, contemporary rival to Juneautown. Speculator Byron Kilbourn refused to align his bridges with Juneautown's, the consequence of which is apparent today. There wasn't much going for the land, other than its location as a transit point to Madison. Other than North Old World 3rd Street, much of the architecture was razed for megaprojects. Highlights in Kilbourntown include the Mediterranean revival Riverside Theater along West Wisconsin Avenue; the Germania Building on West Wells Street, once the site of a German-language publishing empire and notable for its carved lions and copper-clad domes (endearingly dubbed "Kaiser's Helmets"); the odd-shaped Milwaukee County Historical Center; the legendary Turner Hall; the Milwaukee Public Museum; Milwaukee Public Library; and the enormous Grand Avenue Mall.

Brady Street

The newest gentrified sibling neighborhood, Brady Street spans a land bridge connecting the Milwaukee River and Lake Michigan, originally Milwaukee's version of Little Italy. There's an appreciable quotient of hipsters and misunderstood geniuses lining coffeehouse windows. The refurbishing has nice touches, such as the etching of Brady Street history into the sidewalk concrete.

Bronzeville

Bronzeville, an erstwhile African American cultural and entertainment center that has faded, has begun a Brady Street gentrification to make it hip and happening. The district runs from North 4th Street to North 7th Street.

Walker's Point

Immediately north of the Allen-Bradley clock, between 1st and 2nd Streets on West National Avenue, is a stretch of Milwaukee that kinda smacks of a Depression-era photo during the day, but by night becomes one of the city's most underappreciated tip-the-elbow neighborhoods. Walker's Point is also one of the most ethnically mixed neighborhoods in Milwaukee. German, Scandinavian, British, Welsh, Irish, Serb, Croatian, and Polish settlers came in originally, and Hispanics and Southeast Asian immigrants have arrived more recently.

Activated in 1962, the **Allen-Bradley clock,** the second-largest four-faced clock in the world, according to the *Guinness Book of World Records* (it was first until 2010, when an enormous clock in Mecca, Saudi Arabia, dethroned it), has octagonal clock faces twice the size of the clocks of Big Ben in London. The hour hands are 15 feet 9 inches long and weigh 490 pounds; the minute hands are 20 feet long and weigh 530 pounds. It's still crucial as a lake navigation marker. (And I love the nickname: the "Polish Moon.") Stop by **Tivoli Palm Garden,** an original alfresco produce market renovated into a *biergarten* by Schlitz Brewing Company and in the 1980s redone yet again.

North Point District

Virtually all of the North Point District on the city's coastal bight is on the National Register of Historic Places. This longtime exclusive community lies west of North Lincoln Memorial Drive and south of East Park Place to East Woodstock Place.

East of here along the lakefront is **Lake Park,** designed by Frederick Law Olmsted, planner of New York City's Central Park and San Francisco's Golden Gate Park. Prehistoric Native American burial mounds are here. At the top of North Avenue is the **North Point Lighthouse,** a Victorian Gothic structure dating from the 1870s and one of the few extant water towers like it in the United States.

West End

A case can be made that the West End rivals Yankee Hill's opulence. West End became the city's first residential suburb, between North 27th Street, North 35th Street, West Wisconsin Avenue, and West Vliet Street. Yankee bluebloods and prominent German American families competed in building the most opulent mansions. Highland Boulevard was at one time referred to as "Sauerkraut Boulevard." Highlights of the area include the Tripoli Shrine Temple on West Wisconsin Avenue, Central United Methodist Church on North 25th Street, Harley-Davidson's corporate headquarters, and Miller Brewing Company.

Sights

Note that much freeway "gentrification" (sorely needed) is ongoing, so be patient! (The U.S. government says Milwaukee is likely to suffer L.A.-esque traffic death by 2020 without it; good news—the first project finished *early* and *under budget*—Midwestern work ethic rocks!)

Beware: Jaywalking is illegal and strictly enforced in Milwaukee, especially during lunchtime hours. You *will* be ticketed; don't even try it. On the other hand, the police dole out equal numbers of tickets to drivers who don't give way to pedestrians.

From the west, I-94 is the primary thoroughfare; I-894 skirts the southern and western fringes north to south, and I-43 meets I-94 at the Marquette interchange downtown and then heads north.

Off the freeways, most of the sights—save the Historic Third Ward or outlying sights—are concentrated in a rough square bounded by WI 145 to the north, I-43 to the west, I-794 to the south, and the big old lake to the east. The Milwaukee River splits the square down the middle and separates the city into its east and west sections. The river is also the line of demarcation for street numbering, so if you bear in mind where the river is, you should be fine.

A comprehensive skywalk system connects the Frontier Airlines Convention Center, the Federal Plaza, and the Shops at Grand Avenue. When it was built, one stretch, the Riverspan, was the only skywalk in the United States built over a navigable riverway, here the Milwaukee River.

a river scene along the Milwaukee River

© THOMAS HUHTI

MILWAUKEE

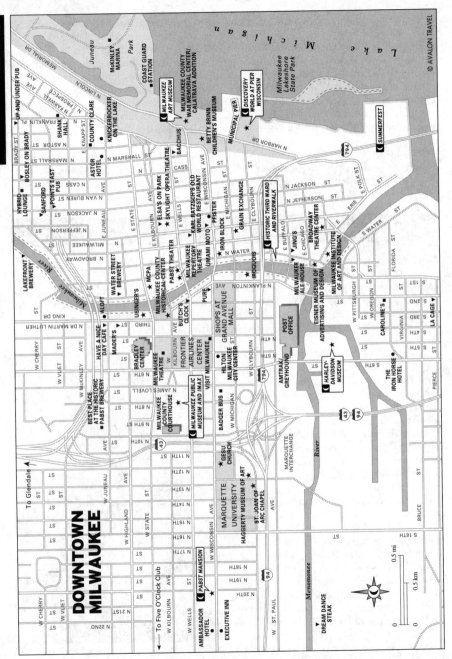

DOWNTOWN MILWAUKEE

© AVALON TRAVEL

Lake Michigan

Milwaukee Lakeshore State Park

To Glendale

To Five O'Clock Club

Juneau Park

McKinley Marina

COAST GUARD STATION

- ▼ UP AND UNDER PUB
- ● COUNTY CLARE
- KNICKERBOCKER ON THE LAKE
- ● BOSLEY ON BRADY
- ▼ POINTS EAST PUB
- ▼ HYBRID LOUNGE
- SANFORD
- ● ASTOR HOTEL
- ★ MILWAUKEE ART MUSEUM
- MILWAUKEE COUNTY WAR MEMORIAL CENTER/ CALATRAVA ADDITION
- ★ DISCOVERY WORLD AT PIER WISCONSIN
- BACCHUS
- BETTY BRINN CHILDREN'S MUSEUM
- ★ MUNICIPAL PIER
- ★ SUMMERFEST
- ★ ELSA'S ON PARK
- ★ SKYLIGHT OPERA THEATRE
- ★ KARL RATZSCH'S OLD WORLD RESTAURANT
- PFISTER
- ▼ UMAMI MOTO
- ● IRON BLOCK
- ★ GRAIN EXCHANGE
- ★ HISTORIC THIRD WARD AND RIVERWALK
- ▼ JING'S
- BROADWAY THEATRE CENTER
- ● IROQUOIS
- ● MILWAUKEE ALE HOUSE
- MILWAUKEE INSTITUTE OF ART AND DESIGN
- ● PURE
- LAKEFRONT BREWERY
- ▼ WATER STREET BREWERY
- ● ALOFT
- ★ USINGER'S
- ★ MILWAUKEE COUNTY HISTORICAL SOCIETY
- ● MCPA
- ★ PABST THEATER
- ★ MILWAUKEE REPERTORY THEATRE
- ▼ HAVE A NICE DAY CAFE
- ▼ MADER'S
- ★ BEST PLACE AT THE HISTORIC PABST BREWERY
- BRADLEY CENTER
- MILWAUKEE THEATRE
- ● BUTCH'S CLOCK
- FRONTIER AIRLINES CENTER
- SHOPS AT GRAND AVENUE MALL
- VISIT MILWAUKEE
- HILTON MILWAUKEE CITY CENTER
- ★ MILWAUKEE PUBLIC MUSEUM AND IMAX
- ★ MILWAUKEE COUNTY COURTHOUSE
- BADGER BUS
- POST OFFICE
- EISNER MUSEUM OF ADVERTISING AND DESIGN
- CAROLINE'S
- ● LA CAGE
- AMTRAK GREYHOUND
- ★ HARLEY-DAVIDSON MUSEUM
- THE IRON HORSE HOTEL
- GESU CHURCH
- MARQUETTE UNIVERSITY
- ★ HAGGERTY MUSEUM OF ART
- ★ ST. JOAN OF ARC CHAPEL
- MARQUETTE INTERCHANGE
- ★ PABST MANSION
- ● AMBASSADOR HOTEL
- ● EXECUTIVE INN
- ▼ DREAM DANCE STEAK

Milwaukee River

King Dr

N Dr Martin Luther King Dr

Menomonee River

0   0.5 mi
0   0.5 km

Milwaukee Angels

Bless the city of Milwaukee for its angels. Not seraphims, but civic altruists officially called public service ambassadors (PSAs around here), they'll happily help with anything.

DOWNTOWN
◖ Historic Third Ward and Riverwalk

The one-time bustling ethnic warehouse district suffered a catastrophic conflagration in 1892 in which more than 500 buildings burned (only one was left standing), displacing thousands of immigrants. Though the area was rebuilt, the earlier verve was always missing.

Until now. Antique stores and art galleries are the norm now, in among dozens of cafés, upscale shops, and a few longtime holdovers. It's also the fruit and vegetable district, quite a sight in the morning as the trucks roll through. A quick tour via historicthirdward.org before arrival would help.

The unofficial "off-Broadway" area of the city, the Third Ward has a new **Broadway Theatre**

© THOMAS HUHTI

Milwaukee's Historic Third Ward

Center (158 N. Broadway, 414/291-7800), which smacks of an 18th-century European opera house; juxtaposed with that is a smaller experimental theater.

The well-regarded **Milwaukee Institute of Art and Design** (MIAD, 273 E. Erie St., 414/276-7889) is housed in an old terminal, rebuilt in the days after the ward fire. *Many* galleries (generally open during sessions 10 A.M.–5 P.M. Tues.–Sat., at times till 7 P.M. Thurs.) display student work.

Run by the MIAD, the around-the-corner **Eisner Museum of Advertising and Design** (208 E. Water St., 414/203-0371, www.eisnermuseum.org, 11 A.M.–5 P.M. Wed.–Fri., from noon Sat., from 1 P.M. Sun., $5 adults) is only the second facility related to this subject in the country, and the only one owned by an art school. Extensive exhibits include the automobile in advertising and beer in ads (natch), along with a half dozen rotating exhibits. You can even record your own radio commercial!

The riverwalk in the Third Ward includes the **Public Market** (414/336-1111, www.milwaukeepublicmarket.org, 10 A.M.–8 P.M. Mon.–Fri., 8 A.M.–7 P.M. Sat., 10 A.M.–6 P.M. Sun.), a year-round farmers market, replete with anachronistic warehouse-style buildings and early-20th-century facades.

The riverwalk's newest attraction is a statue of Arthur Fonzarelli, a.k.a. **"The Fonz"** from the TV show *Happy Days,* which was set in Milwaukee. When announced in 2007, some people sniffed it was a bit low-brow and "serious" art belonged there. Good for the good-humored folks of Brewtown, who have taken to it with pride.

Old World 3rd Street and Water Street

North of I-794 is another modestly gentrified zone along both sides of the Milwaukee River. To the east is Water Street, the happening mélange of microbreweries, sports pubs, dance clubs, restaurants, and cultural attractions. To the west is Old World 3rd Street, with more classic Milwaukee edifices, original old hotels and factories, the Bradley Center, and more

The Fonz greets visitors to the Beer City.

restaurants. The riverwalk here includes **Pere Marquette Park,** with a gazebo, pavilion, and boat dock for tours, along with permanent decks and slips over the water.

Also along North Old World 3rd Street is **Usinger's** (1030 N. Old World 3rd St., 414/276-9100, 8:30 A.M.–5 P.M. Mon.–Sat.), known as the Tiffany of sausage makers. In a city raised on *fleisch,* Usinger's has been the carnivore's heaven since 1880 and partially explains the occasional odd olfactory sensation downtown—the sweet scent of wood smoke mingling with the smell of brewer's yeast. *Food and Wine* has dubbed Usinger's bratwurst the best sausage in America.

Lakefront

Milwaukee sits on the deepest harbor on the western edge of Lake Michigan. For miles, the city rolls like a sideways wave along the lake. You can drive the entire lakefront on WI 32 or bike most of it on separate county park bike paths. You pass nine beaches along the way.

South of the Milwaukee Art Museum and the Discovery World at Pier Wisconsin is one of Wisconsin's newest state parks, **Lakeshore State Park,** a nearly 20-acre parcel of land adjacent to the Summerfest grounds with beaches, fishing, and trails linking it to the entire rest of the state.

◖ Milwaukee Art Museum

Among the tops in the Midwest for visual arts museums is the Milwaukee Art Museum (700 N. Art Museum Dr., 414/224-3200, www.mam.org, 10 A.M.–5 P.M. Tues.–Sun., till 8 P.M. Thurs., $12). The museum holds one of the United States' most important and extensive collections of German Expressionist art—not unimportant, given the city's Teutonic link (the museum is ranked third in the *world* in German art). The museum now houses well over 20,000 paintings, sculptures, prints, and decorative art. Other noteworthy exhibits include a panorama of Haitian art and the repository of Frank Lloyd Wright's Prairie School of Architecture. Pieces date back as far as the 15th century, and the permanent displays are impressively diverse—Old Masters to Warhol through the Ash Can School. The Bradley Wing houses a world-renowned collection of Modern Masters.

MAM is actually one piece of the vast **Milwaukee County War Memorial Center,** a complex comprising several parts of the immediate lakefront and assorted buildings throughout the city. The complex was originally already a landmark, designed by Eero Saarinen. But it's right here at the MAM that the city really put itself on the map. A massive, $50 million architectural enhancement to the museum by international designer Santiago Calatrava is, with zero exaggeration, breathtaking. Or stunning. Or any other superlative you choose. Whatever the description, do not miss it. The addition—gull-like wings, which can be raised or lowered to let sunlight in, soaring above the complex—features a suspended pedestrian bridge linking it to downtown. So important is this addition that no less than *Time* magazine named it "building of the year." Hollywood has even used it in *Transformers 3.*

◖ Discovery World at Pier Wisconsin

Simply overwhelming—in the best possible sense—is this ultra-high-tech (and fetchingly designed) conglomeration of every

© THOMAS HUHTI

the Milwaukee Art Museum's Calatrava addition from Wisconsin Avenue

single science known, all done in an accessible, fascinating manner. Seriously, it's an unbelievable place. Discovery World (500 N. Harbor Dr., 414/765-9966, www.discoveryworld.org, 9 A.M.–5 P.M. Tues.–Fri., 10 A.M.–5 P.M. Sat.–Sun., $17 adults) is the best freshwater education center in the United States—hands down. (I cannot tell you how many museum-resistant kids I've seen who adore this place!) And it's actually limnological as well as the usual natural/human history. It's got 120,000 square feet of exhibits (more than 200 ultimately)—including two massive fresh- and saltwater aquariums—all of them the cuttingest of cutting edge. (And it's not just biology—students have exhibits from communications technology to astronomy, most of it active rather than passive.) My fave is the exhibit on local-boy-done-good (from Waukesha, west of Milwaukee) Les Paul (he is the musician and designer of the same-named famed electric guitar).

Either moored outside or off on some research jaunt is the *Denis Sullivan,* a floating classroom and the only Great Lakes schooner recreation anywhere. Check the website for the un-oft occasions to climb aboard.

Local Architecture

A block from the Milwaukee Public Museum, the distinctive **Milwaukee Public Library** (814 W. Wisconsin Ave., 414/286-3032, free tours 1:30 P.M. Sat.) is an impressive 1895 edifice. You can find it by looking for the dome. Inside, a spacious rotunda displays well-preserved original Old World detail work, while further in finds graceful century-old design, and ambient light (the staircase alone is worth a view!). Oh, and free wireless access too.

In the 200 block of East Wells Street, **Milwaukee City Hall** (414/286-2266, 8 A.M.–4 P.M. Mon.–Fri., free) is a navigational aid for first-timers, with its can't-miss-it Flemish Renaissance design (and also because many remember it from the television sitcom *Laverne and Shirley*). Antechambers there display Old World artisanship. The 10-ton bell in the tower now rings only for special occasions, and it rocks the entire downtown when it does. A $75 million restoration project, finished in 2008, really brought back the amazing luster to the edifice.

On the southeast corner of Water Street and Wisconsin Avenue, the antebellum **Iron Block** is the only example of cast-iron architecture left in Milwaukee, and one of three in the Midwest.

Wisconsin's one-time status as leading world grain producer explains the lavish interiors of the **Grain Exchange** (225 E. Michigan St.). The three-story exchange was built in 1879 (the first centralized trading center in the United States); its atavistic Victorian opulence sports gold motifs and enormous paneled murals within the 10,000-square-foot room.

Breweries, Past and Present

Milwaukee was once home to dozens of breweries churning out the secret sauce of *gemütlichkeit*. The pungent malt scent can still pervade,

MILWAUKEE

© THOMAS HUHTI

the historic Iron Block

and beer does remain a cultural linchpin. **Riverwalk Boat Tours and Rental** (Pere Marquette Park, 414/283-9999, www.riverwalkboats.com) has a fave three-hour brewery tour taking in three local microbreweries on weekends ($25).

Though Pabst, once the sixth-largest (and oldest) U.S. brewer, lives on in name (it's popular in China, of all places), it's no longer made in the United States. Schlitz—the "Beer that Made Milwaukee Famous"—has just made a reappearance, though it's not brewed in Milwaukee. Miller is the lone megabrewing holdout, though Milwaukeeans flipped their collective wig a bit in 2008 when, after a merger with Coors, it was decided to relocate the corporate headquarters to—gasp, of all places, oh the betrayal!—Chicago (worry not, the big ol' brewery itself ain't goin' anywhere).

Microbreweries and brewpubs are now everywhere.

Lakefront Brewery (1872 N. Commerce St., 414/372-8800, www.lakefrontbrewery.com, tours at 3 P.M. most days except Sun., $5) has tours taking in Larry, Moe, and Curly on the tanks, a cheeky start. Lakefront brews include specialty beers such as pumpkin- and cherry-flavored varieties. This generally is voted best brewery tour by local media. The brewery also has a boat dock and lies on the riverwalk.

The brews at **Milwaukee Ale House** (233 N. Water St., 414/226-2336, 11 A.M.–10 P.M. Mon.–Thurs., till 1 A.M. Fri.–Sat., till 9 P.M. Sun., $6–15) are among the best—even better sipped at its great riverside location with double-decker *biergarten*. Great live music here. Local tidbit: This building was once a saddlery and, later, the place where the Hula Hoop was invented!

North of here find Milwaukee's original brewpub at **Water Street Brewery** (1101 N. Water St., 414/272-1195, food served 11 A.M.–9 P.M. Mon.–Sat., $5–15) with an amazing beer memorabilia collection (some 60,000 items).

Beerheads should check out the original

THE BEER CITY

Milwaukee was the place that gave rise to the stereotype. King Gambrinus, the mythical Flemish king and purported inventor and patron of beer, would no doubt have called the city home.

THE BEGINNINGS AND THE RISE

The first brewery in Milwaukee wasn't started by a German. In 1840, Welshmen founded a lakefront brewery. Germans got into the act not much later with Herman Reuthlisberger's brewery in Milwaukee – bang! In 1844, Jacob Best started the neighborhood Empire Brewery, which later became the first of the megabreweries: Pabst. The same year saw Milwaukee's first beer garden – that all-inclusive picnic/party zone with lovely flower gardens and promenades so essential to German culture – open, and this was two years before the city's charter was approved! The next half decade saw the establishment of the progenitors of Milwaukee's hops heritage – in order, Blatz, Schlitz, and the modern leviathan, Miller.

Without question, the primary beer spur was massive immigration. Most influential were the waves of German immigrants, who earned Milwaukee the nickname "German Athens" by the 1880s. Further, when the government levied a whiskey tax of $1 per barrel, tavern patrons immediately began asking for beer instead.

Another factor in Milwaukee's brewery success was location; Wisconsin was a world agricultural player in herbs, hops among them. In addition, Milwaukee's plethora of natural ice gave it an edge over other U.S. brewers. The Great Chicago Fire of 1871 also helped by devastating virtually all of Milwaukee's competition. The city became famous for production and consumption; by the Civil War, there was one tippler's joint for every 90 residents – and *during* the war, the breweries doubled their production yet again. At one time, there were nearly 600 breweries in the state. This led temperance crusader Carrie Nation to declare in 1902, "If there is any place that is hell on earth, it is Milwaukee. You say that beer made Milwaukee famous, but I say that it made it infamous."

The brewers' vast wealth allowed them to affect every major aspect of Milwaukee society and culture; ubiquitous still are the brewing family names affixed to philanthropic organizations, cultural institutions, and many buildings. So popular was Pabst beer that it could afford to place real blue ribbons on bottles by hand; so pervasive were the beers that Admiral Robert Peary found an empty Pabst bottle as he was nearing the North Pole.

THE DECLINE

After the industry's zenith, perhaps 60 breweries at the peak, the number dwindled to only a dozen or so after Prohibition, and today there is just one, Miller.

In the 1950s, Milwaukee could still claim to produce nearly 30 percent of the nation's beer; as of now, the number is less than 5 percent.

Microbreweries and brewpubs (not the same thing) have inevitably cut into the megabrewery markets. And yet microbrews are a throwback of sorts. The first beer brewed in Milwaukee came from neighborhood brewers, most of which put out only a barrel a week, just enough for the local boys. As the major breweries gained wealth, they gobbled up large chunks of downtown land to create open-atrium *biergartens* and smoky *bierhalls*, in effect shutting out the smaller guys.

Most telling of all may be the deconstruction of yet another Wisconsin stereotype: Cheeseheads, despite being born clutching personalized steins, do not drink more beer per capita than any other state – that honor goes to Nevada. (C'mon, though, it's all tourists on benders, right?)

It ain't for Milwaukeean lack of trying; in 2006 *Forbes* called Milwaukee "America's Drunkest City."

MILWAUKEE

interiors of **Horny Goat Brewing & Hideaway** (2011 S. 1st St., 414/482-4628), built in a cool 1930s pump house.

Pabst Mansion

First stop for any historic architecture buff is the grandest of the grand—the Pabst Mansion (2000 W. Wisconsin Ave., 414/931-0808, www.pabstmansion.com, 10 A.M.–4 P.M. Mon.–Sat., noon–4 P.M. Sun., closed Feb., $9 adults). Built 1890–1893 of those legendary cream-colored bricks, it was the decadent digs of Captain Frederick Pabst, who slummed as a steamship pilot while awaiting his heirship to the Pabst fortune. The Flemish Renaissance mansion is staggering even by the baroque standards of the time: 37 rooms, 12 baths, 14 fireplaces, 20,000-plus feet of floor space, carved panels moved from Bavarian castles, priceless ironwork by Milwaukeean Cyril Colnik, and some of the finest woodwork you'll likely ever see. An adjacent pavilion, now the gift shop, was designed to resemble St. Peter's Basilica.

Milwaukee Public Museum and IMAX

Among the most respected nationally and number one nationwide in exhibits is the Milwaukee Public Museum (800 W. Wells St., 414/278-2702, www.mpm.edu, 9 A.M.–4 P.M. Mon.–Sat., from 10 A.M. Sun., closed Tues. in summer, $12 adults.). It initiated the concept of walk-through exhibits in 1882 and total habitat dioramas (with a muskrat mock-up) in 1890; today, its "Old Milwaukee" street life construct is quite possibly Milwaukee's most visited tourist spot. The museum's multi-level walk-through Rain Forest of Costa Rica—featuring its own 20-foot cascade—wins kudos and awards on an annual basis. Among the catacombs of displays on archaeology, anthropology, geology, botany, ethnography, and more are its jewels of paleontology: the world's largest dinosaur skull and a 15-million-year-old shovel-tusk elephant skeleton obtained from the Beijing Natural History Museum.

The museum constantly reworks itself to allow some of the six million-plus pieces in storage to see the light of day. The Live Butterfly

the legendary Pabst Mansion

© THOMAS HUHTI

Garden has become the most popular exhibit with the general public and especially with this author's relatives. The $17 million IMAX theater/planetarium is a big deal, as it is the only place on earth to have such advanced computer projection systems.

Take walking shoes, as the three floors—and you'll want to see every one—will wear you down.

Other Museums

Across from the arts museum in O'Donnell Park, the **Betty Brinn Children's Museum** (929 E. Wisconsin Ave., 414/291-0888, www. bbcmkids.org, 9 A.M.–5 P.M. daily, from noon Sun., closed Mon. Sept.–June, $6) has been rated by *Parents* magazine in the top 10 for best museums for families.

The triangular **Milwaukee County Historical Center** (910 N. Old World 3rd St., 414/273-8288, www.milwaukeecountyhistsoc. org, free) features fascinating explicative displays on the city's legendary Bridge Wars and roiling socialism. A painting alcove displays works of the Panorama painters—an obscure Milwaukee specialty. The center's interiors were closed for renovation at last check; call for hours.

Marquette University

Though the university's namesake was not particularly enamored of the Great Lake coastline, this Jesuit university (Wisconsin Ave., 414/278-3178, www.marquette.edu) was founded in 1881 and christened for the intrepid explorer. (The university purportedly even has bone fragments from the Black Robe.) The university has regular event updates.

The primary attraction here is the **St. Joan of Arc Chapel** (generally open 10 A.M.–4 P.M. daily, from noon Sun., may be closed weekends when school is out), an inspiring, five-century-old relic from the Rhone River Valley of France. Transported stone by stone, along with another medieval chateau, it was reassembled on Long Island in 1927 by a raiload magnate (the French government put the kibosh on cultural relocation after this). It was lovingly redone by some of the nation's premier historic architects and renovators and remains the only medieval structure in the Western Hemisphere where Mass is said regularly. Stories regarding St. Joan and the chapel may or may not be apocryphal; she is said to have kissed one of the stones while worshiping in the chapel during the war between France and England, and that stone has been colder than the surrounding ones ever since.

Another treasure of architecture here is the Brobdingnagian Gothic 1894 **Gesu Church.** The vertiginous heights of the spires are enough, but the gorgeous rose stained glass, divided into 14 petals, is equally memorable.

Also on campus is the **Haggerty Museum of Art** (530 N. 13th St., 414/288-1669, www. marquette.edu/haggerty, 10 A.M.–4:30 P.M. Mon.–Sat., till 8 P.M. Thurs., noon–5 P.M. Sun., free). It is easily one of the city's most challenging galleries and worth it for anyone jaded by excessive exposure to the old masters. It's multicultural and multimedia with a modernist bent. The priciest piece is the Bible series of more than 100 hand-colored etchings by Marc Chagall.

One fascinating item at the **Marquette University Memorial Library** (1415 W. Wisconsin Ave., 414/288-7555) is the world-renowned J. R. R. Tolkien Collection—more than 10,000 pages for *The Lord of the Rings* alone, but also thousands of other documents. You can't just waltz in and paw the collection, remember. Hours vary by semester and are reduced in summer.

Freebies

Bless Milwaukee—there's always free stuff! Downtown, Pere Marquette Park has **free concerts** Wednesday evenings; Cathedral Park Square at Jefferson and Wells features free live jazz Thursday evenings. Virtually every county park has summertime free music, too; check county.milwaukee.gov for schedules.

NORTH OF DOWNTOWN
Charles Allis Art Museum

Overlooking Lake Michigan, the Charles Allis Art Museum (1801 N. Prospect Ave., 414/278-8295, www.cavtmuseums.org,

1–5 P.M. Wed.–Sun., $5 adults, $8 including Villa Terrace) is in a Tudor mansion built by the first president of Allis-Chalmers, a major city employer. It has a superb collection of world art, fine furniture, and nearly 1,000 objets d'art dating back as far as 500 B.C. and covering the entire world. The museum's posh interiors feature Tiffany windows, silk wall coverings, and loads of marble. A special extra: some nights local bands play and your museum entrance ticket gets you in.

◖ Villa Terrace

Within walking distance of the Charles Allis Art Museum, the lavish 1923 Mediterranean Italian Renaissance Villa Terrace (2220 N. Terrace Ave., 414/271-3656, www.cavtmuseums.org, 1–5 P.M. Wed.–Sun., $5 adults) houses an eclectic collection of decorative arts, including art and handcrafted furniture from the 16th through the 20th centuries. A four-year Garden Renaissance program involved the restoration of a variety of botanical collections (organically melding interiors and exteriors). It is now one of the country's only existing examples of Italian Renaissance garden art and design.

University of Wisconsin-Milwaukee

UWM is second in enrollment only to the main campus in Madison; it's well known for its civil engineering program. The **Golda Meir Library** (2311 E. Hartford Ave., 414/229-6282, www4.uwm.edu, 8 A.M.–5 P.M. Mon.–Fri., free) houses the **American Geographical Society Collection,** a priceless collection of more than half a million maps, atlases, logbooks, journals, globes, charts, and navigational aids, including what is reportedly the world's oldest known map, dating from the late 15th century.

Sprecher Brewery

Sprecher was one of the original Milwaukee microbrews, can be found just about anywhere in Wisconsin, and also makes killer root beer and cream soda. Here (701 W. Glendale Ave., Glendale, 414/964-2739, www.

© THOMAS HUHTI

Charles Allis Art Museum

sprecherbrewery.com, $3) you'll find one of the city's favorite microbrewery tours, given its oompah music in a heavily Bavarian-themed lager cellar. Tours (reservations required) are offered at 4 P.M. Friday and at 1, 2, and 3 P.M. Saturday year-round, with occasional weekday tours in summer.

Schlitz Audubon Nature Center

On the far north side of the city, in Bayside, Schlitz Audubon Nature Center (1111 E. Brown Deer Rd., 414/352-2880, www.sanc.org, 9 A.M.–5 P.M. daily, $4) abuts the edge of Lake Michigan on the grounds of an erstwhile Schlitz brewery horse pasture. A six-mile network of trails winds along the beach and through diverse prairie, woodland, and wetland. An observation tower with parapet offers lake views. The interpretive center cost a cool $5.5 million to give it many environmentally friendly features, such as recirculated rain water, sustainable wood resourced from Aldo Leopold's homestead, solar power panels, and low-flow toilets.

© THOMAS HUHTI

Schlitz Audubon Nature Center

Whitnall Park

One of the larger municipal parks in the United States at 600-plus acres, Charles B. Whitnall Park (5879 W. 92nd St., Hales Corners, 414/425-7303, free) is the cornerstone of Milwaukee County's enormous park system and the cornerstone of the state's proposed Oak Leaf Birding Trail, which will eventually have 35 separate parks and forests to view crucial avian habitat. Lush landscaped gardens are found inside the park at **Boerner Botanical Gardens** (414/425-1130, gardens 8 A.M.–sunset daily mid-Apr.–Oct., garden house till 7 P.M. in summer, hours significantly reduced the rest of the year, $5). Forty acres of roses, perennials, wildflowers, and more thrive here; the 1,000-acre arboretum surrounding the gardens includes the largest flowering crabapple orchard in the United States.

Also in Whitnall Park is the **Todd Wehr Nature Center** (9701 W. College Ave., 414/425-8550, 8 A.M.–4:30 P.M., parking $3), designed as a living laboratory of eco-awareness, with nature trails and an ongoing mixed-grass prairie restoration.

SOUTH OF DOWNTOWN
St. Josaphat's Basilica

Just south of downtown, the first Polish basilica in North America is the city's St. Josaphat's Basilica (Lincoln Ave. at S. 6th St., 414/645-5623, tours by appointment, but public welcome to Masses). Parishioners built the structure out of salvaged rubble from the Chicago Federal Building. The capacious dome is modeled after St. Peter's in Rome; inside is a rather astonishing mélange of Polish iconography and hagiography, relics, stained glass, and wood carvings.

Beer Corner

The only-in-Milwaukee award goes to **Forest Home Cemetery** (2405 W. Forest Home Ave.) and its designated sector of eye-catching monuments to the early Milwaukee brewing giants: Blatz, Pabst, Best, and Schlitz rest in peace beneath the handcrafted stones. Kooky or spooky, heritage is heritage. You can usually enter the cemetery weekdays until around 4 P.M. and on Saturday mornings.

Mitchell International Airport

Mitchell International Airport has its **Mitchell Gallery of Flight** (5300 S. Howell Ave., 414/747-4503, www.mitchellgallery.org, 8 A.M.–10 P.M. daily, free) housing a number of aircraft, including a zeppelin. More appealing is the retrospective of the iconoclastic and innovative military aviation pioneer Billy Mitchell, a Beer City native.

Speaking of the airport, a unique, free way to kill time waiting for your plane to depart is to drive your rental car along Layton Avenue to near South Kansas Avenue (the north side of Mitchell International Airport). You'll find a small, relatively unknown viewing area to watch planes take off and land.

WEST OF DOWNTOWN

(Miller Brewing

King of the hill now in Milwaukee is mega-brewer Miller (4251 W. State St., 414/931-2337, www.millercoors.com, tours daily summer, closed Sun. otherwise, hours vary, free). This slick, modern operation is the very antithesis of a neighborhood brewer. Frederic Miller apprenticed and served as a brewmaster at Hohenzollern Castle in Sigmaringen, Germany, before striking out for the United States in 1855 at age 28 and starting a small brewery. His original Plank Road Brewery, bought from the son of the Pabst progenitor and not to be confused with Miller's shrewdly

---

HOG HEAVEN

Beer may have made Milwaukee famous, but to some, Milwaukee-born Harley-Davidson – the bikes, the slavishly devoted riders, and the company – truly represents the ethos of Milwaukee: blue-collar tough, proud, and loyal.

THE COMPANY

William S. Harley and Arthur Davidson, boyhood friends in Milwaukee, were fascinated by the bicycle (and German motorbike) craze around the turn of the 20th century. In 1903, they rigged a single-cylinder engine (the carburetor was a tin can) and leather-strap drive chain onto a thin bicycle frame – with no brakes. Thus began the first putterings of the company known for roaring.

The company incorporated in 1907 and within a decade became the largest motorcycle maker in the world. The Harleys' reputation for sound engineering and thus endurance – the first motorcycle lasted 100,000 miles – made them popular with the U.S. Postal Service and especially police departments. In the first Federation of American Motorcyclists endurance test, a hog scored above a perfect 1,000 points, leading to a Harley dominance in motorcycle racing for decades. Constant innovations, such as the first clutch, also fueled success.

During World War I Harley gained the U.S.

government's devotion – Harleys with sidecars equipped with machine guns also pursued pesky Pancho Villa into Mexico in 1917. Europeans found a great enthusiasm for the machines, too, after the Great War; within five years, 20 percent of the company's business was exported.

Further, no motorcycle maker could claim the innovation or the zeal with which Harley-Davidson catered to its riders. Original dealers were instructed to employ the consumers in as much of the process as possible. Harley-Davidson open houses were legendary. *The Enthusiast*, the company's newsletter, is the longest-running continuously published motorcycle organ anywhere.

THE BIKES

The company hit eternal fame with the goofy-looking, radically designed Knucklehead in 1936, when a public initially dismayed by the bulging overhead valves (hence the name) soon realized its synthesis of art and engineering – it has been called the most perfect motorcycle ever made. The Sportster, introduced in 1957, also gets the nod from aficionados – it's called the Superbike. In the 1970s, the Super Glide – the *Easy Rider* low-rider's progenitor – singlehandedly rescued the company. The modern Softail and Tour Glides are

named contemporary brewing operation, put out 300 barrels per year—no mean feat, but nothing stellar. Today, Miller—now merged as MillerCoors—is the second-largest brewery in the nation, with a total production of *45 million* barrels a year (the warehouse is the size of five football fields). Hour-long tours take in the ultra-high-tech packaging center, the hangar-size shipping center, and, finally, the brewhouse. Tours end at the Caves Museum, a restored part of Miller's original brewery in which kegs of beer were cooled. The ineluctable Bavarian hut dispenses free samples (to those 21 and over, natch) and features an antique stein collection and ornate woodwork.

Harley-Davidson Museum

Harley-Davidson plant tours in the western suburb of Wauwatosa ended in 2009, but that's OK, because to replace it the company has created Paradise for you. You can't say you've seen Milwaukee without a visit to "Hog Heaven" (I ain't seen it elsewhere, so I call dibs on that name)—the massive, 100,000-square-foot facility (Canal and South 6th Sts., 414/343-4235, www.h-dmuseum.com, 9 A.M.–6 P.M. Thurs.–Tues., 9 A.M.–8 P.M. Wed., $16 adults). This $30 million project, the Mecca for Made in America, features an interactive museum and exhibits on the history, culture, and lifestyle engendered by the company and its slavishly devoted riders.

---

considered by Harley-Davidson to be the best ever engineered.

GOOD TIMES, BAD TIMES

By the 1940s, two-thirds of all U.S. bikes were Harley-Davidsons. By the 1950s, swelled by demand, Harley managed to push out its main competitor, Indian Motorcycle. But somewhere along the line, something happened. Harleys had been derisively dubbed "Hardly Ablesons" because of their tendency to break down – or so said owners of archrival Indian Motorcycles.

When AMF (American Machine and Foundry) took control of the company in 1969, sales were plummeting. Whatever the cause, sales hit the wall, morale of the company's workforce hit an all-time low, and things got so bad that manufacturing was doled out to separate factories around the country.

In 1981, a group of about 30 Harley employees bought the company back and virtually reinvented it. With top-of-the-line products, brilliant marketing, and a furious effort at regaining the trust of the consumer, Harley-Davidson moved steadily back into the market. By the late 1980s, the company was again profitable against Japanese bikes. The effects are manifest: There's a veritable renaissance of the Harley craze, an extensive

Milwaukee's new pride and joy: the Harley-Davidson Museum

© THOMAS HUHTI

waiting list for bikes (all 75,000 produced in a year are spoken for up to a year in advance), and Harley groups tooling even the streets of Hong Kong. More than half of Harley owners are senior citizens, married, college educated, and have high incomes.

The contemporary Harley-Davidson headquarters sits very near the site of that shed/workshop that cobbled together the first bike. The company remains firmly committed to its downtown location. It has programs encouraging employees to live in the neighborhood and is one of the most in-touch corporations in town. Its 2008 grand opening of a new Harley-Davidson museum cements it as a Milwaukee brand forever.

Rooms are full of vintage vehicles and, not surprisingly, Elvis' bike probably gets the most attention. And God bless 'em, they stay open 365 days a year, in true blue-collar style.

The best way to experience Harley otherwise is to be around for Harley riders' conventions, when literally 100,000 Harleys descend on the city to fete the metallic beasts. It's an indescribable experience to *hear* and *feel* tens of thousands of Harleys roaring down I-94 toward Miller Park on their way to a Brewers game from the museum—the Beer City becomes a tented Hog City for a glorious summerlong celebration.

Annunciation Greek Orthodox Church

"My little jewel—a miniature Santa Sophia" is how Frank Lloyd Wright described the final major work of his life—the Annunciation Greek Orthodox Church (9400 W. Congress St., Wauwatosa, 414/461-9400). Its imposing rondure is a landmark to Milwaukee architecture—a dramatic inverted bowl into which

Wright incorporated symbolic golds and blues and the Greek cross. The blue-tiled dome rises 45 feet above the floor and spans 104 feet. During the most recent update, the congregation was involved in a heated dispute as to whether the original murals should be changed to more, er, "religious" themes. Individual tours are not possible.

Other Churches

The progressive **Central United Methodist Church** (639 N. 25th St., 414/344-1600, tours by appointment 8:30 A.M.–4 P.M. Mon. and Wed., till 1 P.M. Fri., free) is partially enclosed by earth and incorporates radical energy-saving and solar-energy measures (the tower holds solar panels).

It's not a church per se, but the **Tripoli Shrine Temple** (3000 W. Wisconsin Ave., 9 A.M.–4 P.M. Mon.–Fri., free) is worth a look, if only for the oddly appealing Taj Mahal nature of the place. It was built during a period of "fantasy architecture" and was indeed based on

the distinctive Domes

the Taj Mahal of India. The main dome is 30 feet in diameter and is flanked by two smaller domes. Camels, lanterns, and floral designs are some of the artwork decorating the interiors.

Milwaukee County Zoo

Believe it or not, the Milwaukee County Zoo's (10001 W. Bluemound Rd., 414/256-5411, www.milwaukeezoo.org) innovative designs have been mimicked nationally and internationally for the past five decades. Yep, they set the standard for what many today take for granted in zoological park settings. The animals' five global environments, grouped in specific continental areas with a system of moats, create apparent juxtaposing of predator and prey. Almost 5,000 specimens live here, many of them also residents of the endangered species list. Perennially popular are the polar bears and other aquatic leviathans viewable through subsurface windows. In a century-old barn is a dairy complex—an educational look at milk production. Zoomobiles ($3) roll about the expansive grounds, and minitrains ($1.50) also chug around. On occasion, you can even hop aboard an elephant or a spitting camel. Animal shows take place throughout the day.

It's open 9 A.M.–5 P.M. Monday–Saturday, 9 A.M.–6 P.M. Sunday and holidays May–September, till 4:30 P.M. the rest of the year. The rides and animal shows have varied schedules. Admission is $12 adults; parking is $11. All rides and activities within are extra. Admission rates are lower October–May.

The Domes

Though it's officially the **Mitchell Park Horticultural Conservatory** (524 S. Layton Blvd., 414/649-9800, www.countyparks.com, 9 A.M.–5 P.M. daily, $6.50 adults), everybody knows this complex as "the Domes." You'll know why once you take a gander at the conical seven-story, 148-foot-tall glass-encased buildings. The capacious interiors, totaling about 15,000 square feet, are isolated into arid desert, traditional floral, and tropical rainforest biospheres. One is re-landscaped up to half a dozen times annually. Outside, the conservatory, ringed with more sunken gardens, is the only structure of its type in the world.

Entertainment and Events

NIGHTLIFE

Milwaukee is no Austin, Texas, but there's a lot more music and nightlife than people realize. Then again, it's also the city where sheepshead (a native card game) tournaments might get equal billing with live music in the same bar. Milwaukee has more than 5,000 bars, which is in the top 10 per capita nationwide, so there's something out there for everyone. (*Forbes* also called it "America's Drunkest City.") And it is the City of Festivals: throw a dart at a calendar and you'll hit an enormous festival of some sort. And again, it's top 5 for cultural arts in the United States—surprise!

The deal: These places come and go. The ones in here show staying power.

The free weekly *Shepherd Express* gives a rundown of most of the clubs; the Friday edition of the *Milwaukee Journal-Sentinel* is fairly thorough.

An Oldie Rises Again

In early 2010, the long-defunct and vacant Pabst Brewery complex was rechristened as **Best Place at the Historic Pabst Brewery** (901 W. Juneau Ave., 414/630-1609, noon–midnight daily except Tues., tours $9). It has lost none of its historic charm. One part of the enormous place is the Little Tavern on the Hill, with all classic Milwaukee beers on draught; otherwise, get yer Pabst memorabilia here!

Classic Milwaukee

The folks at **Kochanski's Concertina Beer Hall** (1920 S. 37th St.) certainly have big shoes to fill, seeing as their place was the home of legendary Milwaukee polkameister Art Altenberg, who for decade after decade ran his club to preserve live polka music. Many nights this still lives on here; guaranteed every Wednesday night is traditional polka music. It's real-deal and it's a hoot!

Nightlife Districts

Stretching along the Milwaukee River, aptly named **Water Street** draws a preponderance of Marquette students and lots of downtown business types. Nightlife varies from a microbrewery to sports bars and dance clubs. The **Water Street Brewery** (1101 N. Water St., 414/272-1195, food served 11 A.M.–9 P.M. Mon.–Sat., $5–15) is Milwaukee's original brewpub. Raucous as all get out is **Rosie's Water Works** (1111 N. Water St., 414/274-7213).

More and more shops, boutiques, and restaurants are moving into the **Walker's Point** neighborhood. Nightspots here vary from a pub with a sand volleyball court outside to a Teutonic watering hole, dark sippers' pubs, and a whole lot more. Walker's Point is also the home of Milwaukee's oldest LBGT dance club, **La Cage** (801 S. 2nd St., 414/672-7988); it's also the largest in Wisconsin.

Bar/restaurants such as **Elsa's on Park** (833 N. Jefferson St., 414/765-0615), **Louise's** (801 N. Jefferson St., 414/273-4224), and others, all in the same area, have given **North Jefferson Street** and environs the feel of a subdued scene—all in the ritzy section of town full of boutiques, galleries, and the like. The *yin* to Water Street's noisy *yang*.

Dance Clubs

These come and go, but as of these keys thwacking, the hottest place seemed to be **Decibel** (1905 North Ave., 414/272-3337, www.decibelmke.com), the place where you can act like a VIP (or see one). Indeed, even in the depths of winter you'll see fashionistas stepping gingerly from limousines dressed head to toe in up-to-the-minute wear. The dance floor is hot, but you can escape the low-frequency thumping in the DeepBar, a relaxing vodka lounge.

One with the most staying power locally is the live music/dance club **Mad Planet** (533 East Center St., 414/263-4555), a perennial winner of local awards for best dance club. They have regular dance parties that always

turn into a mix of all local subcultures; here, goths mix with punks. Get there early.

Yeah, I know it's a chain, but **Have a Nice Day Cafe** (1101 N. Old World 3rd St., 414/270-9650) is a fun retro haven for those stuck in the 1970s; their signature goldfish bowl drinks will help you get into the, er, groove.

Live Music

ROCK

Shank Hall (1434 N. Farwell Ave., 414/276-7288) offers a constant barrage of prominent local, regional, and national acts. It was once a stable, so the interior isn't exactly a delight when the lights come up. More good spots for local rock or regional alternative acts and mostly college crowds include **Points East Pub** (1501 N. Jackson St., 414/272-0122) and the acoustically atrocious **Rave** (2401 W. Wisconsin Ave., 414/342-7283). Many readers of local websites and other media have voted the live music—genres and atmosphere—at **Milwaukee Ale House** (233 N. Water St., 414/226-2336, 11 A.M.–10 P.M. Mon.–Thurs., till 1 A.M. Fri.–Sat., till 9 P.M. Sun., $6–15) as tops.

Not here on a weekend? Fret not, for the **Cactus Club** (2496 S. Wentworth Ave., 414/482-0160) has music, often national acts, many weeknights.

LATIN

Real-deal no-frills Mexican food brings in throngs to **Tres Hermanos** (1332 W. Lincoln Ave., 414/384-9050), but you also can't beat the dancing to live Tex Mex and Norteña music Friday and Saturday nights.

BLUES AND R&B

It used to be all blues all the time (in a scuzzy kind of way) at the **Up and Under Pub** (1216 E. Brady St., 414/276-2677); under new owners it's gotten a freshening up and added a nice variety of rock, roots, and more.

The Riverwest neighborhood is a prime spot. A small neighborhood tavern unconcerned with decor, **Linneman's River West Inn** (1001 E. Locust St., 414/263-9844) has blues and some folk.

JAZZ

Serious jazzers should head for the **Jazz Oasis** (2379 N. Holton Ave., 414/562-2040) or a local institution, **Caroline's** (401 S. 2nd St., 414/221-0244), just south of downtown, where you go for the music and atmosphere, not necessarily the decor.

WORLD MUSIC AND ECLECTIC

International flavors—musical and otherwise—are on offer in a comfortable setting at **Nomad World Pub** (1401 E. Brady St., 414/224-8111), part coffee shop, part unpredictable drink-pouring bar where you can get betel nuts while listening to world beat music, sometimes live.

Regular Irish music—along with Irish fare—is available at **County Clare** (1234 N. Astor St., 414/272-5273), set in a retro guesthouse.

Taps, Taverns, and More Nightspots

Along bopping North Farwell Avenue, **Von Trier** (2235 N. Farwell Ave., 414/272-1775) could pass for a German *bierhall* with its long heavy wooden bench seating and a summertime *biergarten*. In true Bavarian and Wisconsin style, there's a buck's head affixed to the wall. They were "refreshing" the place at last check, but it's lost none of its essence. A block away on North Avenue, **Vitucci's** (1832 N. Ave., 414/273-6477) is a quieter place and a personal favorite watering hole—a Milwaukee fave since 1936.

At **Landmark Lanes** (2220 N. Farwell Ave., 414/278-8770), in the bowels of the Oriental Landmark Theater, there's bowling—this is Milwaukee, after all—but mostly it's a happening young nightclub with three separate bars, pool tables, and dartboards. The place has been around forever, and it's great.

If you're looking for a more upscale place, try the **Hi-Hat Lounge** (E. Brady and Arlington Sts., 414/220-8090). With cool jazz wafting in the background, it's got a classy but not showy feel and an older, sophisticated crowd.

Too many neighborhood taverns to count exist in Milwaukee, and everybody's got a different recommendation. The since-1908 **Wolski's** (1836 N. Pulaski St., 414/276-8130) is a corner tavern that defines a Milwaukee tippler's joint. You're an unofficial Beer City denizen if you drive home with an "I closed Wolski's" bumper sticker on your car.

LGBT

The longtime standard for the LGBT community is **La Cage** (801 S. 2nd St., in Walker's Point, 414/672-7988). Just opened is a casually chic new place, **Hybrid Lounge** (707 E. Brady St.).

CULTURE AND THE ARTS

In Rand McNally's *Places Rated,* Milwaukee hit the top 5 percent of big cities for cultural attractions and the arts. Since the 1990s, more than $100 million—and counting—has been poured into downtown arts districts. Per capita, Milwaukeeans donate more to the arts than any U.S. city besides Los Angeles. Four dozen cultural organizations call the city home—23 theater companies alone.

Rundowns for all cultural activities can be found in the Friday and Sunday editions of the *Milwaukee Journal-Sentinel. Milwaukee Magazine* also has a comprehensive monthly compendium.

Cultural Centers

The **Pabst Theater** (144 E. Wells St., 414/286-3663, www.pabsttheater.org), an 1895 Victorian piece of opulence that still today seems as ornate as ever, is a majestic draw in its own right (free public tours are given at noon on Saturdays if show schedules don't conflict), but it also continues to attract national acts of all kinds. The **Marcus Center for Performing Arts (MCPA)** (929 N. Water St., 414/273-7121, www.marcuscenter.org) has a regular season of theater, symphony, ballet, opera, children's theater, and touring specials. It is the home of the Milwaukee Symphony Orchestra, the Milwaukee Ballet Company, the Florentine Opera Company, and much more.

A detailed, painstaking postmillennial restoration of the **Milwaukee Theatre** (500 W.

Kilbourn Ave., 414/908-6000, www.milwaukeetheatre.com), a historic 1909 gem, has created a state-of-the-art facility for concerts and theatrical productions.

Theater

The city has nearly two dozen theater companies performing in many locations. The **Skylight Opera Theatre** (414/291-7800, www.skylightopera.com) and **Milwaukee Chamber Theatre** (414/276-8842, www.chamber-theatre.com) are residents of the lovely Broadway Theatre Center (158 N. Broadway, 414/291-7800) downtown. The Chamber Theatre's language-centered contemporary plays are always a challenge.

The nation's only African American professional theater group is the **Hansberry-Sands Theatre Company,** which performs at the Marcus Center (929 N. Water St., 414/273-7121, www.marcuscenter.org).

The **Milwaukee Repertory Theater** (108 E. Wells St., 414/224-1761, www.milwaukeerep.com) is part of an international network of cooperating organizations and offers classical, contemporary, cabaret, and special performances September–May.

Music

The **Milwaukee Symphony Orchestra** (700 N. Water St., 414/291-6010, www.milwaukeesymphony.org) is one of the nation's top orchestras. No less than *New Yorker* magazine, with an all-too-typical coastal undercurrent of surprise, described it as "virtuoso."

A low-cost alternative is the **Wisconsin Conservatory of Music** (1584 N. Prospect Ave., 414/276-5760, www.wcmusic.org), which offers performances of faculty, students, and guest artists.

A personal favorite is **Present Music** (1840 N. Farwell Ave., 414/271-0711, www.presentmusic.org), a group commissioning and performing eclectic, challenging works from modern composers.

Dance

Milwaukee has a thriving modern dance culture; New York City companies make regular visits to do performances in numerous sites around the city. Ranked among the top ballet companies in the country is the **Milwaukee Ballet Company** (504 W. National Ave., 414/643-7677, www.milwaukeeballet.org).

© THOMAS HUHTI

Milwaukee's historic Pabst Theater

Nationally renowned is Milwaukee's modern **Ko-Thi Dance Company** (414/442-6844, www.ko-thi.org), committed to the preservation and performance of African and Caribbean arts. Wildly popular shows are held in spring and fall at the Pabst Theater.

EVENTS

Another term of endearment for Milwaukee is the City of Festivals. Almost every week of the year brings yet another celebratory blowout feting some cultural, ethnic, or seasonal aspect of the city—and sometimes for no reason at all. The city's festival rundown is one large database. Show up any weekend from late May to early November and you're guaranteed something to do at a festival grounds in town.

The short list: German Fest, the largest multiday festival in the country (July); Bavarian Folk Fest (June); Oktoberfest; Polish Fest (June); Lakefront Festival of Arts (July); Festa Italiana (July); Bastille Days (July); Greek Festival (July); Mexican Spring Festival–Cinco de Mayo (May); Mexican Fiesta (Aug.); Irish Fest (Aug.); African World Festival (Aug.); Serbian Days (Aug.); Indian Summer (Sept.); Asian Moon Festival (Sept.); and Holiday Folk Fair (Nov.).

The largest party of all is early August's **Wisconsin State Fair** (414/266-7000, www.wistatefair.com), at the fairgrounds west along I-94. This fair of all fairs features carnivals, 500 exhibits, livestock shows, entertainment on 20 stages, and the world's greatest cream puffs.

◖ Summerfest

This is the granddaddy of all Midwestern festivals and the largest music festival in the world (so says the *Guinness Book of World Records*). For 11 days in late June, top national musical acts (as well as unknown college-radio mainstays) perform on innumerable stages along the lakefront, drawing millions of music lovers and partiers. Agoraphobics need not even consider it. Shop around for discount coupons at grocery stores and assorted businesses, or consider a multiday pass, available at businesses all around town.

Shopping

There's more to shopping in Milwaukee than the requisite cheddar cheese foam wedge hat and cheese and bratwurst gift packs. (Though these are of course to be on your list!)

SHOPS AT GRAND AVENUE MALL AND ENVIRONS

Virtually everyone starts at the economic (as well as geographic) heart of Milwaukee, the Grand Avenue Mall—a synthesis of old and new. Originally built in 1915 as the Plankinton Arcade, much of its architecture was retained when the four-block area was gentrified into a lower level of shops and an upper level of sidewalk cafés and people-watching heights.

From here, neighborhoods reach out for your wallet. To the immediate north, North Old World 3rd Street has mostly good restaurants but a few long-standing shops, the highlight of which has to be **Usinger's** (1030 N. Old World 3rd St., 414/276-9100, 8:30 A.M.–5 P.M. Mon.–Sat.). Sausage as a souvenir—is that a Milwaukee gift or what? Other highlights include Ambrosia Chocolates and, of course, the Wisconsin Cheese Mart.

OTHER SHOPPING DISTRICTS

The **Historic Third Ward, Jefferson Street,** and **East Brady Street** areas offer the most compelling strolls for shoppers. All are blocks-long areas of carefully gentrified Old World–feeling streets, filled with art and antique galleries, specialty shops, and oodles of places to grab a cup of java or a quick bite in a chic setting to recharge the purchasing battery.

Sports and Recreation

Milwaukee has been rated in the top 10 percent of like-size U.S. cities for recreational opportunities in and around the city. Don't forget too that the Beer City is major league. No exaggeration—it supports three professional teams along with a minor league hockey team.

RECREATION

Looking for something more aerobic? Consider the more than 150 parks and parkways and 15,000 acres of greenland. Milwaukee has more park area per person than any metropolitan city in the United States and won the Gold Medal for Excellence by the National Recreation and Park Association. The place to inquire first is the Milwaukee County Parks System (414/257-6100, www.countyparks.com).

Hiking and Biking

The following is but a thumbnail sketch of what the county has to offer.

The **Oak Leaf Trail** is the diamond of all Milwaukee-area trails. One name but comprising multiple loops, this beauty wends through all the parkways and major parks of the county, topping out at longer than 100 miles (the main section for most is an easy loop around the lakefront)! The trail begins along Lincoln Memorial Drive between Ogden Avenue and Locust Street. Signs from here point your way, though note that not *all* myriad loops are well marked (or even marked). The most popular subroute is a 13-mile marked route, the **Milwaukee '76 Trail,** starting from O'Donnell Park and stretching along the lakefront to the Charles Allis Art Museum and through east-side historic districts. As the Oak Leaf trailhead is along the lakefront, the best thing to do is to explore the littoral scenery after huffing and puffing all day. At 2400 North Lincoln Memorial Drive is the city's most popular beach—**Bradford Beach.**

Henry Aaron State Trail, a new addition to the state's reputable system, is a six-mile path leading from the lakefront, through historic districts, and ending in the near-west suburbs, much of it following the Menomonee River.

Other popular multiuse trails run along the Menomonee River between Good Hope and Bluemound Roads, along the Milwaukee River from Good Hope Road to the lakefront near McKinley Marina, along the Root River from Greenfield Avenue to Loomis Road, and along the south lakefront through Cudahy and South Milwaukee.

Find great ski trails at a number of parks, including Schlitz Audubon Nature Center, Whitnall Park, and, believe it or not, the zoo.

Bike and in-line skate rentals and personal watercraft (and kayaks) are usually available along the lakefront at **Milwaukee Bike and Skate Rental** (414/273-1343, www.milwbikeskaterental.com) in Veterans Park. Just north of McKinley Marina, **Welker Water Sport Rentals** (414/630-5387) rents personal watercraft and kayaks.

The county's website has maps of the Oak Leaf Trail and others, or you may request them.

Charter Fishing

Milwaukee leads the state in charter operations and salmonoids taken. On a scintillating summer day, the marina and harbor areas of Milwaukee appear to be discharging a benevolent, whitewashed D-Day flotilla.

The Convention and Visitors Bureau (414/273-7222, www.visitmilwaukee.org) can provide more detailed information on specific charter operations. Investigating charter operators before sailing can save quite a lot of personality friction; the boats are not that big, and you are the one who'll have to sit out on the big lake with the skipper all day.

Bowling

An apt local joke: Wisconsin's the only state where you can factor your bowling average into your SAT score. The city's 81 regulation bowling centers can take care of your bowling jones, but even better, a couple of neighborhood joints have old-style duckpin bowling. The **Holler House** (2042 W. Lincoln Ave., 414/647-9284) has the two oldest sanctioned bowling lanes (Lanes 1 and 2) in the United States. A tradition of sorts here is to "donate" your bra to the rafters on your first visit! A true Milwaukee treasure is long-standing **Koz's Mini Bowl** (2078 S. 7th St., 414/383-0560), with four 16-foot lanes and orange-size balls; the pin setters still make $0.50 a game plus tips. An aside: Koz's was actually a WWII-era house of ill repute; the lanes were simply a cover to keep locals from asking questions.

Ice Skating and Hockey

The **Pettit National Ice Center** (500 S. 84th St., off I-94, 414/266-0100, www.thepettit.com) is the only one of its kind in the country and one of only five of its scope in the world. National and international competitions are held here regularly. The public can enjoy the 400-meter ovals and two Olympic-size hockey rinks when they're open ($6); you can even jog on a running track. Tours cost $3.

Golf

Milwaukee is often mentioned for its nearly 20 golf courses within a short drive. Most prominent in the near vicinity is **Brown Deer Park** (7835 N. Green Bay Rd., 414/352-8080); for a public course, it's amazing. Whitnall and Oakwood Parks also have excellent courses.

Camping

The best public camping is a half hour to the west via I-94 and south on WI 67 in **Kettle Moraine State Forest** (262/646-3025, open year-round); it's very popular and is often booked, so arrive/reserve early. The nearest private campground is southwest of Milwaukee along I-43 in Mukwonago at **Country View Campground** (S110 W26400 Craig Ave., 414/662-3654, mid-Apr.–mid-Oct., $25). Country View offers a pool, playground, hot showers, and supplies. RVs can camp at the Wisconsin State Fairgrounds, west along I-94 in West Allis, but it's crowded and cacophonic with freeway traffic.

SPECTATOR SPORTS
The Brew Crew

Milwaukee remains something of an anomaly—the smallest of the small markets. And most markets of comparable size support just one major league franchise, not three, as Milwaukee does.

Miller Park, the Milwaukee Brewers' stadium, is absolutely magnificent. It has been described as the most perfect synthesis of retro and techno in the world—do check it out.

Baseball season runs early April–late September, and obtaining tickets is sometimes an issue, especially on weekends or whenever the archenemy Chicago Cubs come to town. This true-blue Brew Crew fan is happy to report that the Brouhas are perennially at least in the playoff hunt!

For ticket information, call 414/902-4400 or 800/933-7890, or log on to www.milwaukeebrewers.com.

Milwaukee Bucks

Except for an occasional woeful hiccup season, the Bucks are generally an upper-tier team in

© YUKI TAKANO

Miller Park, where there are no bad seats

THE BREW CREW

Not a baseball or even a sports fan? It matters not; a Brewers game is a cultural necessity. Consider the following:

TAILGATING

Nobody but nobody parties before a ball game like Wisconsinites, and Milwaukeeans (and Green Bay Packers fans) have perfected the pregame tailgate party. The requisite pregame attraction is the meal of beer, grilled brats, and potato salad, eaten while playing catch in the parking lot. (The *Guinness Book of Records* recognized the Brewers' erstwhile home, Milwaukee County Stadium, as the site of the world's largest tailgate party – the new Miller Park has nearly double the party area!) And the food inside the stadium is superb: NBC Sports commentator emeritus Bob Costas has deemed the stadium's bratwurst tops in the major leagues.

AND IT'S THE BRATWURST BY A, ER, NOSE . . .

But this is not the best reason to go to a game. The Brewers have the coolest stunt in pro sports: the **Sausage Race**. Grounds-crew members stick themselves into big, clunky sausage outfits – a hot dog, a Polish sausage, an Italian sausage, a bratwurst and a Mexican *chorizo* – and lumber around the field to a thrilling finish at home plate. It's so popular that opposing players beg for the opportunity to be a Milwaukee sausage for the day.

the NBA East. Tickets are sometimes hit or miss, but unless the Los Angeles Lakers are in town, you can usually land them. The Bucks offer great deals on their Bonus Nights, when certain seats (and not all of them at nosebleed elevation) are dirt cheap—by NBA standards, anyway. For ticket information, call 414/276-4545 or log on to www.bucks.com.

Accommodations

Most travelers will find lodging in downtown Milwaukee much better than they may have expected, given the historic grace of many buildings.

A good trick is to check the Milwaukee Convention and Visitors Bureau's website (www.visitmilwaukee.org) for constant package deals at local hotels, even in peak seasons.

Note that all rates given are merely the lowest on offer during peak season.

DOWNTOWN

Downtown Milwaukee is full of gracefully aging anachronisms, some wearier than others. One hint: Given Wisconsin's winter, you may wish to note whether your accommodation is linked via the downtown **skywalk system.**

Under $50

Downtown? Are you serious? There's a not-too-far-away hostel in Kettle Moraine State Forest in Eagle (262/495-8794, $25).

$100-150

Once again—good luck. First place to check is the 1920 art deco **Astor Hotel** (924 E. Juneau St., 414/271-4220 or 800/558-0200, www.theastorhotel.com, $99 and up), which has character (and characters strolling about) through and through, down to the original fixtures. It's amazing to hear the contrasting reviews from travelers on this one—some say they had no issues, others insist that it's basically ancient with a bucket of paint slopped on. Meaning—this is one of those places where you'd better be prepared to look at a number of rooms.

Just opening as this was being researched

was **Aloft** (1230 N. Old World 3rd St., 414/226-0122, www.aloftmilwaukeedowntown.com, $99–299), possibly the trendiest place in town—think minimalist boutique. Love the high ceilings and windows. Initial reports are that it has wonderful designs but to keep in mind it caters to a very young—code for boisterous—crowd. It does look smashing and no one disputes the friendliness of the staff.

About the same prices are at the no-it's-not-a-contradiction **Hotel of the Arts Downtown – Days Inn** (1840 N. 6th St., 414/265-5629, www.hotelofthearts.com, $99–179). Ditto with the to-the-sky ceilings and glass walls; the "arts" comes from rotating art exhibits and special package rates for many arts group performances in town. Free parking, unlike many other hotels in town.

The historic apartment/condo building housing **Knickerbocker on the Lake** (1028 E. Juneau Ave., 414/276-8500, www.knickerbockeronthelake.com, $125) overlooks Lake Michigan on a bluff just northeast of the funky Brady Street area—a great location. The lobby sports original marble floors and vaulted ceilings. Individually designed rooms are detailed with antiques, but also have modern amenities such as air-conditioning, Internet access, and more; some rooms have smashing deck views, fireplaces, or other extras. Well-regarded restaurants on-site. Now, honestly, some have found the place to be, well, let's say anachronistically funky, or are miffed that half the building is owner-occupied, but others say, "Hey, that's part of the charm."

The **Hilton Milwaukee City Center** (509 W. Wisconsin Ave., 414/271-7250 or 800/445-8667, www.hiltonmilwaukee.com, $139–240) is perhaps the best example of restored charm downtown. (And yet as of this edition they were still in the midst of another $19 million upgrade!) This incarnation features limestone ashlar, pink granite, and buff terra-cotta; it's Milwaukee's sole Roaring 1920s art deco–style hotel, right down to the geometric marble motifs in the lobby. If Lake Michigan's too chilly, fear not, for in addition to a recreation center, the hotel now sports an island-themed water recreation area with water slides and a real sand beach.

Over $150

Generating lots of well-earned buzz is **Hotel Metro** (411 E. Mason St., 414/272-1937, www.hotelmetro.com, $159 s, $259 d), a posh but cute boutique hotel in an erstwhile art deco office building. Glass sinks from Wisconsin's Kohler Company are among the noticeable design highlights of the 65 oversize suites, replete with steeping tubs or whirlpool baths; downstairs is a chic, seen-on-the-scene bar. The art deco stylings include environmentally friendly practices such as bamboo-wood floorings and wood from sustainable forests. It's also got one of the best cafés in Milwaukee. Among the service highlights—bicycles for guests! (But parking's 25 bucks.)

The granddaddy of Milwaukee hotels—called the "Grand Hotel" in fact—is the **Pfister** (424 E. Wisconsin Ave., 414/273-8222 or 800/558-8222, www.thepfisterhotel.com, $244 s, $264 d), built in 1893. This posh city-state–size behemoth oozes Victorian grandeur. The somewhat overwhelming lobby is done with such ornate intricacy that the hotel organizes regular tours of its displays of 19th-century art. Its state-of-the-art recreation facility outshines most health clubs. The laundry list of attractive features and service accolades could fill a phone book.

NORTH OF DOWNTOWN

Most lodging choices are found off I-43 along Port Washington Road. Best overall rooms and location are at the **Hilton Milwaukee River Inn** (4700 N. Port Washington Rd., 414/962-6040 or 800/445-8667, www.hilton.com, $101), with well-appointed one-bedroom rooms and a gorgeous, quiet river location. The excellent restaurant has an even better river view.

SOUTH OF DOWNTOWN

If you've got an early-morning flight or are just looking for something cheap close to downtown, head south. At least two dozen lodgings are scattered about, most along South Howell Avenue, West Layton Avenue, and South 13th Street, and all save one are neon-light chain options. Of these, close enough to get you off to your plane early is **Howard Johnson** (1716 W. Layton Ave., 414/282-7000 or 800/446-4656, $69).

Over $150

Any hotel that aims to, as they say, mingle business suits with biker leathers and boots is gonna raise a few eyebrows, but **The Iron Horse Hotel** (500 W. Florida St., 414/373-4766 or 888/543-4766, www.theironhorsehotel.com, $225 and up) is an I'll-be-damned near success in that. Honestly—a biker boutique hotel, and appropriately a stone's throw from the new Harley Davidson Museum. Its loft-style rooms are loaded to the gills with chic-but-tough (naturally) design and everything designed, indeed, for someone waltzing in with biker boots or a biz laptop (or, these days, both).

WEST OF DOWNTOWN

Those options listed here are nonchain lodgings inside the western suburbs. Follow the interstates in any direction for most chain options.

$50-100

Adjacent to the Ambassador Hotel, its sister hotel is the more business travel–oriented (but equally worthwhile) **Executive Inn** (2301 W. Wisconsin Ave., 414/342-0000, from $69). Note that it's a bit of a walk to the downtown area.

$100-150

For a B&B, try the 1897 Queen Anne **Acanthus Inn** (3009 W. Highland Blvd., 414/342-9788, $85–120), a 10-room historic mansion that has retained most of its original design. Period lighting and artwork add a nice touch.

Resurrected from the doldrums (and helping the neighborhood do the same) is the **Ambassador Hotel** (2308 W. Wisconsin Ave., 414/342-8400, www.ambassadormilwaukee.com, $129), just outside the western fringes of downtown. Inside a remodeled 1927 art deco structure ($12 million and counting sunk into upgrades, right down to the terra-cotta exterior), this place is historic meets state-of-the-art. I just love to sip a martini in its Envoy Lounge. Its only drawback: location, that is, not downtown.

Food

Gastronomically, you'll be surprised by Milwaukee—a pan-ethnic food heaven spanning the gamut from fish fries in cozy 120-year-old neighborhood taprooms to four-star prix fixe repasts in state-of-the-art gourmet restaurants. That is, no casseroles and meat-and-potatoes monotony here!

DOWNTOWN
Fish Fries

In Milwaukee, you'll find a fish fry everywhere—even at the chain fast-food drive-through and Miller Park during Friday-night Brewers games. Dozens of neighborhood taverns and bars still line up the plank seating and picnic tables with plastic coverings on Friday nights. The tables are arrayed with tartar sauce and maybe pickles (you'd better like coleslaw, because that's what you get as a side dish). Most fish fries come in under $10 for as much as you can stuff in. Or head for a Catholic church; Milwaukee's got 275 parishes, so you'll find a good one. I would head for Lakefront Brewery (1872 N. Commerce St., 414/372-8800, www.lakefrontbrewery. com), where its restaurant, **Palm Garden** (414/273-8300), has a wondrous Friday fish fry. Expect loads of varieties—including bluegill and perch—and they offer a combination platter. Better, it all comes with real-deal tater pancakes—like the old days—and rollicking polka music. Great fun!

FISH FRIES

Cuisine experience number one in Wisconsin is a Friday-night fish fry. Its exact origins are unknown, but it's certainly no coincidence that in a state contiguous to two Great Lakes, featuring 15,000 glacial pools, and undergoing waves of Catholic immigration (Catholics don't eat meat on Fridays during Lent), people would specialize in a Friday-night fish-eating outing.

Fish fries are myriad – it's so popular that even the local fast-food restaurants have them; the American Serbian Hall serves 2,500 people at a drive-through; Chinese, Mexican, and other ethnic restaurants get in on the act; and even Miller Park has fish fries at Friday Brewers games.

Everybody has an opinion on who has the best fish fry, but, truthfully, how many ways can you deep-fry a perch (or one of the other species variants – haddock, walleye pike, and cod)? (You can find broiled options at times.) I've always preferred church basements.

Generally set up as smorgasbords (sometimes including platefuls of chicken, too), the gluttonous feasts are served with slatherings of homemade tartar sauce and a relish tray or salad bar. The truly classic fish-fry joints are packed to the rafters by 5:30 p.m. – and some even have century-old planks and hall-style seating.

Consider yourself truly blessed if you get to experience a smelt fry. This longtime tavern tradition has pretty much disappeared; in the old days, smelt – milk-dipped, battered, and even pickled – were the thing.

Go immediately to http://classicwisconsin. com and hit the link to "Fish Fries" – a list of reviews is maintained.

Coffee and Tea Shops

Those with a java fixation should head immediately for the Brady Street area (http://bradystreet. org), where you'll find an inordinate number of coffee shops of every possible variety.

Watts Tea Shop (761 N. Jefferson St., 414/291-5120, 9 A.M.–4 P.M. daily, tea 2:30–4 P.M.) heads the list for afternoon tea and homemade everything, from scones to chicken salad. The shop is ensconced in the ritzy Watts store, purveyor of prohibitively fragile china, silver, and crystal.

Steak Houses

Staying in the Hilton Milwaukee City Center? Go no farther than your establishment's **Milwaukee Chop House** (633 N. 5th St., 414/226-2467, 5–10 P.M. Mon.–Sat., $18–68); in addition to luscious steaks, the bone-in rib eye is likely the best in Milwaukee.

Some Milwaukee friends howled to include **Butch's Clock Steak House and Martini Bar** (414/347-0142, dinner nightly except Sun., $20–40) for its throwback-to-bygone-days atmosphere.

Water Views

A lovely lake view comes at **Coast** (931 E. Wisconsin Ave., 414/727-5555, 11:30 A.M.–2 P.M. and 5–9 P.M. daily, $8–20), offering absolutely superb vistas of the Milwaukee Art Museum's new Calatrava addition and Lake Michigan. Pan-American in scope, the creative foods here are superbly made but, as with the comfortably designed interiors, unpretentious.

Seafood

Milwaukee's newest place for creative and solid seafood is **Bosley on Brady** (815 E. Brady St., 414/727-7975, 4–10 P.M. Tues.–Sat., till 8 P.M. Sun., $17–33)—seafood with a Key West attitude (it says).

Just north of downtown, the **◖ Roots Restaurant and Cellar** (1818 N. Hubbard St., 414/374-8480, brunch, lunch, and dinner, $10–45) is to be praised for following an ethos of sustainability in ingredients. Better, it's got phenomenal food—classy upstairs, more casual downstairs—and zillion-dollar deck views.

Fine Dining

Nouvelle cuisine is done magnificently at **C Sanford** (1547 N. Jackson St., 414/276-9608, 5:30–9 P.M. Mon.–Thurs., 5–10 P.M. Fri.–Sat., $30–70), one of the state's most original and respected innovators of cuisine and definitely a place to cook up an excuse for a splurge. It's feted by national foodie media and has garnered a wall full of awards—*Gourmet* magazine has more than once named it one of the United States' top 50 restaurants.

Oh, but then you'd miss **C Bacchus** (925 E. Wells St., 414/765-1166, 5:30–9 P.M. Mon.–Thurs., till 10 P.M. Fri., 5–10 P.M. Sat., $11–22), which rivals Sanford in quality, but is the antithesis of stuffy. Small plate menus in the bar are even as memorable as the dining room (which itself is lovely).

Something you'd never expect? How about a remarkable meal in a Milwaukee casino? Indeed, the elegant and creative fare at Potawatomi Bingo Casino's **C Dream Dance Steak** (1721 W. Canal St., 414/847-7883, 5–9 P.M. Tues.–Thurs., 5–10 P.M. Fri.–Sat., $26–39) is worth the trip even for the nonslots players. I was a bit miffed when they switched to a more carnivore-centric menu (hence, steak) in 2009, but it's still one of the best in town.

Vegetarian and Health Food

For takeaway health food, a number of co-ops and natural-foods stores are in the downtown area. This author's favorite is definitely the vegan-friendly **Riverwest Co-op** (733 E. Clarke St., 414/264-7933, 7 A.M.–9 P.M. Mon.–Fri., 8 A.M.–9 P.M. Sat.–Sun., $4–8), especially for a quick, healthy breakfast (and a smoothie in mid-morning). The veggie Korean bibimbop is damned fine, as are the Saturday night vegan pizzas.

Not a veggie restaurant per se, but a Slow Food movement follower is **Comet Café** (1947 N. Farwell Ave., 414/273-7677, 10:30 A.M.–10 P.M. Mon.–Fri., 9 A.M.–10 P.M. Sat.–Sun., $6–12). Your carnivore friend can have the traditional mom (well, Milwaukee mom, anyway) meatloaf with beer gravy, while your vegan friend can have the vegan Salisbury steak. Everyone's happy!

German

Rollicking, boisterous, and full of lederhosen, **Mader's** (1037 N. Old World 3rd St., 414/271-3377, 11:30 A.M.–9 P.M. Mon.–Thurs., till 10 P.M. Fri.–Sat., 10:30 A.M.–9 P.M. Sun., $18–24) has held its position as *the* German restaurant for the hoi polloi since 1902. Purists sometimes cringe at the over-the-top atmosphere (it's packed to the rafters with German knickknacks, not to mention tour buses idling outside), but the cheeriness is unvanquishable. Try the *knudel* (which doesn't taste as if it came out of a box), Rheinischer sauerbraten, oxtail soup, or Bavarian-style pork shank. Mader's also serves a Viennese brunch on Sunday.

However, **C Karl Ratzsch's Old World Restaurant** (320 E. Mason St., 414/276-2720, 11:30 A.M.–2 P.M. Wed.–Sat., 4:30–9 P.M. Mon.–Fri., 4:30–10 P.M. Sat., $8–30) is superbly realized and this author's fave Milwaukee German experience. This decidedly more upscale multiple-award winner is split into two levels. The lower level features a bar with an extensive stein collection and impressive dark interior woodwork. The menu is copious and decidedly carnivorous—sauerbraten, braised pork shank, *rouladen, käse spätzle,* special strudels, and even some vegetarian offerings. Not Teutonic-centered? Even the fish fry is among Milwaukee's best! A pianist tickles the keys nightly.

Italian

The city's best purveyor of *alta cucina* is **Osteria del Mondo** (1028 E. Juneau Ave., 414/291-3770, 5–10 P.M. Mon.–Thurs. and Sun., till 11 P.M. Fri.–Sat., $16–32). The restaurant also has an atmospheric Italian wine bar and thoroughly relaxing patio.

Mimma's Cafe (1307 E. Brady St., 414/271-7337, 5–11 P.M. Fri.–Sat., till 10 P.M. Sun.–Thurs., $11–19) constantly gets national write-ups for its cuisine—more than 50 varieties of pasta and weekly regional Italian specialties.

French

Milwaukee...French food? Absolutely. You can find diminutive eateries fashioned after casual Paris restaurants to Gallic-oriented hot spots whose fare and style rival those of much larger metropolises. Starting it all was Bartolotta's Lake Park Bistro north of Downtown.

The more casual but still creative **Coquette Cafe** (316 N. Milwaukee St., 414/291-2655, 11 A.M.–10 P.M. Mon.–Thurs., till 11 P.M. Fri., 5–11 P.M. Sat., $7–22), modeled after a French or Belgian brasserie, could best be called global French; it's not oxymoronic. The cuisine is hearty yet chic—a wonderful combination.

Latin American

Cempazuchi (1205 E. Brady St., 414/291-5233, 11:30 A.M.–10 P.M. Tues.–Sat., 5–9 P.M. Sun., $11–19) wavers not a bit from edition to edition. A pan-Mexican menu features superbly realized dishes, from succulent moles to light Veracruz seafood dishes.

Asian

First off, yes, yes, we all know Chinese food is better on the coasts. Yet after two decades of living in and traveling around China, this author was impressed by the cuisine at **Jing's** (207 E. Buffalo St., 414/271-7788, 11:30 A.M.–9:30 P.M. daily), a pan-Cathay place but with a specialty of the east and southeast provinces—think sweeter rather than hotter. But, as always, ask for the special menu or beg the owner or cook to give you the real-deal. Trust me.

Venerable **Izumi's** (2150 N. Prospect Ave., 414/271-5278, 11:30 A.M.–2 P.M. and 5–10 P.M. Mon.–Fri., 5–10:30 P.M. Sat., 4–9 P.M. Sun., $6–26), run by a Japanese chef/owner well trained by years of experience in Milwaukee Japanese eateries, tops the choices in town. The food here is impeccably well thought out and executed; this author's fave has to be its chef's remarkable take on the Milwaukee fish fry!

The upscale Asian fusion with a heady concentration of Japanese eclectic at ◖ **Umami Moto** (718 N. Milwaukee St., 414/727-9333, 11 A.M.–2 P.M. Mon.–Fri., 5–10 P.M. Mon.–Wed., 5–11 P.M. Thurs.–Sat., $13–25) is worth any trip. Extraordinary.

NORTH OF DOWNTOWN
Coffee Shops

The **Fuel Cafe** (818 E. Center St.)—great name—is exceedingly young, hip, and alternative; you'll find cribbage players and riot grrls. The decor is mismatched rummage-sale furniture with an arty flair, and the service bills itself as lousy. It isn't—and there's a great menu of coffee drinks, bakery items, salads, sandwiches, even Pop Tarts! Try the Kevorkian Krush: three shots of espresso and mocha.

Custard

Frozen custard is an absolute must of a Milwaukee cultural experience; the dozens of Milwaukee family custard stands were the inspiration for Big Al's Drive-In on the 1970s TV show *Happy Days*. In an informal poll, 20 questions determined a dozen different recommendations for where to experience frozen custard. Most often mentioned (but you really can't go wrong anywhere): **Kopp's** (5373 N. Port Washington Rd., 414/961-2006), which does custard so seriously that it has a flavor-of-the-day hotline.

Vegetarian and Health Food

A longtime standby for a low-key and decidedly body-friendly meal is **Beans and Barley** (1901 E. North Ave., 414/278-7878, 9 A.M.–9 P.M. Mon.–Sat., 9 A.M.–8 P.M. Sun., $4 and up). Very much a hip (though low-priced) eatery, it's housed in what smacks of an old grocery store warehouse encased in glass walls from an attached grocery and small bar. Everything from straight-up diner food to creative vegetarian is on the menu, with Indian and Southwestern options, as well as juices and smoothies.

Soul Food

Mr. Perkins (2001 W. Atkinson Ave., 414/447-6660, 5:30 A.M.–6 P.M. daily, $5 and up) is the place to go for soul food, with tons of down-home specialties—collard greens, catfish, chitterlings, fried apples, turkey legs, and the like, as well as homemade sweet potato pie and peach cobbler like you'll find nowhere else. The owner passed away in 2010 and Milwaukee diners will miss his presence; hopefully his restaurant can keep on going.

Fine Dining

Opened by a prominent local restaurateur and housed in an exquisitely restored century-old park pavilion, **C Bartolotta's Lake Park Bistro** (3133 E. Newberry Blvd., 414/962-6300, 11 A.M.–9 P.M. Mon.–Fri., 5–10 P.M. Sat., 11 A.M.–2 P.M. and 5–9 P.M. Sun., $7–12) has, with each edition of this guide, somehow managed to remain rock-solid as a dining highlight. Its French cuisine is superb and, if nothing else, the view from the drive along the lake is worth the time. It's a popular Sunday brunch spot. Best of all—the interiors are airy, offering plenty of privacy between tables.

A newer, fantastic restaurant in the far northern suburbs is **The Riversite** (11120 N. Mequon Rd., Mequon, 262/242-6050, 5–10 P.M. Mon.–Sat., $19–31), which features remarkable seasonal cuisines to supplement classics—excellent steak and lamb. They've also got *tapas* nights Tuesdays and special menus Thursdays. Of note here are the unusually capacious dining areas—a popular place but one where you're not elbow-to-elbow.

SOUTH OF DOWNTOWN
Fish Fries

For the most one-of-a-kind fry anywhere, head for **C American Serbian Hall** (53rd St. and Oklahoma Ave., 414/545-6030, $10), recognized as the largest in the nation. On Friday night, this hall serves more than a ton of Icelandic-style or Serbian baked fish to more than 2,500 people (make that two tons on Good Friday). The operation got so big that a drive-through has been added, which serves an additional 1,200 patrons. Unreal—watching cars backed up for miles while next to the complex waiting patrons (many chattering in Serbian) engage in fun-spirited bocce ball games.

This author loves the side dishes of beans and rice, *ensaladas,* and the Puerto Rican batter on the fish at the **United Community Center's Café el Sol** (1028 S. 9th St., 414/384-3100, $9).

Bistro

Amazing is the new neighborhood bistro **Pastiche** (3001 S. Kinnickinnic Ave., 414/482-1446, lunch Mon.–Fri., dinners Mon.–Sat., $12–25), a fusion of French Italian and even a bit of Iberian Peninsula. Reserve ahead, as it's tiny but worth the effort.

Custard

The south side has perhaps the most legendary custard in the city. An institution since the early 1940s is **Leon's** (3131 S. 27th St., 414/383-1784); it's got the best neon. The **Nite Owl Drive In** (830 E. Layton Ave., 414/483-2524) has been dishing up ice cream and doling out burgers by the same family for a half century; even Elvis loved to eat here.

Mexican

You'll find the most substantial Mexican menu (not to mention a most unpretentious atmosphere) at **Tres Hermanos** (1332 W. Lincoln Ave., 414/384-9050, 11 A.M.–10 P.M. Sun.–Thurs., 11 A.M.–midnight Fri.–Sat., $9–20), specializing in seafood in virtually every form—particularly a soup that'll knock your socks off. There's rootsy, live Tex Mex and Norteña music on weekends.

Milwaukee's southeast side is a haven for unpretentious authentic Mexican eateries; some Mexican grocers have lunch counters in the back or sell delectable tamales ready for takeout. **Conejito's** (4th and Virginia Sts., 11 A.M.–midnight daily, $4 and up) is a neighborhood bar-restaurant with authentic atmosphere and real-deal Mexican food. The same is true at **Jalisco's,** which has numerous locations (one at 2207 E. North Ave.) but whose original (9405 S. 27th St., 414/672-7070, $5), after perishing in a fire, has a slick new rebuild to go with its great food. Jalisco's restaurants (7 A.M.–3 A.M. Sun.–Thurs., 24 hours Fri.–Sat.) serve creative burritos as big as your head.

Serbian

Enjoy top-notch Serbian food in a delightful Old World atmosphere at 【 **Three Brothers** (2414 S. St. Clair St., Bay View, 414/481-7530, 11:30 A.M.–2:30 P.M. Tues.–Fri., 5–10 P.M. Tues.–Sun., $11 and up). The 1897 turreted brick corner house, an original Schlitz brewery beer parlor, was turned into a restaurant by the present owner's father, a Serbian wine merchant. Not much has changed—the high paneled ceilings, original wood, dusty bottles on the bar, mirrors, and mismatched tables and chairs remain. All of it is charming. The food is heavy on pork and chicken, with lots of *paprikash* and stuffed cabbage. The signature entrée is *burek*, a filled phyllo dough concoction the size of a radial tire; you wait a half hour for this one. The restaurateurs' daughter recently added vegetarian options! The restaurant is difficult to find— this neighborhood is the real Milwaukee—you'll likely wind up asking for directions from a horseshoe club outside a local tavern.

One little-known place for Serbian in south Milwaukee is **Fritz's Pub** (20th St. and Oklahoma Ave., 10 A.M.–1 A.M. Mon.–Tues., 7 A.M.–1 A.M. Wed.–Sat.), with a decent selection of Serbian-style sandwiches.

Polish

Polonez (4016 S. Packard Ave., St. Francis, 414/482-0080, 11 A.M.–3 P.M. Tues.–Fri., 5–9 P.M. Tues.–Sat., 11 A.M.–8 P.M. Sun., $5–17) is a longtime Milwaukee favorite. Since previous editions of this guide, it has transformed geographically and atmospherically— it's now a white-tableclothed fine-dining (but very casual in feeling) experience. The pierogi and cutlets are phenomenal, as is the very good *czarnina* (a raisin soup with duck stock, duck blood, and fruits—seven soups daily). The Sunday brunch is unrivaled.

Indian

Rock-bottom pricing (most of the million choices under $7), outstanding takeout, and mesmerizing smells—you can't beat local unknown **Bombay Sweets** (3401 S. 13th St., 414/383-3553, 11 A.M.–8 P.M. daily).

WEST OF DOWNTOWN

Fish Fries

A good bet is **Tanner Paull Restaurant** (6922 W. Orchard St., 414/476-5701, 4–9 P.M. Fri., $9), in an American Legion Post (how cool!). A half ear of corn is among the unique sides at this place, the first to offer all-you-can-ram-in fish fry in the Beer City.

Steak Houses

【 **Five O'Clock Club** (2416 W. State St., 414/342-3553, 5:30–9:30 P.M. Tues.–Sat., $19–32) has been around forever and is so popular for steaks you absolutely need a reservation. It has the largest portions in town, all simmered in the eatery's legendary meat juice, and old-fashioned touches such as relish trays, but some have opined that its quality doesn't always match its legendary tradition.

Some locals say the best steaks aren't even in Milwaukee itself but in Wauwatosa at **Mr. B's, a Bartolotta Steak House** (17700 W. Capitol Dr., Wauwatosa, 262/790-7005, 5:30–9:30 P.M. Mon.–Sat., 5:30–8 P.M. Sun., $16–37), run by one of Milwaukee's most successful restaurateurs. The steaks are grilled over hardwoods; Italian entrées are also available.

Italian

Hmm, the name Bartolotta in Wauwatosa seems to be omnipresent. Yes, 【 **Ristorante Bartolotta** (7616 W. State St., Wauwatosa, 414/771-9710, 5:30–9:30 P.M. Mon.–Thurs., 5–10 P.M. Fri.–Sat., 5–8:30 P.M. Sun., $16–28) is a warm and friendly eatery run by a legendary Milwaukee restaurateur—definitely worth the trip.

Vegetarian

Loads of restaurants in Milwaukee can accommodate vegetarians, but we all know that that generally means a couple of pasta entrées or something done the same way only they don't throw in the meat. This author's favorite vegetarian restaurant (it's also vegan friendly) is far west of downtown in Brookfield, but worth the drive; it's **Café Manna** (3815 North

Brookfield Rd., Brookfield, 11 A.M.–9 P.M. Mon.–Sat., $6–15). This author would die right now for their Jamaican lentil burger (and he is an avowed carnivore).

Information and Transportation

INFORMATION
Visit Milwaukee (400 W. Wisconsin Ave., 414/908-6205 or 800/554-1448, www.visitmilwaukee.org, 8 A.M.–5 P.M. Mon.–Fri., 9 A.M.–2 P.M. Sat. in summer, weekdays only the rest of the year) is in the Frontier Airlines Center. Additional offices are at Mitchell International Airport (414/747-4808) and by Discovery World at Pier Wisconsin (414/273-3950).

Milwaukee LGBT Center (315 W. Court St., 414/271-2656, www.mkelgbt.org) is a good local organization for the lesbian, gay, bi, and transgendered community.

The local sales tax totals out at 5.6 percent. You'll pay a 9 percent tax on hotel rooms in addition to the sales tax, 3 percent on car rentals, and a 0.025 percent tax on food and beverage purchases.

Media
The *Milwaukee Journal-Sentinel* is a morning daily. The Friday paper has a complete listing of weekend cultural events, music, clubs, and movies. Fans of alternative views pick up weekly copies of the free *Shepherd Express,* which is also a good source of local arts and nightlife info. The local monthly repository of everything Milwaukee is *Milwaukee Magazine.* For online help, check www.onmilwaukee.com, generally the best of the half dozen or so web guides.

Listen to the eclectic, student-run **WMSE** at 91.7 FM—it might surprise you. Local standby has always been **WTMJ** (620 AM) for news and talk radio.

Bookstores
The bookstores-per-capita quotient is pretty high here. Two blocks north of Grand Avenue Mall, **Renaissance Book Shop** (834 N. Plankinton Ave., 414/271-6850) has an amazing six stories of books. It even has a second place at the airport!

GETTING THERE
By Air
General Mitchell International Airport (5300 S. Howell Ave., 414/747-5300, www.mitchellairport.com) is southeast of downtown, near Cudahy. It's best reached by traveling I-94 south and following the signs. From downtown, head south on 6th Street North; it should get you to WI 38 (Howell Avenue). Nearly 50 cities are reached direct from Milwaukee; more than 235 flights per day depart.

Shed a tear for Milwaukee-based Midwest Airlines, which in 2010 was taken over by **Frontier Airlines** (800/432-1359, www.frontierairlines.com). Oh, it's still fine but gone are the double-wide leather seats among other amazing amenities; at least they kept the famed baked-on-board cookies. Nonstop flights are available to all major and minor airports in the nation. The airline offers excellent package deals including airfare, car rental, and accommodations from a dozen major U.S. cities.

Milwaukee County Transit System **buses** run to the airport; almost any bus can start you on your way if you ask the driver for transfer help. A taxi from downtown costs $15–20 and takes 20 minutes. Airport limousines cost half that.

For all ground transportation questions, call the airport's hotline, 414/747-5308.

By Bus
Greyhound (414/272-9949) is at the Amtrak station. Buses leave up to a dozen times daily for Chicago; buses also go to Minneapolis, Madison, and certain points in central

Wisconsin. A few other intercity coaches have offered service to similar areas, but their consistency in scheduling leaves much to be desired.

Up the street from the Greyhound station is the **Badger Bus** (635 N. James Lovell St., 414/276-7490). Buses leave this location for Madison nine times daily (or nightly, depending on season). Badger Bus also serves Mitchell Field International Airport and heads for Minneapolis and St. Paul when universities are in session.

The Southwest Airlines of bus service— **MegaBus** (http://us.megabus.com)—runs from the bus center in Milwaukee to Chicago, as well as Minneapolis. Fares are around sixteen bucks to Chicago, but there are no ticket offices, terminals, or sometimes even service. It is imperative to check the website for pick-up information.

By Train

Amtrak service between Milwaukee and Chicago is oft-debated but never seems to die. With a multimillion dollar facelift to its terminal, it looks to be good to go for a long time.

More than a half-dozen trains operate daily, with hefty fares of $22 one-way on off-peak weekdays, $32 on the weekend. Service to Minneapolis is less imperiled; one train still leaves daily. The Amtrak station (433 W. St. Paul Ave., 414/271-9037) also houses Greyhound.

Discussions have been endless about whether to link Chicago's Metra service through Kenosha and Racine to Milwaukee and, possibly, outlying suburbs; it would be slower than Amtrak but also much cheaper. Other experimental train service west toward Madison is supposedly set for 2013; we'll see.

By Boat

High-speed ferry service from Milwaukee to Muskegon, Michigan, saves you a, well, boatload of hassle with **Lake Express** (866/914-1010, www.lake-express.com). Three round-trips make the zippy 2.5-hour run across the lake: leaving Milwaukee at 6 A.M., 12:30 P.M., and 7 P.M. Rates (one-way/round-trip) are not cheap but the service is outstanding: $85/129 adults, $25/45 children under 17, $92 for your car. Service starts in early May and tapers off in late October. The terminal is in Milwaukee's south-side neighborhood of Bay View. A passenger-only hovercraft service between Milwaukee and Chicago, with a possible stop in Racine, has been proposed from this new pier.

GETTING AROUND
Taxis

Taxis are all metered and have a usual drop fare of around $3 for the first mile and about $1.50 for each additional. **American United Taxicab** (414/220-5010) is the state's largest operation and has GPS-aided guidance.

Buses

The **Milwaukee County Transit System** (414/344-6711, www.ridemcts.com) operates loads of buses. (Save 25 percent by buying a 10-pack of tickets.) The system also has good options for free trolley loops around downtown in summer.

Rental Cars

Every major rental-car agency is represented at Mitchell International Airport and many have a half dozen or so representatives throughout the city. There is a 3 percent tax on car rentals.

Organized Tours

Increasingly popular are Milwaukee River (and occasionally Lake Michigan harbor) cabin cruiser tours, some also offering dining cruises.

The venerable *Iroquois* boat tours of Milwaukee Boat Lines (414/294-9450, www.mkeboat.com, 1 P.M. and 3 P.M. Sat.–Sun., 1 P.M. Mon.–Fri. June–Aug., $14 adults) departs from the Clybourn Street Bridge on the west bank of the Milwaukee River and offers scenic narrated tours. Sporadic evening tours are also offered June–September.

Riverwalk Boat Tours and Rental (Pere Marquette Park, 414/283-9999, www.riverwalkboats.com) offers a number of tours, most of them themed for imbibing, including a weekend brewery tour taking in three local microbreweries ($25). You can also rent your own two-person boat ($15 per hour) or pontoon boat ($55 per hour).

At the Municipal Pier, south of the Milwaukee Art Museum, the replica 19th-century schooner **Denis Sullivan** (414/276-7700, www.discovery-world.org) is Wisconsin through and through, with all lumber culled from northern Wisconsin forests; it is more than 130 feet long with three 95-foot native white pine masts. Technically it's a floating classroom, part of the new non-profit Pier Wisconsin project, but its pricey tours ($25 children, $50–55 adults) are available to anyone interested in maritime history and ecology. They're also jaw-droppingly spectacular, not to mention better-than-any-book

educational. Sailing schedules vary year to year (and by season).

You can do it yourself by hopping aboard an old-fashioned **trolley** (free!) from Milwaukee County Transit System (414/344-6711, www.ridemcts.com). Schedules have varied quite a bit, but service has generally been Wednesday–Sunday, summer only. Note that Summerfest, Brewers games, and other sights outside the downtown are not served (the city has special summer shuttles for these).

Perhaps the most Milwaukee way to tour the city would be aboard a rumbling Harley-Davidson. Organized group tours no longer operate, but **House of Harley** (6221 W. Layton Ave., 414/282-2211, www.houseofharley.com) has the blessings of Harley-Davidson to rent brand-new motorcycles; better, they can offer classes on how to ride 'em too.

Vicinity of Milwaukee

TEN CHIMNEYS

A mere 15-minute drive west of downtown Milwaukee, close to Waukesha, brings you to "Broadway's Retreat" in the Midwest: **Ten Chimneys** (S43 W31575 Depot Rd., Genesee Depot, 262/968-4161, www.tenchimneys.org), the erstwhile home of the Great White Way's legendary Alfred Lunt and Lynn Fontaine. From its creation as a haven for artists in the 1920s, it welcomed legions of actors, writers, singers, and film stars, all seeking spiritual rejuvenation in a bucolic retreat. Having fallen into disrepair, it was nearly razed before an extraordinary renovation effort saved it. The 2003 reopening gave the public a jaw-dropping view of an entirely unknown piece of U.S. cultural history. Inside, the exquisite detailing and furnishings are almost an afterthought, so caught up are visitors by mementos sent to Fontaine and Lunt from Helen Hayes, Noel Coward, and Charlie Chaplin, among others. The sublime 18-room main house sits perched above 60 acres of rolling moraine topography; nearby are a "quaint" eight-room cottage and

Swedish-style log cabin, and a dozen other buildings. Not simply a memorial to a bygone era, Ten Chimneys is a living artists' retreat again—sponsoring workshops, collaborations, teacher-training programs, and public classes.

Tours are available, but don't count on an impromptu visit; officially it's open to the public 10 A.M.–4 P.M. Tuesday–Saturday May–October, but if a special event is taking place you may not get in. The place is also pricey: $35 for a full estate tour, $30 for a main house tour only.

◖ CEDARBURG

What candy-facade original-13-colony spots such as Williamsburg are to the East Coast, Cedarburg is to Old World Wisconsin. It's been seemingly preserved in a time vacuum, thanks to local residents who successfully fought off wholesale architectural devastation from an invasion of Milwaukeeans looking for an easy commute. Cedarburg, about a half hour north of downtown Milwaukee, was originally populated by German (and a few

British) immigrants, who hacked a community out of a forest and built numerous mills along Cedar Creek, which bisects the tiny community, including the only worsted wool mill and factory in what was then considered the West. Those mills, and more than 100 other original Cream City–brick buildings, have been painstakingly restored into the state's most concentrated stretch of antiques dealers, shops, galleries, bed-and-breakfasts, and proper little restaurants. Stop at the visitors center for an excellent booklet on historic-structure walking tours.

The heart and soul of the town is **Cedar Creek Settlement,** an antebellum foundation mill once the village's center of activity but now a several-blocks-long hodgepodge of shops, restaurants, and galleries. The **Cedar Creek Winery** (262/377-8020, 10 A.M.–5 P.M. Mon.–Sat., 11 A.M.–5 P.M. Sun.) is also on the premises; tours take in the aging cellars. West of the main drag (Washington Road), Portland Road features one of the original structures in Cedarburg, the enormous, five-story **Cedarburg Mill,** now home to yet another antique shop. Along Riveredge Drive is the **Brewery Works** (262/377-8230, 1–4 P.M. Wed.–Sun.), a restored 1840s brewery housing the Ozaukee County Art Center.

Three miles north of town is the last extant **covered bridge** in the state, dating from 1876; to get there, head to the WI 143/60 junction on Washington Avenue. This is an excellent bike tour! Southeast of Cedarburg via Hamilton Road is the original settlement of **Hamilton,** with another picturesque creekside mill.

The town has a great **Performing Arts Center** (W68 N611 Evergreen Blvd., 262/376-6161), with a full slate of visiting artists and performances. **Cedarburg Cultural Center** (W62 N546 Washington Ave., 262/375-3676) has regular jazz and folk performances along with art exhibits. The local **visitors center** (262/377-9620 or 800/237-2874, www.cedarburg.org) is here; very friendly and useful staffers will point you in the right direction. A small **general store museum** is also in the complex.

Gorgeous lodging options exist; nobody comes here to stay in a motel. The **Stagecoach Inn and Weber Haus Annex** (W61 N520 Washington Ave., 262/375-0208 or 888/375-0208, www.stagecoach-inn-wi. com, $95–150) is a historic inn and pub on the old Milwaukee–Green Bay stagecoach line. Nine lovely rooms are in the main inn; three are in a restored 1847 frame building across the street where you can stroll in a private garden. Six suites have whirlpools; two have gas fireplaces. Rumors say a benign, black-garbed apparition wafts through the inn.

For food, you can get classic Wisconsin German tavern fare or the casually upscale cuisine found at most gentrified enclaves such as this. It's a chichi name and menu at **Cream and Crepe Café** (Cedar Creek Settlement, 262/377-0900, 10 A.M.–8 P.M. Tues.–Sat., 10 A.M.–5 P.M. Sun.–Mon., $4–10), but the crepes are delectable, as is the creekside dining area.

Galioto's Twelve21 (1221 Wauwatosa Rd., 262/377-8085, 11 A.M.–2 P.M. Mon.–Fri., 5–9 P.M. Mon.–Thurs., 5–10 P.M. Fri.–Sat., 4–8 P.M. Sun., $7–26) is a smashing new eatery housed in an erstwhile classic Wisconsin country tavern. The superb renovation features original beams and flickering flames in an original fireplace. The well-done dishes focus on creative comfort food—the pork chops are legendary.

Landmark Tours (P.O. Box 771, Cedarburg, WI 53012, 262/375-1426) leads group tours through Cedarburg and Ozaukee County.

PORT WASHINGTON

Forty minutes north of Milwaukee is Port Washington, a littoral Lake Michigan community that links up with east-central Wisconsin. Port Washington put itself into the history books with its quixotic anti–Civil War draft riots, when mobs took over the courthouse and trained a cannon on the lakefront until the army showed up and quelled the disturbance. Part Great Lake fishing town and part preserved antebellum anachronism, Port Washington, a declination backing off the lake, is known for its enormous downtown **marina** and fishing

© THOMAS HUHTI

Port Washington's Lake Michigan shoreline

charters. You can stroll along the breakers, snapping shots of the art deco **lighthouse,** now a historical museum. Another renovated lighthouse is home to the **Port Washington Historical Society Museum** (311 Johnson St., 262/284-7240, 1–4 P.M. in the summer). The **Eghart House** (1–4 P.M. in the summer) on Grand Avenue at the library is done up in turn-of-the-20th-century style. Also along Grand Avenue, what's known as the **Pebble House,** site of a tourist center, was painstakingly arranged of stones scavenged from the beaches along the lake. Franklin Street, dominated by the thrusting spire of St. Mary's Church and various castellated building tops, rates as one of the most small town–like of any of the Lake Michigan coastal towns. Upper City Park, on a bluff overlooking the water, affords wondrous views of the lake and horizon.

Port Washington claims to hold the **world's largest fish fry** annually on the third Saturday of July, though it's got a couple of in-state rivals for that title.

The city offers lots of B&Bs, including the huge shingle Victorian **Port Washington Inn** (308 W. Washington St., 877/794-1903, http://port-washington-inn.com, from $125), a gorgeous structure that gets kudos for its environmentally sound practices.

Plenty of good food is available in Port Washington—every place will have a decent fish selection, if not a particular specialty. **Bernie's Fine Meats Market** (119 N. Franklin St., 262/284-4511, 9:30 A.M.–5:30 P.M. Mon.–Fri., 9:30 A.M.–4 P.M. Sat.) is a good place to scout out Wisconsin-style smoked meats—especially sausage varieties.

Farther north is **Harrington Beach State Park** (262/285-3015), unknown to most outside of the Milwaukee area, which is too bad. It's got great lake and limestone bluff views, an abandoned limestone quarry and quarry lake, and hiking trails, some a bit treacherous. A new campground here relieves a serious need for public camping along Lake Michigan's southern shoreline.

MADISON

Perhaps the best way to explain the Mad City: Madison is populated by droves of people who came for college and never left (this humble author included). And those who left probably only did so because of the winters.

A Wisconsin governor's aide once quipped, "Madison is 60 square miles surrounded by reality." His precision is inarguable and the quote has become a proud bumper-sticker slogan in the city. Madison may be reminiscent of other leftist hot spots such as Berkeley and Ann Arbor, but the salad days of revolution are long gone. Financial institutions are rather more conspicuous than cubbyhole political storefronts, and corpulent lobbyists seem to outnumber radicals. The student population rarely raises a fuss anymore, unless to over-celebrate UW sports teams' championships or holidays

in beer-soaked student bacchanalia (tear gas for drinking, not for war protesting).

Still, the capital is a wacky place. Octogenarian Progressives mingle with aging hippies and legions of university professors, and corporate and Capitol yuppies don't seem out of place. The student-body omnipresence is a given—everyone in Madison is considered a de facto student anyway. It remains the "Madtown"—one agreeable, engaging, oddball mix. (Milwaukeeans'—nay, much of the rest of the state's—stereotype of Madison is of a time-warp bunch of radicals gone touchy-feely who think they live at the center of the universe.)

No guidebook hype—Madison is a lovely town, ensconced erratically on an isthmus between two lakes. You'll find endless greenery, a

© THOMAS HUHTI

HIGHLIGHTS

LOOK FOR ◖ TO FIND RECOMMENDED SIGHTS, ACTIVITIES, DINING, AND LODGING.

◖ **State Capitol:** Similarities in size and design were a deliberate in-your-face to the powers that be in D.C. (page 71).

◖ **Monona Terrace:** This striking white edifice melds the land and water distinctly (page 71).

◖ **University of Wisconsin-Madison Campus:** Here you'll find a weekend's worth of museums; the Memorial Union, a nightlife institution in the Mad City; gorgeous lakeside trails; and the best napping spots (page 74)!

◖ **University of Wisconsin Arboretum:** The entire city population gets its blood working here walking and jogging, though few realize it's a restoration project to re-create the landscape of the state in its virgin form (page 76).

◖ **National Mustard Museum:** Though tongue-in-cheek, this is a highly serious foodie heaven (page 77).

◖ **Olbrich Botanical Gardens:** These mammoth, magnificent gardens feature a gorgeous Thai pavilion, donated in part by the royal family of Thailand, under which to sit and gaze at the beauty (page 77).

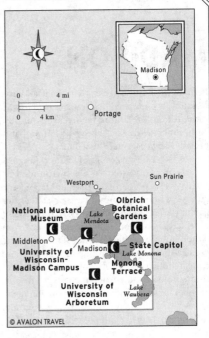

low-key downtown, a laid-back way of life, and a populace appreciably content if not downright enjoying themselves. Civic pride runneth over. No surprise, then, that after years of being a bridesmaid, Madison was finally named by *Money* magazine in 1996 as the best place to live in America; it would repeat the honor two years later. (Just google "Madison" and "best" and see how many media have celebrated the city.)

HISTORY

Perhaps appropriately for such an enclave of iconoclasm, Madison did not even exist when it was picked as the capital site. Judge James Duane Doty lured legislators away from the original capital—tiny Belmont—with offers of free land in what were no doubt termed lush

river valleys to the northeast. Territorial legislators, probably dismayed by the isolation of Belmont, fell over themselves to pass the vote. Not one white person lived in the Madison area at the time.

Four Lakes

Originally dubbed "Taychopera" (Four Lakes), these marshy lowlands were home to encampments of Winnebago Indians. The first whites trekking through the area—most heading for lead mines in the southwest—remarked upon it in journals as a preternaturally beautiful, if wild, location. One early soldier wrote that "the country . . . is not fit for any civilized nation of people to inhabit. It appears that the Almighty intended it for the children of the forest."

MADISON

Madison's Lake Monona in the morning

© THOMAS HUHTI

It remained that way until 1837, when a solitary family set up a rough log inn for workers who arrived to start construction on the Capitol. (Bars doubled as the first churches, this being Wisconsin.)

After Statehood

In 1848, the territory became a state, just as finishing touches were being added to the Capitol; there was still not even a semblance of established roads. A munificent Milwaukee millionaire, Leonard Farwell, showed up and, most likely aghast at the beastly conditions, started on major infrastructure work.

Civil War spending expanded the city rapidly; afterwards, Madison had nearly 500 factories of all sorts. By the 20th century, more than 19,000 inhabitants lived in Madison. Still, despite the numbers, wild animals gamboled through the remaining thickets, and one contemporary Eastern visitor remarked that Madison resembled nothing much more than an exaggerated village, down to a village's mannerisms and conduct.

20th Century

One historian said of most of Madison's past, "The historian finds little of stirring interest; and that little almost always the reflex of the legislature." From the boozy, brawling first legislators, Madison has always had a sideshow accompaniment to its vast cultural arenas. This was perhaps never more manifest than in the 1960s, during implosions over the Vietnam War, when Madison truly became the Mad City—one of the nation's foremost leftist concentrations.

Overtones of radicalism still exist, but the city really doesn't seem to get *too* worked up about much anymore. Everyone's too busy biking around the lakes or people-watching on State Street (if not hustling for that graduate seminar).

PLANNING YOUR TIME

The Mad City makes for a fabulous weekend. Base yourself downtown and spend the first day walking between Lakes Monona and Mendota (i.e., the Monona Terrace to

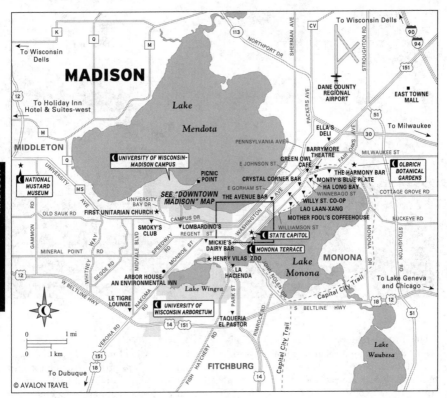

the Capitol to the University of Wisconsin via State Street), and roll to the University of Wisconsin Arboretum and/or the Olbrich Botanical Gardens the second day. If you're rolling through here to otherwheres or only have a day, any of the above make(s) for a great stop-off and leg stretch (you'll also find much better food in downtown Madison than anywhere on an interstate!).

ORIENTATION

You will get lost; trust me. The downtown spreads along a narrow isthmus between two large lakes, which doesn't bode well for traffic (though you're always within eight blocks of lakeside prettiness, I guess).

Given the topography, traffic can be maddeningly circuitous. Always keep an eye on

the Capitol. Also keep in mind that east and west in street names are approximations—it's actually closer to northeast and southwest. *All east-west streets use the Capitol as the dividing point.*

The main thoroughfare down the throat of the isthmus is East Washington Avenue (U.S. 151); it leads directly to, and then around, the massive state Capitol, which is connected to the university by State Street.

The main artery between east and west Madison is the white-knuckled swells of the Beltline—U.S. 12/14 and 151/18 (or any combination thereof). It's unlikely you'll be able to avoid the Beltline altogether; just avoid rush-hour peaks. (A Windy City bro-in-law has said of it, "The only place where Madison traffic ever rivals Chicago's.")

Like everywhere else, parking sucks here. Either not enough or expensive; worse, parking sentinels are thought to be omniscient.

Unlike Milwaukee, *nobody*—drivers, bikers, pedestrians—follows the laws (but we claim we do). Pay attention out there!

Sights

DOWNTOWN AND ISTHMUS
State Capitol

Standing atop the most prominent aerie in Madison, the stately white bethel granite Wisconsin State Capitol (2 E. Main St., 608/266-0382, www.doa.state.wi.us) is the largest in the country and definitely one of the most magnificent. Designed by George Pesi, who also designed the New York Stock Exchange, it sits a stately 300 feet above an already high moraine—a beacon for lost out-of-towners (and a 25-year pain in the butt for yours truly to bike up each morning). The current building (the first two burned) was constructed over 11 years and cost $7.25 million—$0.25 per state resident per year of construction. (Never again would something like this be possible on the public nickel.) It resembles the nation's Capitol from afar: The powers that be in D.C. took this as a sign of homage but then realized plans were to build Wisconsin's Capitol taller than D.C.'s. So ours had to become shorter, though its volume is greater (holds more beer, of course). The interior features 43 different types of stone from eight states and six foreign countries, including semiprecious marble nonexistent today. The mosaics, imported and domestic hand-carved furniture, massive murals, and hand-stenciling make the building priceless. Interesting Capitol tidbit: The Capitol always wins local surveys for cleanest public bathrooms. If you don't arrive in time for a tour, the observation deck is also generally open in summer, with superb views! The building is open 8 A.M.–6 P.M., with free tours hourly 9–11 A.M. and 1–3 P.M. Monday–Saturday, Sunday also in summer.

Monona Terrace

Garish white whale or architectural cornerstone? You be the judge of Monona Terrace Community and Convention Center (1 John Nolen Dr., 608/261-4000, www.mononaterrace.com). Madisonians may never come to terms with their decades-old love-hate relationship with it. Supporters hoped that the structure, which some call Frank Lloyd Wright's masterpiece, partially atop Lake Monona on pylons, would draw attention (and moneyed conventioneers) to Madison; critics moaned that it was yet another civic white elephant—and a monument to someone they considered an egotistical SOB.

Wright's hoped-for design included much, much more than was finally constructed, and only three years after it opened its structures already required repairs. (Sorry, but that's *so*

© THOMAS HUHTI

Wisconsin's grand capitol

MADISON

MADISON

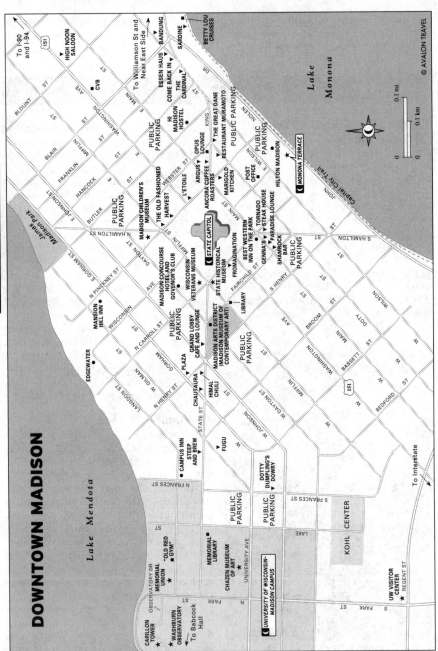

DOWNTOWN MADISON

© AVALON TRAVEL

© THOMAS HUHTI

Monona Terrace, designed by Frank Lloyd Wright

Frank Lloyd Wright, even admirers would have to admit!) But even opponents admit that nothing like it exists in a city of comparative size. Most visitors simply wander about, taking in the views; a photography gallery highlighting Wright's work is inside, as is the **Madison Sports Hall of Fame.** If you get a chance, get a glimpse of it from a canoe in the early morning sun. Wow.

The building is open 8 A.M.–5 P.M. daily. The rooftop garden area is open till 10 P.M. Sunday–Thursday, till midnight Friday and Saturday. Guided tours ($3) are available at 1 P.M. daily. Free concerts are offered often during summer.

State Street and Museum Mile

Bookended by the Capitol on one end and the university on the other, State Street is a quasi-pedestrian mall full of shops, boutiques, coffeehouses, restaurants, bookstores, museums, cultural centers, and much of the downtown's character. People-watching along these seven blocks is a long-standing tradition.

The **Madison Arts District** takes up the 100 block of State Street along with a few blocks on either side of it for a zone of galleries, art spaces, museums, and performance venues. It was brought about by the amazingly generous donation of $50 million—later increased—by a local Madtown philanthropist. This being Madison, it didn't come without vocal opponents. Did Madison really need an arts venue for wine-sipping yuppies? The original plans had, quite unbelievably, planned on gutting the memorable Oscar Mayer Theater inside the Civic Center. The plans were later scaled back, but not enough for some.

Six museums and a couple of other highlights lie along State Street and Capitol Square. On the State Street corner of Capitol Square, the **State Historical Museum** (30 N. Carroll St., 608/264-6555, www.wisconsinhistory.org, 9 A.M.–4 P.M. Tues.–Sat., $4) lets you stroll through commendable, challenging permanent multimedia exhibits that detail the state's geological, Native American, and European settlement history. The lower level is a gallery area featuring revolving exhibits; three more floors feature boatloads of historic exhibits. This museum also has unquestionably the best bookstore for Wisconsin titles.

Kitty-corner from the historical museum, the **Wisconsin Veterans Museum** (30 W. Mifflin St., 608/267-1799, http://museum. dva.state.wi.us, 9 A.M.–4:30 P.M. Mon.–Sat. year-round and noon–4 P.M. Sun. Apr.–Sept., free) has two impressive main galleries of exhibits, dioramas, and extensive holdings tracing Wisconsin's involvement in wars from the Civil War to the Persian Gulf conflict. Even Mexican border campaigns are detailed. Main attractions are the mock-ups of battles and cool aircraft hovering overhead. Children will love the submarine periscope sticking out of the gallery's roof, which allows for a true panoramic view of downtown Madison.

The kid-centric **Madison Children's Museum** (100 N. Hamilton St., 608/256-6445, www.madisonchildrensmuseum.org, 9:30 A.M.–5 P.M. daily, till 8 P.M. Thurs., $7) two blocks east is housed in an old triangular corner edifice. After a couple years of construction, it opened in its new home, in 2010, and features state-of-the-art and cutting edge everything—quite amazing for a city of *any* size. (And yes, this being Madison, it's all recycled, earth-friendly, etc.) Visitors can romp through and get their hands on a variety of traditional and computer-oriented activities. The kid-centered rooftop park is good for anyone!

One block nearer to the university from the historical society museum is the distinctive Madison Civic Center and, within it, the **Madison Museum of Contemporary Art** (211 State St., 608/257-0158, www.mmoca. org, noon–5 P.M. Tues.–Thurs., till 8 P.M. most Fri., 10 A.M.–8 P.M. Sat., noon–5 P.M. Sun., free). The prominent gallery window is always attracting the attention of passersby, most staring quizzically at the art or, occasionally, the performance artist trapped inside. The small galleries are interspersed through three floors of the civic center complex and feature contemporary art—mostly paintings and some photography. A good gift shop is here.

The complex also houses the Overture Center for the Arts, which hosts modern and classical music, touring shows, and Broadway plays. The Isthmus Playhouse inside is a thrust-stage venue.

The remaining museums operate under the auspices of the University of Wisconsin. The first one listed here is only one block off the end of State Street. As State Street runs its final block and melds with the Library Mall, walk past the bookstore and a church and then bear left down a cul-de-sac. The **Chazen Museum of Art** (800 University Ave., 608/263-2246, http://chazen.wisc.edu, 9 A.M.–5 P.M. Tues.– Fri., 11 A.M.–5 P.M. Sat.–Sun., free) contains almost 16,000 holdings, the oldest dating from 2300 B.C. The open, airy design features several levels of permanent collections, including Egyptian and Greek porcelain, Japanese prints, Indian figurines, Russian icons, early European and American art, and a somewhat moody roomful of Renaissance church art. The top floor showcases modern American artists. At the time of writing, the already-wonderful museum was set to unveil its massive $43-million renovation, which would double the exhibition space (the new design itself looks smashing).

University of Wisconsin-Madison Campus

Bascom Hill on the other end of State Street affords a view similar to the one from the State Capitol rise. Crowning this is Bascom Hall, one of the original buildings of the university, established in 1848. North Hall, down the hill toward the lake, was the campus's original building and served until 1850 as a one-room university. A statue of a relaxed Abraham Lincoln sits in a tiled courtyard between Bascom and North Halls; the tiered hill is a favorite sack-out spot for students between (or skipping) classes. From a handful of students and wild animals in 1848, the university has grown to 1,000 acres and more than 50,000 students and faculty; it is a world-renowned institution.

Since its inception, UW has imbued the fabric of the community to a larger extent than even

© THOMAS HUHTI

chilling on Bascom Hill, a UW tradition

the state government has. The campus sprawls gorgeously for nearly two miles along the southern cusp of capacious Lake Mendota.

The nucleus of campus is **Memorial Union** (800 Langdon St., 608/262-1331, www.union.wisc.edu). Perched beside Lake Mendota, it's a must-stop for any visitor. Have but one night in the Mad City? You'll never forget relaxing by the lakeside on the Union Terrace, sipping a refreshment in one of the legendary Union rays-of-the-sun metal chairs as the sun lazily sets.

A **visitors information center** (608/263-2400 or 608/265-9500, http://visit. wisc.edu, 8 A.M.–5 P.M. Mon.–Fri., 11 A.M.– 2:30 P.M. Sat.–Sun.) is available in the "Old Red Gym" next to the Union. Guided tours depart weekdays at 3 P.M. and weekends at noon. (The main visitors center is far south of here at 21 N. Park Street; it's closed weekends.)

Not far from Bascom Hall is a **carillon tower** with 56 bells and sporadic Sunday afternoon performances. Up the hill from the tower is **Washburn Observatory** (1401 Observatory Dr., 608/262-9274), one of the first observatories to use radio astronomy. It was also renovated in 2009 to restore its historic charm. Traditionally it's open at 9 P.M. the first and third Wednesday of each month April–October (every Wednesday mid-June–late July); the rest of the year, it opens at 7:30 P.M. Note that it's open only if skies are at least 75 percent clear. If for nothing else, hike up to the observatory to drink in the views of Lake Mendota. A hundred yards away from the Union along Observatory Drive, at the corner of Babcock Drive, is a conglomeration of 22 gardens on a 2.5-acre Victorian estate that once belonged to the university deans. Another gem is just below Birge Hall on Bascom Hill; **Botany Garden** has nearly 1,000 plants arranged in evolutionary sequence.

The **UW Geology Museum** (1215 W. Dayton St., Weeks Hall, 608/262-2399, http://geology.wisc.edu, 8:30 A.M.–4:30 P.M. Mon.–Fri., 9 A.M.–1 P.M. Sat.–Sun., free) is rather small but has large exhibits, including a scaled version of a limestone cave, a 30-some-foot-long dinosaur, and a mastodon skeleton. Of course, you'll also view the detritus of millions of years of the machinery of fossilization, meteorites, and minerals.

One retreat from throngs of folks that most people don't know about isn't really a museum. But **Wisconsin State Herbarium** (430 Lincoln Dr., 608/262-2792, http://botany.wisc.edu, 7:45 A.M.–4:30 P.M. Mon.–Fri., free), in front of Bascom Hall atop Bascom Hill, is the nucleus of the botany department and its greenhouses are wonderful. The staff asks that you phone first, just to be sure someone knows you're coming.

Lots of UW's departments offer tours; it's best to call ahead and verify it is possible. Or log on to http://vip.wisc.edu for a full list of offerings.

This is the Dairy State, after all, so when you need to refuel, there is *only* the **Babcock Hall Dairy Plant** (1605 Linden Dr., 608/262-3045, 7:30 A.M.–5:30 P.M. Mon.–Fri., 11 A.M.–4 P.M. Sat.), where you can get up-close-and-personal looks at the creation of UW's famed ice cream; the department also makes cheese and other dairy-related products. My personal fave is the legendary fudge-bottom pie, but walking away without an ice cream cone is a cardinal sin! Biotechnology is a new addition to the **agricultural campus.** But the aesthetics of the **Dairy Barn** (1915 Linden Dr.) aren't to be missed. Designed in 1898 by a UW professor, its cylindrical style became a world standard. Tours focusing on the university's crucial role in Midwestern agriculture, biotechnology, and veterinary science can be arranged through the information center at the Old Red Gym.

Where State Street ends and the university begins stands the **Memorial Library** (728 State St., 608/262-3193, hours vary). Ranking in the top five nationwide for its collection (it holds more than five million volumes), it also has a few areas with rare books. A plan to add floors to the library raised a hullabaloo, since it would block the view of the Capitol.

Bus lines (many lines free within campus areas) serve just about everything. For general campus information, call 608/262-2400.

Picnic Point: A lakeshore path runs from the popular terrace of the Memorial Union, bypasses dormitories, boathouses, beaches, and playing fields, and winds up at yet another of the university's gorgeous natural areas—Picnic Point. This narrow promontory jutting into Lake Mendota is split by a screened gravel path and is popular with hikers, joggers, and bikers. You can walk to the tip in under 20 minutes; along the way there are offshoot roads and trails as well as firepit picnic sites. The views of the city merit the stroll/jog.

OUTSIDE OF DOWNTOWN
Henry Vilas Zoo
Still delightfully free to the public is Henry Vilas Zoo (702 S. Randall Ave., 608/266-4732, www.vilaszoo.org, 9:30 A.M.–5 P.M. daily; children's zoo open summers only). For a city of Madison's size, the array of 800 wild animals, representing almost 200 species, is quite impressive, with constantly expanding facilities, especially for big cats and primates. The Herpetarium and Discovery Center offers hands-on entertainment for kids; they can also get free rides and various entertainment Sunday mornings in summer.

◖ University of Wisconsin Arboretum
The UW Arboretum (1207 Seminole Hwy., 608/263-7888, www.uwarboretum.org, 7 A.M.–10 P.M. daily, free) is one of the most expansive and heavily researched of its kind in the nation. Its 1,260 acres comprise stretches of natural communities from wetland to mixed-grass prairie; the restoration work on some is unique—designed to resemble Wisconsin and the Upper Midwest before settlement. More than 300 species of native plants flower on the prairies, some of which are the world's oldest restored tallgrass prairie and the site of the first experiments (in the 1940s) on the use of fire in forest management. The deciduous forests include one virgin stand dating to the time of European settlement in the lower half of the state. Flowerphiles the world over come here to sit beneath the fragrant lilac

stands! In the deciduous forests along Lake Wingra, Native American burial mounds dating as far back as A.D. 1000 can be found. Best of all are the more than 20 miles of trails and fire lanes. *Note that no bicycles or in-line skates are allowed.*

The **McKay Center** (608/263-7888, http://uwarboretum.org, 9:30 A.M.–4 P.M. Mon.–Fri., 12:30–4 P.M. Sat.–Sun.) is a solar-heated visitors center plunked in the midst of the arboretum, surrounded by 50 acres of ornamental gardens and shrubs. It has free guided tours at 1 P.M. Sunday, along with lovely evening walks once per month.

First Unitarian Church

One structure Frank Lloyd Wright designed that attracts many viewers is the First Unitarian Church (900 University Bay Dr.), distinctive for its acclivitous triangles but more so for its new 21,000-square-foot, $9 million addition. The addition is sublime, adding some graceful rondure to the original angular geometry, not to mention a host of cutting-edge design and construction implementations (geothermal heating, mowing-free landscaping, high-tech glass, and more).

National Mustard Museum

Nothing quite like the place where "mustard happens." At the not-nearly-famous-enough Mustard Museum (7477 E. Hubbard Ave., Middleton, 800/438-6878, www.mustard-museum.com, 10 A.M.–5 P.M. daily, free), just outside the gravity pull of Madison's western fringes, you're greeted at the door by cheery, delightfully irreverent hosts, their lapels exclaiming, "Just let us know if you need any condiment therapy." And all this because of one of those accursed, classic Boston Red Sox September Swoons—Bill Buckner's infamous boot of that World Series Game 6 groundball, snatching defeat from the jaws of victory for the hapless Bosox. Barry Levenson, a lawyer before that moment, became an apostate to the game. In a scene from a twisted *Field of Dreams,* Barry wandered into a late-night grocery store where the mustard jars were heard to say, "If you

collect us, they will come." (Umm, OK.) So he opened this eccentric museum featuring the underappreciated spice. What better place to open a mustard museum than a state where bratwurst is king? All kidding aside, this is a serious place, with more than 2,000 mustards on display. It's also the world's largest mustard retailer— 400 to buy and 100 to sample. Ladysmith, Wisconsin's own Royal Bohemian Triple Extra Hot Horseradish Mustard, is the hottest. The museum has even sponsored National Mustard Day, heretofore known as August 5. One of the most enjoyable stops in Wisconsin, the Mustard Museum is a must-see.

Olbrich Botanical Gardens

Along Madison's east side, these mammoth gardens (608/246-4550, www.olbrich.org) feature a tropical forest conservatory with a waterfall inside a 50-foot glass pyramid, along with a botanical education center and seemingly endless gardens covering almost 15 acres. Concerts (free every Tues.) take place in summer.

Thai Pavilion at Madison's Olbrich Botanical Gardens, a gift from the king of Thailand

A highlight for the center—and, incidentally, the place where many of these pages were dutifully scribbled in a morning ritual by yours truly—is a magnificent Thai-style pavilion, donated in part by the royal family of Thailand in recognition of the close relationship between the UW-Madison and Thailand. The conservatory is open 10 A.M.–4 P.M. daily, till 5 P.M. Sunday; the gardens are open 8 A.M.–8 P.M. daily April–September, 9 A.M.–6 P.M. October, 9 A.M.–4 P.M. November–March. Admission to the conservatory is $1, free to all 10 A.M.–noon Wednesday and Saturday. Admission to the gardens and Thai pavilion is always free.

Entertainment and Events

A cornerstone of local culture is the **Overture Center for the Arts** (201 State St., 608/258-4141, www.overturecenter.com), home to myriad performing venues.

Freebies
Grab a picnic basket and head for the Capitol Square on Wednesday evenings for free concerts put on by the **Wisconsin Chamber Orchestra.** Though the weather is incessantly bad for these concerts, they are wildly popular. The **Memorial Union** (800 Langdon St., 608/262-1331, www.union.wisc.edu) at the UW is the most popular place to be Thursday–Saturday for its free concerts.

For family-themed freebies, always check the local *Isthmus.*

NIGHTLIFE
The city's best nightlife is downtown and on the east side; cultural draws are downtown, period. The west side is mostly a zone where Hooters is a draw within megamall sprawl.

Check the free local paper *Isthmus* for club happenings.

Downtown
MEMORIAL UNION
It's free, open to all ages, and a local tradition: an alfresco music mélange Thursday–Saturday on the Memorial Union's outdoor terrace (800 Langdon St., 608/262-1331, www.union.wisc.edu). The whole place really gets bopping Friday and Saturday—the music cranks up and the beer starts flowing. During inclement weather, the whole shebang moves indoors to

© THOMAS HUHTI

Friday night at the UW Memorial Union's terrace

the cavernous Rathskeller (an acoustic death zone). You are supposed have a UW ID *and* valid driver's license to buy beer here; they're strict about it.

BARS AND PUBS
Madison—mostly thanks to the UW, one thinks—pretty much always is at the top 10 in the Princeton Review party schools in the United States; the city definitely leads in binge-drinking. Read: tons and tons of watering holes.

The closer you are to the university, the greater the population of students in the raucous bars. Agoraphobics need not even consider venturing into them, but at least Madison's legendary drink specials keep things cheap. The Capitol Square area, a mere seven blocks from the university, has a much lower undergrad quotient; you'll be rubbing elbows with lots of suit-and-

THE POLKA

Wisconsinites possess a genetic predisposition to polka, established by statute as the state's official dance. Given the state's heady 19th-century influx of Eastern and Central European immigrants – the highest concentration in America at the time – it's only natural that the peasant dance would take root here. Some cultural historians claim Wisconsin harbors more species of polka than anyplace else in the world. Polka music emanates from across the AM dial. At weddings, one polka per hour is virtually an unwritten house minimum. Polka at Brewers games, polka in the Capitol building, even polka Masses in churches! In Wisconsin, polka is king.

They ain't the same. The Swiss did the polka step on the first beat of a bar, while the Austrians did it on the last half beat. The Dutch used a backward swing and omitted the hop, replacing it with only a slight rise or roll of the body. The Poles' polka stepped in measures of four, with the polka lead foot every second step. Czechs did it without a hop. Finns used a 4/4 rhythm and an abrupt heel step and added bits from their own baleful tango. Generally, polka couples turn right continuously without reversing and always move to the right.

The snobbish European elite considered it a madness of the lowest base order but we dug it from the get go. Eastern and Central Europeans also gravitated to the south, where predominantly African American steps were incorporated. A large population of Europeans took their music to Texas and melded border flavors into the music called *conjunto*. Today, some country-western two-steps are being traded back and forth between country and polka camps.

And in Wisconsin, all forms have melded into one eclectic, happy dance. Wisconsin polka is mainly the Polish mazurka and the Dutch, Swiss, and Czech polkas. The best way to experience it is at one of the state's many polka festivals, including the annual Wisconsin Polkafest in mid-May in diminutive Concord. Check out wisconsinpolkamusic.com for a great introduction.

---

tie government wannabe-powers-that-be. For the nonce **Opus Lounge** (116 King St., 608/441-6787) is the place to attempt to be "scene"; pricey drink concoctions and global fusion appetizers are the thing here.

To really escape the students, the *best* views in the city come at **Fresco** (211 State St., 608/663-7374), perched atop the Madison Museum of Contemporary Art. Sit in a chic sofa encased by glass with a panorama of the city. You pay for the view.

It's mostly students at the well-lit and capacious **Plaza,** just off State Street at the corner of Johnson Street, known for its tangy burgers. Two floors of twentysomethings—the upper level looks for all the world like a house party—socialize at **Genna's** (105 W. Main St., 608/255-4770) across from the Capitol along West Main Street. A half block away is the dimly lit **Paradise Lounge** (119 W. Main St., 608/256-2263), once home only to serious hard-core drinkers but now

a hangout for the black-and-flannel crowd. A few doors down is the **Shamrock Bar** (117 W. Main St., 608/255-5029), one of Madtown's three gay bars.

Lots of Capitol suits enjoy good pub grub at the **Argus** (123 E. Main St., 608/256-4141), an antebellum building with pressed-tin coffered ceilings; at night, legions of the netherworld mingle with the late-going yuppies.

Another string of bars—nay, *sports bars*—chock-full of students is found along Regent Street down from Camp Randall stadium. The hordes of students generally don't stray as far as the subdued **Greenbush Bar** (914 Regent St., 608/257-2874), an excellent Italian neighborhood eatery and *the* place in the area for a glass of wine or a scotch.

OOMPAH

Get your personalized mug filled with one of more than 250 beers and join in a boisterous bout of singalong or polka with lederhosen- and dirndl-clad help at the **Essen Haus** (514 E. Wilson St., 608/255-4674, 4–10 P.M. Tues.– Thurs., 4–11 P.M. Fri.–Sat., 3–9 P.M. Sun.). A local tradition is to imbibe a boot of beer—a prodigious amount. Oh, yeah, it is a German restaurant too for the sauerbraten deprived.

If that gets too much, the **Come Back In** (508 E. Wilson St., 608/258-8619), a huge adjoining tavern, is a great place to quaff a tap— for all the world like a subterranean German *bierhall*.

LIVE MUSIC
Always, but always, you can find something at the **High Noon Saloon** (701A E. Washington Ave., 608/268-1112). It was opened by a legendary Madison alt-club owner after her equally legendary alt-club burned down.

Fans of alternative rock head for **The Annex** (1206 Regent St., 608/256-7750) along the sports bar row of Regent Street.

DANCE CLUBS
A perennially fave dance club is **The Cardinal** (418 E. Wilson St., 608/251-0080), heavy on Latin music but you may find a jazz/martini fete or even a fetish night.

Near East Side
The Near East Side begins four or five blocks east of the Capitol, downhill along East Wilson Street to the hairy junction of about six or seven roads at the cusp of Lake Monona. Here, legendary Williamson Street ("Willy Street") begins. Willy Street and its neighborhoods are a pleasant hodgepodge of students and families, with an up-and-coming array of restaurants, clubs, bars, and shops, all still recalling the 1960s salad days, when these blocks were the hippified enclaves of revolution and fighting The Man. The cornerstone is the **Crystal Corner Bar** (the Crystal, 608/256-2953) at the corner of South Baldwin and Willy Streets; this neon-lit bar is a hot blues (especially blues), roots rock, Cajun, and R&B spot in town (though it doesn't have as much music as it used to).

Up the road to the west is funky **Mother**

Fool's Coffeehouse (1101 Williamson St., 608/259-1301), with eclectic music regularly. And a bit further is **Plan B** (924 Williamson St., 608/257-5262), the hippest gay bar in town.

Continuing east of the Crystal, you'll find one of the greatest neighborhood bars in Madison: **Mickey's** (1524 Williamson St., 608/251-9964). It's famous for rock-bottom beer prices, coasters made from well-worn carpeting, and large crowds. But, get this, it also has amazing food. Seriously.

Regular eclectic big-name music acts—roots rock, alternative, hip-hop, folk, international— appear at the neighborhoody **Barrymore Theatre** (2090 Atwood Ave., 608/241-2345), recognizable for its distinctive-hued dome. This old vaudeville hall (which also hosts film festivals) has an endless schedule, so something is bound to be in town.

Folkies definitely should head to the hippified Near East Side. Most acoustic music will be found at Mother Fool's or, inside the Wil-Mar Center, the **Wild Hog in the Woods** (953 Jenifer St., 608/257-4576), which regularly welcomes folk artists and holds barn dances and the like.

West Side
The west side of Madison may be a dreary slice of strip-mall hell, but **Le Tigre Lounge** (1389 S. Midvale Blvd., 608/274-0944) is a time trip back to the Rat Pack.

A bit closer to downtown along Old University Avenue, **Blue Moon Bar and Grill** (2535 University Ave., 608/233-0441), once a classic Whisky tavern, spruced itself up into a cool art deco B&G without losing any of its charm. Burgers are legendary here, but the clam chowder is also luscious.

THEATER AND CLASSICAL MUSIC
The University of Wisconsin's **Vilas Hall** (821 University Ave., 608/262-1500) has two theaters presenting university dramatic and musical productions throughout the year. The long-standing **Broom Street Theatre** (1119

MADISON

DAWN PATROL, OR, THE INSTITUTION

Visiting friends in Madtown over the weekend? Well, you ain't sleepin' in Saturday. No matter how hungover or workweek-weary we are, rising early for a stroll around the Capitol at the **Dane County Farmers Market** (www.madfarmmkt.org) – the largest of its kind in the United States – to pick up goat cheese, salmon, and organic produce (and java) is an absolute must.

More than 200 farmers line Capitol Square April–October and dispense everything you could possibly imagine.

Key word: organic – though not exclusively; everything, however, must be grown/raised in Wisconsin. The only-in-Madison juxtapositions include an organic herb farmer, a free-range-chicken vendor, a Hmong family selling vegetables, jugglers, local politicos pressing the flesh, and a heckuva lot of political or social organizations of many bents. Add to this, zillions of gapers circling counterclockwise (most hauling SUV-size baby strollers). Agoraphobics won't take to it at all.

Just *try* to beg off when your friends shake you awake!

Crowds throng State Street during the Dane County Farmers Market.

Williamson St., 608/244-8338, www.broomstreet.org) is the Midwest's oldest year-round experimental theater group.

A refurbished movie theater is now the **Bartell Theatre** (113 E. Mifflin St., 608/294-0740, www.madstage.com), which also features many of the same local and regional theatrical groups as the Overture Center, including the **Madison Theatre Guild** (608/238-9322).

The popular **Madison Symphony Orchestra** (608/257-3734) performs a dozen or more times during the year at Overture Hall in the Madison Arts District Complex. On campus, the **UW-Madison School of Music** (608/263-9485) has a year-round slate of performances by faculty, students, and visiting musicians; the **Chazen Museum of Art** (800 University Ave., 608/263-2246, http://chazen.wisc.edu) has a popular Sunday Afternoon Live series in autumn and winter.

EVENTS

In June there is **Cows on the Concourse,** a fun way of highlighting Wisconsin's dairy industry; you can get up close and personal with dairy cows, as they're scattered all over the Capitol area.

July's biggie is the now-annual **Rhythm and Booms** choreographed fireworks display on the Fourth—it's the largest in the Midwest and definitely a treat. Later that month, the **Art Fair on the Square** is a huge draw—one of the largest events in the Midwest and one of the largest juried art fairs in the country; the **Dane County Fair** also brings many visitors. October brings the world's largest dairy show, the **World Dairy Expo,** a big-time international event, with agriculturalists and scientists from all over the globe coming to check up on any new dairy industry progress; regular folks can get a lifetime of knowledge about dairy.

© THOMAS HUHTI

Sports and Recreation

You may notice that Madisonians spend all their time jogging, biking, 'blading, skiing, or participating in some other cardiovascular exercise. In fact, this may be why *Outside* magazine has declared Madison a dream spot to live.

RECREATION
Biking and Hiking

No doubt about it, cycling is king in Madison. *Bicycling* magazine called Madison the fourth-best biking city in North America. Second only to Seattle in number of bikes per capita, Madison pedals virtually everywhere it goes. There are—quite seriously—bike traffic jams on certain routes in peak hours since 10 percent of the citizenry commute by bicycle. Mad pedalers will happily discover 25 miles of established pathway on trails and more than 110 miles of interconnected routes along city streets, bike paths, and parkways.

The most popular path is the **Lake Monona loop,** easily accessible along John Nolen Drive, which passes the Monona Terrace Convention Center along the lake; it's about 12 miles long and cruises through residential neighborhoods. A caveat: The route is marked much better if you go clockwise from the Monona Terrace, though the best lake views come if you start counterclockwise.

Many head over to the UW Arboretum for a lovely ride (note that the arboretum's unpaved trails are for feet only).

Here's an outstanding way to combine the two: the Capital City State Trail (trail pass required). You can reach it from the Lake Monona loop where the lakeshore path bisects the Beltline Highway at Waunona Way; signs point you along a spur underneath the overpass, 300 yards to the official trailhead. Follow this through Fitchburg and then turn right on Seminole Highway (bike-friendly) and continue to the entrance of the arboretum.

Should you wish to keep on the Capital City State Trail, it stretches west from Lake Monona all the way to Verona, where it links with the existing Military Ridge State Trail, a grand journey. (Better, it will in the future lead all the way to Illinois and down along Madison's isthmus before heading east to Cottage Grove to link with the Glacial Drumlin State Trail, allowing one to bicycle all the way to Milwaukee.) The Madison segment is part of a visionary project dubbed E-Way, a corridor encompassing more than 3,200 acres for ecological, educational, and recreational use. It isn't just a trail—it's an established "necklace" of linked islands of educational or environmental importance. Madison environmentalists lobbied and fought hard for 25 years to see it established.

All that would be a full day's work. A much easier ride is to start at the UW's Memorial Union, from where a path leads along Lake Mendota to Picnic Point. Gorgeous sunrises.

Budget Bicycle Center (1230 Regent St., 608/251-8413) and **Yellow Jersey** (419 State St., 608/257-7733) both rent bikes. They also stock maps of city bicycle routes.

Any cycling trail in the city is also open to hikers. The UW Arboretum has the most bucolic trails, some of them quite superb for an urban area.

Golf

Madison has four public courses, of which **Yahara Hills** (6701 E. Broadway, 608/838-3126) is the least crowded. Don't even bother trying to get a time at **Odana Hills** (4635 Odana Rd., 608/266-4724), so crowded at times it's like Disney World.

An outstanding course is the University of Wisconsin golf center, **University Ridge Golf Course** (7120 CR PD, 608/845-7700), a championship par-72 course with the tightest slingshot fairways you'll find in town.

Canoeing and Water Sports

Canoeing magazines also rave about the city.

This comes as little surprise since the city boasts four lakes, the larger two of which—Mendota and Monona—are connected by the Yahara River, a superb ribbony urban stream passing through locks and a series of smaller lakes. The Yahara connects to the Rock River, which itself flows through southern Wisconsin. Factoring in tributaries of the Rock leading westward to the Ol' Miss, technically, you could paddle all the way to the Big Easy!

Wingra Boats (824 Knickerbocker St., 608/233-5332) rents boats, canoes, kayaks and sailboats, and also gives lessons; find them at Vilas Park next to the Henry Vilas Zoo.

Camping

The nearest public campground is **Lake Kegonsa State Park** (608/873-9695), approximately 15 miles southeast off I-90 on Highway N. It's not a particularly breathtaking park, but it's large and the lake is nice.

SPECTATOR SPORTS

The UW is what draws the sports nuts to Madison. The university is NCAA Division 1A in all sports, and the cardinal red–garbed citizenry is gaga over the Badgers. Camp Randall Stadium on a football Saturday is an experience you'll not soon forget. If the opponent is a Big 10 foe, forget about a ticket, but for early-season games an occasional ticket may be available. Ditto with the perennial Western Collegiate Hockey Association champion (and six-time national champion) Badgers, who play at the Kohl Center (one of the best hockey facilities in the United States); the fans here may be more rabid than the football legions. (The blasting of "Sieve!" at opposing goaltenders after scores is truly cacophonous.) The men's and women's basketball teams both regularly get to their respective tournaments. For information on ticket availability, call the ticket office at 608/262-1440.

Accommodations

Listings here are but highlights, and chain affiliations are generally eschewed. One bright spot in Madison is that comfortable digs can be had for under $100. Always check ahead—football Saturdays and many UW events max out rooms in town.

DOWNTOWN
Under $50

Madison's **HI Madison Hostel** (141 S. Butler St., 608/441-0144, www.madisonhostel.org, $22 members, $25 nonmembers), a year-round facility, is central, progressive, and very well run. Six-bed dorms and one- to three-person rooms book out in summer so try to make reservations.

$50-100

You may (but probably not) find (barely)-sub-$100 prices with a decent view at the **Best Western Inn on the Park** (22 S. Carroll St., 608/257-8811, $99), which sits opposite the

magnificent Capitol. The hotel is nothing flashy, but it's in a prime spot.

But here's something no one else seems to know about: stay at the you're-gonna-go-there-anyway **UW Memorial Union** (800 Langdon St., 608/262-1583, www.union.wisc.edu/guestrooms, $75–102). Perfectly comfortable rooms with a couple of double beds; higher-end rooms have lake views.

$100-150

Gorgeous vistas of a more natural bent are found at the **Edgewater** (666 Wisconsin Ave., 608/256-9071, www.theedgewater.com, $119), plopped on a small bluff overlooking Lake Mendota a handful of blocks east of the university campus. Rooms are smallish but decent. They don't offer many extras. Health club privileges mean a bit of a hike—but hey, it's got a swimming beach! The dining room is popular with locals for the sunsets as much as the food. This place is at the center of one of those

MADISON

only-in-Madison hoo-hahs about its proposed expansion and rejuvenation.

The towering (for the Mad City, anyway) **Madison Concourse Hotel and Governor's Club** (1 W. Dayton St., 608/257-6000, www. concoursehotel.com, $119) certainly can boast some of the most reputable dining and seen-on-the-scene options in town. Equally up to snuff and with killer views (in some rooms) is the **Hilton Madison** (9 E. Wilson St., 608/255-5100, $125), adjacent to the Monona Terrace.

A spiffy boutique hotel with European stylistic flair just off the State Street corridor is the **Campus Inn** (601 Langdon St., 608/257-4391, www.thecampusinn.com, from $135). It's very distinctive. More than one traveler has raved about the service.

Over $150

Recommended without hesitation is the ◖ **Mansion Hill Inn** (424 N. Pinckney St., 608/255-3999, www.mansionhillinn.com, from $200), an opulent 1858 Romanesque revival on the National Register of Historic Places. Set snugly along a quiet residential street close to downtown, this ornate piece of Victoriana features a distinctive gabled roof and wrought-iron railings encircling the etched sandstone facade. Inside, the opulence is breathtaking, with thrusting round-arched windows, ornate cornices, hand-carved marble, spiral staircase, and a wraparound belvedere. All surrounded by Victorian gardens. The eight rooms vary from Empire style to a Turkish nook, Chinese silk, an Oriental suite, a room done up as a study, and more.

OUTSIDE OF DOWNTOWN

Accommodation zones—mostly chain or mom-and-pop operations, not bad but simply unremarkable—are strung along the Beltline (U.S. 12, 14, 18, 151), the artery linking east and west Madison. Another concentration of motels is found at the junction of U.S. 151 and U.S. 51 and east along U.S. 151 (East Washington Avenue) to East Towne Mall—the major commercial section of the east side. Stick to name brands.

$100-150

Given Madison's progressive environmentalism, it's little surprise to find the ◖ **Arbor House – An Environmental Inn** (3402 Monroe St., 608/238-2981, www.arbor-house.com, $145–230). Its renovation using all recycled materials, from the frames to the beams to the tiling, is but a start; it is about as environmentally progressive as it gets. In a highly respectable and superb location on the near west side, the inn sits directly across from the arboretum and within walking distance of the chichi shop zone of Monroe Street. The extras here—canoeing, sauna, massage, and babysitting, to name a few—run a full page long.

The west side is home to tons of mall zones, and strung along the Beltline are dozens of motels and hotels. Families generally head directly for the ◖ **Holiday Inn Hotel and Suites-West** (1109 Fourier Dr., 608/826-0500, $135), as it's home to Madison's only full-fledged indoor water park. The kids go nuts on the water slides or in the game room; parents relax in the grand piano bar. Some rooms have kitchenettes.

Food

Given the cosmopolitan-minded citizenry that apparently doesn't like to stay home and cook, you'll find something you like.

Supper Clubs

It may be one of the hearts of the state, but you'd hardly know it by Madtown's dearth of mentionable supper clubs; downtown's lack of one is particularly galling. Oh, a couple do exist outside of the Capitol/university area and isthmus, but even locals quibble over whether, due to atmosphere or fare, those are truly deemed supper clubs. Readers' opinions on this matter are most welcome.

DOWNTOWN
Quick Bites

Late spring through early autumn just buy a box from a food cart and sprawl on the mall at the university end of State Street or at the Capitol Square and munch with the ever-friendly squirrels. Best people-watching-cum-meal experience in the city! This author's favorite food cart appears Saturdays during the Dane County farmers market and weekdays at the University Library Mall: the little red cart housing the sublime food from **Ingrid's Lunch Box** (608/345-2132, www.ingslunch-box.com).

Or head for the cheese-lover's nirvana, **Fromagination** (12 S. Carroll St., 608/255-2430), which has extraordinary artisanal cheeses and a few select sandwiches. Well worth it if you know nada about *fromage*.

Burgers, Brewpubs, and Brats

Dotty Dumpling's Dowry (317 N. Frances St., 608/259-0000, 11 A.M.–1 A.M. daily, $4) always wins local surveys for burgers, which really are sublime creations (if a bit pricey). Some Madison radicals frequent the place simply because the owner put up a Pyrrhic battle against

© YUKE TAKANO

Fromagination in downtown Madison

MADISON

the city when it wanted to buy his former location for the city's new arts district.

The Great Dane (123 E. Doty St., 608/284-0000, 11 A.M.–11 P.M. daily, $7–16) is a brewpub occupying what was Madison's landmark Fess Hotel. The interior upstairs is fairly spacious, but it's best known for its great courtyard. The catacomb-like downstairs is a great place for moody swilling. The Great Dane has been ranked in the top 10 brewpubs in the nation in terms of beer consumption; no surprise in a university town in Wisconsin. The food is exceptional, way above basic pub grub, and the place has got a new billiards hall and cigars for aficionados.

It's nearly raucous inside, but stick the brats, burgers, and other pan-Wisconsin-produced fare at ◖ **The Old Fashioned** (23 N. Pinckney St., 608/310-4545, www.theoldfashioned.com, 11 A.M.–9 P.M. Mon.–Fri., 4 P.M.–1 A.M. Sat.–Sun., $5–28) on china on a white tablecloth and it'd pass for fine dining. It's my fave restaurant to take out-of-towners.

Cafés

Not really a café per se but unclassifiable otherwise is the **Grand Lobby Cafe and Lounge** (216 State St., 608/255-2594, 11 A.M.–2 P.M. and 5:30–10 P.M. Tues.–Fri., 9 A.M.–1 P.M. and 5:30–10 P.M. Sat., 10 A.M.–2 P.M. Sun., $6–12) in the lobby of the Orpheum Theater. It's a totally cool take on breakfast, lunch, or dinner, in the stately interiors of a grande dame of Madison. Some items are quite creative; the Sunday brunch is great.

Praise the universe, we now have something other than greasy eggs at a casual place downtown. Extremely understated but heads above others of similar ilk is ◖ **Marigold Kitchen** (118 S. Pinckney St., 608/661-5559, 7–10:30 A.M. and 11 A.M.–3 P.M. Mon.–Fri., 7 A.M.–2 P.M. Sat., $4). This bustling bistro does unique takes on breakfasts and lunch—personalized sandwiches like you've never experienced.

Coffeehouses

State Street is crawling with the places. One venerable institution is **Steep and Brew** (544 State St., 608/256-2902, hours vary with UW's semesters), an initiator of the coffee generation in Madison.

An excellent option is **Ancora Coffee Roasters** (112 King St., 608/255-2900), which has the best interior of any coffee shop downtown. Warm and naturally lit, this is a place to relax with a latte.

Fish Fries

Madison doesn't necessarily live and die for the fish fry, but some good ones are here. Check www.madisonfishfry.com. Generally voted the best fish fry in Madison is an institution, ◖ **The Avenue Bar** (1128 E. Washington Ave., 608/257-6877, 11 A.M.–10 P.M. Mon.–Fri., 8 A.M.–10:30 P.M. Sat., 8 A.M.–9 P.M. Sun., $6), with a number of tables along its huge bar and a newer hall decorated in a pastiche of Badger memorabilia and farm implements. It does a fish boil every day that is worth a try.

Diner

The most classic downscale Madison breakfast place has to be **Mickie's Dairy Bar** (1511 Monroe St., 608/256-9476, lunch and dinner Tues.–Sun.), doling out awesome breakfasts (luscious pancakes) and malts since the 1940s. The atmosphere is super here and the decor real-deal, down to the aging napkin dispensers and anachronistic knickknacks everywhere (the café's name harks back to the establishment's days as one of the largest milk and bread retailers in the city). Try the Scrambler or the Frisbee-size flapjacks.

Custard and Ice Cream

Madison has caught the custard bug so prevalent in Milwaukee, up to a point. Personal favorites include **Michael's Frozen Custard,** with lots of locations, and **Culver's,** found throughout southwestern Wisconsin (the latter's butterburgers are also something to write home about!). However, you'll not find either within walking distance (or even a short drive) of downtown. No worries, for the University of Wisconsin comes to the rescue again: For the obligatory Wisconsin experience, a true Homer

Simpson moment to say "Mmmm," head directly for the UW campus and **❰ Babcock Hall,** where the university cooks delectable batches of its own proprietary ice cream, which is also served at the Memorial Union.

Vegetarian and Health Foods

Many restaurants have vegetarian-friendly food—vegan-friendly is another matter. Check www.vegmadison.com for more. What yours truly does is grab a lunch to go from the **Willy St. Co-op** (1221 Williamson St., 608/251-6776, 8 A.M.–9 P.M. daily), which is technically on the Near East side.

A new entry for this edition is a five-minute drive east from the co-op. At the **Green Owl Café** (1970 Atwood Ave., 608/285-5290, 11 A.M.–9 P.M. Tues.–Sat., till 3 P.M. Sun., $5–10) you'll find only vegan and vegetarian dishes; the soups are worth the trip, as are the faux-meat sandwiches.

Asian and Middle Eastern

Without question among the best restaurants in town is **❰ Restaurant Muramoto** (225 King St., 608/259-1040, 11:30 A.M.–2 P.M. Mon.–Fri., 5–10 P.M. Mon.–Sat., 5–9 P.M. Sun., $7–15). The food is creative pan-Asian with Japanese at its heart. Nothing here disappoints—a cliché, but it's true. Even the service has been far, far above the usual college-town-lethargic, with servers who may still be preoccupied by their master's degree thesis but still do a damn good job.

Wisconsin's only Indonesian restaurant is **Bandung** (600 Williamson St., 608/255-6910, 11 A.M.–2 P.M. Mon.–Sat., 5 P.M.–9 P.M. Mon.–Thurs., 5 P.M.–10 P.M. Fri., 4 P.M.–8 P.M. Sun., $5–15). The Indonesian food is solid, but Bandung also has Thai choices. Service is occasionally erratic here.

Madison's got one of the United States' highest concentration of overseas Chinese students, but not much good Chinese food—till now, that is, with **❰ Fugu** (411 W. Gilman St., 608/286-7277, 11 A.M.–10:30 P.M. Mon.–Sat., 11 A.M.–10 P.M. Sun., $4–9). With two decades around China, this author's pretty

fussy—and this pan-Cathay (and Asian fusion) joint (heavy on Sichuanese food) is the only place in Madison he'll eat Chinese food. More—his Chinese friends like it. 'Nuff said.

The Madison institution for Nepali cuisine has always been **Himal Chuli** (318 State St., 608/251-9225, 11 A.M.–9 P.M. Mon.–Wed., 11 A.M.–9:30 P.M. Thurs.–Sat., noon–9 P.M. Sun.), a great little place with a menu that will never let you down. Lovers of Himalayan food were orgasmic when the owners opened the equally delightful **Chautaura** (334 State St., 608/255-3585, 11 A.M.–9 P.M. Mon.–Wed., 11 A.M.–9:30 P.M. Thurs.–Sat., noon–9 P.M. Sun., $7–14), which serves Nepali cuisine with heavy overtones of Indian and even Tibetan—at higher prices, mind you, given the expansive space.

Steak Houses and Supper Clubs

Grazing vegetarians—a dominant sociopolitical force locally—must have been a bit taken aback by the resurgence of the true carnivorous experience downtown. Steak houses with a true-blue throwback, 1950s martinis-and-slabs-era feel now exist, highlighted by the **Tornado Steak House** (116 S. Hamilton St., 608/256-3570, 5:30–10 P.M. daily, $17–36). This might be the best nouveau take on the old supper club in town. Steaks are the highlight, but the Friday pan-fried perch are a wonderful option for those non-red-meat lovers. Sunday, wonderfully, is homestyle chicken dinner night.

Fine Dining

If you're in town for only one night, the place to choose is definitely **❰ L'Etoile** (1 S. Pinckney St., 608/251-0500, www.letoile-restaurant. com, 5:30–8:45 P.M. Mon.–Fri., 5–9:45 P.M. Sat., $20–35), on Capitol Square directly opposite the Capitol. The creative regional fare has garnered nationwide raves and placed the owners in the national cuisine spotlight—named one of the United States' top 50 restaurants by *Food and Wine*. The restaurant was slow-food and locavorish and whatever decades ago; it also truly strives to reach that esoteric

MADISON

netherworld of the harmony of cuisine, art, and culture. Simply put, the menus are incredible gastronomic representations of the geography and ethos of this place. L'Etoile is highly recommended. The owners also have a wonderful gastropub contiguous to it with delectable bakery and light meals all day and comfort food Sundays to take up L'Etoile's slack.

No places at L'Etoile? Problem solved: Walk one block north to the equally well-realized **((Harvest** (21 N. Pinckney St., 608/255-6075, 5:30–10 P.M. Mon.–Thurs., 5:30–11:30 P.M. Fri.–Sat., $16). The burgeoning slow-food movement—French and American, with local organic ingredients—inspires the culinary experience at this, one of southern Wisconsin's best.

Making a name for itself is the newer **((Sardine** (617 Williamson St., 608/441-1600, 5–10 P.M. Tues.–Thurs., 5–11 P.M. Fri.–Sat., 9 A.M.–9 P.M. Sun., $6–20). It may not consider itself a fine dining establishment (as in posh), but the seafood in a capacious lakeside dining room is really something special. The skate here is sublime.

NEAR EAST SIDE AND NORTH SIDE
Cafés

Best place to take guests when they show up unannounced on a Saturday morning for the farmers market is **((Monty's Blue Plate** (2089 Atwood Ave., 608/244-8505, 7 A.M.–9 P.M. Mon.–Thurs. and Sun., 7 A.M.–10 P.M. Fri.–Sat., $5–9), an upscale diner on the Near East Side with deliciously art deco cool blue interiors. You'll find the best synthesis of American meat and potatoes with trendy off-the-beaten-menu items. The chefs are equally adept with meat loaf and tofu and scrambled egg Mediterranean surprise.

It doesn't feature the usual artery-clogging bar food; hell, it isn't even pub grub. **The Harmony Bar** (2201 Atwood Ave., 608/249-4333, food served 11 A.M.–midnight Mon.–Thurs., 11 A.M.–8:45 P.M. Fri.–Sat., $4) is a wonderful approximation of a very casual neighborhood bar that happens to have good

food. Formerly an early 20th-century east-side tavern and fish-fry server extraordinaire, the current incarnation has a menu varying from homemade pizzas to walnut burgers. The back room features mostly blues and roots rock on Friday and Saturday.

Deli and Ice Cream Parlor

The wildly popular **Ella's Deli** (2902 E. Washington Ave., 608/241-5291, 10 A.M.–11 P.M. Mon.–Thurs., 10 A.M.–midnight Fri.–Sat., $3 and up) is a kosher deli and ice cream parlor—though traditionalists quibble with the revered "deli" moniker (they cavil, this author says). This Near East Side location is very family-friendly—a wild descent into circus kitsch, complete with a carousel outside.

Cajun

A longtime favorite is the takeout-only **New Orleans Take-Out** (1920 Fordem Ave., 608/241-6655, 11 A.M.–9 P.M. Mon.–Sat., $5 and up), with the hottest dirty rice you'll find in Madison and some delectable sweet potato pie.

Southeast Asian

The food will clear your sinuses, but the spices don't dominate the wondrously simple but rich fare at **Lao Laan-Xang** (1146 Williamson St., 608/280-0104, $6–16), which has good specials. Hours are complicated, but essentially lunch and dinner daily.

If they're full, head two blocks east and you'll find the newer **Ha Long Bay** (1353 Williamson St., 608/255-2868, lunch and dinner daily, $6–15), a fusion of Vietnamese-Thai-Lao cuisine. Go for whatever—it's all done well.

WEST AND SOUTH OF DOWNTOWN
Italian

Well, the decor can be a bit garish, what with fountains and all, but Madisonians absolutely remain rock solid behind **Lombardino's** (2500 University Ave., 608/238-1922, 5–9 P.M. Tues.–Thurs. and Sun., 5–10 P.M. Fri.–Sat., $6–21), with a seasonally adjusted menu of freshly prepared high-quality Italian fare.

Mexican

The title of top Mexican eatery now belongs to ((**La Hacienda** (515 S. Park St., 608/255-8227, 8 A.M.–3 A.M. Sun.–Thurs., 8 A.M.–4 A.M. Fri.–Sat., $4–12). The menu is an encyclopedic traipse through home-style Mexican, down to a great daily *comida corrida,* menudo, huge burritos, sweetly tart mole sauce, and a killer *chile de arbol.* The lunch specials are good deals and, best of all, it doesn't close until way, way late every day.

A couple of friends insist I'm a knucklehead and that **Taqueria El Pastor** (2010 S. Park St., 608/280-8898, 7 A.M.–11 P.M. daily, $3–9), a most unassuming little place, is better. They may be right. Just ask for the house specialties.

Thai

Diminutive **Sa Bai Thong** (2840 University Ave., 608/238-3100, 11 A.M.–9 or 10 P.M. Mon.–Sat., 5–9 P.M. Sun., $5–15) is arguably the best Thai restaurant in the state. Ensconced drearily in another of those endless strip-mall hells in the near west side, its menu really isn't extensive, but the food is generally done to perfection. It's so popular that it recently expanded into the suite next door.

Fish Fries

From the west side of town, it may be better to swing toward Middleton, where **The Stamm House at Pheasant Branch** (6625 Century Ave., 608/831-5835, 5–9 P.M. Tues. and Thurs., 5–10 P.M. Wed. and Fri.–Sat., 4–9 P.M. Sun., $6) is a popular supper club housed in a century-old farmhouse. The place is absolutely jam-packed and very festive; given the crowds, service can be spotty, but the atmosphere is unbeatable.

Steak Houses

Ah, ((**Smoky's Club** (3005 University Ave., 608/233-2120, 5–10 P.M. Mon. and Wed.–Sat., $12–35)—one of a dying breed, it's a real charcoal-killer place. The classic supper club-cum-steak house, Smoky's is the type of place where the waitresses have been bustling for four decades and the bartender will remember your drink on your second visit. Big 10 sporting teams make pilgrimages here when they're in town. The decor is simple but homey, and the atmosphere most definitely frenetic. Reservations are essential.

Information and Transportation

INFORMATION AND SERVICES
Visitor Information
The **Greater Madison Convention and Visitors Center** (615 E. Washington Ave., 608/255-2537 or 800/373-6376, www.visit madison.com) is not well located if you're on foot.

Media
The **Wisconsin State Journal** is the thin daily; its sibling *The Cap Times* is the more liberal freebie published twice a week.

Neither of these really compares to the free weekly *Isthmus;* Madisonians dutifully trek to java shops for a scone and a folded *Isthmus* with their lattes. A civic watchdog, it's got the most energetic writing and especially kicks in entertainment scribblings.

For the best all-around coverage of the city, check the *Isthmus* website: www.thedailypage .com.

A delightful mélange of progressivism, half-assed professionalism, at times near-anarchy, and great music, **WORT** (89.9 FM) is a local community-sponsored station. There's little else like it in town.

Bookstores
Madison is an amazing place for a bookworm, with more than 50 bookshops. The country's largest **Barnes and Noble** (7433 Mineral Point Rd., 9 A.M.–11 P.M. Mon.–Sat., 10 A.M.–9 P.M. Sun.) megastore (outside of New York City's

original) has opened on the west side, with more than 150,000 titles in stock.

You'll find more than half a dozen bookstores by strolling along State Street.

Internet Access

Virtually all the downtown coffee shops have wireless Internet access, but if you don't have your own laptop, you're pretty much out of luck. The **public library** (201 W. Mifflin St., 608/266-6300) has free Internet terminals—but count on a definite wait.

GETTING THERE
By Air

The **Dane County Regional Airport** (4000 International Ln., 608/246-3391) has more than 85 nonstop flights daily.

City buses run to the airport. The closest bus stop is a couple of hundred yards after you walk left out the doors of the airport along International Lane.

A taxi ride from the airport to downtown costs $12 minimum.

By Bus

Greyhound (800/231-2222) has lost its Madison terminal and had in one month moved to two different locations; at the time of writing it was opposite the Madison Metro North Transfer station on the north side.

Badger Bus (877/292-8259, www.badgerbus.com, $22) has seven daily departures to Milwaukee: 3:30 A.M.–7:30 P.M., some via Mitchell International Airport. Problem is: some leave from the UW Memorial Union, some from Kelley's Market six blocks or so west of the State Capitol on West Washington Avenue, some from the Dutch Mill Park and Ride near the interstate. They have service to Minneapolis when the university is in session.

For Chicago head to the Memorial Union, where the **Van Galder** bus (608/257-8983 or 800/747-0994) leaves up to eight times daily: 2 A.M.–6 P.M. for O'Hare; some continue to downtown or Midway Airport. A one-way ticket downtown or to O'Hare is $27. The Van Galder also makes stops in Janesville and Beloit.

WATCH YOURSELF

Please accept a local's apology in advance. While on the one hand, *most* Madisonians are some of the politest folks you'll ever meet (Wisconsin, actually, was #2 in the country in a recent Oxford University study), you have to remember that we also think we're the center of the universe. And thus, when many of us are driving, pedaling, or walking, we will simply not pay any attention to anyone else. *All* here are culpable: pedestrians, bikers, drivers. When you're driving, bikers will fly through a stop sign in front of you; when you're biking, pedestrians will walk across a red light in front of you and give you a sniff if you even look like you may question it; when walking, you're fair game (no matter what the signs or laws say).

Now, I know a lot of people are going to dispute this, but yes, we all do it. I also know that many people will laugh and say, "Dude, you should come to . . ." True. However, the goat-getter is the hypocrisy mixed with self-righteousness. We honestly believe we're Mr. and Ms. Polite, yet when we're riding our bikes, stop signs just don't apply to us. We may growl at you to stop at a stop sign on your bike, but we don't have to use our turn signals. Or give a pedestrian right of way in our car. Grr. (Even the cops – one of the best, most patient police forces I've ever witnessed worldwide – never give me and my dog the right of way!)

GETTING AROUND
Taxis

Three taxi services operate in Madison. The most common choice is **Badger Cab** (608/256-5566), since it operates a shared-ride (read: cheaper) service. If that's not an option, **Madison Taxi** (608/258-7458) and **Union Cab** (608/242-2000) are both fine.

Buses

Madison buses (608/266-4466, www.cityof-madison.com/metro) generally run 6 A.M.–10 or 11 P.M., though this varies by line. If in doubt, you can always head to Capitol Square, around which spins just about every bus in town.

Organized Tours

A couple of places offer water tours of Madison lakes, including **Betty Lou Cruises** (608/246-3138, www.bettyloucruises.com, Thurs.–Sun. summers, $25–40), which has dining and sightseeing trips, including a very popular Pizza and Beer cruise.

MADISON

FROM THE WINDY CITY: SOUTHEASTERN WISCONSIN

Driving into the Badger State through Chicago, the centrifugal force of the interstate arcs of the Windy City whip one into a region of prairies, lakes, farms, and lots of people.

Give this region a miss and you'll regret it. Yes, the trees have long since been felled, replaced by agricultural tracts on the fecund glacial till. And its population centers have always battled—unfairly—Rust Belt associations. Yet within a short bike trip one can find bustling city life, ethnic neighborhoods, gorgeous vistas from an enormous expanse of coastline, and, yes, classic pastoral dairyland.

HISTORY

Ironically, this gateway to the state wasn't the first entry point for paleolithic hunters or white explorers. The area didn't beget the state; it simply perpetuated it. Steamships laden with European immigrants landed at Milwaukee and the southern ports, where about 90 percent of Wisconsinites live today.

HIGHLIGHTS

◖ **HarborPark:** Kenosha's got a lovely example of urban gentrification done swell (page 95).

◖ **Racine Art Museum (RAM):** The retro-chic RAM holds the United States's most superlative collections of folk arts (page 100).

◖ **Golden Rondelle Theater:** Racine's gem is an unmistakable piece of Frank Lloyd Wright art (page 100).

◖ **Holy Hill:** Recharge your soul at this cathedral towering over surrounding forests (page 103).

◖ **Horicon Marsh:** Quite literally, millions of birds take flight here on their epic migrations (page 105).

◖ **Octagon House:** Watertown's one-of-a-kind behemoth was the site of America's first kindergarten (page 110).

◖ **Old World Wisconsin:** This is one of the United States' most expansive collections of settlement structures (page 113).

◖ **Hoard Historical Museum and Dairy Shrine:** What would a visit be without a pilgrimage to this temple to the moo-cow state (page 114)?

◖ **Aztalan State Park:** Lake Mills' isolated gem is one of the state's archaeological treasures (page 115).

◖ **Geneva Lake:** A tranquil resort area, it's got one of the loveliest lakepath strolls anywhere (page 122).

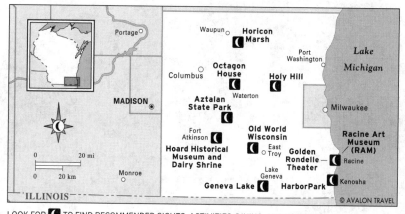

LOOK FOR ◖ TO FIND RECOMMENDED SIGHTS, ACTIVITIES, DINING, AND LODGING.

SOUTHEASTERN WISCONSIN

Major manufacturing industries, reliant on cheap labor and water transportation, also established themselves here, giving the state its only real Rust Belt presence.

PLANNING YOUR TIME

This region could easily be explored in a weekend. The best thing would be to base yourself in **Racine** or **Kenosha** from the east, or **Janesville** or **Beloit** in the west. Then again, **Lake Geneva** is very central! I'd go for Lake Geneva since it is a legendary place of respite.

This author's general tour thereafter is to head for Racine and Kenosha on the first day, then head up to the I-94 corridor and the Horicon Marsh National Wildlife Refuge *or* to Beloit (the Angel Museum and Beloit College) and Janesville (Rotary Gardens) the second day.

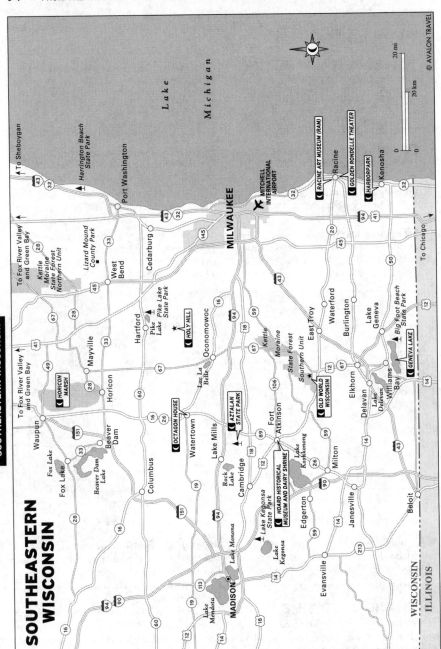

Kenosha

Though its history was one of smokestacks and work whistles and its primary employer for decades was an automobile plant, Kenosha *definitely* belies any blue-collar stereotype. In fact, *Reader's Digest* once declared it the second-best "Family Friendly City" in the United States. (Sheboygan, Wisconsin, was first.) The city owns 8 out of 10 lakefront plots—meaning, parks—and you'll find an appealing array of early-20th-century buildings, anchored by a downtown revitalized by green space, a promenade, a farmers market, and electric streetcar lines.

SIGHTS

Streets run gridlike east-west and avenues north-south. The major arteries into town are: WI 50 (75th St.), WI 158 (52nd St.), and WI 142S.

◖ HarborPark

At the turn of the most recent millennium, Kenosha beaverishly set out to redo its downtown lakefront spectacularly. This is truly one of the freshest-looking Lake Michigan city stretches anywhere. The cornerstone, as it were, is definitely the **Kenosha Public Museum** (56th St. at 1st Ave., 414/262-4140, www.kenoshapublicmuseum.org, 9 A.M.–5 P.M. Tues.–Sat., noon–5 P.M. Sun.–Mon., closed Mon. fall/winter, free). Its most exciting exhibit is on the Schaeffer Mammoth, the oldest butchered mammoth found in the Western Hemisphere; the bones date to 12,000 years ago, and it helped prove human existence during that era—no small detail. More recent archaeological digging in the county, along with sites in Virginia and Pennsylvania, has caused scientists to rethink traditional Siberian land-bridge theories of paleonatives to North America. Definitely check it out!

Right nearby is the **Civil War Museum**

© THOMAS HUHTI

classic "moo-cow" country view outside Kenosha

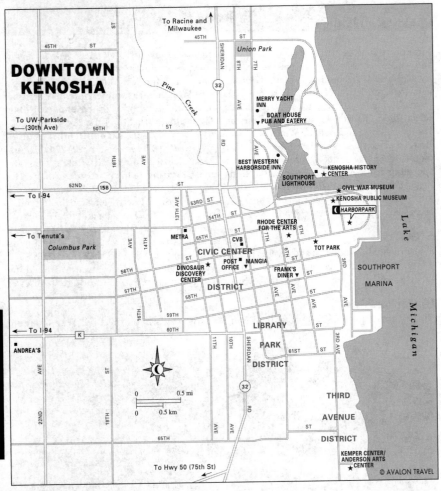

DOWNTOWN KENOSHA

(5400 1st Ave., 262/653-4140, 9 A.M.–5 P.M. Tues.–Sat., noon–5 P.M. Sun.–Mon., closed Mon. fall/winter, $7) focusing on the role of Wisconsin and neighboring states (and Indiana) during the war. A recent reconstruction was done smashingly.

Across the channel next to gorgeous Southport Lighthouse is the **Kenosha History Center** (220 51st Pl., 262/654-5770, www.kenoshahistorycenter.org, 10 A.M.–4:30 P.M. Tues.–Fri., 10 A.M.–4 P.M. Sat., noon–4 P.M. Sun., free). The main museum here focuses fascinatingly on the crucial role transportation, specifically, auto manufacturing, played in the history of the city. Opened in 2010 after years of restoration work, a renovated lighthouse keeper's residence nearby presents the rich, myriad maritime history of the city, the southernmost Lake Michigan port in the state. Lighthouse tours ($10) are available weekends only mid–May–October.

Library Park District

The Library Park District, between 59th and 62nd Streets and 6th Avenue and Sheridan Road, was once the site of homes on the Underground Railroad, now marked by a plaque. Visitors can view the birthplace of Orson Welles at 6116 7th Avenue.

3rd Avenue District

East of the Library Park District and fronting the lake between 61st and 66th Streets, the 3rd Avenue District is the most popular historic stroll, featuring most of the ornate mansions of the wealthy early-20th-century citizens.

Kemper Center (6501 3rd Ave., 262/657-6005, open weekends, free) is a complex of historical structures that sits inside one of seven gorgeous county parks. This park, the largest at 18 acres, is the only one in the nation listed in its entirety on the National Register of Historic Places. The Gothic revival and Italianate antebellum hall was originally a school for girls. Its grounds include an arboretum with more than 100 species of flora (including more than 100 types of roses and a flower and herb garden designed for those without sight). One mansion is open to the public 1–4 P.M. Saturday–Sunday March–October. Also in the park is the impressive French Tudor **Anderson Arts Center** (121 66th St., 1–4 P.M. Tues.–Sun., free).

Civic Center District

Northwest of the Library Park District, roughly between 55th and 58th Streets and 8th and 11th Avenues, the Civic Center District during the late 19th century was the first district to undergo massive experimental civic rejuvenation. As part of a "City Beautiful" campaign, this district has been credited with effecting political reform. Even the post office is a neoclassical revival gem.

Possibly the most favorite museum in town is the kid (of all ages)-friendly **Dinosaur Discovery Center** (5608 10th Ave., 262/653-4460, www.dinosaurdiscoverymuseum.org, noon–5 P.M. Tues.–Sun., free). The usual fab hands-on stuff make it fun; this author loves the on-site working paleontology lab.

ENTERTAINMENT AND EVENTS

Lots of arts performances take place at the grand **Rhode Center for the Arts** (514 56th St., 262/657-7529, www.rhodeopera.org), in a restored opera house. It's also home to the Pollard Gallery, dedicated to two artists, Nan and George Pollard, the latter a portraitist who has painted innumerable figures in world history in the late 20th century.

SHOPPING

Shopping in Kenosha is a sight in itself for **Prime Outlets**, near the junction of I-94 and WI 165.

Downtown **Andrea's** (2401 60th St., 262/657-7732) is a fourth-generation (since 1911!) shop selling all sorts of home items, cards, books—it's even got a tobacco shop and old-timey soda fountain.

RECREATION
Sportfishing

In most years, Kenosha sportfishing rates number one in the state in terms of fish caught per hour, especially trout and salmon. Here you'll find the greatest opportunity to catch all species of coho salmon, rainbow trout, king salmon, brown trout, and lake trout. Contact the **Kenosha Charter Boat Association** (800/522-6699, www.kenoshacharterboat v.com) for all details.

Trails

The **Pike Trail** runs 14 miles south along Lake Michigan to the Illinois border and through **Chiwaukee Prairie** (near Carol Beach), the only unbroken stretch of mixed-grass prairie in Wisconsin. The prairie is home to more than 400 native plant species, including the endangered pink milkwort. The area is now protected as both a National Natural Landmark and a State Natural Area. The trail also goes north to Racine. Eventually one will be able to bike from the Illinois border north through Milwaukee to Cedarburg, Grafton, and who knows how much farther north?

Camping

The closest decent public campground is at the 4,500-acre **Richard Bong State Recreation Area** (262/878-5600), along WI 142, a mile west of WI 75 in Brighton and about 25 minutes northwest of Kenosha. You'll see hang gliders, parasailors, and remote-controlled planes buzzing around; fitting, as it's named for a WWII flying ace.

ACCOMMODATIONS

Unique is the **Merry Yacht Inn** (4815 7th Ave., 262/654-9922, $50). The quaint little place was built into an old firehouse.

A few of the 115 units at the **Best Western Executive Inn** (7220 122nd Ave., 262/857-7699, $89) are multiroom patio suites. Expect solid amenities here.

You'll get great views at the **Best Western Harborside Inn** (5125 6th Ave., 262/658-3281, $109–199), right on the lake. Some have opined it's not as good as the former, but it's been put under new management who seem to be on the ball.

FOOD

[**Mangia** (5517 Sheridan Rd., 262/652-4285, 11:30 A.M.–2 P.M. Tues.–Fri., 5–9 P.M. Tues.–Sat., 4–9 P.M. Sun., $9–30) fits Italian heavy Kenosha to a T. This basic trattoria pushes out lovely wood-fired pizzas and exquisitely done pastas, meats, seafoods, and roasted entrées. Oh, and Barack Obama has been quoted calling the owner his favorite chef.

Some, however, say the most nostalgiac Kenosha Italian experience comes from long-time fave [**Tenuta's Deli** (3203 52nd St., 262/657-9001, 9 A.M.–9 P.M. Mon.–Sat., 9 A.M.–6 P.M. Sun., $4–9). A good place to stop if you're in a hurry, it's got a smattering of pastas, salads, and ready-made entrées. It's also an outstanding Italian grocery store.

This author, long favoring scuffed news-print-on-Formica-kind-of-eating, has always adored [**Frank's Diner** (508 58th St., near HarborPark, 262/657-1017, 7 A.M.–2 P.M. daily, $3–10), a place where factory workers coming off shift and misunderstood genius writers pour each other's coffee. It's housed in the oldest continually operating lunch car diner in the United States (pulled here by six horses!). Forget the train car aspect; this is simply roots eating, plain and simple, in a warm and welcoming Midwestern atmosphere.

Oh, yeah, if you catch a lunker, take it to the **Boat House Pub and Eatery** (4917 7th Ave., 262/654-9922, 11 A.M.–2 A.M. daily), where the staff will grill it for you!

INFORMATION AND SERVICES

You'll encounter solicitous and chatty folks at the Kenosha Area Convention and Visitors Bureau (812 56th St., 262/654-7307 or 800/654-7309, www.kenoshacvb.com, 8 A.M.–4:30 P.M. Mon.–Fri.).

GETTING THERE AND AROUND
Getting There

Kenosha is connected to Milwaukee via Racine by **Wisconsin Coach Lines** (877/324-7767, www.wisconsincoach.com), which runs numerous buses daily; it stops at the Metra station among others.

You can also hop aboard Wisconsin Coach Lines' **Airport Express** (877/324-7767, www.wisconsincoach.com), which goes north to Milwaukee via Racine and south to Chicago (but it stops way out west of town at the Brat Stop on the interstate).

Metra (312/322-6777, www.metrarail.com) offers train service between Kenosha and Chicago's Madison Street Station. Trains depart the METRA Commuter Rail Center (5414 13th Ave., 262/653-0141) up to eight times daily.

Getting Around

Kenosha's utterly cool electric streetcar rumbles through the downtown area to the Metra train station and back; best, it whips through two of the historic districts. And costs all of a quarter!

Racine

Like its de facto sister city to the south, Kenosha, Racine suffers somewhat from its association with manufacturing. But the city lakefront, once a true-to-form, ugly-as-hell mill town with a horizon of gas tanks and brown sloughs, was *mostly* razed in the early 1990s and spruced up. Now, it's full of landscaped parks and plenty of public boat launches, and the city sports the largest marina on Lake Michigan—more than 100 acres.

Ethnically, while in the early 20th century the city boasted the nation's most appreciable Bohemian influence, it is now known for its Danish contingent—it's got the largest Danish population outside of Denmark—and West Racine is even referred to as "Kringleville," for

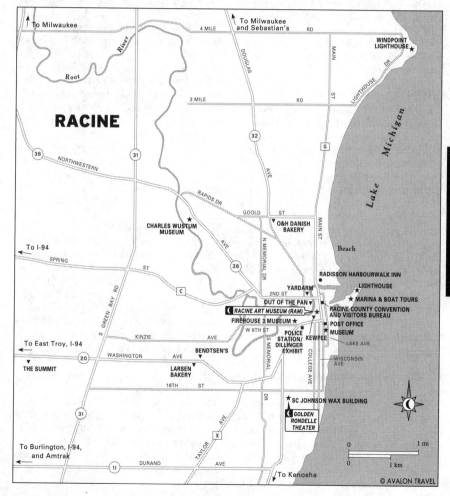

SOUTHEASTERN WISCONSIN

© AVALON TRAVEL

the pastry produced in huge numbers by local bakeries.

History

The Root River, named by early Native Americans for its gnarled, knife-resistant roots, so unimpressed French voyageurs in the 1670s that they up and decamped. In 1841 the town incorporated under the name Racine ("root" in French). Like Kenosha, Racine was plagued by the maddeningly shifty river mouth and resultant sandbars, so citizens had to dig out and construct the first piers in 1843–1844. Initially, lake traffic was the lifeblood of the city, but by the turn of the 20th century, Racine was a leading national figure in farm-implement and wagon production.

SIGHTS
◖ Racine Art Museum (RAM)

This impressive museum (441 Main St., 262/638-8300, www.ramart.org, 10 A.M.–5 P.M. Tues.–Sun., $5), in a scintillating, chic edifice (yet meshed superbly with its 1860s structure) in the city center, is, with little hyperbole, one of the best in the Midwest. Holding one of the top three collections (more than 4,000 pieces) of Works Progress Administration's traditional arts and crafts in the United States, it is rivaled only by the Smithsonian and the American Craft Museum in New York. As an aside, this building, once a bank, was the place John Dillinger robbed in 1933.

◖ Golden Rondelle Theater

It's hard to miss the globular-shaped (with 90-foot arching columns) Golden Rondelle Theater (1525 Howe St., 262/631-2154) on the city's south side. The most distinctive of Racine's architectural landmarks, it was unveiled at the New York World's Fair in 1964–1965. Afterwards, Taliesin Associate Architects was commissioned to bring the theater to Racine and incorporate it near the SC Johnson Wax administration building, also designed by Wright. Free tours of the SC Johnson administration building depart the theater at various times on Fridays only; *reservations are necessary.* The Great

Workroom is worth the tour itself. Worth the visit as well is the company's new (as of 2010) Fortaleza Hall, a gorgeous, glass new employees' hall with a small museum to company history and works by Frank Lloyd Wright.

Other Museums

Brother to the RAM, the **Charles Wustum Museum** (2519 Northwestern Ave., 262/636-9177, 10 A.M.–5 P.M. Tues.–Sat., free) displays regional art in a historic 1856 Italianate farmhouse on a 13-acre spread of park and formal garden.

A former fire station full of antique equipment constitutes the **Firehouse 3 Museum** (700 6th St., 262/637-7395, 1–4 P.M. Sat., free), right downtown and easily visited.

The **Dillinger Exhibit** isn't a museum but a fun look at the bad old days of cops and robbers. On November 20, 1933, four brazen robbers held up a downtown Racine bank, stole $27,700, and relieved a security guard of his machine gun. When Dillinger was finally taken down in Arizona, the gun was recovered—complete with Dillinger's signature on the stock. It's now on display in the Racine Police Department lobby (730 Center St.).

Windpoint Lighthouse

Many visitors associate Racine with the eye-catching red beacon atop the breakwaters across from Reefpoint Marina. Racinians would likely rather be associated with Windpoint Lighthouse, north of town between Three Mile and Four Mile Roads. Believed to be the oldest (built in 1880) and tallest (112 feet) lighthouse on the Great Lakes, it is still in use today. You can't go inside, but you can stroll the grounds at most hours of the day.

Scenic Drives

The city of Racine boasts a historic chunk of roadway. Three Mile Road, beginning at 108th Street and running east to 80th Street, was laid out in the early part of the 19th century and has remained virtually untouched (and unwidened). It still has old oaks and rail fences at its verges and makes a beautiful tour.

© WALTER ARCE/123RF.COM

Racine's Windpoint Lighthouse

State Rustic Roads are everywhere you look. One heads north of town along Honey Lake Road, Maple Lane, and Pleasant View Road to Highway D and WI 83, passing along the way a woodland preserve, dairy farms, and marshes with muskrat houses. Backtrack to Highway DD and it picks up with another Rustic Road adjacent to the **Honey Creek Wildlife Area.** This route also passes the **Franklyn Hazelo Home,** which is on the National Register of Historic Places. Southeast of Burlington off WI 142 via Brever Road or Wheatland Road, a Rustic Road passes under an expanse of oak and black walnut trees. Highlights include old barns, an old farmhouse, marshes, and lots of great fishing along the Fox River, accessible from Hoosier Creek Road.

Northeast of Waterford, via WI 164 and WI 36, is Loomis Rustic Road, originally an 1840 territorial road that's little changed. Along the way, you'll pass Colonel Heg Memorial Park, commemorating Wisconsin's highest-ranking Civil War officer. A park museum describes the region's settlement by Norwegians, and an 1830s cabin sits nearby.

Burlington

The town of Burlington sits about 25 miles west of Racine. For a town of only 8,900 people, it's sure got a bunch of damn liars. The home of the world-famous Burlington Liar's Club, it hosts an annual yarn- and fib-spinning festival and also distributes a brochure about the town's **Tall Tales Trail.** Also called Chocolate Town USA (a Nestlé plant is here), Burlington has many streets named after candy bars and, of course, the **Chocolate Experience Museum** (113 E. Chestnut St., 262/763-6044, 9 A.M.–5 P.M. Mon.–Fri., 10 A.M.–2 P.M. Sat., free).

The **Spinning Top Exploratory** (533 Milwaukee Ave., 262/763-3946, www.topmuseum.org, $5) has more than 1,500 examples of yo-yos, tops, and anything else that revolves. *With reservations only,* you get a tour featuring videos, demonstrations, and game-playing, as well as a look at prototype tops used in a feature film on the subject.

ENTERTAINMENT AND EVENTS

On Memorial Day weekend, little Burlington whoops it up during **ChocolateFest** (www.chocolatefest.com).

Racine's **Fourth of July** celebration (www.racine.org) is the largest in the state, replete with the longest parade in Wisconsin. (If you're very lucky, it'll be a year when 19th-century mock clipper ships are prowling about.)

The granddaddy of all events is mid-July's **Salmon-a-Rama** (www.salmon-o-rama.com), during which more than 4,000 anglers from 25 states land about 18 tons of fish and another 200,000 people crowd the lakefront for a huge blowout of a festival. It's the largest freshwater fishing festival in the world.

RECREATION
Charter Fishing

Racine has one of the most productive charter operations on Lake Michigan; it also has the largest marina on the Great Lakes—more than 100 acres. Six different species of salmon and trout cohabit near three reefs lying outside the harbor. In July 2010, a man caught a Wisconsin-record and (likely) world-record 41.5-pound brown trout off Wind Point!

For more information, contact the **Fishing Charters of Racine** (800/475-6113).

Biking

The county has a 117-mile on-road bicycle trail marked; sections are on a multiuse trail. Six county scenic multiuse trails exist; the North Shore Trail links to Kenosha and links up with the Racine/Sturtevant Trail.

Canoeing

The Root and Fox Rivers and Honey Creek west of Racine are good for canoeing. **Riverbend Nature Center** (3600 N. Green Bay Rd., 262/639-0930) rents canoes.

Camping

Sanders County Park (4809 Woods Rd., 262/886-8400, closed in winter) has 50 campsites, along with a playground and hiking trails.

ACCOMMODATIONS

The only over-the-water hotel on southern Lake Michigan is a goodie. The (**Radisson Harbourwalk Inn** (223 Gaslight Circle, 262/632-7777 or 800/333-3333, $139 s, $149 d) has rooms affording gorgeous lake views, and suites with whirlpools on balconies. Boaters can dock at slips and the restaurant on-site is well regarded. Extras include 24-hour room service, in-room coffeemakers, airport transportation, and more.

FOOD
Fish Fries

The **Yardarm** (920 Erie St., 262/633-8270, 11 A.M.–10 P.M. Sun.–Thurs., 11 A.M.–midnight Fri.–Sat., $6 and up) has fish fries nightly.

Burgers

Not a greasy spoon per se, (**Kewpee** (520 Wisconsin Ave., 262/634-9601, 7 A.M.–6 P.M. Mon.–Fri., 7 A.M.–5 P.M. Sat., $1 and up) rates a nod as the best burger joint in perhaps all of southern Wisconsin. Devotees regularly come from as far away as the Windy City. Decades old (it started in 1927), this erstwhile teen hangout doesn't have much in the way of ambience now. It's as fast as fast grub gets, but you can't beat the burgers or malts. It's standing-room-only at lunchtime.

Kringle

Racine is still lovingly called Kringleville, for good reason. Almost all travelers leave town with white wax-paper bags stuffed with *kringle,* a flaky, ovoid kind of coffeecake filled with a variety of fruits and almond paste or pecans. Family bakeries vie annually for top honors of best *kringle,* and they still make it the Old World way—some taking three days to prepare the dough alone. Aficionados who have written in with advice say: 1) pecan *kringles* are best; and 2) always go for the thinnest slice on the plate, since it always has the most filling.

O&H Danish Bakery (1841 Douglas Ave., 262/637-8895, 5:30 A.M.–6 P.M. Mon.–Fri., 5 A.M.–5 P.M. Sat.) does the most advertising and probably ships the most *kringles,* and

President Obama did make a stop here in 2010! But most readers have opined that **((Larsen Bakery** (3311 Washington Ave., 262/633-4298, 6 A.M.–5 P.M. Mon.–Fri., 6 A.M.–4 P.M. Sat.) or **((Bendtsen's** (3200 Washington Ave., 262/633-0365) have the best.

Another Danish highlight is *aeblewskiver,* a lovely spherical waffle.

Bistro

((Sebastian's (6025 Douglas Ave., 262/681-5465, 5–9 P.M. Mon.–Sat., $6–18), just north of downtown, has long been a fine bistro. Cuisine varies from grouper to Thai chicken, much using produce from its adjacent garden.

An outstanding casual spot for, oh, let's call it world-fusion food is **Out of the Pan** (550 State St., 262/632-0668, 11 A.M.–3 P.M. Mon.–Fri., 5–10 P.M. Tues.–Sat., brunch Sun., $9–26). The restaurant is creative, hip, and friendly (and the Sunday brunch is simply superb).

Supper Clubs

The Summit (6825 Washington Ave., 262/886-9866, lunch and dinner daily, $6–18) has lunches and dinners in a casual atmosphere, but you might want to check out its incredible Sunday brunch, if only for the extraordinary array of *kringle* available.

INFORMATION AND SERVICES

The Racine County Convention and Visitors Bureau (345 Main St., 262/884-6400 or 800/272-2463, www.visitracine.org) is open regular business hours (with weekend hours in summer).

GETTING THERE
By Train

There's no Amtrak service directly to Racine, but trains do stop at 2904 Wisconsin Street in Sturtevant to the west. Racine city buses travel to Sturtevant. Kenosha's Metra trains still haven't been extended north to Racine though everyone wants them to.

By Bus

Airport Express (877/324-7767, www.wisconsincoach.com) makes stops in Racine on its routes to and from Chicago's O'Hare Field and Milwaukee's Mitchell International Airport.

Wisconsin Coach Lines (877/324-7767, www.wisconsincoach.com) also stops in Racine on its run between Milwaukee and Kenosha.

Buses stop at the **Racine Transit Center** in the 1400 block of State Street.

GETTING AROUND
Trolleys

One buck gets you as far north as Reefpoint Marina and as far south as 7th Street. The trolleys run daily Memorial Day–Labor Day (usually); on Friday and Saturday, the city has at times offered "pub and grub" runs stopping at restaurants and bars downtown till late.

From Milwaukee to Madison

((HOLY HILL

Even recovering Catholics might appreciate a side trip to Holy Hill (262/628-1838), with the neo-Romanesque church dominating the skyline, simply because, as one visitor noted, there is nothing like the sound of Holy Hill's bells tolling through the Wisconsin countryside. In 1855, a disabled mendicant hermit experienced a "cure" atop the 1,340-foot bluff and established Holy Hill as a pilgrimage site. One of the church spires, 180 steps up, affords commanding views of variegated kettle moraine terrain and, on clear days, the downtown Milwaukee skyline. A $5 million (plus) renovation replaced the roof with Vermont slate that matches the surrounding hills; the priceless interiors were painstakingly reappointed.

Then again, some say, get there while you

© YUKI TAKANO

sunset near Holy Hill

can. The nearby town of Erin is showing every sign of suburbia, so much so that Scenic America placed Holy Hill on its 10 Most Endangered Landscapes list.

Around the church are 400 heavily wooded acres crossed by the National Ice Age Scenic Trail; the grounds also contain a half-mile trail and a grotto. The monastery has guest rooms and retreat facilities; reservations are required. There is also a cafeteria open weekends year-round and daily June–October; the Sunday brunch is another nice reason to visit. To get there, head 30 miles north of Milwaukee via U.S. 41/45, then west on WI 167.

HARTFORD

Little Hartford is a few miles north of Holy Hill via WI 83. It's worthy of a stop just to see the art deco interiors and smashing pieces of auto history at the **Wisconsin Automotive Museum** (147 N. Rural St., 262/673-7999, 10 A.M.–5 P.M. Mon.–Sat. and noon–5 P.M. Sun. in summer, less the rest of the year, $7 adults). The museum displays more than 80

antique automobiles, motorcycles, farm equipment, and other engine-driven machines in pristine condition, including Wisconsin-produced Nash automobiles and high-caliber Kissels, which were built in Hartford 1906–1931.

East of town is **Pike Lake Unit** (Hwy. 60, 262/670-3400), a relatively unappreciated chunk of glacial terrain. The large park is dominated by 1,350-foot-high Powder Mountain. (Well, actually, it's a "kame"; that's all right, the lake is a "kettle!") A brand-new 160-foot-high tower makes for wonderful views. The park has close to a dozen miles of trails on six primary loops. A stretch of the National Ice Age Scenic Trail cuts through the park.

WEST BEND

The **Museum of Wisconsin Art** (300 S. 6th Ave., 262/334-9638, 10 A.M.–4:30 P.M. Wed.–Sat., 1–4:30 P.M. Sun., $5) boasts a large holding of early-19th-century Wisconsin art. In addition to the works of Milwaukee-born German Carl von Marr, an antique dollhouse spans an entire room. This smashing $12 million renovation was finished in 2010 and designed by the same folks who brought you the lovely Discovery World complex in Milwaukee.

An aside about those kitchen appliances. The West Bend Company has untold thousands of original appliances in storage, with no repository to show them, choosing to keep them locally (rather than in Madison at the State Historical Society) in hopes that the historical museum might find a wing for them. The Smithsonian has gushed about the collection, saying it far surpasses its own.

North of town on WI 144 and Highway A is the awe-inspiring **Lizard Mound County Park** (2121 Hwy. A, 262/335-4400, daily Apr.–Nov., free), along with Aztalan State Park, one of the state's most important archaeological sites. The Mississippian Indians here predated Aztalan's by perhaps 500 years and built amazingly detailed earthworks in geometric and animal forms. It's well worth a trip.

◖ HORICON MARSH

One of nine nodes of the National Ice Age Reserve, the Horicon is divided into two parts: the National Wildlife Refuge in the north and the Horicon Marsh Wildlife Area in the southern tier of the greenery. Spreading over 32,000 acres, the marsh was formed by the Green Bay lobe of the Wisconsin Glacier beginning around 70,000 years ago. The result was a shallow glacial lakebed filled with silt—the largest freshwater marsh in North America, often called the "Little Everglades of the North." (And it's the largest cattail marsh in North America.)

The marsh was populated originally by nomadic Paleo-Indians, who hunted animals right along the edge of the receding ice floes. In turn, Hopewell tribes, mound builders, Potawatomi, and Winnebago all lived in or around the marsh. Europeans showed up and began felling the region's deciduous forests. A dam was later built to facilitate floating timber logs on the Rock River and to create mill power. The water levels rose nine feet, resulting in the world's largest artificially-made lake. Around the time of the Civil War, far-thinking conservationists succeeded in having the dam removed and reconverting the marsh to wetland. It became a legendary sport-hunting paradise; private clubs removed whole wagonloads of birds after hunts.

Around the end of the 19th century, agricultural interests once again lobbied to drain the marsh and reestablish farming. What couldn't be drained off was going to be used for profit-rich muck farming or moist-soil agriculture. The efforts failed, though the dikes the companies built still exist in a gridlike pattern today. Citizens' groups finally organized in the 1920s to call for legal designation of the marsh as a refuge. In 1927, the state legislature passed the bill, which officially protects the lower one-third; the federal government still maintains the upper two-thirds.

The marsh has a few Indian mounds along the east side, accessible by a driving route, as well as a four-mile-long island, an educational barn, and plenty of fishing.

great egret surveying Horicon Marsh

© CHAS. E. MARTIN/DREAMSTIME.COM

AMERICA'S DAIRYLAND

Surprise, surprise: Dairying was not the first gear in the state's agricultural machine – wheat was. Wisconsin was a leading world wheat producer and exporter through the 1870s.

Inauspiciously, the state's initial forays into home butter (and cheese) were derisively called Western Grease. Wisconsin cattle were initially miscegenational hybrids of hardier species. Milk production was hardly a necessity.

THE BIRTH OF A STEREOTYPE

In the 1850s, transplanted New York farmers organized the first commercial cheesemaking factory systems. In addition, the first experiments in modern herd management and marketing were undertaken. One New Yorker, Chester Hazen, opened a cheese factory in Ladoga and in 1864, its first year, produced 200,000 pounds. Within a half decade, the state had nearly 50 factories, and in some spots the demand for milk outstripped the supply.

Immigrants followed up, finding the topography reminiscent of home and the glacial till profoundly fecund (one spot of Dane County has been termed the world's richest agrarian soil).

Old World pride mixed with Yankee ingenuity created an explosion of Wisconsin dairying. The first dairy organizations were founded after the Civil War; a dairy board of trade was set up in Watertown in 1872. The state's dairies shrewdly diversified the cheesemaking and took the western markets by storm. By the 20th century, a stereotype was born: Jefferson County, Wisconsin, was home to 40,000 cows and 34,000 people.

W. D. HOARD

A seminal figure in Wisconsin's rise to dairy prominence was theretofore unknown W. D. Hoard. In 1870, Hoard began publishing *The Jefferson County Union*, which became the mouthpiece for Wisconsin farmers. The only central source for disseminating information, the paper's dairy columns transmogrified into *Hoard's Dairyman*. It was the most influential act in Wisconsin's dairy industry.

Hoard had never farmed, but he pushed tirelessly for previously unheard-of progressive farm techniques. Through Hoard, farmers learned to be not so conservative, to keep records, and to compare trends. Most significantly, Hoard almost singlehandedly invented the specialized, milk-only cow. He became such a legend in the industry he was elected governor in 1889.

The University of Wisconsin followed Hoard's lead and established its College of Agriculture's experimental stations in 1883. The renowned department would invent the butterfat test, dairy courses, cold-curing processes, and winter feeding.

HOW YOU GONNA KEEP 'EM DOWN ON THE FARM?

Dairying in Wisconsin is a $26.5 billion industry, accounting for a tenth of the state's total economic output (and nearly half of all agricultural). It is more crucial to the state's economy than citrus is to Florida ($9.3 billion) or potatoes are to Idaho.

Nearly three-tenths of all the butter and cheese in the United States is produced in Wisconsin. It produces 2.3 billion pounds of milk per year on average; that's fourth highest of any *nation*. Wisconsin cheesemakers have won 33 percent of World Cheese Championship first prizes; California, less than 5 percent. At the 2009 US Cheese Championship,

But birds are the big draw. Annually, more than one million migrating Canada geese, ducks, and other waterfowl take over the marsh in a friendly—if histrionic and cacophonic—invasion. The geese alone account for three-quarters of the total.

The marsh has an established 30-mile-long **Wild Goose Parkway,** a drivable loop that takes in the whole of the marsh and offers some spectacular vistas. There are innumerable pulloffs with educational displays. The gates open 8 A.M.–3 P.M. Monday–Friday and some Saturdays mid-April–mid-September.

yup, Wisconsin won 11 of 15 championships and a state cheese took top honors overall. And it took 114 out of 192 awards; California won, that's right, nine.

Look, Wisconsin is the only state to require a master's license to make cheese! (Also, 90 percent of state milk is used for cheese and small herds on family farms raised stress free – on good soil – will produce quality milk.)

Wisconsin has more than 26 percent of the U.S. cheese market today, while California has 20.4 percent (experts have for decades predicted California would eclipse Wisconsin). Wisconsin keeps its lead in specialty cheeses with 650 varietals, California less than half of that. And yet, things have been far from easy.

In 1993, the unspeakable occurred: California edged ahead of Wisconsin in whole-milk output – egads. California's dairy output is now hovering around seven percent more per annum than Wisconsin's. Further, Wisconsin has seen its family dairy farm numbers dwindle from post-WWII figures approximating 150,000 to less than 15,000 in 2010; at one grim point the state lost an average of 1,000 dairy farms annually. This hurts when 99 percent of your farms are family owned. Apparently, "America's Dairyland" is a title under siege.

Badger State politicians on Capitol Hill blame the dairy problems on outdated – nay, absurd politically uneconomic insanity – federal milk-pricing guidelines, which pay other states higher rates than Upper Midwest farmers. Eau Claire, Wisconsin, is the nucleus; the farther you get from that point, the higher the price – up to $3 more per 100 pounds (milk paying a farmer $1.04 per 100 pounds in Wisconsin fetches a South Florida farmer $4.18!). Wisconsin farmers even resurrected "milk strikes," dumping milk in protest. Recent legislation has even strengthened the system and solidified regulations favoring corporate farms.

Not to be completely apocalyptic, Wisconsin, though in a decline, is in little danger of completely losing its cultural underpinnings of rural Americana. Supplying so much of the cheese in the United States still equals a huge market – and predicted U.S. cheese consumption rises will help. And Badger farmers are finding ways to stem the wave of disappearing farms. One innovative program involves rural villages' banding together, pooling resources, and buying family farms to keep them operational. Recently, the numbers of cows in the state has begun to rise.

Economists also say that California's cheese industry is dangerously tied to the stock market, since many of its consumers are Double Income No Kids types – every time the stock markets hiccup, California's markets quake, but not Wisconsin's. (Wisconsin's have been around for more than a century.) California cheesemakers, also, are mostly huge factory operations, as opposed to small family operations in Wisconsin. Seventy-five percent of Wisconsin cheesemakers grew up in an operation in which a grandparent had worked in the industry; only 20 percent of California's cheesemakers can say that.

One thing Wisconsin will never have to worry about is water – something that California agriculture constantly has to face, and projections paint a fairly dire picture for enormous farm operations in the Golden State.

Thus, it may not be able to compete in whole numbers, but on a per capita basis, Wisconsin is still America's Dairyland.

SOUTHEASTERN WISCONSIN

Wildlife

Wetlands, upland grassy fields, and deciduous woodlands harbor a panorama of flora and fauna. The deep marshes are flooded every year except during severe droughts; water levels can rise four feet—crucial for nesting waterfowl, especially diving ducks, grebes, and fish-eating fowl. The denser vegetation brings security in nesting, breeding, and rearing young. Even wild rice grows again in the great marsh.

Some of the more than 260 species of birds include mallards, blue-winged teals, coots, ruddy ducks, cormorants, herons, and terns. The marsh is the largest nesting area east of the Mississippi River for red-head ducks, almost 3,000 of which show up each year. Birds are most often spotted during spring and fall migrations. Rookeries—particularly one on Cotton Island—attract egrets, herons, and cormorants. In 1998, for the first time in more than 100 years, trumpeter swans returned to the marsh. No state has spent more time or money to bring trumpeter swans back to native areas, and after years of preparation, a dozen swans were released. The goal is to have 20 nesting pairs eventually.

What of those honking geese? They come from the watery tundra near Hudson Bay in northern Canada. Some begin arriving by mid-September, with a gradual increase through October and sometimes into November. Upon arrival, they establish a feeding pattern in surrounding fields, eating waste corn and grass. Picture-perfect mass takeoffs occur right around sundown. The geese remain until dwindling temperatures freeze their water supply.

Recreation and Tours

The Horicon Marsh Wildlife Area, in the southern half of the marsh, has several established **canoe trails** through the wetlands, Mieske Bay, and along the east branch of the Rock River.

More than six miles of **hiking trails** are accessible on the south side of WI 49. The trails spin deep into the marsh, occasionally on boardwalks, sometimes shrouded by cattails.

Canoes can be rented at the **Blue Heron Landing,** WI 33 at the bridge in Horicon, also the place to get aboard a **pontoon boat tour** of the marsh with **Blue Heron Tours** (920/485-

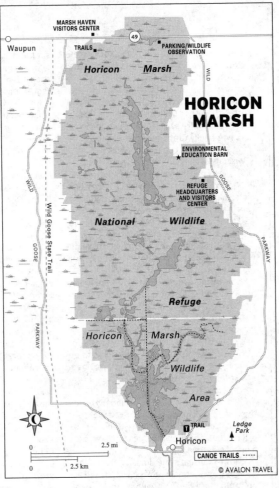

4663, www.horiconmarsh.com). Tours run daily at 1 P.M. May–September, weekends only in the off-season. A one-hour tour is $10 adults. A special two-hour tour, taking in the largest heron and egret rookery in Wisconsin, is twice the price. Canoe and kayak tours and rentals can also be arranged.

Tons of special events take place throughout the year. One of the best in North America is early May's **Bird Festival;** check horiconmarshbirdclub.com for information.

Marsh Haven Visitors Center

Three miles east of Waupun along WI 49 is the marsh's **visitors center** (920/342-5818, 10 A.M.–4 P.M. Mon.–Fri., 9 A.M.–5 P.M. Sat.–Sun., $1). It has a theater, art displays, exhibits on the natural history of the marsh—including a live display of birds—and trail access from the parking lot.

Marsh Headquarters

The DNR Headquarters (920/387-7860) of the Horicon Marsh Wildlife Area is along WI 28, open weekdays. The National Wildlife Refuge Headquarters (920/387-2658) is open weekdays and is housed in a $5 million education center, with nearby hiking trails and wildlife-viewing area. Plans include a 6,500-square-foot education center between Horicon and Mayville.

Horicon

The small town of Horicon has camping ($8), its own hiking trails, and Indian caves under the bluff line at **Ledge Park,** east of town via WI 28 and Raasch's Hill Road. Truly a spectacular place to hang out, it's the western edge of the Niagara Escarpment, which stretches all the way up to Niagara Falls.

Horicon also has an access trail to the **Wild Goose State Trail,** a 30-mile multipurpose trail skirting the western edge of the marsh all the way north to Fond du Lac. Brief sections of the trail allow horses, ATVs, and snowmobiles. Trail passes, which are available at the Marsh Headquarters, are required.

Waupun

Even with a maximum-security prison casting a shadow over the town, Waupun somehow manages to maintain an attractive, if somewhat subdued, downtown. (It was described by the old WPA Wisconsin guidebook as "almost oppressively pleasant.") Noteworthy are its five life-size bronze statues scattered throughout town, presented to Waupun by a late industrialist/sculptor, some of whose own sculptures are also seen about. One of the life-size statues, on Madison Street, is the first casting of James Earl Fraser's *End of the Trail,* part of a series

commemorating the genocidal expansionism of the frontier.

Geese are everywhere in Waupun, both as decoration and physically during migration. The city fetes all those geese the first week of October during **Wild Goose Days.** Great ethnic festivals in Waupun include the **Klompen Fest,** a Dutch fair in June in which townsfolk literally "klomp" through town and scrub the streets in one particularly memorable parade; and **Volksfest,** a German blowout the first week of September.

Waupun has an access trail leading east to the Wild Goose State Trail.

Mayville

East of the marsh in the town of Mayville—whose city water has been judged by certain scientists as some of the best tasting in the United States—is the **White Limestone School** (N. Main St., 920/387-3474, 1:30–4:30 P.M. second and fourth Sun. May–Oct., free), known mostly for its collection of rural Wisconsin photographs taken by Edgar Mueller. The local historical society operates the **Hollenstein Wagon and Carriage Factory** (11 N. German St., 920/387-5530, 1:30–4:30 P.M. every second and fourth Sun., free), an old factory that once produced wagons. Several wagons are on display.

One of the best inns in Wisconsin—for eating and sleeping—the ◖ **Audubon Inn** (45 N. Main St., 920/387-5848, www.audubon-innjamhospitality.com, from $120) dates from 1897 and you'll feel you're in bygone days when you enter.

COLUMBUS

Given the name, it's no surprise that the community is home to the **Christopher Columbus Museum** (239 Whitney St., 608/623-1992, www.columbusantiquemall.com, 8:15 A.M.–4 P.M. daily, free), one of two in the world, though this is suspiciously housed within the state's largest antiques mall (more than 72,000 square feet of old stuff—one of the largest collections of glassware in the United States is here).

Otherwise, the downtown has intriguing,

small-town architecture, the most significant example of which is the **"Jewel Box"** (159 W. James St.), or, the 1920 Farmer's and Merchant's Bank, a lovely example of Louis Sullivan's Prairie School style and now a quasi-local museum full of banking and architectural stuff upstairs.

WATERTOWN

Watertown justifies its name: It lies at the bifurcation of the Rock River as it wends through an oxbow bend in the valley. Yankee settlers appeared as early as 1836 and harnessed the channel's water power—it drops 20 feet on its course through town—for grist- and flour mills, some of which still stand.

Historically, besides water power, Watertown was known for geese and Germans. Watertown goose livers were the top of the pâté de foie gras line. The city exported up to 25 tons of the rich organ to eastern markets annually. (Watertown perfected the art of "noodling"—force-feeding the geese with noodles to fatten them up.) The local high school's team nickname is the Goslings—not exactly ferocious, but at least historically relevant.

Until quite recently, the town's name was rendered Wasserstadt on a few business signs, a remnant of the heavy immigration of enlightened freethinkers fleeing political and social persecution in 1848 Germany. Most notable was Carl Schurz, a political reformer who arrived in Watertown in 1855 and eventually left his mark on U.S. politics. His wife put the town on the map, though, in contemporary terms; hers was the first kindergarten in the United States, which continues to be one of the city's primary tourist draws. At a critical transportation point in southern Wisconsin, Watertown was rumored at one time to be on the short list for state capital relocation.

◖ Octagon House

This house (919 Charles St., 920/261-2796, docent-led tours 10 A.M.–4 P.M. daily May–Oct., 11 A.M.–3 P.M. Labor Day–Memorial Day, $7 adults) may be the most impressive in the state. It is certainly the largest pre–Civil War

Watertown's enormous Octagon House

© THOMAS HUHTI

family residence in the Midwest, with more than 8,000 square feet of floor space and 57 rooms (although only one fireplace!). Built during the course of 13 years by John Richards—who owned three mills on the river below the vertiginous hill upon which the house sits—the house sports one of the nation's only cantilevered spiral staircases, a basswood and cherry marvel that pirouettes 40 feet to the upper levels. This baby was so well built that reportedly not one of the stairs on the staircases creaks! Behind the house on the large grounds is the nation's first kindergarten.

Practicalities

Lodging-wise, go south eight miles on WI 26 to I-94, where there are tons of chains.

The (**Upper Krust** (1300 Memorial Dr., 920/206-9202, 6 A.M.–9 P.M. Mon.–Sat., 9 A.M.–1:30 P.M. Sun., $3–8) is a creative breakfast/sandwich/hot plate kind of place, but it's absolutely famed for its killer pies. You can't get near this place at lunch; it's so popular that traveling businesspeople will phone a day ahead to reserve pies and then take away a dozen at a time!

The building housing **Elias Inn** (200 N. 2nd St., 920/261-6262, 5–10 P.M. Mon.–Thurs. and Sat., 4–10:30 P.M. Fri., $6 and up) has come a long way from the days when it was a German-style *bierstube*. Farmers coming into town to do their banking on Friday would stop off to quaff a brackish tap in a cloudy glass while suit-and-tie types from the bank munched head cheese or homemade venison sausage. Its present incarnation is straight-up supper club with hints of Midwestern regional cuisine.

(**Mullen's** (212 W. Main St., 920/261-4278) is a southeastern Wisconsin landmark. Well into its sixth decade, it's got the best homemade ice cream you'll ever taste and an interior reminiscent of bygone times.

OCONOMOWOC

That's oh-KAHN-uh-muh-wahk (sometimes that first syllable sounds an awful lot like "uh"). It's the only city in America with a name spelled with five o's, one in every odd-numbered position in the word. Oconomowoc is another trim, spread-out Victorian city, this one wound around Lac La Belle and Fowler Lake, with other lakes in chip-shot range.

Oconomowoc is primarily a strolling town, and the local chamber of commerce along East Washington Avenue has brochures for a **historical walking tour.** If you don't have any time to actually take the tour, go to the lobby of the First Bank of Oconomowoc (155 W. Wisconsin Ave., 262/569-9900), where you'll find paintings of many of the homes in town.

Food

Spinnaker's (128 W. Wisconsin Ave., 262/567-9691, lunch and dinner daily, $6–11), right on Lac La Belle serves casual food, from burgers to seafood and prime rib. Live entertainment is offered Wednesday–Saturday nights. It's one of the best places to take the brood for a step above average family-style restaurants. A nice screened porch is a perfect spot to unwind.

Purportedly the oldest dining establishment in Wisconsin is the (**Red Circle Inn** (262/367-4883, 5–9:30 P.M. Tues.–Sat., $18–25), established in 1848. Enjoy gourmet American and some French country cuisine. You'll find it along WI 16 east of Oconomowoc Lake at the junction with Highway C.

KETTLE MORAINE STATE FOREST-SOUTHERN UNIT

The Kettle Moraine State Forest-Southern Unit is sibling to the northern tier. Debate continues—gets a bit bristly at times—over plans to acquire sufficient private lands to link the two (and the Ice Age National Scenic Trail), creating a green buffer against Lake Michigan suburban expansion and, thus, preventing the destruction of southern Wisconsin's glacial topography. The Wisconsin DNR hoped to add more than 16,000 acres by the time this edition is finished (or it may be too late).

The state's oddball glacial heritage pops up everywhere—residual kames, eskers, and the eponymous kettles and moraines. Also within the forest are weatherbeaten homestead log cabins, now one-eyed and decaying in the tall grass, and a handful of bluff-line panoramas taking in all the glacial geology. In 2002, the forest literally returned to life. Original prairie seeds dormant for 150 years bloomed again; the resurgence happened because of agricultural lands lying fallow long enough. With time DNR hopes to bring back 5,000 acres of phoenixlike seeds, which would make it the largest natural prairie area east of the Mississippi River.

The **KMSF Headquarters** (S91 W39091 WI 59, 262/594-6200, 8 a.m.–4:30 p.m. daily) has detailed maps of the whole shebang.

Recreation

You'll hear cyclists muttering about the parking lots being chockablock with autos, but those same whiners seem to forget innocent hikers, who can barely take a step without checking for gonzo mountain bikers. Yes, Kettle Moraine is popular, so be prepared.

The forest offers 160(!) miles of trails, some hiking, some biking, some both; most of these are groomed for cross-country skiing in winter. The National Ice Age Scenic Trail cuts through the park from the Pine Woods Campground to Rice Lake—about 30 miles (usually cut into four segments). The rough but popular John Muir Trails boast incredible blooms of pasque flowers in spring and some of the best biking—diverse, challenging, and designed specifically for mountain bikes. (Look at the twists and turns of the blue loop's southernmost point, stretching into a mature hardwood forest, and you'll see the outline of a squirrel.)

Camping

Primitive camping is allowed at three Adirondack backpacking shelters along the Ice Age Trail—free, registration necessary. The forest also has four campgrounds, some with walk-in sites. There is also a fully accessible camping cabin. For tranquility, head directly to Pine Woods Campground; not only does it have the most isolated, shaded campsites, but it also has 32 sites where radios are banned (a godsend—respite from the yahoos)!

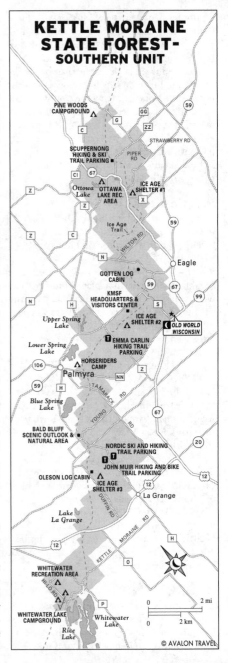

on the trail in the Kettle Moraine State Forest-Southern Unit

You can also get to boat-in campsites; check at the ranger station.

Food
Impressive is **Union House** (262/968-4281, dinner from 4:30 P.M. Tues.–Sat., $17–32), in Genesee Depot. There's great heartland fare buttressed by unique entrées such as quail—lots of wild game, actually.

Supplies and Rentals
La Grange General Store (N1242 WI 59, 262/495-8600, www.backyardbikes.com) is a welcome little gem dispensing a luscious array of deli, café, and natural-food items. You can also get items such as buffalo burgers, organic chicken from Oconomowoc farms, and other meats from local producers. It also rents mountain bikes and cross-country skis.

◖ OLD WORLD WISCONSIN
Say "Eagle, Wisconsin," and even natives say, "Where?" But say, "Old World Wisconsin" and everybody's eyes light up. City-size Old World

Wisconsin (Hwy. 67, 262/594-6300, www.wisconsinhistory.org, 10 A.M.–5 P.M. Mon.–Sat., noon–5 P.M. Sun. in summer, shorter hours May–Nov., $16 adults), a 575-acre outdoor museum run by the state historical society, comprises more than 65 immigrant structures relocated from around the state and organized here into Polish, Danish, Norwegian, Yankee, Finnish, and, not one but two, German homesteads. Its collection of original log and wood buildings is the largest in the United States and considered the best. Newer are reconstructed buildings and a cemetery from Pleasant Ridge in Grant County in southwestern Wisconsin (five miles south of Lancaster); this was among Wisconsin's first African American communities. The complex is so big that trams ($2) make a circuit continuously.

Walking the whole route is about 2.5 miles; to save your legs, nature trails cut through woods or across meadows.

Despite this, attendance has been plummeting. New proposals to incite interest include relocating an original Wisconsin beerhouse here, constructing a Native American village, and even loosing buffalo and elk on-site! Worse, in 2010 a massive tornado hit the grounds, causing a worrisome amount of damage; you'll be able to see damage for some time (especially a sad dearth of trees now).

Very popular is the **Clausing Barn Restaurant,** an octagonal 1897 barn designed by a Mequon immigrant. It offers casual cafeteria-style dining with an emphasis on heritage cuisine.

FORT ATKINSON
Bisected by the Rock River, which flows sluggishly south and west of town into Lake Koshkonong, the town was hastily erected by soldiers during the 1832 Black Hawk War. Dairying truly put the town on the map. William Dempster Hoard, the sort of patron saint of Wisconsin's dairy industry, began *Hoard's Dairyman*, a newsletter-cum-magazine, here in 1873. Fort Atkinson is a trim slice of Americana. It's been called by *Money* magazine one of the "hottest" small towns in the country.

© THOMAS HUHTI

HER LIFE BY WATER

Absolutely unknown to Wisconsinites – except those in her hometown of Fort Atkinson – Lorine Niedecker's simplistic, haiku-like poetry (life and place among the common) is arguably the most evocative interpretation of the ethos of a place in the canon of Wisconsin literature. Overlooked as most poets are, she has been included by no less than the *Norton Anthology* as one of the 20th century's most significant American poets.

Lorine Niedecker was born in 1903 on her beloved Blackhawk Island, a peninsular marshy swale with a rustic collection of minor resorts and fishing families in shotgun shacks. Blackhawk Island's isolation and tough life – the river flooded, her father seined carp in scows, and her mother developed deafness – caused her to leave Beloit College early.

Reading Louis Zukofsky's "Objectivist" issue of *Poetry* magazine in 1931 changed her profoundly. The objectivist doctrine of viewing a poem as a pure form through which the things of the world are seen without the ambiguity of feeling resonated deeply in her. Like those of other prominent Wisconsin writers – among them Zona Gale, John Muir, Aldo Leopold – Niedecker's works were ecological in every sense. Her attention to the "condensory" (her word) called for using only words that contributed to a visual and aural presentation. Resolutely hermitic, Niedecker cloistered herself in her small hand-built cottage. This sense of isolation is fundamental to appreciating her passionately understated writing.

Niedecker never sold many books but was not interested in teaching, so she supported herself by scrubbing floors at Fort Atkinson General Hospital, scriptwriting for WHA radio in Madison, and proofreading for *Hoard's Dairyman*. Her greatest work may have been as field editor for the classic Wisconsin guidebook – the 1942 WPA guide to the Badger State.

An unhappy first marriage ended in 1930. She remarried happily in 1961 and traveled widely throughout the Midwest for the first time. It was this travel that raised her poetry to another level; for the first time she wrote extended poems. Her output was prolific as she lived quietly on the island until her death in 1971.

MUST-READS
What many consider her greatest poem, "Lake Superior," was included in the great *North Central*, published in 1968 in London, followed two years later by the classic *My Life By Water: Collected Poems 1936-68.*

◖ Hoard Historical Museum and Dairy Shrine

No visit to America's Dairyland would be complete without a look-see at the Hoard Historical Museum (407 Merchants Ave., 920/563-7769, 9:30 A.M.–4:30 P.M. Tues.–Sat. June–Labor Day, shorter hours the rest of the year, free), housed in a Gothic revival/mission oak–style mansion. The museum displays a restoration of the Dwight Foster House—the area's first frame house, built in 1841—along with two rooms of exhibits, the anchors of which are an extensive, 15,000-piece Native American artifact collection—so extensive the Smithsonian once eyed it—and a wealth of information on the Black Hawk War. Even Abe Lincoln, who traveled through the county in 1832 with the militia chasing Black Hawk, gets a nod.

The museum is also the site of the **Dairy Shrine,** an assemblage of audiovisual displays, dioramas, and artifacts tracing the history of Wisconsin dairying.

Lake Koshkonong

The second-largest lake in Wisconsin, Lake Koshkonong is fed by the Rock River. The lake's entire circumference is lined with restaurants, inns, resorts, and marinas. For a small village town, Newville's got a lot of action, especially in the way of restaurants and pubs. You'll also find county parks with trails bypassing effigy mounds, covered bridges on bike trails, and canoe rentals.

Accommodations and Food

A favorite place of mine in these parts is the ⟨ **Cafe Carpe** (18 S. Water St., 920/563-9391, www.cafecarpe.com, hours vary—but it stays open late, $4–12), one of the best casual eateries in the state. The food is a carefree, delicious blend of Midwestern diner and downscale café. But "the Carp" is even more famous as Wisconsin's best venue for folk music. Low-key and friendly, this is one place you'll revisit.

Side Trip: Jefferson

The next town north of Fort Atkinson (via WI 26) is Jefferson, worth a visit for its natural beauty. The **Jefferson Marsh Wildlife and Natural Area,** east of Jefferson via Highway Y, is a 3,129-acre tamarack preserve—the state's largest—and a sanctuary for endangered egrets. It's even got effigy mounds.

⟨ Aztalan State Park

Aztalan State Park (920/648-8774), a skip off the interstate, is completely overlooked by 99 percent of passing travelers. Or, for the moment it is. The state has plans to upgrade facilities, reclaim surrounding farmland, add a chic new visitors center, and increase attendance by 700 percent. Visit while it's still an isolated gem.

Surrounded by agrarian stretches, the park feels eerily historic; the Rock River rolls by silently, and the only sound audible is the wind shuffling through the leaves of the corn. One of the largest and most carefully researched archaeological sites in Wisconsin, Aztalan covers almost 175 acres and features remnant stockades and hiking trails snaking in and around the large burial mounds. Scientists theorize that this spot was a strategic northern endpoint of a Middle Mississippian culture, whose influence stretched south to New Orleans and into Mexico. If the solitary—if not lonely—park superintendent is around, you may get an impromptu tour.

Lake Mills is an engaging classic small Victorian town. Encircling a central park, it has wide tree-lined avenues, mansions, and droopy willow trees. Visitors can enjoy Lake Mills' free Bartles Beach or, for a fee, Sandy Beach, on the other side of Rock Lake. (An

new and old at Aztalan State Park near Lake Mills

SOUTHEASTERN WISCONSIN

aside: There are those who believe—this is no joke, universities have sent research teams—that there are pyramids beneath the black surface of Rock Lake. Apparently, these structures were produced by copper-mining expeditions from Asia and Europe several thousand years ago. Why they would halt mining and create pyramids hasn't been explained.) The less leisure-minded should head to the junction of WI 89 and Highway A, a node for the **Glacial Drumlin Trail,** a 47-mile multipurpose recreation trail spanning from Waukesha to Cottage Grove east of Madison. The Lake Mills segment may be the most picturesque along the entire trail, with an old depot and trestle at the trailhead not far from Rock Lake. There's also a good wildlife area south of Lake Mills.

Cuisine-wise, the community arguably has the best burgers in the state—butter-filled little heart-attack patties called **sliders** served all summer by the American Legion (129 S. Main St., Lake Mills, 920/648-5115) right downtown.

CAMBRIDGE

A perfect day trip from Madison, Cambridge lies along U.S. 12/18 to the east. Actually a mosaic of communities around the minor resort-area nucleus of Lake Ripley, Cambridge is now mostly associated with its myriad pottery shops, antique stores, and quaint architecture.

Nonantiquers can head to the innumerable parks, including Ripley Park on the west end of Lake Ripley. Better is the **Cam-Rock Park System,** consisting of three parks with tons of trails around small ponds and lakes. The Glacial Drumlin Trail passes north and west in Deerfield.

Janesville

General Motors bought out a local factory in 1919 and began Janesville's first assembly line. Within a decade, more than half of the city owed its economic fortunes to GM. And did until the shocking economic collapse of 2009 left its final GM plant shuttered. But blue-collar doesn't mean generic—you'd be amazed how trim and architecturally special the city can be (approximately one-fifth of all of Wisconsin's buildings on the National Register of Historic Places can be found in Janesville!).

SIGHTS
Rotary Gardens

One slice of the city's 2,100 acres of park, these gardens (1455 Palmer Dr., 608/752-3885, www.rotarygardens.org, dawn–dusk daily year-round, $5 adults, $3 children) spread over a dozen acres and encompass several landscaping techniques—Japanese rock, English cottage, French, Italian, sunken, and perennial, all united by a theme of Dialogue: World Peace Through Freedom.

Across the street you'll find a segment of the Ice Age Trail.

Not far from Rotary Gardens is **Palmer Park** (2501 Palmer Dr.), a large green space with a wading pool, tennis courts, and the CAMDEN Playground, the largest fully accessible playground in the United States.

Lincoln-Tallman House

The Lincoln-Tallman House (440 N. Jackson St., 608/752-459, 9 A.M.–4 P.M. daily June–Sept., weekends year-round, $8 adults), the 1855 home of a prominent abolitionist, is the only private residence in Wisconsin in which Abe Lincoln hung his hat. Architecture mavens have called it one of the finest of its kind in America. Also on-site are the original horse barn and a Greek revival stone house used by servants.

A million-dollar-plus renovation added heating and air-conditioning to preserve the original decorations and interiors, including the bed in which Honest Abe slept. The house offers lots of special holiday tours.

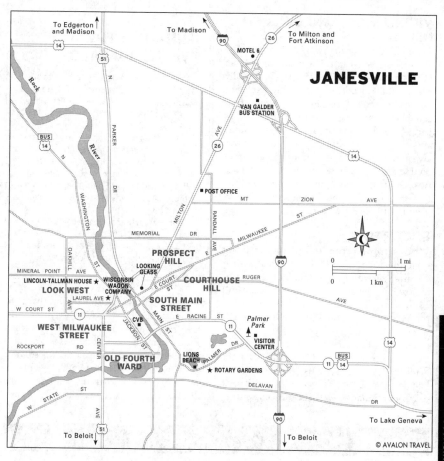

Wisconsin Wagon Company

This Janesville company (507 Laurel Ave., 608/754-0026, tours by appointment, $3) makes replicas of wooden American Classic coaster wagons—an outstanding bit of Americana brought to life, since the original factory went out of production in 1934 and the Sears-Roebuck catalog was never the same.

ACCOMMODATIONS AND FOOD

Cheapest dependable digs are without question at the local **Motel 6** (3907 Milton Ave.,

608/756-1742, $40). A number of other chain motels are nearby.

Looking Glass (18 N. Main, 608/755-9828, 11 A.M.–9 P.M. Mon.–Fri., 11 A.M.–6 P.M. Sat., noon–4 P.M. Sun, $3–7) has pub grub. The interior is a rustic blend of original high, pressed-tin ceilings and polished brass and dark wood bar.

GETTING THERE

Van Galder buses (608/752-5407) stop in Janesville en route to Madison and Chicago up to 10 times a day. The bus stops at the terminal at 3120 North Pontiac.

VICINITY OF JANESVILLE
Milton
At the junction of highways WI 26 and WI 59 in flyspeck Milton is the **Milton House Museum** (608/868-7772, 10 A.M.–5 P.M. daily Memorial Day weekend–Labor Day, weekends only spring and fall, $6 adults), a 20-room hexagonal erstwhile stagecoach inn once used as part of the Underground Railroad—the stone and earth tunnels still lie beneath it. It was also purportedly the first building made from poured grout "concrete" in the United States. Also on the grounds is an 1837 log cabin (the terminus of the subterranean tunnel) and plenty of 19th-century artifacts.

EDGERTON
Whiz through the fields surrounding Edgerton and you'd swear you were in North Carolina or eastern Virginia by the odor of tobacco on the air. Edgerton is Wisconsin's "Tobacco City." Thus it makes sense that the **Tobacco Heritage Days** (608/347-4321, www.tobaccoheritagedays.com) are held here in mid-July. For a few years there, apparently PC-dom had run amok (they likely thought filtering down from Madison) and the name had dropped the, er, "T" word. Now, it's back to tabacky, proudly. Well, the tobacco-spitting

---

MIRACLE: THE WHITE BUFFALO

In 1994, an extraordinarily rare white buffalo – Miracle – was born on the Heider Farm near Janesville. It was the first white buffalo in the United States since 1933. Spiritually significant to Native Americans, it became a pilgrimage point. Amazingly and admirably, the family refused to profit off it and instead opened its farm to all comers just to share in such a blessing. Miracle died in 2004, but amazingly, another white calf was born in 2006, though it lived only a few months.

The **Heider Farm** family continues to greet visitors (2739 River Rd. S, 608/741-9632, whitebuffalomiracle.homestead.com) daily, but call first to confirm.

---

contest has been discontinued, but that's another matter entirely.

Otherwise, check out Rascal, as in the raccoon of the eponymous classic children's book, which was written by local Sterling North, whose home (409 W. Rollin St., 608/884-7589, 1–4:30 P.M. Sun., $3) is pretty much as the family left it (he really did keep a raccoon in his room!).

Beloit

Beloit lies along a wide expanse of the Rock River at its confluence at Turtle Creek. It is a lovely spot, explaining in part the migration of virtually the entire village of Colebrook, New Hampshire, to this town in 1837.

The city's founders erected a college (respected Beloit College, patterned after eastern religious seminaries) and a church before much of anything else and landscaped the town around designs of a New England village with a square. It must have had a positive effect. In the rough-and-tumble 1840s, a traveler wrote of it as "an unusual community, amid shifting pioneer conditions already evincing character and solidity."

Anthropologist Margaret Mead once called busy and vibrant Beloit "a microcosm of America."

SIGHTS
The following are but a small sketch—this city has an inordinate amount of great historic attractions!

Angel Museum
The world's largest privately held collection of angel artifacts is on display at Beloit's Angel Museum (656 Pleasant St., 608/362-9099, www.angelmuseum.com, 10 A.M.–4 P.M. Thurs.–Sat. Apr.–Dec., $7 adults), housed

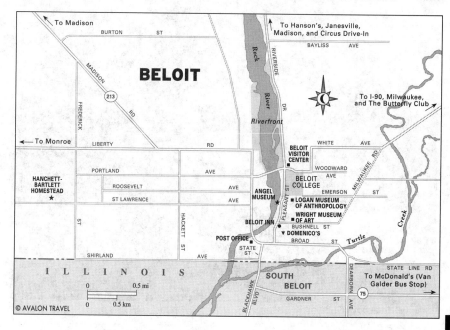

in a restored church right on the Rock River. Angels of all sorts are on display—more than 12,000 and counting—but the highlight is no doubt the nearly 600 African American angels donated by Oprah Winfrey.

Beloit College

Founded on the Rock River's east bank as Beloit Seminary, Beloit College (www.beloit.edu) is the oldest college in Wisconsin. Its founding philosophy was to preserve eastern mores and culture in the heathen "West"—though it could pay its two professors only $600 a year "if they can raise it." The Middle College building, dating from 1847, is the oldest college building north of Chicago. Beloit College's Victorian Gothic **Logan Museum of Anthropology** (College and Bushnell Sts., 608/363-2677, 11 A.M.–4 P.M. Tues.–Sun., free) is now one of the most respected museums in the state, with almost a quarter of a million artifacts from around the globe, including the most extensive Stone Age and paleolithic collections outside of Europe. There are those who believe, incidentally, that a

certain Beloit College professor was the inspiration for Indiana Jones. Hmm.

The **Wright Museum of Art** (Bushnell St. and Prospect St., 608/363-2677, 11 A.M.–4 P.M. Tues.–Sun., closed during campus holidays, free) has permanent holdings, including American and European paintings and sculpture, Asian decorative arts, and graphics.

The new **science building** is just off Pleasant Street and offers a telescope on top of the building (the erstwhile observatory may be relocated). Also, more than two dozen Indian burial mounds dot the campus.

Historic Buildings

The **Near East Side** has more than two dozen structures east of Beloit College; the **Bluff Street** area is also good. Houses in the Near East Side include the unique cobblestone Rasey House, Beloit College's original president's home, and a mélange of mid- to late-19th-century styles. The Bluff Street area across the river also features some houses with delightful cobblestone construction.

© THOMAS HUHTI

Tiffany Bridge outside Beloit

Hanchett-Bartlett Homestead

This limestone Greek revival and Italianate mansion (2149 St. Lawrence Ave., 608/365-7835, 1–4 P.M. Sat.–Sun. June–Sept., $3 adults suggested), built from locally quarried stone, sits on 15 acres and has been restored to period detail, with special attention to the original color schemes. A great limestone barn filled with farm implements sits on the property, along with a smokehouse nearby. A rural school has been relocated here, and the gray shed-planked Beckman-Howe mill (608/365-1600), on the National Register of Historic Places and dating to the post–Civil War period, is a five-minute drive west on Highway H. The mill has been selected as one of the 10 most endangered historic sites in Wisconsin.

Side Trips

Tough-to-find little **Tiffany** lies northeast of Beloit on Highway S, but it's worth a search; it's got one of the most unusual **bridges** anywhere, a remnant five-arch iron-truss span

based on Roman architecture. Built by the Chicago and Northwestern Railroad in 1869, the structure was modeled after a bridge in Compiegne, France. Each arch spans 50 feet with a 26-foot radius. To reach Tiffany, head east on Highway S from Shopiere and turn left onto Smith Road. You can really view the bridge only from the Smith Road iron truss bridge, built in 1890. Tiffany is a personal favorite, an anachronistic relic in the dewy midst of nowhere. The **Tiffany Banquet Inn** (5842 E. Creek Rd., 608/365-7600) is a wonderful place for dinner—the fish fry is amazing, and they polka down Friday and Saturday.

Back in Shopiere, check out the village's antique weight-driven timepiece adorned with four lion heads.

ENTERTAINMENT AND EVENTS
Nightlife

Young visitors will want to head straight for the **C House** (608/363-2804), a.k.a. Coughy Haus or CHAUS, on the Beloit College campus. A dark but cozy hall, there are bands at times, from grunge to jazz-fusion.

Events

The summer brings July's **Riverfest** (608/302-5256, www.beloitriverfest.com) a four-day music fest that's one of the largest of its kind in the country, with more than 50 national acts performing. Only Milwaukee's Summerfest is larger in Wisconsin.

Turtles in the Park (www.visitbeloit.com) in August is just precious—all turtles, everywhere. Check it out!

RECREATION
Camping

The **Turtle Creek Campground** (608/362-7768) is two miles northwest of town just off of I-90.

Spectator Sports

The **Beloit Snappers** (608/362-2272) are a farm team of the Minnesota Twins. The Snappers' logo-adorned paraphernalia are among the country's most sought-after souvenirs.

ACCOMMODATIONS

Given the proud architecture of Beloit, it's a tad surprising that the city lacks a historic inn or B&B.

Contemporary cool meets with historic touches at the newish **Beloit Inn** (500 Pleasant St., 608/362-5500, www.beloitinn.com, $99) right downtown. This attractive place has studio and one-bedroom suites with lots of extras. Many have opined it's worth the money.

FOOD

Enjoy *huge* burgers (and assorted "Roadkill") at **Hanson's** (615 E. Cranston Rd., 11 A.M.–variable hours daily, $2–8) on the river along U.S. 51. It's also the place to experience local flavor, hands down.

The **Circus Drive-In** (3525 Riverside Dr., 608/362-9375, 11 A.M.–8 P.M. daily, from 4 P.M. Mon., $2–5) is a classic, complete with trays hooked on half-open windows. Interestingly, new owners had trouble coming up with a loan to refurbish it and banks wouldn't touch 'em. So a generous local just gave 'em the cash—howzat for good small-town neighbors?

Domenico's (547 E. Grand Ave., 608/365-9489, 11 A.M.–11 P.M. daily, $6–9) is the pizza joint of choice, with a good veggie pie. Also featured are Italian goodies such as chicken primavera, veal *a'dominico,* and lots of shrimp and seafood.

Equally traditional, casually ritzy, and open for over seven decades is ◖ **The Butterfly Club** (Hwy. K east of town, 608/362-8577, 5–9:30 P.M. Mon.–Sat., noon–8 P.M. Sun., $9–23). Enjoy supper club dining on a patio and likely the best fish fry around (available Wednesday nights as well as Friday). You gotta love fresh-baked cinnamon rolls with your meal. Live entertainment is featured on Friday.

INFORMATION

The **Beloit Visitor Center** (500 Public Ave., 608/365-4838 or 800/423-5648, www.visitbeloit.com) is near the Beloit Inn.

GETTING THERE

Van Galder buses (608/752-5407) stop in Beloit on their forays to and from Madison and Chicago (O'Hare airport and downtown). The 10 daily buses (each way) stop at the McDonald's in South Beloit, at the junction of IL 75 and U.S. 51.

The local **Greyhound** (3001 Milwaukee Rd., 608/365-7808) has daily departures to Madison and Chicago.

Lake Geneva and Environs

Of Wisconsin's three lakes regions, the southernmost playground is the gateway resort city of Lake Geneva (not to be confused with the lake itself, Geneva Lake!).

It's visited by quite a few Windy City summertime refugees who'd prefer not to tackle the five-hour drive all the way to the northern woods. About 60 percent of annual visitors in fact call Chicago home. In the town and around the entire perimeter of the lake are eye-catching anachronistic residences, cautious development (a modicum of ersatz New England does exist), a state park, and sites of historical interest.

History

The lake was originally settled by Potawatomi Indians on its western cusp. Big Foot State Park is named for a Potawatomi chief—bleakly ironic since the Potawatomi were forcibly relocated to Kansas. Minor milling days lasted

until the Iron Rooster steamed into town on freshly laid tracks, carrying Chicago's elite for a summertime respite. The Great Fire of 1871 cemented the city's status as a getaway when it became a retreat for Chicago's refugees. So many magnificent estates lined the shores it was dubbed "Newport of the West," a moniker still applicable today.

A note: Lake Geneva is one piece of the Geneva Lake area mosaic. Actually composed of four lakes—Delavan, Comus, Como, and Geneva—the area forms a rough triangle with the city of Lake Geneva to the east, Delavan 10 miles to the west, and little Fontana to the south on the western cusp of Geneva Lake. Williams Bay is also included, along the northern perimeter of Geneva Lake. Lakeless little Elkhorn lies to the north, outside the immediate area.

◖ GENEVA LAKE

With a surface area of 5,262 acres (7.6 miles long by 2.1 miles wide) and a depth of 135 feet, Geneva Lake is one of the larger lakes in southern Wisconsin. Spring-fed, it was carved out by the Michigan glacier during the ultimate glacial epoch. Today one can't help but love its loopy mix of restored Victorian and low-key resort, natural splendor, and most of all, its accessibility in circumference to the public.

The coolest activity in southern Wisconsin? Lake Geneva residents still get their mail delivered by boat, just as in the 1930s. Visitors can also hop on the mail boat, the *Walworth II* (Riviera Docks, 262/248-6206 or 800/558-5911, www.cruiselakegeneva.com), in operation for more than 100 years, seven days a week in summer, albeit for $29 adults.

Then again, busy-as-a-bee types with itchy feet absolutely insist the most fun is a 26-mile-long **footpath** that circles the lake via linked ancient Native American footpaths. (Truly remarkable, given the century the place has been a tourist haven; the law actually requires its preservation.) You can reach it at any park along the

LAKE GENEVA

MAXWELL · MADISON ST · BROAD ST · 120 · NORTH ST · To Kettle Moraine State Forest · ▼ MEDUSA · SAGE ST · WISCONSIN ST · ST · To Delavan · GENEVA ST · ★LAKE GENEVA MUSEUM · To Kenosha · T.C. SMITH INN B&B ● · MAIN ST · 50 · LIBRARY ■ · ■ POST OFFICE · CHAMBER OF COMMERCE ■ · ANNIE'S ICE CREAM PARLOR AND RESTAURANT · SCUTTLEBUTT'S ▼ · BOAT TOURS · POPEYE'S · ◖ GENEVA LAKE · H · S LAKE SHORE DR · WELLS ST · 0 0.25 mi · 0 0.25 km · SEVEN OAKS · 120 · To Big Foot Beach State Park and Illinois · © AVALON TRAVEL

Lake Geneva

lakefront. Along the way, the path passes those same gargantuan summer homes (palatial manors), a state park, and loads o' natural beauty. Ultimately, the one big typical draw is **Yerkes Observatory** (373 W. Geneva St., Williams Bay, 262/245-5555, tours 10 A.M., 11 A.M., and noon Sat., free), which has the world's largest refractor telescope. The observatory, now obsolete (though lovely from the outside), has been shopped around by its owner, the University of Chicago. One plan included—gulp—building a luxury resort around it (it was quashed due to public outcry).

Opened only in 2008 after a massive $1.2-million renovation is **Black Point Estate** (262/248-1888, www.blackpointmansion. com). (Bless the family for this—they could have sold it off for bazillions in subdivision cash.) One state historian has called it the most perfect example of a summer mansion in the state. In order to see it, you should arrive the way residents here always did: by boat. *You'll need to climb about 100 stairs to scale the bluff.*

The easiest—and thus most popular—way to experience the lake is on a tour in either a replica Mississippi paddle wheeler or lake steamer from **Geneva Lake Cruise Lines** (Riviera Docks, 262/248-6206 or 800/558-5911, www.cruiselakegeneva.com). Tours leave six times daily mid-June–early September, less otherwise. Full tours range from one hour up to just under three hours and cost $21–59 adults; the higher-cost tours are daily lunch, dinner, or Sunday brunch cruises. In peak summer season boats seem to depart constantly. Other boats in the cruise line include genuine lake steamers, including one still using a steam engine from the early 1900s, the only large steamboat left in Wisconsin.

SIGHTS

For a great freebie, head for the **library** (918 W. Main St., 262/249-5299, 9 A.M.–8 P.M. Mon.–Thurs., 9 A.M.–6 P.M. Fri., 9 A.M.–1 P.M. Sat.), which has comfy chairs and a four-star view of the lake. You can also peruse detailed county guidebooks on historical structures and local history. Beyond that, head immediately for **Big Foot Beach State Park** (262/248-2528), where you'll find sublimely cool waters for dipping.

ENTERTAINMENT AND EVENTS

The third weekend of August, the community has **Venetian Nights,** when the town and lake turn into an ersatz Venice with torch-lit boat rides and lots of fireworks.

RECREATION
Boating

The Geneva Lake region has more marinas than you can imagine, including **Gordy's** (320 Lake Ave., 262/275-2163) in Fontana, with ski boats, ski schools, sailboats, and cruises.

Golf

Who said marinas? The list of golf courses is the size of a small phone book. Noteworthy is **Geneva National** (1221 Geneva National Ave. S., 262/245-7010), four miles west of Lake Geneva town on WI 50. Rated in the state's top 10 by *Golf Digest,* it's got championship courses designed by Arnold Palmer and Lee Trevino. Fees are extravagant.

Camping

Just outside of Lake Geneva to the south along WI 120, **Big Foot Beach State Park** (262/248-2528) features great swimming and picnicking. The short trails make for easy strolls and great cross-country skiing. It has too many campsites, however, for a 270-acre park.

ACCOMMODATIONS

Dozens of motels, hotels, inns, bed-and-breakfasts, and resorts line Geneva Lake and fill downtown Lake Geneva town as well as the small communities surrounding the lake—you definitely need to call ahead for summer weekends.

Sadly, though finding something sub-$100 is technically possible in high season, finding something worth recommending in Lake Geneva itself has become nearly impossible. Opinions are welcome.

$100-150

I've found the rustic (but modern enough) cottages and welcoming folks of **Duffy's** (W4086 Lake Shore Dr., 262/248-7100, www.duffpub.com, from $100) to be a treasure, like the way things used to be. It's a ten-minute drive northwest, but worth it. There's a good pub here as well.

Bugs Moran used to hang out at the **Waters Edge of Lake Geneva** (W4232 West End Rd., 262/245-9845, www.watersedgebb.com) in the 1920s and 1930s. Seven suites full of antiques—each with its own private deck—are available in a bucolic, quiet setting. You may get lucky and find a sub-$150 room here; it'd be worth it in Lake Geneva.

Over $150

Central to Lake Geneva, a block off Broad Street, is the **T. C. Smith Inn B&B** (834 Dodge St., 262/248-1097 or 800/423-0233, www.tc-smithinn.com, $175–215). It's got the most authentic historical feel—an eclectic mélange of architectural styles in an 1845 mansion set amidst a formal courtyard, gardens, and a waterfall. The posh interiors feature oriental carpets, antiques, artwork, original gasoliers, and an original trompe l'oeil (a still-life painting designed to give the illusion of reality), as well as fireplaces everywhere. It's pricey, but you get breakfast in bed!

The **French Country Inn** (WI 50 W, 262/245-5220, www.frenchcountryinn.com, $175–275) was partially constructed in Denmark and shipped stateside more than a century ago to serve as the Danish pavilion in the 1893 World's Fair; the house later did time as a Chicago rumrunner's joint during Prohibition. All rooms have TV and air-conditioning; some have fireplaces. There is a swimming pool and a modest but reputable French country-style dining room serving excellent steaks, fresh fish, and from-scratch cooking.

The **Abbey Resort** (269 Fontana Blvd., Fontana, 262/275-6811 or 800/558-2405, www.theabbeyresort.com, from $240) is an enormous spread of 13 parlors and 140 villas, some fireplace suites, and standard rooms—all of which got a $40 million renovation (renovation, not the original cost!). Amenities include indoor and outdoor pools, a health club, water-skiing, tennis, bicycling, and golf. It has four restaurants, four lounges, and, perhaps its most attractive offering, a sybaritic European spa.

The multidiamond, polystarred **(** **Grand Geneva** (U.S. 12 and WI 50, 262/248-8811 or 800/558-3417, www.grandgeneva.com, $239–389) is worth every penny if every media outlet is to be believed. A three-story lodge with more than 300 rooms, its amenities include indoor tennis, a 36-hole golf course, driving range, boat and ski rentals on-site (a downhill ski mountain is adjacent), bicycles, skeet shooting, a recreation room, indoor exercise facilities, massage therapists, weights, whirlpools, sauna, and steam room. Its private land holdings include almost 1,500 acres of diverse meadow and forest, along with its own lake.

That said, many insist that the best of all isn't even a resort. At **(** **Seven Oaks** (682 Wells St., 262/248-4006, www.sevenoakslakegeneva. com, $259), think cottage layout with boutique hotel interiors, though folks adore this place universally as much for the caring, welcoming owners. It's a genuine retreat.

FOOD
Quick Bite
The best option for dessert—for the last half century—is **Annie's Ice Cream Parlor and Restaurant** (712 Main St., 262/248-1933, $3–5). The interior is done up in late-19th-century style, and the light menu offers fresh sodas, lots of waffles, salads, quiches, and big sandwiches.

Waterfront
Legions keep coming back to **Popeye's** (Broad St. and Wrigley Dr., 414/248-4381, lunch and dinner daily, $5–11) for fare from the roaster, which smokes chicken, pork, and lamb (each on a different day). The menu also features Yankee pot roast, Middle Eastern salad, liver and onions, pot pies, and veggie burgers. Adjacent is **Scuttlebutt's** (831 Wrigley Dr., 262/248-1111, 7 A.M.–9 P.M. daily, $5–15),

another American joint with, interestingly, some Swedish specialties.

Steak Houses and Supper Clubs
An institution on the lake is the tavern downstairs at **Chuck's** (352 Lake St., 262/275-3222, lunch and dinner daily, breakfast Sat.–Sun.) on Lake Street in Fontana. The "seven-mile view" is legendary.

Worth a side trip just for the ambience is **Fitzgerald's Genoa Junction Restaurant** (772 Hwy. B, 262/279-5200, 5–9 P.M. Wed., Fri., and Sat., 3–7 P.M. Sun., $7–13) in Genoa City, approximately 10 minutes southeast of Lake Geneva. Housed in a historic octagon house, the supper club is famed for fish boils Friday; ribs, fish boil, and chicken on Wednesday and Saturday; and fish, ribs, and chicken Sunday.

Finer Dining
One needn't head to a city-state resort to get fabulous food. A Mediterranean-centric (but not solely) menu is absolutely solid at the lively bistro **(** **Medusa** (501 Broad St., 262/249-8644, 5:30–10 P.M. Fri.–Sat., $18–35). Trust the chef's specials and do try the homemade gelato.

Most of the resorts have their own restaurants. Of note are **The Abbey Resort** (269 Fontana Blvd., Fontana, 262/275-6811 or 800/558-2405, www.theabbeyresort.com); the **French Country Inn** (WI 50 W, 262/245-5220, www.frenchcountryinn.com); and the **Grandview** (2009 S. Lake Shore Drive, 262/248-5680) at the Geneva Inn.

INFORMATION
The **Lake Geneva Chamber of Commerce** (201 Wrigley Dr., 262/248-4416 or 800/345-1020, www.lakegenevawi.com) is well versed in helping tourists out.

VICINITY OF LAKE GENEVA
Elkhorn
This trim village up U.S. 12 northwest of Lake Geneva lies splayed around a somnolent tree-shaded square. It's sometimes called "Christmas

SOUTHEASTERN WISCONSIN

Card Town"—and you'll know why if you show up anytime around Christmas. It's the kind of place where local businesses list their home phone numbers as well as their business phones. The oldest municipal band in the state, established in the 1840s, still toots it out summer Friday evenings at Sunset Park. This seems singularly appropriate, because five primary industries of the town are related to the manufacture of musical instruments.

One rumor running rampant around Elkhorn concerns the existence of a large-eared, werewolf-type beast said to prowl the surrounding forests. During the last century, many sightings have been reported; the local humane officer once even had a file labeled "werewolf."

While in Elkhorn don't miss **Watson's Wild West Museum** (off U.S. 12/67—look for the sign, 414/723-7505, 10 A.M.–5 P.M. Tues.–Sat., 1–5 P.M. Sun., May–Oct., $5 adults). This is the lifelong labor of love of the proprietor, who's got a serious Western obsession. Over 35 years his collection has grown to museum-worthy proportions. Branding irons seem to be a specialty, but there are also thousands of assorted knickknacks. The owner may even show up dressed like Wyatt Earp.

Delavan

Delavan's two lakes are great reasons to visit—excellent fishing on Delavan Lake—but for nonhydrophiles, Delavan is also home to a bit of clown history. For about 50 years in the 19th century, Delavan was the headquarters for most of the country's traveling circuses, including the prototype of P. T. Barnum's. Local cemeteries at the end of 7th Street are full of circus performers and workers dating from this time; Tower Park is chock-full of colorful circus memorials and statuary.

Visitors can wander about trails at the **arboretum** north of town along the shores of Lake Comus. Delavan Lake was once one of the most polluted in Wisconsin, heavily soiled by phosphorous runoff; however, an aggressive rehabilitation campaign has turned it into one of the southeast's cleaner lakes, leading to the establishment of the **Turtle Valley Wildlife Area** just north of town. Restored from fallow farmland, these 18,000 acres are a good example of Wisconsin's aggressive wetlands restoration programs. Hike through dark peat...and mint!

Believe it or not, Delavan is becoming known for Mexican food. **Hernandez El Sarape** (212 S. 7th St., 262/728-6443, lunch and dinner daily, $2–6) has excellent versions of food from San Luis Potosí state.

It's worth the trip to the expansive, farmlike settings of **Millie's** (N2484 Hwy. O, 414/728-2434, breakfast, lunch, and dinner daily July–Aug., closed Mon. rest of the year, $5–8) for the kitsch factor—a servers-in-costume kinda place. The touted Pennsylvania Old World–style, from-scratch cooking is amazing in scope but some have opined a bit generic.

DOOR COUNTY

Hold your left hand up for a moment, palm out. The thumb is, as the Depression-era WPA Wisconsin guidebook put it, "the spout, as it were, of the Wisconsin teakettle." That's the Door Peninsula. Early French inhabitants called the watery cul-de-sac formed by the peninsula La Baye (later, La Baye Verde, and finally, Green Bay). "Cape Cod of the Midwest" and other silly likenings (I've even heard "California of the North," and that *really* gets me going) are the rule here.

Incessant comparisons to Yankee seaside villages don't wholly miss the mark, though in spots the area smacks just as much of chilled, stony Norwegian fjords. Bays in all the colors of an artist's palette are surrounded by variegated shoreline—250 miles (more than any other U.S. county) alternately rocky beach, craggy bluff, blossom-choked orchard, bucolic heath, and meadow. Door County's established parkland acreage—county, state, and municipal—is staggering, considering its size. Generation upon generation of shipbuilders, fishers, and farmers benefited from the magical microclimate here, and there's a predisposition within the populace not to get worked up about much.

HISTORY

Limestone bedrock here rises 220 feet out of Lake Michigan; it's part of the same Niagara Escarpment that stretches south to Lake Winnebago (and east all the way to Niagara Falls). Eons of waves have carved rough sea caves into the multihued red and smoky black cliffs. (The shores on the western side of Green Bay are dramatic in contrast—mostly

HIGHLIGHTS

LOOK FOR 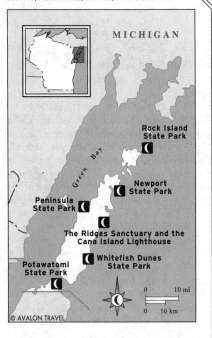 TO FIND RECOMMENDED SIGHTS, ACTIVITIES, DINING, AND LODGING.

◖ Potawatomi State Park: Overlook the historic waterways of the Door – all from a high perch atop the Niagara Escarpment (page 138).

◖ Whitefish Dunes State Park: On the wilder side, splendid dunes and critical habitat are here, formed by the rough wave action (page 139).

◖ The Ridges Sanctuary and the Cana Island Lighthouse: A beloved sanctuary, it contains the grand, brilliantly white Cana Island Lighthouse (page 144).

◖ Newport State Park: Find preserved wilderness in one of the Midwest's most traveled vacation destinations. Yup, escape the madding crowds here (page 146).

◖ Peninsula State Park: This park is somnolent and picturesque, despite having tourist numbers rivaling Yellowstone's (page 153)!

◖ Rock Island State Park: This is as far as you get from anywhere in the state, an unparalleled "getaway" spot (page 168).

MICHIGAN

Green Bay

Rock Island State Park

Newport State Park

Peninsula State Park

The Ridges Sanctuary and the Cana Island Lighthouse

Whitefish Dunes State Park

Potawatomi State Park

0   10 mi

0   10 km

© AVALON TRAVEL

low-slung topography crawling toward the shore through marsh or beach.)

Porte des Mortes

At the tip of the peninsula is the only major gap in the escarpment, Porte des Mortes, the fabled "Door of Death"—so named by petrified early French explorers. The ferocious local climate has devoured hundreds of ships here. Accounts vary wildly (travelers will believe anything—and pass it along at the next inn) regarding which tragedy gave rise to the name Door of Death, but all are remarkably harrowing. Most accounts point to a band of 300–500 Potawatomi—some say Winnebago—who were dashed against rocks. Before the advent of modern navigation and large, diesel-driven screws, most ships could not overcome the shifting currents or conflicting wind shears (and shoals).

Human History

Human habitation at what today is Whitefish Dunes State Park dates back to 100 B.C. to judge by traces of the North Bay People, who spread from the mouth of the bay all the way to Rock Island. Woodland Indians arrived in the mid-1600s, when hostile, large-scale Iroquois expansion in Acadia forced the Hurons to flee. They likely arrived on Rock Island, which had been populated by Potawatomi, who would later return to open the doors to the Europeans. With the aid of Winnebago and Ottawa Indians, one of the largest ramparts in the New World was constructed on Rock Island to repel Iroquois invaders. (The U.S. government would later forcibly evict the Potawatomi from Rock Island so lumbermen could enter.)

On Washington Island in the late 17th century, the Potawatomi would initiate commercial

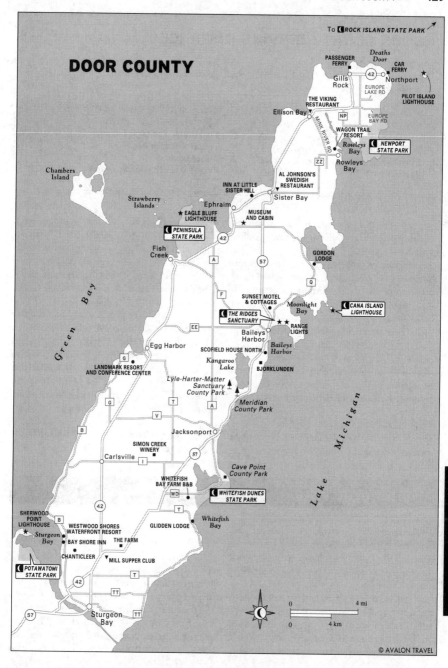

DOOR COUNTY

To ◖ROCK ISLAND STATE PARK ↗

Deaths Door

PASSENGER FERRY
Gills Rock
CAR FERRY
42
Northport ★
EUROPE LAKE RD
PILOT ISLAND LIGHTHOUSE

THE VIKING RESTAURANT
Ellison Bay
NP
EUROPE BAY RD
WAGON TRAIL RESORT

MINK RIVER RD

Rowleys Bay
ZZ
Rowleys Bay
◖NEWPORT STATE PARK

AL JOHNSON'S SWEDISH RESTAURANT

Chambers Island

Strawberry Islands

INN AT LITTLE SISTER HILL
Ephraim
Sister Bay

★ EAGLE BLUFF LIGHTHOUSE
MUSEUM AND CABIN ★

◖PENINSULA STATE PARK
42

Fish Creek
A
GORDON LODGE
57
Q

F
SUNSET MOTEL & COTTAGES
Moonlight Bay
◖CANA ISLAND LIGHTHOUSE

◖THE RIDGES SANCTUARY
★★ RANGE LIGHTS
EE
Baileys Harbor

Egg Harbor
SCOFIELD HOUSE NORTH
Baileys Harbor
G
BJORKLUNDEN

LANDMARK RESORT AND CONFERENCE CENTER
Kangaroo Lake

Lyle-Harter-Matter Sanctuary County Park
A
Meridian County Park

G

V
B

Jacksonport

SIMON CREEK WINERY
Carlsville
I
57

Cave Point County Park

WHITEFISH BAY FARM B&B
WD
◖WHITEFISH DUNES STATE PARK

Lake Michigan

T

SHERWOOD POINT LIGHTHOUSE
B
GLIDDEN LODGE
Whitefish Bay

WESTWOOD SHORES WATERFRONT RESORT
★ Sturgeon Bay
BAY SHORE INN
THE FARM
CHANTICLEER
42
MILL SUPPER CLUB

◖POTAWATOMI STATE PARK

42
TT
TT

57
Sturgeon Bay
TT

Green Bay

0   4 mi
0   4 km

© AVALON TRAVEL

DOOR COUNTY

DOOR COUNTY DRIVING DISTANCES

TO THE DOOR
Chicago-Sturgeon Bay: 231 miles (4.5 hours)
Milwaukee-Sturgeon Bay: 145 miles (2.75 hours)
Madison-Sturgeon Bay: 184 miles (3.75 hours)

WITHIN THE DOOR (LAKESIDE)
Sturgeon Bay-Jacksonport: 15.4 miles
Jacksonport-Baileys Harbor: 7 miles

Baileys Harbor-Rowleys Bay: 15.5 miles
Rowleys Bay-Gills Rock: 7.5 miles

WITHIN THE DOOR (BAYSIDE)
Sturgeon Bay-Egg Harbor: 19 miles
Egg Harbor-Fish Creek: 6 miles
Fish Creek-Ephraim: 5 miles
Ephraim-Sister Bay: 4.3 miles
Sister Bay-Ellison Bay: 5.6 miles
Ellison Bay-Gills Rock: 3.9 miles

operations with Pierre Esprit Radisson, who considered the island one of his favorite sites in all New France.

Fishermen were the first to occupy most points along the Lake Michigan coast, including Rock and Washington Islands. Some of the largest fish ever caught on Lake Michigan were landed off Rock Island. Those communities, which also began commercial shipping and shipbuilding, cemented the regional economy in the 1830s. In shipbuilding, Sturgeon Bay always played second fiddle to Manitowoc farther south, but it still managed to parlay its ship factories into one of the major facilities on Lake Michigan.

PLANNING YOUR TIME

It's the quintessential weekend escape, yet let's make it a lazy, spiritual-battery-recharging week, which makes eminently more sense. If possible, try to schedule your arrival during the preternaturally lovely blossom season (generally beginning in very late April or very early May) or during an open-lighthouse period (generally concurrent with the blossoms)—wow!

Choose one place as a base of operations—**Sturgeon Bay,** for less driving time when leaving, or **Fish Creek,** for its centricity and because it's so darn cute. The county is also set up so that you go up one side and return along the other. (This author prefers to go up the more congested bay side and return along the more subdued lake side.) And please, don't forgo the somewhat forgotten county sibling—**Washington Island,** which itself leads to must-see **Rock Island.**

Sturgeon Bay

The anadromous leviathans for which Door County's gateway community is named once crowded the harbor waters in such plenitude that ships would literally run aground atop heaps of them.

Whether or not Sturgeon Bay is properly the heart and soul of the county, it lies at a most strategic location: It was used for eons by Native Americans as a portage point. When the 6,600-foot-long canal was blasted, chiseled, hacked, and dug through to link the bay with Lake Michigan, the town of Sturgeon Bay was set. Besides the shipbuilding, most of the county's cherries are processed here.

More: The genuine graciousness of the folks is palpable. Sturgeon Bay was voted Wisconsin's Friendliest Small Town by those who really know—the readers of *Wisconsin Trails* magazine. Some jaded and wearied city dwellers are made uneasy by these folks, who

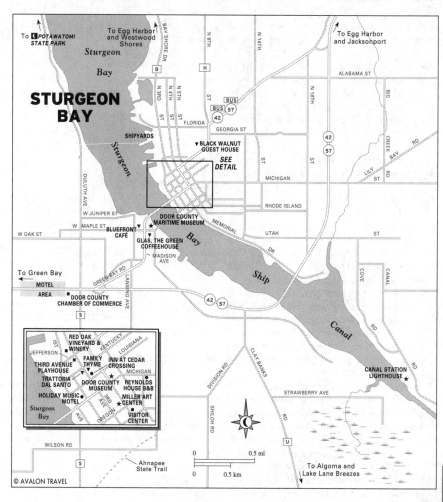

To Egg Harbor and Westwood Shores
To POTAWATOMI STATE PARK
Sturgeon Bay
STURGEON BAY
To Egg Harbor and Jacksohport
ALABAMA ST
BAY SHORE DR
N 8TH ST
N 14TH ST
B
H
BUS 42
BUS 57
N 3RD ST
N 4TH ST
N 5TH ST
ST
FLORIDA
GEORGIA ST
N 18TH ST
42
57
BIG CREEK RD
LILY RD
BAY
ST
SHIPYARDS
Sturgeon
▼ BLACK WALNUT GUEST HOUSE
SEE DETAIL
MICHIGAN
ST
DULUTH AVE
W JUNIPER ST
W MAPLE ST
DOOR COUNTY MARITIME MUSEUM
RHODE ISLAND
W OAK ST
W
BLUEFRONT CAFÉ ▼
MEMORIAL
UTAH
ST
Bay
GLAS, THE GREEN COFFEEHOUSE
DR
COVE
CANAL
To Green Bay
MADISON AVE
Ship
MOTEL AREA
GREEN BAY RD
LANSING AVE
DOOR COUNTY CHAMBER OF COMMERCE
S
42 57
Canal
RD
CANAL STATION LIGHTHOUSE ★
RED OAK VINEYARD & WINERY
KENTUCKY
LOUISIANA
JEFFERSON
FAMILY THYME ▼
INN AT CEDAR CROSSING
THIRD AVENUE PLAYHOUSE
MICHIGAN
TRATTORIA DAL SANTO
DOOR COUNTY MUSEUM
REYNOLDS HOUSE B&B
CLAY BANKS
STRAWBERRY AVE
HOLIDAY MUSIC MOTEL
3RD AVE
MILLER ART CENTER
Sturgeon Bay
AVE
OREGON
VISITOR CENTER
DIVISION RD
SHILOH RD
RD
U
WILSON RD
S
0   0.5 mi
Ahnapee State Trail
0   0.5 km
To Algoma and Lake Lane Breezes
© AVALON TRAVEL

once pumped gas for this exhausted traveler while he rested in front of the station because he simply looked bushed.

SIGHTS

To while away some time pick up a map for a wondrous **National Register Walking Tour** of Sturgeon Bay, detailing more than 100 neighborhood edifices. Another personal fave freebie is to wander north of downtown to **Bay Shipbuilding**—a great place to espy behemoth

vessels as they're being launched or brought in for fixing. You can't get in the grounds but you can still get some good views.

Also check out great scenery along Lake Forest Road and Highways T and TT east of town. Wow!

Lighthouses

One of the oldest of its kind, dating from 1899, the **Canal Station Lighthouse** originally used an experimental design in which only latticework guy wires supported the tower and lantern. The station was redone after the turn of the 20th century, constructing the skeletal steel framework around the 100-foot-tall light. Access has become restricted now to the annual Lighthouse Walk weekend, but you can also see it from boat tours from Sturgeon Bay. If you arrive on wheels, the north breakwall is supposedly accessible, though views aren't all that great.

Ditto the restrictions on access for the **Sherwood Point Lighthouse** nearby.

Wineries

Given the county's proclivity for fruit production, perhaps it's not surprising that wineries have sprouted up every which way. Technically the only one *in* Sturgeon Bay itself is **Red Oak Vineyard & Winery** (325 N. Third Ave., 920/743-7729, www.redoakvineyard.com, hours vary), or at least the tasting room is downtown, where you can sample the wines from California grapes—and one local cherry wine. It's co-owned by a local Sturgeon Bayer who studied law before finally seeing the light and returning home to follow his passion, and good on him for it!

Eight miles north of Sturgeon Bay, in Carlsville, **Door Peninsula Winery** (5806 WI 42, 920/743-7431, www.dcwine.com, from 9 A.M. daily year-round, $3 tours) is housed in an old schoolhouse. Tours take in the cellars and winemaking rooms where 40 Door County California-style fruit wines are produced. A good eatery is attached.

An additional couple of miles along WI 42 to CR I (turn right) brings you to **Simon Creek Winery** (5896 Bochek Rd., 920/746-9307, www.simoncreekvineyard.com, 10 A.M.–6 P.M. Mon.–Sat. mid-May–late Oct., free tours), the county's largest and newest winery. There's an added bonus of live music Sunday afternoons. I love their Peninsula cream sherry!

Door County Maritime Museum

The Door County Maritime Museum (120 N. Madison Ave., 920/743-5958, www.dcmm.org, 9 A.M.–6 P.M. daily Memorial Day–Labor Day, less often the rest of the year, $7.50 adults) is in a sparkling, 20,000-square-foot complex with splendid views of the bay. It synopsizes the shipbuilding industry, and kids love the periscope from a nuclear submarine; it's part of an ambitious exhibit on the crucial role Manitowoc played in building subs in World War II. Outside, you can also tour (10 A.M.–3:30 P.M. every half-hour during peak season, $5) the big ol' *John Purves,* a restored 1919 cherry-red tug.

Door County Museum

At 4th Avenue and Michigan Street you'll find a small museum (18 N. 4th Ave., 920/743-5809, 10 A.M.–4:30 P.M. May–Oct. daily, free) originally built by the WPA during the Great Depression. The *Chicago Tribune* called it the "Best Small Museum in the Midwest." The most popular attraction is the old-time firehouse, complete with refurbished pumper vehicles, including a horse-drawn model predating the end of the Civil War. Climb-aboard, hands-on vehicles are great for the urchins.

Miller Art Center

This fine art center (107 S. 4th Ave., 920/746-0707, www.millerartcenter.org, 10 A.M.–8 P.M. Mon., 10 A.M.–5 P.M. Tues.–Sat., free) is in the Sturgeon Bay library. The top floor houses the permanent collection, with an emphasis on 20th-century Wisconsin artists. One room houses Gerhard Miller's works.

The Farm

The Farm (N WI 57, 920/743-6666, www.thefarmindoorcounty.com, 9 A.M.–5 P.M. daily Memorial Day weekend–mid-Oct., $8 adults) bills itself as a living museum of rural America, and it lives up to that. On 40 acres of an original homestead, various old-style dwellings and structures dot the compound, and pioneer implements line the walls. The primary draw for families is the menagerie of farm animals—you can simply never tire of milking a goat, can you? You'll also find nature trails and informative displays about the diverse peninsular ecology.

DOOR COUNTY SPECIALTIES

BLOSSOMS

Flowers show up in mid-May and you're likely to be plowed under by camera-toting tourists here for blooming season. Cherry trees are lovely enough, but much of the county's cutover land and agricultural pasture has been left to regrow wild, and the county contains five state parks and the Ridges National Natural Landmark, a wildflower preserve with 13 species of endangered plants. The county is now also making a concerted effort to become one of the daffodil capitals of the world, planting more than 100,000 bulbs annually. Look for the white-and-peach-colored daffodil – I mean, doorfodil (seriously), developed locally.

Generally by the second or third week of May, blooms are peeking out. The bay side blooms first; the lake side follows a week to 10 days later. As soon as the blossoms are out, it's time for the **Festival of Blossoms,** a monthlong shindig of blossom field trips, midway rides, pageants, fish boils, shipyard tours (your only chance to see the operations up close), lighthouse tours, parades, and special cherry-centered celebrations.

LIGHTHOUSES

Door County has more lighthouses (people like to quiz you on this around here) than any other county in the United States. Starting in 1836 with Rock Island and in 1858 on Pilot Island (which can be toured only from the water), 10 lighthouses were constructed along the coasts and canals to hold Lake Michigan's stormy temperament somewhat in check. Almost all are still in some recognizable condition, and tours of some are offered regularly.

TOURS

A few resorts or lodges offer boat tours from their marinas; **Door County Fireboat Cruises** (120 N. Madison Ave., 920/495-6454, www.ridethefireboat.com, $20 adults) depart from the Maritime Museum and use a retired Chicago fireboat to chug along for two-hour cruises at 10:30 A.M. and 12:30 P.M. Memorial Day–Labor Day. The 10:30 tour travels through the Sturgeon Bay Ship Canal to Lake Michigan, while the 12:30 tour travels out into Sturgeon Bay to Sherwood Point and past its lighthouse. In July and August these trips definitely leave unless the wind is howling; in May, June, September, and October call ahead.

Harbor Lady (920/707-5239, www.harborlady.com) leaves from a resort and conference center complex opposite the Holiday Music Motel. For $15 to $20 you get a sightseeing cruise or a lunch (burgers and chicken) or dinner (buffet) cruise aboard a much plusher ride!

North of town, the **University of Wisconsin agricultural research station** is open for public perusal. Individuals can obtain a map for a self-guided tour of the 120-acre fruit and potato research center.

Too tired to hoof it? **Door County Trolley** (920/868-1100, www.doorcountytrolley.com) has an array of fun tours (historical, themed, culinary, and more, $14–65) on an old-fashioned streetcar. Check their website or phone for pickup points, which vary by tour.

ENTERTAINMENT

Sturgeon Bay is not a happening place when the sun goes down, to be sure, but there are options. The **Third Avenue Playhouse** (239 N. 3rd Ave., 920/743-1760, www.thirdavenueplayhouse.com) has a year-round slate of theatrical and musical performances in a renovated movie house.

One consistent place for catching live music is **GLAS, the Green Coffeehouse** (67 E. Maple St., 920/743-5575), with live music regularly but not on a set schedule. Oh, and in addition to good coffee and a lovely vista of Sturgeon Bay waters, it's got menu items as well. (The name, by the way, is Gaelic for "green"—yes, they get asked a lot.)

SHIPBUILDING

Given its welcome promontory jutting into the waters, 425 miles of shoreline, the safe haven of Green Bay, innumerable bights offering linked harbors, a plethora of native oak and, most important, a channel toward the outside world, it's no surprise that Door County became so important in shipbuilding.

As early as the 1830s, Manitowoc began to turn out oak sailing ships sturdy enough for the travails of the Great Lakes on the way to the St. Lawrence Seaway: the Wisconsin crowning achievement the Great Lakes schooner, a wooden ship with tight ends front and back that met below the water, a shallow draft, and a raisable centerboard, designed specifically to tackle Lake Michigan.

Door County to the north, meanwhile, had newer shipyards which didn't have to go through later refitting pangs – converting facilities to turn out steamships instead of clippers.

Sturgeon Bay churned out ships in amazing numbers. The first one left Sturgeon Bay shipyards in the mid-1850s, but it wasn't until the prime of the schooner days, in the mid-1860s, that the town really hit the big time. In the decade following the Civil War, perhaps two dozen famed ships were manufactured in the new shipyards.

The first major shipbuilder in Sturgeon Bay was Leathem and Smith, predominantly a ship-repair facility that opened in the 1880s. By World War I, it had expanded its operation into a prosperous boatworks and, during the Great

War, produced more tugboats than any other outfit. Now called Bay Shipbuilding, it is still in operation in Sturgeon Bay. In fact, it's the number one operation, comprising a number of Sturgeon Bay builders in one grand merger, and can handle boats up to 1,100 feet long.

Many shipbuilders relocated here for the environment and abundant resources. In 1896, Riebolt and Wolter moved an entire drydock from Sheboygan. During the past half century, various corporate mergers have resulted in most of the Sturgeon Bay Michigan Street Bridge area's being an arm of one or more subsidiaries of the same company. Despite the decline in shipping brought about by the advent of railroad and autos, about 40 ships were still constructed during the decade and a half leading to 1986.

Peterson Builders, Inc., started just after the turn of the 20th century and constructed yachts, fishing tugs, and rowboats. Business boomed during the 1930s and the war years – 24-hour operations cranked out sub chasers and minesweepers. Today, the output includes wooden naval minesweepers, gunboats, torpedo retrievers, steel tugs, and landing craft.

The final jewel in Sturgeon Bay's shipping crown is Palmer-Johnson. Devoted to racing craft and custom yachts, it puts out million-dollar private vessels and acts as a repair facility. So renowned for yachts is Palmer-Johnson that offices and facilities have opened in four countries.

Up the road a piece, **Roadhouse** (5790 WI 42, 920/743-4966, Tues.–Sun.) in Carlsville, about eight miles north of Sturgeon Bay, has food, yeah, but it has often offered live blues performances Saturday nights July–October, though not last time we passed through town.

RECREATION
Rentals

Outdoor recreation equipment which doesn't require an engine can be rented from several outfitters. **Bay Shore Outfitters** (27 South Madison Ave., 920/818-0431, www.bayshore-outfitter.com) downtown opposite—sort of—the Maritime Museum and other locations has rentals as well as guided tours. Figure $25 for a daily bike rental, more for a kayak.

Boats, canoes, and other outdoor gear can be rented from **Boat Door County** (920/743-3191), with several locations in Sturgeon Bay—the easiest being the Maritime Museum (120 N. Madison Ave.). Potawatomi State Park also has rentals, including kayaks.

Charter Fishing

Sturgeon Bay's sportfishing charter fleet ranks near the top five in the state in total salmon takes on a seasonal basis, but that's in numbers only. Factoring in relative populations, the Door Peninsula's communities are way ahead of the pack. Around here, lunkers prevail. The Wisconsin DNR says Sturgeon Bay charters have more fish per trip than any other north of Milwaukee, and a record 44.92-pound chinook salmon was landed (by a 16-year-old) off Sturgeon Bay near the legendary fishing spot called the Bank (as in bank reef); however, Algoma won't let you forget that it was from an Algoma charter boat. Most people don't know that the smallmouth bass and walleye fishing around here can be some of the best in Wisconsin, especially for flyfishing in late spring. As always, obtain a local list and do some advance work.

You can also contact the **24-hour fishing hotline** (920/743-7046).

Biking

Pick a direction and you'll find grand bike touring. This author loves to head up the lake side in the morning (starting from the Coast Guard Lighthouse—note that there can be lots of traffic on Highway T!) and then head back along the bay in the afternoon. The **Ahnapee State Trail,** best suited for mountain bikes but road bikes can handle it fine, starts just south of town and runs to Algoma. For non-deadly off-road riding, simply head to Potawatomi State park south of town.

ACCOMMODATIONS

Expect multiple-night minimums during peak season (and year-round if your stay includes a Saturday night). Unless specified otherwise, all listed accommodations are open year-round.

$50-100

A few of the cheapest motels may offer high-season rates in the $65–85 range for a single in summer; these dip much lower (as low as $45) in nonpeak times. However, most places cost much more than that.

Among the best budget choices—and yours truly's home away from home for more than a decade—is the (**Holiday Music Motel** (30 N. 1st Ave., 920/743-5571, www.holidaymusicmotel.com, $75). In 2007 a group of musicians—local and national, including Jackson Browne, I kid you not—came here to write songs for a benefit for the Michigan Street Bridge. Long story short, they loved the experience and the place was for sale, so what the heck, they bought it and rejuvenated it into a budget boutique kinda joint. You likely won't need the recording studio (don't worry—it's quiet), but your room has a fridge and new appointments. This is truly one of the best budget choices in Door County, odd history notwithstanding.

Then again, folks come here for cottage life, no? All the higher-end resorts have isolated cottages high on creature comforts. On the economical end, **Lake Lane Breezes** (5647 Lake Ln., 920/743-3463, www.lakelanecottages.com, $80 per day, $420 per week) sleeps 2–4 people. A very family-friendly operation, it's even got a tree house outside for the kids, and pets are welcome. It's southeast of town via Highway U (Clay Banks Road).

$100-150

At the (**Reynolds House B&B** (111 S. 7th Ave., 920/746-9771, www.reynoldshousebandb.com, $100–165), the ersatz anachronism of spinning parasols is eschewed here—it actually feels like a century ago in this antique-adorer's paradise. It emphasizes small but gorgeous rooms, superb service, and, was voted as having the best breakfast in the Midwest by no less than the knowledgeable readers of *Midwest Living* magazine.

A century-old commercial building (and erstwhile soda fountain), the **Inn at Cedar Crossing** (corner of 3rd Ave. and Louisiana St., 920/743-4200, www.innatcedarcrossing.com, $115–195) would best be described as Victorian country; the owner's flair and passion for folk art decoration is expressed in the rooms (room 6 is particularly warm and spacious). The inn also has a fabulous dining room.

DOOR COUNTY

You're not likely to find more welcoming proprietors than those at the splendid ◖ **Black Walnut Guest House** (454 N. 7th Ave., 877/255-9568, www.blackwalnut-gh. com, $145–160). The inn's four relaxing rooms are entirely different from one another—hmm, do you want the one with the spiral staircase to the hot tub in a tower, or the one with the double-sided fireplace?—but all are delightfully well-conceived. This guest house is very highly recommended.

North of Sturgeon Bay five miles via Highway 57, **Whitefish Bay Farm B&B** (3831 Clark Lake Rd./Highway WD, 920/743-1560, www.whitefishbayfarm.com, $125), a 1908 American farmhouse, has four sunny rooms. Instead of quotidian day jobs, the transplanted Milwaukeeans now raise Corriedale sheep. The farm covers 75 acres of meadow and orchard and with all that wool the owners, accomplished weavers, give spinning and weaving demonstrations in their barn-cum-art gallery.

Over $150

The restored farmhouse **Chanticleer** (4072 Hwy. HH N/Cherry Lane Rd., 920/746-0334, www.chanticleerguesthouse.com, $170–280) sits on a 30-acre orchard with gardens and sheep—yep, sheep. Find multilevel suites with 15-foot vaulted ceilings and private terraces, lofted suites with bisque pine ceilings and rafters, and a head-shaking array of amenities in each. Notable extras include a solarium, sauna, hiking trails, and a heated pool. I never met a person who didn't adore this place.

The **Bay Shore Inn** (4205 Bay Shore Dr., 920/743-4551, www.bayshoreinn.net, $199–310) has long been known as one of the most family-friendly resorts in the United States; it has three dozen luxurious kitchenette suites overlooking the bay, with a private beach. Just follow Highway B north out of town.

Not far away, quite a few folks have dropped a line to rave about **Westwood Shores Waterfront Resort** (4303 Bay Shore Dr., 800/440-4057, www.westwoodshores. net, $200-plus), with one- and two-bedroom suites with full kitchens, all of which have

commanding views of the bay. The suites have absolutely everything you could wish for, and staff friendliness is as noticeable as the views.

The 1930s **Glidden Lodge** (4676 Glidden Dr., 920/746-3900 or 888/281-1127, www. gliddenlodge.com, $235–390) was the epitome of hedonistic delight at the time—a massive, fieldstone main building offering stunning lake views. On the "quiet side of the peninsula," it's got a prime peninsular location. It's all suites, which all offer breathtaking lake views and magnificent sunrises. Follow WI 57 north to Highway T and turn right to Glidden Drive.

FOOD

The **Mill Supper Club** (4128 WI 42/57 N, 920/743-5044, dinner Tues.–Sun., $10–25) is a basic supper club with fish boils Tuesdays and Thursdays. Nothing flashy about it, but the food is great and the service has always been chipper as only found in a small town.

I'm most impressed with the newest restaurant in the Door: **Family Thyme** (136 N. 3rd Ave., 920/818-0520, 10:30 A.M.–8 P.M. Sun.–Thurs., 10:30 A.M.–9 P.M. Fri.–Sat., $8–15). A simple straight-up menu ranges from crafted (I think it's apt) burgers to southwestern-style kabobs and even a Thursday night world cuisine with, best of all, prices that won't break the bank. Better, it had taken over a bistro and the interiors will surprise you with some elegance considering the budget-worthy food!

West of the ship canal and a casually chic, energetic place, **Bluefront Café** (86 W. Maple St., 920/743-9218, lunch and dinner daily, brunch Sun., $8–18) defines eclectic. Where else in town to find pan-fried locally caught walleye next to a Thai vegetarian wrap? Yup, here. Try the fish tacos—it brings 'em in.

Phenomenal Northern Italian cuisine in a cozy but contemporary setting is right downtown at **Trattoria dal Santo** (147 N. 3rd Ave., 920/743-6100, 5–9 P.M. Mon.–Thurs., 4–9 P.M. Fri.–Sun., $12–25). This wonderful place has been honing its cuisine for nearly two decades and they've never overlooked anything in atmosphere. For this edition they added a new wine bar.

DOOR COUNTY FISH BOIL

Just when travelers think they've come to understand Wisconsin's predilection for fish fries, Door County throws them a curveball on the fish fetish – the fish boil, which is not at all the same thing.

Though Scandinavian immigrants came with their own recipes for fish soups and stews, the fish boil likely came from pure practicality. Door County had few cows or pigs, but it was rich with whitefish; potatoes and onions, hardy vegetables, were also abundant.

The modern version is a different story. As some tell it, the proprietor of Ellison Bay's Viking Restaurant concocted the first modern fish boil back in the 1960s, ostensibly searching for something unique to serve at the restaurant. It was an immediate hit that snowballed into the de rigueur culinary experience of Door County. Whatever the historical genesis of the boil, it has become a cultural linchpin for the peninsula community, almost a county ordinance.

THE WORKS

A Door County fish boil requires only a couple things: a huge witch-quality iron cauldron, firewood sufficient to blaze a light for Great Lakes ship traffic, and the innards – fish steaks, small potatoes, onions, and a heck of a lot of salt. Whitefish is for purists, but don't let that stop you from trying other varieties such as trout.

Add salt to the water and bring to a boil (the salt raises the boiling temperature of the water and helps keep the fish from flaking apart in the water). Add potatoes and boil for 15 minutes. Add onions and boil another 4-5 minutes. Add fish, which is often wrapped in cheesecloth to prevent it from falling apart, and boil for another 10 minutes. Now, here's the fun part: Right before the fish is done, use kerosene to jack up the flame to space shuttle-launch proportions. The kerosene induces a boil-over, which forces the oily top layers of water out of the cauldron to be burned off in the fire. Drain the rest and slather it with butter. The requisite side dishes are coleslaw, dark breads, and, this being Door County, cherry pie or cobbler for dessert.

An epicurean delight is the ◖ **Inn at Cedar Crossing** (corner of 3rd Ave. and Louisiana St., 920/743-4200, 7:30 A.M.–9 P.M. Sun.–Thurs., 7:30 A.M.–9:30 P.M. Fri.–Sat., $8–32). Though quite modern and posh, the inn features original decor down to pressed-tin ceilings and ornate glasswork, and a fireplace roars in each dining room. The menu, heavy on fresh fish and seafood, emphasizes regional ingredients—as many foods as possible come from Wisconsin. Patrons swoon over the desserts with a somewhat alarming passion.

INFORMATION

The **Sturgeon Bay Visitor Center** (36 S. 3rd Ave., 800/301-6695, www.sturgeonbay.net) is downtown.

The **Door County Chamber of Commerce** (1015 Green Bay Rd., 920/743-4456 or 800/527-3529, www.doorcounty.com), just south of town, is generally full of all the information you're likely to need. It's got a 24-hour touch-screen information/reservation service. Otherwise, you'll find boatloads of local papers and other media.

One good website (www.doorcounty-wi.com) has links to other businesses and local media; another good website (www.doorcountynavigator.com) is as much a sounding board for those who've tried local attractions, lodgings, and dining (that is, locals as well as travelers!).

GETTING THERE

Door County well represents the American antipathy toward public transportation. Hoi polloi disembarking from a Greyhound evidently doesn't fit well in a Cape Cod sunset postcard scene. There are no buses, no trains, and no ferries from points south. (Technically,

legendary views from Potawatomi State Park

one entrepreneur has floated a proposal to run a passenger-only ferry to Menominee in Michigan's Upper Peninsula from here, but this has been a rumor for years.) Sounds great? Wait till you see the traffic on a peak weekend.

Very small and very limited air shuttles from Chicago to Sturgeon Bay have occasionally popped up (none at present), but your real choice is to fly into Green Bay and rent a car or take the **Door County-Green Bay Shuttle** (920/746-0500, www.doorcountygreenbay-shuttle.com, reservations necessary), whose service does have a super-cool retro checker taxi!

POTAWATOMI STATE PARK

Unfolding along the western edge of Sturgeon Bay and flanked by Sherwood and Cabot Points, Potawatomi State Park (920/746-2890) is known for rolling birch-lined trails atop the limestone ridges scraped off the Niagara Escarpment. The geology of the park is significant enough that Potawatomi marks the beginning of the Ice Age National Scenic Trail. You won't need a science background or superlative designations to appreciate its inspiring vistas and solitude; it is, simply, one of the peninsula's magical, not-to-be-missed natural retreats.

Almost 11 miles of trails wind through the park. An eight-mile **off-road bicycle trail** also meanders through grassy meadows. The great **Tower Trail** quickly ascends the ridges through thicker vegetation, leading to a 75-foot-tall **observation tower** and a belvedere vantage point of Michigan's Upper Peninsula on a good day (check out sunsets!). Islets rimmed in hues of blue and gray pepper the outlying reaches off the park (bring a polarizing camera lens on a sunny day). Fishing in the naturally protected bay is some of the best in the lower Door. The chilled waters also offer some fantastic scuba diving, with wrecks seen below.

Popular are the 14 miles of cross-country skiing trails and winter **camping** areas. Camping is popular as hell, so reserve the first day possible the winter before your trip; I'm not kidding. A camping cabin is available for disabled travelers. A park sticker is required in addition to the campsite fee.

For a quick road trip, head back toward WI 42/57 but turn right onto Highway C and then right onto Highway M, which takes you all the way to the **Sherwood Point Lighthouse** (it's a bit tough to spot). Built in 1883, this one took precisely one century to finally become automated! The 38-foot-high house guarding the bayside entrance into Sturgeon Bay was constructed with a 10-sided cast-iron light. Closed to the public, it and the old keeper's house are used today as a retreat for the Coast Guard. It is also open only during designated festival times, generally late May or early June.

Lakeside

Otherwise known as the "quiet side," this area shows less commercial development than the rest of the peninsula. The lakeshore side of the Door is a wonderland of pristine heath, healed cutover forest, rocky sea caves, some of Lake Michigan's finest beaches, biome preserves, picture-postcard lighthouses, and two of Wisconsin's best state parks.

The quick way into the area is WI 57, branching off WI 42 north of Sturgeon Bay. Farther off the beaten path, get right above the water along the coast starting southeast of Sturgeon Bay at the Sturgeon Bay canal North Pierhead Lighthouse. From there, an established State Rustic Road hugs the coastline all the way to Whitefish Dunes State Park, bypassing Portage and Whitefish Points and the Lilly Bay curve. Don't worry about getting lost once you find Highway T; there are no other roads!

◖ WHITEFISH DUNES STATE PARK

Some say Whitefish Dunes State Park (920/823-2400), approximately eight miles northeast of Sturgeon Bay, is the most pleasant park in the state system. The beach is indisputably so—miles and miles of

© DOOR COUNTY CHAMBER OF COMMERCE

Whitefish Dunes State Park

mocha-colored dunes sculpted into ridges by the prevailing winds.

The littoral site's proximity to inland lakes and creeks (nearby Clark Lake is more than 800 fish-rich acres) was likely the primary reason for settlement; eight temporary encampments or small villages date as far back as 100 B.C. European settlers arrived in 1840, when a commercial fishing operation on Whitefish Bay was begun by the Clark brothers (who lent their name to the nearby lake), working side by side with the Winnebago.

Today, everybody comes for the big dunes—among the highest on Lake Michigan, east or west. They were formed by numerous advances and retreats of ancient lakes and, later, Lake Michigan, and zillions of storms. Sand banks first closed off Clark Lake in what is now the mainland, and as vegetation took hold three millennia ago, wind deposits began piling up atop the sandbar. The result is a microcosm that couldn't possibly occur on the bay side of the peninsula—a wide beach rising to forested dunes. The tallest, Old Baldy, stands 93 feet high.

The one rule to follow dutifully is *stay off the dunes.* Many of the grasses holding together the mounds are peculiar to this park, and once they're gone, the dunes are done for (just take a look at the lifeless gashes created by motorcyclists before the park was established). Plank-and-rope boardwalks allow beach access on the **Red Trail;** at the midpoint, it branches away from the water to link with longer trails through mixed hardwood, red pine, or oddball wooded dune areas—13 miles in total. Continuing on the Red Trail to its southern end, hikers can reach the only climbable dune—Old Baldy, which offers panoramas of Lake Michigan and Clark Lake inland. From there, it's possible to link with longer trails. Farthest to the north, a short access trail to the White Trail leads to **Cave Point County Park,** likely the most photographed parkland in Door County.

From south to north in Whitefish Bay, the geology shifts from dunes to mixed sand and stone and, finally, at Cave Point, to exposed limestone ledges thrusting up to 50 feet above the water of the Niagara Escarpment—the bedrock of the peninsula. Eons of crashing waves have hewn caves and cenotes that show up as blowholes of sorts as the surf pounds and crashes, echoing like rolling thunder. The whole effect is not unlike the crumbled parapets of a time-worn castle. Sea kayakers have a field day snooping around this small promontory. Straight-faced old-timers tell of a schooner that slammed into the rocks at Cave Point in 1881 (true). Laden with corn, the ship cracked like a nut and spilled its cargo (true), and within a few days, corn had mysteriously appeared in Green Bay on the other side of the peninsula (hmm).

A caveat: Do not take swimming lightly here. The concave bend of Whitefish Bay focuses all the current, forming tough riptides. Predicting where these form is never entirely possible and *lifeguards are never on duty.*

This park is day-use only; no camping. Great picnicking, though, is found right atop the limestone ledges overlooking the lake. Do check out the nature center for its exhibits on the geology and anthropology of the area.

JACKSONPORT

You can always tell those who have explored the bay side of the peninsula first and then backtracked through Sturgeon Bay to come back up this side. Generally, these are the ones who race right through Jacksonport as if they didn't know it was there and then turn around to try to find what they missed.

At one time, Jacksonport rivaled Fish Creek as epicenter of economic booms on the Door. Once the local lumber was depleted, Jacksonport's docks were relegated to fishing boats. The last community to be settled in the county, Jacksonport caught one of the Germanic immigrant waves, and its annual **Maifest** (www.jacksonport.org/maifest) is among the larger shindigs held throughout the summer.

Somnolent Jacksonport today sports a few

shoreline view near Jacksonport

© THOMAS HUHTI

antique shops and gift cottages selling wares and crafts from dozens of Door County artists. A lazy strand of sand acts as a beach, and top-notch fun comes in the form of the sweets at the **Town Hall Bakery** (6225 WI 57, 920/823-2116).

Right downtown is the pinnacle of Jacksonport's developmental ambition: the **Square Rigger Lodge and Cottages** (6332 WI 57, 920/823-2404, www.squarerigger-lodge.com, from $80/100 s/d). More than a dozen basic but comfortable modern motel/condo units overlook the water (some do not), and most have private balconies or patios. One-to three-bedroom cottages also line the waterfront. They have lively fish boils here nightly in July and August, and four times a week in the off-season.

The supper club of choice is **Mr. G's** (5890 WI 57, 920/823-2899, lunch and dinner daily, $6–14), with a ballroom that has in the past had live entertainment, though most entertainment today comes from tall tales at the joint's Tiki Bar, part of the local bars' Yacht Club,

which is more Jimmy Buffett than America's Cup to be sure.

If that's too sedate, you may also have time for a margarita and some homemade salsa at **J.J.'s** (6301 WI 57, 920/823-2700) nearby!

BAILEYS HARBOR

Lake Michigan sportfishing really shows itself as you enter Baileys Harbor, every inch of road chockablock with trucks and boat trailers and a glistening new marina. It's a fitting legacy, actually. In 1844, a Captain Bailey and crew were foundering in a sudden squall when they espied this cove and took shelter. They were amazed to find a deep, well-isolated harbor and gorgeous cedar stands backing off the beach. So enthralled was the captain that he and the shipping company owner persuaded the U.S. government to construct a lighthouse at the entrance some years later. Thus, the first settlement in Door County was established. Its harbor remains the only designated Harbor of Refuge on the peninsula's lake side.

DOOR COUNTY

CALMER NEAR THE LAKE

Jacksonport, Door County, is on the 45th parallel, exactly halfway between the equator and the north pole, but don't let that fool you – the peninsula's climate is far more temperate than in other northerly Wisconsin areas. The ferocious waters of Lake Michigan, legendary for their unpredictability and furor, can also ameliorate the weather, keeping things cool in the dog days and taking the bite out of winter's Alberta Clippers. (Early weather accounts from Door County point out that the northern tip is generally a few degrees warmer than the southern end, though the bayside vs. lakeside difference is more important climatically.) This in part explains the rather one-sided habitation of the Door; most of the residents live on the western, or bay, side. With Lake Michigan in a huff, blowing fog, spray, and mist, Green Bay, in the lee of 15 miles of limestone windblock, remains sedate (if a bit cloudy). (Another oddity exists. Anyone visiting the vicinity of one of the Great Lakes will soon learn of "lake effect" snow, which is exactly as it seems. The waters can dump much more snow on the littoral edges than even a few miles inland, especially for those on the eastern shores. Looking at a map of Door County, surrounded by all that water, and you'd think it'd snow like a sonofagun here. Nope, Green Bay is not actually large enough to produce the necessary conditions, and as a result, Door County receives some of the lowest amounts of precipitation in the state!)

Sights

Before you come barreling into town, know that the sights around here are mostly south of town coming from Cave Point County Park. South of town along WI 57 at the southern end of Kangaroo Lake are my absolute undiscovered gems—**Lyle-Harter-Matter Sanctuary and Meridian County Parks,** which sandwich the highway and feature rough undeveloped trails past Niagara Escarpment rocks and one of the largest dunes in the county. (And remember as you sit and munch your granola bar, you're halfway to the North Pole!)

A bit south of town and along a splendid stretch of beach is a decidedly different kind of vacation, an educational seminar (from $1,000 with superb food, far less if living off-site) at **Bjorklunden** (7590 Boynton Ln., 920/839-2216), more a relaxed, soul-searching means of personal growth than a for-credit school experience (though it is the northern campus of Lawrence University in Appleton). Participants can live in a recently reconstructed Norwegian-style lodge built of local fieldstone and undertake courses in humanities and natural sciences. Some midweek seminars are also cheaper. Just to stay at the lodge, which looks like a Viking ship, is around $400 a week, meals included.

Visitors can tour from 1–4 P.M. Monday and Wednesday ($4) and check out the Norwegian *stavkirke* (church).

During the summer, the gardens of the estate host **Door Shakespeare** (920/839-1500, www.doorshakespeare.com), with evening performances daily except Wednesday.

In town itself, this author loves a simple pooch-led stroll along one of the county's longest sand beaches at **Baileys Harbor Park.**

The Town Hall (can't miss it) has the local **visitors information center** (corner of WI 57 and CR F, 920/839-2366, www.baileysharbor.com), open daily in summer and fall.

Recreation

Chinook salmon and rainbow and brown trout are the quarry for local charter boats, and the fishing in Baileys Harbor is some of the best in the county—Lilliputian Baileys Harbor (pop. 780) boasts a salmon harvest one-half the size of Milwaukee's.

Accommodations

Baileys Harbor has a couple of basic, modestly priced motels. I stumbled into the **Sunset Motel & Cottages** (8404 WI 57, 866/406-1383, www.baileysunsetmotelandcottages.

© DOOR COUNTY CHAMBER OF COMMERCE

Baileys Harbor

com, $75 and up) once and was most impressed by what you get for what you pay—as confirmed by a couple of other guests staying there. It's casual, rustic, but comfortable, with friendly proprietors—the way things used to be everywhere in these parts. It's just north of the Highway Q turnoff.

On the south side of town, there are above-average motel rooms and a lovely littoral setting to boot at the **Beachfront Inn** (8040 WI 57, 920/839-2345, www.beachfrontinn.net, from $90). In addition to a private beach, indoor heated pool, and regular campfires, this place gets many, many kudos for being so pet-friendly (they even have their own rescue dogs).

What may be the most enviably sited lodging in all of Door County is ◖ **Gordon Lodge** (1420 Pine Dr., 920/839-2331, www.gordon-lodge.com, $160–425). Spread across the tip of a promontory jutting into Kangaroo Lake's north bay, the long-established Gordon Lodge sprouted in the 1920s as an offshoot of a popular Sturgeon Bay doctor's summer home. The main lodge has a lake view, while villas with fireplaces creep out right atop the water. Some original cottages are set back and nestled under the pines, which also drape over fitness trails. The dining room is casually elegant, and the Top Deck lounge, originally a boathouse, is unsurpassed for after-dinner dancing. Go north out of town and follow Highway Q toward the lake to Pine Drive.

The 1860s-era log home **Scofield House North** (920/839-1503 or 877/376-4667, www.scofieldnorth.com, $135–285) was painstakingly dismantled near Pulaski, Wisconsin, and relocated to the village, where it has become a showpoint lodging option. The gorgeous two-story log home has two bedrooms with skylights, two fireplaces, cathedral ceilings, and a lovely sunroom.

Food

The town has gone from basic fare to two road-trip-worthy eateries. Newest is **Harbor Fish Market and Grille** (8080 WI 57, 920/839-9999, breakfast, lunch, and dinner daily, $6

DOOR COUNTY

and up), a casually fine place in a 120-year-old building offering wondrous atmosphere. All comers will be happy; you gotta try the Wednesday and Friday (Friday only off-season) lobster boil! There's great custard and espresso next door.

(Restaurant Saveur (8041 WI 57, 920/839-2708, 11:30 A.M.–3 P.M. and 5:30–10 P.M. Tues.–Sun., $17–35), very close by, is fabulously creative in its entrées that, despite flitting about the globe, are firmly rooted in the co-owner's South America (Chile to be precise). If nothing else, the restaurant would get my business for eternity for promising, when they opened, to be "creative, ambitious, elegant," and all those other usual things, but also to be "completely unpretentious." Done and done, and so it's become possibly the best new restaurant in Door County for this edition.

That said, some of us are old-school. If so, or if you're a Packers fan (rhetorical?), head immediately to **Weisgerber's Cornerstone Pub** (WI 57, 920/839-2790, breakfast, lunch, and dinner daily May–Oct., shorter hours off-season), which has three squares of solid comfort food (pan-fried perch since 1926) and quite honestly the best service during the last trip to the Door!

(THE RIDGES SANCTUARY AND THE CANA ISLAND LIGHTHOUSE

Baileys Harbor is sandwiched between the strategic safe harbor on Lake Michigan and Kangaroo Lake, the peninsula's largest inland lake. Travelers are so preoccupied with these two sights that it's easy to miss the two large promontories jutting off the peninsula just north of town, forming **Moonlight Bay.** These two capes may be the state's most awesome natural landmarks and definitely have the most inspiring lighthouses. North along Highway Q is a critical biotic reserve, **The Ridges Sanctuary** (Ridges Rd., 920/839-2802, www.ridgesanctuary.org, trails open daily, $4 adults), 1,000 acres of boreal bog, swamp, dune, and a complete assortment of

wildflowers in their natural habitat. The eponymous series of ancient spiney sand ridges mark the advance of ancient and modern Lake Michigan. All 23 native Wisconsin orchids are found within the sanctuary's confines, as are 13 endangered species of flora. The preserve was established in the 1930s by hardcore early ecologists (such as Jens Jensen) in one of the state's first environmental brouhahas, incited by a spat over plans for a trailer park. The U.S. Department of the Interior recognizes the site as one of the most ecologically precious in the region; it was the first National Natural Landmark in Wisconsin.

The famed **Baileys Harbor Range Lights** are a pair of small but powerful lighthouses: a shorter, wooden octagonal one across the road on the beach, the other 900 feet inland—raised in 1869 by the Coast Guard. Three easy trails, ranging from just under two miles to five miles, snake throughout the tamarack and hardwood stands—20 miles in all and well worth the effort. Also on the grounds you'll find a nature center. Many have found the educational programs some of the best in the state.

Continue on Ridges Road to additional sites deemed National Natural Landmarks by the Department of the Interior and dedicated by The Nature Conservancy. **Toft's Point** (or Old Lighthouse Point) is along a great old dirt road that winds through barren sands with innumerable pulloffs. A few trails are found throughout the 600-plus acres that take up the whole of the promontory and include almost three miles of rock beach shoreline. To the north of the Ridges, the **Mud Lake Wildlife Area** is more than 1,000 acres protecting the shallow lake and surrounding wetlands. A prime waterfowl sanctuary, Mud Lake and its environs may be even more primeval and wild than the Ridges. Canoeing is also very popular, as Reibolts Creek connects the lake with Moonlight Bay.

And the bays don't end yet. North of Moonlight Bay is isolated North Bay, site of a handful of cottages and resorts. On the southern promontory you'll find undoubtedly the one lighthouse on the peninsula that everyone

Cana Island Lighthouse, one of Wisconsin's most famous lighthouses

simply must visit, the **Cana Island Lighthouse** (10 A.M.–5 P.M. May–Oct., $4, and another $4 to climb the tower), accessible via Highway Q to Cana Island Drive to a narrow spit of gravel that may be under water, depending on when you get there. (Please note that this is a residential area, so really go slowly—blind curves are everywhere—and never, ever park inappropriately.) Impressively tall and magnificently white, the lighthouse is framed naturally by white birch. One of the most crucial lighthouses in the county, it stands far off the coast on a wind-whipped landform. Built in 1870, it was obviously considered a hardship station during storm season. North Bay is also the site of **Marshall's Point,** an isolated stretch of wild land completely surrounded by private development oft touted as a possible state park for its remarkable microclimate.

ROWLEYS BAY

Out of Baileys Harbor, WI 57 swoops back toward Sister Bay to WI 42. The next lakeside community, Rowleys Bay, is mostly a massive

and well-established resort and nearby campground, **Rowleys Bay Resort** (1041 Hwy. ZZ, 920/854-2385 or 888/250-7666, www. rowleysbay.com, May–Oct., $119–319 lodge/ cottages). First of all, everyone still calls it "Wagon Trail," which until this edition was what it was called (the campground nearby was part of the operation). Originally a bare-bones fishing encampment and later a rustic lodge, the city-state has transmogrified into what is certainly the most comprehensive operation on the upper Door Peninsula. From semi-rustic lodge rooms (though these, with new management, will likely be gone) to posh suites, somehow the place does it all and does it well. Two- and three-bedroom rustically upscale vacation villas are set on wooded or waterfront sites; some can house a dozen folks comfortably, and all have whirlpools and fireplaces.

The contiguous, more or less, **campground** (920/854-2818, www.wagontrailcampground .com, from $37 for tents), spread throughout 200 acres along the bay, is really quite fastidious and professionally run. (It also

DOOR COUNTY

offers cabins and even yurts!) Reservations are recommended.

Several miles of trails wend through the resort's acreage; one leads to Sand Bay Beach Park on Rowleys Bay, another to the Mink River Estuary. On the bay, the resort's marina offers bicycles, canoes, kayaks, paddleboats, charter fishing boats, and scenic excursions.

The reason most folks show up at the resort, though, is **❰ Grandma's Swedish Bakery,** a magnet for sweet tooths from around the country hungry for 10 kinds of homemade bread, cardamom coffee cake, cherry pie, Old World–style bread pudding, and scads of muffins, cookies, and pastries. The specialty is Swedish sweets—*limpa* and *skorpa* (thinly sliced pecan rolls sprinkled with cinnamon sugar and dried in the oven). The resort's restaurant features all-you-can-eat fish boils Saturdays in summer.

Mink River Estuary

Stretching southeast from Ellison Bay to the edge of Newport State Park, the Mink River Estuary acts, by grace of The Nature Conservancy, to protect the river system as it empties into the bay through marsh and estuary. Primarily a crucial ornithological migratory site, the waters also act as a conduit for spawning fish. The topography of the 1,500 acres is astonishingly diverse and untouched; two threatened plant species—the dune thistle and dwarf lake iris—are found within the boundaries, and more than 200 species of birds pass through.

❰ NEWPORT STATE PARK

Not much is wild in Door County anymore, but the state's only designated wilderness park is here (go figure); this rough, isolated backwoods park (920/854-2500) constitutes half of the tip of the county, stretching for almost 12 miles along the Lake Michigan coast through an established scientific reserve—I might say it's a perfectly realized park. A remarkable diversity of hardwood and conifers, isolated wetland, bog, and even a few hidden coves along the lakeshore make the hiking appealing. Once

your best spot for isolation in Door County – Newport State Park

an up-and-coming lumber village in the 1880s, the town decayed gradually as the stands of forests became depleted. (Ghostly outlines of foundations are still scattered about in the underbrush.)

From wasted white pine cutover, the inner confines of the park are now dense tracts of bog forest. The southern section of the park is an established scientific reserve on 140 acres of mixed hardwoods. The park's magnificent ecosystem draws one of the planet's highest concentrations of monarch butterflies, which make a mind-boggling trip from Mexico's Yucatán Peninsula to San Juan Capistrano and then all the way here. Unfortunately, biologists have noted a dramatic drop-off in monarch numbers, mostly due to pollution and logging.

Trails

The park maintains nearly 40 miles of trails, along which you'll find wilderness campsites. By far the most popular area of the park is the northern tier and the two trails along Europe Lake—one of the largest of the county's inland lakes—a pristine, sandy gem uncluttered by development. With sandy forests and rocky beaches with great views of Porte des Mortes and the surrounding islands, it's got it all. Gravel Island, viewable from Lynd Point, is a national ornithological refuge.

In the southern section of the park, the **Newport, Rowleys Bay,** and **Ridge Trails**

alternately pass through meadows, wooded areas, and along limestone headlands on the coast, mostly along old logging roads. Spider Island, viewable from the Newport Trail, is another wildlife refuge for nesting gulls.

Fifteen of the park's trail miles allow mountain bikes, and bike camping is possible, though the park warns of porcupine damage to bikes overnight! Note that the trails are for the most part hardpacked dirt, but are regularly pocked with bikers' land mines—potholes of quicksand, python-size tree roots hidden under leaves, and more than a few spots of gravel (and porcupines). Essentially, anywhere that hikers go a bike can get to, just not always on the same trail. The most conspicuous off-limits areas are the shoreline routes—it's too tempting for bikers to whip down onto the fragile sands.

Camping

Here's the reason outdoor aficionados pilgrimage here regularly—there's no vehicular access to campsites. Sites are strictly walk-in (a modestly strenuous hike to some, a serious pack to most, but it sure beats the traffic death of Potawatomi and Peninsula; the shortest hike in is one-half mile, the longest nearly four miles). Two sites on Europe Lake are waterside, so canoes can land and camp; the Lake Michigan side has plenty of lakeside sites. Winter camping is outstanding here. As always, reserve way early.

Bayside

A preface, or perhaps, a caveat: WI 42 and WI 57 have been slated for (or, really, are endlessly being debated about) widening and straightening for years. South of Sturgeon Bay the road has already turned into mad swells of multilane madness. Thereafter, the leviathan transportation bureaucracy began eyeing stretches north of town. Grimly efficient, WI 42 north of Sturgeon Bay is approaching interstate whooshing.

WI 42 has perhaps the most intriguing history

of any country road. Not your average farm-to-market remnant, it was hewn from a tundralike wilderness in 1857 by starving millers and fishers desperate when winter arrived earlier than expected and froze supply boats out of the harbor.

On the way to Egg Harbor out of Sturgeon Bay, a great on-the-water side trip is along Highway B. Eventually, it merges with Highway G around Horseshoe Bay and leads directly to Egg Harbor.

EGG HARBOR

There's something of a contrived (officially, "revitalized") feel to Egg Harbor, back on WI 42. A couple of structures smacking of the early days are now redone with fresh facades. But there's more than a little new development, including an ersatz-Victorian strip mall that could have been plunked down in any city suburb or fringe sprawl in America.

This isn't to denigrate the lovely village at all, built on a rise overlooking one of the most accessible and well-protected harbors along either coast. The harbor had long been in use by the Winnebago before military materiel and trade ships necessarily anchored here—the only safe spot between Fish Creek and Little Sturgeon Bay. In the 1850s, Jacob and Levi Thorp, two brothers of the founder of Fish Creek, collaborated to build a pier to allow transport of local cordwood. By the 1890s, a rivalry with Fish Creek was born.

Oh, and that name. It doesn't stem from any ovoid land configuration but from a legendary 1825 battle between vacationing rich folk. While rowing to shore in longboats, boredom apparently got the best of the well-to-do, who started winging picnic-packed eggs back and forth. When the shells settled, a name was born. And they do celebrate this with occasional staged—and eminently delightful—egg throws, whether individuals or locally sponsored. (Yes, they do call the place—get ready to groan—an "eggscape.")

Sights and Activities

As you wind off WI 42 and down the hillside, your first sight is probably the most picturesque **village park** in the county, this one with a small strand of smooth-stoned and sand beach. There are free concerts Thursdays and Sundays in summer—lovely! Farther south a couple of miles you'll find an even better view of Horseshoe Bay and another very sandy beach at **Frank E. Murphy County Park.**

Just east of town a quaint, aged dairy barn now houses the **Birch Creek Music Center** (Hwy. E, 920/868-3763, www.birchcreek.org). Acoustics are extraordinary, considering the moo-cows who once lived here. Evening concerts by budding students and national names in the big barn are regularly scheduled (generally mid-July–Labor Day) and are something of an institution in the area—the big band series is particularly popular. Percussion performances are the specialty.

Sight of sights and a landmark for denizens of the Door is the Gothic revival **Cupola House** (7836 WI 42, 920/868-3941), a massive building constructed in 1871 by Levi Thorp, as local cordwood made him among the wealthiest men in the county. During the summer, resident artists at the Birch Creek Center give performances at the house; the mansion houses an assortment of shops and boutiques.

Ultra-premium wines (through micro-vinification, their word, not mine) are at **Stone's Throw Winery** (3382 Hwy. E, 920/839-9660), in a cool old barn.

The local library has a small visitors information center (920/868-3717, www.eggharbordoorcounty.org).

Accommodations

The cheapest accommodations to be found in Egg Harbor will run you $90 or more, including the **Lullabi Inn** (7928 Egg Harbor Rd./WI 42, 920/868-3135, www.lullabi-inn.com, $89–199) on the north end of town, the cheapest available, but you can expect a welcoming atmosphere despite the low bucks. Stay in small but clean value doubles, or upgrade through an array of larger rooms and apartments.

One of the largest resort complexes in the entire county, in fact Door County's largest resort, **Landmark Resort and Conference Center** (7643 Hillside Rd., 920/868-3205 or 800/273-7877, www.thelandmarkresort.com, $125–400) has myriad condo options, but all proffer spectacular views. You'll need both hands to count the swimming pools, another two for the tennis courts. There's also an excellent restaurant. It's easy to find this one—you can't miss it.

You'll find award-winning rooms at **Ashbrooke Suites** (7942 Egg Harbor Rd., 920/868-3113, www.ashbrooke.net, $154–249), with one- and two-bedroom suites done up in a French country atmosphere. It's just up the road from the Lullabi Inn.

Nonresort options abound in town. Try **Woldt's Intown Farmette** (7960 Church St., 608/873-8884, www.richwoldt.com, $125 daily, $500 weekly). This two-story cottage is adjacent to a reconstructed Dutch colonial barn and windmill. Turn east on Highway E, then a quick north jaunt onto Church Street.

Or, coming into town on WI 42, turn east onto Highway T for one mile to **The Cottage Retreat** (4355 Hwy. T, 920/743-4420, www.cottageretreat.com, $100–485 daily, $450–2,300 weekly). It has a reconstructed main cottage, lovingly put together from collected fieldstone. In fact, this place was green before green was in—built into earthen berms with southern glassed exposure, two of the main retreats are as cozy as can be. The sun-soaked two-bedroom cottage can sleep six and offers a combined kitchen/dining room/living area and a boardwalk to a Finnish wood sauna.

Food

All of the following are right on the main drag.

The early meal (and lunch) of choice is at the longstanding **Village Cafe** (7918 WI 42, 920/868-3342, 8 A.M.–10 P.M. daily) at the north end of town, a from-scratch place where you might find a vegan burger chicken fried steak tarted up Door County style with cherries and pecans.

Shipwreck's (7791 Egg Harbor Rd., 920/868-2767) has good pub grub but is really known as the county's only microbrewery (watch 'em brew as you quaff and you must try the Cherry Wheat Ales). Al Capone supposedly loved to hang with the lumberjacks here and used the subterranean caverns to beat a retreat.

The restaurant for gourmands in town, however, is ◖ **Trio** (4655 Hwy. E, 920/868-2092, dinner daily till 9 P.M. Memorial Day weekend–late Oct., $11–18), an eclectic and ambitious Italian and country French eatery serving fantastic antipasti and entrées. No bones about

it, this place gets raves from visitors for its Italian and French dishes. It's subdued in a lovely setting, yet kids are welcome and the staff have always been much praised. It's very well-done, and has been for many years now.

The **Log Den** (6626 WI 42, 920/868-3888, lunch and dinner daily, brunch Sun., $8–25), just south of Egg Harbor on WI 42, is a 10,000-square-foot place that actually feels less immense than that. The name is no misnomer, with wood everywhere, much of it ornately—at times cheekily—carved into a menagerie of anthropomorphism (I love sitting by the large lolling black bear). The menu runs from great—and moderately priced—burgers and sandwiches to ahi tuna, bluepoint oysters, and prime rib. The families that run the place have been along these shores and in these woods for more than a century and really give you an introduction to the place. And it's one of the most fun places to watch a Packers game, as well!

Then again, **Casey's Smokehouse & BBQ** (7855 WI 42, 920/868-3038, from 11 A.M. daily) is just about the perfect place to gorge on brisket or ribs after a long day of paddling or pedaling.

FISH CREEK

This graceful community offers visitors the anticipated coffee-table pictorials. It may be the soul, as it were, of the county, and yet, it's also "just" another Door County village—with a population right at 200.

Arguably the most picturesque view in the county is along WI 42 as it winds into the village from a casual bluff. The official village history describes the town's situation succinctly—"with its back to a rock and its face to the sea." A treasured stretch of road with a few hairpin perils, a roller-coaster gut-lifter, and suddenly you're in a trim and tidy Victorian hamlet that could have come out of a Currier and Ives print. Fish Creek boasts the most thoroughly maintained pre-20th-century architecture on the entire peninsula, about 40 historic structures.

In 1844, trader Increase Claflin, the first non-native permanent settler in Door County,

© DOOR COUNTY CHAMBER OF COMMERCE

Fish Creek marina

DOOR COUNTY

left Sturgeon Bay after a few less-than-propitious incidents with the Potawatomi and wound up here. About this time, an Eastern cooper afflicted with terminal wanderlust, Asa Thorp, made his way to Door County, searching for his fortune. With his two brothers, Thorp constructed a loading pier and began a cordwood cutting business to supply steamships plying the coast. Later, Fish Creek transformed itself into the hub of commercial fishing on the Door Peninsula. Tourism was fortuitously there to take up the slack when the steamship supply industry petered out. By the late 1890s, locals were already putting out "Tourist Home" signs. Within a decade, even the home of Asa Thorp had been transformed into the Thorp Hotel.

Sights and Activities

Most visitors to Fish Creek prefer to simply stroll about, getting a look-see at the original architecture in an old county. The harbor area also has remnants of the earliest cabins. Even the remains of an 1855 cabin built by the

founding Thorp brothers stands on the grounds of the newfangled Founders Square mélange of shops and restaurants in the village center; they were rebuilt after a fire as closely as possible to the original designs. Another landmark structure is its famous "haunted house," the 1875 Greek revival **Noble House** (intersection of WI 42 and Main St., 920/868-2091, noon–5 P.M. Fri.–Sat. mid-May–mid-June, noon–5 P.M. Mon.–Sat. mid-June–Labor Day weekend, $3). The Gibraltar Historical Association (920/868-2091) has **historic walking tours.**

The country's oldest summer theater, the **Peninsula Players** (north of Fish Creek off WI 42 on Peninsula Players Rd. inside Peninsula State Park, 920/868-3287, www.peninsulaplayers.com) perform a spate of Broadway plays and musicals in a gorgeous garden setting with bayside trails late June–mid-October, a tradition in its seventh decade. Reservations are recommended. Even better: relatively recent renovations include heated floors!

Less than half as old, but with boatloads of attitude, the tongue-in-cheek **American Folklore Theatre** (920/839-2329, www.folkloretheatre.com) is an acclaimed theater-and-song troupe as likely to perform their own rollicking originals (as in "Cheeseheads: the Musical" or "Guys on Ice," a paean to ice fishing) or a ghost story series as they are the works of the Bard. Performances are held May–mid-October, also in Peninsula State Park, and now include an autumn Town Hall Series performed around the county. Mixed with the zaniness, as the name suggests, is an admirable amount of state and national heritage.

During August, professional musicians from across the country assemble in Fish Creek for the annual **Peninsula Music Fesival** (920/854-4060, www.musicfestival.com), which offers Renaissance, Reformation, baroque, and chamber ensembles, along with an array of thematic material. Nationally known folk musicians and touring troupes make an appearance at **Door County Auditorium** (3926 WI 42, 920/868-2787, www.dcauditorium.com); theater and dance performances are also held regularly.

At the north end of town, the **Skyway Drive In** (3475 WI 42, 920/854-9938, www.doorcountydrivein.com) is a throwback movie experience—it's charming to catch a flick under the stars with a Green Bay breeze wafting.

Perhaps the most, er, accessible winery in Door County, and one that focuses on the county, **Orchard Country** (WI 42 S, 866/946-3263, www.orchardcountry.com, 9 A.M.–5:30 P.M. daily, till 6 P.M. Fri.–Sat.) is a fave. The winery has award-winning county fruit wines, pick-yer-own fruits, sleigh rides, and a bunch more.

Without chartering a boat or flying your own plane, the easiest way to take in (but not actually step onto) **Chambers Island** across the Strawberry Channel is via twice daily **sailboat rides** (920/256-9042, www.friendlycharters.com, $40 per person).

The **Fish Creek Information Center** (4097 WI 42, 920/868-2316 or 800/577-1880, www.fishcreekinfo.com) is fully equipped to deal with your travel snafus or last-minute needs; trust me—I've given it lots of practice.

Recreation

Boat and bike rentals are available in town at **Nor Door Sport and Cyclery** (4007 WI 42, 920/868-2275) near the entrance to Peninsula State Park, which is the place to get a hybrid bike, mountain bike, or a single-speed cruiser. Plenty of other equipment is also for rent. In winter, you can rent cross-country skis and even snowshoes and ice skates. At **Edge of Park Bikes and Mopeds** (Park Entrance Rd., 920/868-3344) your moped rental includes a state park sticker.

Accommodations

The cheapest rooms in prime season are likely at two places. **Julie's** (4020 WI 42, 920/868-2999, www.juliesmotel.com, $79–106), near the state park, has basic but good rooms (and a super-duper café) and gets a nod for being pet friendly; well, they're friendly in general but you know what I mean. Figure ten bucks more for the most inexpensive but nice rooms at **Applecreek Resort and Cottages**

DOOR COUNTY CHERRIES TAKE ON THE NATION

In early 2010 ABC's *Good Morning America* set out in search of the best breakfast in America. After interminable hoo-hah that that generally involves, it came down to four, Fish Creek's White Gull Inn (specifically, its tear-of-joy-inducing cherry-stuffed French toast) pitted against three other friendly-though-they-should-have-known-better-than-to-try eateries nationwide. Come on, are you serious? The White Gull, natch, came out on top. Score one for the Cheeseheads (or Cherryheads up here)! In celebration, the inn also serves it daily now. It comes with a night's stay; you can substitute but honestly, why on earth would you?

(WI 42 and Hwy. F, 920/868-3525, www.applecreekresort.com, $90 and up); they've got loads of other room choices.

I've always had a soft spot for the **Fish Creek Motel and Cottages** (920/868-3448, www.fishcreekmotel.com, $98–245) at the end of Cottage Row, a block and a half past the stop sign off WI 42, given it was the first place I ever stayed in the county way back when. This amazing motel was actually built in Ephraim and boated around the point in 1981. Free bikes are a nice touch here. They had just completely finished remodeling the motel section at the time of writing.

Travel media scour every inch of the peninsula annually, looking to scoop others on an undiscovered gem, though they generally rehash the same old thing: the stately grace and charm of the ◖ **White Gull Inn** (4255 Main St., 920/868-3517, www.whitegullinn.com, $155–295). A proud old guesthouse since 1897, it's truly the grande dame of Door County. Rooms—a couple with private porches—are anachronistic but still plush; a few cottages and rooms in a cliff house are also available.

The dining room serves a spectacular array of continental, creative regional, and seafood in a country inn atmosphere that's not at all stuffy. And then there's that legendary fish boil, so popular that people swear they've made the return trip just to experience the boisterous one here, where it's made extra special by the boilmasters, who often preside over impromptu singing.

You'll find the most history of all at the **Thorp House Inn and Cottages** (4135 Bluff Rd., 920/868-2444, www.thorphouseinn.com, $125–205 rooms, $125–185 cottages), on lands originally belonging to Freeman Thorp, nephew to Fish Creek's founding father. The inn is backed up along the bluff overlooking the harbor. When Thorp perished in a 1903 shipwreck, his widow was forced to convert their new Victorian into a guest home. You'll get anachronistic-feeling B&B-style rooms at the inn or a great beach house, or quaint but modernized (just enough) cottages.

A main rival to the White Gull Inn is the **Whistling Swan** (4192 Main St., 920/868-3442, www.whistlingswan.com, $135–205). This one has the best local history—it was originally constructed across Green Bay in Marinette and scudded across the winter ice in 1907 to its present site. Five period rooms and two suites are available; the arched windows, fireplace, and high ceilings of the lobby are a draw for casual browsers in the shops on the main level.

The most unusual place you'll likely find in Door County is the four-floored **Silo Guest House** (3089 Evergreen Rd., 920/868-2592, $110), near the state park. It's got two bedrooms and is fully furnished. The top floor is the living room, which offers a grand view of the surrounding areas. July–August it rents by the week only ($525).

Food

Yours truly groaned upon hearing in 2008 that ⟨ **The Cookery** (WI 42, 920/868-3634, lunch and dinner daily, breakfast Sat.–Sun., $4–26), a sunny café with great, healthy takes on standards, had suffered a devastating fire.

Thank God all were well and they decided to fight on. The low-key place is now a tad more upscale, but snobby it ain't—it's simply a well-thought through and well-run place that's always trying to do the right thing, whether for the earth, the village, or the customers. Breakfast packs the place on Saturdays and Sundays, and healthy options abound; even vegetarians aren't forgotten.

An admission: yours truly is no fan of pizza (he loathes tomato sauce). Surprising as heck then that he can't get enough of the pizzas at ⟨ **Wild Tomato** (4023 WI 42, 920/868-3095, 11 A.M.–10 P.M. Sun.–Thurs., 11 A.M.–midnight Fri.–Sat.). Seriously, I've even had persnickety outstater foodie types rave about these za's. Eat local, act local and all that—they just taste incredible.

After weeks of supper clubs, this author was overjoyed to find **Mr. Helsinki** (Main St. above the Fish Creek Market, 920/868-9898, 5–11 P.M. daily, $7–22)—and not just because yours truly is of Finnish stock! Rather, this international fusion bistro specializes in, well, everything from crepes to a dash of Latin and a lot of Asian tastes and it does it well, right down to homegrown kaffir limes and Mexican epazote spice. You can even get a luscious vegan squash curry. It's a bit funky and irreverent and a whole lot of something else.

The food at the historic **Summertime Restaurant** (1 N. Spruce St., 920/868-3738, 7:30 A.M.–10 P.M. daily in season, $4–30) runs from fish to steaks, with a bit of Italian thrown in. The specialty of the house is South African back ribs. Seating? Your choice of a large hall, a loft dining room, or an outside patio. Built in 1910 as one of the original village cafés, it's definitely still got that old-fashioned feel.

Moving into the site of a longstanding supper club, **Cooper's Corner** (4172 Main St., 920/868-2667, 7 A.M.–11 P.M. daily, $7–30) fills those big shoes well and definitely takes the cuisine up a big notch. As many local products as possible are used in the creative dishes; they also smoke their own fish. The interiors were finished off with a lovely waterfall and al fresco dining. It's owned by the proprietors of the Door Peninsula Winery in Carlsville. (All that fine dining verbiage aside, their scrumptious breakfasts are very reasonably priced!) Having only been open a while, it'll have a break-in period for service, but it's off to a great start.

The White Gull Inn gets much-deserved press around the state—and, recently, nation—for its dining, yet for dinner you may not be able to beat the 【 **Whistling Swan** (4192 Main St., 920/868-3442, www.whistlingswan.com, dinner daily, $18–36). Expect gorgeous environs, gorgeous food (which of course is impeccably done), and a top-notch staff. This is a genuine treat.

【 PENINSULA STATE PARK

Consider: 3,800 variegated acres stretching from the northern fringe of Fish Creek, past Strawberry Channel, past Eagle Bluff, past Nicolet Bay, and finally to Eagle Harbor and Ephraim. All of it magnificent. Deeded to the state for a state park in 1909, Peninsula is the second-oldest park in the state system, and with no statistical manipulation the park is numero uno in usage in Wisconsin. (Heck, it even draws more folks per annum than Yellowstone National Park!)

The peninsula, rising 180 feet above the lake at Eagle Bluff, is a manifestation of the western edge of the Niagara Escarpment, here a steep and variegated series of headlands and reentrants. The ecosystem here is unparalleled. Near Weborg Point in the southwest, the Peninsula White Cedar Forest Natural Area is a 53-acre stand of spruce, cedar, balsam, and hemlock, and the boggy residual tract of an ancient lake. South of Eagle Tower is the larger, 80-acre Peninsula Beech Forest Natural Area. Not only is this a primitive example of northern mixed hardwood, but it is a relatively uncommon stand of American beech. Within both confines is a handful of threatened species, including the vivid dwarf lake iris. Other rarities include gaywings, Indian paintbrush, blue-eyed grass, and downy gentian. Not impressed? You will be if you ever witness a sunset here!

© DOOR COUNTY CHAMBER OF COMMERCE

Peninsula State Park

WORKING UP A SWEAT, DOOR COUNTY STYLE

For generations the Door was for weekend art browsers, beach lollers, or leaf-or-cherry-peepers, yet today you're as likely to see Lycra-clad gonzo type-T travelers with bike/kayak/ski racks atop the Subarus or Moby Dick-chasing boats behind the Suburban. Yep, Door County is actually a sublime place to get into or onto the land (or water).

Hiking is available pretty much everywhere, from nature trails to relatively ambitious backcountry hikes in the northern swaths of the county. One dream of this author's is to simply walk up one side of the peninsula, then head back on the other side, camping at public parks along the way. It's very doable.

Fishing has always been key here, whether it's a grandpa tossing a line for a smallmouth bass (this being one of the best places in the United States for the species), or, more commonly, a tourist heading out on a charter for trout or salmon (Sturgeon Bay especially for the latter). A real treat is helping the locals net tasty smelt around late April. There are far too many options for a book of this size; the county's chamber of commerce website (www.doorcounty.com) has very good links to whatever you need.

Then, there's **biking.** Yers truly is a biker, on and off the pavement. Really nothing in life is better than tossing away the book and map and just heading up any road in the county – you can't get lost. Better: the roads are mostly level here. Traffic is rarely too problematic, even on the main highways here, so you've also got Peninsula and Potawatomi State Parks for gorgeous and challenging on-road biking. The best off-road cycling in Wisconsin may come at Newport State Park.

The hidden gem to be sure is **kayaking.** It took some time to catch on, but there are more and more guides and outfitters in the county to help you experience the gorgeous waters around these parts. The rule, generally, for me is to stick to the bay side 'cuz I'm chicken of taking a kayak on a Great Lake, though Washington Island has wondrous paddling.

History

As usual, the first European, Increase Claflin, was a squatter; he parked his cabin high above the Strawberry Islands in 1844. But Plano Indian encampments have been examined and dated to 7000–4000 B.C., and the Menominee, Fox, Winnebago, Iroquois, and Potawatomi Indians have all occupied littoral sites. The Native American presence—and for once, overtly harmonious relations—is symbolized by the **Memorial Pole.** This 40-foot totem pole commemorates Potawatomi chief Simon Khaquados, laid to rest here in 1930 before thousands of admirers. Unfortunately, the settlers didn't love him enough to preclude building a golf course around his grave; the pole today sits between the number 1 and number 9 fairways.

Sights and Activities

Obligatory is the **Eagle Bluff Lighthouse** (920/421-3636) built during the Civil War by U.S. lighthouse crewmen as the second of the peninsula's lighthouses, a square tower about 45 feet tall attached to the keeper's house. It stands atop the bluff and can be seen for 15 miles; the views from its top stretch even farther. The prized assignment for lighthouse keepers in the peninsula, it had a commanding view and the best salary, the princely sum (for 1880) of $50 per month. Public interest prompted local historical societies to peel off 80 layers of paint and set to work refurbishing it in the late 1950s. Tours ($5 adults) are given in early summer and autumn every half hour 10 A.M.–4:30 P.M. Monday–Friday, with shorter hours the rest of year.

Two 75-foot towers were erected at the park's inception and used as fire-spotting towers (one was later removed because of dry rot). **Eagle Tower** was placed where it is simply because so many people wanted to spot a pair of long-term nesting eagles—the two for whom

© DOOR COUNTY CHAMBER OF COMMERCE

Eagle Bluff Lighthouse, Peninsula State Park

the bluff, the harbor, and the peninsula itself were eventually named. Ambitious visitors can take Minnehaha or Sentinel Trails in lieu of driving.

Before hiking, most visitors head to the **White Cedar Nature Center** (Bluff Rd., 920/854-5976, 10 A.M.–2 P.M. daily Memorial Day–Labor Day, shorter hours rest of the year) to walk a nature trail and view a host of exhibits covering the park's natural history.

Golf

Deemed by the golf press one of the gems of Midwestern courses, this 18-holer is plunked right in the eastern swath of the park. (It was built by a group of Ephraim businessmen in the early 1900s as a nine-hole course with sand greens.) Tee-time reservations are obviously necessary—as early as you can make them. Call 920/854-5791 for information.

Other Recreation

More than 20 miles of hiking trails network through the park and along the shores of the bays. Fifteen miles of on- and off-road bike trails exist, and a state trail pass is required on certain marked routes. What may be the most heavily traversed recreational trail—**Sunset Trail**—roughly parallels Shore Road for five miles through marsh and hardwood and conifer stands. At dusk it is definitely not misnamed. An extra few miles take in the littoral perimeter of Nicolet Bay and lead back to Fish Creek via back roads.

The toughest trail, but also the most rewarding, the **Eagle Trail** covers two miles skirting the harbor and a couple of natural springs and affords challenging scrambles over 200-foot bluffs. The easiest hike is the three-quarter-mile **Minnehaha Trail,** linking Nicolet Bay Campground and Eagle Trail.

You won't forget a kayak or canoe trip to **Horseshoe Island,** which has its own mile-long trail. A bit rugged and definitely isolated, it's a fave getaway.

Peninsula State Park has its own bike and boat rentals (920/854-9220) at Nicolet Beach.

Camping

Originally, camping was generally allowed in any direction the ranger waved his hand and cost from free to $0.50 per week. Today, the DNR receives up to 5,000 applications for summer reservations *in January*. At last count there were, let's see, tons of campsites—469 to be exact, separated into four sectors, but it'll still be tough to show up without a reservation and get one. Only one sector is open year-round.

Incidentally, this is one of the state parks that tacks on an extra fee for camping 'cuz it's so damned used.

EPHRAIM

As the map tells it, five miles separate Fish Creek and Ephraim, but you'd hardly know it. On the way north, as you pass the north entrance of Peninsula State Park, a modest jumble of development appears, and then vanishes, and shortly the fringes of beautiful Ephraim appear.

By the way, that's EE-frum. Another of those endlessly long Door County villages along a vivid harbor, Ephraim isn't the oldest community in the county, nor are its structures the most historically distinguished. But aesthetically it may have them all beat, and in many other respects, the community is the most perfectly preserved slice of Door County. The quaintness isn't accidental—for a while the village dictated via social pressure that all structures were to be whitewashed in proper fashion. And it stuck. The town is set along gorgeous Eagle Harbor. An enclave of pious fortitude, it was settled by Norwegian Moravians and christened Ephraim, which means "doubly fruitful" in Hebrew.

Sights and Activities

The oldest church in the county, the **Moravian Church** (9970 Moravia St., 920/854-2804), built out of necessity when the village founder's living room no longer sufficed, is, appropriately enough, along Moravia Street. It was built in 1857 out of cedar from the Upper Peninsula (local logs were too rough for such a sacred house); they offer free tours of this church on Thursdays at 1:30 P.M. Also on Moravia Street, the **Pioneer Schoolhouse Museum** (9998 Moravia St.) doubles as a repository of local history. Local art displays, with various media represented from juried shows and chosen by local arts associations, are worth a view. The final historic structure along the street is the **Thomas Goodletson Cabin,** an 1857 original (inside and out) and one of the peninsula's first cabins.

Down off the bluff are the **Anderson Barn and Store.** The ruddy barn was built in 1870. During the summer, it's open for browsing; the salient square silo is a rarity. Built in 1858 by Aslag Anderson, one of the original Scandinavian settlers, it sports old-time store items along with museumlike pieces. All structures save for the church operate as one museum (920/854-9688, 11 A.M.–4 P.M. Mon.–Sat. mid-June–Aug., Fri.–Sat. Sept.–Oct., $3, $5 including tour).

Summertime **walking tours** of all the historic structures depart at 10:30 A.M. Tuesday–Friday (usually, but call to verify) from the Anderson Barn.

Recreation and Events

South Shore Pier, in the heart of the village, has a large number of water-based recreation and tour opportunities. Hour-plus catamaran cruises (starting at $28), including a sunset cruise, depart seven times daily aboard the *Stiletto* (920/854-7245). Or rent your own pontoon boat, kayak, Waverunner, paddleboat, or fishing boat from the **South Shore Pier** (920/854-4324). Other operations offer kayak and windsurfing lessons and rentals; one even has parasail rides, which was only a matter of time.

The highlight of the entire year in Ephraim is the Scandinavian summer solstice celebration **Fyr Bal Festival.** Bonfires dot the shoreline and fish-boil cauldrons gurgle to commemorate the arrival of summer. A "Viking chieftain" is crowned and then blesses the ships and harbor. The accompanying art fairs are less Norse in nature.

Ephraim's information center (920/854-4989, www.ephraim.org or www.ephraim-door-county.com), is right along WI 42. A 24-hour kiosk is there in season for last-minute motel scroungers.

Accommodations

Understated and good for the wallet, **Trollhaugen** (WI 42, 920/854-2713, www.trollhaugenlodge.com, $79–169) just north of the "action" in the village is part motel, part lodge and log cabin. It's in a quiet wooded setting with updated lodge decor. Splurge for the log cabin, though the rooms are what you'd expect (not bad at all).

Not far away from here, there are those who have insisted to me that the **Eagle Harbor Inn** (9914 WI 42, 920/854-2121, www.eagleharbor.com, $98–269) is, for dollar spent, the best inn in Door County, if not the Midwest. Now that's saying a whole big mouthful but if they're wrong, it's not by much. The elegant nine-room inn (with two multiperson suites) is antique-strewn and offers a sumptuous country breakfast in the garden. The one- to three-bedroom cottages on nicely wooded grounds are also very appealing.

I quite like—no, love—**◖ Lodgings at Pioneer Lane** (9998 Pioneer Ln., 920/854-7656 or 800/588-3565, www.lodgingsatpioneerlane.com, $169 and up), which has themed rooms. This often results in embarrassing tackiness, but these are impeccably executed with kitchenettes, fireplaces, private porches or balconies, and superb detailings. And the owners get rave reviews from pretty much everybody. (So be nice to 'em!) By far this is the best new entry for this edition. It's north of Wilson's ice cream parlor, then right onto Church Street.

Food

There are precious few restaurants here; the lodges and resorts take most of the food business.

I'm generally on the manic run and so really appreciate **Good Eggs** (9820 Brookside Ln., 920/854-6621, 7 A.M.–1 P.M. daily May–Oct.,

$5–9), set back off WI 42, where you can build your own omelet, wrap it up in a tortilla (try the cilantro), and dash. Or sit at their tables and relax with the water view.

A step-up in price is the casually creative **Chef's Hat** (Hwy. Q, 920/854-2034) off the main highway. Pear and pumpkin soup and a sandwich pretty much sums it up.

The **Old Post Office** (10040 WI 42, 920/854-4034, breakfast and dinner only, $5–10) in the Edgewater Resort is known mostly for one of the biggie fish boils in the county, but also for Belgian waffles.

Another touted lodging dining room is **The Second Story** (10018 Water St., 920/854-2371, 8 A.M.–8 P.M. daily May–Oct., $5–12) at the Ephraim Shores Motel, offering family-style soups, sandwiches, quiches, seafood, a salad bar, and wondrous Norwegian meatballs. Foodie friends have opined that the dessert tray is worth a visit!

It's nearly a Door County law that you stop at **Wilson's** (9990 Water St., 920/854-2041, from 11 A.M. daily May–Oct.) old-fashioned ice cream parlor, right in the heart of the village. Opened in 1906 and serving pretty much ever since, it's got ice cream cones as big as bull-horns, as well as burgers and homemade soups and salads. (Stick to the ice cream.) You'll feel as if you're in a Norman Rockwell painting hanging out on the white-framed porch.

SISTER BAY

Sister Bay can sure get congested on a typical summer Saturday—symbolic of its status as the largest community north of Sturgeon Bay (though the population is a mere 695). It's also the only spot north on the peninsula where a minor mall reveals itself. Named for twin islands offshore, the bay—not offering quite the wind-break of Eagle Harbor—never got much notice from southbound steamers until Scandinavian settlers discovered the dense forest land in the surrounding hills and erected cabins in 1857.

Activities

Sister Bay's quaint village park, with one of the prettiest stretches of beach around, hosts

Sister Bay's Fall Festival

the huge **Fall Festival** and is the linchpin of a fine community network of parks, which offer regular doses of free big band, jazz, country, and folk concerts—one definitely each summer Wednesday afternoon. Also on the south edge of town is the **Old Anderson House Museum** (intersection of WI 57 and Fieldcrest Rd., 920/854-7680, tours: weekends and holidays mid-May–mid-Oct., free), a restored house dating from 1895; this baby was built in Marinette, Wisconsin, and dragged across the ice to get it here.

Bayshore Outdoors (920/854-7598, www.kayakdoorcounty.com) has daily guided kayak tours, along with rentals of cross-country skis, snowshoes, and bikes.

Accommodations

Getting a room for around $60 isn't too hard in Sister Bay—a Door County rarity! One of the cheapest motels on the Door is the delightfully rustic **Century Farm Motel** (10068 WI 57, between Sister Bay and Ephraim, 920/854-4069, $60 and up). A real country farm, it's got four individual units with TVs and refrigerators. There are no frills here, but it's almost homey nonetheless.

Also good is the rustic, century-old **Liberty Park Lodge** (north on WI 42, 920/854-2025, www.libertyparklodge.com, $99–144). The main lodge has rooms dating back to the Door's tourism beginnings, now lovingly redone. Also available are Cape Cod–style woodland and shore cottages. Overall, a rich balance of old and new. And for the price, you cannot beat it.

A definite hop up, and perhaps a steal, **Little Sister Resort** (10620 Little Sister Hill Rd., 920/854-4013, www.littlesisterresort.com, $115–220) sits in a cedar forest setting south of Sister Bay off WI 42 near a gorgeous bay. These very comfortable surroundings also cater to families. You'll need to brew some coffee to go through the mind-boggling array of cabins and chalets, but this place is worth the money.

Forty-five large (up to 600-square-foot) and attractive rooms are available at the

Country House Resort (715 N. Highland Rd., 920/854-4551 or 800/424-0041, www.country-house.com, $120–337). All feature refrigerators and private waterside balconies, and some have whirlpools and other miscellaneous amenities. The grounds cover 16 heavily wooded acres with private nature trails and a 1,000-foot shoreline. It's *just* south of the main "drag" off WI 42, then toward the bay.

Food

For the "only in Wisconsin" file: The **Sister Bay Bowl and Supper Club** (504 Bay Shore Dr., 920/854-2841, daily April–Jan., Sat.–Sun. otherwise, $4 and up) right downtown does have bowling. But, believe it or not, it offers one of the better fish *fries* around—great if you're wearying of fish boils!

Or, right nearby, the best sandwiches in the county, this author says, come at the **D.C. Deli** (10663 WI 42, 920/854-4514, 9 A.M.–8 P.M. Mon.–Sat., 9 A.M.–3 P.M. Sun., $9), a smokehouse and restaurant that had a brisket so good that it once made my legs wobbly.

The **Mission Grille** (intersection of WI 42 and WI 57, 920/854-9070, breakfast, lunch and dinner daily, $5–25) at the junction of the two big highways is an early-20th-century church-turned-cozy restaurant. It features unpretentious but superb New American cuisine and atmosphere (and wine list). Vegetarians aren't ignored. The summertime dining on a trilevel patio and veranda is one of the most relaxing dining spots around.

The name **Sister Bay Cafe** (611 WI 42, 920/854-2429, breakfast and dinner with varying hours Apr.–Nov., $3–14) is misleading. It's got your basics, but better, the creative dinners shine, and then there's a whole slew of authentic Scandinavian fare, including a Norwegian farmer's stew; red fruit pudding with cream; and beef and pork patties styled after a Danish dish.

The most famous ethnic eatery in the county, if not the state, is ◖ **Al Johnson's Swedish Restaurant** (702 WI 42, 920/854-2626, 6 A.M.–9 P.M. daily, $5–18), where cars regularly screech to a halt when drivers see the legendary live goats munching the sod roof. The menu offers Swedish and American food. Pound after pound of Swedish meatballs is served nightly, and other favorites are the Swedish beefsteak sautéed in onions and lingonberry pancakes for breakfast. It's often standing room only, and the restaurant doesn't take reservations. It's so lively it prob'ly ain't yer best bet for a romantic anniversary dinner. On a sad note, famous Al passed away in 2010, a great loss for the county.

You'll find impeccably well-thought-out and executed "regional international" cuisine, and certainly a meal worthy of splurging on, at the ◖ **Inn at Kristofer's** (734 N. WI 42, 920/854-9419, from 5 P.M. Wed.–Mon. May–Oct., $15 and up). Tiny in size but eminently dependable in its fare, the inn is a highlight of any true culinary experience in Door County. Just a recent heavenly example: Chicken Roulade with local cherries and Japanese herb bread crumbs with a lingonberry (local) reduction. This place will wow you. The inn also gives gourmet cooking lessons.

On the north end of town, the **Waterfront** (10947 N. WI 42, 920/854-5491, 5–9 P.M. Tues.–Sun., $24–37) is run by a couple with three decades in the Door's restaurant business and is well-known for its seafood.

Information

Sister Bay has a quaint tourist information center (416 Gateway Dr., 920/854-2812, www.sisterbay.org) in a refurbished log schoolhouse.

ELLISON BAY

Plunked along the decline of a steep hill and hollow tunneling toward a yawning bay, Ellison Bay's facade isn't initially as spectacular as Ephraim's, the architecture isn't as quaint as Fish Creek's, and it's a fifth of the size of Sister Bay. Nonetheless, there is something engaging about the place. It begins with what may be the best view from the highway in the whole county. Atop the 200-foot bluff on the south side of town, you can see clear to Gills Rock, farther up the peninsula. Founded in the early 1860s, the village originally served as a hub for lumber, courtesy of the operations in nearby

© DOOR COUNTY CHAMBER OF COMMERCE

Ellison Bay's Bluff County Park

Newport State Park. As recently as the 1930s, the town's commercial fishery led Wisconsin in tonnage—perhaps the reason a local restaurant is credited with the first fish boil.

Sights

The name is often misinterpreted as an approximation of the 130 lovely acres overlooking the northern fringe of Ellison Bay (north on WI 42, then left on Garrett Bay Rd.), but in fact, **The Clearing** (12171 Garrett Bay Rd., 920/854-4088, www.theclearing.org) refers to something a tad more metaphysical—closer to "clarity of thought." A contemplative retreat for the study of art, natural science, and the humanities—philosophy is ever-popular—the school was the result of a lifetime's effort by famed landscape architect Jens Jensen. Much like contemporary Frank Lloyd Wright, Jensen's maverick style and obdurate convictions grated against the entrenched elitism of landscape architecture in the early 20th century. His belief in the inseparability of land and humanity was considered foolish, if not outright heretical, in

those early days. A Danish immigrant, Jensen arrived in the United States in 1884 and became more and more enamored of the wild Midwestern landscape while simultaneously cultivating his radical notions of debt to the earth and the need to connect with it despite living in a rat race. While in Chicago creating the parks that made his name, he began buying land around Ellison Bay. By the 1930s, everything had jelled into a cohesive plan, and he spent the next 15 years establishing his retreat according to folk educational traditions in northern Europe.

The grounds contain a lodge, a library, a communal dining area, and cottages and dormitories for attendees. Summer classes are held May–October and last one week, though some day seminars are also offered. Meals are included. Lots of group work, outdoor exploration, campfires, and other traditional folk systems are the rule. Fees, including room and board (except Thursday supper, when attendees are encouraged to explore the town for a fish boil), are around $500 a week in the dormitory, $550 a week in a double room. Nonparticipants can visit on weekends 1–4 P.M. mid-May–mid-October.

Ellison Bay has the grand **Bluff County Park,** three miles southwest along WI 42 and then off toward the lake. Nearly 100 wild acres atop 200-foot bluffs overlook the lake. There is no camping, but some rough trails (none to the water) wind through the area. You'll find some wowser views!

Accommodations

The best places to stay are actually in the vicinity of Ellison Bay. Just north of "downtown" and very good for the price is the **Parkside Inn** (11946 WI 42, 920/854-9050, www.theparksideinn.com, $89–129). The main lodge has basic but very clean motel-style rooms; there's a more upmarket guest house with one or two bedrooms as well.

Food

The eatery of choice in town—it is in fact the heart of the village—has for a long spell been **The Viking Restaurant** (12029 WI 42, 920/854-2988, 6 A.M.–9 P.M. in summer, till 7 P.M. thereafter, $4–15). Credited with filling that first iron cauldron with whitefish, potatoes, and onions, and brewing up a culinary tradition, The Viking sadly was damaged severely by a fire in September 2010, quieting the roaring kettle fire for the first time in decades. At the time of writing, the staff (and many locals) were feverishly working on reconstruction and expected to have it reopened by spring 2011.

◖ **T. Ashwell's** (east of WI 42 on Mink River Rd., 920/854-4306, 5–10 P.M. Wed.–Mon. May–Mar., $20–34) is another Door County bistro worthy of an extra nickel or two. Creative comfort food, unique nouvelle cuisine, and yes, it features sustainably raised local food as much as possible, and much more, all in a cheerily casual environment. Take in a Thursday, or *tapas* night; otherwise, it'd be a lovely surprise if you got there on a Chef's Choice night and let him do it all for you.

Information and Services

The smallest visitors center on the peninsula might be the closet-size information kiosk in Ellison Bay (920/854-5448, May–Oct.), across from The Viking Restaurant.

GILLS ROCK AND NORTHPORT

Out of Ellison Bay, WI 42 cuts east and then changes its mind and bends 90 degrees north again into the tightly packed fishing village of Gills Rock (pop. maybe 75) and the first of the ends of the road. Parked high atop 150-foot Table Bluff overlooking Hedgehog Harbor across from Deathdoor Bluff, pleasant Gills Rock is as far as the tourist road goes on the Door—that is, until you hop islands. Sleepy and quaint and known as the tip or top of the thumb, Gills Rock has the feel of an old tourist camp from the 1930s. Up WI 42 a couple of miles is truly the end of the line, Northport. (Incidentally, the sine wave turns of the highway leading to the ferry offer some splendid autumnal scenery!)

© THOMAS HUHTI

Gills Rock harbor

Sights and Activities

Door County's "other" maritime museum (this is an offshoot of Sturgeon Bay's) is parked on a little dusty side road in Gills Rock—the **Door County Maritime Museum** (12724 W. Wisconsin Bay Rd., 920/854-1844, 10 A.M.–5 P.M. daily May–Oct., $4.50 adults). This one features gill nets and more gill nets—or rather, the commercial fishing industry. The highlight is an old fishing tug, and there is plenty of other equipment. Admission includes a chatty guided tour.

Capt. Mariner (920/421-1578) is ubiquitous in Gills Rock for wetting a line. Chinook salmon and German brown trout are the specialties, and the rates of $80 per person aren't bad at all. You fish virtually the entire time and with this set-up, solo travelers and novices can take advantage of Great Lake sportfishing, a service difficult to find on other charters.

You'll find the best views of the bay and solitude at the largest park in the county, **Door Bluff Headlands,** almost 200 acres of wild trails and woodland. From WI 42, take Cottage Road to Garrett Bay Road.

Scuba divers come to Gills Rock for underwater archaeology. No joke—beneath the surface of local waters lie more than 200 wrecks, and the State Historical Society has ongoing "digs" on its Wisconsin Maritime Trails project. (If you can't suit up, the local visitors centers have maps of land-based information markers pointing out wreck sites from shore; link up at maritimetrails.org.) The **Shoreline Resort** (920/854-2606, www.theshorelineresort.com) has dive charters, though you must have your own gear and already be certified. The resort also offers daily narrated **scenic boat tours.**

Washington Island Ferries and Cruises

The most luxurious way to Washington Island is a narrated cruise aboard the *Island Clipper* (920/854-2972, www.islandclipper.com), a 65-foot cruiser specifically designed by a Sturgeon Bay boatbuilder for the Death's Door crossing. A basic crossing ($12 adults) is available, as is a ferry plus "Viking Train" island tour ($24).

There are up to 10 departures 10 A.M.–5 P.M. daily in peak summer season.

Northport exists solely to accommodate the second of the ferry lines to Washington Island. This pier was established as an escape from fierce prevailing winds on the Gills Rock side. Northport, in fact, has eclipsed Gills Rock as a departure point to Washington Island, as it is virtually always free of ice and saves precious crossing time. Those who wish to drive their cars over to Washington Island will have to come here for the **Washington Island Ferry** (920/847-2546 or 800/223-2094, www.wisferry.com), which takes autos and passengers. It also hooks up with the Cherry Train tour of the island if you take the 9:45 A.M. or earlier crossing from Northport, 11 A.M. from Gills Rock. The schedule for the ferry is staggering; check the wall map. In high season, July–late August, 21 round-trips depart to and from the island beginning at 7 A.M. from the island, 7:45 A.M. from Northport (no early trip on Sundays!). The farther you are from this zenith chronologically, the fewer trips depart. December–January, only four trips depart per day; February–March there are only one or two per day, and vehicle reservations are mandatory. Call anyway for verification in the off-season. A car costs $25 (passengers not included), each adult is $12, bicycles are $4, and motorcycles are $15—all prices are round-trip.

Accommodations

Prominent in Gills Rock, the **Shoreline Resort** (12747 WI 42, 920/854-2606, www.theshorelineresort.com, $119) offers waterfront rooms with patios and a popular rooftop sun deck; the views are grand! Charter fishing tours and assorted sightseeing cruises (the sunset cruise is perennially popular) also leave the on-site marina. It also rents bikes.

Unheard-of **On the Rocks Cliffside Lodge** (849 Wisconsin Bay Rd., 920/854-4907, www.cliffsidelodge.com, Apr.–Nov., $350 and up) is possibly the most private Door County experience; you simply have to eyeball it for yourself. This jewel is a massive 3,500-square-foot A-frame lodge with fieldstone fireplace atop a

60-foot cliff. It was overwhelming enough for *National Geographic* to feature it. Rates start at $350 a night for two people, but this sucker holds up to 18 (for $775)!

Food

The best food you're going to get in Gills Rock is some of that grand smoked Lake Michigan fish at **Charlie's Smokehouse** (12731 WI 42, 920/854-2972), whose proprietor or family have been doing it since 1932. The **Shoreline Resort** (12747 WI 42, 920/854-2606, www.theshorelineresort. com, lunch and dinner daily May–Oct.) is the other dining option, with good whitefish and basic hearty fare.

Washington Island and Rock Island

Rustic, time-locked Washington Island, an easy (and safe) ferry ride from the mainland across Death's Door, very nearly wasn't included as part of the Door, but in 1925, the Supreme Court ruled in Wisconsin's favor in a border dispute with Michigan. At issue were a number of the dozen or so islands in the Grand Traverse Chain, of which Washington and the surrounding islands are a part.

The island isn't what most expect. Many envision a candy-facade Mackinac Island, full of historically garbed docents or fudge sellers every two steps. Not at all. It's populated by 650 permanent residents, and development is absolutely unobtrusive. The place has a pleasant weatherbeaten seaside look to it, rather than the sheen of a slick resort. Best of all, Washington Island has the feel of a small Midwestern town, right down to the well-used community ballparks. This explains the island's perfectly apt PR tout line: "North of the Tension Line."

HISTORY
Natural History

Beyond Washington Island is one of the Niagara Escarpment's longest gaps as it stretches under the waters to Michigan and on to Ontario. Of the islands stretching across the lake to Michigan's Upper Peninsula, Washington is the granddaddy, geologically and historically. With 36 square miles, the island's circumference is just over 25 miles. The escarpment is on a consistent, gradual declivity (2–5 degrees), a mere 160 feet above the lake's surface, surrounding Washington Island's rough, wave-battered exterior. Nowhere on the Door Peninsula does nature manifest itself with more force—wind-whipped stretches of open meadow or scattered hardwoods equally wind-bent—than on this tough island.

Human History

The Door, a macabre caveat of death for those foolhardy enough to attempt the savage waters here, fits Washington Island, truly the door to Wisconsin. Washington and Rock Islands were populated long before the rest of northeastern Wisconsin. Before vandals and thickets of ambitious brush got ahold of the sites, the island was one of the richest Native American archaeological time capsules in the Midwest. The original island dwellers were likely the Potawatomi and later the Huron (the island's original name was Huron Island), among others, who arrived in flight from the bellicose Iroquois in modern Quebec.

Island-hopping voyageurs plying the expanses of New France found a ready-made chain of havens and temporary fishing grounds stretching from Michigan to the Door Peninsula, and thus to the Fox and Wisconsin Riverways. Purportedly, Jean Nicolet himself was the first European to set up camp on Washington Island. Pierre Esprit Radisson, who wintered here with the Huron, dubbed it the most pleasant place he had experienced in the Great Lakes. The most famous European presence still lends itself to the murky legends swirling in the cruel straits. In 1679, Robert

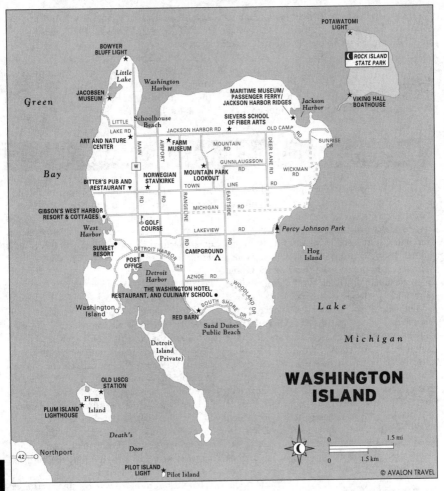

La Salle sailed the *Griffin* into Detroit Harbor, where he met and bartered fur and iron wares with the Potawatomi and then left, destined for Mackinac Island. The ship vanished, and mariners have regaled the gullible with stories of a shrouded ship matching its description haunting the shoals around the Door ever since.

A large-scale European presence appeared in the early 1830s, when immigrants into Green Bay heard of trout the size of calves being taken from the waters around the island. The first fishers were Irish, but the true habitation mark on Washington Island is pure Icelandic—richest in the United States. Several thousand of the nation's first Icelandic settlers arrived, took readily to the isolation, and set down permanent roots. Their heritage is clearly manifest in the *stavkirke*—the wooded stave church—being built gradually by island residents, one massive white pine log at a time, and by the proud Icelandic horses roaming certain island pastures.

SIGHTS

There is a lighthouse on Washington Island, the **Bowyer Bluff light** on the northwest side. Unfortunately, you can't see it, but you may wish you could—at 210 feet, it's the tallest on the Great Lakes.

Art and Nature Center

A mix of natural and cultural island history is displayed here (1799 Main Rd., 920/847-2025, 10:30 A.M.–4:30 P.M. Mon.–Fri., 11:30 A.M.–4:30 P.M. Sun. mid-June–mid-Sept., shorter hours after Labor Day, $1 adults), at the corner of Main and Jackson Harbor Road in an unassuming building resembling an old schoolhouse. Permanent artwork displays are housed within, and nature trails branch from the rear. Art classes are offered, and regular musical events are held during a weeklong midsummer festival.

Museums

The top stop for museum hoppers is the **Maritime Museum** (10 A.M.–4 P.M. Mon.–Fri. Memorial Day–Oct., with some weeks open daily in summer, donations) at the east end of Jackson Harbor Road, opposite the ferry landing. The museum retains a significant presence—what little remains of the island's commercial fishing industry operates out of secluded Jackson Harbor. You'll find a reconstructed fish shed, a couple of ice houses, an old fisherman's house, some outdoor displays (a Kahlenberg engine, an old Coast Guard boat, and remnants of a wreck), and the site itself, housed inside two fishing shacks.

The **Jacobsen Museum** (920/847-2213, 10 A.M.–4 P.M. daily Memorial Day weekend–mid-Oct., donations) is housed in a vertical log building owned by early settler Jens Jacobsen, on the south shore of Little Lake. The packrat progenitor collected a huge number of natural history artifacts, mostly Native American arrowheads and beads. Also inside you'll find Danish scrollwork, maps, models of shipwrecks, fossils, and tools. There's also a whole bunch of weird stuff lying out front, such as an ancient leviathan rudder from the steamer

Louisiana, which ran aground in 1913; ice cutters; and huge capstans for raising anchors.

The smallest of all is the **Farm Museum** (920/847-2577, hours vary, June–Oct., free), a spread of pioneer structures off Airport Road along Jackson Harbor Road. A pioneer log home, a double log barn and shed with a collection of hand tools, 15 pieces of horse-drawn machinery, a forge and blacksmith shop, a reconstructed stone building, and a popular petting zoo are on the grounds. Regularly scheduled kids' and families' farm activities starting on Wednesdays after July 5 and running through mid-August are a hoot.

Sievers School of Fiber Arts

In its second decade, the Sievers School of Fiber Arts (Jackson Harbor Rd., 920/847-2264, www.sieversschool.com) is the most intriguing of island highlights. It's less a school than a retreat into weaving, papermaking, spinning, basketweaving, batik, tapestry, drafting, Scandinavian woodcarving, and any other number of classes in vanishing folk arts. On any given day, the solitude is accentuated by the thwack of looms or the whirring of spinning wheels. Classes are offered May–October, and weekend or one-week classes are available. Fees range $190–340, plus up to $120 for dorm fees for a weeklong class. A downtown consignment shop displays and sells the works created as well as cherrywood looms.

Dunes

No visit to the Maritime Museum is complete without a stroll on the nature trail through the ecosystem of the **Jackson Harbor Ridges,** a 90-acre State of Wisconsin Scientific Reserve. The fragile mix of shore meadow, dune, and boreal forest is not found anywhere else in the peninsula. Northern plant species such as the rare dwarf lake orchid and arctic primrose, along with white cedar, fir, and spruce, are found here. A part of the ridges was established with a Nature Conservancy tract. There is an isolated and generally underpopulated beach adjacent to the reserve.

More great Lawrence of Arabia dunescapes

DOOR COUNTY

are found across the island, southeast of Detroit Harbor along South Shore Drive at **Sand Dunes Public Beach.**

Parks

The generally gravelly shoreline is rimmed with parks and beaches: **Schoolhouse Beach** in Washington Harbor, with tough and chilly swimming in a secluded setting (and extraordinarily smooth stone!); the Ridges in Jackson Harbor; and **Percy Johnson Park** on the eastern side at the tip of Lakeview Road, offering vistas of Hog Island and a nesting sanctuary. None allow camping.

Inland is where you'll find the two interesting parks. A small picnic area and park is adjacent to the airport, of all places, and people head out with a lunchtime sandwich to watch the odd plane arrival. To get there, take Main Road north, then Town Line Road east to Airport Road. The most commanding views of all are at the 200-foot heights of **Mountain Park Lookout,** just about the geometric center of the island.

Entertainment

The **Red Barn,** south of Gislason Beach along South Shore Drive, features a regular assortment of local talent—musicians or whoever else can be drummed up. The **Art and Nature Center** (1799 Main Rd., 920/847-2025) offers a weeklong midsummer music festival during which concerts and programs are offered.

RECREATION

With 75 miles of paved roadway, Washington Island was made for biking. A weekend here is just about enough time to spin around the main perimeter and nose off on a few side roads. Much of the eastern littoral roadway is gravel, as is the main artery, Michigan Road, in the center of the island. Bikes can be rented at a couple of places at the ferry dock, and trails are marked by green signs.

Field Wood Farms (one-half mile west of Main Rd. on W. Harbor Rd., 920/847-2490) offers trail rides on descendants of original Icelandic stock horses—a rarity

anywhere—and the oldest registered herd in the United States. Pony rides, riding instruction, and horse-drawn wagon rides are also available by appointment.

Fishing for 30-pound salmon is not unheard of in the sheltered waters around the island's bays; other big takes include perch, smallmouth black bass, rock bass, and especially northern pike, right in Detroit Harbor. A number of charter operations run about, including salmon and bass charters.

ACCOMMODATIONS

Washington Island features a patchwork of lodging options, stemming from its isolation. You'll find basic motels, intriguing and microscopic kiosk-cottages, spacious but threadbare cabins that look like deer-hunting shacks heated with oil furnaces, even the odd resident's spare bedroom. Finding a cheap room (as in under $100) is generally no problem. For a blast from the past, and a really cheap sleep, there's **Gibson's West Harbor Resort & Cottages** (920/847-2225, gibsonwh@itol. com, $30 s, $40 d), about halfway up the west shore from the ferry landing. Yep, they've got basic housekeeping cottages ($90 average), but the coolest of all are the sleeping rooms—tiny but tidy—with shared bathrooms above the main building, an erstwhile logging boarding house; it's all of $30 for a single and $40 for double—they even have a five-person room for $65. Absolutely nothing like it elsewhere these days.

A slight step up, the **Sunset Resort** (Old W. Harbor Rd., 920/847-2531, www.sunsetresortwi.com, $75) is a longstanding island getaway, run by the fifth generation of the inn's original Norwegian (1902) founding family. Cupped by spinneys of pine, the inn offers knotty pine cottages and one super loft cabin. Rooms are simple but clean; impromptu campfires typify the family atmosphere. Breakfasts here are legendary.

North up the road from the ferry landing at the mouth of the harbor is another smattering of no-frills accommodations, restaurants, and services. The best-known lodging here is something that has put the island squarely on the map for those searching for something a bit different. The 🄲 **Washington Hotel, Restaurant, and Culinary School** (Range Line Rd., 920/847-2169, www.thewashingtonhotel.com, $125–280) is more a retreat than a lodging option. This renovated 19th-century hotel features amazing touches such as organic linens and handmade beds. Some rooms even share baths with chuffing steam showers. How about breakfast baked in an old-fashioned brick oven? Even better is the food—simply, simply worth every mile of the drive or boat to get here. Such positive feedback came from delighted lodgers that the restaurant is also a culinary academy! And rarely will you find proprietors who will work as conscientiously or heroically to solve what has caused someone to be less than happy (not me, but I've seen it and it was real-deal, not obsequious). That said, at times the hotel is booked with events and so closed to tourists, so phone or email ahead!

FOOD AND DRINK

Food for the obvious reasons, drink because you'll hear quite a bit about the potent "bitters"—an antifreeze-proof Scandinavian tradition still served in local pubs. If you can stomach a shot, you're in the club.

An island delicacy is a "lawyer." No, not the counselors, but rather another name for the burbot, a mud-dwelling gadid fish with barbels on the chin.

To-live-for Icelandic pancakes and Norwegian *barkram pankaka*—cherry and cream filled pleasures—are the house specialties at breakfast at **Sunset Resort** (Old W. Harbor Rd., 920/847-2531, 8–11 A.M. daily July–Aug., Sat.–Sun. only June and Sept., $2–7). This local hot spot serves morning grub, including homemade breads.

Landmark **Bitter's Pub and Restaurant** (Main Rd., 920/847-2496) is in Nelson's Hall, a century-old structure in the center of the island. Famed for its Bitter's Club, initiated in 1899, it draws about 10,000 visitors annually. Bitter's is the best elbow-rubbing option on the

island; the restaurant is classic Americana—steaks, seafood, and chicken. A $5 breakfast buffet, lunch, and dinner are served daily. Fish boils are held three days per week.

INFORMATION

The Washington Island Chamber of Commerce (920/847-2179, washingtonislandwi.com or washingtonislandchamber.com) has all the information you might want; it often has folks to greet you on the mainland side.

GETTING THERE AND AROUND
Getting There

Ferry lines run to and from Washington Island via the "top of the thumb." Ferries have made the seven-mile crossing somewhat quotidian, but it wasn't always so. Winter crossings used to be made by horse-drawn sleigh or—unimaginably—car, but weather conditions could change the ice or eliminate it altogether within a relatively short period. Today the ice freezes the crossing nearly solid for just more than 100 days each year, but modern ferries can take much of the ice thrown at them. When ice floes pile up during extreme cold, the ferries either "back up" and try to make an end run, or "back down" and run right at the ice. At those times, ferry service is preciously light and reservations are necessary to cross with an automobile.

You could theoretically paddle a sea kayak from Northport all the way to Washington Island—and it has been done. The lunatic fringe aspect of that notwithstanding, it would be the most breathtaking way to meet the Porte des Mortes head on. Obviously, you'd better be a damn good—and experienced—paddler.

On Island

If you've come over sans car, **Dor Cros Inn** (1922 Lobdell Point Rd., 920/847-2126) has bikes for rent; problem is, you'll have to hoof about a mile-and-a-half north up the road to get there.

A few tours/shuttles depart from the ferry dock regularly, linking with the ferries from

Northport and Gills Rock. Lots of folks rave about the **Cherry Train** (920/847-2039, www.cherrytraintours.com, $15), essentially a Chevy Suburban pulling carriages, which offers four tours daily.

Or rent your own moped for $90 per day at **Annie's** (920/854-2972) at the Island Clipper Dock.

Head up Main Road from the ferry dock to **Bread & Water Bakery & Café** (1275 Main Rd., 920/847-2400, breadandH2O@gmail.com) where they have great food, but more, where, as they say, "Kayak is spoken." Yup, the island has great kayaking, and this is your place to find a guide, a rental, or both.

◖ ROCK ISLAND STATE PARK

Less than a mile from Washington Island's Jackson Harbor as the crow flies is one man's feudal estate-turned-overgrown state park. Getting to Rock Island (920/847-2235), the most isolated state park in Wisconsin's system, necessitates not one but two ferry rides. When you get there, you've got a magnificent retreat: a small island, yes, but with delicious solitude, icy but gorgeous beaches, and the loveliest skies in Wisconsin, stars and sunrises-wise.

Native Americans lived in sporadic encampments along the island's south shore from 600 B.C. until the start of the 17th century. In approximately 1640, Potawatomi Indians migrated here from Michigan; allied Ottaway, Petun, and Hurons fleeing extermination at the hands of the Iroquois nations followed in the 1650s. The Potawatomi were visited in 1679 by Rene Robert Covelier, Sieur de la Salle, whose men built two houses, the remains of which are still visible amid the weed-choked brambles off the beach. Eventually, the French and the Potawatomi returned, establishing a trading post that lasted until 1730. Until the turn of the 20th century, the island was alternately a base camp for fishers and the site of a solitary sawmill. Rock Island is thus arguably the true "door" to Wisconsin, and a ready-made one at that—the first rock on the way across the temperamental lake from Mackinac Island.

Flora and Fauna

Here's why the isolated island is so great—no ticks, no pesky raccoons, no skunks, and no bears. In short, no perils for backpackers. The worst thing out there are the rather pernicious fields of poison ivy (though these are usually well marked). There are white-tailed deer, lemmings, foxes, and a few other small mammals and amphibians. Plenty of nonpoisonous snakes can also be seen.

The northern hardwood forest is dominated by sugar maple and American beech. The eastern hemlock is gone. The perimeters have arbor vitae (white cedar) and small varieties of red maple and red and white pine.

Sights

Two of the most historically significant buildings in Wisconsin, as deemed by the Department of the Interior, are Thordarson's massive limestone **Viking Hall** and **boathouse.** Patterned after historic Icelandic manors, the structures were cut, slab by slab, from Rock Island limestone by Icelandic artisans and workmen ferried over from Washington Island. Only the roof tiling isn't made from island material. That's a lot of rock, considering that the hall could hold more than 120 people. The hand-carved furniture, mullioned windows, and rosemaling-like detail, including runic inscriptions outlining Norse mythology, are magnificent.

The original name of Rock Island was Potawatomi Island, a name that lives on in one of the original lighthouses in Wisconsin, **Potawatomi Light,** built in 1836. The original structure was swept from the cliffs by the surly lake soon after being built but was replaced. Unfortunately, it's not open to the public except for ranger-led tours. The house is accessible via a two-hour trail.

On the east side of the island are the remnants of a former fishing village and a historic water tower—don't laugh—it, too, is on the National Register of Historic Places. The village dwelling foundations lie in the midst of thickets and are tough to spot; there are also a few cemeteries not far from the campsites.

THE MAN OF THE ROCK

In 1910, Milwaukee inventor Chester H. Thordarson plunked down $5,725 for 775-acre Rock Island. In the next 55 years, Thordarson gradually tamed the wilds and carefully transformed at least part of the island into his own private retreat.

Thordarson initially restored a few squat settlers' cabins while he pondered his masterpieces – a boathouse hewn meticulously from island limestone and, later, his grand mansion (it was never built), as well as gardens and other experiments in horticulture.

This was no simple exercise in a rich man's indulgence. As prescient as he was entrepreneurial (he made his fortune inventing more than 100 patentable devices), Thordarson developed only 30 acres of the island, with the full intent of leaving the remaining 745 as an experiment in ecological preservation. With a profound knowledge of the natural world, much of it the result of self-educated sweat, he spent the rest of his days analyzing the biological minutiae of his island. Because of this, in 1929 the University of Wisconsin gave him an honorary Master of Arts degree. The school also purchased his entire island library, containing one of the world's greatest collections of Scandinavian literature.

These are the resting spots of the children and families of lighthouse keepers and even Chief Chip-Pa-Ny, a Menominee leader.

Otherwise, the best thing to do is just skirt the shoreline and discover lake views from atop the bluffs, alternating at points with up to half a mile of sandy beach or sand dunes. Near campsite 15, you'll pass some carvings etched into the bluff, done by Thordarson's bored workers.

Recreation

At one time a sawmill buzzed the logs taken from the island; the wheel-rutted paths to the mill turned into rough roads. Thordarson let them grow over during his tenure on the island, but today they form the basis for a few miles of the park's 9.5 total hiking miles. The island is only 900-plus acres, so you've got plenty of time to cover everything, assuming you're not just spending an afternoon. If that's the case, you can do double-time and cover the perimeter in just under three hours. You'll see all the major sights and an additional magnificent view on the northeast side—on a clear day you can see all the way to Michigan's Upper Peninsula. For those less aerobically inclined, just head for the **Algonquin Nature Trail Loop,** an hour-long (maximum) traipse.

No wheeled vehicles are allowed in the park.

The dock does allow private mooring for a fee of $1 per foot.

Camping

The camping at Rock Island is absolutely splendid (next to the Apostle Islands, the best in the state), with sites strung along a beachfront of sand and, closer to the pier, large stones. Many of the sites farthest from the main compound are fully isolated, almost scooped into dunes and, thus, fully protected from wind but with smashing views (site 13 is a favorite). The island holds 40 primitive campsites (all reservable) with water and pit toilets: 35 to the southwest of the ferry landing, another 5 spread along the shore farther southeast—these are isolated backpacker sites. Two additional group campsites are also available. Reservations are a good idea in summer and fall (and essential on weekends during those times).

Note: The park is a pack-in, pack-out facility, so plan wisely.

Access

If you're not sea kayaking over, the **Karfi** (it means "seaworthy for coastal journeys" in Icelandic, so fear not; 920/847-2252) has regular service. Boats depart Jackson Harbor on Washington Island daily May 25–mid-October (usually Columbus Day for some reason); the

DOOR COUNTY

boat leaves hourly 10 A.M.–4 P.M. in high season (June–Aug.) with an extra trip at 6 P.M. Friday. Round-trip tickets cost $9 adults and $11 campers with gear. In the off-season, you can arrange a boat, but it's prohibitively expensive.

Private boats are permitted to dock at the pier, but a mooring fee is charged.

OTHER ISLANDS
Plum and Pilot Islands

Before the establishment of the lighthouse on Plum Island, more than 100 ships were pounded into the shoals of the Door. In one year alone, Plum Island became the cemetery for 30 ships. Though safer than any U.S. highway today, it will never be sweat-free; as recently as 1989 a ship was thrown aground by the currents. The U.S. Lighthouse Service established the **Pilot Island Lighthouse** in 1858. It stands atop what an early guidebook described as "little more than a rock in the heavy-pounding seas." Two brick structures stand on Pilot Island and are about the only things still visible. Once-dense vegetation has been nearly killed off, turned into a rocky field by the ubiquitous and odoriferous droppings of federally protected cormorants, which long ago found the island and stuck around.

Plum Island had to wait until 1897 to get its imposing 65-foot skeletal steel light, after which the mortality rate within the Door dropped significantly. Plum Island—so-called for its plumb-center position in the straits—is home to an abandoned Coast Guard building on the northeast side, an old foghorn building on the southwest tip, and yet another decaying Cape Cod–style lightkeeper's residence near the range lights.

Neither island is accessible—unless your sea kayak runs into trouble—except for boat tours given during the Festival of Blossoms, usually offered three times daily from Gills Rock.

Detroit Island

Steaming into Detroit Harbor on Washington Island, look to the starboard side. The island with the crab-claw bay is Detroit Island, one of the largest satellite islands surrounding Washington Island. Settlers built the first permanent structures on the island in the early 1830s and gradually forced the displacement of the resident Ottawa and Huron Indians, who had been there for generations. Once the island was an archaeological gem, but thieves have laid waste to it. Today it is privately owned and not accessible.

GATEWAY TO DOOR COUNTY: EAST-CENTRAL WATERS

Forsaken by travelers winging to the north woods or the Door Peninsula, the East-Central Waters region is, surprisingly to many, the most historically significant region of Wisconsin. The initial and one of the most important doorways to the state later became the site of the first permanent settlements and the state's timber-and-water commercial nucleus.

When the Portage Canal linking the Upper Fox and Lower Wisconsin Rivers was completed, two of the most crucial waterways in the Great Lakes system were finally joined, allowing transport from the Atlantic Ocean all the way to the Gulf of Mexico. (The Fox River is one of the few rivers in North America to flow north.) The Fox River engineering was no mean feat for the time—it

required 26 locks and dams to corral the rapids and negotiate a 200-foot drop. Within a century, though, the decrepit condition of the Fox River locks in Kaukauna earned them the distinction of being one of the 10 most endangered historic sites.

Thus, Wisconsin established the **Fox-Wisconsin Riverways Heritage Corridor** to preserve what was left. The entire length of the Fox River is being eyed by the National Park Service as a National Heritage Corridor. In addition to the locks, some of the only extant French-style agricultural developments can still be seen—they're recognizable by their long, narrow drawbacks from the river, as opposed to the usual patchwork parallelograms of the other European immigrants.

© THOMAS HUHTI

HIGHLIGHTS

☾ Kohler: An erstwhile corporate employee town, the state's most reputed (if not astonishing) resort is also here (page 179).

☾ Wisconsin Maritime Museum: Learn about everything from wooden schooners to WWII submaking at this wowser (page 184).

☾ Point Beach State Forest: Relax along a grand littoral stretch and amid ecological precious zones (page 187).

☾ The Pack: 'Nuff said (page 188).

☾ The History Museum at the Castle and A.K.A. Houdini: Learn the secrets of Harry Houdini's escape tricks (page 199).

☾ High Cliff State Park: It's worth a stop for its magnificent perch above Lake Winnebago (page 204).

☾ EAA Air Adventure Museum and Fly-In Convention: The museum is fabulous; the convention is jaw-drop kid-in-all-of-us amazing (page 207)!

☾ The Little White Schoolhouse: Donkey-blue Wisconsin founded the elephant party, believe it or not (page 213).

☾ Wolf River: This natural beauty features dells, rapids, misty cascades, all surrounded by depths of public lands (page 218).

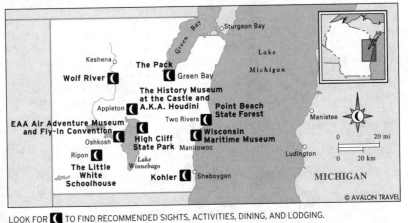

LOOK FOR ☾ TO FIND RECOMMENDED SIGHTS, ACTIVITIES, DINING, AND LODGING.

HISTORY

Early nomadic Paleo-Indians arrived as the glaciers retreated; this was well before Jean Nicolet came calling in 1634. The Jesuits thereafter attempted to found the westernmost fringe community of New France. Later, immigrants began pouring in, harvesting the timber treasures for the rapacious needs of a burgeoning nation. For a while, with the hinterlands timber industry and the prodigious fishing harvests and shipping receipts, this was the richest section of the state.

Though the timber has slowed to a less heady trickle and the shipbuilding and fishing fleets are mostly gone, the region still juxtaposes some great recreation with the zenith of Wisconsin's early economic triumvirate.

PLANNING YOUR TIME

A weekend is out of the question, unless you center yourself somewhere in the historic **Fox Cities** area and pick and choose—by region or activity. Otherwise, you could spend a night and day in either Oshkosh or Appleton and

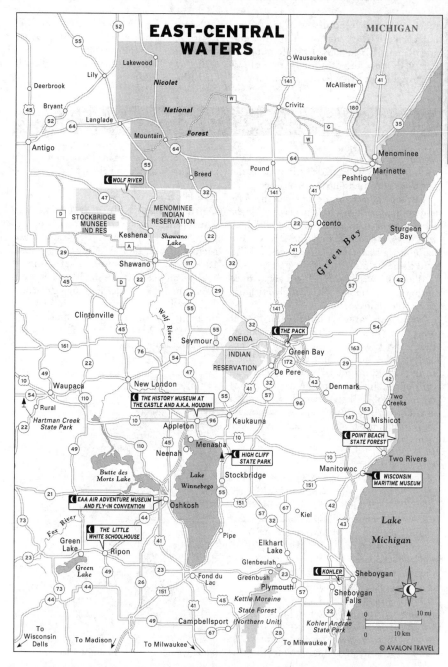

EAST-CENTRAL WATERS

MICHIGAN

52

55

Lakewood

Nicolet

Deerbrook

Lily

Wausaukee

141

McAllister

41

Bryant

45

52

64

Langlade

National

Crivitz

180

35

W

Forest

Mountain

64

G

Antigo

64

Pound

141

W

Menominee

55

Breed

Marinette

WOLF RIVER

32

141

41

Peshtigo

47

32

MENOMINEE INDIAN RESERVATION

D

22

Oconto

Sturgeon Bay

STOCKBRIDGE MUNSEE IND RES

Keshena

Shawano Lake

A

41

Green Bay

57

42

29

Shawano

117

32

45

22

D

Clintonville

Wolf River

47

29

55

141

THE PACK

54

45

Seymour

55

ONEIDA

32

163

161

76

54

INDIAN

Green Bay

29

22

47

RESERVATION

172

De Pere

42

10

49

Waupaca

110

New London

41

32

43

Denmark

54

Rural

THE HISTORY MUSEUM AT THE CASTLE AND A.K.A. HOUDINI

55

57

96

163

Two Creeks

22

Hartman Creek State Park

10

96

Kaukauna

147

Mishicot

49

110

Appleton

POINT BEACH STATE FOREST

45

Menasha

HIGH CLIFF STATE PARK

Neenah

10

Two Rivers

Butte des Morts Lake

Lake Winnebago

Stockbridge

Manitowoc

WISCONSIN MARITIME MUSEUM

21

EAA AIR ADVENTURE MUSEUM AND FLY-IN CONVENTION

55

151

73

Fox River

THE LITTLE WHITE SCHOOLHOUSE

Oshkosh

44

57

67

Kiel

42

Lake

Green Lake

41

Pipe

32

43

Michigan

23

Elkhart Lake

73

Green Lake

49

Ripon

Glenbeulah

KOHLER

Sheboygan

44

44

73

23

Fond du Lac

Greenbush

23

Plymouth

Sheboygan Falls

26

151

57

32

45

Kettle Moraine State Forest (Northern Unit)

Kohler Andrae State Park

0   10 mi

To Wisconsin Dells

49

Campbellsport

0   10 km

67

28

To Madison

To Milwaukee

To Milwaukee

© AVALON TRAVEL

then spend the second in any of the following: Oshkosh (EAA Air Adventure Museum) and Ripon (Birthplace of the Republican Party); High Cliff State Park to Kohler/Sheboygan; the Wolf River; or Manitowoc (Wisconsin Maritime Museum) and Two Rivers (Point Beach State Forest). This author would just spend the whole two days salivating over Packerdom at Lambeau Field in Green Bay . . .

Sheboygan

Sheboygan has come a long way, touristically speaking. This phlegmatic, gritty industrial town was once anything but a must-see.

Fast-forward two decades. Herculean efforts and millions of dollars have made possible the renovation of marinas, promenades, lighted walkways, bike trails, building facades, and harbor breakwaters. It's almost nearing postcard cliché realms.

(Progress? Well, *Reader's Digest* once named Sheboygan the number one "Family Friendly" city in the United States.)

Sheboygan has never lacked fame for one other thing: bratwurst. It's the self-proclaimed Bratwurst Capital of the World and nobody touches Sheboyganites and their brats. Innumerable neighborhood butchers still turn out family-secret-recipe bratwurst (everyone is slobberingly devoted to his or her own butcher), and Brat Days (www.bratdays.org) in summer is one of Wisconsin's largest food festivals.

History

Nearby cascades inspired the Ojibwa name Shaw-bwah-way-gun, "the sound like the wind of the rushing waters." Due to its fortuitous location, equidistant from Milwaukee and Manitowoc, the village erected one of the first decent piers along Lake Michigan, allowing lake schooners and ferries to bring tens of thousands of German, Dutch, and English immigrants, many dairy farmers, to town.

During the final wave of German immigration, between 1880 and 1890, some areas hereabouts were (and are) 95 percent German. Most of the immigrants were woodworkers, so several furniture and wood-product factories opened. Thus, Sheboygan also became known as the city of cheese and chairs.

SIGHTS
John Michael Kohler Arts Center
This superlative arts center (608 New York Ave., 920/458-6144, www.jmkac.org, 10 A.M.–5 P.M. Mon.–Fri., also till 8 P.M. Tues. and Thurs., 10 A.M.–4 P.M. Sat.–Sun., free) is one of Sheboygan's cultural landmarks. The wondrously progressive, eclectic grouping of galleries is devoted to contemporary art in all media, including galleries devoted to self-taught artists. The center has been nationally recognized for its unusually broad scope and its efforts to

Sheboygan's distinctive lighthouse

© THOMAS HUHTI

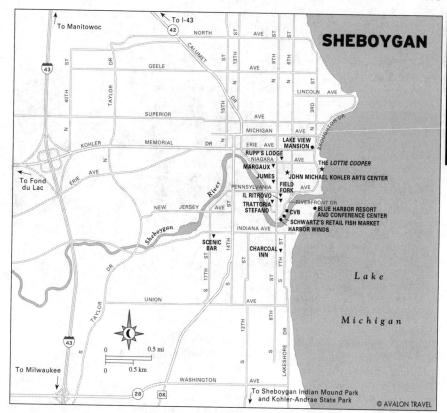

incorporate the community—no PR-speak, it means *the whole community*—in its undertakings. This explains its consistent ratings by industry groups in the top 10 nationwide.

The Boardwalk

The city center's gem is this winding walkway alongside the Sheboygan River and Riverfront Drive, trailing gentrification as it goes. The old fishing shanties have been transformed into antique shops, art galleries, restaurants, and other retail outlets. A few old weatherbeaten shacks remain.

The *Lottie Cooper*

One of 62 wrecks near Sheboygan, the *Lottie Cooper,* a three-masted lumber schooner, went

down in a gale off Sheboygan on April 9, 1894, killing one. Including one of the longest salvaged keels of a Great Lakes wreck, the vessel now rests in Deland Park, near the North Pier. It's along a lovely lakefront promenade.

Sheboygan Indian Mound Park

An archaic relic (5000 S. 9th St., 920/459-3444, free) along the Black River region in south Sheboygan, this place is eerily impressive. The 18 Native American effigy mounds, in myriad geometric and animal shapes, date from A.D. 500. A beautiful nature trail runs along a creek.

Kohler-Andrae State Park

A personal favorite, this may well be the best stretch of beach along Wisconsin's Lake

© THOMAS HUHTI

Kohler-Andrae State Park near Sheboygan

Michigan shoreline (1020 Beach Park Ln., 920/451-4080). It includes two miles of wind-swept beach and a plank trail that meanders through the fragile Kohler Dunes Natural Area, one of the state's rarest habitats (an interdunal wetland). I've never *not* stumbled across white-tailed deer among the dunes. The chilly waters off the park are home to about 50 shipwrecks (a diver's paradise). Many of the recovered wrecks are on display at the Sanderling Center here.

Henning's Wisconsin Cheese

Nobody makes 'em anymore like they do at the too-cool Henning's Wisconsin Cheese (20201 Point Creek Rd., Kiel, 920/894-3022, www. henningscheese.com, 7 A.M.–4 P.M. Mon.–Fri., 8 A.M.–noon Sat.), northeast of Sheboygan in little Kiel. The operation is enormous enough, complete with an outstanding museum of cheese-making. You'll snap lots of images on your mobile phone of the gigantic 12,000-pound wheels of cheddar cheese, this being the only remaining place in the United States to make 'em!

RECREATION
Charter Fishing

Sheboygan's 300-slip **Harbor Centre Marina** (821 Broughton Dr., 920/458-6665) offers great fishing with about 35 licensed skippers operating out of Sheboygan. Prices vary, but it's generally around $300–450 (not including tip or a Wisconsin fishing license) for 1–4 people for a half-day charter; some outfits offer minicharters.

Old Plank Road Trail

In 1843, the territorial legislature, hoping to effect permanent settlement in today's Sheboygan County region, began building the first plank road to reach all the way to Fond du Lac. It was completed in 1852. Today, the Old Plank Road Trail is a paved 17-mile-long multipurpose recreation trail running from western Sheboygan to Greenbush and the Kettle Moraine State Forest's northern unit (and thus the Ice Age Trail), via Kohler and Plymouth, a lovely ride in spots.

BRATWURST: THE WISCONSIN DISH

Bratwurst, a Germanic legacy of Wisconsin, is the unofficial state dish. The brat (pronounced to rhyme with "plot," not "splat!") is pervasive here. Supermarkets devote entire lengths of freezers to accommodate sausage-makers. Many towns still have old butcher shops that string up homemade flavors.

THE IMMIGRANT EPICURE

Strictly speaking, the bratwurst is but one of hundreds of varieties of sausage, according to official (and draconian) German food law. Actually, sausage-making was here with the Native Americans, who had long stuffed deer intestines and hides with wild rice, grains, meats, offal, and herbs to produce pemmican, which is, technically, a sausage.

From the earliest settlement of the state, immigrants did make their own sausage. Wisconsin's bratwurst, unlike some varieties, is almost strictly made from pork. The internal mixtures would consist of meat, fat, and seasonings, along with occasional starches such as rice and bread. Concoctions were and are highly secret – similar to the recipe for Coca-Cola.

INFINITE VARIETIES

The main categories of Wisconsin sausage follow. In addition, the Czech method includes a rice sausage and head cheese; the Norwegians make *sylte*, which is spiced and salted in brine.

German: There are a zillion kinds of German sausage. Bratwurst are most often seasoned with marjoram, pepper, salt, caraway, and nutmeg.

Italian: Italian sausage is sweeter and hotter. Fennel gives it its trademark flavor.

Polish: Think garlic-heavy ring of two-inch-thick, dark pink bologna-esque sausage is traditionally steam-fried for dinner (and then cut into sandwiches for leftovers and lunchboxes). Polish recipes often call for red cabbage and mustard sauces.

BRATS IN SHEBOYGAN

The place to go is **Miesfeld's Triangle Market** (4811 Venture Dr., two blocks north of the intersection of I-43 and WI 42, 414/565-6328), where Chuck and the gang have been putting out national-award-winning sausages (15 varieties of bratwurst have thus far garnered 68 national awards) for as long as anybody can remember. The town has a celebratory fit of indulgent mayhem come August with its Bratwurst Days.

Some brat-related Sheboygan-only tips:

- "double" – you simply cannot eat just one brat

- "fryer" – whatever thing you cook the brat on (Cheeseheads otherwise say "grill")

- "fry out" – used as both a noun and a verb

- "hard roll" – it looks like a hamburger bun but it's bigger and harder (sometimes called sennel roll)

PREPARATION

Microwave a brat and you'll incur the wrath of any Wisconsinite. Frying one is OK, but traditionally a brat must be grilled. Brats work best if you parboil them in beer and onions for 10-15 minutes before putting them on the grill. Sheboyganites absolutely cringe at parboiling, so don't tell them I told you. Another no-no is roughage crammed in the bun – lettuce, tomatoes, and so on; even sauerkraut, loved by Milwaukeeans, is barely tolerated by Sheboyganites.

Another option: Parboil brats briefly. Sear in butter in a frying pan. Set aside. Pour two cups dark beer into fry pan and scrape residue. Combine a finely chopped onion, some beef stock, juice from one lemon, and maybe one chopped green pepper. Put brats back in and boil 12-15 minutes. Remove brats and place on hot grill. Sauce can be thickened with flour or cornstarch and poured over the top. A Cheesehead will stick the sauce in a bun alongside the brat with mustard.

ACCOMMODATIONS

Nothing is cheap in Sheboygan, if you can even find a place; Sheboygan for some reason lacks myriad motels—and enough nearby camping. Best bet would be east of I-43 at nearly every exit.

The **Harbor Winds** (905 S. 8th St., 920/452-9000, www.pridehospitality.com, $79) is the only place on the water in Sheboygan. An observation deck affords a great view, the staff is friendly, and residents get a free morning newspaper and breakfast.

The **Blue Harbor Resort and Conference Center** (725 Blue Harbor Dr., 920/452-2900, www.blueharborresort.com, $229–689) is a four-level Victorian replica with an indoor water park. The self-enclosed place boasts spas, fitness centers, two enormous restaurants, arcades, and more.

With a commanding view above Lake Michigan is the **Lake View Mansion** (303 St. Clair St., 920/457-5253, www.lakeviewmansion.com, $159–249), a gorgeous historic structure. The five rooms all have private baths and a view of the lake.

FOOD
Brats

To sample the "best of the wurst" (they say, not me!)—you've got myriad options. For me, it's the **Charcoal Inn** (1313 S. 8th St., 920/458-6988, 6 A.M.–9 P.M. Tues.–Fri., 6 A.M.–7 P.M. Sat., and 1637 Greele Ave., 920/458-1147, 5 A.M.–7 P.M. Tues.–Sat., $4–8), where they still fire up a fryer every morning to supplement its unpretentious Midwest fare.

Fish Fries

The **Scenic Bar** (1635 Indiana Ave., 920/452-2881, 4–9 P.M. Tues.–Thurs. and Sat., 11 A.M.–2 P.M. and 3:30–10 P.M. Fri., 4–8 P.M. Sun., $5) has standard supper-club-in-a-tavern fare, with a fish fry Friday at noon and night (pike, bluegill and perch in addition to standard cod). Most locals point this place out as the place for unpretentious fare.

It's takeout only at **Schwarz's Retail Fish Market** (828 Riverfront Dr., 920/452-0576), the best place in town for fresh fish.

American

Jumes (504 N. 8th St., 920/452-4914, 6 A.M.–7:30 P.M. daily, $3 and up), a retro diner, is the place to go to rub shoulders with the locals, read the compendious menu, and enjoy the dirt-cheap heart-stopping breakfast. My Sheboyganite friends swear by this one.

Margaux (821 N. 8th St., 920/457-6565, 11:30 A.M.–1:30 P.M. Tues.–Fri., 5–9 P.M. Mon.–Sat., $8–18) is a casually upscale place for pan-world cuisine and the spot to get away from the red-meat-heavy fare of these parts.

Enjoy rib-sticking American food at **Rupp's Lodge** (925 N. 8th St., 920/459-8155, 11 A.M.–2 P.M. and 5–9 P.M. Mon.–Fri., 4–9 P.M. Sat.–Sun., $5–25), which has been around for six decades. Aged, hand-cut steaks are the specialty here, along with standard supper club fare. Through a glass partition, you get to watch the food being prepared in the kitchen. On Friday and Saturday nights, patrons join in singalongs at a piano.

Italian

Dishing up the best Italian is the ever-friendly ◖ **Trattoria Stefano** (522 S. 8th St., 920/452-8455, 5–9 P.M. Mon.–Thurs., 5–10 P.M. Fri.–Sat., $12–28), a casually upscale place with a bright pastel (and handmade brick) environment. For years a foodie must-stop, comments from readers have begun to mention a bit of a dip here. Hopefully it's an aberration. BTW, for a more subdued Italian experience, across the street is another of the owner's ventures: **Il Ritrovo** (515 S. 8th St., 920/803-7516, lunch and dinner Mon.–Sat.), dinner with pizza good enough for Naples' authorities to have certified it as OK! If that weren't enough, Stefano has also opened **Field to Fork** (511 S. 8th St., 920/694-0322, 7 A.M.–3 P.M. Mon.–Sat.) next door to the pizzeria—think locavore deli and light lunch place (love the coney dog!).

INFORMATION

The **Sheboygan County Convention and Visitors Bureau** (712 Riverfront Dr., Ste. 101, 920/457-9497 or 800/457-9497, www.visitsheboygan.com) is along the Boardwalk.

GETTING AROUND

If the city budget allows, Sheboygan has a quaint, battery-propelled replica **trolley** that buzzes about the downtown area during summer.

Vicinity of Sheboygan

◖ KOHLER

A planned workers' community surrounding the operations of the Kohler Company, Kohler is trim and attractive—thoroughly inspiring for a sense of community. Kohler also houses the state's most incredible resort/restaurant and puts on unforgettable factory tours.

Sights

The **Kohler Factory** and, to a lesser extent, **Kohler Design Center** (101 Upper Rd., 920/457-3699, www.kohler.com, 8 A.M.–5 P.M. Mon.–Fri., 10 A.M.–4 P.M. Sat.–Sun. and holidays, free) are must-sees. The international manufacturer of bathroom fixtures here showcases in its 2.5-hour tour the company's early factory and factory-town history, along with its wares in an incredible "Great Wall of China." Also featured are a theater, ceramic art gallery, and more. Tours of the factory itself are on weekdays only and require advance registration.

Waelderhaus (House in the Woods) (1100 W. Riverside Dr., 920/452-4079, tours 2, 3, and 4 P.M. hourly, free), a dwelling based on homes from the mountainous Austrian Bregenzerwald region commissioned by a daughter of the Kohler founder, contains antique furnishings and highlights such as candle-reflected water-globe lighting.

Hands down the best golf in Wisconsin—and some say the Midwest—is found in Kohler at the **American Club** resort (Highland Dr., 920/457-8000, www.destinationkohler.com). **Blackwolf Run** offers two PGA championship courses—one of them was the highest-rated gold medal course in the United States according to *Golf* magazine. Newer are the preternaturally lovely courses of **Whistling Straits**, designed to favor the old seaside links courses of Britain; it's even got sheep wandering about! There are the Straits Course and a challenging Dunes Course, both PGA championship courses. In 2000 Whistling Straits unveiled its new Irish Course, a companion course to the first Straits course; among other things it features some of the tallest sand dunes in the United States. It's all good enough for the PGA Championship to have been played here—twice. Call 920/457-4446 for details; it's neither cheap nor easy to golf these courses.

Accommodations and Food

Easily Wisconsin's most breathtaking resort, ◖ **The American Club** (Highland Dr., 920/457-8000, www.destinationkohler.com, $260–1,210) is the Midwest's only AAA five-diamond resort. The 1918 red brick facade of an erstwhile workers' hostel and dormitory has been retained, along with the original carriage house, though both have been poshly retrofitted. A full slate of recreation is offered, of note two championship Pete Dye golf courses (one of them considered one of the most perfect examples in the world of a shot-master's course). There's also a private 500-acre wildlife preserve to explore. If that's not enough, the seven dining rooms and restaurants include the state's best—the Immigrant Room, winner of the prestigious DiRoNa Award. Here, various rooms offer the ethnic cuisine and heritage of France, Holland, Germany, Scandinavia, and England. The food is created with regional Wisconsin ingredients. Jackets are required.

If ever you splurge in Wisconsin, this is one of the places to do it; if not, consider the tours offered Monday–Saturday at 2 P.M. for a look-see.

SHEBOYGAN FALLS

Sheboygan actually got its start near these somewhat thundering falls of the Sheboygan River. The town has a great riverwalk with views of the falls and two very historic districts. Among the grandest bed-and-breakfasts in the area is **◖ The Rochester Inn** (504 Water St., 920/467-3123 or 800/421-4667, $109 s or d), a massive 1848 general store. The rooms all have parlors with wingback lounges, and there are four split-level luxury suites and a grand internal spiral staircase.

Richard's (501 Monroe St., 920/467-6401, lunch Tues. only, dinner Mon.–Sat., $6–35), in an 1840s stagecoach inn, features excellent finer dining.

PLYMOUTH

Plymouth lies just west of Sheboygan and would definitely be on a National Register of Quaint Places—the aesthetics of its early Yankee settlements remain amazingly intact. Initially a solitary tavern-cum-stage stop, as all rail traffic passed through the little burg, it eventually became the center of the cheese industry in eastern Wisconsin (the first Cheese Exchange was here).

Sights

The local chamber of commerce has an impressively mapped and detailed historical and architectural walking tour highlighting about 50 buildings. The visitors center is itself an architectural highlight: the **Plymouth Center** (E. Mill St., 920/893-0079, 10 A.M.–2 P.M. Sun.–Thurs.), a restored 1920s edifice that also houses a historical museum and art galleries.

Accommodations and Food

Historic bed-and-breakfasts are everywhere you turn. A structure woodworkers will want to see is the **52 Stafford Irish Guest House** (52 Stafford St., 920/893-0552, www.52stafford. com, $100). The 19 guest rooms are decent, but the main attraction here is the food. The limited but ambitious menu changes a lot; the signature meal is an Irish beef brisket basted in Guinness—it'll wow you. The rich woods, ornate stained glass, and original fixtures give the place a special atmosphere. Do drop by Wednesday evenings for rousing Irish music.

ELKHART LAKE

Northwest of Sheboygan is one of the region's first resort areas (www.elkhartlake.com). In the early 20th century, well-to-do Chicagoans sought out the quiet getaway and, later, so did high-profile mobsters such as John Dillinger. Another major draw is the international speedway **Road America,** North America's longest natural road-racing course. (And a couple of, um, subdued local museums.)

Accommodations and Food

One of the oldest and most established lodgings (family-run since 1916) is **Siebkens** (284 S. Lake St., 920/876-2600, www.siebkens. com, $139–459 weekends), a turn-of-the-20th-century resort with two white-trimmed main buildings (open only in summer) and a year-round lake cottage. A nod to modernity in their plush new condos is also available. The classic tavern and dining room serve up regional fare on an old porch.

Much posher is the **◖ Osthoff Resort** (101 Osthoff Ave., 920/876-3366, www.osthoff. com, $170–625), with lavish comfort and fine lake views. Lola's dining room and the Aspira spa are superb (good enough that they have a cooking school here now). This is a real *wow* experience.

One of the most extraordinary meals of late has come at the newer **◖ Paddock Club** (61 S. Lake St., 920/876-3288, 4 P.M.–close Tues.– Sun., closed March, $18–38). You'll find indescribably good new American cuisine in another erstwhile gangster hangout.

KETTLE MORAINE STATE FOREST-NORTHERN UNIT

A crash course in geology helps preface a trip through the 29,000 acres of the northern unit of the Kettle Moraine State Forest (262/626-2116). The northern unit was chosen as the site of the Henry Reuss Ice Age Interpretive Center—on the Ice Age National Scenic

enjoying splash time in a lake in the Kettle Moraine State Forest-Northern Unit

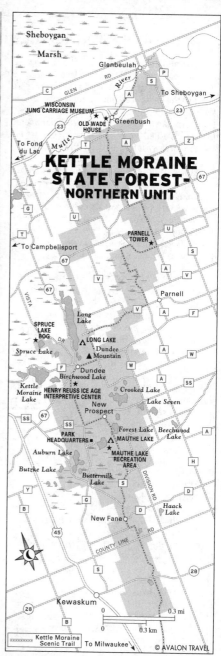

Trail—given its variegated topography of kettles, terminal moraines, kames, and eskers, and all that other geological vocabulary. Surrounded by suburban expansion, it somehow manages to hold 12 State Natural Areas inside its borders.

This northern swath of forest is the complement to its sibling southwest of Milwaukee. Supporters of the forest have always envisioned the two sections of forest as a quasi-superforest, concatenate segments of lands acting as an urban buffer zone along a 120-mile ecocorridor.

Henry Reuss Ice Age Interpretive Center

Along WI 67 near the Highway G junction is the Henry Reuss Ice Age Interpretive Center (920/533-8322, 8:30 A.M.–4 P.M. Mon.–Fri. and 9:30 A.M.–5 P.M. Sat.–Sun. Apr.–Oct., shorter hours in winter). The back deck has outstanding vistas of the whole topographical shebang. The exhibits and documentary theater are well worth a stop. A self-guided

ICE AGE NATIONAL SCENIC TRAIL

Glaciation affected all of the Upper Midwest, but nowhere is it more exposed than in Wisconsin. Southwestern Wisconsin's Driftless Area is also the only purely unglaciated region on the planet surrounded by glacial till.

Wisconsin's epic Ice Age National Scenic Trail is a 1,200-mile course skirting morainic topography left behind by the state's four glacial epochs. It's also an ongoing project, started in the 1950s and still being pieced together. When county chapters have finally cobbled together enough municipal, county, and state forest land with donated private land for right-of-way, Potawatomi State Park in Door County will be linked with Interstate State Park on the St. Croix National Scenic Riverway via one continuous footpath.

THE ICE AGE SCIENTIFIC RESERVE

Technically, the trail is but a segment of the Ice Age National Scientific Reserve, established by congressional fiat in 1971 after decades of wrangling by forward-thinking ecologist Ray Zillmer of Milwaukee.

The reserve's nine units are scattered along the advance of the glacial periods and highlight their most salient residuals. Numerous other state and county parks, equally impressive geologically, fill in the gaps. Kames, eskers, drumlins, moraines, kettles, and all the glacial effects are highlighted in the units on the east side of the state. An interpretive center is planned for Cross Plains, Wisconsin, west of Madison.

THE TRAIL

As of 2010, around 700 miles of *official* trails had been established either by the National Park Ser-

vice, county chapters, or state parks; the rest are link-up trails, roads, or even Main Street USA's. The longest established stretches come in the Chequamegon and Nicolet National Forests, along the Sugar River Trail in southwest Wisconsin, through the Kettle Moraine State Forest, and along the Ahnapee State Trail in the Door Peninsula. Hiking the whole thing is possible, though it takes about three months and oodles of patience attempting to circumvent cityscapes where segments have not yet opened.

Camping is a problem along the route if you're outside an established park or forest. Do not trespass or private landowners may stop any progress.

INFORMATION

View the National Park Service's website (nps.gov/iatr) or contact the Ice Age National Scenic Trail (608/441-5610, www.iceagetrail.org) in Madison.

40-mile auto geology tour starts from the center. A short nature trail winds from the building outside.

Wade House and Jung Carriage Museum

Along WI 23 in Greenbush the **Old Wade House** (Hwy. T, 920/526-3271, 10 A.M.–5 P.M. daily mid-May–mid-Oct., $11 adults) sits along the oak plank road that stretched from Sheboygan to Fond du Lac. The state historic site is a wondrous, detailed reconstruction of the 1848 original sawmill—note the post and beam work—one of few like it in the United States. Environmentally friendly construction was used—as in the original.

Perhaps the Wade House's biggest draw is the impressive **Wisconsin Jung Carriage Museum,** with the state's largest collection of hand- and horse-drawn vehicles (many rideable).

Scenic Drives

The forest offers a smashing scenic drive. As you drive along ribbony highways (including official Rustic Roads), you'll trace the oldest geology in Wisconsin, 10,000-year-old outwash of the last glacial period.

The scenic drive is linked in the south with other great back roads all the way to the Southern Unit, about 40 miles away. It's hard to get lost; just follow the acorn-shaped road signs. From Sheboygan Marsh in the north to Whitewater Lake in the southern unit, the road totals about 120 miles and passes through six counties.

Recreation

More than 140 miles of trails snake through the forest's narrow northern unit, including the highlight, the sublime 31-mile segment of the **Ice Age National Scenic Trail.** It runs the length of the park and hooks up with five other forest trails for plenty of options. Five shelters are along the way. Backpackers must have permits (generally easy to obtain, but plan early for high season).

The best-known trail is the 11-mile **Zillmer Trail,** accessible via Highway SS; there's one tough ridge with a great vista.

Some say the best view (1,300 feet above sea level, plus 450 feet above the tower) is the one from **Parnell Tower,** two miles north of WI 67 via Highway A.

Parkview General Store (262/626-8287), north of the Mauthe Lake Recreation Area entrance, has bicycle, paddleboat, canoe, and rowboat rentals.

Camping

In all, 400 campsites are available, lots of them reservable. Primitive shelter camping is possible along the Glacial Trail. **Mauthe Lake** also has a tepee for rent.

Manitowoc and Two Rivers

These Lake Michigan quasi-sister cities were originally home to tribes of Ojibwa, Potawatomi, and Ottawa. The tranquil harbors attracted fur traders, and by 1795, the Northwest Fur Company had built its post here. Under Europeans, the area prospered during the heady early decades of whitefish plunder and shipbuilding, the latter still around.

Charter Fishing

Charter fishing is big business. Coho and king salmon, along with lake and brown trout (and some rainbow), are most popular for skippers in these waters.

MANITOWOC

This small bight was a port of call for weary Great Lakes travelers—the earliest ones in birchbark canoes—heading for Chicago. Drive out into the countryside and you can still see smokehouses and bake ovens on early farmsteads, log threshing barns large enough to drive machinery through, split-rail fencing, and unique cantilever house designs.

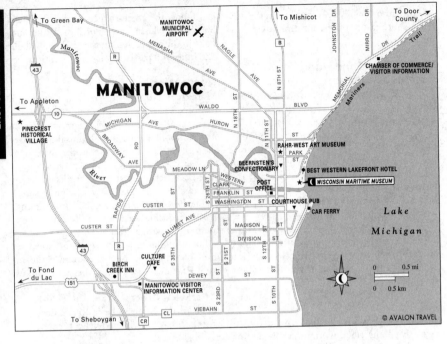

An enormous fishing industry came and, thanks to overfishing through injudicious use of drift nets and seines, went. However, the so-called Clipper City shifted to producing ships beginning in the 1800s, peaking around World War II, when Manitowoc's shipyard became one of the most important naval production facilities in the country.

Wisconsin Maritime Museum

At peak WWII production, Manitowoc eclipsed even major east coast shipbuilding centers. Its legacy is remembered at the Wisconsin Maritime Museum (75 Maritime Dr., 920/684-0218, www.wisconsinmaritime.org, 9 A.M.–6 P.M. daily Memorial Day weekend–Labor Day weekend, until 5 P.M. the rest of the year, $12 includes access to the *Cobia*). Flanked by the USS *Cobia* submarine (a National Historic Landmark, one of 28 built here, and one reason Manitowoc is the only U.S. city with streets named after subs!), the museum is an amazing conglomeration of Great Lakes (especially local) maritime history.

Other Sights

The **Pinecrest Historical Village** (Pine Crest La., 920/684-5110, 9 A.M.–5 P.M. daily May–Oct., $6 adults) is an ensemble of more than 25 extant buildings brought here and painstakingly restored on 60 acres. Structures date from as far back as the 1840s.

The **Rahr-West Art Museum** (610 N. 8th St. at Park St., 920/683-4501, 10 A.M.–4 P.M. Mon.–Fri., till 8 P.M. Wed., 11 A.M.–4 P.M. Sat.–Sun., free) is an 1891 Victorian with intricate woodworking and grand beamed ceilings housing one of the finer collections of art in the Midwest. A tidbit: The brass ring in the street out front is where a piece of Sputnik hit in 1962.

Stretch your legs on the **Mariners Trail,** a 12-mile-long paved recreation trail between Manitowoc and Two Rivers.

© THOMAS HUHTI

USS *Cobia* standing guard over Manitowoc's harbor

Accommodations

Most motels and hotels, including several chain operations, are clustered around the I-43/U.S. 151 interchange. The **Birch Creek Inn** (4626 Calumet Ave., 920/684-3374 or 800/424-6126, www.birchcreekinn.com, $50 s or d) put $1 million in renovations to turn itself into a quaint little spot: a 1940s motor inn with a cottage complex—unique!

The luxury accommodation in town is the **Best Western Lakefront Hotel** (101 Maritime Dr., 920/682-7000 or 800/654-5353, $99), the only place right on the lake and adjacent to the maritime museum.

Food

Superb sandwiches with homemade breads and healthful insides are to be had at **Culture Cafe** (3949 Calumet Ave., 920/682-6844, $4–11).

Boisterous is the **Courthouse Pub** (1001 S. 8th St., 920/686-1166, 11 A.M.–9 P.M. Mon.–Fri., 3:30–9:30 P.M. Sat., $5–15), which handcrafts its own brews and has above-average pub grub in a painstakingly restored 1860s Greek revival.

Chocolate fanatics and the dessert-minded should not miss **Beernsten's Confectionary** (108 N. 8th St., 920/684-9616, 10 A.M.–10 P.M. daily), a renowned local chocolatier for about 50 years.

Information

The super Manitowoc Information Center (920/683-4388 or 800/627-4896, www.manitowoc.info) is prominently housed on the western highway junction and has a 24-hour kiosk.

Getting There

Originally one of seven railroad and passenger ferries plying the route between here and Ludington, Michigan, the **SS *Badger*** (800/841-4243, www.ssbadger.com) is a wonderful anachronism. Though it's technically a steamship—the last of its kind on Lake Michigan—you can hardly tell thanks to modern pollution controls. Crossings take four hours and depart daily mid-May–mid-October, with two departures June–late August from Manitowoc.

Round-trip fares are $109 per person, $59 per car. Some intriguing deals are available.

TWO RIVERS

Two Rivers is, they say, the fishing capital of Lake Michigan. But residents are even prouder of another claim to fame: The ice-cream sundae was invented here in 1881 at a 15th Street soda fountain. (Yes, yes, we know—it's in a friendly rivalry with another not-to-be-mentioned-here U.S. city for this honor.) The mammoth historic **Washington House Museum and Visitor Center** (17th St. and Jefferson St., 920/793-2490, 9 A.M.–9 P.M. daily May–Oct., 9 A.M.–5 P.M. daily Nov.–Apr., free), once an immigrant hotel-cum-dance hall/saloon, dispenses information as well as great ice cream at a mock-up of the original fountain that made the town famous.

Sights and Recreation

Across from Washington House is the fascinating **Woodtype/Printing Museum** (1619 Jefferson St., 920/794-6272, 9 A.M.–5 P.M. Tues.–Sat., free), with vintage equipment for international woodtyping. The **Two Rivers History Museum** (1810 Jefferson St., 920/793-1103, 10 A.M.–4 P.M. daily, free) two blocks away was once a convent.

At **Rogers Street Fishing Village** (2102 Jackson St., 920/793-5905, 10 A.M.–4 P.M. Mon.–Fri. and noon–4 P.M. Sat.–Sun. May–Oct., $4 adults), artifacts include those from the regional U.S. Coast Guard, especially its lighthouse operations. There is a lot of shipwreck memorabilia—folks say it's Wisconsin's largest shipwreck exhibit—and plenty of retired vessels.

Excellent are the **Woodland Dunes** west 10 miles along WI 310. The eponymous spiny mounds were the littoral edges of a glacial lake.

Accommodations

Farthest south from town toward Manitowoc, the **Village Inn on the Lake** (3310 WI 42, 920/794-8818 or 800/551-4795, www.villageinnwi.com, $99) is a decent, family-run operation—a two-level motel (with RV sites) with a coffee shop and minigolf course on the premises.

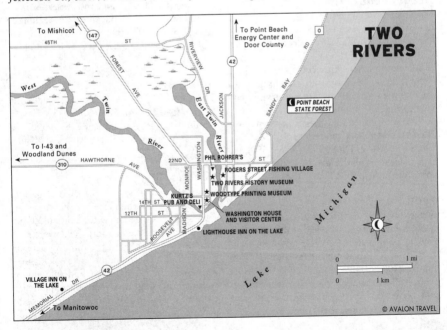

© THOMAS HUHTI

Point Beach State Forest's gorgeous lighthouse

The **Lighthouse Inn on the Lake** (1515 Memorial Dr., 920/793-4524 or 800/228-6416, $124) is showing its age but still fine. The standard rooms aren't exactly capacious, but they do have magnificent vistas of Lake Michigan—and some higher-priced rooms *are* quite large.

Food
Hole-in-the-wall **《 Phil Rohrer's** (1303 22nd St., 920/794-8500, 7 A.M.–8 P.M. Mon.–Sat., from under $1) serves classic diner fare. One of my personal favorites, it has a handful of swivel seats, fewer booths, and since 1962 has had some of the state's greatest "ho-made" soups with the slider burgers and rib-sticking comfort food specials. Try the raw fries.

One of the best-known restaurants in this region is **Kurtz's Pub and Deli** (1410 Washington St., 920/793-1222, 11 A.M.–10 P.M. Mon.–Sat., $4–11). It was established in 1904 to serve the rollicking sailors hopping off Great Lakes steamers and clippers. Today, let's call it an "upscale pub."

Don't forget: The dessert tray is at the visitors center!

《 POINT BEACH STATE FOREST
Just north of Two Rivers is a gorgeous tract of state forest—Point Beach State Forest (920/794-7480), off Highway O, six miles east of town. You can't miss it: The majestic white lighthouse towers above the sandy pines. The wind-whipped 2,900 acres spread along latte-colored sandy beaches; the wicked shoals offshore have pulled plenty of ships to their graves. The lighthouse is functional, but public access is sporadic. The preserved ridges along the shoreline are residual effects of a glacial lake last seen retreating 5,500 years ago, one reason the entire forest is a State Scientific Area. One of Wisconsin's official **Rustic Roads** stretches along the park—Highway O, a.k.a. Sandy Bay Road.

Up the road farther is the **Point Beach Energy Center** (6600 Nuclear Rd., 920/755-6400, 9:30 A.M.–4 P.M. Tues.–Sat., free). The Point Beach nuclear plant has caused some controversy in Wisconsin because of plans to store waste aboveground in concrete casks. Nonetheless, the energy center features worthwhile hands-on exhibits on energy, as well as a nature trail and observation tower.

One of nine Ice Age National Scientific Reserves in Wisconsin is the **Two Creeks** area, a few miles north of here. Two Creeks contains the remnants of a 12,000-year-old buried glacial forest.

DENMARK
Also a hop off the interstate on the way to Green Bay is the Danish enclave of Denmark, known heretofore as Copenhagen. There's lots of old Danish architecture downtown, and more cheese shops per capita than anywhere else.

Green Bay

La Baye

Not only colorful, *La Baye Verte* was a haven from the volatility of Lake Michigan. In 1669 New France established under Jesuit overview an official settlement—the first permanent settlement in what would be Wisconsin—at the mouth of the bay near the present-day suburb of De Pere.

The bay region's explorers and trappers found a wealth of beavers and new networks of inland waterways—meaning trees; the wilderness from here to the Fox River Valley produced more than any other region in New France.

After a century of changing hands, the bay was the transportation conduit, for both commerce and immigration, to the rest of Wisconsin and, via the Mississippi, the country.

The City

Forts erected by the French, mostly during periods of Native American unrest, gave permanence to east-central Wisconsin's most populous community, Green Bay.

The fur trade made up the bedrock of the city's fortunes early on, but Green Bay began growing in earnest upon completion of the Erie Canal in 1825, when the state's first European immigrants descended en masse into Wisconsin, most via Green Bay. Many put down roots immediately, working in Green Bay's burgeoning agricultural, logging, and iron smelting industries; the paper and lumber industry quickly surpassed the beaver trade.

Enormous amounts of ship and railroad transportation still muscle through this to-the-core blue-collar town of tight working-class bungalows.

But remember: History and subtle gentrification notwithstanding, if there is one dominant cultural ethos underpinning the city, it is the *beloved* Green Bay Packers. *The Sporting News*—among many, many other national media—has rated the entire city the number-one

sports fans in the National Football League, literally in a league of their own. Need more proof? The waiting list for season tickets is longer than a phone book in a midsize city; at present if you apply now, you'll get tickets in about 200 years. This is a city where 60,000 people pay to watch a *practice*.

Orientation

Cupping Green Bay and bisected by the Fox River, streets can sometimes be a confusing jumble. Always keep in mind which side of the river you're on, and when in doubt, head for Lake Michigan and start over.

◖ THE PACK

One of the oldest professional football teams in the United States—and the only community-owned team in professional sports—the Green Bay Packers are *it* in this town; check out the glazed-eyed, slobbering Packer fans from around the globe jumping in glee in renovated-but-still-classic Lambeau Field's parking lot. Perhaps no stadium mixes tradition with modernity more than this national treasure. Fans care only that they can visit the stadium virtually every single day of the year! The atrium and its restaurants and shops are open 8 A.M.–9 P.M. daily except game days (till midnight Friday and Saturday); you'd be surprised how many people are wandering around at 8:30 A.M.

Tourists and locals often crowd the free, twice-a-day practices (usually 8:15 A.M. and 2:30 P.M.-ish) during the Packers' late-summer **training camp,** held at the practice facility along Oneida Street across from Lambeau Field. Sometimes practices are held indoors in the team's state-of-the-art Hutson Practice Facility. Practices begin in mid-July and run until preseason games begin in late August. There are usually morning practices and less strenuous post-lunch workouts. In mid-July too is the **Packer Hall of Fame Induction Ceremony,** a very big deal to Packers fans.

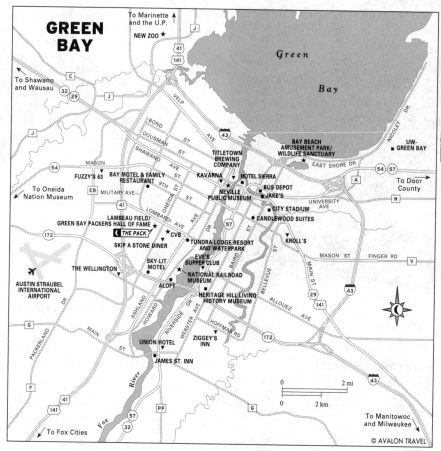

(You can also catch a glimpse of initial mini-camps, which open as early as April.)

A perfect Packer Country day would go as follows. Start by watching some of the practice sessions; those standing along the fence line to watch are known as "railbirds," and it's a tradition for Packer players to ride local kids' bikes to and from the playing field. Offer your handkerchief to a weeping Packer fan who's come from afar to realize this dream.

You *can't* miss the **Lambeau Field** tour. Visitors explore virtually every corner of this local landmark (except—sadly—the Packers' locker room), including the pressbox, the visitors' locker room, the skyboxes, and even the field itself. Hour-long tours are given 10 (or 11) A.M.–4 P.M. daily on nongame days; cost is $11 adults.

The number-one Packer destination is the Lambeau Field Atrium, home to the **Green Bay Packers Hall of Fame** (9 A.M.–6 P.M. daily, hours vary for home games, $10 adults). Packers, Packers, Packers. That's all that's here. It's an orgy of fandom. Most fans weep at the life-size re-creation of the 1967 Ice Bowl—the defining moment in making the team the real "America's Team;" kids will have to push adults out of the way to go wild in the interactive zone!

© WISCONSINART/DREAMSTIME.COM

Lambeau Field

Here's the essential stuff for up-to-date information: 888/442-7225 or packers.com!

Other Packer Sights

True fans will also head to **Fuzzy's 63** (2511 W. Mason St., 920/494-6633, www.fuzzys63. com), a bar owned by retired Pack legend Fuzzy Thurston.

The most unusual sight? How about **Skip a Stone Diner** (2052 Holmgren Way, 920/494-9882) in Ashwaubenon. It preserved the stool sat in regularly by a Packer linebacker, the ferocious Ray Nitschke. (The street name Holmgren Way, incidentally, comes from a Packer coach.)

In 2002, a plaza was dedicated at **City Stadium** (1415 E. Walnut St., behind Green Bay East High School), where the Packers played 1925–1956.

Believe it or not, in Packer-nuts (and utterly anti-Chicago *anything*) Green Bay there exists a *Chicago Bears bar!* The **Lorelei Inn** (1412 S. Webster St., 920/432-5921) was originally owned by a Bears fan (and the decor tells it), but his kids are Packers fans! You can expect good-natured ribbing. It's closed Sundays except when the Pack and Bears clash.

For all things Packers, here are some good websites: packersnews.com, packerforum.com (a global fan site), southendzone.com, packersbars.com (find a Packer bar wherever you are), oldbagofdonuts.com (Packers fans will fill you in on the name), jsonline.com (Milwaukee's newspaper is kicks for Packers coverage), packers.scout.com (for real football draft geeks), and greenbaypressgazette.com.

During training camp and on select game days, a cheery way to take in the Pack is aboard the **Legends of Lombardi Tour** on a red double-decker bus imported from England. It leaves from the Convention and Visitors Bureau (1901 S. Oneida St., across the street from Lambeau Field, 920/494-9507 or 888/867-3342, www.greenbay.com).

OTHER SIGHTS
Museums

The staggering **National Railroad Museum** (2285 S. Broadway Ave., 920/437-7623, www.nationalrrmuseum.org, 9 A.M.–5 P.M. Mon.–Sat., 11 A.M.–5 P.M. Sun., $9 adults), with more than 80 railroad cars and locomotives, has a respected collection rivaling any in the nation. Available for close-up inspection is personal fave Big Boy, the world's largest steam locomotive. Of course, train rides are also available, five times daily in summer. Included in the admission is a mile-long jaunt on a narrow-gauge railroad.

Perhaps the most unusual state park in Wisconsin is **Heritage Hill Living History Museum** (2640 S. Webster Ave., 920/448-5150, www.heritagehillgb.org, 10 A.M.–4:30 P.M. Mon.–Sat., noon–4:30 P.M. Sun., Apr.–Oct., $8 adults). More than 25 historic buildings from around Wisconsin have been reconstructed at this 50-acre site. Separated into four distinct thematic areas—Pioneers, Military Life, Small Towns, and Agricultural—the buildings include mock-ups of flimsy original sapling-and-bark dwellings of the Jesuits and some of the oldest extant buildings in Wisconsin. All areas are accessible via wagons.

TITLETOWN

It is ever the same: Sunday morning, 11:59 A.M. The network feed fades to black. Then, as always, a still shot of Him. And, slowly, with the melodrama of sports announcers, the voice-over: "The Man. Vincent T. Lombardi." Or, even more powerfully, "Titletown..." It incites goosebumps, followed by the shakes of unvanquishable dumbbell belief.

THE RELIGION

If there are any awards for professional sports fandom, the Pack and its beloved legions sweep – hands down. One grizzled sportswriter wrote, "The Dallas Cowboys were only another football team; the Packers were a practicing religion." If he only knew the ambivalence, the bittersweet...well, *curse* of being born a Packerbacker. (This author was unlucky enough to be born on the demise of the last Packer empire, after Super Bowl II, back in 1968, and don't think his family hasn't reminded him of the lethal coincidence.)

The Green Bay Packers are the only passively proselytizing franchise in all of professional sports. Hard-core travelers and football aficionados will find Packer bars and Packer fan clubs in every state in the union – as far away as jolly old England. I've even found scads of Packer faithful bellowing for Sunday satellite-dish equity as far away as Taiwan and Thailand.

EARLY YEARS

The Packers were founded in 1919 as one of the handful of teams that would eventually make up the National Football League. The team was born in the back room of the *Green Bay Press-Gazette*, where the cigar-chomping sports editor, George Calhoun, and legendary ex-Notre Damer Curly Lambeau agreed to found a local team. They convinced a local industry bigwig to supply a practice field and uniforms, thus obligating the team to call itself the Indian Packing Company Footballers. This was later shortened to you-know-what. Going 10-1 its first season, the dynasty had begun.

After literally passing the hat in the crowd for the first season, the Packers, in need of financial stability, hit upon one of the most unusual money angles in sports. The community issued $5 nondividend public shares in the team; almost beyond logic, the citizens scooped up the stocks.

The *only* nonprofit, community-owned team in professional sports, the Green Bay Packers have become a true anomaly: a small-market team with few fiscal constraints on finding and wooing talent. And they can never desert the town – if they try to move, the organization is dissolved and all money goes for a Veterans of Foreign Wars memorial.

TITLETOWN'S TITLES

After the Packers whomped their opponents in the first season, they became the first NFL team to win three consecutive NFL titles, and they did it twice – 1929-1931 and 1965-1967. In all, they won 11 championships through 1968 and the Lombardi years. In fact, though the Lombardi-led teams get all the glory, the teams of the early years were even more dominant, amassing a 34-5-2 record.

Then the well went dry. Before the 1990s brought in more forceful management, the Packers suffered through their longest drought ever between NFC Central Division Championships: 24 years. Twenty-four long, unbearable, embarrassing years. Still, the fans dutifully packed the stadium every Sunday. They always believed.

But after all those doormat decades, the Packers finally won the Super Bowl again in 1997, which began an always-in-the-playoffs run culminating in yet another notch in the Titletown belt on February 6, 2011, when the Packers defeated the Super Bowl-seasoned Pittsburgh Steelers 31-25 for their record 13th NFL championship and fourth Super Bowl title. The headline in the *Milwaukee Journal-Sentinel* said it all: "Titletown Again." (Although the most apt quote oft-heard after the game was, "The Lombardi trophy is coming home!")

The **Neville Public Museum** (210 Museum Pl., 920/448-4460, www.nevillepublicmuseum.org, 9 A.M.–4 P.M. Mon.–Tues. and Fri.–Sat., 9 A.M.–8 P.M. Wed.–Thurs., noon–5 P.M. Sun., $4 adults) contains art, history, and science exhibits. The outstanding main hall exhibit "On the Edge of the Inland Sea," a 7,500-square-foot diorama of a retreating glacier, is worth admission, as is the impressive view of the city skyline.

Bay Beach Amusement Park

One of my favorites in Green Bay is the anachronistic gathering of more than a dozen rides along the bay shoreline at the Bay Beach Amusement Park (1313 Bay Beach Rd., 920/391-3671, 10 A.M.–9 P.M. daily June–Aug., Sat.–Sun. May and Sept.). The best part: Rides cost as little as *$0.25.*

Bay Beach Wildlife Sanctuary

Up the road from the amusement park is the excellent Bay Beach Wildlife Sanctuary (1660 E. Shore Dr., 920/391-3671, www.baybeachwildlife.com, 8 A.M.–7:30 P.M. daily Apr.–Sept., shorter hours the rest of the year, free), a 700-acre spread with exhibits on Wisconsin fauna, including the very popular timber wolf house.

NEW Zoo

The well-regarded NEW Zoo (4378 Reforestation Rd., 920/448-4466, 9 A.M.–6 P.M. daily Apr.–Oct., less often the rest of the year, $4 adults, free Wed.), eight miles north of Green Bay, allows the animals greater freedom to roam. Animal compounds include Prairie Grassland, Wisconsin Native, and International—you're as likely to see a Galápagos tortoise as you are a Wisconsin red fox. The zoo has tripled in size in recent years and added many new exhibits, including a black-footed penguin zone. A children's area allows interactive experiences.

Side Trip

West of Ashwaubenon is zany **Seymour,** which bills itself as the "Home of the Hamburger,"

purportedly invented here. The townsfolk fete their title with the annual **Burger Fest** the first Saturday in August; they pretty much try to fry a world-record burger (some three tons!) annually. Just check out the enormous burger and Hamburger Charlie on Depot Street, west of WI 55.

ENTERTAINMENT AND EVENTS

For local entertainment listings, check the schedules in the *Green Bay Press-Gazette.*

The Arts

On the University of Wisconsin-Green Bay campus, the smashingly modern **Weidner Center for the Performing Arts** (920/465-2217, www.weidnercenter.com) showcases national and regional musicians, plays, musicals, dance performances, and the annual Green Bay jazz fest. The city boasts its own symphony orchestra and two community theater groups.

Events

Green Bay's hootenanny, **Bayfest** (www.artseventsinc.com), takes place at the UW-Green Bay campus at the beginning of June. The festival includes five musical stages, some 25 international cuisine tents, games, a carnival, and a huge fireworks display.

There's *always* something Packer-oriented going on in late summer as the city gears up for the NFL season.

RECREATION

Trails

The **Fox River Trail** is a 14-mile multipurpose trail stretching along the Fox Valley corridor to Greenleaf. The city is also the departure point for the **Mountain Bay Trail,** an eight-miler linking to trails west to Wausau.

Camping

The camping nearest to Green Bay is toward Door County north on WI 57, 15 miles out of town: **Bay Shore County Park** (920/448-4466, May–Oct.).

Spectator Sports

It's virtually impossible to get *face price* tickets to regular-season Packers games, especially if the Pack's success continues; preseason games are another matter. Call 920/496-5700 for ticket information.

ACCOMMODATIONS

A caveat: Don't even think of showing up in Green Bay on a weekend when the Packers are playing at home with any hope of getting budget lodging, or any lodging for that matter. Try the visitors bureau's website (www.greenbay.com) for links and deals or even the local lodging association's (www.greenbay-getaways.com).

Downtown

It's been surprisingly possible to scare up a $75 room (though most are more) at the extended-stay **Candlewood Suites** (1125 E. Mason St., 920/430-7040, $60–189), which has a phenomenal number of amenities.

Brand-new upmarket digs are right nearby at the much-raved about **Hotel Sierra** (333 Main St., 920/432-4555, www.hotel-sierra.com, $139–179). It's more or less a self-contained city, so everything you need is here, including a free breakfast in the morning.

Southwest: Airport and Stadium

At the **Sky-Lit Motel** (2120 S. Ashland Ave., 920/494-5641, www.skylitmotel.net, $50–85) you get what you pay for, though it's fine for a cheap sleep.

Where Lombardi Avenue swings around to hook up with Military Avenue to the west is the step-up (and this author's home away from home) **Bay Motel** (1301 S. Military Ave., 920/494-3441, $45–75), where all rooms have free movies; some have mini refrigerators.

A boutique hotel for chic youngsters in Packerville? Yup, **Aloft** (465 Pilgrim Way, 920/884-0800, www.aloftgreenbay.com, $95) is a new boutique hotel that is contrapuntal to blue-collar. It's zen chic and very friendly.

Have a family? The only place to head is the **Tundra Lodge Resort and Waterpark** (Lombardi Ave. and Ashland Ave., 920/405-8700, www.tundralodge.com, $129–399), just a hop, skip, and jump from Lambeau Field. Indoor/outdoor waterparks let the kids work up a sweat; then let 'em gorge in the buffet-style restaurant.

De Pere

De Pere has a couple of interesting lodging choices. A new boutique hotel overlooking the Fox River, the **James St. Inn** (201 James St., 920/337-0111, www.jamesstreetinn.com, $74–220) is in a historic mill. Andrew's Restaurant on-site here is fabulous, especially for fish.

FOOD

Don't forget that De Pere also has some fine eateries, especially the ever since-1918 **Union Hotel** (200 N. Broadway, 920/336-6131, $15–30), the most absolutely anachronistic environment (in a good way) you can find in the state.

Vegetarian

No, it's not oxymoronic to be a vegan in Green Bay; it just seems that way. **Kavarna** (143 N. Broadway, 920/430-3200, breakfast and lunch daily, brunch Sat.–Sun., $5–10) is more of a coffee shop with a café complex, but the yam fries (baked!) are worth a trip.

Heartland Fare

If you really want to rub elbows with the locals, check out (**Kroll's,** the best family restaurant in town, with two locations. The more convenient one is on Main Street (1658 Main St., 920/468-4422, 10:30 A.M.–11 P.M. daily, until midnight weekends, $4–11). The other (S. Ridge Road, closer to Lambeau Field, 920/497-1111) is the older of the two and appears to have come straight out of the movie *Diner.* They serve great walleye and perch along with legendary burgers. This Kroll's also features wall buzzers that customers can use to summon the wait staff.

Kroll's competition is **Bay Family Restaurant** (Military Ave. and 9th St.,

920/494-3441, breakfast, lunch, and dinner daily, $6–11). The Bay uses ingredients direct from family farms and serves homemade pies and piles of hash browns the size of encyclopedias. There are two other locations: 1245 East Mason Street and 1100 Radisson Street. All are open for three squares per day.

Supper Clubs and Fine Dining
Green Bay has every right to argue that it does the supper club as well as Milwaukee in numbers and quality. For exquisite rib-eye steak, **Ziggey's Inn** (741 Hoffman Rd., 920/339-7820, 5–9 P.M. Tues.–Sun., $7–18) can't be beat. Even better is the time-warp aspect of the place—you can imagine Packer teams of the 1960s sitting around digging in.

The Wellington (1060 Hansen Rd., 920/499-2000, lunch and dinner Mon.–Fri., dinner Sat., $8–28) is a Green Bay institution of sorts. An exclusive spot done up as an English drawing room, it specializes in beef Wellington (no surprise) and excellent duck, steer tenderloin, and seafood dishes.

◖ **Eve's Supper Club** (2020 Riverside Dr., 920/435-1571, lunch and dinner Mon.–Fri., dinner Sat., $12–50) has the grandest view of any dining establishment, perched atop the 2020 Riverside office building overlooking the Fox River, almost directly across from the railroad museum. You most certainly pay for your view.

Brewpubs
Green Bay's got a couple of lively brewpubs. Right downtown at the west end of the Fox River Bridge along WI 29 is **Titletown Brewing Company** (200 Dousman St., 920/437-2337, 11 A.M.–11 P.M. daily, $8–15), with an above-average menu of quite creative fare. It's housed in a grand old depot with a soaring clock tower—great environs! To be fair, virtually across the street, the **Hinterland** (920/438-8050, dinner daily, $8–18) has great beer and phenomenal, way-above-pub-grub food—even caribou, wild boar and the like. The food is not just for kicks; it's professionally well made.

Italian and Pizza
Italian restaurants are the dominant ethnic specialty in Green Bay. One of the best-known is **Victoria's** (2610 Bay Settlement Rd., 920/468-8070, lunch Mon.–Sat., dinner daily, $5–15). Let's not quibble over that stupid word "authenticity"—the portions are outrageously huge; vegetarians also have good options.

The best pizza in town is at **Jake's** (1149 Main St., 920/432-8012, 4 P.M.–midnight Mon.–Sat., 2 P.M.–midnight Sun., $4–6). You'll have to wait up to half an hour for a seat at times, but it, too, is well worth the time.

INFORMATION
The Packer Country Tourism Office (1901 S. Oneida St., 920/494-9507 or 888/867-3342, www.greenbay.com) is across the street from Lambeau Field. It actually serves Green Bay east to Two Rivers, Kewaunee, and Algoma.

The *Green Bay Press-Gazette* is Wisconsin's oldest newspaper, started in 1833 as the *Green Bay Intelligencer;* it's a great source of local goings-on.

GETTING THERE
By Air
Austin Straubel International Airport (920/498-4800), in southwest Green Bay off WI 172, is served by six airlines and more than 50 flights daily to Milwaukee, Chicago, Cleveland, Denver, Detroit, Milwaukee, and Minneapolis.

By Bus
The **bus depot** (800 Cedar St., 920/432-4883) is served by Greyhound (and two on-off regional lines) to most points in southern and western Wisconsin and west to Minnesota.

GETTING AROUND
Organized Tours
The *Foxy Lady* (920/432-3699, Tues.–Sun. mid-Apr.–mid-Oct.), docked behind the Holiday Inn City Centre, offers sightseeing, lunch, cocktail, sunset, dinner, and moonlight cruises. Rates start at $15 for a narrated cruise and go up to $38 for a sunset dinner.

Reservations are required for all but the sightseeing cruise.

ONEIDA NATION

West of Green Bay are the 12 square miles making up the **Oneida Indian Reservation.** Known as the "People of the Standing Stone," the Oneida were members of the League of the Iroquois and once a protectorate of the Stockbridge-Munsee bands on the east coast. They moved westward en masse (save for a small band still in New York) not long after the turn of the 18th century.

One of the only repositories of the history of the Oneida is the **Oneida Nation Museum** (W892 EE Rd., 920/869-2768, 9 A.M.–5 P.M. Tues.–Fri., 10 A.M.–5 P.M. Sat., $2 adults, $1 children). Exhibits in the main hall focus on Oneida history and culture; a longhouse and stockade are outside, as well as a nice nature trail. The Oneida **powwow** takes place on or near the Fourth of July.

The Bottom of the Door

For many folks, Door County begins only when they have buzzed the bridge spanning Sturgeon Bay's Lake Michigan canal; others claim that you're not in the county until WI 42 and WI 57 bifurcate into bayside and lakeside routes northeast of town. Still, Door County proper includes a chunk of 15 or more miles south of the ship channel, and the *peninsula* comprises underappreciated Kewaunee County, east of Green Bay, as well.

Note that WI 57 has been undergoing dramatic changes and this will likely continue as long as tourists flock to the Door. The road bends away from the lake and into a hyperdrive four-lane divided highway. And up the peninsula this may creep. (Somehow transportation engineers have to figure out a way to plat the road and not damage archaeological sites, wetlands, and threatened species, all of which have slowed the project.) For now, along WI 57, you'll find an easy-to-overlook little county wayside. At **Red Banks** wayside, a statue to Jean Nicolet stands a few hundred yards from the red clay bluffs overlooking the serene bay. Those in the know agree that it was here that Jean Nicolet first came sloshing ashore in 1634, cracking his harquebuses to impress the Winnebago.

But WI 57 leaves much to the imagination. More adventuresome travelers might attempt to find Highway A out of Green Bay; it spins along the same route, but right atop the lake. Bypassing Point Sable—once a boundary between Native American tribal lands—the road offers views of a state wildlife area across the waters. Farther up, you can see Vincent Point and, immediately after that, Red Banks itself. This byway continues through Benderville before linking with WI 57 again (there's camping in a county park up the road) before crossing the Kewaunee-Door County line into Belgian territory.

BRUSSELS AND VICINITY

Brussels and surrounding towns such as Champion, Euren, Maplewood, Rosiere, and Forestville constitute the country's largest Belgian-American settlement. The architecture of the region is so well preserved that more than 100 buildings make up Wisconsin's first *rural* National Historical Landmark. Right along WI 57, the homes and Catholic chapels show distinctive Belgian influences along with a lot of reddish-orange brick and split cedar fencing. On alternating weekends through the summer, the villages still celebrate *Kermiss,* church Mass during harvest season.

Brussels is the area's capital of sorts, with **Belgian Days** the first week of July—plenty of Belgian chicken, *booyah* (thick vegetable stock), *jute* (boiled cabbage), and tripe sausage. You'll find Belgian fare in a few places in Brussels, including **Marchants Food, Inc.** (9674 WI 57, 920/825-1244, 8 A.M.–8 P.M. Mon.–Fri., 8 A.M.–6 P.M. Sat., 8 A.M.–12:30 P.M. Sun.), open daily for 50 years.

A quick side trip takes in lots of Belgian architecture. In Robinsville, a mile and a half east of Champion along Highway K, sits the **shrine grotto,** a home and school for disabled children founded by a Belgian to whom the Virgin Mary is said to have appeared in 1858.

Not Belgian per se but north of Luxemburg, itself south of Brussels, near the junction of Highways A and C is ◖ **Joe Rouer's** (920/866-2585), a classic bar with legendary burgers that this author would love to eat right now. The cheese curds are pretty darned good, as well.

North of Brussels along Highway C, the **St. Francis Xavier Church and Grotto Cemetery** is representative of

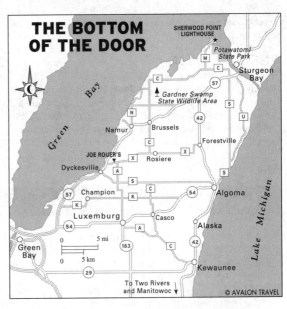

THE BOTTOM OF THE DOOR

Belgian rural construction; farmers contributed aesthetically pleasing stones from their fields to raise a grotto and crypt for the local reverend.

Three miles northeast of Brussels via Highway C is the **Gardner Swamp State Wildlife Area** along Keyes Creek.

KEWAUNEE

Perched on a hillside overlooking a lovely historic harbor, Kewaunee was once bent on rivaling Chicago as maritime center of the Great Lakes and could likely have given the Windy City a run for its money when an influx of immigrants descended after hearing rumors of a gold strike in the area. But Chicago had the rail, while Kewaunee, despite its harbor, was isolated and became a minor port and lumber town.

Sights

Kewaunee is Wisconsin's Czech nerve center. Outlying villages show a Czech/Bohemian heritage and you'll often hear Czech spoken. Five miles south of town via WI 42 is

a new **Heritage Farm** (920/388-0604), an 1876 Czech homestead renovated into a sort of cultural center; open by appointment or during events (of which there seems always to be one).

The chamber of commerce has maps of a nifty **walking tour,** taking in about three dozen historical structures. Everybody snaps a shot of the 1909 **Kewaunee pierhead lighthouse.** The structure consists today of a steel frame base and steel tower with a cast-iron octagonal lantern about 50 feet high. At the harbor you can take a tour ($3) aboard a retired World War II **tugboat.** The central **Old Jail Museum** (Vliet and Dodge, 920/388-4410, noon–4 P.M. daily in summer, free) is near the courthouse in an old sheriff's home, part of which doubled as the jail, with gruesome dungeon cells. Statues of Father Marquette and solemn, pious Potawatomi are likely what you'll be shown first. Head, too, for the replica of the USS *Pueblo.* The ill-fated Navy ship, involved in an incident with North Korea in the 1950s, was built in Kewaunee during World War II.

Three miles west of town, the Wisconsin Department of Natural Resources operates a state-of-the-art **Anadromous Fish Facility** (N3884 Ransom Moore Ln., 920/388-1025, 10 A.M.–5 P.M. daily, free). Detailed are the spawning practices of anadromous fish, viewed through underwater panels.

Southwest of town in Montpelier township is a **Rustic Road** scenic drive involving parts of Hrabik, Cherneysville, Sleepy Hollow, and Pine Grove Roads. Close to here, south of Krok, is the only known Wisconsin rooftop windmill, a granddaddy of a historic structure.

At **Svoboda Industries** along WI 42 North, you'll see what is purportedly the world's largest grandfather clock—39 feet tall.

The local visitors information center (920/388-4822 or 800/666-8214, www.kewaunee.org) is right on WI 42, north of downtown, near a great marsh walk.

Accommodations

On the harbor is the **Harrison Harbour House** (920/388-0606, $35!), built for a former governor and best described by the proprietors as a "hunting cabin for fishermen," with bunk beds, stone walls, rough-hewn board ceilings, and a definite feel of lake life. It isn't for everyone, but some folks just groove on it.

The **Historic Karsten Inn** (122 Ellis St., 920/388-3800, www.karsteninn.com, from $90) is a B&B rebuilt from a real inn; they've also got a bistro-esque dining room.

If Door County camping is too far away, $15 gets you a basic site at **Kewaunee Village** (333 Terraqua Dr., 800/274-9684), north of town along WI 42; a nature area has trails.

Food

The local specialty is Czechoslovakian and Bohemian food, including *kolace* (yeast buns with fruit filling) and *buhuite* (pronounced bu-ta—thin dough filled with seeds or fruit), sauerkraut rye bread, and *rohlik*. These delectable baked goods are available at **Tom's Pastry Shop** (409 WI 42, 920/388-2533), which is also a deli. Near the bridge in town are a couple of places for great smoked fish.

ALGOMA

The whole drive along WI 42 from Manitowoc to Algoma is spectacular—a resplendent, beach-hugging route. As you swoop into Algoma from the south, seemingly endless miles of wide, empty beach begin, both road and beach unencumbered by travelers. This freshly scrubbed little community of friendly folks might be said to be a wonderful poor man's Door County (were one to approve of such distinctions).

The small town is known today mostly for its killer sportfishing, and its marinas account for the state's most substantial sportfishing industry with four—count 'em—state records.

At the time of writing, a new passenger ferry between Algoma to Frankfort, MI, was being bandied about; once a pipe dream, it's actually gaining traction as of late.

Sights

Von Stiehl Winery (115 Navarino St., 920/487-5208, www.vonstiehl.com, guided tours 9:30 A.M.–4:30 P.M. daily May–Oct., 2 P.M. Sat. rest of year, $3.75 adults) is the oldest licensed winery in Wisconsin, housed in what was once the Ahnapee Brewery (named after the local river), built in the 1850s, whose three-foot-thick limestone walls are a ready-made underground catacomb system. The house specialty is cherry wine; many other Wisconsin fruit wines are produced, all guarded by a patented system to prevent premature aging and light damage.

Algoma is also the southern terminus of the **Ahnapee State Trail,** a section of the Ice Age National Scenic Trail stretching 18 miles partially along the Ahnapee River to the southern fringe of Sturgeon Bay. Another trail runs from Algoma to Casco.

Algoma once had a legendary "fishing mayor," Art Dettman. His name lives on in a restored fish shanty—a quasi-museum to fishing—on the National Register of Historic Places. It's open by appointment only; call 920/487-3443 for information.

Algoma has, without a doubt, the cutest

movie theater in Wisconsin—my living room is larger.

Charter Fishing

Second in the state for fish taken, this is a prime place to smear on the zinc oxide and do the Ahab thang. Early-season lake trout are generally hot in May, but June is Algoma's biggest month; rainbow trout and chinook salmon are everywhere. Steelhead and especially king salmon are added to the mix come July, and brown trout get big in August. September fishing is great.

Camping

Ahnapee River Trails Campground (E6053 W. Wilson Rd., 920/487-5777, $18) is on the Ahnapee River Trail.

Accommodations

A basic motel that may not be right atop Lake Michigan (it's all of across the road), the **Algoma Beach Motel** (2221 Lake St., 920/487-3214, $79) has clean rooms and a very welcoming owner.

Food

Several family restaurants and diners in town serve Belgian *booyah* and Belgian pie. For espresso, coffee, tea, or light food—along with live music—in a trendy atmosphere, you can't beat **Caffe Tlazo** (607 WI 42, 920/487-7240, 6 a.m.–8 p.m. Mon.–Fri., 7 a.m.–8 p.m. Sat., 7 a.m.–7 p.m. Sun., $5 and up). Casual dining is at the historic **Hotel Stebbins** (201 Steele St., 920/487-5526, www.thehotelstebbins.com, 4:30–10 p.m. daily during peak season, 5–9 p.m. Tues.–Sat. rest of year, $8–25), where they often have live music.

For a picnic basket, **Bearcat's** (WI 42 and Navarino St., 920/487-2372, 9 a.m.–5 p.m. daily year-round) has great smoked fish for dirt cheap prices!

Information and Services

The tourist information center (920/487-2041 or 800/498-4888, www.algoma.org) is on the south edge of Algoma along WI 42. It is also the departure point for historical walking tours of downtown—on your own or guided ($3).

Appleton

I've seen it referred to as the Queen of the Fox Cities and the Princess of Paper Valley (though one local thought a bit and pointed out that if you said that here, no one would know what city you were talking about!). Bisected by the Fox River, this spread-out city hardly seems paper-centered industrial when you're traipsing about the gentrified downtown area.

One civic nucleus is well-respected Lawrence University, a small liberal-arts college that was the state's first co-ed institution of higher education and also the first to initiate a postgraduate papermaking institute.

Appleton grew up around a mill, but wheat production was far more profitable than floating log rafts. Not until after the Civil War did local industrialists turn their attention to Wisconsin's ready-made paper wealth. It is still so—the region is known alternatively as Paper Valley.

The Fox Cities and Fox Valley

Between Neenah and Kaukauna along Lake Winnebago's northwestern cap lie a dozen concatenate communities making up the Fox Cities region—a region part of but distinct from the Fox River Valley, which itself stretches along the Fox River–Lake Winnebago corridor and takes in all communities between Green Bay and Oshkosh. Appleton is the region's economic anchor; the smallest town is Combined Locks. All take their inspiration from the Fox River—one of the few rivers in North America to flow north. Together, the Fox Cities constitute the third-largest metropolitan area in the state (pop. 180,000), a statistic many Wisconsinites find surprising.

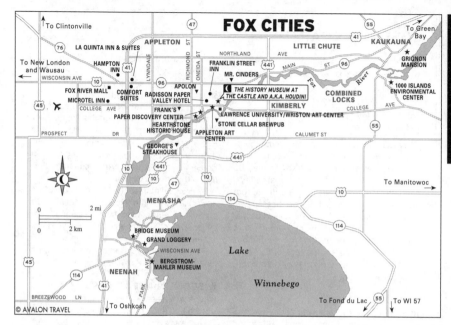

SIGHTS
◖ The History Museum at the Castle and A.K.A. Houdini

Paper may be the raison d'etre, but folks just can't get enough of that Houdini magic. Born Ehrich Weiss in Hungary in 1874, the enigmatic Houdini spent most of his life in Appleton. A.K.A. Houdini (330 E. College Ave., 920/735-8445, www.myhistorymuseum.org) is maintained as part of The History Museum at the Castle. The foremost collection of Houdini artifacts anywhere includes the Guiteau handcuffs, which bound President Garfield's assassin and from which the magician later escaped. The center has prepared a detailed walking tour of the city (marked with brass plaques), taking in the sites of his childhood. Magic shows, hands-on exhibits, and more thrill kids (and parents).

The museum (330 E. College Ave., 920/735-9370) itself contains an excellent and award-winning exhibit ("Tools of Change") on the workers and economic history of the Lower Fox region.

The museums are open 10 A.M.–4 P.M. Tuesday–Saturday, till 8 P.M. Thurs., noon–4 P.M. Sunday June–August, closed Monday the rest of the year. Admission is $7.50.

Paper Discovery Center

Where else should the Paper Industry Hall of Fame (425 W. Water St., 920/749-3040, www.paperdiscoverycenter.org, 10 A.M.–4 P.M. Mon.–Sat., $5) go but the Fox River Valley, of which Appleton is the queen? In a renovated paper mill, experience every facet of paper, start to finish—with lots of activities for the kids.

Hearthstone Historic House

Hearthstone Historic House (625 W. Prospect Ave., 920/730-8204, 10 A.M.–3:30 P.M. Tues.–Fri., 11 A.M.–3:30 P.M. Sat., 1–3:30 P.M. Sun., $6 adults) is a massive 1882 Victorian. Within Appleton's city limits, the old Fox drops almost 40 feet, much of it in angry rapids. In the late 1880s the Hearthstone, the city's major

JOSEPH MCCARTHY

I have in my hands a list of 205 names that were made known to the Secretary of State as being members of the Communist Party and who nevertheless are still working and shaping policy in the State Department.

Uttered by Senator Joseph McCarthy (a Fox Cities native) in Wheeling, West Virginia, these words – in what became known as the 205 Speech – thrust him into the national political spotlight. Before he shot himself in the foot politically, he dominated U.S. politics, electrified the nation, aided Tricky Dick, and inspired a new word. Wisconsinites still wonder how they feel about one of their most infamous native sons. (And after passage of the post-9/11 Patriot Act, his name was being brought up again and again.)

TAIL GUNNER JOE

After a lifelong struggle with education, McCarthy graduated from Marquette Law and astonished everyone by winning a judgeship in 1938 through sheer grassroots, flesh-pressing toil.

He was not, shall we say, a widely respected judge. He further infuriated opponents by stumping for higher office – by exaggerating, some say – from the South Pacific, while in World War II; Tail Gunner Joe was born.

THE JUNIOR SENATOR

McCarthy was swept up in the GOP wave of 1946 and made it to Washington, besting a La Follette (the name is legendary here). He incessantly angered the Senate with his intractable attitude, personal attacks, and rules violations. By 1949, the congressional leadership loathed him, and most assumed he was simply a lame-duck embarrassment.

What no one counted on was his shrewd prescience about the national paranoia over Communism. In part, McCarthy concocted the Red Scare. He was once again reelected. His path culminated in his antics in the Special House Committee on Un-American Activities. McCarthyism was born.

By 1953, he had reached the pinnacle of his powers, attacking his peers and fending off censure attempts from his many Senate enemies. One charge finally stuck – a kickback scheme. On December 2, 1954, he was officially censured, diminishing the blindly firing junior senator from Wisconsin.

WISCONSIN AND MCCARTHY

Was he a nutcase obscenity? A prescient, passionate Red fighter? Strident opposition to McCarthy was everpresent throughout his reign. The large press in Madison and Milwaukee lobbed as many editorial shells as it could to bring him down. "Joe Must Go" recall petitions collected with almost half a million signatures statewide.

Ask Wisconsinites today about McCarthy and they'll likely dodge the question or roll their eyes and shudder. There *are* still those who support him.

Perhaps most tellingly, Appleton, his adopted hometown, removed his bust (and all other signs) from the courthouse, while favorite resident Harry Houdini is celebrated with Houdini Plaza and its huge memorial sculpture smack in the city center.

---

architectural draw, was the first home to be lighted by a self-contained hydroelectric plant (the United States' first mostly electric streetcar line went up simultaneously). The rich original appointments have been preserved, down to period electroliers and light switches designed by Thomas Edison. Hands-on displays teach visitors about electricity and allow you to operate the controls of a power plant.

Art Galleries

Lawrence University's **Wriston Art Center** (E. College Ave., 920/832-6621, hours vary Tues.–Sat., free) features rotating and permanent exhibits of student and guest artists in traditional and mixed media. If for no other reason, go to see the building's otherworldly design.

The **Appleton Art Center** (130 N. Morrison St., 920/733-4089, www.appletonartcenter.

org, hours vary Mon.–Sat., free) has three galleries, with an emphasis on regional artists, and hosts the largest summer art fair in the state. The Fine Art Exhibition showcases Fox River Valley artists.

Side Trips

In nearby New London, along the Wolf River, the **Mosquito Hill Nature Center** (N3880 Rogers Rd., 920/779-6433) offers some good hiking trails and the very intriguing Wisconsin Butterfly House, showcasing Wisconsin's native butterfly species. The American water spaniel, bred by a local resident, also originated in New London.

Among the oldest paved trails in Wisconsin is hard-to-find number 53 on Wisconsin's Rustic Road system. Beginning in 1857, work was done on what today are Garrity, McCabe, Greiner, and Bodde Roads, northwest of Appleton along U.S. 41 at Highway JJ. (Keep your eyes peeled—it's somewhat confusing.) Along the way, you'll pass scenic double-arch bridges, a stone silo, and a wildlife conservation area.

ENTERTAINMENT AND EVENTS

Pick up a copy of the free monthly *Scene,* which has a good listing of entertainment and cuisine. Also check out appletondowntown.org.

Pubs and Nightspots

Park Central (318 W. College Ave., 920/738-5603) comprises a half dozen bars, comedy clubs, and sports bars. Closer to Lawrence University, one place to check out is **Houdini's Lounge** (117 S. Appleton St., 920/832-8615), a pub with Houdini as a central theme (no surprise) and more than 60 beers available.

Packed to the rafters is **Cleo's Brown Beam** (205 W. College Ave.), which bills itself the "Cheers of Appleton" and has an amazing display of Christmas lights all year. **Bazil's** (109 W. College Ave., 920/954-1770) features an amazing 135 microbrews.

The **Stone Cellar Brewpub** (1004 Olde Oneida St., 920/735-0507) is an 1858 brewery that whips out a few tasty brands—one named for Houdini.

USA Today called **The Wooden Nickel** (217 E. College Ave., 920/735-0661) the best sports bar in Wisconsin, and it's hard to argue with that.

But yours truly loves **Olde Town Tavern** (107 W. College Ave., 920/954-0103) for its wonderful beers of yesteryear (Schlitz? Really? How grandfatherly!).

Cultural Events

Lawrence University has almost always got something happening, from a remarkable speaker series to regular performing arts productions at the Memorial Chapel and Stansbury Theatre, in the Music-Drama Center. For information, contact the Office of Public Events (920/832-6585).

SHOPPING
Malls

Appleton is mall country, with so much mall space that bus tours make regular pilgrimages here. (The city sported the nation's first indoor mall—though it was demolished partially in 2006 for a new complex.) The unity of the **Fox River Mall** (4301 W. Wisconsin Ave., 920/739-4100), the state's second-largest indoor mall, is admirable (add up the shops surrounding it, and it's the highest concentration in the state!).

SPORTS AND RECREATION
Spectator Sports

Goodland Field (2400 N. Casaloma Dr., 920/733-4152) is the home of the Wisconsin Timber Rattlers, a single-A minor league franchise of the Milwaukee Brewers. It's typical family-friendly fun with zany promotions and dirt-cheap prices!

ACCOMMODATIONS

West of downtown are most lodgings, including the value **Microtel Inn** (321 Metro Dr., 920/997-3121, $52 s or d), with an exercise room and whirlpool. The Appleton **Hampton Inn** (350 Fox River Dr., 920/954-9211, $95) has been rated one of the top 10 Hampton Inns nationwide.

One of the largest recreation centers in the state is at the Appleton **Comfort Suites Comfort Dome** (3809 W. Wisconsin Ave., 920/730-3800, $100). Some rooms have kitchens and microwaves.

A few blocks north of the Avenue Mall is the 1897 Victorian **Franklin Street Inn** (318 E. Franklin St., 920/739-3702, www.franklinstreetinn.com, from $99). Original pocket doors, oak and maple hardwoods, and original chandeliers give the place—one of the stateliest mansions in town—a nice feel.

Trim **La Quinta Inn & Suites** (3730 W. College Ave., 920/734-9231, $99 s or d) was just refurbished and offers two pools, sauna, whirlpool, a dining room, and continental breakfast.

Downtown, newest is the European-style boutique hotel **CopperLeaf Boutique Hotel** (300 W. College Ave., 877/303-0303, www.copperleafhotel.com, from $140), a great deal considering the location, the freshness of the place, and amenities. Folks rave about it.

Just a skip across the street, the **Radisson Paper Valley Hotel** (333 W. College Ave., 920/733-8000, $209) features more than 400 rooms of all types. Take a look at some before checking in.

FOOD

Man, downtown Appleton has just an amazing array of eateries. Just stroll a few blocks and you'll pretty much cover the world!

Pizza

Frank's (815 W. College Ave., 920/734-9131, 4 P.M.–3 A.M. daily, $4–9) has been making every ingredient of its pizzas from scratch for more than 40 years—including the sausage—and it's still going strong. If nothing else, head for the 18-piece brass big band blowouts, held October–May.

Heartland Fare

Popular with Appleton residents is **Mr. Cinders** (1309 E. Wisconsin Ave., 920/738-0100, 10:30 A.M.–late daily, $4–9). You can't go wrong with the burgers or the delicious grilled steak sandwich. Best of all, there's a fish fry all day Friday.

Steaks and Supper Clubs

Open for 50 years and still going strong is **❲ George's Steak House** (2208 S. Memorial Dr., 920/733-4939, lunch and dinner Mon.–Fri., dinner Sat., $5–20). It's strictly steaks and seafood here, with piano music nightly.

Others point out that this is Packerland, after all, so a visit to **Vince Lombardi's Steakhouse** (333 W. College Ave., 920/380-9390, 4–10 P.M. Mon.–Sat., till 9 P.M. Sun., $15–45) in the Radisson Paper Valley Hotel is a requisite—and in fact the steaks are sublime!

Well, hold on, there is also the coolly upscale **Black and Tan Grille** (300 W. College Ave., 920/380-4745, lunch Mon.–Fri., dinner nightly, $20–32) for contemporary American with great steaks and seafood.

Asian

For an upscale Pacific Rim-Asian fusion meal, head directly to **❲ Cy's Asian Bistro** (208 W. Wisconsin Ave., 920/969-9549, lunch and dinner Mon.–Fri., dinner Sat., $10–16), whose remarkable food has heavy overtones of Thai. And Cy is one of the friendliest proprietors you'll ever chat with at your table.

Mediterranean

One of the best dining experiences of late has come at **Apolon** (207 N. Appleton St., 920/939-1122, 5–10 P.M. Mon.–Sat., $9–20), a pan-Mediterranean (Hellenic heavy) restaurant, famed for their flaming cheese.

INFORMATION AND SERVICES

The Fox Cities Convention and Visitors Bureau (3433 W. College Ave., 920/734-3358 or 800/236-6673, www.foxcities.org) is actually quite far west of downtown, but the staff is definitely helpful.

GETTING THERE
By Bus

Greyhound (100 E. Washington St., 920/733-

2318) has frequent daily departures to major regional cities. **Lamers** bus line (800/261-6600) also has one departure daily to Milwaukee's Amtrak station and one to Wausau.

By Air

The **Outagamie County Airport** (www. atwairport.com) is the fourth-busiest in Wisconsin (60 flights daily).

Vicinity of Appleton

NEENAH-MENASHA

The twin cities of Neenah-Menasha are casually regarded as one entity, though their governments are separate. They share Doty Island, where Little Lake Butte des Mortes of the Fox River empties into Lake Winnebago.

Two Fox River channels flowing past the island and two minor promontories made available ready-made water power and gave rise to the birth of both villages by the 1840s. Depressed industries spurred papermaking, and within three decades Neenah-Menasha ruled the powerful Wisconsin papermaking region.

Bergstrom-Mahler Museum

This massive dwelling was once home to early area industrialist John Bergstrom. The highlight of the museum (165 N. Park Ave., 920/751-4658, 10 A.M.–4:30 P.M. Tues.–Fri., 9 A.M.–4:30 P.M. Sat., 1–4:30 P.M. Sun., free) is a world-renowned collection of paperweights, many dating from the French classic era of 1845–1860. The glass menagerie, as the museum calls it, is made up of 2,100 exquisite pieces.

Downtown Neenah and Menasha Riverfront

The scenic, landscaped Fox River north channel sports walkways with a kid-friendly fountain and summer concerts; the rest of the twin towns feature a marina and more than 30 picturesque historic buildings, many straight neoclassical in design. The best view is from the still-hand-operated lock on the canal. A new museum along Tayco Street, the **Bridge Tower Museum** (10 A.M.–7 P.M. daily May–Nov., free), is in an 80-year-old bridgetender's tower.

Downtown Neenah's East Wisconsin Avenue gives the best glimpse into 19th-century opulence and great river vistas. The mansions along this stretch were the partial setting for Wisconsin native Edna Ferber's novel *Come and Get It.*

Neenah's Doty Park contains a reconstruction of **Grand Loggery** (noon–4 P.M. daily June–Aug.), the home of James Doty, the state's second territorial governor. Artifacts of family and area history are scant, however.

Menasha's **Smith Park** has a few Native American burial mounds. **Kimberly Point Park,** at the confluence of Lake Winnebago and the Fox River, has a great lighthouse and some good views of the river. The big draw is the world-class **Barlow Planetarium** (1478 Midway Rd., 920/832-2848, fox.uwc.edu, $6 adults for public shows), on the campus of UW-Fox Valley. It has virtual reality exhibits and new public shows every week; no reservations required.

Adjacent to the planetarium is the **Weis Earth Science Museum** (1478 Midway Rd., 920/832-2925, hours vary, $2), the official mineralogical museum of the state. You wanna know what's what about glaciers and the stunning sandstone formations of the state? Right here's the place.

An FYI: in Menasha, the **Club Tavern** (56 Racine St., 920/722-2452) is one of this author's favorite low-key taverns. Lots of off-beat beers on tap and friendly proprietors.

KAUKAUNA

The word *gran ka-ka-lin* is a French-Ojibwa pidgin hybrid describing the long portage once necessary to trek around the city's 50-foot cascades, which ultimately required five locks to tame. A bit more amusing: In 1793, the area's land was purchased—the first recognized deed in the state—for the princely sum of two barrels of rum.

Sights

Not far from the pesky rapids of old stands **Grignon Mansion** (Augustine St., 920/766-3122, noon–4 P.M. Fri. and Sun., $4 adults). Built in 1838 by Augustin Grignon, to replace the log shack lived in by rum-dealing city founder Dominique Ducharme, the house became known as the mansion in the woods. It has been thoroughly renovated, down to the hand-carved newel posts and imposing brick fireplaces—the apple orchard still stands. (Though from the outside it doesn't look much like a "mansion.") Several of Kaukauna's legendary locks can be reached via the grounds.

Across the river at a bight is the aptly named **1000 Islands Environmental Center** (700 Dodge St., 920/766-4733, 8 A.M.–4 P.M. Mon.–Fri., 10 A.M.–4 P.M. Sat.–Sun., free), a vital stop on the Mississippi Flyway for waterfowl and predatory birds. A huge number of mounted animals are displayed, and live versions include plenty of native Wisconsin fauna, such as great blue heron, coot, and bitterns. The acreage also supports a stand of chinquapin oak, rare in the state. Plenty of great trails run along the Fox River here.

◖ HIGH CLIFF STATE PARK

The vista from this sheer escarpment northeast of Lake Winnebago is truly sublime. The cliff is actually the western edge of the Niagara Escarpment, a jutting, blufflike dolomite rise stretching almost 1,000 miles to the east, through Door County and beyond to Niagara Falls. From the top, almost 250 feet above the waters, you can see all of the Fox River Valley—Appleton, Oshkosh, Neenah, Menasha, and Kaukauna. Perhaps we should do as Chief Redbird of the Ojibwa did; he loved to sit on the cliff and "listen" to the lake—his statue still does today.

High Cliff was founded on an old limestone quarrying and kiln operation. Extant

© THOMAS HUHTI

Grignon Mansion, modest but historically perfect

© THOMAS HUHTI

lime kilns aging gracefully, High Cliff State Park

materiel and former Western Lime and Cement Company structures still stand. Effigy mounds (28–285 feet long) found along trails originated from an unknown prehistoric Native American tribe.

Recreation

Southeast of Appleton approximately 12 miles, the park (920/989-1106, day use 6 A.M.–11 P.M. daily) maintains both a swimming beach and an 85-slip marina. Hikers have seven miles of somewhat steep trails to choose from, and cross-country skiers have access to four of those come winter. The **Lime-Kiln Trail** is just over two miles and runs from the lime kiln ruins to the lake and then up the east side of the escarpment. The longest is the **Red Bird Trail,** mostly gentle and passing by the family campground.

Camping

The park's 1,200 acres have 112 fairly isolated campsites (920/989-1106), most occupied early in the high season.

Oshkosh

Former President Jimmy Carter once said in a speech at the University of Wisconsin-Oshkosh campus, "I have never seen a more beautiful, clean, and attractive place." He was referring to this Fox River Valley city of 55,000—the one with the weird name. Situated on the western bight of Lake Winnebago and bisected by the Fox River, the city is often associated, by both Wisconsinites and outsiders, with two disparate images—bib overalls and bizarre airplanes. Since 1895, Oshkosh B'Gosh has turned out functional, fashionable bib overalls and children's clothing and launched the city's tongue-twisting name onto the international

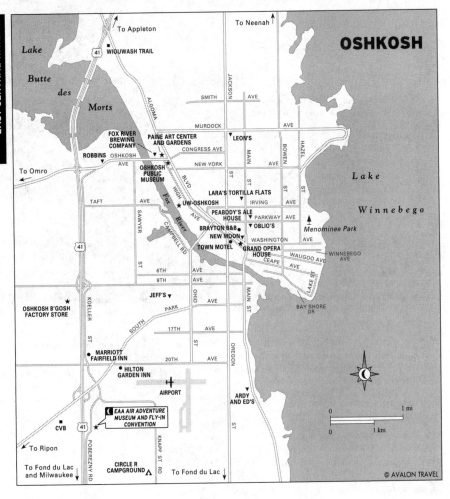

scene. (And, yes, they *have* heard people say things such as "Is this Oshkosh, b'gosh?") As for bizarre airplanes, the annual Experimental Aircraft Association's Fly-In is the largest of its kind, a not-to-be-missed highlight of itinerant edge-dwelling avionics.

History

Strategically located, waterwise, Oshkosh had always been a historic gathering spot for Native Americans. The primary Jesuit Black Robe himself, Father Jean Claude Allouez, even came in 1670 to preach to the Fox and Menominee Indians.

SAWDUST CITY

More than a century and a half ago, the north woods of Wisconsin extended much farther south than today. In 1848, the first large-scale sawmills appeared. By the close of the Civil War, about 35 factories were roaring. The result was constant light showers of wood dust—at times an inch thick on the back streets. Hence, Oshkosh earned the moniker "Sawdust City." Excavations along Oshkosh riverbanks still reveal marbled layers of compacted sawdust.

This sawdust condemned the city to a painful series of conflagrations; an 1875 fire was so bad that the city—built of the cheap local timber—finally rebuilt with stone. Ironically, some of this stone came from Chicago, itself recently devastated by fire and rebuilt mostly with wood from Oshkosh sawmills!

◖ EAA AIR ADVENTURE MUSEUM AND FLY-IN CONVENTION

The state has officially decreed this museum (3000 Poberezny Rd., 920/426-4818, www. airventuremuseum.org, 8:30 A.M.–5 P.M. Mon.–Sat., 10 A.M.–5 P.M. Sun., $12.50 adults) a state treasure, a consequence no doubt of the 800,000 or so visitors who converge on Oshkosh for the annual fly-in sponsored by the Experimental Aircraft Association (EAA). More than 250 airplanes of every possible type are displayed in the museum—aerobatics, home-built, racers, and more. Five theaters, numerous display galleries, and tons of multimedia exhibits make this well worth the admission; kids (of all ages) absolutely adore the many, many hands-on exhibits in the Kidventure Gallery. (I still can't recover from the g-force machine.) Be there when flights are offered in old-timey planes, complete with the leather hat, goggles, and wind-blown hair. The museum is located off U.S. 41 at the WI 44 exit, next to Wittman Regional Airport. All in all, this is perhaps the best money spent for a family in the region.

EAA International Fly-In Convention

Oshkosh aviation pioneer Steve Wittman designed and built racing planes, one of which is on display at the Smithsonian. He was so impressive he drew the attention of Orville Wright and other airplane aficionados. Soon

EAA Fly-in Convention participants roaring by

after the EAA moved to Oshkosh, a tradition began: the gathering known as the Fly-In, now a legendary, jawdropping display of airplanes that draws hundreds of thousands of people from around the world.

And it's certainly a spectacle. The skies in the last week of July and into August are filled with planes and pilots who'll never shake their appetite for aviation the way it used to be done—strictly by the seat of your pants. Handmade and antique aircraft are the highlights, but lots of contemporary military aircraft are also on show. Thrilling air shows go on nonstop. In all, almost 12,000 aircraft and more than 750,000 people are on hand for this one. Remember to wear good shoes, a hat, and sunscreen, and carry water.

The Fly-In is held the last week of July and/or first week of August and runs 8 A.M.–8 P.M. daily; air shows start at 3 P.M. It doesn't come cheap; for nonmembers, prices are $37 a day adults.

OTHER SIGHTS
Paine Art Center and Gardens
A lumber baron's Tudor revival house, this museum (1410 Algoma Blvd., 920/235-6903, 11 A.M.–4 P.M. Tues.–Sun., $9 adults) displays meticulously appointed rooms showcasing period furnishings and antiques, along with 19th-century French Barbizon and U.S. art. Outside lie acres and acres of gardens; one, modeled after the Dutch Pond Garden at Hampton Court in England, features more than 100 varieties of roses. Legend has it the place is haunted, but the caretakers disavow any knowledge.

Oshkosh Public Museum
In a grand 1907 English-style home, this is one of the best public museums you'll see in a town of Oshkosh's size. Permanent holdings range in subject from local and natural history, china, and pressed glass to Native American ethnology and archaeology. One highlight is an eight-foot-tall Apostles Clock designed and built in the late 1800s by a German immigrant; it's considered one of Wisconsin's

THE REPUBLIC OF WINNECONNE

In 1967 the state of Wisconsin issued its annual highway map. Puzzled taverngoers in Winneconne – let's get this out of the way now, it's west of Oshkosh – tried to find their village. Gone, absent, forgotten, ignored.

With tongues nudged a bit into cheek, the village board voted to secede from the state; then it declared war. The new Republic of Winneconne's banner boasted: "We like it – where?" To which the governor, in Madison, said smiling, "By the way, where *is* Winneconne?" The brouhaha continued as the little village that wouldn't be ignored went through machinations of re-creating itself as a sovereign nation; all of this as the nation chuckled along with the resulting media barrage. They've never been overlooked since.

most treasured pieces of folk art. The museum (1331 Algoma Blvd., 920/424-4731, 10 A.M.–4:30 P.M. Tues.–Sat., 1–4:30 P.M. Sun.) is still, respectably, free.

Grand Opera House
Try to visit this architectural gem (100 High Ave., 920/424-2355), an 1883 edifice designed after majestic halls in Italy.

Oshkosh B'Gosh
This clothier, established in 1895, put Oshkosh on the map, fashion- and functionwise. Tours of the factory, where the dandy pinstriped bib overalls come together, are sadly no longer offered. (Darn insurance companies.) Instead, head for the **Oshkosh B'Gosh factory store** (Prime Outlets, 3001 S. Washburn, 920/426-5817), which features outlet prices.

ENTERTAINMENT AND EVENTS
The free monthly *The Scene* also lists Appleton and Green Bay happenings.

Bars and Music
Peabody's Ale House (544 N. Main St., 920/230-1110) has live music—blues to rock and jazz. For a basic watering hole without the cacophony of college students downing shots, try **Oblio's** (434 N. Main St., 920/426-1063). It's got a pressed-tin ceiling, an antique wood bar, and photos of old Oshkosh.

Cultural Events
Stage and theater shows are found on the campus of UW-Oshkosh at the **Frederic March Theatre** (926 Woodland Ave., 920/424-4417).

RECREATION
Fishing
Winnebago-region specialties are the white bass run (generally mid- to late May) and sheepshead. For a one-of-a-kind, only-in-Wisconsin experience, be here in February for the sturgeon spearing season.

Parks and Beaches
Asylum Point Park, a wildlife restoration area, has trails running from marshland to prairie to lakefront.

For swimming, jump in Lake Winnebago itself at **Menominee Park** along Millers Bay at Hazel and Merritt Streets. While there, sample the great zoo and "Little Oshkosh," one of the country's largest playgrounds and kiddie amusement parks.

Trail Systems
Of the 75 or so miles of multipurpose trail in the area, the main route is the **WIOUWASH Trail,** a crushed limestone surface meandering through woods, marshes, farm fields, and tallgrass prairie from Oshkosh to the Winnebago County line.

Camping
No state or county park camping options are very close. A private option is **Circle R Campground** (1185 Old Knapp Rd., 920/235-8909, $17); take exit WI 26 from U.S. 41 to Hwy. N and go east one mile.

ACCOMMODATIONS
Downtown
The least expensive option in downtown Oshkosh is the **Town Motel** (215 Division St., 920/233-0610, $50). Fresh coffee is the only extra.

STINKING WATER

Lake Winnebago dominates east-central Wisconsin. At 10 miles across and 30 miles north to south, this shallow lake – once a glacial marsh – is among the largest freshwater lakes fully locked within one state. It totals 88 miles of shoreline comprising 138,000 acres formed more than 25,000 years ago by a lobe of the Wisconsin glacier.

The lake was always crucial to Native Americans as a part of the water transport system along the Fox and Wolf Rivers. The name purportedly comes from a linguistic mix-up – or deliberate pejorative snub – from the French, who dubbed the Native American tribe they discovered here the "stinkers" (an updated transliteration); "Stinking Water" was a natural follow-up.

Lake Winnebago today is heavily populated with fishers and pleasure-crafters. In winter, up to 10,000 cars park on the frozen lake at any one time; if you're around in February, do not miss the annual throwback to Pleistocene days – the sturgeon-spearing season.

Wind east out of Fond du Lac via U.S. 151 to skirt the eastern shoreline along what locals call "the Ledge," the high breathtaking rise above Deadwood Point. The small town of Pipe along this route is home to an awesome 80-foot tower. Farther north is Calumet County Park, with six rare panther effigy mounds. (At the entrance to the park, stop at The Fish Tale Inn to see the largest male sturgeon ever caught on the lake.) An even better place to experience the lake is High Cliff State Park, along the northeastern edge.

There is another hotel lodging centrally located but it cannot be recommended for the price. What can be recommended, however, are the truly lovely rooms and welcoming proprietors of **Brayton B&B** (143 Church Ave., 920/267-0300, from $89).

West

Most Oshkosh accommodations are spread along the highway interchanges of U.S. 41 west of town. Cheapest of these is the always-economical **Marriott Fairfield Inn** (1800 S. Koeller Rd., 920/233-8504 or 800/228-2800, $70), off the 9th Street exit and offering a pool, whirlpool, and game room.

The **Hilton Garden Inn** (1355 W. 20th Ave., 920/966-1300, $84) is equidistant from attractions west and downtown and has a full slate of amenities.

FOOD
Supper Clubs and Fine Dining

The proprietors may dispute categorization as a supper club, but **Robbins** (1810 Omro Rd., 920/235-2840, 11 A.M.–10 P.M. Mon.–Sat., from 8 A.M. Sun., $7–19) closely fits the bill. Casual or formal, it's steaks and fresh fish; it also follows the Wisconsin tradition of in-house sausage-making and meat smoking.

Family Fare

Spacious but cozy, the **New Moon** (N. Main and Algoma Blvd., 920/232-0976, 7 A.M.–way late daily, $3–6), in a renovated 1875 beaut, is the place for coffee or a light meal. Sandwiches to creative soups (not your average offerings) are typical here—emphasizing local and state ingredients and products. It also offers live music and poetry readings.

Not far from Oshkosh, in little Omro, is the **Main Street Restaurant** (103 E. Main St., 920/685-5980, 5 A.M.–9 P.M. Mon.–Sat., 6 A.M.–8 P.M. Sun., $4 and up), housed in an 1881 grocery, shoe, and millinery store. Expect the occasional 40-pound turkeys and outstanding dressing to supplement the hearty family fare. You can also pick up a fishing lure at Al's Lure Shop, in a corner of the restaurant.

Drive-Ins

Oshkosh has two *classic* drive-ins. **Leon's** (121 W. Murdock Ave., 920/231-7755, 11 A.M.–11 P.M. Sun.–Thurs., till midnight Fri.–Sat. in summer) is a classic neon kind of place with delectable custards (and turtle sundaes!) and a mouthwatering homemade sloppy joe–style concoction. **Ardy and Ed's** (2413 S. Main St., 920/231-5455) has been around since 1948 and does not appear much changed. It still plays 1950s tunes, and the waitstaff still gets around aboard roller skates.

Fish Fries

Hands down, locals pick **Jeff's** (1005 Rugby St., 920/231-7450, dinner till 10 P.M. Mon.–Sat., lunch Fri. and Sun., breakfast Sun., $4–20) as the place to go for great seafood simultaneously down-home and cutting edge. The traditional perch at the Friday fish fry simply heads the list of seafood and steaks.

Brewpub

Fratello's Cafe is part of the complex of the **Fox River Brewing Company** (1501 Arboretum Dr., 920/232-2337, 11 A.M.–10 P.M. Mon.–Fri., 11 A.M.–11 P.M. Sat., 11 A.M.–9 P.M. Sun., $5). The attractive café interiors overlook the river; you can even boat up to the outdoor deck. Service has been iffy. Brewery tours are available Saturday.

Mexican

Head for **Lara's Tortilla Flats** (715 N. Main St., 920/233-4440, 11 A.M.–10 P.M. Mon.–Sat., $5–12), a real-deal family affair turning out excellent *norteño* food—the recipes came up with grandma from her Salinas boardinghouse a century ago. (Everything's made from scratch.) The decor features images of the clan's role in the Mexican Revolution as well as great-grandpa's role in capturing legendary *bandito* Gregorio Cortez.

INFORMATION

The Oshkosh Convention and Visitors Bureau (920/303-9200 or 877/303-9200, www.visitoshkosh.com) is southwest of the U.S. 41 and WI 44 interchange along Waukau Avenue.

GETTING THERE

The local **Greyhound** stop is at Wittman Regional Airport (920/231-6490). Not too many buses serve Oshkosh.

Lamers bus line (800/261-6600) runs between Milwaukee and Wausau, with stops in Stevens Point, New London, Appleton, Oshkosh, and Fond du Lac.

Fond du Lac

Fond du Lac often refers to itself as "First on the Lake"—sort of a loose take on the French, which translates literally as "bottom (or far end) of the lake."

History

Three separate Winnebago villages predated European permanent arrival in 1785. Despite its strategic location—at the base of a big lake and equidistant to the Fox-Wisconsin riverway—the town grew painfully slowly. Everywhere-to-be-seen town father, and later Wisconsin's first territorial governor, James Doty, had the town platted in 1835.

Boomtown status effectively eluded the place—timber was too far north and receding fast. The local constabulary, the story goes, couldn't afford a pair of handcuffs! However, a plank road, laboriously laid down from Sheboygan, became a vital channel of transportation from the Lake Michigan coast.

SIGHTS
Galloway House and Village

The stately mid-Victorian Italianate villa Galloway House (336 Old Pioneer Rd., 920/922-6390, 10 A.M.–4 P.M. daily Memorial Day weekend–Labor Day, $7 adults), originally finished in 1847, features 30 rooms, four fireplaces, and much Victorian opulence. Behind is a turn-of-the-20th-century village containing 23 restored regional dwellings and structures, including the Blakely Museum, an assortment of pioneer and early-20th-century Fond du Lac stuff, including an extensive local private Native American collection—even a mounted passenger pigeon.

FOND DU LAC

To Oshkosh
Lake Winnebago
To Green Bay and HIGH CLIFF STATE PARK
STRETCH EAT AND SLEEP
To Oshkosh and Green Bay
Supple's Marsh
Lakeside Park
W SCOTT ST
E SCOTT ST
JUKEBOX CHARLIE'S
JOHNSON ST
To Sheboygan
To Ripon and Eldorado Marsh
SCHREINER'S
DIVISION ST
RAMADA PLAZA HOTEL
ST. PAUL'S CATHEDRAL
PIER 15
JOHNSON ST
DIVISION ST
CVB
GROVE ST
OCTAGON HOUSE
BELLAFINI'S
ROGERSVILLE RD
MICROTEL INN AND SUITES
SEBASTIAN'S STEAKHOUSE
HOLIDAY INN HOLIDOME
PIONEER RD
GALLOWAY HOUSE AND VILLAGE
To Milwaukee
To Madison
To Milwaukee
0   1 mi
0   1 km
© AVALON TRAVEL

Octagon House

This 12-room private home (276 Linden St., 920/922-1608, www.octagonhousefdl.com, $15) was originally raised as a stockade against Native American attack. Later, it became a node on the Underground Railroad (you can add almost a dozen secret places to the number of rooms, including secret passages, tunnels, and one hidden room). And it wouldn't be complete without the requisite ghost reportedly wafting about. Tours must be arranged in advance.

St. Paul's Cathedral

This Episcopalian English Gothic stone cathedral (51 W. Division St., 920/921-3363, www. stpaulsepiscopalcathedral.org, 9 A.M.–4 P.M. Tues.–Fri., $2) houses the Oberammergau unified collection, a priceless assemblage of wood carvings. Tours are by appointment.

Lakeside Park

One of the better municipal parks anywhere is this 400-acre tract. The eastern part's eye-frying-white sentinel lighthouse is probably Fond du Lac's most recognizable symbol. Nearby are landscaped islands, a deer park, a minitrain, a harbor, and a marina, among other things. A carousel dating from the 1920s is one of the few extant wooden merry-go-rounds left in the state; it still runs on a simple two-gear clutch. All the horses are pegged—constructed wholly without nails.

Eldorado Marsh

Just a few miles west of Fond du Lac along WI 23 and Highway C is an unknown canoeists' paradise, the 6,000-acre Eldorado Marsh, which subsumes the 1,500-acre shallow flowage marsh. Locals refer to it as the "Everglades of the North." I'm not sure about that, but it is a tranquil, solitary spot.

EVENTS

Though it might get some argument from Port Washington to the southeast, Fond du Lac purports to hold the world's largest fish fry in June—more than 5,000 fish dinners and sandwiches are generally consumed in one gluttonous three-day **Walleye Weekend** (www. fdlfest.com).

RECREATION
Biking

The city has a balanced system of rural trails, including the great **Ledge Lookout Ride,** 45 miles on the eastern shore of Lake Winnebago along the Niagara Escarpment. Better yet is the **Wild Goose State Trail,** of which Fond du Lac is the northern terminus. The screened limestone trail stretches 34 miles south to the Horicon National Marsh, the city of Horicon, and beyond. A trail pass, which can be acquired at bike shops and some trailheads, is necessary.

Fishing

Fond du Lac is the southernmost access point for fishing on Lake Winnebago, the most popular fishing lake in the state. You gotta be here during sturgeon season!

ACCOMMODATIONS

Cheapest on the west side is the spartan **Stretch Eat and Sleep** (Pioneer Rd. at Hwy. OO and U.S. 41, 920/923-3131, $45–75), featuring air conditioning, a restaurant, and in-room computer access.

Microtel Inn and Suites (649 W. Johnson St./WI 23, 920/929-4000 or 888/771-7171, $59) has a health club, whirlpool, and more.

The **Holiday Inn Holidome** (625 Rolling Meadows Dr., 920/923-1440 or 800/465-4329, $109) offers its usual amenities.

There's only one option near the central area, the full-service **Ramada Plaza Hotel** (1 N. Main St., 920/923-3000 or 800/272-6232, $119 s, $129 d). It has an indoor pool, whirlpool, lounge, restaurant, health club, covered parking, and some suites. And, according to a few visitors, some possibly paranormal activity!

FOOD
Burgers and Ice Cream

The teenybopping **Jukebox Charlie's** (248 N. Hickory St., 920/923-8185, open at 4 P.M.

Tues.–Sun., $5) features poodle-skirted waitresses, 1950s music on the jukebox, and a dance club, with occasional revue-type shows. There are burgers, malts, and the like, along with homemade tater chips! Outside, under a 35-foot jukebox sign, carhops move on wheels.

Since the Civil War, the family of **Kelley Country Creamery** (W5215 Hwy. B, 920/923-1715, daily) has been a dairy mainstay in these parts. You'll love their ice cream, especially sitting on a porch looking at the cows the milk came from! Head south on U.S. 41, then east on Highway B.

Supper Clubs and Fish Fries

If it's steak you want, head for **Sebastian's Steakhouse** (770 S. Main St., 920/922-3333, dinner daily, $4–14), which is certainly good for the number of choices it gives you and for the excellent value.

Jim and Linda's Lakeview (W3496 Hwy. W, 920/795-4116, www.jimandlindas.net, dinner daily in high season, dinner Tues.–Sun. off-season, $12–45) serves four-course dinners (and fish fries). If nothing else, come for the view of the lake—the place is 30 feet from the eastern shoreline. It's in little Pipe; take U.S. 151 east to Highway W and then west.

Italian

Bellafini's (7 14th St., 920/929-8909, dinner Tues.–Sat., $5–12) is a gem for Italian food and friendliness—so have said more than one Italian! That said, it can get a bit busy, so be patient.

Family Dining

Arguably *the* Lake Winnebago culinary institution is **❰ Schreiner's** (168 N. Pioneer Rd., 920/922-0590, 6:30 A.M.–8:30 P.M. daily, $3–9), a hearty American-style family restaurant serving meals since 1938. The menu is broad, the servings copious, and the specials Midwestern. But the real highlight is the bread, made fresh on-site in the bakery. The New England clam chowder is also superb—so good it's on the restaurant's website (www.fdlchowder.com).

INFORMATION

The Fond du Lac Area Convention and Visitors Bureau (171 S. Pioneer Rd., 920/923-3010 or 800/937-9123, www.fdl.com) is well stocked to help.

GETTING THERE

The local **Greyhound** stop (920/921-4215) is at the Mobil gas station, 976 South Main Street. **Lamers** (800/261-6600) also stops here on its run between Wausau and Milwaukee.

West of Winnebago

RIPON

One of the most picturesque small towns anywhere, winding Ripon has an oddball and fascinating heritage. Founded in 1844 by an organization called the Wisconsin Phalanx as an experiment in communal living, it was named Ceresco, after the Roman goddess of agriculture, and attempted to implement in pure form the democratic principles of French social progressive François Charles Marie Fourier. A decade later, it came to fame as the birthplace of the Republican Party. (This claim, incidentally, is hotly disputed by a few other communities in the United States, but hey, in 2004, the U.S.

Senate passed a bill recognizing Ripon's status, and even the U.S. Postal Service commemorated it with a postmark.)

Later, Ripon became the birthplace of another political pioneer—Carrie Chapman Catt, one of the founders and first presidents of both the American Women's Suffrage Association and the League of Women Voters; it was under her lead that the 19th Amendment to the Constitution was finally passed.

❰ The Little White Schoolhouse

Along the 300 block of Blackburn Street (WI 44) stands the birthplace of the Republican

© THOMAS HUHTI

the Little White Schoolhouse

Party, the Little White Schoolhouse (303 Blackburn St., 920/748-4730, 10 A.M.–4 P.M. daily June–Aug., weekends spring and fall, $1). This official national monument doesn't hold much more than a few mementos, but it's still fun to poke around in.

At the time of writing, rumor had it that adjacent to this a new **Republican Presidents Museum** was planned.

Other Sights

Ripon College (300 Seward St., 920/748-8364) overlooks the town from a hill and houses the C. J. Rodman Center for the Arts, containing two paintings by Sir Anthony Van Dyck.

Five miles or so south of town on WI 44/49, then east along Reed's Corner Road, is **Larson's Famous Clydesdales** (W12654 Reeds Corner Rd., 920/748-5466, Mon.–Sat. May–Oct., tours $15). More than a dozen of the equine giants made famous by sentimental Budweiser beer commercials are bred and raised here, including a national champion six-horse hitch. Demonstrations are given at 1 P.M.,

and visitors can pet the horses. Reservations are required.

GREEN LAKE

Green Lake is approximately one-sixth the size of Ripon, but this flyspeck town pulls in tons of visitors, all coming for the eponymous 7,320-acre lake—the deepest in the state, if not the largest. In 1867, the first resort west of Niagara Falls was built here. When Chicagoans heard about it, the rush was on. Within three decades, posh resorts had begun to dot the shores. Despite its granddaddy status as a resort, the tourists are neither condescending bluebloods nor so numerous that the small-town charm is obliterated.

Sights

Explore local history in Friday Park (along Mill St.) at an old **railroad depot** housing historic artifacts; architecturally even more appealing are the historic 1910 **Thrasher Opera House** (506 Mill St.) and 1898 **Green Lake County Courthouse** (492 Hill St.).

On the water, Heidel House Resort operates the popular **Escapade Tours** (643 Illinois Ave., 920/294-3344, $13). Brunch, cocktail, dinner, and sightseeing excursions are also offered.

Scenic Drive

Rustic Road 22, also known as White River Road, ends at Highway D, north of Princeton, but affords the experience of two original plank bridges and views of mostly DNR-protected wetlands. From Green Lake, head west along WI 23 to Princeton, then north on Highway D.

Speaking of Princeton, do check out this little treasure. It's a time-locked little burg plunked along the Fox River and has plenty of anachronistic architecture, worthy galleries, and the state's largest weekly flea market. Princeton is also site of the long-running **Cattle Fair.** For ice cream and light foods, you can check out, let's see, a refurbished gas station or renovated general store; or find excellent Italian food (along with tarot cards) in a 19th-century Victorian at **Mimi's** (523 Water St., 920/295-6775, lunch and dinner daily, $6–15).

Or how about a drive with an eco-bent?

A number of miles west of the little town of Montello, then south on Highway F, takes you to **Muir Park and Fountain Lake Farm,** the boyhood home of John Muir as well as a birder's paradise. Many sandhill cranes can be seen here—the Fox River Unit of the Horicon National Wildlife Refuge is across the road. It's estimated that Marquette County alone holds one of North America's highest concentrations, about 1,100.

Recreation

There's an awful lot to do in Green Lake, but fishing tops the list (though the golf ain't bad either). The **Green Lake Marina** (485 Park Dr., 920/294-6221) rents all craft.

For land-based recreation, there may be more golf courses per capita in the Green Lake vicinity than anywhere in Wisconsin. The Scottish links style **Golf Courses of Lawsonia** (WI 23 W, 920/294-3320) have been rated as among America's top public courses, according to *Golf Digest* magazine, which gave the elevated tees and merciless bunkers four stars. The **Tuscumbia Country Club** (680 N. Illinois

BIRTH OF THE REPUBLICAN PARTY

By the early 1850s, regarding slavery the powers within the contemporary political parties were impotent, willfully ignorant or hamstrung by both sides. Antislavery activists within the Whig Party in Ripon ultimately grew tired enough to call for action. In 1852, Alvan Earle Bovay visited Horace Greeley in New York City to discuss matters. The Whigs were waning, but what was next?

Then, Senator Stephen Douglass of Illinois provided an opportunity for a minor revolution with his Kansas-Nebraska Bill; the proposal was to extend slavery beyond the perimeters of the earlier Missouri Compromise.

Bovay immediately and quietly summoned 53 other voters back to Ripon to devise a battle plan for opposing the slavery proponents. Ripon had long been a nerve center of the abolitionist movement. So strong was its opposition, in fact, that the city was the site of what's known as "Booth's War," a guerrilla skirmish between Milwaukee abolitionist Sherman Booth, who helped escaped slaves along the Underground Railroad, and the federal authorities; local citizens helped Booth and frustrated the authorities for a five-year period.

Bovay hoped to organize the abolitionists into a cohesive force to be called Republicans ("a good name...with charm and prestige," he said). His oratory was effective, and the Republican Party was born on March 20, 1854, in the Little White Schoolhouse in Ripon. Official declaration of its platform came two years later in Pittsburgh; standing near the podium was Abraham Lincoln, who, four years later, would become the party's first successful presidential candidate.

Ave., 920/294-3240) is Wisconsin's oldest course; it's known as one of the best-manicured courses in the Midwest.

Accommodations

Rates are *really* high around here during the summer.

A motel with a resort complex sums up **Bay View** (439 Lake St., 920/294-6504, $105), a good deal for the money. Anglers love this place—there's plenty of fishing and boat rentals. Some kitchenettes and suites are available.

One of Wisconsin's best and best-known resorts is the (**Heidel House Resort** (643 Illinois Ave., 920/294-6128 or 800/444-2812, www.heidelhouse.com, $165–615), a 20-acre, self-contained sybaritic universe. More than 200 guest rooms, including some estate buildings, run the gamut of luxury—it even plunked down $200 million for a new spa. The dining is superb.

Both **Miller's Daughter** (453 North St., 920/294-0717, www.millersdaughter.com, $155) and **Angel Inn** (372 S. Lawson Dr., 920/294-3087, www.angelinns.com, from $115) are superb bed and breakfasts—truly special, each of them, so take your pick.

Food

A local favorite is **Norton's** (380 S. Lawson Dr., 920/294-6577, lunch and dinner daily, $9–28), the only supper club on the lake accessible by water. Norton's has grand alfresco dining on a lakeside deck.

Ready to splurge? Rated one of the best restaurants in Wisconsin is the (**Grey Rock Mansion Restaurant** (643 Illinois Ave., 920/294-6128 or 800/444-2812, www.heidelhouse.com, dinner Tues.–Sat., brunch Sun., dinner Thurs.–Sat. in off-season) in the Heidel House Resort and Conference Center. Housed in an 1890s building, the charming rich woods interiors and fireplaces support the food. The walleye here will knock your socks off.

Information

The **Green Lake Area Chamber of Commerce** (550 Mill St., 920/294-3231 or 800/253-7354, www.visitgreenlake.com) is in town.

WAUPACA AND THE CHAIN O' LAKES

The Waupaca area lies at the western edge of the east-central waters region and qualifies as hydrophilic: 22 spring-fed lakes southwest of Waupaca form one of the longest recreational stretches in the lower half of Wisconsin—240 lakes in the county alone. Settlement began in the region around 1848; the first flour mill went up a year after the state's birth. The city was named for an altruistic Potawatomi chief, Sam Waupaca, who collapsed and died after convincing local Natives not to kill the white settlers.

Sights

The most popular activity in the Chain O' Lakes is to take a breezy ride aboard an authentic sternwheeler, the former flagship of a brewery, the *Chief* (or on the more sedate motor yacht *Lady of the Lakes*). The 90-minute tours take in 8–11 lakes of the chain. Sunday champagne brunch tours ($14) are available. **Tours** (715/258-2866) begin running Memorial Day weekend and depart four times daily 11:30 A.M.–4 P.M. for the eight-lake tour aboard the *Chief;* rates run $10 adults. There are fewer departures during the weeks before Memorial Day and after Labor Day. The 11-lake tour on the *Lady of the Lakes* costs the same and lasts two hours; it departs at 4 P.M.

Just southwest of Waupaca along WI 22 lies tiny **Rural,** honest to goodness a town that time forgot. It's a Yankee town stuck in the middle 1800s. Virtually the entire city, along the switchbacking banks of the Crystal River, is on the National Register of Historic Places. The architectural renaissance is impressive; it's gotten so popular that WI 22 was rerouted *around* the town to avoid spoiling it. It's also a good spot to pick up antiques. Check out the unbelievable selection at **Walker's Barn,** a converted chicken farm that now seems to have about half the antiques in Waupaca County.

Another short jaunt out of the city via Highway K takes you to **Red Mill.** The biggest waterwheel in the state, it's been converted into a hodgepodge of shops offering handicrafts, antiques, and lots and lots of scented candles in an original interior. One of the few extant covered bridges in Wisconsin is also there (400 handcrafted oak pegs were used in its construction), along with the Chapel in the Woods. Red Mill lies along a beautiful stretch of the Crystal River with a picturesque park.

Scenic Drives

Two of those farm-to-market narrow country lanes in the area are **Rural Road** and **Emmons Creek Road,** both jutting westward out of Rural toward Hartman Creek State Park. The former serpentines across the Crystal River several times; the latter takes in a tributary trout stream of the Crystal and lots of woodland.

South of Waupaca along Highway E (itself fairly narrow) is Saxeville and, still farther south, **26th Road,** along Highway W out of town; 26th Road stretches to Highway H along the Pine River Valley, a Class II trout stream. This drive passes several dwellings—one a log cabin—predating the Civil War.

Recreation

A segment of the National Scenic Ice Age Trail is in **Hartman Creek State Park** (715/258-2372); the county section totals 20 miles and links on both ends with Portage County's segment. The park has a hike-in primitive cabin offered on a first-come, first-served basis. The state park also maintains off-road bike trails. The park is also popular with canoeists and boaters, since most of the upper Chain O' Lakes are either in or adjacent to state park lands.

The lolling, tranquil Crystal River is perfect for canoeing. Organized excursions leave from **Ding's Dock** (along Hwy. Q, 715/258-2612), which also rents decent cottages.

This is prime touring area for bikers; trails run along waterways and through some Amish farmstead areas. Northwest of the city, the topography shifts to rolls of kettles and moraines.

Camping

Hartman Creek State Park is the best bet for camping. Otherwise, in or near the city are six private campgrounds, including some in town: **Waupaca Camping Park** (E2411 Holmes Rd., 715/258-8010, $20) has separate tent areas.

Accommodations

This is another resort/cottage area, so despite the large numbers of places, few are cheap. More upscale lodging is at the **Best Western Grand Seasons** (110 Grand Seasons Dr., junction of WI 10 and 54, 715/258-9212 or 887/880-1054, $79), which has a pool, health club, sauna, and enormous game room.

In anachronistic Rural (*the* place for a quaint getaway) is the **C Crystal River Inn** (E1369 Rural Rd., 715/258-5333 or 800/236-5789, www.crystal-riverinn.com, $70–168), an old farmstead. The six original farmhouse guest rooms (with myriad styles and amenities) are done with antiques and brass beds. All the rooms have views of either the river, a wildwood garden, or the backyard garden. You'll also find cottages and a "Little House on the Prairie." Superb.

Food and Entertainment

The Clear Water Harbor (N2757 Hwy. QQ, 715/258-2866, www.clearwaterharbor.com, from 10 A.M. daily, $3), known locally as the "Har Bar," serves a menu varying from pub grub sandwiches (try its famous 'shroomburger) to salads and a Friday fish fry. It's also popular for summer entertainment, with a huge deck on the lakeside. It's open seasonally. From here, you can do the Wally Walk up the road into King to the very local **Wally's Bar** (N2702 County Rd. QQ, 715/258-2160), where you can get a Lunch Box shot: beer with amaretto and orange juice. (It's tasty if you can down it quickly.)

A respectable eatery (a place you'd take your grandma) is **Simpson's** (222 S. Main St., 715/258-2330, lunch and dinner daily, $4 and up), a subdued supper club also known as the Indian Room. Simpson's has been serving lunch and dinner since the 1930s, specializing in chicken with mushrooms and wine sauce.

Information

The **Waupaca Area Chamber of Commerce** (221 S. Main St., 715/258-7343 or 888/417-4040, www.waupacamemories.com) has all the info you need.

The Wolf River Region

MENOMINEE INDIAN RESERVATION

The Menominee nation represents the oldest established inhabitants of the territory of Wisconsin. Unlike the diasporic nature of many U.S. tribes, the Menominee are strictly Wisconsin residents. The reservation lies a chip-shot north of Shawano and abuts the southern perimeter of the Chequamegon-Nicolet National Forest and the northern edge of the much smaller Stockbridge Indian Reservation. All Wisconsinites nod at its crown jewel, the Wolf River, one of the region's top draws.

History

Anthropologists have surmised that the Menominee, an Algonquian-speaking tribe, may have been in the Wisconsin territory as far back as 10,000 years ago. The tribe and its many bands once controlled regions of the Upper Great Lakes from as far south as Milwaukee to the Escanaba River in Michigan's Upper Peninsula and the entire breadth of Wisconsin.

Beginning in 1817, a series of breached federal treaties gradually eroded Menominee sovereignty until, by 1854, they were allowed only 12 townships on the present-day reservation; some of the ceded land was turned over to the Oneida and Stockbridge Indians for their own reservations. Almost 10 million acres dwindled to 200,000.

The Menominee, who had been given reservation status by a treaty signed near the Wolf River's Keshena Falls, asked for their status as natives to be terminated in 1961 in an attempt at federal assimilation. It was a dismal failure, and reservation status was reinstated in 1973. The tribe today numbers approximately 6,500, more than half of whom live on the reservation.

Menominee Indian Reservation Forest

The 223,500 acres of forest surrounding the reservation include some of the most pristine stands of hardwoods, hemlock, and pine in the Great Lakes region; it's regarded as an invaluable ecosystem. The tribe has had a lumber operation since 1908, one of the first and largest Native-owned in the United States; they had been trading lumber with the Winnebago long before European contact. Their high-tech present-day plant is the largest and most modern in the region. More than two billion board feet have been removed from the forest—more than twice the entire yield. Yet the Menominee have been lauded by international environmentalists for instituting a radical sustainable ecosystem model, now being examined by Indian bands from the Atlantic Coast to the Nuu-chah-nulth group of tribes from Vancouver Island. Forestry experts from as far away as Cambodia and Indonesia have come to the tribe's new forestry institute.

🌊 Wolf River

Meandering through the reservation from its headwaters in Lily to the north is the nascent Wolf River, a part of the Fox River system, which includes the Fox and Wolf Rivers headwaters, the lower Fox River, and Lake Winnebago. Quiet at its source, it picks up steam as it crosses through Langlade, and by the time it hits the reservation, it's got a bit of a dander up. This stretch of the state-designated Outstanding Water Resource and federally-designated wild river is perhaps the most spectacular. It drops almost 1,000 feet as it crosses the reservation, from the multihued juttings and white water of Smokey Falls to the eerie canyons of the Wolf River Dells. Water conditions range from placid—below Post Lake—to hair-raising—in sections near Smokey Falls.

The colorful toponymy describes it well: Little Slough Gundy, Sherry Rapids, Horse Race Rapids, Twenty Day Rips, and more. The stretch of river between Gilmore's Mistake and Smokey Falls—the lower terminus for most rafters—can be rife with midrange rapids, some up to eight feet.

So pristine are these waters that the Wolf River was the inspiration for the state's most enduring environmental debate—whether or not a mine to the northwest in Crandon would endanger the ecology. And in terms of recreation—these waters are, indeed, blue ribbon for rafters and kayakers.

The river has sections for neophytes and for hard-core river runners. (During high-water periods, operators shut down trips—proof it can be serious business.) Outfitters in these parts generally don't supply guides or captains, so you're on your own. White-water enthusiasts also note: The Red River nearby—Gresham, especially—is also quite good for kayaking.

There are a handful of tour operators in the area; many just rent boats, while others run full six-hour trips. Most offer camping. **River Forest Rafts** (715/882-3351, www.wolfriver-camping.com) has watercraft/bike rentals and has trails for mountain bikes.

Operating out of Keshena on the Menominee Indian Reservation is **Big Smokey Falls Rafting** (715/799-3359), with three runs between the W. W. Bridge paralleling WI 55 through three falls areas.

For a one-of-a-kind lodging option, try **Jesse's Historic Wolf River Lodge** (W2119 Taylor Rd., 715/882-2182, www.wolfriverlodge.com, $100–300) in White Lake. Rustic deep woods relaxing best describes it. There are lodge rooms, various cabins, even a funky tree house that is beyond description. All rooms come with a rib-sticking breakfast.

Off the river and aside roads, the Wolf River is worth investigating on foot. **Wolf River Dells** has a short nature trail leading to rough multicolored granite cliffs overlooking the Wolf for hundreds of yards along both the upper and lower dells. The Dells are four miles from a well-marked turnoff from WI 55 along a road that alternates from hardpack gravel to nerve-wracking. A footbridge crosses the 40-foot gurgling Smokey Falls to a small midriver island. Purportedly, the mist from the waters is actually smoke from the pipe of a spirit living within the falls. **Spirit Rock,** a couple of miles above Keshena Falls, is also significant.

According to legend it's really a petrified Menominee warrior who angered the earth. This warrior, Ko-Ko-Mas-Say-Sa-Now, allegedly asked for immortality and was thrust into the earth forever. Some believe kind spirits come to offer rings of tobacco, and their willowy vapors can be observed flitting among the trees in the dusky night.

Oh, don't forget fishing. One of Wisconsin's designated fly-fishing-only stretches of blue-ribbon trout waters is near Hollister.

Menominee Logging Camp Museum

The Menominee Logging Camp Museum (Hwy VV, north of Keshena, 715/799-3757, 9 A.M.–3 P.M. Tues.–Sat., 11 A.M.–4 P.M. Sun., May 1–Oct. 15, $10 adults), at Grignon Rapids along the Wolf River, north of the Wolf at Highway VV along WI 47, is the largest and most comprehensive exhibit of timber heritage in the United States (it is also pricey). Seven hand-hewn log buildings and more than 20,000 artifacts re-create an early 1900s logging camp. The rustic feel adds to the experience. Of note are the 12-to-a-bunk bunkhouse and the 1,000 pairs of oxen shoes, not to mention a 400-year-old pine log.

Powwows

Two powwows are held annually. On (or close to) Memorial Day weekend, the **Veteran Powwow** honors the reservation's military veterans. Larger is the **Annual Menominee Nation Contest Powwow,** held the first weekend in August. This is one of the largest cultural events in the Upper Midwest. Both are held in the natural amphitheater Woodland Bowl.

STOCKBRIDGE-MUNSEE INDIAN RESERVATION

The Stockbridge-Munsee are an Algonquian-speaking band of the Mohican Indians. The three tribes composing the band (along with a fourth, which eventually opted for assimilation) stretch throughout the Connecticut and Hudson River Valleys. This band is one of the best traveled of any in the state, though that's hardly of its own doing; the word "Mohican" means, aptly enough, "people of never-still waters." They first appeared in Wisconsin in the early 1820s, living in the Fox River Valley (hence, the town of Stockbridge on the eastern shore of Lake Winnebago; the Stockbridge cemetery there is a National Historic Site) along with the Munsee, a Delaware tribe also forced west by European expansion. Some Stockbridge Indians decamped to Indiana Territory in Kansas; others moved to Red Springs, Wisconsin, to live on land ceded to them in 1856 by the Menominee (who got $20,000 for 2.5 million acres). The tribe numbers about 1,500.

Sights

The **Stockbridge Munsee Historical Library Museum** (715/793-4270, 8 A.M.–4:30 P.M. Mon.–Fri., free) has one of the best archives of Native American material in Wisconsin, including maps dating from the 1600s (not on public display). Most exhibits are on the day-to-day life of the Stockbridge and the later fur trade. Of note is the section on the missionaries—those stoic Jesuits—including a catechism written in Mohican and a 1745 Bible presented to the Stockbridge by an emissary of the Prince of Wales. The library and museum are four miles east of Bowler.

SHAWANO

Shawano lies along the proud Wolf River at one of its widest points and serves as the recreational heart of the Wolf. The lake bearing the name Shawano sits to the east, full of fish.

The name (pronounced SHAW-no) is another mellifluous result of the Menominee term for the large lake: Sha-Wah-Nah-Pay-Sa, "Lake to the South."

Settlers first came to work in lumber mills built in the 1840s and then to serve traffic on an old military road (Main Street was part of it). The city now has one of the country's largest milk-products plants and a leading artificial breeding cooperative.

But it's recreation that draws most

visitors—fishing on Shawano Lake and whitewater rafting on the wild Wolf River. This is true-blue, mom-and-pop, basic family-style resort country.

Sights

The **Heritage Park Museum** (524 N. Franklin St., 715/526-3536, 1:30–4:30 P.M. Sat.–Sun. in summer, $3 adults) adjoins the Wolf River and Sunset Island downtown on a somewhat dusty compound. The museum features cheesemaking exhibits and a collection of early street lamps, among other buildings. The downtown also has a restored old depot with assorted historical flotsam.

Seven miles south of town, the almost unknown **Navarino Wildlife Area** is a restored 1,400-acre glacial lakebed, once a swamp and wetland that was drained and farmed for a century. Fifteen dikes have re-created the wetlands—sedge meadow to cattail marsh. Prairie and oak savanna restoration work is ongoing. The marshes support a resident family of sandhill cranes; the best wildlife-viewing is along the Wolf River drainages on the western fringes, near McDonald Road. A nature center (715/526-4226, Mon. and Fri. only) is at the site. Get to the wildlife area via WI 156 and McDonald Road.

The **Mielke Theater** (715/526-6171) stands in an isolated, bucolic setting with a country garden and offers year-round cultural events varying from an arts and crafts fair (a good time to scout for Midwestern handicrafts) to children's theater and plenty of concerts. Go a mile north on WI 29 and then follow signs along Highway HHH.

Scenic Drives

Definitely pick up a great map of the *Pineries to the Present* state heritage tours (four!). The tours are fully detailed and worth a whole day of checking out extant sights in two counties!

West of Shawano approximately 25 miles is tiny **Wittenburg,** the endpoint of one of Wisconsin's Rustic Roads, this one Highway M, which ends in **Tigerton.** There are lovely scenes on this route—historic round barns and stone buildings (including a gas station), and closet-size historical museums in both Wittenburg and Tigerton.

Tigerton was also the home of Wisconsin's first antigovernment militia, the Posse Comitatus, who made some waves in the early 1980s before retreating into obscurity after several of its leaders were jailed. They've been pretty quiet since, though there are definitely still members out there. An important thing to remember in these days of militias under every rock is that these folks have always been around.

Events

Every August, Shawano hosts three days of fiddlin' and pickin' during the **Folk Festival** (www.shawanoarts.com) at Mielke Theater and Park. Featured in prior years have been national folk acts, along with such diverse activities as Japanese *koto* and tea ceremonies.

Recreation

The **Mountain Bay Trail** is a 65-mile multiuse trail connecting Green Bay, Shawano, and Wausau. It's a grand trail and leads to numerous other trails. Ditto with the **WIOUWASH Trail,** which intersects with the Mountain Bay Trail in Eland.

Closest public **camping** is on the north shore of Shawano Lake, via Highway H, with 90 campsites in a decent wooded area with a great big beach. Sites run $11.

Accommodations

A good budget option is the strictly motel **Pine Acre** (1346 E. Green Bay St., 715/524-6665 or 800/730-5236, $45), with few amenities but excellently appointed rooms (and one cottage) and low prices. It's on a nicely wooded lot.

Most of Shawano is classic Wisconsin rustic lodging country—cabins and cottages that are clean but very, very simple. Rates vary: You can find a cabin for four folks for as low as $600 a week—not a bad deal. A good example of Shawano lodging is **Bamboo Shores** (W5873 Cedar Ave., 715/524-2124 or 800/969-2124, $1,000–2,000 per week), which has cottages that can sleep 6–10.

Food

A popular supper club with a few creative twists on the menu (duck confit, for example) is **Cotton Patch** (W4890 Lake Dr., 715/745-2101, dinner Wed.–Sun., brunch Sun., $8–22); they also have live entertainment Friday and Saturday.

It's strictly German food at **Sigrid's Bavarian Trail** (Hwy. H on Loon Lake Dr., 715/745-2660, lunch and dinner Tues.–Sun., $6–12), which also has live entertainment and a German deli, all overlooking Loon Lake.

Information

The visitors center of the chamber of commerce (213 E. Green Bay St., 715/524-2139 or 800/235-8528, www.shawanocountry.com) is well-stocked for you!

WOODS AND WATERS: NORTHEASTERN WISCONSIN

With one of the planet's highest ratios of lakes to land—37 percent of the total surface area is water—cartographically, this region is more blue than green. So it's of little wonder this place is such an "escape."

Escape *is* the key. Local populations run in inverse proportion to the saturating numbers of tourists. Two counties, Iron and Florence, are among the least-populated in the entire state; Florence County has precisely zero incorporated towns.

Somewhere among the few highways crisscrossing the region is a north-south division oft discussed by Wisconsinites—a Thoreau-esque zone of tranquility rather than a Great North Woods Mason-Dixon line. A popular Northern Wisconsin wordsmith once said, "Well, we basically consider everything south of U.S. 2 to be Confederate." That's pretty far north.

PLANNING YOUR TIME

Well, a weekend is tough, particularly if you plan to blaze a trail from the south for the weekend. If so, your place of rest would be either **Minocqua, Woodruff, and Arbor Vitae**

HIGHLIGHTS

LOOK FOR ◖ TO FIND RECOMMENDED SIGHTS, ACTIVITIES, DINING, AND LODGING.

◖ **Peshtigo Fire Museum:** On the same day as the Great Chicago Fire, an even greater and deadlier conflagration vanquished Peshtigo (page 225).

◖ **Peshtigo River Parkway:** Marinette County has more waterfalls than any other in Wisconsin, many along this wilderness Rustic Road (page 227).

◖ **Eagle River Chain of Lakes:** A resort area with endless recreation, its jewel is the world's longest chain of lakes (page 240).

◖ **Snowmobile Alley:** Explore local ethos at a rousing championship sled race, a 'biling

museum, and a hall of fame to the rocket riders (page 243).

◖ **Waswagoning:** Perhaps the most precious cultural educational spot in Wisconsin is this reconstructed living-history Ojibwa village (page 255).

◖ **Turtle-Flambeau Flowage:** Ah, visit that glorious Wisky wilderness – the Badger State's Boundary Waters (page 256).

◖ **Iron County's Waterfalls:** Not quite as many as in Marinette County, but these are (shhh!) higher and have a bit more thunder (page 260).

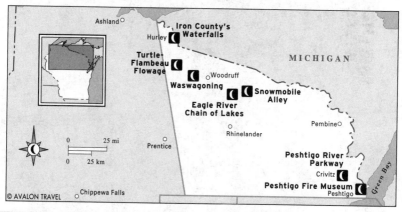

(it's all one place up here) or **Eagle River,** and pick one or two of the highlights. This is vacation land, so that's why so many resorts are by-the-week. You spend two days doing not a damn thing but sit by your cabin's lake and snooze, then get squirrelly and start

exploring—this author does it counter-clockwise, based in either of the above: a day and a half each in Marinette County (Peshtigo River region), the Nicolet National Forest, Northern Highland American Legion State Forest, and Iron County.

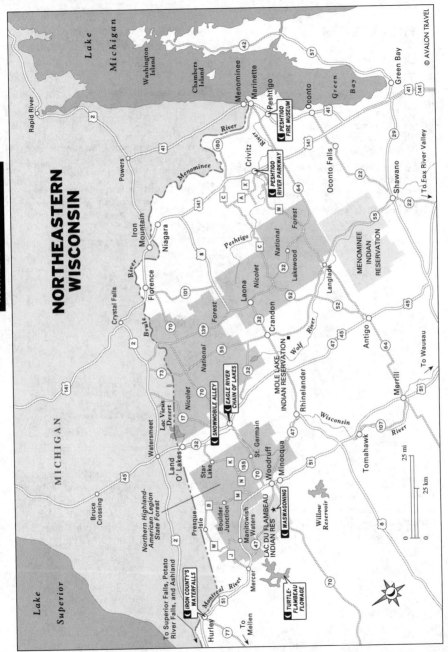

NORTHEASTERN WISCONSIN

© AVALON TRAVEL

Green Bay to Marinette

For the most part, the great old bay isn't visible at all. If you want a lakeside tour, Highways J, S, and Y, in that order, really track the bay.

OCONTO

This little community was home to the Archaic period's Copper Culture Native Americans five millennia ago, their burial site now a state park. Great Lakes historians debate whether Oconto—not De Pere—actually became the initial settlement site of the St. Francis Xavier Mission in 1669.

At the corner of Chicago and Main Streets is the first church ever built by the Christian Science religion.

Copper Culture State Park (920/826-7304) lies on the north bank of the Oconto River. The site has yielded 45 ceremonial burial sites from 4,500 years ago, during the Old Copper period. These early denizens were the first to develop commercial wares (some have been found as far away as New Mexico) and to fashion copper into tools. The park is quite understated (show up in winter and you'll probably be alone) and contains a minuscule museum, open relatively sporadically.

Practicalities

Consider a swing north to Peshtigo and **Schussler's Supper Club** (Hwy. B West, 715/582-4962, dinner Tues.–Sun., $6–12) which looks a bit weary inside but has copious German (real schnitzel) and Old World European fare (plus steaks and prime rib) and fresh bakery and desserts.

A good side trip to quaff a brew, **Hunters and Fisherman's Bar** (133 W. Main St., 920/829-5228) in Lena, is chock-full of unbelievable taxidermy. While in Lena, stop by the great **Kugel Cheese Mart** (Old Hwy. 141, 920/829-5537, www.kugelscheese.com), too.

C PESHTIGO FIRE MUSEUM

A—make that *the*—highlight here is the old church turned into the Peshtigo Fire Museum

THE GREAT PESHTIGO FIRE

October 8, 1871, was quite literally a day from hell. Most of the country was shocked at the news of the Great Chicago Fire and the incipient fame of Mrs. O'Leary's cow. But on the very same day, diminutive Peshtigo, Wisconsin, suffered an even more devastating fire, one unknown to most Americans.

Incessant dry weather sparked repeated minor fires for hundreds of miles around Peshtigo. Merging due to stiff winds, a virtual tornado descended on Peshtigo – vulnerable, *wooden* Peshtigo – and engulfed it seemingly within minutes. Many of Peshtigo's 2,000 residents died asleep. The fire eventually raged up the Green Bay coast, into Menominee, Michigan, and grazing Marinette, scorching 400 square miles in all.

Every building in the community save one (and a cross in the cemetery) was destroyed. Despite the steaming waters, helpless victims leapt into the Peshtigo River and thereby saved their lives. In Peshtigo alone, 800 (or more) people perished. The total regional death toll has been estimated at 1,200, though no official tally will ever make certain. Whatever the sum, Peshtigo was one of the worst conflagrations in United States history.

(Oconto Ave., 715/582-3244, peshtigofire.info, 10 A.M.–4:30 P.M. daily June–Oct. 8—the fire's anniversary, free). The museum is rather spartan—scant objects survived the furnace heat—but as such is quite a powerful encapsulation of the grim 1871 Peshtigo fire. A few pictures in particular offer a powerful look at the tragedy. There's a somber cemetery adjacent, in which several hundred of the victims are interred.

To reflect on the horror of the fire, wander through the **Peshtigo Wildlife Area,** six miles southeast on Highway BB, on Peshtigo Point.

Marinette and Vicinity

MARINETTE

The sister cities of Marinette, Wisconsin, and Menominee, Michigan, flank the Menominee River as it merges into Lake Michigan. The Wisconsin sibling was named for Queen Marinette, the daughter of a Menominee chieftain and the Chippewa-French wife of a local fur trader in the late-18th century. It provides all the incentive the locals need to affix *Queen* to everything, including the city's name.

The city once served as Wisconsin's lumber hub (producing more white pine than anywhere else in the world). A staggering 10.6 *billion* board feet of timber floated to town down the Menominee River—even more astonishing given the region's pervasive waterfalls.

Ah, waterfalls. For sheer number of cascades in a county, Marinette County can't be beat.

Sights

The **Marinette County Logging Museum** (715/732-0831, 10 A.M.–4:30 P.M. Tues.–Sat. June–Labor Day, $2 adults), by the river in Stephenson Island Park, contains replicas of two logging camps, a stable, and a blacksmith shop (all done by one dedicated man). One can't help being impressed by the old sled-load of about 50 pine logs out front being consigned and hauled to the mills.

The area rivers—the Peshtigo and the Menominee—both make for good rafting with some adequate white water. Contact the local tourist office or the County Parks Office (715/732-7530) for maps and information.

Accommodations

Marinette Inn (1450 Marinette Ave., 715/732-0593, www.marinetteinn.com, $55) has spruced itself up and now offers lots of amenities. This is a great value for the price.

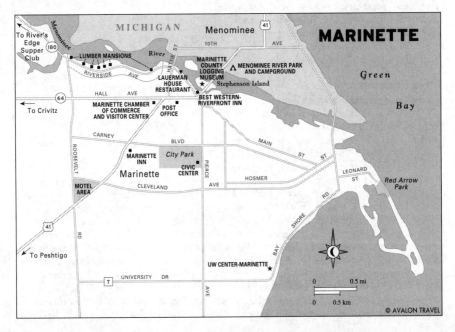

© THOMAS HUHTI

one of Marinette County's many waterfalls

Right in the heart of downtown, left off U.S. 41 onto Riverside Avenue along the Menominee River, the **Best Western-Riverfront Inn** (1821 Riverside Ave., 715/732-0111, $79) offers rooms with river views.

Food

Marinette is close to yooper country—a yooper would be a resident of Michigan's Upper Peninsula—so pasties, a regional specialty, are pervasive.

The **River's Edge Supper Club** (N4178 Hwy. 180, 715/735-7721, dinner daily Mon.–Sat., $10–25) has a glorious riverine location and some surprising creativity to bolster its supper club menu (good veal, for once). Even auslander food snobs were modestly impressed when taken here.

Perhaps one of the best foodie experiences in the northeast is ◖ **Lauerman House Restaurant** (1975 Riverside Ave., 715/732-7800, www.lauermanhouse.com, lunch Tues.–Fri., dinner Mon.–Sat., $18–36), a French fusion bistro tucked into a stately Queen Anne B&B.

Information

The **Marinette Chamber of Commerce and Visitor Center** (601 Marinette Ave., 800/236-6681, www.marinettecounty.com) is in a bright little house.

◖ PESHTIGO RIVER PARKWAY

Dropping in latitude faster than any river in the state and featuring one of the longest stretches of active white water in the Midwest, the winding Peshtigo River begins in the north-central part of Wisconsin near Crandon, bisects the Nicolet National Forest, and really gathers steam as it crosses into Marinette County. So special is it that the state in 2001 officially cobbled together major chunks of privately held but wild lands, creating the 9,200-acre **Peshtigo River State Forest** (715/757-3965) and the contiguous **Governor Thompson**

State Park (715/757-3979; locally, lots still say "Caldron Falls Park").

The river links small communities (and outstanding natural areas) before emptying into Green Bay. Best of all, even private landowners in the flowage area had always kept it wild, so shoreline visual clutter is minimal.

To be frank, this stretch isn't much for white water aside from the county parks. Unless you're going to experience the river from a raft, the Peshtigo is more accommodating to the fisher along this route.

Most everything is accessible via officially designated Rustic Road 32. Its 26.5 miles start at Goodman Park Road in the north, thence to Parkway Road, and end at Highway W in the south. A half dozen good county parks and campgrounds are passed, along with the Peshtigo and Thunder Rivers and lots of established forest land. The only downside is the egregious plastering of signs along the route.

The northwestern section of the county, approximately 20 miles northwest of Crivitz, combines stands of forest, acre after acre of white water, and flowages chock-full of fish.

Beginning near the Athelstane County Forest Area, the white water starts at **Taylor Rapids.** There's camping available here at **Goodman Park** (featuring Strong Falls) as well as farther downstream at **McClintock Falls Park.** The latter park has a unique stand of hemlock and, if you're up for it, a 600-foot-long beaver dam (but it's a tough, wild, hour-long hike to see the dam—ask any local there which way to go).

The river then passes through Wilson Rapids and the river-runner's big-gulp, Roaring Rapids, before reaching the apex, Caldron Falls and 1,200 acres of flowage deemed Class-A1 muskie fishing. A few state records have been plucked from the area in past years. (Near here is the newish Governor Thompson State Park.)

After passing **Old Veteran's Lake Campground,** you'll come to **Twin Bridge County Park.** This is the best spot besides the High Falls Dam to check out the 1,750 acres of blue-ribbon fishing in the High Falls Flowage.

You'll see more intimidating cascades at Veteran's Falls in **Veteran's Memorial**

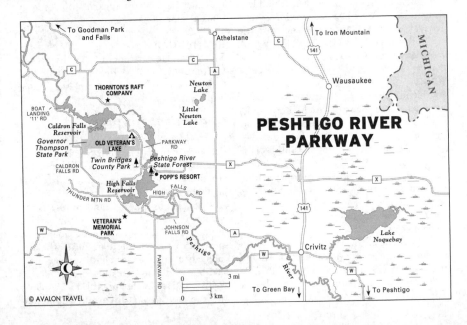

Park, off Parkway Road along the Thunder River. The river's roaring section closes out at Johnson Falls and Sandstone Flowage, a wilderness-quality fly-fishing-only stretch along Medicine Brook.

River Running: The Peshtigo is popular with kayakers, canoers, and rafters. The **state park office** in Crivitz (N10008 Paust Ln., 715/757-3965) and the **Marinette County Outdoor Recreation Office** (715/732-7530, www.therealnorth.com) have more information.

Private operators rule the river. One, **Thornton's Raft Company** (Parkway Rd., Athelstane, 715/757-3311, www.thorntonsresort.com, $27), is a campground-cum-resort offering cottages, a bar and restaurant, a swimming beach, and the like.

Practicalities

The area between Caldron Falls Reservoir and High Falls Flowage will likely have more tourists. Small resorts, restaurants, bait shops, and so on are found all over this area, the only place where the visual litter of touristdom unfortunately takes over. The entertainment runs the gamut from basic country-music-and-fish-fry to world-famous hog wrestling at the **Caldron Falls Bar** (W12326 Parkway Rd., 715/757-3467). Yup, Jackson Hole this ain't.

THE REST OF MARINETTE COUNTY

The waterfalls and other natural areas in the rest of this gargantuan county are really why we're here. It's a great place to leaf through the priceless county-road *Wisconsin Atlas and Gazetteer* and nose out all the waterfalls and white-water photo ops. The **Marinette Chamber of Commerce and Visitor Center** (601 Marinette Ave., 800/236-6681, www.marinettecounty.com) has maps (which you'll need); better, highway signage, once woefully inadequate, has improved.

Crivitz

It's hard to believe tiny Crivitz is the hub of the county. It's the center for supplies and communications in the area, and most resorts use the town as a base. Besides the Peshtigo River resorts and camping areas, Crivitz is the main town for big Lake Noquebay to the east. There's plenty of good fishing, and east of the lake you'll find a state wildlife area and a stretch of county forest, not to mention oodles of resorts.

Wausaukee

The nearest community to Newton Lake and Little Newton Lake, Wausaukee has limited tourist offerings.

Local gas stations have motels adjoining them; keep that in mind about lodgings around here. The **Wausaukee Bowl** (326 Main St., 715/856-5531, $6–12) serves a perch and walleye fish fry.

East of town on the Menominee River, **Bear Point Motel and Yacht Club** (W5154 State Hwy. 180, 715/856-5092, $35–40) is notable mainly because it's the "hook-and-line" sturgeon fishing center of Wisconsin.

Amberg and Pembine

Amberg's fantastic **Dave's Falls,** south of town on Highway V, was named after a 19th-century lumberman who lost his life clearing a logjam in the river.

The **Amberg Museum** (Hwy. V, 1–4 P.M. Fri. and 10 A.M.–4 P.M. Sat. in summer, free) displays the town's granite quarrying story (cool old derrick!), and an always-awesome old fire truck, among zillions of other things.

Northwest of town on Town Corner Lake (and in the Town Corner Lake Wildlife Area) are rock formations adorning the banks and a whole series of rapids, and a few winding trails.

Midway between Amberg and Pembine on U.S. 141 is most folks' favorite area for waterfalls. **Twelve Foot Falls** offers campsites, banner trout fishing on the Pike River, and access to other great cascades; **Eighteen Foot Falls** is about a mile away. The problem is, you're going to get lost trying to find them all—Bull Falls, Eight Foot Falls, Horseshoe Falls (great, but really tricky to find), and Twelve and Eighteen Foot Falls. For a surefire way to get to Twelve

NORTHEASTERN WISCONSIN

and Eighteen Foot Falls, just head to Lily Lake Road off U.S. 8 and follow the signs down the gravel, dirt, and occasionally paved road.

A personal favorite, Long Slide Falls, is along a leisurely drive northeast out of Pembine on Morgan Park Road. A quarter mile from the pulloff area, the Pembonwon River is channeled over a 50-foot drop, and the water's great in summer. You can climb down right atop the main roaring channel—magnificent. Smalley Falls is just upstream. A few miles east you'll find **Morgan Park,** a county park with campsites.

The best, or at least most isolated, rapids aren't even in Wisconsin—at least the access road isn't. Journey up the remaining leg of U.S. 141, and just before you reach Niagara, veer onto U.S. 8 and cross into Michigan. Just south of Norway, Michigan, **Piers Gorge**

offers a secluded, fantastic hike alongside the Menominee River, especially early in the morning. Imagine ramming three *million* board feet of lumber through here!

If ya wanna hang yer hat where some shady characters used to, head for the **Miscauno Island Four Seasons Resort** (N16800 Shoreline Dr., 877/324-5244, www.fourseasonswi.com, $159) near Pembine. Twice owned by purported "criminal elements" dating from the 1930s, its recent incarnation is as a comfy resort.

Marinette County Biking

Marinette County information centers have a good brochure on great bike routes throughout the county. Routes range 20–50 miles, and if you don't mind a few miles of gravel here and there, you can cool off in all those waterfalls.

Chequamegon-Nicolet National Forest: Nicolet Side

The Nicolet—named for the first intrepid European to arrive in Green Bay in 1634—section of Wisconsin's capacious national forest is very nearly the state's perfect approximation of the "Great North Woods experience"—about 666,000 acres in all, with 1,400 miles of fishable stream and more than 1,200 lakes, many grade A1 for lunkers. The "Nick" today encompasses five primitive wilderness areas (about 44,000 acres) holding stands of majestic trees—some just a scant few—that somehow managed to escape logging a century ago; trees 200–400 years old are found in the forest.

A personal observation is that the Nicolet National Forest is less cluttered than the Chequamegon. Often the backroads sectors of the forest are absolutely vacant, and even on weekends, precious few folks are around. Hike into one of the admirable wilderness areas and you're guaranteed seclusion.

Francophiles and smarty-pants tourists will do the "neek-oh-LAY" take on the name, though it's mostly "nick-uh-LAY." Don't be

surprised, though, to hear "nickle-ETT" from more than a few—mostly puzzled—visitors, but I swear I've heard a couple of locals utter it at gas stations.

Cradle of Rivers

The moniker "Cradle of Rivers" is not a misnomer here, the forest acts as the headwaters (or at least major conduit) for several of the state's renowned wilder rivers, including the Pine, Popple, Pike, Wolf, Wisconsin, and Peshtigo. The more sedate Brule is a canoeist's dream. This forest gave rise to the Wisconsin Wild River System.

Recreation

More than 820 miles of trails wind through the 666,000 acres on 32 trails (for all uses) of varying length, and there are miles of logging skid roads, old railroad grades, and abandoned truck trails to explore on your own.

Fishing? With the headwaters of the Wolf River, and the Wisconsin, the lazy Brule, fishy Popple and Oconto, and wild Peshtigo Rivers running through it, Nicolet is an angler's paradise.

Cradle of Rivers canoeing is sublime. Most parts of the Pine and Brule Rivers are good for beginners, as well as part of the Peshtigo segment. More advanced paddlers usually head for the Wisconsin, Deerskin, Popple, Oconto, and Wolf Rivers. The Wolf is nationally recognized for its aggressive fast waters (and thus is better suited for rafts). The closest rentals are in Lakewood, but **Hawk's Nest Eagle River Canoe Outfitters** (1761 Hwy. C, St. Germain, 800/688-7471, www.hawksnestcanoe.com) also has overnight trips into North Woods destinations.

Camping

Twenty-four campgrounds are established within the national forest, most in the northern half, fewer in the south around Lakewood. Reservations (www.recreation.gov) are available at some "established" campgrounds. Rates range from free to $30, averaging $12 per site.

A handful of primitive hike-in sites are found in the wilder regions of the wilderness areas. Less ambitious "walk-in" sites are also found at Fanny Lake in the Lakewood District and Perch and Lauterman Lakes in the Florence District. Wilderness and walk-in sites are $5 a day or $20 a year, and no water is available. That said, wilderness areas are open year-round. Common sense and zero-impact camping rules must prevail. *Whatever you do, contact the local ranger station if you plan to crash through the underbrush to sleep with the Sasquatches.* A few ill-planned camping forays could ruin it for everyone.

Fees

In addition to campsite fees, a $5 parking fee is necessary for boat landings, beaches, trailheads, and some remote campsites.

Information

The Nicolet National Forest section is parceled into two districts: Lakewood/Laona, and Florence/Eagle River. Florence has a visitors center; the main headquarters is in Rhinelander (500 Hanson Lake Rd., 715/362-1300). Other offices are in Eagle River, Glidden, Hayward, and Medford.

LAKEWOOD DISTRICT

Lakewood is considered the heart of this district, perhaps because within a short radius of Lakewood are more than 60 prime fishing lakes. The only highlight besides the auto tour is a restored 1881 logging camp at McCauslin Brook Golf Club. Apparently, the camp is one of the oldest of its kind in the United States, though I suspect one in Minnesota may be older. Two miles south of Lakewood are a number of gingerbread houses, special for their country architecture, built from local wood and stone. Another unknown sight, the **Woodland Trail Winery** (Big Hill Rd. and WI 32, 715/276-3668, www.woodlandtrailwine. com, 9 A.M.–6 P.M. daily) makes wine out of Wisconsin-grown fruit, including some interesting whites. Free samples are available.

There are not many places to stay, and five miles east of town along Highway F is **Waubee Lodge Resort-Motel, Supper Club, and Cocktail Bar** (715/276-6091 or 800/492-8233, www.waubeelodge.com, from $89, expect multiday minimums in summer), a much better choice than anything in Lakewood. The supper club is particularly popular.

Recreation

Eight trails are scattered throughout the southernmost of Nicolet's districts; merely highlights are here. The 1.25-mile **Quartz Hill Trail,** south of Carter via WI 32, takes hikers along somewhat steep McCaslin Mountain and passes a marker describing the quartz-quarrying operations of early Ojibwa and one of the few remaining fire-spotting towers left in the forest.

For the Thoreau in all of us, the wondrous **Jones Spring Area** is a hands-off, motors-off, wild area accessible most easily from Highway T, west of Lakewood, to Fanny Lake. These 2,000 primitive acres feature three lakes,

LAKEWOOD AUTO TOUR

Seventeen highlighted natural and historical points dot these 65 miles in and around Lakewood, Townsend, and Mountain. (Factoring in getting lost, it's a conservative 80 miles.)

Cathedral of Pines is an impressive name for some of the oldest standing wood in the Nicolet, if not Wisconsin. Even more appealing, around 100 nesting pairs of great blue herons predominate.

My personal favorite is stop number 9, the **Mountain Fire Lookout.** Go into Mountain on WI 32, left onto Highway W, and then another immediate left onto Old 32. A handful of miles later, you'll come to the access road. This is one of only a couple of the network of 20 New Deal-era fire-spotting towers throughout the region. The total height of the tower plus elevation is 880 ear-popping, creaky feet.

The **Waupee Flowage,** stop number 11, is off Highway W and Grindle Lake Road. It's serene and isolated – you'll likely be alone here – and there are painters' aesthetics and a tranquil platform designed to expedite the nesting of osprey (also drawing bald eagles).

Head back to Highway W and then left on La Fave Road. Turn left onto Holts Ranch Road (the maps say right) to stop number 14 – the **Logging Camp.** These eerie stone ruins of a late-19th-century logging camp are now choked with weeds and brambles. The white pines across the road were untouched in the last century.

After crossing the steel-framed girder bridge spanning the Oconto River, you reach a prime jumping-off spot for hiking the Lakewood Trails, just east of Lakewood.

overlooks, an Adirondack shelter, pack-in hiking campsites, and wood duck boxes. The wildlife is truly puzzled by the sight of hikers.

If nothing else, hike the 22-mile abandoned railroad grade of the Chicago-Northwestern Railroad.

The Wolf River technically does not flow through the Nicolet, but it skirts the far southwest boundary; with no kinetic energy yet, rafting is best here.

Do not canoe beyond Markton and into the Menominee Indian Reservation without checking local regulations first.

The Oconto River flows through the area, but extended trips should really be tackled only by advanced canoeists. As the rangers point out, "Many a canoe has been totaled on these stretches."

Camping

The campground at 362-acre (and walleye-rich) **Boulder Lake** is the Nicolet's largest and most popular.

Boot Lake is approximately half the size and also has nice lakeside sites. A hiking trail leads across the highway to **Fanny Lake,** in tranquil,

primitive Jones Spring Natural Area, 2,000 acres of semi-wild land (with pack-in sites).

Bagley Rapids, south of Mountain along WI 32, has 30 sites and not much else. It's primitive but great for rafting and canoeing as it's on the Oconto River.

Information

The **Lakewood Ranger Station** (15805 WI 32, 715/276-6333) is on the south edge of Lakewood.

LAONA DISTRICT

One rather mundane story explicating this town's name has it that it was the name of the daughter of a local businessman (sigh). The number one highlight in town is the Lumberjack Special at the **Camp Five Museum Complex** (715/674-3414, www.camp5museum.org). Getting to the museum necessitates clambering aboard a railway buff's dream—the wheezy old Vulcan 2-6-2 steamer. The center houses a 1900s general store and rail memorabilia everywhere, a nature center, a surrey forest tour operation, and a farm corral (hands-on for the children). Visitors can even buzz through rice banks and a natural bird refuge on the Rat River via pontoon boats. Four departures leave 11 A.M.–2 P.M. Monday–Saturday mid-June through the last Saturday of August. Museum and train cost $19 adults.

You may want to pay some respects, then. The once-majestic **MacArthur Pine** (west of Newald off Forest Rd. 2167) was a 420-year-old white pine that narrowly sidestepped the buzzsaws but couldn't escape fire. Once the tallest of its kind in the world at more than 175 feet, it boasted a 17-foot circumference and 7,500 board feet of lumber. In 2001 the tree succumbed to a suspicious fire. Many do still come.

West of Laona near Crandon is the heart of the Forest County Potawatomi Native American tribe (Neshnabek, or "original people" is what they call themselves, www.fcpotawatomi.com), one of eight Potawatomi bands in the United States and Canada. A splendid cultural education comes at the **Forest County Potawatomi Cultural Center and Museum** (5460 Everybody's Rd., 715/478-7474, www.potawatomimuseum.com, 9 A.M.–4 P.M. Mon.–Fri., $3 adults). Of particular interest is the Wall of Treaties—43 of them, more than any other U.S. tribe. This linguist author loves the language kiosk.

Recreation

Trails spiderweb around Laona. Minor trails include the **Halley Creek Bird Trail,** off Highway H east of Laona via Forest Road 2136, a one-miler traversing four distinct habitats; the **Knowles Creek Interpretive Trail** (east of Wabeno on Hwy. C) is less than a mile along a 200-acre wetlands impoundment with viewing platforms.

The **Michigan Rapids Trail** is a pretty hike along the Peshtigo River north of Laona via U.S. 8 and Forest Road 2131.

The only trail in this district for skiers and bikers in addition to hikers is the **Ed's Lake National Recreation Trail,** via Highway W, a six-miler following old railroad grades.

One section on the Peshtigo River nearby is prime for novice to experienced paddlers: It starts two miles northwest of Cavour off WI 139 and ends at the Cavour CCC bridge, a trip of about 7.5 miles. After this it can be downright dangerous.

A new 33-mile **Wolf River State Trail** from Crandon to White Lake in Langlade County is under construction. Bypassing Lake Metonga, the Bog Brook Natural Area, wetlands, the Wolf River, and plenty of rapids, it'll be a dream when done.

Camping

The largest and most popular of the district's five campgrounds is secluded **Laura Lake.**

Along WI 32 near Hiles, tiny **Pine Lake** lies on the sandy shore of one of the forest's largest lakes.

Southwest of Wabeno, along WI 52, isolated **Ada Lake** is a peaceful campground of 20 sites, as is **Bear Lake,** and both have good trout fishing; the latter offers good walk-in sites and great views.

Information

The **Laona Ranger Station** (715/674-4481) is west along WI 8.

FLORENCE AND EAGLE RIVER DISTRICT

Phelps

About the only community of any size in the Eagle River District is Phelps, offering, in this author's humble opinion, the best community lake view in the forest.

Whatever you do, don't miss the **Lac Vieux Desert,** the Wisconsin River's headwaters, north on Highway E. Muskie anglers go berserk in these waters, haunted by the most ferocious of lunkers.

Florence and Spread Eagle

Spread Eagle sits at the tip of one of the most diverse ecosystems in the state—one of the few remaining plains areas. There is also a small chain of nine lakes, reportedly frequented by Al Capone and other nefarious underworld figures during Prohibition. On U.S. 2/141, actually closer to Florence, you'll find **The Chuck Wagon** (715/696-6220, lunch and dinner daily), a rustic log structure once part of the northland's tourist camp network and now a rustic tavern and eatery. Florence, the under-populated-county's seat, has one of the small-est, oldest, and not-to-be-messed-with county jails in Wisconsin—a scant 24 by 30 feet—built like a tomb in 1889.

Florence's **Wild Rivers Interpretive Center** (corner of U.S. 2/141 and Hwy. 101/70, 888/889-0049, www.florencewisconsin.com) is also the best source of information in the region, shared by federal, state, and county offices. Stop by just to see the albino buck display.

Scenic Drive

Officially-designated Wisconsin Rustic Road 34 departs Alvin and traverses parts of Lakeview Drive, Carey Dam Road, and Fishel Road. It's secluded and a nice northern forest experience on the whole, but it is unpaved and narrow as hell.

Recreation
FLORENCE AREA

A personal favorite for canoeing is the Brule River, which also forms the northern border of the **Whisker Lake Wilderness,** the district's mammoth spread of almost primeval wilderness. The tract covers about 7,500 acres, and there is a stand of virgin pine and hardwood. Whisker Lake is the area for dispersed camping.

The district's highlight, the grand **Lauterman National Recreational Trail,** offers nine total miles for hikers, bikers, and skiers, connecting Lauterman Lake with Perch Lake in the north. Lauterman Lake has five walk-in campsites available and an Adirondack shelter.

The aptly named **Ridge Trail** west of Florence winds along an aspen ridge and the Pine River. **Assessor's Trail** plunges deep into hemlock stands so thick you'll feel the light fading.

Not to be confused with the Bois Brule River in far northwestern Wisconsin is the sedate, comfy Brule River. Doubling as the Wisconsin-Michigan border, the river runs through splendid wilderness areas and offers killer trout fishing. The Brule is decidedly lazy for most of its length and has the most dependable water levels of any in the forest but *never* take a canoe past the Brule River Dam.

The Pine and Popple Rivers run through the district, and sections of both are part of Wisconsin's own Wild River System. They also traverse what might be the state's most primitive wilderness. If you can swing some sightseeing in addition to the frenetic rapids, the residuals of old logging dams are found en route. *Neither river should be explored without first checking with Florence's Wild Rivers Center or the Florence Ranger Station regarding water conditions and possible regulatory changes.*

EAGLE RIVER AREA

Seven miles northeast of Eagle River is the 5,800-acre **Blackjack Springs Wilderness Area.** Highlights include four large clear springs forming the headwaters of Blackjack Creek, along with a lake and assorted streams, some of which produce Brobdingnagian trout.

The wonderful 20,000-acre **Headwaters Wilderness,** 16 miles southeast of Eagle River (producing the wild Pine River), holds some of the largest and oldest trees in the national for-est and Wisconsin. The area is characterized by muskegs and bogs alternating with forested swamps and a few dense uplands.

The most popular trails are undoubtedly those of the **Anvil Lake National Recreation Trail,** east of Eagle River via WI 70, 12 excel-lent miles of CCC trails for hikers, skiers, and mountain bikers. Dramatic plunges and tons of rutted tree roots will dismount you or snag your ski tip. Watch for the woodland warbler.

Connected to the Anvil system is the easier **Nicolet North Trail System,** 15 miles of trails which in turn connect to the **Hidden Lakes Trail.** Hard-core hikers can forge on all the way to the Anvil Trail, though the North Branch of the Pine River must be forded, as there is no bridge.

The **Franklin Nature Trail** is only one mile long, but it's impressive—some of the hard-wood and hemlock spinneys are more than 400 years old.

The **Sam Campbell Memorial Trail** (inter-pretive), off Forest Road 2178 north of WI 32, is named for a local naturalist and writer who used nearby Vanishing Lake for inspiration and contemplation. It's eerie how you can still see residuals of a 1986 fire.

The half-mile **Scott Lake Trail** winds through 300-year-old stands of white pine and then via a short trail to Shelp Lake and outstanding bog environments. You'll be alone except perhaps for an ornithologist or two.

Finally, you can witness how the USFS manages timber resources on the **Argonne Experimental Forest Trail,** a so-called living laboratory of less than a mile with more than a dozen markers explaining (or justifying) in some detail how the forest is used. The road is east of Three Lakes via WI 32.

The Eagle River District's **Natural History Auto Tour** is an 80-mile mélange of natural history, topographical sights, and the historical museum in Three Lakes.

For those without much time, just take a spin through the forest nine miles east of Eagle River off WI 70 via the old **Military Road,** Forest Road 2178, and **Butternut Lake Road,** a nice forest-in-a-nutshell trip through splendid scenery. Old Military Road, once called the Lake Superior Trail, is the modern result of a trail that's been in use for millennia—first by the nomadic early Native American tribes, then by explorers, trappers, and miners, and, finally, of course, by the U.S. military.

Most of the Pine River is tranquil from the put-in site along Pine River Road, but there are some notable rapids after WI 55, and a few portages are mandatory. The Eagle River District section offers a few looks at the remnants of old sawmills on the banks.

Camping
FLORENCE AREA
Super is the carry-in **Brule River** campground, on the Wisconsin-Michigan border north of Alvin via WI 55 and set in a lovely red pine and balsam grove.

Contiguous **Chipmunk Rapids Campground** and **Lost Lake Campground** off WI 70 via Forest Road 2450 are 18 miles southwest of Florence. Tiny Chipmunk is adjacent to

Lauterman National Recreation Trail and offers its own legendary artesian drinking well at a carry-in site along the Pine River. The latter has a 150-year-old stand of hemlock and pine. No motors allowed, so it is quiet.

EAGLE RIVER AREA
Popular but mediocre **Anvil Lake** is nine miles east of Eagle River right atop WI 70; at least there are the grand Anvil Lake trail systems here.

Huge is **Franklin Lake,** along the Heritage Drive Scenic Byway (Forest Rd. 2181), with tons of diversions for kids; trails also connect this to Anvil Lake Campground and to the nearby **Luna-White Deer Lake Campground,** with sites sandwiched between the *motorless* lakes.

The largest lake in the Nicolet, Lac Vieux Desert's 2,853 acres were fished by the Ojibwa before Europeans found these headwaters of the Wisconsin River. You'll see lots of rustic resorts dotting the shoreline. This is one of my favorite areas for exploring and taking photos. The muskie fishing is great here, too.

Sister campgrounds **Spectacle Lake** and **Kentuck Lake** are 16 miles northeast of Eagle River via WI 70. Spectacle is a family favorite for its 500-foot beach.

The primitive but free ($5 forest fee, however) **Windsor Dam** campsites are semi-carry-in and secluded along the North Branch of the Pine River.

Information
The **Florence Ranger Station** (WI 70 and U.S. 2, 715/528-4464) shares an office with the Florence County Parks Department and a tiny nature center. The **Eagle River Ranger Station** (1247 Wall St., 715/479-2827) is on the north end of town.

VICINITY OF NICOLET NATIONAL FOREST
Antigo
Twenty miles west of the lower reaches of the forest, little Antigo marks your entry into ginseng country near Marathon County. It's worth a side trip for any angler—pretty much everyone in these parts, right?—checking out

Sheldon's Inc. Mepps Fishing Lures (626 Center St., 715/623-2382). (Any fisher worth his weight knows who they are.) Tours of the fishing lure plant are offered year-round, and anglers spend most of the time ogling the lunkers on display. Free tours are offered five times a day, 9:15 A.M.–2:30 P.M. Monday–Thursday May–December, less often the rest of the year.

Mole Lake Indian Reservation

The Sokaogon (Mole Lake) Band of Lake Superior Chippewa occupies the smallest reservation in Wisconsin—3,000 acres west of the national forest. It's known informally as the "Lost Tribe" for its lengthy peregrination before arriving here and battling the Sioux for control of the area (and because the 1854 federal treaty signed was lost in a shipwreck on Lake Superior). The name "Sokaogon" means "Post in the Lake" and refers to the appearance of a petrified tree in the midst of a nearby lake, perhaps auguring the end of the band's wandering.

A ferocious battle with the Sioux in 1806— more than 500 died—produced a significant home for the Sokaogon. The land here is the most abundant in *manomin* (wild rice) in Wisconsin. The beds around the village of Mole Lake are among the last remaining ancient stands of wild rice.

Right along WI 55 is an 1870s **cabin** once used as a postal layover and trading post. The cabin is known as the Dinesen House and was the home of Wilhelm Dinesen, father of Isak Dinesen ("Out of Africa"), who named it "Frydenland" or "Grove of Joy." It is being refurbished to house a small cultural/visitors center.

The Lakes District: Northeast

From Tomahawk in the south, draw a line northwest to Hurley. Make another line from Tomahawk northeast to Land O' Lakes. The area outlined is one of Wisconsin's two northern "lakes districts," essentially one spread of water, with seemingly a lake for every resident (many lakes remain unnamed). In terms of lakes per square mile, the region is surpassed only by areas in northern Canada and Finnish Lappland. In the three major counties in the district (Iron, Vilas, and Oneida), lakes or wetlands make up almost *40 percent* of the surface area. Considering that these primeval pools of glacial hydrology are ensconced almost wholly within state and county forest land, the area is a perfectly realized Great North Woods escape.

TOMAHAWK

Somnolent Tomahawk lies on the mighty Wisconsin River and is a cheery, modest resort town, nestled near the confluence of four northern rivers. Named for an oddly configured nearby lake, Tomahawk's lumber industry at one time rivaled any town's to the north.

The **Tomahawk Chamber of Commerce** (4th St., 715/453-5334, www.gototomahawk. com) is always helpful. Adjacent to the chamber office, a small **historical center** showcases lumber history, but most interesting are the regularly scheduled nature seminars, outdoors workshops, and scientific courses at **Treehaven** (715/453-4106, www.uwsp.edu), a natural resources education and conference center on 1,500 acres, about 15 miles east of Tomahawk via Highway A. Sporadic naturalist-guided hikes, family nature courses, and even concerts are ongoing.

Harley-Davidson has a plant here and **plant tours** (611 S. Kaphaem Rd., 414/343-7850, 10 A.M.–2 P.M. Mon.–Fri., free) take place June–mid-September. If you're here in fall, check out the plant's sponsored Colorama tours—and there's also the excellent Yesteryear ethnic festival.

Scenic drives abound. The wondrously scenic WI 107 hugs the Wisconsin River south to Merrill—a great stretch of eye candy. Along the way, you'll pass by the trailhead to the seven-mile multipurpose **Hiawatha Trail.** You could also depart east of town via Highway D, Highway B, and then WI 17 to Merrill—along here you pass by two nature areas, classic moraine topography, and Lookout Mountain (the highest point on the Ice Age Trail) before whipping by Gleason, a.k.a. the Trout Fishing Capital, and ending up at Haymeadow County Park and the gorgeous Prairie Dells Scenic Area.

Southeast of Rhinelander about 20 miles are tiny Pelican Lake and Jennings. The latter features the 1899 **Mecikalski Stovewood Building** (County Trunk B, Jennings). Also called "cord wood" or "stack wall," the style of architecture refers to the short end-cut logs, which are "stacked" and bonded with mortar or clay. Economical and practical, it didn't require entire log lengths. The practice is decidedly American, and 19th-century Wisconsin was prime country for it; more than 60 structures were built using this method, though this is the best example and the only commercial building of this style.

Accommodations and Food

The pinnacle of Tomahawk lodgings is undoubtedly **Palmquist Farm** (N5136 River Rd., Brantwood, 800/519-2558, www.palmquistfarm.com, from $66). Generations of Finns on this 800-acre beef, deer, and tree farm have welcomed guests to their cozy North Woods cottages and man, what a grand place it is. You can indulge in myriad trails, luscious breakfasts (what pancakes!), deep hospitality, and yes, a real-deal sauna; a fave are the winter by-the-fire hootenannies. It has worthy weekend package deals, a steal at the price.

The dining room at **Bootleggers** (Bus. 51 N at Hwy. L, 715/453-7971, from 5 P.M. Tues.–Sat., from 4 P.M. Sun.) is right on Lake Nokomis, and plenty of snowmobiles pull right up at the door.

RHINELANDER

Rhinelander is also a gateway of sorts—to water (the confluence of the Wisconsin and Pelican Rivers in town and all those lakes

Have a picnic alongside a great North Woods legacy in Rhinelander.

© THOMAS HUHTI

to the north) and to forests (the Northern Highland American Legion State Forest to the northwest, the Nicolet National Forest to the northeast).

The Sioux used the rivers' confluence for a base; in 1870, young explorer Alexander Brown spied the same spot and found himself the owner of a town. A bit of expedient glad-handing (naming the town for a railroad magnate) paid off and soon opening one sawmill each year was the town's average.

Sights

The **Rhinelander Logging Museum** (off Bus. 8, 715/369-5004, 10 A.M.–5 P.M. daily in summer, free) is an assemblage of lumber-era detritus exhibited in an old logging camp dining hall and the old Rhinelander depot. The **Civilian Conservation Corps Museum** is also on site. You'll find a large assortment of logging flotsam and an outstanding antique outboard engine museum section strewn about the grounds.

The easiest freebie is the **Oneida County Courthouse** downtown: by day, scope out the murals of homesteading life; by night, the Tiffany glass on the dome radiates an amber light.

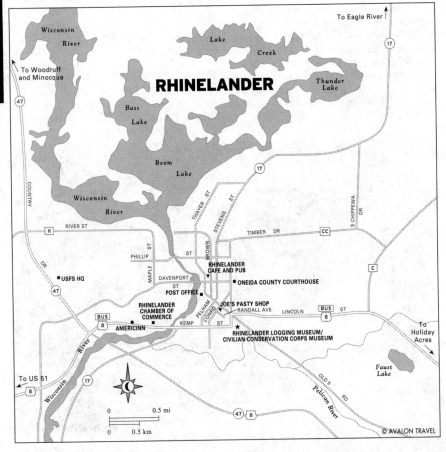

© AVALON TRAVEL

HODAG

Not of the mythical proportions of big-toed Sasquatch, yet Rhinelander's own crafty backwoods prehistoric relic, the Hodag, has been legendary in its own right, akin to the jackalope – that hybrid of horned and long-eared fauna populating tourist towns everywhere west of the Mississippi, though, oddly enough, spotted only by the grizzled denizens of local shot-and-a-beer joints. Something monstrous, something mysterious, populates the Great North Woods around Rhinelander.

In 1896, local Gene Shepard showed up with a photograph of a ferocious beast that had sprung at him in the forest – seven feet long, half reptilian and half leonine, sharpened walrus-esque tusks, razor-sharp claws, a coniform row down the back worthy of a triceratops, and Brahma bull horns.

Wildfire rumors spread – supposedly the beast had been caught licking up the last offal of a white bulldog, its favorite meal. A lumberjack posse led by Shepard supposedly captured it, with chloroform and a long pike, yet oddly nobody but he could look at it. When the jig was about up, Shepard claimed the Hodag escaped but ultimately, somewhat reluctantly, admitted the hoax.

It never quite left the psyche of the local community, however: The Hodag is everywhere. Hodag is the high school nickname and mascot. Parks and businesses are named after it. Check out the history and the hoax at Rhinelander's Logging Museum. The coolest souvenir in the northlands is a Hodag sweatshirt.

The Wisconsin Legislature once even discussed a bill that would make it the "official mythical beast" of Wisconsin.

Accommodations

Just west of downtown the **AmericInn** (648 W. Kemp St., 866/538-0817, $99) is the best regular hotel.

◖ Holiday Acres (U.S. 8 E, 715/369-1500 or 800/261-1500, www.holidayacres.com, $99–289) is a high-gear family resort well known among generations of North Woods vacationers. The more than 1,000 acres feature a motor lodge, spiffy cottages (many with fireplaces), and the Three Coins, a dining room among the most popular in the north. The resort's recreational list boggles the mind.

Food

Tip of the cap to the third-generation pasty makers at **Joe's Pasty Shop** (123 Randall Ave., 715/369-1224, 10 A.M.–6 P.M. Tues.–Fri., 8 A.M.–3 P.M. Sat.) downtown—they make 'em from scratch daily (no mean feat) using environmentally friendly practices.

◖ Rhinelander Cafe and Pub (30 N. Brown St., 715/362-2918, 7 A.M.–11 P.M. daily, $5–25) has been in business since 1911 and today is the must-see dining experience in the region. The huge, hall-style dining room is buttressed by the original diner counter. Prime rib, steaks, and duck are still the specialties. SRO (standing room only) is the norm.

Holiday Acres – Three Coins Dining Room (U.S. 8 E, 715/369-1500, 5:30–9:30 P.M. daily, 9 A.M.–1:30 P.M. Sun. brunch, $8–16) specializes in seafood and offers a consistent slate of jazz. Believe it or not, international jazz stars have tooted in little Rhinelander, Wisconsin.

Information

The **Rhinelander Chamber of Commerce** (Sutliff Ave., 715/362-7464 or 800/236-4386, www.rhinelanderchamber.com) is just off U.S. 8.

Getting There

The **Rhinelander/Oneida County Airport** (3375 Airport Rd., 715/365-3416) has service to the Twin Cities and Milwaukee.

◖ EAGLE RIVER CHAIN OF LAKES

Eagle River's status as a tourism head honcho was perhaps a foregone conclusion, given that it lies along a chain of 28 lakes following the Eagle River—considered the longest such interlinked chain of freshwater lakes in the world. Because precious few portages exist after linking up with the Wisconsin River, you could paddle all the way to the Big Easy.

An interesting self-guided water tour is a boathouse tour; the local chamber of commerce has a detailed brochure. Head for the **Burnt Rollways Reservoir,** made up of 20 of the lakes. At more than 7,626 acres, with 106 miles of shoreline, it's one of the region's most popular boating and fishing areas. These lakes are in turn linked to the Eagle chain of eight lakes by way of the historic Burnt Rollways boat hoist—dating from 1911—at a dam site between Long Lake and Cranberry Lake. (By the way, the name Burnt Rollways comes from the revenge exacted on a work boss who couldn't pay some loggers; they torched his logs stacked on the rollway.)

The **Otter Rapids Dam and Hydroelectric Power Plant** is a late-19th-century power plant still cranking out electricity. This is the beginning of the long series of dams and assorted river blocks on the Wisconsin River, which have given it the nickname "Hardest-Working River in the Country."

EAGLE RIVER

Some would say that the *town* Eagle River isn't properly within the lakes district—the Nicolet National Forest even named one of its districts for the town, after all. They cavil, I say. Eagle River splits the two regions apart, so it could go either way.

Eagle River was apparently named in the 1850s by a pair of itinerant trappers camped along the river who marveled at the number of eagle pairs along the river. Yet another lumber babytown, it got the drop on northern Wisconsin in reshaping itself into a major tourist destination.

It is winter, and in particular, snowmobiling,

© RACHEL FRIEDMAN

canoeing on endless chains of lakes, Eagle River

that really sets Eagle River apart from the rest of the dime-a-dozen summer retreat towns. The community's absolutely frenetic international snowmobile races in January are simply not to be missed.

Sights

The **Trees for Tomorrow Resources Education Center** (611 Sheridan St., 715/479-6456, www.treesfortomorrow.com) is worthwhile. On the south bank of the Eagle River, this WPA-funded facility dates from the 1930s. A self-guided nature trail snakes through a demonstration forest and the Tuesday morning/afternoon family activities and Tuesday evening free lectures are popular.

The **Northwoods Children's Museum** (346 W. Division St., 715/479-4623, 10 A.M.–5 P.M. Mon.–Sat., noon–5 P.M. Sun., $6) has lots of hands-on activities for kids; they can even harvest cranberries from a bog.

In Three Lakes, south of town, **Three Lakes Winery** (6971 Gogebic St., 715/546-3080, www.fruitwine.com, 9 A.M.–5 P.M. daily,

hit with the crowds, as have vintage
nd the fact that fans can pony up some
and roar around the track.

weekend sees dozens of manufactur-
r operators, and sponsors bringing in
-the-art equipment for demonstrations
ne hands-on opportunities. The loudest
erupt when a member of the Green Bay
shows up.

ermain

f Eagle River, St. Germain's **Snowmobile
g Hall of Fame** (8481 W. WI 70,
2-4488, www.snowmobilehalloffame.
ours vary by season, free) is without
the most *essential* stop in the North
s, should you wish to understand the
ethos. The cool memorabilia includes
ds and uniforms. You can also watch
-packed videos of famous races, focus-
gically on the granddaddy race over in
River in January. Naturally, you can sled
to the entrance in winter; better, if you
p in mid-January, you can ride off on a
our with celebrity racers.

ner

bop up WI 155 five miles to the place
it all began: Sayner. 'Bilers head directly
e **Vilas County Historical Museum**
155, 715/542-3388, 10 a.m.–4 p.m. daily
orial Day—the town's Colorama weekend
tumn, $2 donations) and the exhibit on
ride and joy of the area, local eccentric-
-good Carl Eliason, the inventor of the
ymobile back in 1924. Also interesting is
ook at the area's fishing guide history.
the museum is closed for the season, the
are at **The Carl Eliason and Company**
(274 Main St., 715/542-3233, 7:30 a.m.–
p.m. Mon.–Fri., 8 a.m.–noon Sat.), where
first sled was assembled (old models are on
lay); next door is the **Sayner Pub** (stop in
e the old ski hill mural on the ceiling).
One lodge folks have mentioned for genera-
s is **Froelich's Sayner Lodge** (715/542-
1 or 800/553-9695, www.saynerlodge.com)
Plum Lake. The resort has been offering

vacationers a place to crash since the 1890s, and
the Froelich family has operated the lodge since
the 1950s. Nothing fancy—*remember that,
please*—but a wonderful slice of Wisconsin tradition. Open late May–September, the lodge
has simple rooms ($69–109 daily) and one- to
three-bedroom cottages ($105–262 daily).

You'll find the oddest dining experience
around at **Weber's Wildlife Game Farm** (W
155 at Hwy. C, 715/542-3781), a weird amalgam of taxidermy display, private zoo, and
wildlife show, and a favorite pit stop of local
snowmobilers. The farm is a mile south o
Sayner.

NORTHERN HIGHLAND AMERICAN LEGION STATE FOREST

Most of the lakes region is subsumed by th
largest of Wisconsin's state forests—225,00
acres. Its proximity to the frenetic tourist tow
of Minocqua and Woodruff bring an estimat
two million visitors per annum. Today, a
glers rival pleasure boaters and canoeists
the 54,000 acres of surface water on 930 lak
and 250 miles of rivers and streams.

This is muskie country. Other anglers m
claim to be looking for other lunkers, but
erybody knows that most are secretly lobb
and reeling, hoping for that Moby Mus
trophy. The region is at friendly war with
Hayward area for bragging rights.

Recreation

This is a canoeist's dream. Three separate
chains lie within the forest, and the Eagle R
chain of 28 lakes lies to the east. Nineteen
derness lakes in the Vilas and Oneida Co
sections of the forest are absolutely free o
sual shoreline pollution and have no road
cess (85 percent of the region is governi
owned); a good example is Salsich Lake
Star Lake. An additional 40 lakes are dev
ment-free, but have some road access; the
popular is probably Allequash.

The most popular canoe trip in the for
doubtlessly on the **Manitowish River,**
ning 44 miles from High Lake, northe

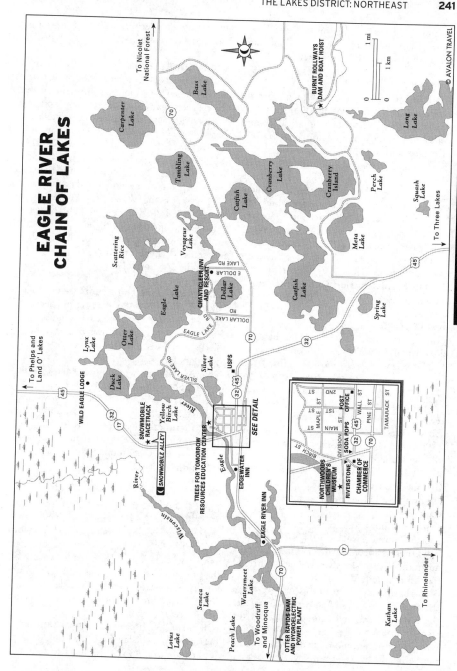

EAGLE RIVER CHAIN OF LAKES

shorter hours for tours) is in an old railroad depot. Tours and tastings are free, and there are some fantastic local cranberry wines.

Events

A follow-up event to the snowmobile world championships is the **Klondike Days** festival, generally held at the end of February. Everyone comes to see the World Championship Oval Sled Dog Sprints—billed as "the fastest sled dog racing in the world"—on the same track as those monster machines. This is not some tongue-in-cheek laugh-fest; teams compete over two days in three classes for more than $20,000 in purse money—no small potatoes. Otherwise, it's as if the whole town were transported back a century ago. Very cool.

Anglers own the summer, and their own crown jewel is August's **National Championship Muskie Open**—the largest amateur muskie tournament anywhere.

Recreation

Fishing first. Muskie, walleye, and bass predominate. (Hint: The Lac du Flambeau chain of lakes has world-class muskie fishing.) Your best bet is to contact **Eagle River Area Guides** (715/479-8804, www.eagleriverguides.com).

If you're heading out on your own, boat rentals are available from **Heckel's** (437 W. Division St., 715/479-4471, www.heckels.com).

Pick up a copy of *Fishing Hot Spots*, an angling guide series published in the area.

The excellent **Razorback Ridge** ski trails (12 miles) are a short drive west of Sayner along Highway N. These double as mountain-bike trails.

If you're not up for paddling the 28 lakes yourself, **Hawk's Nest** (715/479-7944, www.hawksnestcanoe.com) offers tranquil runs down the Wisconsin River and does outfitted tours throughout Wisconsin.

It is beyond the scope of this guide to detail the massive networks of snowmobile trails to the east and west (and through) Eagle River. **Decker Sno-Venture Tours** (715/479-2764, www.sno-venture.com) is rated number one almost annually by *Snowgoer* magazine, beating out weighty competitors such as Yellowstone Tour and Travel and Togwotee's Sno World.

Accommodations

Resorts, resorts everywhere, though in town there are a few basic motels, some right on the Eagle River, many with boat docks and to-the-door sled access. Many of the motels are friendly and not too pricey, considering, including **Edgewater Inn** (5054 U.S. 70 W, 715/479-4011, www.edgewater-inn-cottages.com, $85 rooms, $125 cottages), with charming rustic rooms and cottages overlooking the water.

Also west along WI 70, the **Eagle River Inn** (5260 WI 70 W, 715/479-2000, www.eagleriver-inn.com, $119–249) has basic rooms, "bunk bed rooms" great for families, condos, and some kitchenette units available—they can handle 2–6 (or more) folks. Full recreation amenities are here.

Chanticleer Inn and Resort (1458 Dollar Lake Rd., 715/479-4486, www.chanticleerinn.com, $129, more for cottages and houses) offers motels, cottages, and town houses right on the chain of lakes. The dining room is exceedingly popular.

North of downtown on Duck Lake **(Wild Eagle Lodge** (4443 Chain O' Lakes Rd., 715/479-3151 or 877/945-3965, www.wildeaglelodge.com, from $200) is just about the most smashingly rustic yet sybaritic place in the region. There are raves about this place, its one- to three-bedroom lodge homes, and its friendliness.

Food

The **(Riverstone** (219 N. Railroad St., 715/479-8467, dinner daily, brunch Sun., $6 and up) takes you back to logrolling days with its 1880s oak back bar and vintage ceilings and floors. Then it lurches you forward into the present with a state-of-the-art exhibition kitchen and awards for its wine cellar and cuisine, which it precisely describes as from comfort to creative.

Jump back in time but in a much more light-hearted way at the fab **(Soda Pop's** (125 S. Railroad St., 715/479-9424, lunch and dinner daily, $4–9), where you've never tasted such delicious bygone-days "fast food" (that's a positive, BTW) sammiches and, better, about 200 varieties of, yes, soda pop. The 1800s interiors—all original—were redone well enough to win an award from the state of Wisconsin.

Folks rave about the dining room/supper club of the **Chanticleer Inn** (1458 Dollar Lake Rd., 715/479-4486, breakfast and dinner daily, $4–13). The casually elegant atmosphere is nice, and you can't beat the waterside view.

Information

The chamber of commerce's depot **information center** (201 N. Railroad St., 715/479-8575 or 800/359-6315, www.eagleriver.org) is phenomenally well organized.

Getting There

The airport offers **Trans North Aviation** (715/479-6777, www.transnorth.com), with regularly scheduled (though to and from Chicago's Palwa

(SNOWMOBILE A
Eagle River

Every January throngs of Wisconsin's de facto pastiming—descend on Eagle River cacophonic, boisterous revelr supercharged sleds—the **Worl Snowmobile Derby** (715/479 bytrack.com, figure $65 for with daily passes also availa "Best Little Racetrack in the most important snowmobile c in the world—almost 400 rac Getting a pitside seat is truly a ence: The ice kicked up by the siles stings your face and word ground, smoke, and steam fr

The Thursday-night quali E rig pu tra

SNOWMOBILE CENTRAL

Something inspired Carl Eliason to strap a small gas-powered boat engine onto a toboggan, pound on some turnable skis, and let himself loose across the ice near Sayner, Wisconsin, in 1924. Voilà! – the first modern snowmobile was patented in 1927.

Wisconsin's populace sleds more than any state. More than 25,000 miles of well-tracked trails are maintained by dozens and dozens of snow clubs throughout the north – the nation's most extensive network. And these are just maintained trails; Wisconsin Trail number 15 bisects the state southeast to northwest – a seeming million frozen miles aboard a sled. One quarter of the nation's 2.7 million sleds are in Wisconsin, and tourism for 'biling equals that generated by certain western states' ski industries (some northern resorts make 85 percent of their income from snowmobilers). *Snowgoer* magazine readers consistently rate northeast Wisconsin tops in the country.

Buzzing machines scrape to a halt next to you at the gas station. Businesses post advertisements along snowmobile trails. Lodgings cater to snowmobilers exclusivel als, linked trails on-site (they ca door), and more.

Some regard 'biling aficionad browed Cro-Magnons who despo landscape. And yes, in a time-hono making "pit stops" can translate as About 25-40 snowmobilers die ev

However, True 'bilers cringe at the few yahoos fueled on Leinenk Snowmobile clubs are actually a bunch who do as much charity wor trail maintenance. Snowmobile c ones who best bring together lo and landowners and even work w mental groups to share access – that Wisconsin's club trail networ cially recognized highway system true that an engine is an engine – ing hydrocarbons into the air – te reducing emissions annually. And t of snowmobiles is still far lower t pollution machines of other folks' S mowers, leaf blowers, powerboats,

a s
ra
m

St
W
Ra
71
co
do
W
lo
ol
ac
Ea
rig
pu
tra

Sa
Tl
wl
to
(W
M
in
th
m
sn
th

sle
sto
4:
th
di
ti
32
tie

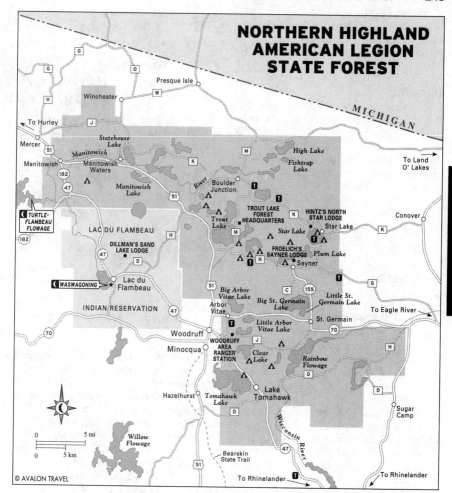

NORTHERN HIGHLAND AMERICAN LEGION STATE FOREST

Boulder Junction, all the way to the Turtle-Flambeau Flowage through extras such as wild rice beds.

The top draw to the forest is the 18-mile **Bearskin State Trail** for hikers/bikers, linking Minocqua and Harshaw in Oneida County via an old railroad grade.

Nine primary hiking/skiing trails wend their way through the forest, ranging in length from 2 miles (the appropriately named **Schlecht**—that's "bad" in German—a bruising trail, with steep inclines) to 13 miles on the **Lumberjack Trail,** a wilderness track through the oldest timber in the forest as well as some recently logged areas. Many say their favorite is **Statehouse Lake,** a couple of miles of excellent riverside views along a section of the Manitowish River.

Four cross-country/hiking trails do triple duty as off-road cycling options within the forest—**McNaughton, Madeline Lake, Lumberjack,** and **Shannon Lake.**

But these are only the established trails. Myriad logging trails wind throughout the forest, and these are definitely on-limits for bikes.

Camping

There are almost 1,100 sites at 20 campgrounds in the forest; surely you'll find something. Modern family campgrounds have reservable sites; wilderness camp areas are also available, and, unlike most places, they can also be reserved. Most impressive is the network of primitive wilderness canoe campsites—nearly 100 in all (a dozen sites can be reserved).

With a (free) permit, dispersed camping is also allowed along the Lumberjack Trail or along any of the labyrinthine network of snowmobile trails.

Information

The most visited ranger station in the forest is the **Woodruff Area HQ** (8770 Hwy. J, Woodruff, 715/356-5211). But the main HQ is actually the **Trout Lake office** (northeast of Woodruff, off U.S. 51 and Hwy. M, 715/385-2727). The DNR website has a PDF attachment with all possible information within.

Mercer

One of the most photographed sights in the state, **Claire de Loon** is a gigantic loon guarding the roadway outside Mercer's tourist information cabin (715/476-2389). Mercer is definitely "loony" (sorry) if that means friendly as hell and is most often used as the northern entry point into the amazing Turtle-Flambeau Flowage.

Manitowish and Manitowish Waters

These sister communities (though they don't refer to themselves as such) lie a handful of miles apart via U.S. 51 at the far northwestern corner of the state forest and were named in a linguistically bastardized way for *manitous*, the spirits that according to the Ojibwa populate the region. Set on a minor chain of 10 lakes and assorted wetlands (totaling 4,265

Claire de Loon welcomes you to the Turtle-Flambeau Flowage.

© THOMAS HUHTI

acres), the area is a tourism center in summer, and the other economic base is cranberries. The cranberry marshes near Alder and Little Trout Lakes outside of town are some of the highest-producing bogs in the nation. Free one-hour tours are available at 10 A.M. Friday the first week of July through the second week of October; meet at the Manitowish Waters Community Center (Airport Rd., a mile south of Hwy. W, 715/543-8400). No reservations needed and the juice provided is luscious!

The **Manitowish River Trail** is a 20-mile novice-level canoe trip from the U.S. 51 bridge in Manitowish Waters into the wild Turtle-Flambeau Flowage. Rustic campsites (no water) are found on the way.

On Statehouse Lake is the **North Lakeland Discovery Center** (a mile north of U.S. 51 on Hwy. W, 715/543-2085, www.discoverycenter.net), a nonprofit ecology center with lots of trails and a wonderful array of programs and events throughout the year.

Also south of town, off Powell Road, the

Powell Marsh Wildlife Refuge contains native grains and grasses luring one of the only groups of sharp-tailed grouse in northern Wisconsin.

But people really know little Manitowish Waters as the local hideout of John Dillinger. **Little Bohemia Lodge** (142 U.S. 51 S, 715/543-8800, dinner daily year-round, lunch Fri.–Sun. seasonally, $11–23)—a.k.a., "The Hideout"—is where Dillinger, Babyface Nelson, and two others blazed their way out of an FBI raid in 1934, killing two mobsters, an FBI agent, and a local constable, and catching national attention. Bullet holes and assorted gangster detritus are still visible, and the lodge is still in operation. (Incidentally, Dillinger wasn't the inspiration for .30/.30 Road in town—it was the Northland's obsession with hunting.)

An excellent lodging option with an equally fabulous dining room, **Voss' Birchwood Lodge** (south on U.S. 51, 715/543-8441, www.vossbl.com, from $85 daily) has been in the same family since 1910. The stately, rustic main lodge has a large, warm fireplace and there are also large guest cottages.

Pine Baron's (Hwy. W, 715/543-8464, dinner daily in season, $7–23) serves roast duck, venison, pheasant, and buffalo, and is likely the nicest place in the area.

After all your fish fries, the Creole and Cajun at the **Blue Bayou Inn** (288 U.S. 51, 715/543-2537, 5–9 P.M. Mon.–Sat. May–Oct., $15–25) will do you well.

If that weren't enough fine dining, the newest is the outstanding **Smokey's** (Hwys. K and W, 715/543-2220, dinner Tues.–Sun., from $10) with fabulous steaks, seafood, and pastas.

The **Pea Patch** is a saloon/motel/and so on good for Saturday's Peanut Day: Throw the shells on the floor.

The **Manitowish Waters Chamber of Commerce** (U.S. 51 N, 715/543-8488, www.manitowishwaters.org) is staffed by *great* folks!

Presque Isle

Northeast of Manitowish Waters and technically outside the state forest, Presque Isle was dubbed "Almost an Island" by French explorers. The mazelike streams and lake chains gave the land a resemblance to an island within a flowage. It calls itself Wisconsin's "Last Wilderness."

The world's largest **walleye hatchery** (8 A.M.–4:30 P.M. Mon.–Fri. year-round) produces millions of walleye for transplanting to area lakes—great, as it is the number one game fish in the state. It's a popular place to visit.

On an isolated promontory with more than 4,000 feet of shoreline—the **Bay View Lodge** (Bayview Rd., 715/686-2448, www.bayviewlodge.biz, $90 daily low season, $800–1,200 weekly) offers year-round one-, two-, and three-bedroom cottages.

The family-oriented **Lynx Lake Lodge** (Hwy. B, 715/686-2249 or 800/882-5969, www.zastrowslynxlakelodge.com) has weekly rentals from around $800 for a two-bedroom cottage with two meals daily. The dining room at the Lynx has brunches and smorgasbords worth the money.

More famous for its copious German food, the **Carlin Club Lodge** (715/686-2255 or 800/562-5900, dinner Mon.–Sat., $8–17) is a year-round lodge and boisterous dining room. You may even find a polka band around.

The **Presque Isle Chamber of Commerce** (715/686-2910, www.presqueisle.com) is right along Main Street.

Boulder Junction

One word: muskie. That's pretty much the obsession around Boulder Junction, locked in mortal, if benign, competition with Hayward in northwestern Wisconsin. The town touts itself as the "Muskie Capital of the World" (*sic,* I know, I know, they say "Musky"), as does its rival, and with nearly 200 lakes surrounding the town, you'll get the chance to meet your Pleistocene match somewhere.

Suddenly here you're in a zone of chichi coffee shops (no more silty campfire cowboy coffee!), boutiques, cafés, and even—gasp—a bookstore. And yet it's as North Woods as it gets. This refreshing mix impelled *Sports Afield* to dub Boulder Junction one of "America's Greatest Outdoor Sports Towns."

Something totally different: for some reason,

WISCONSIN'S WHITE WHALE

Every year, the well-nigh-impossible pursuit of the white whale of Wisconsin, the muskellunge (hereafter muskie) ineluctably turns the most rational of anglers into raving Ahabs. It's more than just a fish. It's a mental or mythical construct that life can only rarely approximate. Once hooked, these primeval behemoths can imitate the acrobatics of any marlin – or play smart and lie low on the bottom, sailor-knotting your test line. Averaging an hour or more to spot from the boat when hooked, the muskie is a formidable opponent.

Boulder Junction and Hayward are locked in a friendly competition over bragging rights to the title of "Muskie Capital of the World." Wisconsin's Vilas County and its western lake groupings now make a fairly decent living on frothing anglers looking for 50-inchers.

Good luck. It takes an average of 100 hours just to get a nibble, and the average required 10,000 casts is too much for all but the most obsessed. (Packer great Brett Favre purportedly hooked one on his second cast; it happened during the Packers' blessed 1996–1997 Super Bowl season, so it makes sense.) Once hooked, a muskie can toy with you for up to 45 minutes, tugging at but never quite taking the bait; once it does, you'd better not have anywhere to go in the near future.

THE CREATURE
The word "muskie" is still of doubtful etymology. The Ojibwa had a close cognate, which essentially translated as "ugly fish." Musk-

ies migrated eons ago from oceans to inland seas. Three basic types of muskie exist: the aforementioned basic species, or Great Lakes muskie; an Eastern, or Ohio, version; and a loathed mutation of a muskie and the northern pike, the Tiger Muskie. The mouth contains a jaw wrapped halfway around the head and the largest canine teeth of any freshwater fish. Those teeth can be used to attack mammals and birds as large as a muskrat (or a finger); more than one puzzled fisher has pulled out a skeletal smaller fish chewed up by a muskie while on the line.

The state record is a whopping 69-pounder taken in 1949 from a dammed section of the Chippewa River near Hayward; thus began the rivalry with the Boulder Junction area, which probably has more muskie in more of its lakes.

Extreme popularity among anglers, heavily sedimented lakes, and lakeshore overdevelopment hurt numbers, but catch-and-release imperatives and stocking (despite the insane cost to raise fingerling muskie) have ameliorated things somewhat. One-quarter of the current population has been raised through stocking.

And if you do land a legal muskie (32 inches), consider letting it go anyway. Only 10 percent of muskies reach that legal limit, and only a small percentage live 15 years. Exact replicas can be built for show. And certainly don't eat a Moby Dick: Old-time muskies can be laced with PCBs.

---

the area's whitetail deer herd has a recessive gene causing albinism, so don't be surprised if you espy one of the local "ghost herd."

Boulder Junction, in an admirable display of civic ambition, maintains its own **Boulder Area Trail System** for mountain bikes and hikers, and more are being created all the time. The trails start right at the visitors center, including a new 13.5-mile paved route to Crystal Lake. Near Boulder Junction is the largest wilderness area donated to The Nature Conservancy in the country. At 2,189 acres with 15 wild lakes

the **Catherine Wolter Wilderness Area** is open to low-impact recreation.

Dirt-cheap mom-and-pop operations to cushier condo-esque digs line the surrounding 20-odd lakes. Here's a tip: Trout Lake, the largest and deepest in the county, is almost wholly owned by the state, so shoreline clutter is kept to a minimum. Peruse the very few local options there for solitude.

A bit rustic but comfy and charming (I love how they call themselves a "C&B"—cabin and breakfast), the **Evergreen Lodge** (6235

Evergreen Ln., 715/385-2132, www.evergreenlodgewi.com, $650–1,500 weekly) is on Little Crooked Lake. Very cozy and modern housekeeping cabins are available, sleeping up to six people, with quite reasonable high-season rates.

White Birch Village (8764 Hwy. K, 715/385-2182, www.whitebirchvillage.com, $850–1,800), east of Boulder Junction, offers clean, modest homes with decks, and some with fireplaces—great cathedral ceilings in one! The owners have been in and around these parts for over 50 years.

The **Guide's Inn** (Hwy. M and Center St., 715/385-2233, 5–10 P.M. Mon.–Sat., $9–23) has long been a standard for continental cuisine. That said, though some still rave, others have opined strenuously that service has gone downhill.

Other fare goes from the simple to the eclectic at the wondrous ◖ **Outdoorsman** (Main St., 715/385-2826, closed Mon. nights), with a Bible-sized breakfast menu, great lunches, and some of the most wonderful casual-fine dining in the North Woods.

For a worthy Friday fish fry in a true Wisconsin atmosphere, **Pope's Gresham Lodge** (4042 Pope Rd., 715/385-2742) sits on Lower Gresham Lake and loads of taxidermy perches about you.

You can't miss the **information center** (Hwy. M, 715/385-2400 or 800/466-8759, www.boulderjct.org) in a renovated log cabin. Besides lots of information, the center's got a cozy living room atmosphere, so pull up a chair and peruse the brochures.

Star Lake

Check out the **Star Lake Forestry Plantation** on the remains of an old lumber camp. The plantation, begun in 1913, was the first attempt at silviculture in northern Wisconsin, a phenomenally successful venture, considering the forest is still around. Also in the area you'll find the **Star Lake-Plum Lake Hemlock Natural Area,** one of the state forest's 14 state natural and scientific areas.

A lodge of some repute in Wisconsin, and excellent for its range of economical to extravagant lodgings, ◖ **Hintz's North Star Lodge** (Hwy. K, 715/542-3600 or 800/788-5215, www.hintznorthstar.com) was once a grand old logging hotel, catering later to the Chicago railroads. The lodge offers housekeeping units, villas, and two lake homes, both with whirlpools. The lodge, however, is most popular for its creative Midwestern cuisine—a homey eatery since before the 20th century. Rates start at a promising $95 per night way up to $1,500 week for a historic home in Minocqua, with multi-night minimums during peak periods.

For classic but updated North Woods Wisconsin lodging—the kind of cabins oft-described as "well and sturdily built"—try **Camp Edna and Bear Cottage** (715/736-9696, www.campedna.com, $850–1,500 weekly), on Star Lake between Star Lake and Boulder Junction. They offer a year-round woodsy home and cottage (housing eight and six, respectively).

Lake Tomahawk

The **Shamrock Bar** (7235 Bradley St., 715/277-2544) houses what is supposedly the world's longest muskie; if that doesn't wow you, it's also got karaoke. Lake Tomahawk also hosts a semilegendary **duck race.** North of town via WI 47 to the state forest campground you'll find the **Lake Tomahawk Mounds,** four earthen mounds dating from A.D. 1000.

Land O' Lakes

Although aptly named Land O' Lakes is technically outside the auspices of the Northern Highland American Legion State Forest, it is pulled spiritually thataway by its own chains of lakes linking it with its state forest brethren.

To the east is Lac Vieux Desert, the headwaters of the not-yet-toiling Wisconsin River. To the west (actually, in full circumference) are an almost incalculable number of those famous little pools of water lined with resorts and summer cottages, including the 17-lake, 150-mile-long Cisco Chain, the second-longest chain of lakes in Wisconsin (and a historic route of natives and early explorers). West of Land O' Lakes along Highway B is the true continental divide and separation point for watersheds flowing to the Mississippi, Lake Superior, and Lake Michigan. A marker near Devils Lake shows the precise spot.

Crossing over into Michigan off Highway B via Highway Z, Highway 535 leads you into the **Sylvania Wilderness Area,** an established recreation area about 21,000 acres large, dotted with almost 40 lakes. Camping is available. While in Watersmeet, you could check out the puzzling **mystery lights** that have been intermittently observed during the past few decades. Go north on U.S. 45 out of Watersmeet to Paulding and then west on Robbins Pond Road. Park anywhere and head for a hill. The freaky lights appear to wisp up and out of the woods, where they hang for up to 15 minutes; some say they resemble a star but are very amber-colored.

Rohr's Tours (715/547-3321, www.rwt-canoe.com) offers guided wilderness tours (hours or days), heavy on canoeing. The service maintains its own primitive campground (and lodge) and offers complete outfitting and paddling instruction courses.

True history is at the **Gateway Lodge** (U.S. 45 and Hwy. B, 715/547-3321 or 800/848-8058, www.gateway-lodge.com, $85 studio, $95 suite), a landmark (great lobby with colossal fieldstone fireplace) in the 1930s and 1940s, when Hollywood big shots and presidents used to hang their hats here. A face-lift has left it comfy yet still rustic; now you don't have to worry about mice chewing holes in your bags! Modern amenities include an indoor pool, hot tub, and redwood sauna.

The **Sunrise Lodge** (5894 West Shore Dr., off Hwy. E, 715/547-3684 or 800/221-9689, www.sunriselodge.com, from $100), on the west shore of Lac Vieux Desert, has a fresh-scrubbed woodsy feeling in its 20 one- to seven-bedroom units. Plenty of home-cooked food is offered in the dining room and bakery. Recreation abounds, with its own exercise and nature trails in addition to the 4,600-acre lake. American Plan packages are necessary in summer.

You'll be hard-pressed to have a better time than at the always boisterous **Bear Trap Inn** (Hwy. B, 715/547-3422, 4–9 P.M. Tues.–Sat., $5–13), a couple of miles west on Highway B. It's one of the oldest eateries in Land O' Lakes, so you'll still hear expressions such as "wet your whistle" while waiting at the bar for a table. When you do sit down, go for the garlic stuffed tenderloin. Lively big band music may complete the effect.

Speaking of wetting one's whistle, for a true-blue North Woods experience, head along the South Shore Road of Lac Vieux Desert, out of Phelps, to the **Hillside Resort** (715/547-3646). It's about as woodsy as it gets. (From Land O' Lakes, take U.S. 45 south to Highway E and head east to South Shore Road.)

MINOCQUA, WOODRUFF, AND ARBOR VITAE

Location, location, location. That pretty much sums up these contiguous communities set amid the lush public verdance and 3,200 lakes. Only about 8,000 souls occupy the three burgs (Minocqua dominates—heck, it even seems cosmopolitan compared to Woodruff and AV), but they're drowned annually by a sea of southlanders come summer, with minor relief after Labor Day before the first snows and the ineluctable advance of the buzzing hordes of snowmobilers. Though it's not as well known as Minocqua and Woodruff, the town of Arbor Vitae—literally, "tree of life," named for the plethora of white cedar all around used by French explorers to ward off scurvy—is also considered part of the group.

Expect minivans and more minivans (and boat trailers). Lots of them. Along with Wal-Mart-size gas stations every which way. Though you might anticipate a foot-first leap into price-gouging or polluted gridlock, it's pretty low-stress for such a popular place.

History

Minocqua too was once a Sawdust City full of timber cutters and sawhogs. Never quite a risque conglomeration of speakeasies and poker games, the city had enough fast money to make things interesting. Next, squatters in rough camps to the north were thrown out by the

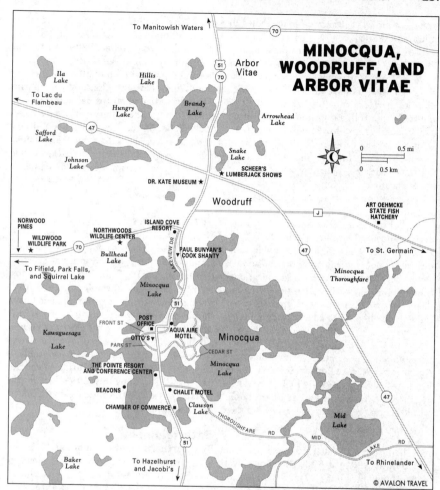

railroad, which set about platting Woodruff. Sister cities were born.

Almost serendipitous was the "discovery" of the towns as summer getaways. Trains chugging out of Chicago became known as the "Fisherman's Special" and "Northwoods Hiawatha." Since then, it's been Tourism (capital "T" intended) all the way. And with the paradisiacal location—more than *90 percent* of the area is in federal hands—it's hard to imagine a bust cycle.

Sights

In Woodruff, the **Dr. Kate Museum** (923 2nd Ave., 715/356-6896, 11 A.M.–4 P.M. Mon.–Fri. mid-June–Labor Day, free) showcases a real *Dr. Quinn, Medicine Woman*. Kate Pelham Newcomb, the "Angel on Snowshoes," was a hardy country doctor early in the 20th century. Trying to raise funds for a hospital, schoolchildren throughout the township and beyond initiated what became known as the "Million Penny Campaign." Enter that newbie television and the world was galvanized—more than $20 million was raised.

Kids—well, parents too, trust me—go nuts for **Scheer's Lumberjack Shows** (1126 1st Ave., 715/356-4050, www.scheerslumberjackshows.com), also in Woodruff. World champion lumberjacks run through the tricks of the trade in a rollicking show of logrolling, canoe jousting, ax throwing, chopping, all with Yanko the camp cook doing his spiel of gabbing and singing. Showtimes are at 7:30 P.M. Tuesday, Thursday, and Saturday, with matinees at 2 P.M. Wednesday and Friday, early June–late August. Admission is $10 adults.

Tucker the kiddies out more at the wonderful **Wildwood Wildlife Park** (W. WI 70, 715/356-5588, 9 A.M.–5:30 P.M. daily in summer, fewer hours spring and fall, $12 adults), a cross between a petting zoo and educational center. More than 110 species of fauna are dispersed across the spacious grounds. Boat rides, nature hikes, and educational programs are offered.

Others prefer to witness wildlife rehabilitation and wilderness return facilitation at the **Northwoods Wildlife Center** (8683 Blumstein Rd. and WI 70 W, 715/356-7400, 10 A.M.–4 P.M. Mon.–Sat., free), designed as equal parts hospital and education/research center. Free but they could use a few bucks, right?

Or check out one of the planet's largest and most high-tech cool-water fish hatcheries, the **Art Oehmcke State Fish Hatchery** (WI 47 and Hwy. J, 715/358-9213, 8 A.M.–4 P.M. daily, free) in Woodruff. The hatchery goes at a rate of almost 50,000 per year. King muskie holds court here—it ought to—this hatchery developed methods to "farm" these fish. Guided tours are given weekdays at 11 A.M. and 2 P.M.

Completing the scene is a slew of family amusement centers, replete with cacophonic go-carts or interminable holes of mini-golf and indigestible hot dog stand–style food. Not much is cheap.

Both the Rainbow and Willow Reservoirs offer thousands of acres of true wilderness areas, which are dwindling in the state. Between them lie 10,000 primeval water acres and 150 miles of unadulterated shoreline. **Rainbow Flowage** has an almost unheard-of concentration of eagles and osprey, with up to 20 pairs of osprey alone. **Willow Flowage** has nearly a dozen pairs of osprey and an almost equal number of eagles; it also has the county's only waterfall—**Cedar Falls,** on the Tomahawk River. To get there, take Cedar Falls Road out of Hazelhurst. You may even see the odd wolf pack. In 1998 the state of Wisconsin plunked down nearly $10 million to buy the Willow Flowage to retain its wilderness status.

Scenic Drives

West of Minocqua along WI 70 brings you to Mercer Lake Road, one endpoint for another grand Rustic Road, this one offering access to the Bearskin State Trail. It loops for almost 10 miles along innumerable lakes and hardwood spinneys before crossing the remains of the old railroad tracks that carried in the early throngs of tourists. Mercer Lake Road eventually links with Blue Lake Road (head east) and crosses the Tomahawk River; in the middle is an optional length of Sutton Road, which leads back to WI 70. Along this section look for the remains of early-20th-century cabins built by homesteaders.

Entertainment

The **Northern Lights Playhouse** (715/356-7173) performs Broadway musicals and some nonmusicals June–October in Hazelhurst. Brand-new is the **Campanile Center** (141 Milwaukee St., Minocqua, 715/356-9700, www.campanilecenter.org) in an old Catholic church building; it offers tons of stuff, including Broadway shows, ragtime music, and big brass bands.

Recreation

A true gem of Minocqua is the **Minocqua Winter Park and Nordic Center** (12375 Scotchman Lake Rd., 715/356-3309), rated in the top 10 in the Midwest and offering 70-kilometer tracks for striding and skating, as well as three short loops for children. Some weeknights a 1.5-mile loop is lighted. It also operates an open telemarking slope.

Guided **fishing** is a serious industry in Minocqua. In Vilas County alone, which encompasses much of the forest land and tons of the lakes, during one Muskie Marathon anglers registered 1,672 muskies totaling 22,000 pounds. Many local pros stake their livelihoods on bringing up lunker muskies or walleye; some also dabble in bass or northern pike.

Accommodations

More than 32 lakes lie within the parameters of Minocqua; it's a mind-boggling array of accommodations out there. But do your homework and reserve early for summer.

Minocqua, Arbor Vitae, and Woodruff have around a dozen basic motels, including the best bet for budget travelers, the **Chalet Motel** (715/356-3003, $45), just north of the visitors information center on U.S. 51. It's clean, quiet and cheap, all year.

Meticulously clean rooms overlooking Lake Minocqua are at the **Aqua Aire Motel** (806 U.S. 51 N, 715/356-3433, www.aquaaire.com, $80 s, $90 d). Some rooms have refrigerators and microwaves and it's got some extra offerings.

Within the Minocqua city limits is **The Pointe Resort Hotel and Conference Center** (8269 U.S. 51 S, 715/356-4431, www.thepointeresort.com, from $129), a first-class condo resort on a minor hillock overlooking Minocqua Lake Bay. Spacious studio and one- or two-bedroom condo suites are excellently appointed and have private lakeside balconies or patios. A full list of recreational extras is available.

Along similar lines is the more venerable **Beacons** (8250 Northern Rd., 715/356-5515, www.thebeacons.com), with its landmark boathouse on Minocqua Lake. Around in some fashion since the early 1900s, today it's a lakeside condo resort with one- to three-bedroom units, town houses, condos, and great cottages available. Nightly rates (don't count on it) start at $125, weekly rates around $650.

One resort that is daily-stay (though that may change during peak seasons) is **Island**

Cove Resort (8616 Lakeview Dr., 715/356-5026, www.islandcoveresort.com) with some motel-type rooms from $75, along with more expensive lakeside units and cabins. Some of the units on the lake have fireplace suites. The sunset views are worthwhile. Weekly rates start at around $440.

Food

Best burgers in the North Woods are at **Otto's** (U.S. 51, 715/356-6134, from $5), a Bavarian-style lunch and dinner joint with great brats (from Sheboygan, no less) and friendly folks. (The **Little Musky Bar** on U.S. 51 in Arbor Vitae has equal burgers, but this Packers fan saw a few too many Chicago sports items within—kidding, people, kidding!)

Another fine choice is █ **Jacobi's** (9820 Cedar Falls Rd., 715/356-5591, 5–9 P.M. daily in summer, much less often off-season, $15–25), a quarter mile from downtown in Hazelhurst in a classic backwoods inn (upscale tavern, more like it) dating from the 1930s.

Norwood Pines (W. WI 70, 715/356-3666, 4:30–9 P.M. daily, $9–20) is a supper club (there have been piano singalongs known to break out here) that has great food served on a screened deck over Patricia Lake.

Superb Sicilian-style food is served at **Mama's** (W. WI 70, 715/356-5070, 5–10 P.M. daily, $6–16), which has been doling out sustenance on Curtis Lake to visitors from tots to seniors. Try the pepper steak. There's also good pizza, and the (off-season) Wednesday buffet is a treat for the wallet.

Copious feeds are at **Paul Bunyan's Cook Shanty** (U.S. 51 between Minocqua and Woodruff, 715/356-6270, breakfast, lunch, and dinner until 9 P.M. daily May–Oct., $7–11), the place with the gargantuan Paul and Babe the Blue Ox out front. Expect lumberjack-style meals and old-style cook-shack decor.

Information

The **Minocqua-Woodruff-Arbor Vitae Area Chamber of Commerce** (U.S. 51, 800/446-6784, www.minocqua.org) is right on the highway and well-stocked.

TROUBLE IN PARADISE

It all began in the early 1970s, with the arrest of two members of the Lac du Flambeau Ojibwa Reservation who had crossed reservation borders to fish walleye. A class-action suit followed, and the debate set forth: What, if any, residual fishing rights do Wisconsin Native Americans possess in ceded territory?

Cases that followed focused on spearfishing. Ultimately, a federal appeals court ruling stated the Native Americans had the right to exercise treaty rights granted in the 1830s and 1840s; one treaty said unequivocally that the Natives have rights to use off-reservation lands "until required to move by the President," which never happened.

The Ojibwa have ever since, come spring and fall, returned to the waters and, using traditional-style tridents, harvested walleye and a few muskies. In essence, the decision stated that Native Americans are entitled to first fishing and to a 100 percent take of off-reservation lakes, so long as the practice doesn't harm the resources.

Then came the protests. The most famous group was Stop Treaty Abuse (STA), which garnered the most press coverage. The basic arguments against Indian spearing are that it's unfair special privilege, the night-fishing disrupts the spawning of walleye (in fact, most lakes in the 1840s didn't even *have* walleye), and that if the Ojibwa take their limit, the result would be a zero limit on walleye for non-Indian anglers. (In the Great North Woods, that is tantamount to treason.)

Shell-shocked resort owners, anglers, and citizens didn't know what to do. Some contacted legislators, some organized committees, some went so far as to actually communicate with the Ojibwa, and still others squared off with the Indians at boat landings, where tension ran thick and more than a few incidents of violence ensued. Millions of dollars were spent in police overtime, and hundreds of arrests were made. At one point, the Wisconsin governor had to appear on television to beg the protesters to stay away from the landings. (*Mother Jones* magazine nailed it, calling it "Wisconsin's Walleye War.")

Things calmed down until 1995, when things flared up again. Among other issues, the Menominee Nation in the southeast expressed a desire to reassert treaty rights over commercial fishing. Another group added increased walleye harvesting. In 2000, federal courts blocked the tribes' plans.

This can be expected to reoccur *ad infinitum*.

Though the government denies it, the Ojibwa claim the state tried to railroad them into dropping their walleye limit by suggesting it would start looking closely at casino revenues. Many believe opposition to Indian spearfishing at present has less to do with the walleye than it does resentment over nouveau-riche Indians with loaded casino coffers.

Getting There

Trans North Aviation (715/479-6777) operates out of both Eagle River and Minocqua/Woodruff during summer to Chicago's Palwaukee Airport.

LAC DU FLAMBEAU INDIAN RESERVATION

Wisconsinites unfortunately got to know the Lac du Flambeau Reservation all too well in the late 1980s during furious confrontations between Ojibwa spearfishers and local sportfishers. Edgy and tense in the beginning, while federal courts pondered old treaties, disputes over spearing rights versus nonnative rights reached a head with ugly episodes of violence at boat landings and scores of arrests.

Tensions have eased somewhat, though at times the Ojibwa alarmed northern residents again with their claims to take 100 percent of their limit of walleye, which Wisconsin DNR said would effectively eliminate any sportfishing in the region other than catch-and-release. The Ojibwa in turn were angered by what they considered railroading by the state government, which demanded the Ojibwa drop the quota or the state would start meddling into gaming receipts. Though it never came to pass, it did shed light once again on things that seemingly never change.

The Sioux Indians originally controlled the current Ojibwa reservation. A strategic location at a midpoint between the Montreal River route from the Wisconsin River to Lake Superior as well as the Chippewa River to the Mississippi, it was finally wrested by the Ojibwa around 1650. Lac du Flambeau ("Lake of the Torches") is what the bewildered French first said when they saw the Ojibwa spearfishing in birchbark canoes in the inky black night, lit only by their torches. The largest Native American group never to be forcibly removed from their state territory, the Ojibwa reservation status was established in 1854 with the LaPointe treaty, signed on Madeline Island. It became a general case of federal mismanagement, as usual. The Depression-era WPA guide to Wisconsin took the government to task for conditions on the reservation:

> *In a report published in 1934 the Land Planning Committee...discusses this as an outstanding example of mismanagement of Indian affairs.... For 25 years the reservation was held in trust by the Government, which permitted outsiders to log off the timber, thus depriving the Indian owners of the only valuable property they had. By 1914 lumbering ceased, and the Indians were left unemployed on denuded land. Eventually each Indian received a small tract, virtually worthless for farming, not large enough to be used for grazing or forestry.*

Life on the reservation is better today, though certainly not perfect, judging from the events surrounding spearfishing sites. The Ojibwa population today hovers around the 2,500 mark, with tribal enterprises including a well-respected traditional Ojibwa village, a cultural center and museum, pallet manufacturing, a mall, a fish hatchery, and a casino.

◖ Waswagoning

In 2005, vandals torched a great deal of one of northern Wisconsin's most wondrous cultural offerings—Waswagoning (wa-SWAH-gahning), a meticulous re-creation of an Ojibwa village spread over 20 acres along Moving Cloud Lake on the Lac du Flambeau Indian Reservation. In a credit to the founder, the young arsonists underwent cultural sensitivity training in lieu of a harsh jail term. Hate, in essence, will not be allowed to soil this place.

It remains today an amazing place after a rebuild, devoid of tackiness—and quite possibly the most significant cultural attraction in the north—its name means the same as the Francophone Lac du Flambeau. Various birchbark lodges dot the landscape, connected by trails, each lodge offering demonstrations on aspects of Ojibwa culture—winter maple camps, tanning, birchbark canoe building, wigwam making, specialty dances or weaving, among others. There's a teaching lodge designed for instructional purposes; the directors even delve into Ojibwa philosophies and the sacred side, including the sweat lodge. With the isolated trails and moving lake-edge scenery, the whole is quite effective. There is precious little like it for itinerant tourists. Tours are available 10 A.M.–4 P.M. Tuesday through Saturday, from mid-May through late September, with rates of $8 adults. To get there, go west on WI 47 to Highway H and then a third of a mile. For information, call 715/588-3560 or log on to www.waswagoning.org.

Other Sights

The separate **George W. Brown, Jr. Chippewa Museum and Cultural Center** (603 Peace Pipe Rd., 715/588-3333, 10 A.M.–4 P.M. Mon.–Fri., until 7 P.M. on powwow nights, March–October, $4 adults) is in downtown Lac du Flambeau. The history and culture of the Lac du Flambeau Band of Chippewa is detailed through the most comprehensive collection of Ojibwa artifacts anywhere, with most emphasis from the French fur trade days. Exhibits are sectioned into four seasons. A century-plus-old 24-foot dugout canoe is the favorite attraction, as are ceremonial drums and some clothing. A record sturgeon pulled from the Flambeau lakes is also on display. Tours are available and occasional workshops are conducted, with hands-on demonstrations.

Lac du Flambeau Reservation operates its own **fish hatchery** (N. WI 47, 715/588-3303), raising millions of walleye, muskie, and trout. Scheduled tours are available by appointment. Trout fishing for a fee is available daily, with no license required.

Events

The Lac du Flambeau Indian Bowl hosts **powwows** at 7 P.M. Tuesday mid-June–mid-August. I *love* the invitation tagline: "Don't bring a watch, a business suit, a schedule, or a rain cloud!"

In August, the **Great Western Days Rodeo** is a real-deal competition.

Recreation

The Lac du Flambeau **marina** has access to the 10-lake chain Lac du Flambeau sits on. The Bear and Trout Rivers are good ways to explore most of the lakes, which are very canoe friendly. The Lac du Flambeau chamber of commerce has a good map marking sites of historical interest along the routes, from the crucial water routes via the Bear River to sites of early trading posts, Indian camps from earliest settlement periods, battle sites, forts, Indian boarding schools, and the largest lumber yard in Wisconsin. You can also pass by Medicine Rock, on which Ojibwa made offerings, and the legendary "Crawling Rock," a series of rocks that were purportedly dropped as stepping stones by a warrior fleeing a charging bear; others say it's because one rock seems to move across the water.

The mesotrophic, spring-fed lakes of the Lac du Flambeau chain are also prime muskie waters—three world-class records for line fishing have been recorded around here.

Lac du Flambeau

The town of Lac du Flambeau is virtually in the middle of the reservation, set amid five lakes. For information on the whole area, the chamber of commerce's website (www.lacduflambeauchamber.com) is quite good.

Approximately 30 lodging choices are spread throughout the 10 lakes in the vicinity of the reservation. The venerable **Dillman's Sand Lake Lodge** (13277 Dillman's Way, 715/588-3143, www.dillmans.com) is synonymous with North Woods Wisconsin. The lodge offers condo efficiencies in addition to comfortable cabins perfect for families. And there's always something to do at Dillman's—the lodge often sponsors bike tours, and the Dillman's Creative Arts Foundation sponsors wonderful arts workshops and exhibits. All the amenities would take a page to list; over its 250 acres is everything one could want to do. There's also a sports program for children come summer. Rates run $110–400 daily, up to $2,900 weekly.

TURTLE-FLAMBEAU FLOWAGE

Bookending the western side of the Northern Highland American Legion State Forest is the "Crown Jewel of the North"—also called Wisconsin's version of the Boundary Waters Canoe Area of northern Minnesota. Of all Wisconsin's numerous flowages, reservoirs on major river chains, the Turtle-Flambeau is perhaps the wildest and most primitive. The majority of its shoreline is in state hands and thus off-limits to development—in fact, many of the lakes in the flowage have only one (or no) resorts or cottages on them.

The area was originally dammed in 1926 by endless public and private endeavors to regulate water supply and secondarily supply power. With the Turtle backed up behind the "Hoover Dam of Iron County," the waterways of the Bear, Manitowish, Turtle, and Flambeau Rivers became enmeshed. The resulting 20,000-plus acres, one of the larger bodies of water in the state, has never gotten the same attention as other regions of Wisconsin—thankfully so, say many. To keep it as close to wilderness as possible, in 1990 the state of Wisconsin bought the whole mess, lock, stock, and barrel. Nine lakes, numerous

LOONS

The shrill call of a loon dancing across placid lake waters: unforgettable. Yet these gorgeous birds are threatened by, in order, shoreline development, pollution, and even unknowing harassment by recreational lake users.

The Wisconsin counties of Vilas and Oneida have close to 2,000 loons. The Turtle-Flambeau Flowage has the largest number of common loon nesting sites found anywhere. The common loon, found on Wisconsin waters, is one of four species and the only one outside of northern Canada and Alaska. It is the head that is most striking – an obsidian green, with a narrow, pointed beak. The neck will be ringed in a thick band of white. Usually black and white, with an angelic wingspan of about five feet, its streamlined-but-oddly-configured body is decidedly not for landlubbing – loons often have to remain half-in, half-out of the water, resting their chests on the shore.

A loon can dive as deep as 200 feet for a full 10 minutes searching for aquatic delicacies. When it wants air, it "sprints" across the water surface for almost a quarter mile, gathering speed for flight. Ferociously territorial, only one nesting pair of loons will occupy a lake, except for unusually large lakes, which might have two.

Scientists have classified loon "speak" into four categories: wails, hoots, tremolos, and yodels. The former two are what you'll probably hear at your campsite. The wails and hoots both indicate either concern or interest. The latter two are defensive cries.

creeks, three rivers—backcountry lovers find it all orgasmic. Virtually all flora and fauna native to the state are here in spades, with the granddaddy sportfish, the lake sturgeon, also prowling the waters. The highest numbers in the state of nesting pairs of eagles, loons, and osprey are on the property.

The flowage is broached primarily via Mercer and Manitowish Waters on the north side, Springstead in the east, and Butternut/Park Falls on the west.

Note: Highway FF is a grand bicycle route stretching between Butternut and Mercer. Winding, rustic, and not too heavily laden with traffic, it has some wearied sections of road, but overall it isn't too bad.

Canoeing

The canoeing is superlative in the flowage—as close to alone as you could hope to be. The north fork of the Flambeau River is a 26-mile trip from the flowage to Park Falls; almost two dozen rapids are transgressed en route.

The **Bear River Trail** is a 25-mile trip, reasonable for novices, that leaves southwest of Lac du Flambeau on Flambeau Lake, with one easy rapid; eventually it joins with the Manitowish River and lolls into the town of Manitowish.

The heart of the flowage is traversed by two popular trails: the **Manitowish Route** and the **Turtle River Route.**

It goes without saying that you should do your homework before sliding the canoe into the water. Conditions and water levels vary, so check ahead.

Accommodations

Many simple North Woods–style cabins, lodges, and resorts line the southwestern section of the flowage, essentially trailing Highway FF from Butternut to Mercer. The places are no-frills, precisely the way it's supposed to be. Included within is **Deadhorse Lodge** (4125 N. Popko Circle West, 715/476-2521, www.deadhorselodge.com, $110–200 daily with three-night minimum). Get past the name and check out the nine newer vacation cabins of all sizes and varieties, some with whirlpools and fireplaces. Others have loved **Flambeau Vista Retreat** (Park Falls, 715/762-4612, www.flambeauvista.com, from $140 with two-night minimum), which has two multi-person cabins.

For those who would rather rough it, more than a dozen established campsites are found along the flowage, many on little islets dotting the reservoir—that's the best camping. The eastern bulbous section of the Chequamegon National Forest is also right nearby. Contact any of the area's chambers of commerce for specifics on regulations and precise locations—some of the sites are not easy to find. Sites are first-come, first-served.

Information

The Wisconsin DNR actually has little useful information. Better would be to contact the chambers of commerce in Mercer (5150 N. U.S. 51, 715/476-2389, www.mercerwi.com), Hurley (316 Silver St., 715/561-4334, www. hurleywi.com) and Park Falls (400 S. 4th Ave., 715/762-2703 or 800/762-2709, www.park falls.com). Also try a compendium site: turtle flambeauflowage.com.

The Iron Range

Hurley and even smaller Montreal lie in the midst of the mighty Penokee Iron Range as well as the over-the-border Gogebic Iron Range, the last and most massive of the Upper Peninsula's three prodigious iron deposits, long since depleted. The range, for many Wisconsinites, has been unfairly relegated to backwater status—too many news reports in southern Wisconsin mentioned the population flight from Iron County in the bad old days of economic decline. And while it is true the county ranks pretty low in population and thus doesn't have the infrastructure taxes to pretty things up as the richer areas to the southeast do, Iron County has important history and even some outstanding topography. The Turtle-Flambeau Flowage is one of the most wildernesslike stretches of any northern river, and Iron County competes squarely with across-the-state rival Marinette County for numbers of cascades. Marinette may have more, but no falls beat Iron County's for sheer height and isolation.

The Flambeau Trail

Native Americans followed a route from Saxon Harbor northwest of Hurley, portaging canoes and beaver pelts between their villages and Northwest Fur Company Trading Posts. The 90-mile trail from Madeline Island to Lac du Flambeau became the crucial Flambeau Trail, followed in due course by explorers, trappers, traders, and the U.S. military. The whole thing

is mapped out now, passing Superior Falls at the first take-out point. **Little Finland,** one of the last and best bastions of hardy *Suomi* mining heritage in the Upper Midwest, houses the National Finnish-American Cultural Center— here check out the Finnish-style fish-tail construction of adhering beams, which once stood in Ashland's bay as an ore dock. Also, head five miles south of Hurley to the corner of Dupont and Rein Roads, where you'll see a huge stone barn designed by a Finnish stonemason. The trail later passes the **Continental Divide;** the northern waters above the divide were unnavigable, necessitating this 45-mile portage to southern-flowing streams. Finally, the trail reaches the Turtle-Flambeau Flowage area at the reconstructed **Mercer Depot**—now a historical society office—before heading into Manitowish and the trail's debouchment toward Lac du Flambeau.

HURLEY

Living museum Hurley sure had some big britches in its headier early days. The little town—more or less a sister city to boomtown Ironwood, Michigan, across the border—arose more than a century ago on the iron riches taken from the subterranean veins of the mammoth Gogebic and Penokee Iron Ranges, the former accounting for almost 40 percent of the Upper Peninsula's economy at its zenith (about 350 mines tore through the subterranean stretches). White pine wealth followed

© THOMAS HUHTI

the largest of its kind remaining: the Plummer Mine head frame, west of Montreal

later. "Lusty infants on a diet of lumber and iron ore," the old WPA guide noted.

What really set Hurley apart from other boomtowns was its unimaginable bacchanalia, for which it became legendary. At its sybaritic zenith, more than 75 saloons lined the aptly named Silver Street, wooing the 7,000-odd salty miners and loggers. The same WPA guide quotes the prevailing wisdom along the logger/miner transient railway: "The four toughest places in the world are Cumberland, Hayward, Hurley, and Hell, and Hurley is the toughest of 'em all." It is against a background of such legend that Wisconsin native and Pulitzer Prize–winner Edna Ferber set the harrowing, only slightly fictionalized account of the brutal Lottie Morgan murder, *Come and Get It,* in Hurley.

Things tamed somewhat with the waning fortunes of ore and receding lines of timber—not to mention Prohibition. Many saloons and dance halls boarded up tight. The rest, however, went backroom or simply hibernated while the mobsters used Hurley as a haven

during Prohibition. When Prohibition was repealed, the town again saw a throwback to drinking and debauchery—even *more* drinking halls lined the raucous Silver Street.

Things have finally cooled off in tough-as-hell Hurley; in fact, you'd be hard-pressed to find anything rowdier along Silver Street than an occasional argument over a Packer game in a local tavern. (To be sure, though, Silver Street hasn't lost all of what made it infamous.) Otherwise, Hurley finds itself wrapped in lore and history—proudly so—and as the nucleus of a winter recreation paradise.

Sights

The grande dame hereabouts is the somewhat wearied but eminently proud **Iron County Courthouse Museum** (303 Iron St., 715/561-2244, 10 A.M.–2 P.M. Mon., Wed., and Fri.–Sat., free). It is indeed a leviathan—turreted and steepled—built in 1893 for a princely $40,000 and sold later to the county. It is worth most of an afternoon. A personal favorite is the mock-up of a Silver Street saloon on the top floor, using carved bars from one of those that made the town legendary. Or visit on a Saturday and you might see volunteers using original late-19th-century Scandinavian-style rag-rug weaving looms. Local artisans have also built replicas of, well, darn near everything. The basement has a morgue—seriously—with a tin casket, cooling board, altar, and requisite old Bible.

A mile west of town is the art deco **Cary Mine Building** (west on WI 77 to Ringle Dr.), the epicenter of mining operations for 80 years.

Finns came in waves to these regions, and their heritage is feted daily at **Little Finland** (U.S. 2, west of U.S. 51 junction, www.littlefinland.com, 10 A.M.–2 P.M. Wed. and Sat., Apr.–Dec., free), home to a museum to Finnish immigration and homesteading, and a great opportunity to scope out traditional Finnish "fish-tail" building construction—and note that some of the timber used to build the center came from the massive Ashland ore docks.

◖ Iron County's Waterfalls

Iron County boasts more than 50 waterfalls, from the wilderness-accessible to the roadside. It's got six of the state's 10 tallest and boasts the highest concentration in the Midwest. Show up during spring snowmelt and these bad boys simply roar.

A note: Things change. Land changes hands and suddenly access roads are no longer, well, accessible. Definitely contact the Hurley chamber of commerce (316 Silver St., 715/561-4334, www.hurleywi.com). It's also got *precise* directions (it would require 10 pages to do so in this guide), right down to GPS coordinates (though it apologizes for taking them from the riverbanks and not in the middle of the falls!).

The highest are personal favorites **Potato River Falls** and the hard-to-find **Superior Falls,** both a respectable 90 feet. To reach the Potato River Falls, head west; south of U.S. 2 in Gurney is a sign to Potato River Falls along a gravel road. Magnificent upper and lower falls don't see many folks, so the trails are great for exploring. There's also rustic camping.

Continuing down WI 169 will bring you to **Wren Falls,** with great trout fishing and more primitive camping, though a meager 15-foot drop for the falls. Superior Falls is west of Hurley 12 miles and then north on WI 122 for 4.2 miles. Cross the Michigan border, go half a mile, and turn left on a gravel road (it's easy to miss—keep your eyes peeled). There's a parking area and signs to the great, chuffing 90-foot cascade raining into Lake Superior.

The east branch of the Montreal River has **Peterson Falls** (35 feet) and **Spring Camp Falls** (20 feet). The west branch has **Kimball Park Falls,** with a series of riffles, and 15-foot **Gile Falls** (check out the large waste rock tailing piles, residual of iron ore mining, across the way).

The Turtle River in the Mercer area also has three oft-visited falls, including the ever-popular **Lake of the Falls,** with rustic camping. The Upson area has two cascades, **Rouse Falls** and **Little Balsam Falls,** which are accessible only with some orienteering. Easier and equally lovely falls can be found along the

one of Iron County's waterfalls

Black River Parkway north of Ironwood and Bessemer, Michigan, north of Hurley in the Upper Peninsula.

Entertainment and Events

Bars and taverns worth mentioning line the historic five blocks of the downtown Silver Street area, yet be careful: There is a red-light district in the nether reaches!

The oldest marathon in the state and second-oldest in the Midwest (dating from 1969) is the **Paavo Nurmi Marathon,** named, appropriately, for a Finn—dubbed the "Flying Finn" for his numerous Olympic gold medals—and run in August. It's a good place to feast on pasties and *mojakaa,* a beef stew. Thanks to all the snow, Hurley holds its **Red Light Snowmobile Rally** earlier than most, in mid-December.

Recreation

This is Big Snow Country, so snowmobiling is king—bigger even than skiing. More than 350 miles of groomed trails are spread throughout the vicinity, and rentals are available in Hurley. The town even maintains a **24-hour recreation hotline** (715/561-3866) for updates on snow conditions.

Three cross-country trails are maintained in the vicinity, totaling about 40 miles. Contact the Iron County Development Zone Council (715/562-2922) for information. The trails are maintained by donations.

A magnificent trail network for bikers is the 300-mile **Pines and Mines Mountain Bike Trail System,** operated jointly by Michigan, Wisconsin, and the USFS and running through the carpets of forests in Iron County and the Upper Peninsula. Michigan has two good ones—the **Ehlco Tract Complex** and **Pomeroy/Henry Lake** set of gravel roads. Iron County has the third section, an amazing spiderweb of trails and roads leading along old railroad grades, logging roads, and roadways, passing historical sites (in particular the Plummer mine head frame) and tons of forests, streams, and even waterfalls. Those in incredible shape could even make it all the way to Mercer, or west to Upson and beyond.

Thirteen of the best waterfalls are accessible via this system. For info or maps, contact the Hurley chamber of commerce.

For type-T expert—read, expert—kayakers, the rare north-flowing Montreal River is a dream between Saxon Falls and the top of the dam before Superior Falls—a once-you're-committed type of white-water adventure through spectacular canyons over 200 feet high.

For **camping,** the closest county park is **Weber Lake,** west of town on WI 77, right on Highway E. Another is at **Saxon Harbor,** at Lake Superior off U.S. 2 onto WI 122. This is really for RVs, though.

Accommodations and Food

Hurley's got a few budget motels, but you'd do best to head east into Ironwood, Michigan, along U.S. 2; there you'll find some good $40 rooms, even in summer, and many of those motels have Finnish-style saunas. In Hurley the **Anton-Walsh House** (202 Copper St., 715/561-2065, www.anton-walsh.com, $119–139) is in a century-old American foursquare craftsman home. But for real historic lodging, head for Montreal.

So close to the Upper Peninsula of Michigan are you that it'd be a shame not to indulge in that epicurean delight of the Yoopers—the pasty. Honestly, this half-Yooper can claim that Hurley's cafés and diners make the closest approximation to a pasty as you'll find in Wisconsin.

The **Liberty Bell Chalet** (109 5th Ave., 715/561-3753, dinner daily, lunch Mon.–Thurs., $6–12)—I've never not heard it as "The Bell"—has been dishing up Italian and American for nearly a century; most go for the pizza. The most, um, sophisticated meal for a county is without question at the **Kimball Inn** (154 Hwy. 2, 715/561-4095, dinner Tues.–Sun., from $12), with is-this-a-real-bistro? food. Only problem is they close up shop in winter.

Information

Visit the **Hurley Chamber of Commerce** (316 Silver St., 715/561-4334, www.hurleywi.com) for information on the area.

VICINITY OF HURLEY
Montreal

Along the way to Montreal, note exceedingly diminutive Pence, with more than 20 log structures of all sorts visible from the road. This is one of the largest concentrations of such architecture in Wisconsin.

Once peopled by company miners living in squat white shotgun shacks, Montreal today is a living microcosm of the area's heritage. Long ago it was the site of the world's deepest iron ore mine, memorialized with a marker along WI 77. Once the only completely planned and platted company town in Wisconsin, the whole place is on the National Register of Historic Places. Mining is gone but not forgotten—it lives on west of town in the only extant mining head frame, the **Plummer Mine Headframe.** Eighty feet tall and imposing as ever, it's one of the truer pieces of history you'll see around. An interpretive park surrounds it, highlighted by the **Cary Building,** the art deco main office of the mine.

Accommodations in Montreal include **The Inn** (104 Wisconsin Ave., 715/561-5180, $85), a 1913 B&B built by the Montreal Mining Company for workers. It has lovely interiors and fantastic hosts. A couple of other historic dwellings are now quasi-B&Bs as well.

INDIANHEAD COUNTRY: NORTHWESTERN WISCONSIN

The northwestern reaches have been dubbed (by whom it's never been made clear) as Indianhead Country, ostensibly because the northern stretch of the St. Croix River and the Bayfield Peninsula form a Native American chief gazing westward. That may be a bit of a stretch, but it does lend a touch of romanticism to the region.

Consider that within one chapter we're talking about Amish tours and muskie fishing nearly simultaneously, it shows you that, honestly, enormous northwestern Wisconsin defies any attempts to capture it in thumbnail sketches. Simply this: within one grand region, the northwest offers everything that the rest of the state can boast.

One consortium of northwestern counties (www.wisconsinindianhead.org) has information on the entire region.

PLANNING YOUR TIME

One look-see at a map will help you forget about a do-it-all weekend. No problem, as **Bayfield** (and the across-the-water Apostle Islands) is quite possibly the most perfectly realized weekend getaway spot in the state. Otherwise, the Chequamegon National Forest has some of the most isolated camping in Wisconsin. To even attempt the madness that is seeing it all in a short time, this author bases himself in kinda-central **Hayward** and barrels about in a grand radar sweep!

And even driving like a mad trucker, a week is tough for this author. Why not give it two weeks? Come on, tell your boss, you deserve it!

© SCOTT NESVOLD/123RF.COM

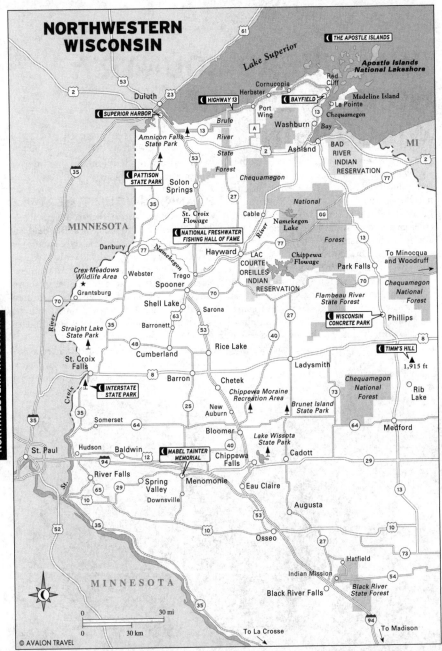

NORTHWESTERN WISCONSIN

THE APOSTLE ISLANDS

Lake Superior

Apostle Islands
National Lakeshore

Duluth

HIGHWAY 13

Cornucopia
Herbster

Red
Cliff

Madeline Island

BAYFIELD

La Pointe

SUPERIOR HARBOR

Port
Wing

Chequamegon

Brule

Washburn

Bay

MI

Amnicon Falls
State Park

River

A

Ashland

BAD
RIVER
INDIAN
RESERVATION

State

PATTISON
STATE PARK

Solon
Springs

Forest

Chequamegon

National

MINNESOTA

St. Croix
Flowage

Cable

Namekegon
Lake

GG

Forest

NATIONAL FRESHWATER
FISHING HALL OF FAME

River

Danbury

Hayward

LAC
COURTE
OREILLES
INDIAN
RESERVATION

Chippewa
Flowage

Park Falls

To Minocqua
and Woodruff

Crex Meadows
Wildlife Area

Webster

Trego

Chequamegon
National
Forest

Grantsburg

Spooner

Flambeau River
State Forest

Shell Lake

Sarona

WISCONSIN
CONCRETE PARK

Phillips

Straight Lake
State Park

Barronett

TIMM'S HILL

1,915 ft

St. Croix
Falls

Cumberland

Rice Lake

Ladysmith

Chequamegon
National
Forest

Rib
Lake

INTERSTATE
STATE PARK

Barron

Chetek

Chippewa Moraine
Recreation Area

Brunet Island
State Park

Medford

Somerset

New
Auburn

St. Paul

Hudson

Baldwin

MABEL TAINTER
MEMORIAL

Bloomer

Lake Wissota
State Park

Cadott

Chippewa
Falls

River Falls

Spring
Valley

Menomonie

Eau Claire

Downsville

Augusta

Osseo

MINNESOTA

Hatfield

Indian Mission

Black River
State Forest

Black River Falls

0   30 mi

0   30 km

To La Crosse

To Madison

© AVALON TRAVEL

HIGHLIGHTS

 Mabel Tainter Memorial: Menomonie's memorial is a superb example of what lumber wealth did right (page 271).

◖ Interstate State Park: The St. Croix National Scenic Riverway is best viewed from the rugged ridges of this spectacular park (page 276).

◖ Superior Harbor: Some of the world's largest ore docks will really make you skid to a halt (page 283).

◖ Pattison State Park: None of the state's cascades are as splendid as the towering cascade here (page 284).

◖ Bayfield: This town could have stepped out of a picture postcard; you'll likely not want to leave (page 286).

◖ Highway 13 from Bayfield to Superior: Passing through some of the most charming villages you'll ever see, this tour may be the one that you remember the most (page 289).

◖ The Apostle Islands: One of the state's great treasures, these, of the eponymous national lakeshore, are worth a week of sea kayaking and exploring (page 297).

◖ Wisconsin Concrete Park: Folk art of a quiet, inspirational kind is at this author's fave roadside attraction, in Phillips (page 309).

◖ Timm's Hill: This is the state's highest point. Big deal? Show up when the riotous colors of autumn appear (page 310)!

◖ National Freshwater Fishing Hall of Fame: Partly inside a leviathan muskie, this has to be seen to be believed (page 315).

LOOK FOR ◖ TO FIND RECOMMENDED SIGHTS, ACTIVITIES, DINING, AND LODGING.

NORTHWESTERN WISCONSIN

Eau Claire and Vicinity

The city of "Clear Water" is the largest community in northern Wisconsin and lies at a strategic point in the Chippewa River Valley. Busy and pretty, it's bigger (56,000 and change) than Wisconsinites realize.

Timber opportunists came snooping, here as everywhere, as early as 1822. In total, Eau Claire

would process 46 million board feet of lumber, which explains its nickname, "Sawdust City."

Eau Claire went through the usual lumber boomtown throes—a saloon for every five residents, internecine timber squabbles, and violent flare-ups. The city fought with upstream rival Chippewa Falls over water rights. Eau Claire's

EAU CLAIRE

© AVALON TRAVEL

0   1 mi

0   1 km

powers had the forethought to harness the local rapids for hydroelectric power, one reason it would eventually eclipse Chippewa Falls up the river when the timber vanished.

SIGHTS
Carson Park

The touristic hub is a 134-acre peninsular playground west of downtown jutting into Half Moon Lake.

The primary attraction is the **Chippewa Valley Museum** (715/834-7871, www. cvmuseum.com, 10 A.M.–5 P.M. Mon.–Sat. and 1–5 P.M. Sun. summer, shorter hours otherwise,

$4 adults) with award-winning displays on the valley's Ojibwa culture. Of note are the 21-room dollhouse and an anachronistic ice cream parlor. Also on the grounds is the Anderson Log House, an 1850s Swedish-style home.

The **Paul Bunyan Logging Camp** (715/835-6200, paulbunyancamp.org, 10 A.M.–4:30 P.M. daily Apr.–Oct., shorter hours otherwise, $5 adults), a replica of an 1890s camp, features an interpretive center with unusual and wonderful logging file footage and flotsam, including a mini-village of structures, Brobdingnagian heavy equipment, and, of course, the requisite Paul Bunyan and Babe the Blue Ox statue.

The **Chippewa Valley Railroad** offers rides on a half-mile 16-gauge line through the park. The two coal-fired steam engines pull all-wood 1880s passenger coaches, among other beauts, some the best of their kind in the state. Trips run noon–5 P.M. Sunday, Memorial Day–Labor Day, and cost $2 adults.

Carson Park is also the home of the **Eau Claire Cavaliers** and **Eau Claire Express** amateur baseball teams. Eau Claire has fielded semipro teams since the early 1900s and boasts a couple of Hall of Famers. Hammerin' Hank Aaron got his baseball start in Eau Claire in 1952 playing for the then–Eau Claire Bears. Burleigh Grimes, a local-boy-done-good, also pitched for the Bears.

University of Wisconsin-Eau Claire

Lovely UW-Eau Claire (105 Garfield Ave., 715/836-2637) is south of the Chippewa River and downtown via State Street. On campus, the **Newman Clark Bird Museum** (715/836-4166) is an odd, circular structure housing a respected ornithological collection of 530 species. An **arboretum** sprawls over 200 acres and has self-guided trails.

Side Trips

Plenty of outstanding road trips snake throughout the Eau Claire area. The most promising is to Augusta, 20 or so miles to the southeast via U.S. 12. Easily one of the most photographed gems along the route is **Dells Mill** (Hwy. V, 715/286-2714, 10 A.M.–5 P.M. daily May–Oct., $7 adults), three miles north off WI 27 on Highway V. This eye-catching 1864 mill and museum, set along engaging Bridge Creek, is predominantly a museum, but some grinding is still done on-site. The remarkable thing about the mill is that its five structures are constructed solely of hand-hewn timber joined only by wooden pegs. Inside you'll find more than 3,000 feet of belting and 175 waterforced pulleys.

Augusta is in a region rich in Amish culture. **The Wood Shed** (105 W. Lincoln St., 715/286-5404, Mon.–Sat.) has 15,000 square feet of folk art and Amish woodwork, quilting, wall hangings, baskets, rugs, dolls, and furniture. The store arranges tours of the Amish countryside.

One of the top 10 supper clubs in the state, according to more than one foodie publication, is the **Black Bear Supper Club** (WI 27 N, 715/286-2687, dinner Tues.–Sat., lunch and dinner Sun., $6–18) in Augusta. It's got a solid slate of ribs, steaks, seafood, and chicken.

Cadott is approximately 15 miles east of Chippewa Falls on WI 29, at the junction with WI 27. You'll find a **veterans' tribute** featuring 43 flags, the first to honor Asian veterans of the Vietnam War. Another martial marker is along Highway X in Cadott, this one honoring Lansing Wilcox, Wisconsin's last Civil War veteran. Four miles north from Cadott on WI 27, a trademark local sign informs you you're exactly halfway between the North Pole and the equator.

ENTERTAINMENT AND EVENTS

A vaudeville "palace" and movie house in the Roaring 1920s, the **Regional Arts Center** (316 Eau Claire St., 715/832-2787, www. eauclairearts.com) is now home to regional cultural groups.

Eau Claire is not exactly a hotbed of nightlife. The **Cabin** (715/836-4833), at the university, is the oldest coffeehouse in Wisconsin, with folk, blues, jazz, and occasional comedy.

The largest country hoedown in Wisconsin is **Country Jam USA** (www.countryjam.com) in Eau Claire, held the third week of July. The biggest names in country music turn Eau Claire into something decidedly different from its usual self.

RECREATION
Chippewa River Trail

This nearly three-mile-long multiuse path runs through Eau Claire's urban river corridor. The river trail in turn joins with the larger **Chippewa River Valley Trail,** which eventually leads through prairie, mixed forest, and agrarian patchworks to Menomonie and the

Red Cedar State Trail. (Eventually, the **Old Abe Trail** from Chippewa Falls also will lead into the city.) You can reach the river trail at Carson Park (a spur trail) or at UWEC. No trail pass is needed in the city, but a $4 daily pass is needed on the state trails.

Camping

Your best bet is to head for Lake Wissota State Park near Chippewa Falls.

ACCOMMODATIONS

The **Green Tree Inn Suites** (516 Galloway St., 715/832-3411 or 800/236-3411, $55–110) is close to the convention center and offers many two-room suites. Many have written accolades about its good service. Ditto the raves for **Grandstay Residential Suites** (5310 Prill Rd., 877/388-7829, from $119), which has wonderful standard suites and fabulous service.

Then again, for that second price you can score a wonderful room and passes to Chaos waterpark and "action rooms" at the intriguing **Metropolis Resort** (5150 Fairview Dr., 888/861-6001, www.metropolisresort.com, $119). This place defies categorization: let's go with "boutique family resort." There are great service and amenities here.

FOOD

Come here and you can't not hear about the dining and dinner theater combo at the **Fanny Hill Inn** (3919 Crescent Ave., 715/836-8184, 5–9 P.M. Thurs.–Sat. in summer, brunch and occasionally dinner Sun., $13–26). The dining room view is certainly worth the kudos, offering superb views of the Chippewa Valley.

Best breakfast in northern Wisconsin is at the 🄲 **Nucleus Café** (405 Water St., 715/834-7777, breakfast and lunch, from $5). This isn't your parents' Northern Wisconsin café; everything is done with a creative twist. Applewood bacon rather than bacon, hash browns with poblano peppers, and the like. I can't travel without wolfing a Cajun crab omelette.

On par for sandwiches is the **Acoustic Cafe** (505 S. Barstow St., 715/832-9090,

8 A.M.–10 P.M. daily, $3–7). Plus, it's got reliable live music.

You could almost call the fare at the great **Sweetwater's** (1104 W. Clairemont Ave., 715/834-5777, 11 A.M.–9 P.M. Mon.–Sat., 4–9 P.M. Sun., $8–22) eclectic American. It serves gourmet wood-fired pizzas, lots of pasta, and creative takes on the usuals, including prime rib.

On the "other" side of the park, **Mike's Smokehouse and Roadhouse BBQ** (2235 N. Clairemont, 715/834-8153, 11 A.M.–9:30 P.M. daily, $4–12) has way-above-average barbecue and excellent side dishes.

INFORMATION

The well-stocked **Chippewa Valley Visitor Center** (3625 Gateway Dr., 715/834-2345 or 800/344-3866, www.chippewavalley.net) has a 24-hour vestibule and the cleanest restrooms for miles.

GETTING THERE
By Bus

There's a **Greyhound** station (6251 Truax Ln., 715/874-6771) in town.

By Air

The **Chippewa Valley Regional Airport** (3800 Starr Ave., 715/839-4900) is north of town and has daily flights to the Twin Cities and Chicago.

Eau Claire Passenger Service (715/835-0399) also operates ground transportation between Eau Claire and the Minneapolis–St. Paul airport. Nine trips leave daily, and a one-way ticket costs $34.

CHIPPEWA FALLS

Eau Claire may be named the city of clear water, but its chief competitor today is the "City of Pure Water," so called for the natural springs that still feed into the beer that made it famous—Leinenkugel's ("Leinie's").

Good drinkin'? The water in Chippewa Falls is claimed as the "purest" in the United States—just ask the locals. A private laboratory in Minneapolis was called in to settle a friendly feud between Deming, New Mexico, and Chippewa Falls in 1969. The lab gave a nearly perfect quality rating to Chippewa Falls' water—and it's been boasting about it ever since. Chippewa Falls has also been noted by preservationists as one of the country's best preserved, in part due to this: *Time* magazine rated it one of the country's top 10 small towns. The National Trust for Historic Preservation has called it one of the United States' top 10 "Distinctive Destinations."

Sights

In North Woods Wisconsin taverns, the beer of choice is indisputably Leinie's (and that's *never* "Leinenkugel's" if you're trying to fit in). The **Jacob Leinenkugel Brewing Company** (WI 124 N, 715/723-5557, www.leinie.com, tours 9 A.M.–4 P.M. Mon.–Sat., 11 A.M.–4 P.M. Sun., free) has been using the crystal-clear waters of Chippewa Falls to brew beer since 1867. It went from one brand of beer (400 barrels) its first year to nine premium brands, today sold throughout the region. No reservations are necessary for the tours, but it's a good idea.

You can actually view the primevally pure gurgling springs at the **Chippewa Spring House** (600 Park Ave., 715/723-0872), one of the oldest landmarks in the valley and the community's first structure, built in 1836. A glass dome caps the icy water as it rises to flow toward the river, and you can still espy century-old hand-carved graffiti on the walls. Across the street is the **Chippewa Water Company bottling plant,** started by poet Ezra Pound's grandfather and still in operation after more than a century.

Chippewa Falls' modern history is partially chronicled at the **Chippewa Falls Museum of Industry and Technology** (21 E. Grand Ave., 715/720-9206, 1–5 P.M. Tues.–Fri., 10 A.M.–3 P.M. Sat., $3 adults). People are fairly surprised how important Chippewa Falls has been to the computer revolution; Cray Computers, builder of the world's most powerful supercomputers, was founded in Chippewa Falls. Besides the fascinating Seymour Cray Supercomputer Collection, visitors get a look at the history of manufacturing and processing in the city since the 1840s.

Lake Wissota State Park sits opposite the eponymous lake; from here the **Old Abe Trail** starts and runs 20 miles to Brunet Island State Park in Cornell.

Food

The family restaurant of choice is absolutely ◖ **Olson's Ice Cream Parlor and Deli** (611 N. Bridge St., 715/723-4331, 11 A.M.–8 or 9 P.M. daily, $2–5), a landmark since 1923 for its "Homaid" ice cream. Ice-cream aficionado magazines have rated this place in the top 10 in the United States; you can observe the ice cream–making process through large windows.

Candlelight dining and even cruise dinners ($75 per couple) are found at **High Shores Supper Club** (17985 Hwy. X, 715/723-9854, 4–10 P.M. Mon.–Sat., 11 A.M.–10 P.M. Sun., $6–20). As fine as the cuisine are the splendid lake views of Lake Wissota from a garden-side deck table.

Or, right downtown, world fusion food at a great new (for this edition) bistro: **Duncan Creek Wine Bar** (213 Bridge St., 715/723-7000, dinner Tues.–Sat., $7–15).

OSSEO

Osseo draws scads of travelers from *around the world* to an unassuming, big-britches eatery, the world-renowned ◖ **Norske Nook** (7th St., 715/597-3069, 5:30 A.M.–9 P.M. Mon.–Sat., 8 A.M.–8 P.M. Sun. in summer, fewer hours the rest of the year, $3 and up), which arguably bakes the world's best pies. Celebrated by road-food gourmands (and feted by many, many national media appearances), the place could not be more underwhelming when first you walk through the door, as it looks like nothing more than a classic diner. But the food is unreal. It's got the obligatory heart-stopping breakfasts and the requisite Midwestern hot beef sandwiches. Occasionally a dinner special might feature something Scandinavian such as lutefisk or *lefse*. But the pies! The pies are really the thing—a whole page of them. The strawberry pies have up to five pounds of strawberries. The Nook is *the* stop between Eau Claire and the Mississippi.

Since you're already in Osseo, stop by the **Northland Fishing Museum** (1012 Gunderson Rd., 715/597-2551, 9 A.M.–5 P.M. daily, free), an awesome repository of classic and antique fishing equipment, featuring one of the most extensive (and kitschy and hip) fishing lure collections in the world. You want a rusted Evinrude? You got it.

MENOMONIE
One of the ubiquitous oddly spelled Wisconsin towns with the same pronunciation,

Menomonie (muh-NAH-muh-nee) was still one more lumber town alongside a floating log highway. But this was not your ordinary lumber town; it was *the* lumber town, the site of the world's largest lumber corporation at the time, processing more than five million feet of lumber, with 1,200 employees on 115,000 acres of land.

University of Wisconsin-Stout
Fantastically wealthy—and perceptive—lumber magnate James Stout foresaw incipient timber unemployment and founded the Stout Manual Training School, today's

© AVALON TRAVEL

university. It was the first in the country to offer a curriculum designed specifically for industrial arts, helping shift local schools' emphasis toward vocational education. UW-Stout today has a one-of-a-kind Hmong Culture Studies program (the Chippewa Valley has a large number of Laotian immigrants from the Vietnam era).

C Mabel Tainter Memorial

This enormous dark sandstone theater (205 Main St., 715/235-9726, 10 A.M.–5 P.M. Mon.–Sat., 1–5 P.M. Sun., self-guided tours $1) was deliberately contrived by its designer and builder in 1890 to do no less than "advance American architecture, society, education, and religion." It's a lofty, if not quixotic, memorial to the builder's daughter, a local aesthete, who died at 19. In Romanesque style, it smacks of a Thames-side opera house—the interior is downright eye-popping. In relatively rare (for Wisconsin) Moorish style, the ornate auditorium has extraordinary detailing, a Steere and Turner Tracker pipe organ, and very pricey old paintings.

Russell J. Rassbach Heritage Museum

This museum (1820 Wakanda St., 715/232-8685, 10 A.M.–5 P.M. Wed.–Sun. summer, shorter hours the rest of year, $4 adults) has a replica of the kitchen of the Caddie Woodlawn house, a 1931 four-door Nash sedan built in Kenosha, and displays on local Dunn County celebrities, in particular ex-major leaguer Andy Pafko.

Scenic Drives

WI 25 to the south is a great little road trip, paralleling the Red Cedar River State Trail. Downsville, six miles south, offers the **Empire in Pine Museum** (WI 25, 715/644-8452, noon–4 P.M. Tues.–Sat., 1–5 P.M. Sun., May–Oct., $2). A huge, award-winning collection of lumbering artifacts and displays is housed on two floors. A multimedia display portrays Knapp, Stout and Company's massive operations.

Eight miles south you'll find **Caddie Woodlawn Historic Park.** The character in the famed children's book *Caddie Woodlawn* was actually Caroline Augusta, who moved here with her family in 1857; her granddaughter, Carol Ryrie Brink, wrote the book.

Twenty-two miles west on I-94 and then north a hop brings you to little **Baldwin.** The town's **Dutch windmill,** erected to memorialize the town's heritage, is worth the trip. An antique farm equipment museum can also be found in town.

Recreation

The **Red Cedar State Park Trail** departs the historic depot along the west edge of WI 29 in Menomonie and stretches nearly 15 miles south along the Red Cedar River to the **Dunville Wildlife Area.** The Menomonie depot dispenses trail passes and can tell you of the dozen bridges, a "weeping" rock wall and legendary gold buried along the riverbank by fleeing French soldiers, an old cutstone quarry, the wildlife area, accessible via Highway Y, and an old 860-foot-long railroad bridge. You can link up at the end with the Chippewa River Trail to Eau Claire. You can also canoe, kayak, or tube the Red Cedar River from Menomonie. Rentals are found at the Menomonie trailhead; a good option is to canoe down the river and bike back.

Accommodations

A large dose of chain motels comes at the junction of I-94 and WI 25, including the super clean and utterly friendly **Super 8** (1622 N. Broadway, 715/235-8889, $53–129). Bike trail access is a couple blocks away!

Food

A breath of fresh air is C **Zanzibar** (228 Main St. E, 715/231-9269, 4–11 P.M. Tues.–Sat., $12–29). On one menu you'll find tapas, quail, and *ahvosh* (an Armenian flatbread). And it's all well done with friendly, attentive, and knowledgeable service. The martinis are otherworldly as well.

◖ The Creamery (E4620 County Rd. C, 715/664-8354, www.creameryrestaurant -inn.com, 11 A.M.–9 P.M. Mon.–Sat., 11 A.M.– 8 P.M. Sun., $11–25) in Downsville is one of the top-shelf eateries in the state. The menu is "imaginative American" and varies season to season according to the vagaries of farmers markets (yes, it is slow and locally focused here) and the whims of the talented chef (a veteran of respected eateries statewide). The structure itself was a genuine cooperative creamery, constructed in 1904; there are also a few B&B rooms.

Information

You'll find local tourism information at the **Menomonie Area Chamber of Commerce** (700 Wolske Bay Rd., 715/235-9087 or 800/283-1862). The best website is the one covering the whole valley (chippewavalley.net).

Black River State Forest and Environs

The Black River Valley contained the most pine trees per settlement in the state when the first sawmill was opened in 1839. More than 50 sawmills whined away 24 hours a day, processing 4.9 *billion* board feet of lumber. Iron ore mining and smelting has also been a local industrial linchpin since 1856.

The forest was once the prime hunting grounds for the Winnebago, whose hegemony once stretched west throughout the region. Forcibly relocated to northeastern Iowa and later a South Dakota reservation before making a long migration back to Wisconsin, they defied attempts to remove them again.

Green Gold

One Jackson County economic oddity—speaking on a national scale now—is sphagnum moss, commercially produced nowhere except this pocket of western Wisconsin. Rejuvenating itself rapidly in the boggy and marshy areas on the western fringe of the Sand Counties, it can hold 20 times its weight in water and keeps nursery plants and flowers alive during shipping and hydroponic gardening, not to mention being used for surgical dressings.

Wazee Trail

The Wazee Trail is a 62-mile auto tour through the Black River region along historic Native American routes. Twelve miles of the trail— Highway O (North Settlement Rd.)—are established as an official Wisconsin Rustic Road.

RECREATION
The River

The Black River—named for the water's black hue, caused by a high iron content—cuts across Wisconsin's central plain and western upland regions. Unlike most glacially carved waterways, the river cuts for the most part through a steep trench with relatively few marshy areas or lakes (though it is surrounded by those moss-rich swamps). Most visitors come to paddle; 75 river (or tributary) miles are canoeable in the immediate vicinity. Trips are most common out of Hatfield. A trip all the way to the Mississippi River is possible, requiring about five very casual days.

One of the most popular stretches of water is the float upstream from Black River Falls between Hall's Creek to a dam. Ultracasual tubers generally take two hours to leisurely float from Irving Landing to Lost Falls.

Wazee Lake

A number of miles east of Black River Falls is primevally icy Wazee Lake, a glacial lake that is 350 feet deep with no outlets; it's also incredibly clear, so expect to see scuba flags and snorkel gear about. There's plenty of camping available here.

Other Recreation

The Black River State Forest has 35 miles of mountain-bike trails. Cross-country ski trails—highly rated by ski bums, by the way— are five miles north of Millston. *Trail passes are required;* they cost $3 per day.

The county is constantly establishing more trail routes along iron mine trails in county forest land. Hundreds of miles of state and county forest logging roads are open to bikes.

State Forest Camping and Backpacking

Three family campgrounds are in the state forest. You'll also find canoe campsites south of Black River Falls.

Primitive backpacking is also available, and a permit is necessary. You can't camp anywhere you want, so get details from the forest HQ. Though the forest looks small and rather mundane as a "working forest" (meaning that it's managed for timber extraction), it is easy to get off-track here.

INFORMATION

The **Black River State Forest HQ** (715/284-1406) is at the junction of WI 54 East and I-94. The **Black River Falls Chamber of Commerce** (336 N. Water St., Black River Falls, 800/404-4008, www.blackrivercountry.net) also maintains some information.

BLACK RIVER FALLS

Black River Falls is your quintessential Our Town kind of community, set beside the river. (Gotta love the town's greatest ambition—raising an enormous beer stein–shaped office building! Absotively Wisconsin!) The chamber of commerce can point out a few area highlights such as the scenic views from **Bell Mound** or the Native American **petroglyphs** at Gullickson's Glen. The atavistic **Sand Creek Brewing Company** (intersection of East 4th and Pierce Sts., 715/284-7553) was the first brewery in western Wisconsin and then a turkey factory and landmine manufacturing plant during the Korean War. Free tours are available 8 A.M.–4 P.M. Fridays and Saturdays but call first—the staff may be busy bottling (seriously!).

West of town on WI 54 is the **Rustic Mill** (S. WI 54, 715/284-4913, 5–10 P.M. Wed.–Mon., $7–21), a fetching reconverted 1866 feed and flour mill. Try the apple-cranberry pie.

Molly's Grill (715/284-9284, 11 A.M.–10 P.M. Tues.–Sat., $4–11) in downtown Black River Falls is rousing, but I love the **Country Café** (18 Main St., 715/284-1636) nearby, the kind of place that creates and names dishes after regulars.

HATFIELD

Sitting on popular Lake Arbutus, one of the few dam-formed lakes along the Black River, the town is the gateway to numerous resorts in the area (all of which help the town's population swell from 50 to nearly 5,000 in summer). Most resorts are on the southwest perimeter of the lake, along Highway K and Highway J. Also along the shore is the **Russell Park Campground,** a county park with a sandy beach. A state forest campground is on the lake's east side, as is another county campground.

West of Hatfield in Merrillan is the coolest little museum ever—the **Double T Quick Stop and Barbershop.** Say what? It's a 1920s gas station/barbershop—and not much has changed. Not open often, but it's cute to look at.

CATARACT

South of Black River Falls through Cataract to the east, the **Little Falls Railroad and Doll Museum** (Hwy. B to WI 11, 608/272-3266, www.raildoll.org, 1–5 P.M. Thurs.–Sun. May 1–Oct. 31, $5) has hundreds of dolls in rotating exhibits. The working train displays are cool, as are the thousands of old, old books and magazines. Some prefer the **Paul and Matilda Wegner Grotto** not far away from Cataract via WI 27 south and then west on WI 71. It's a garden of concrete sculpture decorated with thousands of glass shards in the usual grotto theme of religion and patriotism.

INDIAN MISSION

The Ho Chunk Nation (Winnebago) has no reservation lands but holds title to about 2,000 acres of land in the Jackson County area. Over Labor Day, Memorial Day, and Thanksgiving weekends, the nation holds **powwows** at Red Cloud Memorial Park. There is also a small cultural museum.

Northwestern Lakes

Erect a radar base in Eau Claire, where U.S. 53 branches north from the interstate, and the sweep of the beam as it rotates clockwise between nine and noon reveals another massive concentration of primeval glacial pools. Second in density only to Wisconsin's other lake district, in the northeast, but second to none in sheer numbers, the area features arguably the state's best muskie fishing and the country's first established scenic riverways.

ST. CROIX NATIONAL SCENIC RIVERWAY

The St. Croix National Scenic Riverway is one of a dozen so designated in the federal Wild and Scenic Riverway System. It was also the first, officially promulgated in 1968 by Congress, containing 252 miles of the Upper and Lower St. Croix Rivers and the entire Namekagon River. Though not technically a part of the system, the Brule

River was and is a de facto link in the chain. With only a short portage between the Brule and St. Croix, this was the most crucial waterway between the Great Lakes and the Mississippi River. Though brown for most of its length in the south (tannic acid leaches into the water from decaying pine and tamarack needles), the riverway is one of the "healthiest" in the United States in terms of biology and biodiversity.

The St. Croix is a schizophrenic river, split into regions at St. Croix Falls. The Upper St. Croix and Namekagon Rivers are the more challenging and isolated for canoeists, drifting and paddling through an expansive river valley streaked with creeks and dotted with thousands of glacial lakes and tracts of second-growth forest. The Lower St. Croix, by the time it departs St. Croix Falls, has become an old man—somnolent and wide, full of sandbars and backwater sloughs.

a tour boat chugging along the St. Croix River

The National Park Service's website (www.nps.gov) has excellent information on the entire riverway, along with local links.

Upper St. Croix and Namekagon Rivers: Along the Route

The St. Croix River begins as a humble, ribbony creek flowing from Upper St. Croix Lake in a muskeg forest between Gordon and Solon Springs. It navigates 102 miles on its course to Prescott, but after just 20 miles it links with the Namekagon River, its main tributary. The Namekagon starts as a chilly trout stream at a dam northeast of Cable, within shouting distance of the Chequamegon National Forest. Both wend through forested valleys in relatively primitive conditions. For pure backwoods isolation, the Namekagon can't be beat.

Near the St. Croix headwaters, a county park in Solon Springs offers an established campground. The park also contains Solon Springs' claim to fame—the **Lucius Woods Performing Arts Center,** a rustic outdoor amphitheater featuring established musical acts on weekends.

The Namekagon changes from an icy, extremely isolated trout stream in dense conifers to a wider channel through marshes and swamps. The river contains one hairpin turn after another, and that's why canoeists love it so much—no boaters.

Hayward to Trego is the most developed 34 miles on the whole upper stretch. It has few rapids, but these can be tough for novices.

Trego, at the Great South Bend of the river, was once a ready-made campsite, used by the original Ojibwa inhabitants. Johnathan Carver in 1767 and Henry Schoolcraft in 1831 also slept on sandbars here. A huge number of **river outfitters** are here, with rentals and shuttles for a minimum of $17. These include **Namekagon Outfitters** (715/635-2015 or 800/547-9028). The **Namekagon Visitor Center** (U.S. 63, 715/635-8346, daily in summer, weekends only spring and fall) is north of town.

Below Trego, a narrow-channeled, twisty trip of 40 miles spins to Riverside. The most backwoodsy part of the entire system, it's thus the most popular weekend excursion.

Confluence

Near Riverside, the two rivers join and form the Upper St. Croix National Scenic Riverway proper, a wider, more sedate, but no less scenic stretch leading to St. Croix Falls. Just south of Danbury, and stretching all the way past Grantsburg, is the long, sinuous **Governor Knowles State Forest,** with 33,000 acres of great canoeing and hiking (about 40 miles total on two 20-mile trails that trace the bluff line above the river), and some primitive campsites along the river.

East of Danbury and easily missed are the 11 separate communities spread through four counties and composing the **St. Croix Indian Reservation.** Often called the "Lost Tribe" because of its dispersion, another tribal community is across the St. Croix River in Minnesota, and the tribal headquarters is to the southeast, near the village of Hertel. Casinos in Turtle Lake and Danbury are tourist attractions, and an annual late August **Wild Rice Powwow** is a popular draw. The whole region east of Danbury along WI 77 is dubbed the "Fishbowl" for its preponderance of glacial pools and the teeming panfish in them.

For a good side trip, head for the thoroughly captivating **Crex Meadows Wildlife Area** east of the landing near Phantom Flowage along Highway F. This 30,000-plus-acre spread features 250 species of birds, including nesting herons, sharp-tailed grouse, sandhill cranes, trumpeter swans, rare colonies of yellow-headed blackbirds, and a dozen species of duck. You may even espy the "Crex Pack," a pack of timber wolves that moved here from Minnesota (no Minnesota jokes, I promise). The prairielands contain more than 200 of the last vestiges of pure prairie plant in the state. There is a wonderful interpretive center on-site, with a new birding trail and self-guided auto tours. Visitors can also canoe, and some limited camping is allowed September–December.

Grantsburg itself is a pleasant one-horse town. The only tourist trap is the nearly eight-foot talking wooden statue of "Big Gust," the likeness of a local historical figure; check him out at the Village Hall. The village also hosts its summertime **Snowmobile Watercross** in July, when snowmobile pilots attempt to skim their machines across a downtown lake. Awesome.

Five miles east of Grantsburg in tiny Alpha is the **Burnett Dairy Cooperative** (11631 WI 70, 715/689-2748), a group of almost 300 local dairy farmers and the former World Cheese Championship winner. Twenty-one miles east and north near Webster you'll find **Forts Folle Avoine** (8500 Hwy. U, 715/866-8890, www.theforts.org, 9 A.M.–5 P.M. Wed.–Sun. in summer, $7), a historical park comprising mock-ups of the 1802 fur trading posts of XY Company and the Northwest Fur Company, along with a reconstructed Ojibwa village. Costumed docents banter in period lingo—right down to bad Cajun chatter. The dining room on special occasions serves up synchronous fare, from wild rice pancakes to "wilderness stew."

Fish Lake Wildlife Area appears three miles south of Grantsburg; the 15,000-acre refuge covers eight flowages and one natural lake, all in a glacial lake basin, and offers walking and driving tours.

Wisconsin's newest proposed state park—it's visitable but not even official yet—is **Straight Lake State Park**, three miles north of Luck (midway between—and a bit east of—Grantsburg and St. Croix Falls) via WI 35. There's great birding as you tramp around sloughs; the Ice Age Trail will call here eventually.

St. Croix Falls

Your arrival in St. Croix Falls, the largest community along the river, is marked by the brand new **River Headquarters** (401 N. Hamilton St., 715/483-3284). It's generally open daily year-round, and inside you'll find maps, exhibits, toilets, and plenty of information.

The **Polk County Information Center** (WI 35, 800/222-7655, www.polkcountytourism.com or, better, www.saintcroixriver.com) south of town on WI 35 is the terminus for the **Gandy Dancer Trail** (named for the "Gandy

Dancers," or railroad workers who used Gandy tools), a multiuse trail atop an abandoned rail line stretching 98 miles to Superior (where the Saunders State Trail cuts in), crossing over the St. Croix River and into Minnesota before cutting back into Wisconsin; one trail highlight is a 350-foot bridge crossing the river. The trail passes through nine cities and villages, and a trail pass is required.

In St. Croix Falls, the **Fawn Doe Rosa Park** (WI 8, 715/483-3772, www.fawndoerosa.com, 10 A.M.–5 P.M. Mon.–Fri. and 10 A.M.–6 P.M. weekends and holidays mid-May–Labor Day, only weekends in the fall, $7.75 adults) is a rehabilitation and education center which contains a wildlife display featuring "Big Louie," a 1,200-pound Kodiak bear, a petting area and pony rides! It's two miles east on WI 8.

Foie gras in St. Croix Falls? You bet, at the foodie haven **Grecco's** (115 N. Washington St., 715/483-5003, lunch and dinner Thurs.–Sun., dinner only Wed., $10–20), best called a global bistro. Try the venison. Or just go for the "Chef's Discretion" and let him guide you!

Interstate State Park

Interstate State Park is south of the "falls." (Before you ask, there are no falls, at least not since the construction of the dam.) Wisconsin's first state park, established in 1900, Interstate has perhaps the most magnificent examples of glacial topography outside of Devil's Lake or Door County. Glacial runoff was so ferocious that it sluiced superb river gorges right through the area's billion-year-old basaltic lava. The parks—one each in Minnesota and Wisconsin—were formed in part to prevent Minneapolis opportunists from exploiting the traprock in the gorge walls for road building. The gorges here in the mid-19th century held the world's largest logjam—150 million board feet, jammed together for three miles upriver, taking 200 men six weeks to disentangle.

The Dalles of St. Croix, a 200-foot gorge of basalt palisades below the falls, draws Spiderman climbers. The **Potholes Trail** is a funky traipse along rounded chasms formed by glacial backwash. Along other trails, oddball hoodoo

climbing along the St. Croix River at
Interstate State Park

formations appear; the most photographed is probably **Old Man of the Dalles,** and you'll see why. Other formations are seen from the river south of here, including a 60-foot-high Devil's Chair (well, what's left—it actually tumbled in 2004!); The Cross, about 15 feet high; and Angle Rock, at the sharp bend in the river. A dozen trails snake for a total of eight miles through the 1,400-acre park. The final link in Wisconsin's **National Ice Age Scientific Reserve,** the park has an interpretive center (715/597-3069, 8:30 A.M.–4:30 P.M. daily Memorial Day weekend–Labor Day, shorter times the rest of the year) with exhibits, films, displays, and even a mural or two. The family campgrounds have great isolated camping and a nice sandy beach not far away. No organized tour boats leave from the Wisconsin side, but the Taylor Falls, Minnesota, docks have tour boats.

Lower St. Croix River

Beginning at the St. Croix Falls Dam, this stretch runs 52 miles to Prescott, where it flows into the Mississippi River.

Osceola, five miles downstream from St. Croix Falls, was named for an Indian chief. The name was originally Leroy, and old Leroy wouldn't allow the change until he was paid two sheep. Downtown, a flight of wooden stairs climbs to **Cascade Falls,** or you can just wander through the charming town and stop for a look-over at the **Emily Olson House** (715/294-2480), which doubles as the local historical society quarters. The **ArtBarn** (1040 Oak Ridge Dr., 715/294-2787) is a renovated barn housing galleries, a theater, workshops, and more. There's a statue of **Chief Osceola** and a large **state fish hatchery** (2517 93rd Ave., 715/294-2525) also in town. The chugging steam engines of the **Osceola and St. Croix Railway** (800/643-7412) depart from the old depot just off WI 35 downtown. The old trains steam on fantastic 90-minute round-trips to Marine-on-St.-Croix, Minnesota, at 11 A.M. and 2:30 P.M. weekends, Memorial Day weekend–late October. Fares are $17 for adults.

Two miles below Osceola, a sharp left cut in the river marks the dividing line between the Sioux and Ojibwa nations under 1837 treaties. The river spins for 10 more miles, passing a Minnesota state park and great old Marine-on-St.-Croix, Minnesota, before the mouth of the Apple River appears. Canoeists should disembark here or try going up the Apple River. Tons and tons of tubers will be winding their way downstream against you; so many people "tube the Apple" that *Life* magazine put the event in its pages in 1941, and the press has dutifully shown up ever after. You'll pass through the **St. Croix Islands Wildlife Refuge** before entering the Apple River, and if you can make it against the current, little **Somerset** waits upstream a handful of miles. There's not much in Somerset, historically known for its moonshine operations, but today the town has frog legs and pea soup; it's famed for both culinary delights. The former culinary concoction can be sampled at **River's Edge** (River's Edge Dr. off WI 64, 715/247-3305, www.riversedgeappleriver. com, 9 A.M.–5 P.M. daily) in town, the latter at an annual town festival.

Beyond Stillwater, Minnesota, the river widens into what is known as **Lake St. Croix**—at times up to 7,400 feet across. The next Wisconsin community above Lilliputian size, **Hudson,** so called for the area's close resemblance to the Hudson River Valley of New York, started as a trading outpost and steamship supply point. This eye-catching river town, Wisconsin's fastest-growing municipality, has a relatively famous **octagon house** (1004 3rd St., 715/386-2654, tours 11 A.M.–4 P.M. Tues.–Sat., 2–4:30 P.M. Sun., May–Oct., $7 adults), dating from 1855. This erstwhile home of a local judge is done in period style, and a Victorian garden surrounds the outside and leads to the carriage house.

The chamber of commerce offers free maps to other 19th-century structures in the downtown area. Off Buckeye Street downtown is an outstanding cliffside park. To the east, **Willow River State Park,** 2,800 modest acres along the eponymous river, offers a few waterfalls. The area was once used as an entryway to burial grounds. Three dams form three separate flowages in the park. A nature center doubles as a ski hut come winter, and this is one of the few parks with winter camping.

Cozy B&Bs are found in every direction. Dominating the historic district architecture is the huge and wonderful **◖ Phipps Inn** (1005 3rd St., 715/386-0800 or 888/865-9388, www.phippsinn.com, $179–209), not far from the octagon house. Built in 1884, this beaconbright white, 1884 Italianate has more fireplaces than most B&Bs have rooms.

For food, there's a fairly wide variety. **Barker's** (413 2nd St., 715/386-4123, 11 A.M.–11 P.M. daily, $8–16) is a spacious place in a historic building with booths. It has lots of burgers and sandwiches, along with lots of beers. Sandwich specials are creative—such as chicken with peanut-chipotle sauce. The author's traveling companion insists that the **San Pedro Cafe** (426 2nd St., 715/386-4003, www.sanpedrocafe.com, 7 A.M.–11 P.M. daily, $8–17) simply must be mentioned for its luscious pan-American cuisine! It has lovely patio dining.

Or go for gut-busting Teutonic food at **Winzer Stube** (516 Second St., 715/381-5092,

dinner daily), in a gorgeous old opera house. This author thought of his grandmother with their Saturday *sauerbraten.*

River Falls

The St. Croix River doesn't run through or even near River Falls, but WI 35 does, and you'll likely pass through if you're traveling the St. Croix Riverway or the Great River Road. Ten miles southeast of Hudson along WI 35, the town of 10,000-and-change got its start when the first settler, a Connecticut Yankee, wrote back to the East, "I think I have found the New England of the Northwest." That part is debatable, but the settlers came in droves, creating yet another sawmill town, with a few brick kilns and sauerkraut factories thrown in for good measure.

It's an attractive town, and the *other* river in these parts, the Kinnickinnic, is blue-ribbon trout-worthy all the way (look for all the rods). The Kinnickinnic River pathway passes historical sites and developments on its traipse through the town. The stone buildings—the bricks baked right here—have their original superficialities, down to glass transom windows. Downtown, catch a flick at the quaint **Falls Theatre** (105 S. Main St., 715/425-2811) where, the folks are proud to say, prices haven't changed since the 1960s.

The most Wisconsinesque local lodging is found not far from town at **Kinni Creek Lodge and Outfitters** (545 N. Main St., 715/425-7378, www.kinnicreek.com, $109), a lodge with a B&B complex plunked along the Kinnickinnic River. There's log furniture (smallish but clean rooms), class I trout fishing, and even fly-tying seminars—now that's Wisconsin!

Unique is **UW-River Falls Falcon Foods** (410 S 3rd St., 715/425-3702, 1–5 P.M. Mon.–Fri.), a student-operated dairy and meat facility with 65 flavors of wonderful Wisconsin ice cream, fresh cheese, and delicious smoked meats.

THROUGH THE FISHBOWL: U.S. 53 TO SUPERIOR

Along the route to Superior, U.S. 53 bypasses little "node" communities, each on its own string of lakes dotted with rustic family and fishing resorts. Veer west off the highway and you'll pass through the "Fishbowl," an area with one of the highest concentrations of glacial lakes in Wisconsin, full to the brim with panfish.

New Auburn

Nine miles east of New Auburn on Highway M, the **Chippewa Moraine Unit** is one of the nine reserve chain links on the trans-state scientific reserve. And also a horribly underappreciated gem. Nearly six miles of nature trails wend through 4,000 acres; a blue heron rookery is visible on an easy one-hour hike. The rest of the trails present you an obvious glacial topography, and a few glacial pools are canoeable. The superb **interpretive center** is perched on an ice-walled lake plain; it won a Governor's Award for design, and it's apparent why when you get there. From the deck, you can get a view of South Shattuck Lake, a kettle or ice-block lake.

To the east, the reserve is connected to **Brunet Island State Park** by a 20-mile segment of the Ice Age Trail. It's a great riverine thumb of a park, set between the confluence of two rivers, south of the Holcombe Flowage. You can knock off the trails without breaking much of a sweat. Chippewa County Forest lands line the area between the state park and the Ice Age Reserve Unit, offering dozens of miles of trails, most of which are unfortunately open to braying off-road vehicles. The canoeing's lazy and fine.

Chetek

Once a community with one of the country's largest lumber companies, Chetek is much more tranquil today. Dozens and dozens of local resorts line 128 miles of lake shoreline on a six-lake chain. There's little else unless you count the **Hydro Lites,** a local water-ski team, as an attraction, or the **ice races** across the lake, held every Sunday after the ice freezes.

Inexplicably, one of the most luxurious inns in Wisconsin is found in Chetek: **Canoe Bay** (115 S. 2nd St., 715/924-4594, www. canoebay.com, $325–490). The architecture of the cottages was inspired by—but not done

by—Frank Lloyd Wright. Better—rooms and cottages are sprinkled through a sublime, isolated setting. The fixed-price menu ($75/person) is to die for in this area. Pricey, but you're not paying for posh—you're paying for peace of mind, and you've got it here. This could be the most splendid isolation you'll find in the state.

Barron

Them ain't chickens you see, but tom turkeys. Seemingly millions of them are kept at the **Jerome Foods processing plant** (34 N. 7th St., 715/537-3131), one of the largest on the planet with 1,800 employees.

Rice Lake

Rice Lake is named for the ancient beds of *manomin* that once lined the shores of the lake. The **Bayfield Trail,** along Lakeshore Drive, is an old Indian pipestone and wild rice trade route. Also along Lakeshore Drive you'll find a burial mounds park with a dozen extant mounds—there were once almost 70.

Rice Lake is the terminus of one of Wisconsin's newest multiuse trails; the **Wild Rivers Trail** stretches 96 miles through three counties. North of Rice Lake on Highway SS is the western endpoint of the **Tuscobia State Trail,** another rails-to-trails project. This one is the longest in Wisconsin, stretching 76 miles east from U.S. 53 to Park Falls. Part of the route is an official Ice Age Trail segment. Golfers might like the **Tagalong Golf Course and Resort** (2855 29th Ave., 715/354-3458), modeled after St. Andrews Course in Scotland. The resort is nice, but it accepts only travelers on package plans in summer. And since golf is the topic—*Golf Digest* lauded the **Turtleback Country Club** (1985 18½ St., 715/234-7641) with four stars for its lovely course.

Of the oodles of lodging choices, **Currier's Lakeview** (2010 E. Sawyer St., 715/234-7474, $60–145) warrants a nod for an ersatz A-frame and a dizzying variety of rooms. Boats and a dock are right out back on the lake. There's also a sauna and continental breakfast is included.

Northeast of Rice Lake, the land is peppered with more lakes and flowages, all dotted with family resorts. Among them, legendary **(Stout's Lodge** (U.S. 53 and Hwy. V, 715/354-3646, www.stoutslodge.com, $179–249) sits on an island in Red Cedar Lake. Constructed laboriously by hand in 1900 out of logs and imported four-inch-thick floor planks and carved beams, the lodge was modeled after famous Adirondack resorts. Massive boathouses, servant and guest quarters, a pistol range, a bowling alley, and a central hall were constructed. It is 26 acres of prime seclusion—so secluded that you have to be ferried out to the island property. Wander its bird sanctuary and look for eagle nests. The resort's **restaurant** is highly regarded, offering the finest dining in the area using fresh local produce and game. Important: its isolation is the draw, so you need to entertain yourself at night.

Try the newer branch of Osseo's famed **(Norske Nook** (2900 Pioneer Ave., 715/597-3069, www.norsenook.com). It remains to be seen if it can duplicate the culinary feats of its Osseo location, but even an approximation of that legendary place still outpaces most others. **Lehman's** (2911 S. Main St., 715/234-2428, 11 A.M.–10 P.M. Tues.–Sun., $5–23) is the local supper club of choice, with good steaks since 1934.

The Blue Hills

Blue Hills Country lies due east of Rice Lake and into Rusk County. These hills are far older than either the Rockies or the Appalachians and were at one time higher than the Rockies—at least until the glaciers lumbered in and shaved them down. The best place to see them is northwest of Weyerhauser, which will also lead you to the endpoint of the Blue Hills segment of the **Ice Age National Scenic Trail.** Tracing the edge of the Chippewa Lobe, from the last glacial period, it's also part of the Tuscobia State Trail. Along the way, the oddball topography of felsenmeer (literally, "sea of rocks") can be seen, formed by excessive frost, which created 100-foot, steep, rocky grades. More than 12 miles of trails lie in the Blue Hills, open for biking, hiking, and cross-country skiing.

Cumberland

Cumberland is a beautiful side trip west from Rice Lake via WI 48 if for no other reason than all the lakes in the area. That's not to mention the late-August celebration of the underappreciated orange tuber at rollicking **Rutabaga Days** (www.cumberland-wisconsin.com).

Spooner

With 350 lakes and the wild and woolly Namekagon River within shouting distance, Spooner is yet another gateway to family North Woods resorts. It's the kind of place where the shops are housed in those ersatz log structures—but on the whole done with a dose of charm.

Since 1953, Spooner's annual zenith has come during the second week of July when it hosts the **Heart of the North Rodeo** (www.spoonerrodeo.com). Wisconsin isn't exactly prime rodeo country, but this PRCA-sanctioned granddaddy is legitimate, drawing top professional rodeo champions. It is among the nation's top 100 rodeos and one of the oldest in the Mississippi Valley.

A couple of alternative attractions exist during other times or for PETA members. Downtown Spooner's **Railroad Memories Museum** (715/635-3325) is filled with the usual stuff, but seven rooms of it.

Spooner had a grand opening of their **Canoe Heritage Museum** (312 N. Front St., 715/635-5002, 10 A.M.–4 P.M. Wed.–Sun. in summer, weekends only in Oct., free) in May 2010 and there's nothing else like it in the state, to be sure.

The **state fish hatchery** (U.S. 70, 715/635-4147, tours 10 A.M. and 2 P.M. Mon.–Fri. May–Labor Day, free), a half mile west of U.S. 63 on U.S. 70, is now among the world's largest freshwater rearing stations.

Spooner is also on the 96-mile-long **Wild Rivers Trail,** which stretches through three northern counties on an old railroad bed. Long Lake is one of the largest and most popular resort zones in the area.

Side Trips
Nearby Shell Lake has the wondrous **Museum of Woodcarving** (U.S. 63 N, 715/468-7100, 9 A.M.–6 P.M. daily May–Nov., $4 adults). This is the largest collection of wood carvings in the world, all done by one person—a local teacher—over a span of 30 years; the masterpiece is the incredibly detailed *Last Supper,* which took four years to finish. Joseph Barta, the inspired artisan, also fancied himself something of a poet. Not kitsch, but wondrous folk art.

Superior

The tip-of-an-arrowhead where Wisconsin and Minnesota share Lake Superior comprises Wisconsin's blue-collar harbor town, Superior. To become the "Pittsburgh of the West," an old guidebook recalls, was Superior's ultimate goal, with hopes of steel mills raised adjacent to the railroad and docks. But Duluth's direct access to larger ore ranges to the west gave it a strategic advantage. Superior's shipyards would, however, develop the first "whaleback," a massive ore carrier.

Poor Superior, many jaded travelers sneer, proffers not much more than mile after mile of drab, eye-level aesthetics typical of an ore town—endless coal foothills, the forlorn natural graffiti of iron oxide, a clunky patchwork of rail lines, ore docks and cranes, and too much fencing. Worse, owing to its lower elevation, Superior seems to catch all of the climatic flotsam that slides off the bluffs and across the harbor. While the sun shines on the crown of Duluth, Superior sulks in a shroud of fog and a perceived shortage of trees.

That said, the phlegmatic port town is one of the busiest deepwater harbors in the nation. And, it sniffs, off the industrial straightaways,

© THOMAS HUHTI

a laker steaming for Lake Superior

NORTHWESTERN WISCONSIN

NORTHWESTERN WISCONSIN

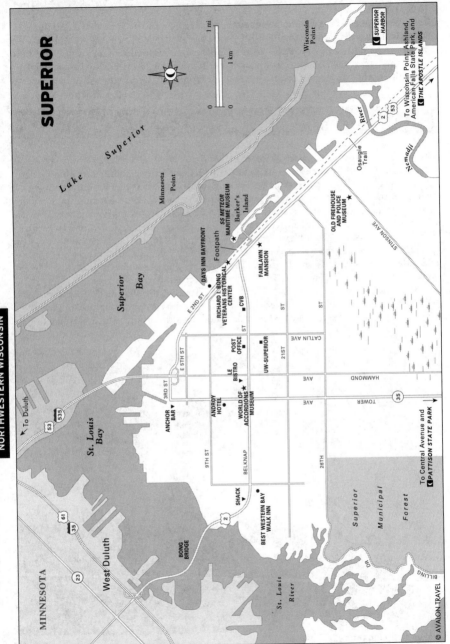

SUPERIOR

MINNESOTA

To Duluth

West Duluth

Lake Superior

Minnesota Point

Wisconsin Point

SUPERIOR HARBOR

To Wisconsin Point, Ashland, American Falls State Park, and THE APOSTLE ISLANDS

St. Louis Bay

Superior Bay

Nemadji River

Osaugie Trail

St. Louis River

Superior Municipal Forest

BONG BRIDGE

BEST WESTERN BAY WALK INN

SHACK

ANCHOR BAR

ANDROY HOTEL

WORLD OF ACCORDIONS MUSEUM

LE BISTRO

POST OFFICE

UW-SUPERIOR

RICHARD I. BONG VETERANS HISTORICAL CENTER

CVB

DAYS INN BAYFRONT

Footpath

SS METEOR MARITIME MUSEUM

Barker's Island

FAIRLAWN MANSION

OLD FIREHOUSE AND POLICE MUSEUM

To Central Avenue and PATTISON STATE PARK

BELKNAP

E 2ND ST

E 5TH ST

3RD ST

9TH ST

CATLIN AVE

21ST ST

ST

ST

TOWER AVE

HAMMOND AVE

28TH

STINSON AVE

BILLING DR

23

61

35

535

53

53

2

2

35

0   1 mi

0   1 km

© AVALON TRAVEL

Superior reveals not only grand stretches of classic Lake Superior history but, real truth be told, tons of trees—it's got the second-largest municipal forest in the United States. And don't let the curmudgeons sully Superior's image—it was nice enough for President Calvin Coolidge to move the White House here in 1928.

A by-the-way: Arnold Schwarzenegger himself graduated from UW-Superior (hotel/restaurant major)!

SIGHTS
◖ Superior Harbor

One of the farthest-inland and deepest freshwater ports worldwide and the largest harbor on the Great Lakes, shipping up to *75 million tons* of ore and grain annually, Superior is thus the hardest-working port on the Great Lakes. So don't overlook it.

Unreal vistas come from the frenetically busy port and the 17 miles of massive docks, grain elevators, and flotillas of monstrous ships. The **Burlington Northern Ore Docks** are indeed the largest in the world. Not all are available

© THOMAS HUHTI

gorgeous Lake Superior

for public viewing, sadly, but the Burlington docks have occasionally allowed observation. Inquire at the visitors center for land access. Also check duluthshippingnews.com for lists of ship arrivals/departures.

Imagine yourself a whaleback ore sailor, drifting by 1,000-foot-long "lakers" and "salties" blowing their horns, as your ship prepares to take on unfathomable amounts (60,000 tons!) of cargo. Do it via the myriad tours of the **Vista Fleet** (715/394-6846, www.vistafleet.com), which actually leave from Duluth's DECC arena and take in the Duluth Aerial Lift Bridge, the Duluth Ship Canal, Port Terminal dock, all of Barker's Island, the Blatnick Bridge, and the world's largest coal docks, and then passes into the St. Louis River to watch taconite being loaded at the Mesabi Iron Ore docks. Two-hour cruises depart late May–mid-October. Rates for basic sightseeing cruises are $14 adults.

Richard I. Bong Veterans Historical Center

Local boy (well, from nearby Poplar, Wisconsin) Richard I. Bong became the United States' greatest WWII ace in his swift and deadly P-38 Lightning. After years of neglect, a P-38 is now on display at this smashing new historical center (305 Harbor View Pkwy., 715/392-7151, www.bvhcenter.org, 9 A.M.–5 P.M. Mon.–Sat., noon–5 P.M. Sun., $9 adults). The P-38 is an intriguing welcome, sitting next to the Bong Bridge to Duluth.

Barker's Island and SS *Meteor*

From the Bong Veterans Historical Center, the few hundred yards to and around Barker's Island, tracing Superior Bay, are a ready-made traveler's leg stretch. The island's state-of-the-art **marina** is the largest marina on the Great Lakes and among the largest freshwater marinas in the world.

Moored permanently and gracefully on the west end of the island, its anchor rammed into the earth, is the crown jewel of the island. The **SS *Meteor* Maritime Museum** (715/392-5742, www.superiorpublicmuseums.org,

NORTHWESTERN WISCONSIN

9 A.M.–5 P.M. Mon.–Sat., 11 A.M.–5 P.M. Sun., mid-May–Labor Day, $6 adults) is the only extant whaleback freighter on the Great Lakes of the type designed and built in Superior's early shipyards. The massive "lakers" that prowl the channels of the Twin Ports are direct descendants of the leviathan 1896 Superior shipyards product.

Need more exercise? From the island, Osaugie Trail continues for five miles along the harbor past some lovely natural areas, and those in super shape could walk all the way to Wisconsin Point.

Wisconsin Point

Just east of Superior, off U.S. 2 at Moccasin Mike Road, a narrow sandbar breakwater acts as a protective lip to the large harbor. The formation is the largest seminatural breakwater in the world and offers a wild, off-the-beaten path snoop into the great harbor. It's a quiet, isolated place with innumerable forks, pulloffs, dead ends, and where-the-hell-am-I turnoffs. The highlight of the excursion is the **Superior entry lighthouse.** No tours are available, but you can get fairly close.

Fairlawn Mansion

Directly opposite Barker's Island stands what is undoubtedly one of the most opulent mansions constructed during northwestern Wisconsin's heyday. Built in 1890, it was home to lumber and Vermilion Range iron ore magnate Martin Thayer Pattison, later Superior's second mayor. The 42-room mansion-cum-landmark (906 E. 2nd St., 715/394-5712, www.superiorpublicmuseums.org, 9 A.M.–5 P.M. Mon.–Sat., noon–5 P.M. Sun., Memorial Day weekend–Labor Day, less the rest of the year, $8 adults), with a distinctive steeple worthy of any basilica, serves as the historical museum of Douglas County—and what an extraordinary cornucopia of regional history it holds!

Other Museums

Superior's early-20th-century firehouse has been turned into the **Old Firehouse and Police Museum** (23rd Ave. E and 4th St., 715/392-2773, Thurs.–Sun. 10 A.M.–5 P.M., $5 adults). The museum houses a whole bunch of kid-friendly antique equipment including a 1906 pumper, some police vehicles, lots and lots and lots of guns, more guns, an old jail cell—did I mention guns?—photos, and a thorough collection of photographs.

Here's something you won't see anywhere but Wisconsin: the **World of Accordions Museum** (1401 Belknap St., 715/395-2787, museum.accordionworld.org, $4 adults). Inside the Harrington Arts Center, the museum is the real thing, the States' only postsecondary-level certification and training program for repair and technician specialists of the accordion family. Seriously. You'll find a great collection of accordions and concertinas and perhaps a delightful concert in the concert hall. (No joke: This is Wisconsin, after all, where the polka is the official state dance!) Contact them to set up a visit.

◖ Pattison State Park

It wouldn't be a trip to Superior without a side trip to this jewel of the state park system, featuring the graceful, thundering 165-foot Big Manitou Falls. It's the highest cascade in Wisconsin—and one of the highest in the eastern United States.

Bisecting the park, the Black River actually looks like dark beer, at times even refracting reddish hues due to oxides in the area's soil. Flowing 22 miles toward Lake Superior from Black Lake, along the Wisconsin-Minnesota border, it was dammed in the 1800s by lumbermen to avoid damaging logs by tumbling them over the great falls. Though it doesn't affect the park's lake, the DNR dumps lampricidic chemicals above Big Manitou Falls regularly to kill sea lampreys, which infest the tributaries of Lake Superior.

Ten miles of trails head in all directions. The must-do **Big Falls Trail** at half a mile is a minor traipse to get a good photo of the big beast waterfall. Trailing the west side of Interfalls Lake, formed by a CCC dam on the Black River, is **Little Falls Trail,** a longer trail at three miles round-trip, but to decidedly smaller falls—about 30 feet.

cascades at Pattison State Park

The southern region has spur trails to the **backpack camping area.**

Of the 50-odd species of mammal in the park, the rare timber wolf and moose have been sighted—very rarely.

Amnicon Falls State Park

Twelve miles southeast along well-traveled U.S. 2/53 is Amnicon Falls (also on the Tri-County Recreational Trail), another prime piece of geology. The weak-tea-colored Amnicon River splits around an island and flows over three impressive falls, each nearly 30 feet high; the river drops precipitously on its course through the park—180 feet in just over one mile. The river's "root beer" color is caused by tannic acid leached from decaying vegetation in the nearby bogs—great for reflecting sunlight, shutterbugs. The watershed contains the only native muskie population in northwestern Wisconsin, and the warm Amnicon itself is a primary spawning run (the name even means "place where fish spawn") for coho, chinook, rainbow trout, and with smelt from Lake Superior.

Leading to the island is the park's famed bowstring covered bridge. A minor, sweatless loop trail begins here, and a **nature trail** leaves from the campground and heads toward a decaying sandstone quarry that dates from the late 1880s.

RECREATION
Charter Fishing

You wouldn't expect anything less than a thriving business catching lake lunkers. Most guides depart Barker's Island for half- and full-day trips and return laden with walleye, lake trout, steelhead, German brown, and king and coho salmon. Many also offer guided river excursions for trout and salmon, particularly on the Brule River toward Ashland and the Root River. The St. Louis River estuary also boasts some of the best walleye takes in North America.

Superior Municipal Forest

The second-largest municipal forest in the United States spreads across the western fringes of Superior. Easily accessible via Billings Drive, which parallels the St. Louis River, or Wyoming Avenue off 28th Street, or even Tower Avenue heading south, the 4,500-acre spread includes 28 kilometers of hiking/ski/mountain-bike trails.

Tri-County Corridor

The corridor is a multiuse recreational trail paralleling U.S. 2 east to Ashland. The best part of the trail is just east of Superior at Wisconsin Point. The trail is a major link to a handful of other trails in Douglas, Bayfield, and Ashland Counties.

Camping

The closest public camping is at Amnicon Falls State Park, the next closest at Pattison Falls State Park; both have reservable sites (advisable).

ACCOMMODATIONS

It ain't the Ritz (keep that in mind) but rather a blast from the (real) past at the **Androy Hotel** (1213 Tower Ave., 715/394-7731, www. androyhotel.com, from $35), from 1925 a cheap sleep option. Some adore its anachronicity; others shudder. I dig it.

A good choice on the west side, near the Bong Bridge and thus an easy skirt into Duluth, is the newer and modestly upscale **Best Western Bay Walk Inn** (1405 Susquehana Ave., 715/392-7600, $75). To get there, continue west of the U.S. 2/Belknap Street bridge split-off.

FOOD

The **Anchor Bar** (413 Tower Ave., 715/394-9747, 10 A.M.–2 A.M. daily, $4–10) is a basic corner bar, but it has the best burgers—and a huge variety (hey, even a cashew burger)—in the region!

You'll find straight smokehouse classics alongside supper club fare at the very good **Shack** (3301 Belknap St., 715/392-9836, 11 A.M.–9 or 10 P.M. daily, $6–18), with more

solid seafood and steaks. Locally, this place owns bragging rights to barbecued ribs and Caesar salads.

Bistro food at decent prices at **Le Bistro** (1409 Hammond Ave., 715/399-3220, lunch Tues.–Fri., lunch and dinner Sat., $10–25), the best place if you need a wine list kind of place.

INFORMATION

The **Superior and Douglas County Convention and Visitors Bureau** (Belknap St., 715/392-2773 or 800/942-5313, www.visitsuperior.com) is just west of U.S. 2/53 along Belknap Street. Another office is adjacent to Fairlawn Mansion.

GETTING THERE

The city is no longer served by Greyhound; you'll have to go to Duluth.

The Lake Superior Coast

Wisconsin is capped in the far north by the serpentine Lake Superior coastline. There are those who say that the entire Wisconsin experience can be had in but two counties—albeit biggies—Bayfield and Ashland, whose perimeters enclose a national lakeshore (including an archipelago), two Indian reservations, arguably the best concentration of waterfalls in the state, and a chunk of the massive Chequamegon National Forest.

The Snow Belt

Lying on the wrong side of Lake Superior as far as weather is concerned, most of Bayfield County sits in the massive cleft of a promontory extending dangerously far, climatically speaking, into Lake Superior. The peninsula watches helplessly as Alberta Clippers race unimpeded across the Canadian Plains, swoop down the precipitous Minnesota escarpments along the north side of the lake, and drop about 120 inches of snow each year, if not more. Bayfield County has been known to get two feet in March, when the rest of the

state—including parts just 30 miles inland—gets less than an inch. During the other minor seasons, a day of azure skies and high clouds can be followed by a shrouded, spitting gale racing out of nowhere.

Yet the big lake is also palliative to the climate. The layering effect around the oversized county moderates things enough to allow for a multihued patchwork of farm and fruit orchards in the bucolic agrarian stretches, with zillions of apple blossoms blazing come spring and fruit stands in every direction in summertime.

◖ BAYFIELD

This gateway village is right out of a Currier and Ives print, the sandstone bluff offering a commanding view of the Apostle Islands. The town is gatekeeper to superlative Bayfield County, a mix of island-dotted seascapes, Great Lakes thunderheads, and pastoral dairyland. It is quite likely the most aesthetically realized village in the state; the *Chicago Tribune* has dubbed it the "Best Little Town in the

Bayfield Harbor

reserved seats; some big-name acts command higher prices.

Downtown Bayfield also has a couple of tiny museums. Better of the two is the **Bayfield Maritime Museum** (1st St. between U.S. Coast Guard Station and City Hall, 715/779-9919, www.apostleisland.com, 10 A.M.–5 P.M. daily Memorial Day–Oct. 5, $5 adults) with displays on the ecosystem and species of Lake Superior, knot tying, Native American fishing, and local history. You can also ogle an original Chequamegon Bay tug and parts from other local boats.

Entertainment and Events

Everybody's pretty much tuckered out from paddling come nightfall, so there's not a lot to do nightclub wise.

The coolest event, personally speaking, is late February's **Apostle Islands Sled Dog Race.** May brings **Bayfield in Bloom,** a monthlong celebration of the coming of blooms in natural areas and orchards. The biggie is October's **Apple Fest,** a blowout feting apples, a fruit integral in all its forms to the local economy. Earlier, in September after Labor Day, a more subdued event (though it's getting fairly sizable now), the **Apostle Islands Lighthouse Celebration** (www.lighthousecelebration. com), showcases the area's lighthouses.

Recreation

Bayfield is home to the country's largest fleet of bareboat charter operations. There is also no shortage of local fishing charters. Other options include biking up and around the coastal interior behind Bayfield. A magnificent day trip on a bike wanders the uplands overlooking the town—take Washington, Rittenhouse, or Manypenny Avenues. All of these roads afford grand views and, one way or the other, lead to the golf course and Highway J; from here Betzhold Road to the north and WI 13 take in many of Bayfield's orchards and 500-foot lake views and provide a cool breeze the whole way.

The easiest trail otherwise is the gorgeous **Iron Bridge Trail,** winding up into the hills

Midwest." Most of the hillside mansions, virtually all on the National Register of Historic Places, were built from the earthtone and pastel brownstone underlying the Apostle Islands archipelago, and every hairpin turn on WI 13 reveals a spectacular lake panorama.

Sights

The "Carnegie Hall of Tent Shows" is a wondrous way to relax after a day of island exploring. The **Lake Superior Big Top Chautauqua** (Ski Hill Rd. at base of Mt. Ashwabay Ski Hill, 715/373-5552 or 888/244-8368, www. bigtop.org) is equal parts vaudeville, minstrel and thespian troupe, and folkways preservation. It all takes place under Big Blue, a 60- by 150-foot tent (so revered was the original that when replaced they actually sold hats made out of it!). A night's slate of entertainment might feature national folk, country, or bluegrass artists; guest lectures; and dramas recounting Chequamegon Bay history. Plenty of food and drink is available on-site. Performances cost $18 adults, $8 children 12 and under for

© MARK HERREID/123RF.COM

NORTHWESTERN WISCONSIN

from the north end of Broad Street, offering a superlative view from a wooden bridge and landscaped terraces.

Tours are myriad to the Apostle Islands. You can go wreck-diving near the islands—there are 25 established hulls littering the lake bottom; several around Sand, Long, and Stockton Islands are popular. The *Coffinberry* is still visible on the surface and is a popular snorkeling destination. All divers must register with the NPS headquarters.

Camping is a hodgepodge of public and private—and pretty tough to get on weekends, so arrive early. At Little Sand Bay of the mainland unit of the Apostle Islands National you'll find a campground. Between Washburn and the Red Cliff Indian Reservation, you'll find a dozen campgrounds.

Accommodations

Bayfield doesn't come cheap after April. A multi-night minimum stay is often necessary in peak periods, particularly on weekends.

The **Seagull Bay Motel** (325 S 7th St., 715/779-5558, www.seagullbay.com, $75–105) is a clean and comfy place with conscientious owners; it has unheard of reasonable prices for these parts. Most rooms have lovely views, and a trail leads to town. Off-season rates are a steal. Some units have kitchenettes.

Arguably the grandest view of the lakeshore is found south of town at the cozy country-style **Apostle View Inn** (83285 WI 13, 715/779-3385, $90–140), with six units set far back from the road. A sister property, the **Winfield Inn** (225 E. Lynde Ave., 715/779-3252, www.winfieldinn. com), is on three acres just a few blocks north of town with rooms, cabins (of myriad size), and cottages—virtually all completely redone with nice detail (and similar rates).

Throw a rock in Bayfield and you'll hit an 1850s brownstone refurbished into a creature-comforts-outfitted B&B. The quintessential Bayfield experience is at the **Old Rittenhouse Inn** (Rittenhouse Ave. and 4th St., 715/779-5111 or 888/644-4667, www. rittenhouseinn.com, $109–299), an enormous old place with 20 meticulously restored rooms

spread through three Victorians, all with working fireplaces. The dining here is internationally regarded.

Food

While in Bayfield, indulge in at least one of the area's two culinary trademarks—whitefish livers and fish boils. Eating whitefish livers started as a tradition a century ago when boats were landing millions of pounds of whitefish. The livers are generally sautéed with onions and sometimes green peppers, though individual styles vary.

The landmark of sorts in Bayfield is funky old **Greunke's** (17 Rittenhouse Ave., 715/779-5480, lunch and dinner daily, $4–15). The place that purportedly started the whole whitefish liver thing is still the place in the village to sample it. The Civil War–era structure still has a sheen of originality to it—down to the heavy wooden doors and a century or more of detritus on the walls. Greunke's is the place for the local fish boil, served Thursday–Sunday in season.

A recent addition, the **Wild Rice Restaurant** (84860 Old San Rd., 715/779-9881, 6–10 P.M. daily, $23–34) is a major plus for foodies. The food here is eclectic and inspired, all in a superbly designed dining room.

An enthralling epicurean experience, the five-course, all-night meals from the **Old Rittenhouse Inn** (Rittenhouse Ave. and 4th St., 715/779-5111 or 888/644-4667, www. rittenhouseinn.com, 5–9 P.M. daily, $45) have been called the most memorable in the state. The fare spans the culinary spectrum but gives a hearty nod to creative Midwestern fare, made with as many area ingredients as possible. The remarkably ambitious menu changes constantly.

Information

The **Bayfield Chamber of Commerce** (Manypenny Ave. and Broad St., 715/779-3335 or 800/447-4094, www.bayfield.org) has lengthy resource lists for accommodations and assorted tours.

Getting There

The **Bay Area Rural Transit (BART)** (715/682-9664, till 6:45 P.M. Mon.–Fri.) bus system, offering service from Red Cliff south to Ashland, has a stop in Bayfield.

◖ HIGHWAY 13 FROM BAYFIELD TO SUPERIOR

Here's where the windshield vistas become worthy of Ansel Adams—the modest Bayfield County mosaic of orchards, multihued patches of unidentified crop, enormous rolls of hay, dilapidated one-eyed shotgun shacks weathering by the side of the road, or even an abandoned Chevy truck rusting in the cattails. WI 13 eases out of Bayfield and whips along the coastline, coming out almost as far west as Superior—about 80 miles and totally worth the effort. These parts were settled predominantly by Finnish and other Scandinavian immigrants pushing west out of Michigan's Upper Peninsula around the middle of the 19th century. They would eventually spread through the ore docks and shipyards of Superior and into the mines of the Mesabi and Vermilion Iron Ranges in Minnesota. A number of their homesteads can still be seen poking through the weeds along the route.

West of Red Cliff and the mainland unit of the Apostle Islands National Lakeshore, lots of tiny side roads poke their way north from WI 13, leading to assorted points and promontories. Some end at established picnic areas near beaches, others offer miles of gravel just to reach an overrated boat landing.

Red Cliff Indian Reservation

Less than 10,000 acres in size, the Red Cliff Reservation (www.redcliff-nsn.org) of the Lake Superior Chippewa hugs the shoreline, starting three miles north of Bayfield, and wraps around the point of the peninsula, a magical stretch of lakefront property. The reservation was established by the legendary Ojibwa chief Buffalo, who stoically and respectfully resisted U.S. federal attempts to appropriate Ojibwa lands thought to contain a wealth of copper ore. At one point, this band of Ojibwa and the

band at Bad River belonged to the La Pointe Band, which separated in the 1840s to the present locations. The reservation has its **Isle Vista Casino** (715/779-3712), as well as a **marina** and adjacent **campground** ($25–35) with resplendent views of Basswood and Madeline Islands. Another campground (privately owned but technically on reservation lands), farther from the madding crowds, is at Point Detour. The reservation's **pow-wow** takes place the first weekend in July.

Cornucopia

The Depression-era WPA state guidebook described Cornucopia thus: "stiff gray fishing nets hang drying on big reels; weathered shacks crowd to the shore line with its old docks; thousands of gulls flash white against the sky." The northernmost community in Wisconsin, edging out Red Cliff by a scant few feet, Cornucopia features hands-down the best sunsets on Lake Superior—this is the place in Wisconsin everyone thinks is his or her secret getaway. There is a marina and a public harbor. Cornucopia is also becoming something of an artists' colony. The best sight not relating to the lake is the onion dome of a Greek Orthodox church; you can also snoop around their small but fun **museum.** Get your postcards stamped here, at the northernmost post office in the state!

The **Village Inn** (22270 Hwy. C, 715/742-3941, www.villageinncornucopia.com, rooms $75) is a little country inn and restaurant that may offer the most quintessential Lake Superior experience—whitefish livers. Also try the fish chowder.

Fish Lipps (715/742-3378) has basic sustenance (try the trout and whitefish in curry) and arranges charters; it's a good spot to rub shoulders with locals.

Herbster

Unincorporated Herbster, at the mouth of the Cranberry River, features a small **recreation area** right on the lake. Exit Herbster via Bark Point Road, which leads to a tall promontory overlooking Bark Bay and far into the lake.

This, the **Bark Bay Slough,** is a unique conservation area, home to quite a few localized plant and animal species. There is also gorgeous scenery to the west of town. In Herbster proper, the beachfront park offers outstanding **camping** (first-come, first-served only) and a fishing dock and boat launch.

Port Wing

More cabins, camping, and boat moorings can be found at Port Wing to the west. This long-established farming town was heavily settled by Finnish immigrants expanding westward from their original bases in Michigan. Other than that, the town boasts the state's first consolidated school district (a radical idea for 1903) and the first school bus, both of which—or at least decent mock-ups thereof—are displayed in a town park. Today, it offers mostly sportfishing charters, a couple of B&Bs (an equal number of bars), and some stores and gas stations. West of Port Wing a marked detour leads to **Brule Point,** down a pocky gravel road scratched out of rough lakeside wetland. There are lots of pulloffs along the way, and a picnic area and great beach at the end. The place is isolated and usually less than populated, even in high summer season.

A few miles west of Port Wing, at the junction with Falls Road, the Iron River crosses WI 13. A left turn on Falls Road leads to **Orienta Falls** of the Orienta Flowage.

Brule River State Forest

For no apparent reason, WI 13 turns sharply to the south and trims the edge of this relatively unknown (though 50,000 acres!) Wisconsin state forest, punctuated by lowland spruce, paralleling the deep Brule River channel from its headwaters near the St. Croix Flowage into Lake Superior.

The river was the most vital link in the chain of waterways between Lake Superior and the Lower Mississippi River, requiring only a short portage from the Brule to the St. Croix River. Daniel Greysolon, Sieur du Lhut, made the river well known in his 1680 writings. More recently, five U.S. presidents have fished its blue-ribbon trout waters (thus, the nickname "River of Presidents"). So enamored of the Brule was Calvin Coolidge that in 1928 he essentially relocated the already relocated White House to a nearby lodge.

Today canoeists and trout aficionados make up the bulk of casual users. The area betwixt U.S. 2 and Stone's Bridge is the most popular, with proud stands of trees and lots of tranquility. Not surprisingly, this is where the presidents summered. Contact the ranger station (715/372-8539) in Brule, south of the U.S. 2 and WI 27 junction, for maps and camping information.

Hikers will find one super nature trail at the Bois Brule Campground, south of U.S. 2, and extended snowmobile/ski trails to trek almost the entire length of the river; one 26-miler heads to St. Croix Lake. Old logging trails branch out in myriad patterns throughout Douglas County.

Two (primitive) campgrounds are in the forest.

To Superior

There's nothing dramatic along the rest of the route until the road graces the banks of the Amnicon River. A couple of miles before the intersection with U.S. 2, you'll find a pulloff offering a great view of a traditional **Finnish windmill.** Built in 1904 and used to grind wheat, it's not in operation but hasn't been allowed to decay.

WASHBURN

Washburn seems to get little respect from the tourism community. Consider that the town of Washburn isn't even in Washburn County. It's in Bayfield County—it's the county *seat*—though most visitors would never guess it. It's a good place to stay for budget-conscious travelers scared off by Bayfield's prices (and full rooms).

Sights

The best thing to do is walk along the town's **lakeshore parkway walking trail,** stretching from Pump House Road in the northeast of town to Thompson's West End Park. Downtown, the **Washburn Historical Museum and Cultural Center** is an unmistakable soft brownstone that was once a bank. **Stagenorth** (123 W. Omaha, 715/373-1194, www.stagenorth.com) is a modern performing arts theater where you might get jazz, you might get a play; even if nothing's on—stop by for a drink at the bar.

On Bayfield Street in the central part of town you'll find an odd biological specimen—the **Lombardy Poplar.** This state champion tree has defied odds by living—and growing—for 80 years, despite the fact that this species is generally short-lived. This one, an exotic European import, has hung on to produce a trunk 52 inches in diameter.

Accommodations and Food
The cheapest rooms, quite a decent deal, are the recently refurbished rooms at the **North Coast Inn and Chalets** (26 W. WI 13, 715/373-5512, $70). There are basic rooms, some with kitchenettes.

There are a couple of great USFS campgrounds north and south of town, but most don't know about the **Big Rock County Campground** on the Sioux River; to get there go three miles northwest of town on Highway C and then right on Big Rock Road. Two fine public campgrounds are right on the water in Washburn; neither takes reservations.

A couple of "bistros" exist in Washburn. Simpler but better for this roadhog are the wood-fired pizzas at **DaLou's** (310 W. Bayfield St., 713/373-1125, lunch and dinner Tues.–Sat.).

Getting There
Washburn is served by the **Bay Area Rural Transit (BART)** (715/682-9664) buses that run between Ashland and Bayfield.

NORTHERN GREAT LAKES VISITOR CENTER
The grand Northern Great Lakes Visitor Center (junction of U.S. 2 and WI 13, 715/685-2680, www.northerngreatlakescenter.org,

9 A.M.–5 P.M. daily), west of Ashland, is without question the best educational experience in northwestern Wisconsin, and it has even better views of the big lake. Best: It's still free. An impressive piece of architecture and construction, it's a multileveled educational center focusing on the region's ecosystem and history. A multimedia introduction produced by Bayfield's Big Top Chautauqua musically chronicles the area's cultural history. Other exhibits also examine cultural history and environmental issues; they all put the lie to the derisive nickname once applied to the region: "The Godforsaken Waste." The center runs admirable educational programs; even exciting on-the-water paddle programs are common.

ASHLAND
Ashland became a transportation point for millions of tons of ore extracted from the Penokee-Gogebic Range of Hurley and Michigan's Upper Peninsula. Pierre Esprit Radisson entered Chequamegon Bay as far back as 1659. Father Claude Allouez built the first mission among the Ojibwa, abandoned in 1669. The propitious bay location engendered transport, and by the 1890s Ashland was shipping twice the tonnage of Milwaukee, Duluth, and Superior combined.

All that has changed, though the town's 9,000 hardy souls hang on to one of the bay's best recreational fishing locations. Touted as the "Garland City of the Inland Seas"—not an exaggeration but not exactly noticeable—it's a sedate town chock-full of old rail lines, stained wood docks, aging trestles, and some superb lakeshore vistas.

Sights and Recreation
Northland College (715/682-1233, www.northland.edu) along Ellis Avenue (WI 13) south of downtown is, given the name, ensconced in the North Woods, a primary inspiration for its eco-minded course work. Locals refer to the school's students as tree huggers—a term of endearment. Case in point: The **Sigurd Olson Environmental Institute** (8 A.M.–4 P.M. Mon.–Fri. when school is in session) is here, a

think-tank and educational center (with great nature photography and other exhibits) for environmental studies, named in honor of the pioneering ecologist who was born and raised in the Ashland area. Lovely Ashland brownstone is scattered across the campus in early-20th-century buildings.

Along U.S. 2 East in Ashland off Bay View Park is **Tern Island,** an island producing two-thirds of the common terns in the Lake Superior region. Jutting into the waters from the park is a reconstructed section of the Ashland Pier, one of the five ore docks built in the 19th century.

Ashland's **parks** spread along the lip of the lake. Most contain absolutely frigid-looking beaches and great picnicking. Maslowski Beach on the west side offers the best views, arguably the best sand stretches, and a bubbling artesian spring. West of town off Turner Road you'll find Prentice Park, connecting with Superior via the **Tri-County Recreation Trail,** a 60-mile biking, hiking, and snowmobile trail that spins through Fish Creek Slough. There are more artesian wells here for the parched (if you're into artesian wells, the Ashland Water Utility oversees one of the largest in North America) and some decent camping.

Ashland and Iron Counties boast one of the highest concentrations of **waterfalls** in the state. Almost two dozen are within a quick drive of Ashland; Potato River Falls is especially worth seeing.

Accommodations

Just drive along U.S. 2 and you'll drive by a half dozen very clean and very good motels for around $50 in high season—best is **Crest Motel** (115 Sanborn Ave., 800/657-1329, $55). The former grand dame **Hotel Chequamegon** (101 U.S. 2 W, 715/682-9095, www.hotelc. com, $135–175) was rebuilt after a 1950s fire, but you'd swear this remake is the original. You'll find rooms of various incarnations, all appointed in period detail. Some say anachronistic, others say that's the point.

Food

The casual brewpub **LC Wilmarth Deepwater Grille and Southshore Brewery** (808 W. Main St., 715/682-4200, 11 A.M.–10 P.M. daily, $6–18) has great views and good food. Peruse the menu with one of six homebrews and then sample the food: walleye (Fridays it's a must) or one of the creative takes—perhaps a wild duck quesadilla?

Tucked away just outside of town is the wonderful **Platter** (315 Turner Rd., 715/682-2626, 4:30–10 P.M. daily, $5–30), the region's most established restaurant, housed in a graceful 19th-century house.

Oh, and best java (organic) and healthful food seemingly *crafted* with thought behind it after the long highway journey from down south is at the **❮ Black Cat** (211 Chapple Ave., 715/682-3680, 6:30 A.M.–9 P.M. Mon.–Fri., 7 A.M.–7 P.M. Sat., 8 A.M.–7 P.M. Sun.) coffeehouse; God, I love this place.

Getting There

Ashland is the southern terminus for **Bay Area Rural Transit (BART)** (715/682-9664), which stretches north to Bayfield and beyond.

BAD RIVER INDIAN RESERVATION

The Mauvaise ("Bad") River was aptly named by the French, disgusted at its treacherous navigation. The Treaty of 1854 allowed The Loon Clan of Lake Superior Ojibwa to settle here along the river, which they renamed Mushkeezeebi, or Marsh River, along with a small contingent on Madeline Island. The 1,800 descendants of the clan live on the largest Indian reservation (123,000 acres) in Wisconsin. It stretches for 17 miles along Lake Superior and more than 100 miles inland, including the superb Kakagon Sloughs, a 7,000-acre wetland of virginal wild rice beds, noted as a National Natural Landmark for its *manomin* (wild rice) and its waterfowl population. Some have called it "Wisconsin's Everglades," and it isn't much of a stretch.

Apostle Islands National Lakeshore

If the Bayfield peninsula in the north is Wisconsin's crown, then the jewels of that crown (a cliché, but befitting) are the nearly two dozen pastel-hued sandstone islands of one of the nation's few national lakeshores. This coastal treasure, misnamed by overzealous or perhaps arithmetically overwhelmed French Jesuits, is to many the most precious region in Wisconsin. In the inverse of the fierce nor'easters tearing across the lake, during the periods when Lake Superior appears placidly equable, spirits seem to appear to deposit droplets of mercury atop the surface of a glistening mirror. Extraordinary.

Natural History
GEOLOGY

The flat-topped, waxy looking islands appear scraped into horizontal symmetry by ice floes. The islands do show a simple "veneer," as one geologist has noted, of imperious glacial wash, yet the remainder of their composition, save for

diminutive Long Island, is billion-plus-year-old pre-Cambrian bedrock. As the last glacier retreated almost 10 millennia ago, all but one of the islands were covered by enormous lakes, precursors to Lake Superior. Superficial wave and wind carving actions molded the islands into their present appearance.

CLIMATE

The islands take the brunt of legendary Superior storms squarely on the chin. To this day, ships still drop their "hooks" in the lee-ward, rain-shadow side of any of the islands to escape fierce nor'easters that might suddenly swell up. Thence, you can expect capricious weather patterns and, as on the mainland, a hell of a lot of snow—around 120 inches average in these parts. But Gitchee Gumee (a Native American–derived name for Lake Superior) can also have a positive spin—those gale-producing waters ameliorate unpleasant

© THOMAS HUHTI

sea caves of the Apostle Islands National Lakeshore

NORTHWESTERN WISCONSIN

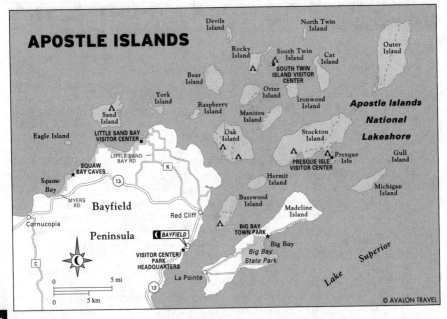

heat. Hands down the best summertime sleeping climate for campers anywhere in Wisconsin is found in the Apostle Islands.

Average high temperatures in summer rarely top 80°F, with nighttime lows in the 50s. Winter temperatures can plunge into the negative teens (and worse with wind chill), though the mean temperature is moderated somewhat by the lake. Spring and fall are the toughest seasons to peg. One day will offer halcyon warmth and azure skies, followed by a pelting slush the next day with winds in excess of 30 knots and six-foot swells on the lake.

FLORA AND FAUNA

The islands support a remarkable ecological diversity, amazing considering how ravaged they were by humans for more than a century. Some of the most pristine stands of old-growth northern mesic and boreal forest and not a few threatened or endangered plant species thrive in the unique island microclimate. In all, 16 Wisconsin State Natural Areas, officially off-limits, are interspersed through the islands.

They contain myriad northern forests, bogs, lake dunes, and lagoons.

Migratory birds have become a primary reason for many tourists to visit the islands. More than 100 species in all inhabit the islands; 98 percent of Wisconsin's herring gull and tern population lives on the Lake Superior coast in and around these islands. Great blue herons and two species of cormorants are protected in two areas, and bald eagle nests can be found in a couple of spots. Even pelicans have been introduced. Wolves, exterminated in the 1950s, are expected to return from Minnesota any day now (they are on the mainland). Deer overran the islands to the extent that organized hunting charters were hired to thin the herds early in the 20th century (but they are managing a slow comeback). A delight on Stockton, Sand, and a few other islands are beaver colonies—a pertinent mammal, so crucial to the settlement and exploration of the region.

The most salient species on the island is the black bear, found on a handful of the islands,

SMOKEY BEAR AND FRIENDS

Wisconsin's secondary mammal is the lumbering, doe-eyed *Ursus americanus*, the black bear. In the north, chances are damn good you'll spot one.

Now, is this a good thing or a bad thing? No one's ever been killed by a black bear in Wisconsin, but attacks do happen. (Some two dozen people have been killed by black bears in the U.S.)

Traditionally Wisconsin's black bears have been found roughly north of a line from St. Croix Falls along the Mississippi east to Green Bay. Numbers have exploded from 5,000 to between 22,000 and 40,000 (so an astonished DNR admitted in 2010 – they had thought just 15,000), so they're migrating south again and have been spotted just a county or two from Illinois.

RUN OR CLIMB . . . OR NEITHER?

The old joke: The black bear will come up the tree after you; the grizzly bear will just knock it down. Seriously, knowing what to do and what *not* to do is paramount. Inquire about recent bear activity. Look for bear activity on the trail: scat, diggings, torn-up logs (they love mealy ants and worms), turned-over logs. Carry a bandanna, shirt, or hat to drop or distract the bear. Leave your backpack on for added protection. Also pray that you never come between a mama bear and her cubs.

Camp in open areas away from trails, thick brush, berry patches, or spawning streams. At the campsite, food is what can kill you. Store food and all odorous items by hanging at least 10 feet above the ground, four feet from the top and side supports, at least 100 yards from your tent. Strain all dishwater and store with garbage; dump water and store garbage 100 yards from your tent. Do not sleep in the same clothes you cooked in. Do not take anything odorous – such as chocolate, toothpaste, and so on – into your tent, or don't be surprised if a bear sticks his head in and says, "Got any chocolate?"

If you meet a bear, *do not run; it may incite aggression.* (They can run 30 miles per hour.) Chances are a black bear will be more afraid of you than you are of it. Talk to the animal in a calm, low voice while slowly backing away. If it attacks, try to scare it away by shouting, making noise, or throwing small stones. Always fight back with a black bear.

including Stockton, which has one of the highest concentrations in the United States. Most of the islands have abundant blueberries, so it isn't quite a surprise to find Smokey and pals swimming the straits in search of food.

Human History

Paleo-Indians entered the region perhaps as soon as the glaciers left the horizon. The chain of islands has seen occupations—permanent or otherwise—of Huron, Sioux, Fox, and later Iroquois, all arriving to exploit the phenomenal wealths of game and fish. But it was indisputably the Ojibwa whose hegemony mostly shaped the human history of the Apostles. Before the enraptured Jesuits christened the islets biblically, Ojibwa myths recounted the creation of the islands—a nature-creator hurled enormous sticks or stones (accounts vary) at a fleeing animal, splashing into the glacial lakes and creating the archipelago.

BLACK ROBES AND BEAVER

Once the wealth of beaver became apparent (and Paris dandies made them the fashion rage), the race was on between the Quebec governor, who wanted to woo the Natives with iron goods, and the Black Robes, who wished to save those Natives from fire and brimstone.

Call it a draw in the long run, but the early sway fell to buck-toothed tree-cutters. The Apostles would eventually become the westernmost shipping point for beaver pelts along the fabled "Voyageur's Highway" along the northern Lake Superior coast. Another route crossed Lake Superior to the area west of Hurley, leading 4,000 miles to Montreal. The fur trade reached its zenith before the Revolutionary War and didn't ebb until the 1840s.

FISHING

The economic linchpin to Lake Superior's south shore was commercial fishing, catching on after the beaver's demise. Enormous stocks of whitefish and herring were netted, processed, and shipped from the islands; despite the dearth of overland transportation, the Apostles were a mainstay in the U.S. fishing industry. Semi-permanent fish camps dotted the islands, net sheds lined the shores, and it became such an industry that a thriving cooperage (barrel-making) industry also developed. An annual fishing season would net almost eight million pounds of fish. The last fishing camps withered away on the islands in the 1950s, when invasion of the Great Lakes by the parasitic sea lamprey choked off fish populations. As with Lake Michigan, sportfishing has become popular because of lake stocking.

QUARRIES

Sandstone from the Apostles helped rebuild Chicago after the Great Fire. Buildings from the Milwaukee County Courthouse to entire city blocks in Chicago and other Midwestern cities owe their construction to the ruddy brownstone culled from quarries on a handful of the Apostle Islands. Hermit Island has the best residual quarry; a visit to the Apostle Island HQ in Bayfield offers an up-close peek at the lustrous stone, dubbed second-best in the United States by architecture and construction firms.

SHIPPING

Mention Lake Superior and associative synesthesia sets in: foghorns, hurricane force gales, flickering ship lights, and rocks littering shoals. The Apostle Islands have the highest concentration of lighthouses in the United States, due in large part to the necessities of fish delivery to eastern and southern population centers and the sociopathic nature of the lake. A lighthouse keeper in the Apostles once reported more than 125 ships in deep-water lanes at the same time. One gruesome tale pre-lighthouse days involved a ship in a fierce storm washing ashore with the frozen corpses of sailors lashed to the masts, surviving the winds but not the hypothermia that followed. Twenty-five documented wrecks litter the lake bottom.

The first lighthouse went up in 1857 on Michigan Island; by 1891 a half dozen lights had been constructed on the islands, which made them the primary shipping landmark across Lake Superior. Today, the Apostles are still a vital link in the North American shipping chain. Iron ore, wheat, and coal are the primary cargoes of the massive beasts prowling the shipping lanes. But they are far surpassed by more modern pursuits—pleasure crafters.

LOGGING

Seemingly incongruous but bitterly ironic is the fact that the Apostle Islands today have some of Wisconsin's most breathtaking old-growth northern forest. This despite the fact that by the 1930s most islands had been depredated by the lumber saw during the dreadful timber epoch. Virgin tracts of red and white pine and hemlock lay yards from a natural waterway; in winter, logs could be stacked atop the ice and floated toward shore come spring. Eventually, the sawyers set their sights on the hardwoods, which required transport. Only those particularly steep-sided islands—North Twin, for example—managed to bedevil the cutters. In 1930, when the National Park Service made research inquiries into national park status at Herbert Hoover's behest, so denuded were the islands (fires subsequent to clear-cutting all but moonscaped most islands) that the National Park Service said they were unrecoverable.

The logging heritage made a return in the mid-1990s, when an entrepreneur log salvager got permits to raise, one by one, the millions of red oak, maple, birch, hemlock, cherry, and elm logs that sank during transportation a century ago but haven't rotted on the lake bottom because of the cold and low oxygen levels. Up to 30,000 logs per year can be raised; once surfaced, old tie hack engravings and markings are still visible. These pristine logs are in high demand from woodworking and timber industries worldwide.

TOURISM AND NATIONAL LAKESHORE STATUS

Great Lakes mariners and many well-to-do shipping bigwigs became enamored of the place (and its salubrious environment) and began making pilgrimages here as early as the 1850s. (The first newspaper travelogues appeared at about the same time.)

As far back as 1891, Northwestern Wisconsin communities had been pushing for the establishment of the islands as a national park. Calvin Coolidge, who relocated the White House to Superior in the late 1920s, wholly supported the idea. The initiative was initially rejected because the NPS feared the islands would never heal sufficiently from logging. Nothing much came about until the 1960s, when U.S. Senator and former Wisconsin Governor Gaylord Nelson, founder of Earth Day and the same man who would later help spearhead the National Ice Age Scenic Trail, brought John F. Kennedy to the Apostles to trumpet federal recognition—one of the earliest environmental speeches by a U.S. politician. Richard Nixon eventually signed the documents on September 26, 1970.

In homage to this prescient and passionate fighter for the land, in April 2004 80 percent of the lakeshore become federally protected wilderness. Better, it was renamed the Gaylord Nelson Wilderness.

◖ THE APOSTLE ISLANDS

Sure, everyone, but everyone, lands in Bayfield and up the coast for the obligatory *lakeshore* experience, yet how many actually see the islands? Don't be one of those folks; make the effort to at least get out onto the lake—if not hop off onto one of 'em for a stroll—and witness them for yourself.

Twenty-two islands—drops of geological history—comprise the Apostle Islands chain. Twenty-one of them, along with a 12-mile chunk of shoreline, belong to the National Lakeshore. They range in size from three-acre

Gull Island to 10,000-acre Stockton Island. Madeline Island is not included, as it's got year-round residents.

All but two of the islands are open for some sort of exploration—those that aren't are off-limits as flora or fauna preserves. Some are primitive and wild, others are almost like a mini-state park. Some are reached daily via Bayfield shuttles, while others are off the beaten track and require a kayak, private boat, or an expensive water taxi from Bayfield.

More than 60 miles of hiking trails can be found on the islands (and mainland), mostly on old overgrown logging roads. Looking at the map of an island, you're likely to presume that skirting the perimeter would be a great day hike. Don't bet on it. Not only are many shoreline areas off-limits to protect flora or fauna, but many of the islands aren't as tame as they look. Explorers and hikers have been dizzyingly lost in a gorge overnight. If you want to hack your own trail, be prepared to sleep with the bears.

Stockton Island

Stockton Island and its twin, Presque Isle, make up the largest island in the National Lakeshore. At just more than 10,000 acres it is easily the most developed and highly visited island; half of the camping in the archipelago is done here. Historically it has always drawn the largest crowds, beginning 3,000 years ago with Native Americans and ending with post–Civil War logging and fish camps and a sandstone quarry operation. For a spell, plans to establish ranches were also considered, giving an indication as to its size. Stockton Island features a beach, 15 miles of hiking, 21 campsites (primitive sites on the north side at an early-20th-century logging camp), a ranger station, and one of the superlative sights in the chain—the **Stockton Island Tombolo State Natural Area.** (*Tombolo* is Italian for "mound," but really translates as "overgrown sandbar.") A visitors center, open when it can be, is also on the island. As a protected area it provides refuge for two threatened sedge species and the English sundew, all thriving in a diverse

680-acre ecosystem. The highest concentration of black bears in the United States is found on Stockton Island: around three dozen!

Oak Island

Shh, this is your author's Wisconsin "escape"; nothing in the world beats camping with Bambi and Smokey on Oak Island.

It's the tallest of the chain, with steep-sided 250-foot ravines etched across its surface and a maximum elevation approaching 500 feet—so tall it protruded above the postglacial lake that submerged the chain. Oak Island's 5,100 or so acres are the inverse of Stockton Island's development. Rustic and tough, this spunky island is the one crowd-haters should head for. There are only about 11 miles of trail, but it's a nice mishmash of leisurely and unforgiving, and all great fun. Before modern upgrades, hikers could be lost for days at a time wandering the minigorges. *Note: Not only is off-trail trekking possibly hazardous, but it may be illegal, as some areas are sporadically off-limits to protect nesting eagles.*

Historically of interest are the pirates who plagued the shoreline, hiding in Oak's rugged topography. Frustrated loggers later followed and established five separate lumber camps. (One guy took up residence on a sand spit for 25 years, becoming known affectionately as the "King of Oak Island.") Their artifacts still lie about the island. The cliffs are ringed by sandy spits and some superb beaches. Black bears are ubiquitous, so take care with food supplies. Oak Island is also the best place in Wisconsin for winter camping!

Raspberry Island

Small at only 296 acres, Raspberry is one of the most popular islands. Its 1860s **lighthouse** is the second-tallest in the region and, after re-opening in 2007 after a needed face-lift, one of the purdiest, too. The cliffs here include uncommon clay-lined sandstone. Sand spit campsites are now closed because of the establishment of an 11-acre protected Sand Spit Natural Area. This is the one tour where the NPS really pulls out all the stops, down to the period-costume detail and a re-creation of the

lighthouse keepers' gorgeous gardens. Docents lead tours on-site constantly late May–late September.

Sand Island

On the western fringe of the chain and fully out of any peninsular windbreak, Sand Island's ecosystem supports a thriving, oddball flora. It's also got a commanding stretch of sea caves on the east side. Sand Island, almost 3,000 acres, was the only island besides Madeline to support a village, this one a community of 100, mostly fishing families—big enough to have a post office. Sand Island was also home to a thriving resort, in operation 1885–1910; historically significant structures are still visible. One trail runs along a one-time Bayfield County Road, past a rusted auto hull to an 1881 Norman Gothic brownstone **lighthouse.** A State Natural Area is predominantly northern wet mesic forest, holding 250-year-old white pine. Still more black bears live here.

Manitou Island

This 1,300-acre island is one of the flattest and least enthralling topographically. The island's fishing camp rivals the one on Little Sand Bay in its exhaustive renovation. A short trail leads from the dock past archaeological excavation sites of Woodland Indians. At the time of writing Manitou had dropped off the radar (and transport schedules), so contact the headquarters to see what's what.

Basswood Island

Basswood Island was the granddaddy (from 1868) of this archipelago's brownstone quarries, shipped around the country for major construction projects. The nearly 2,000-acre island was also temporarily populated by homesteaders and fishers in semipermanent camps up through the late 1930s. Seven total miles of trails wend through the island. Along the coast you'll see hoodoo-like rock formations.

Devils Island

The northernmost island—and as far north as Wisconsin goes—takes it squarely on the chin from Gitchee Gumee come storm season. It's a crucial, and tricky, turning point on shipping lanes on the way to the Duluth-Superior harbors. The rough waters and mercilessly pounding waves are responsible for the prime draw of the island, the **Devils Island Cliffs State Natural Area**—five acres of exposed cliff, subterranean blowholes, and bluff-top boreal forest. The underground chasms underlining the island produce rhythmic booms and whumps that reportedly scared the bejesus out of early visitors; lighthouse keepers reported ferocious extravasations of foamy water during high wave storms. Endangered plants clinging to the cliffs include butterwort and hair-like sedge. An 1891 third-order fresnel lighthouse sits atop the cliffs; there was a huge hullabaloo when the Coast Guard announced plans to dismantle it (it was restored instead). The rest of the island is preserved as part of the Apostle Islands Maritime Forest Natural Area, with old-growth boreal forest in stands across the extent of the island. There is only one campsite, and no well for water is provided.

Outer Island

Outer Island is perhaps the one Apostle most littered with the detritus of human occupation. At 8,000 acres, it's the second-largest in the group. The south end of the island is the best place to hang out, with sand dunes and spits forming a lagoon nearly a mile long. The entire spit area is part of the protected 232-acre Apostle Islands Sandscape Natural Area, a bizarro mélange of coniferous forest, lagoon, pine barrens, and bogs, containing the rare dragon's mouth orchid; migrating birds also use the spit in spring and fall. Another 200-acre spread, of old growth northern mesic hemlock, may be the most extensive in the Great Lakes to survive logging and deer damage.

Rocky Island

Tadpole-shaped Rocky Island is well named for the cliff-walled shoreline on the southern end. A smattering of extant structures from fish camps still lie in the weeds and along an established trail. Twenty acres of the island are protected as

the Rocky Island Cuspate Unit Natural Area, juxtaposing beach dune and bog.

Rocky Island is a chip shot across the channel from South Twin Island, and the two are one of the most popular pairs of islands in the archipelago, despite the fact that South Twin already has a twin.

South Twin Island

In precise topographical contrast to Rocky Island, this sister-of-sorts sits across the narrow channel. The least rocky island in the chain, it's mostly flat and sandy—and diminutive, a mere 360 acres. Despite the lack of craggy belvederes or yawning sea caves, enough folks still visit to warrant a visitors center next to the dock on the west side, though "visitors center" may be overstating it somewhat.

Hermit Island

Hermit Island, if for no other reason than its name, is a perennial favorite of visitors plying the waters on boat cruises. The island is named for a cooper who arrived from the upper peninsula of Michigan. Wilson (just Wilson) had been jilted severely there, and many took that to be the source of a certain pernicious misanthropic nature. During his spell of solitude, only one man, an Indian from Red Cliff, was allowed to visit him. All others were driven off by gunfire, including tax collectors, who had come nosing around after apocryphal-or-not stories surfaced that "Wilson" had squirreled away a fortune on the island. Upon his death the island was swarmed with booty-hunters who dug it up en masse, but to no avail. Later, a brownstone quarry was established, and a few gargantuan blocks of stone lie tumbled about on shore. On the southern side on calmer days the old ribs from a loading pier can be seen in the shallow brownish water.

The Untouchables

Eagle Island is an off-limits protected Critical Species Natural Area, with large numbers of sensitive nesting herring gull and double-breasted cormorant colonies. **Gull Island**'s three acres is also part of this unit, and a

500-foot buffer zone is strictly enforced for boaters May 15–September 1 during prime nesting season. Warmly rufescent **North Twin,** an almost perfect example of northern boreal biome (inhospitable to logging and thus untouched), is also hands-off.

Remaining Islands

The largest remaining island, **Michigan Island,** at almost 1,600 acres, has a mile or so of trails and a lighthouse to snoop around, along with one sand spit campsite (no water) on a small lagoon. Relatively undisturbed, this island is good for those with a Robinson Crusoe bent, hoping to camp on an isolated sand spit and hack through unmarked trails.

Ironwood Island really did once have ironwood, but once the local timber industry got going, it didn't last long.

Otter Island contains historically significant Native American encampments, along with the usual logging and fishing camps.

Cat Island used to house a modest hotel and resort, along with a quarry. There's nothing much now except for a few beaches in the south, some roads, and more weatherbeaten old dwellings. The dispersed camping here is quite good.

Sometimes one island, sometimes two over time—water levels fluctuate—**York Island** is essentially a long, narrow spit popular with kayakers.

Bear Island is geologically noteworthy as the second-tallest island in the chain behind Oak Island, 250 feet above water. More than 400 acres of the island are protected old and recovering northern mesic and wet-mesic forest.

Not an island but a peninsular oddity, **Long Island** smacks more of a breakwater or displaced sand spit, precluding entrance to Chequamegon Bay south of Madeline Island. A breeding ground for endangered piping plover (the only such place in the state—five chicks survived in 2006!), it isn't technically possible to visit.

MAINLAND UNIT

Little Sand Bay is the beginning of the federally protected shoreline on the other side of the peninsula, 13 miles northwest of Bayfield and directly across from (and with nifty views of) Sand Island. Here you'll find yet another National Park Service **visitors center** (715/779-7007, 9 A.M.–5 P.M. Memorial Day–Labor Day and the last three weeks of September). Featuring a dock and scattered displays on fishing, shipping, and tourism, the center particularly rehashes the story of the *Sevona,* a 3,100-ton steamer that was slammed to a watery grave in 1905. Adjacent to the visitors center is the restored **Hokenson Brothers Fishery.** Free 45-minute ranger-led tours depart regularly.

Slowly the National Park Service is forging a mainland **hiking trail** toward Bayfield; it's slightly over half finished. A community **campground** is cheap and has good views, though you're pretty close to neighbors.

Squaw Bay

A trail is being blazed, leading along the 13-mile coastline surrounding Squaw Bay, northeast of Cornucopia; get there by driving along WI 13 and cutting down one of a few roads that dead-end at or behind the waterline—none are developed. The best way to see the two-mile-long spread of absolutely wild sea caves and natural arch-shaped hoodoos in the sandstone is from a kayak, paddling right into the yawning chasms. Easily one of the most photographed sights in the peninsula, the caves soar to heights of 65 feet in some sections.

PRACTICALITIES
Fees

No more fees for reserving campsites (yay!), but there are fees for guided interpretive sessions ($3) and parking ($3–5).

Camping

Eighteen of the archipelago's islands (and one site on the mainland unit) are accessible for campers. All are primitive sites, and some islands have dispersed camping. Stockton Island now has one wheelchair-accessible site.

All campers must register at the Apostle Islands HQ (June–Sept. register also at the Little Sand Bay Visitor Center). Sites cost $10 per night

LYME DISEASE AND WEST NILE VIRUS

Since the first diagnosed case of Lyme disease was isolated in Lyme, Connecticut, in 1975, it has spread across the United States; it is the number one (and fastest growing) vector-borne infectious disease. In 2009, 2,584 cases were reported in Wisconsin – 7th most in the nation and more than four times higher than a decade earlier.

The cause of Lyme disease is *Borrelia burgdorferi*, carried and transmitted to humans via the *Ixodes dammini*, or deer tick. The deer tick is *not* the only tick (or, some think, insect) to carry the bacterium, but in Wisconsin it is the primary carrier. Distinguishing the maddeningly small deer tick from the more ubiquitous dog tick is easy. The deer tick is exceedingly small – the head and body, 2–4 mm, are only slightly larger than a sesame seed – and reddish brown and black. Dog ticks are twice the size and brown, usually with white markings on the back.

Lyme disease diagnosis and treatment are *enormously* controversial; I couldn't begin to go through it all.

West Nile virus has appeared from literally out of nowhere, with more than 4,000 cases and 240 deaths per annum within a half decade. At the time of writing, Wisconsin had had no 2010 cases confirmed; then again, once, Colorado went from none to the country's hot spot in one year. Spread by mosquitoes who feed on infected birds, the virus generally affects those with weakened immune systems and affects the spinal cord and brain membranes, causing encephalitic symptoms. The virus is not transmitted by person-to-person contact. No vaccine exists.

PREVENTION

Lyme disease is highly preventable. Deer ticks are active year-round, so you've always got to be aware. Deer ticks cannot fly or jump. They cling to vegetation and attach themselves to objects pushing through. Always wear light-colored clothing, long sleeves, and long pants, and tuck the cuffs into your boots. A hat is always a good idea. Walk in the center of trails and avoid branches and grasses whenever possible. Check yourself and others *thoroughly*, paying particular attention to the hair. Children are always candidates for tick attachment. Check everybody every 24 hours, even if you haven't been in the deep woods. Studies have indicated that the deer tick must be attached to your skin 24–72 hours before the bacterium is spread. Pet owners beware: Domestic animals can develop Lyme disease, and this is not limited to hunting dogs, so check them as well.

West Nile virus is spread by common mosquitoes, so it's imperative you don't walk around at night in shorts and flip-flops without insect repellent.

People swear by insect repellents using DEET. But remember that DEET's cocktail of toxicology has caused death in children, and unsubstantiated reports have shown that high concentrations of it for long exposures can do very bad things to your nervous system. If you use DEET, buy it in concentrations of no higher than 20 percent for kids, 30 percent for adults. I don't care who disagrees: so-called "natural" repellents aren't worth a tinker's damn.

A Lyme disease vaccine was pulled from the market in 2002 (class-action suits persist); it's still in canine form for pets.

Paramount: Do not panic every time you pull a tick out. The chances are good it's a dog tick, and even if it is a deer tick, it doesn't automatically guarantee Lyme disease. The best way to remove it if you do find one is to grasp it with tweezers as close to the skin as possible and tug it out gently. (Do not jerk or twist, because the head will come off and cause infection. Also, avoid the old method of using a match to "burn" them out; all this does is crisp it and leave the head in.) Disinfect the area thoroughly. You may want to save the tick's body in a plastic bag with a cotton ball soaked in alcohol. Wash your hands after removing the tick.

and a few islands have group sites. *Reservations are probably virtually guaranteed to be necessary if you want to camp on a weekend.* Call (no more than one month early) 715/779-3397 or 715/779-3398.

Most beaches, unless stated otherwise, are off-limits. No impact, blah blah—in short, if you wonder about it, you probably can't. Always ask first.

Garbage and fires are also big problems. Be prepared to go sans flames and pack out your garbage. Water is available at some, but not all, campsites.

The mainland unit of the Apostle Islands Lakeshore does not have an established campground, which always seems to puzzle travelers (but one kayak site is available on the shoreline). Just southeast of the visitors center in Russell, you'll find a community park with campsites. There are 10 others on the peninsula.

Information

The **Apostle Islands National Lakeshore Headquarters** (4th St. and Washington St.,

715/779-3398, www.nps.gov/apis, 8 A.M.–4:30 P.M. daily late May–early Sept., shorter hours the rest of the year) is in the huge and funky Bayfield County Courthouse.

Getting There and Around

Three main ways get you to the Apostle Islands: kayak, tours, or a charter. None are exactly cheap.

Most hikers and campers hop aboard the shuttles of **Apostle Islands Cruise Service** (800/323-7619, www.apostleisland.com) to Stockton and Raspberry Islands. But these are the only islands served.

Thus, your options are paddling/sailing yourself or a *prohibitively* expensive charter (and the latter are tough to find).

TOURS AND DO-IT-YOURSELF TRANSPORTATION

Kayak and equipment rental is available in Bayfield, but head a mere two miles north to Red Cliff and the very progressive and welcoming **Living Adventure** (866/779-9503, www.

water shuttle to the Apostle Islands

© THOMAS HUHTI

NORTHWESTERN WISCONSIN

livingadventure.com). All the equipment you need is here and it offers great tours.

You could paddle the entire **Lake Superior Water Trail,** which stretches 91 miles along the coast between Port Wing and Ashland; this is part of an ambitious 3,000-mile-long trail taking in three U.S. states, Ontario, and many sovereign tribes. The Wisconsin section is a *tough* paddle, so make sure you're up to it.

Rent sailboats and find instruction—you'll be seaworthy in three days of lessons—from **Sailboats Inc.** (800/826-7010, www.sailboats-inc.com).

Apostle Islands Cruise Service (800/323-7619, www.apostleisland.com) also offers a half dozen tours from Bayfield. The main trip for sightseers, the Grand Tour, leaves Bayfield at 10 A.M. daily and spins around all 22 of the islands. You'll see every sight possible without actually getting off the boat. The cost is worth it at $40 adults. During peak season, there is lovely a sunset cruise from Bayfield at 5:30 P.M. Tuesday–Saturday.

Twenty-two wrecks lie in the shallow waters in and around the Apostles. No real dive tours are organized in the archipelago. Divers must register with the park's headquarters.

Warnings: Open canoes are not permitted on Lake Superior, and you'd be nuts to think you could use one. Even kayakers had better know what they're doing before they venture out. When Lake Superior looks placid, it still can hold lots of dangerous surprises—lake levels do change with barometric pressure and wind direction. In combination, a wind-set (caused by winds pushing water to one side of the lake) and extremely low-pressure area will create a "saiche," a three- or four-foot drop in water level, followed by a sudden backflow. Rare, but it could be a killer. Storms are severe and can crop up suddenly. Most occur in November, when the water is still warm and mixes with arctic air, but they can occur at any time.

MADELINE ISLAND

Settled around 1490 by Ojibwa as their permanent tribal home and center of their creation-based religion, Madeline Island later became the most crucial island link in New France. The post would ship such a wealth of beaver pelts that the market in Paris dipped.

The treacherously multisyllabic Moningwunakauning, or "Home of the Golden Shafted Woodpecker," was removed in 1830; a British trader married the daughter of a local chieftain and the church christened her Madeleine.

A permanent population on Madeline Island precluded its inclusion in the National Lakeshore. Year-round numbers hover around 180, but it can swell 15-fold in summer, when residents—mostly well-to-do from the Twin Cities—flock to their seasonal homes. Though it is one of the fastest-growing tourist destinations in northwestern Wisconsin, don't go expecting Cape Cod or the Maine coastline. It is, rather, a humble "island getaway"—15 minutes from the mainland, but thoroughly rustic and with a great state park to boot.

La Pointe

La Pointe is not much more than an assemblage of minor structures housing basic restaurants, a museum, taverns, accommodations, and the few island services. There is the **Historical Museum** (226 Colonel Woods Ave., 715/747-2415, 9 A.M.–5 P.M. daily Memorial Day–early Oct., less thereafter; $5.50 adults, $2.75 children 12 and under). The holdings include real "black robes" worn by Jesuits and John Jacob Astor's accounting papers.

Big Bay State Park

Two millennia ago, the land this park occupies was a shallow bay, what is now canoe-worthy Big Bay Lagoon, another of the archipelago's remarkable ecosystems. The best trail is the **Bay View Trail,** which traces the eastern promontory of the park, bypassing spectacular wave-hewn sandstone formations, sea caves, and plenty of crashing Lake Superior waves. The picnic area at the apex, where the trail hooks up with the **Point Trail,** might be the most popular in Wisconsin. The beach is the most popular spot in the park, a mile and a half of isolation.

Most campsites are isolated from each other—awesome! Some sites are pack-in, though I'd hesitate to call them backpacking. The Madeline Island Ferry dock posts site availability notices—get there way early July–early September. Reservations are available.

Other Sights

Heading east out of town along the main road, turn north on Old Fort Road to Madeline Island's **Indian Burial Ground,** which is returning to its natural state. Farther east, **Memorial Park** features a warming pond and is the burial place of O-Shaka, son of legendary Chief Buffalo, who preserved Native rights to lands on Lake Superior and Madeline Island in 1854 treaties with the federal government. Interred in the cemetery are many of the original 20,000 Ojibwa who populated the island when the French arrived. Michel Cadotte himself, the son of a local trader and the man who married Madeleine, is also buried here. Some of the graves date back three centuries—there should be no need to mention walking softly and acting dignified.

Recreation

Mopeds and mountain bikes are the most popular way to take in the island. To the right of the ferry landing in the large blue building are mopeds for rent. Five minutes on you'll find kayaks for rent.

The Robert Trent Jones–designed course of the **Madeline Island Golf Course** (498 Old Fort Rd., La Pointe, 715/747-212) is a gem, known for lake vistas and double greens; reservations are most likely a necessity in summer.

Vans for two-hour **island tours** generally greet the Madeline Island Ferry.

Besides Big Bay State Park, the island has **Big Bay Town Park,** seven miles out of La Pointe and north of the state park. Campsites are available, none reservable. Rates are $15 per site.

Accommodations

The most basic lodging is **Madeline Island Motel** (715/747-3000, $90 s, $95 d) directly opposite the ferry landing, with rather hefty rates.

For that kind of moolah, consider a little splurge for the luxury accommodations at **The Inn on Madeline Island** (715/747-6315 or 800/822-6315, www.madisland.com, $125–500). The inn is actually a mind-numbing, island-wide assemblage of lakefront properties of all sorts: cabins in the woods, golf course cottages, and some apartments and condos downtown. Truly, this is the one place in Wisconsin where you can say, lingering in the sybaritic digs of a bayview cottage, you've "escaped."

Food

Expect a lack of pretentiousness in the fare on the island. It's simple and straightforward, but good. You want nouvelle cuisine? Minneapolis is to the south.

That said, a casually comfy bistro, **Lotta's** (corner of Main St. and Middle Rd., 715/747-2033), comes darned close to something special. Expect fresh, local ingredients, a daring menu—Cajun whitefish?—and a charming, fresh atmosphere. Lovely.

Then, something out of left field but wholly appropriate for the island's laid-back ethos: Out of the smoldering ruins of an erstwhile island café has arisen **Tom's Burned Down Cafe** (715/747-6100). Part pub, part art gallery, part café, mostly make-it-up-as-you-go-and-have-fun, you never know what's available here—but don't miss it!

Information

The **Madeline Island Chamber of Commerce** (715/747-2801 or 888/475-3386, www.madelineisland.com) operates only in season, Memorial Day weekend–Labor Day. The ferry dock kiosk in Bayfield has all the straight dope if you show up sans reservations (or even a clue).

Getting There

Late January usually until sometime in April, WI 13 becomes the state's only "ice highway"—a real, established state road plowed and maintained across the ice. During the holidays, Christmas trees mark the borders. At the bookend seasons when ice is forming or breaking up and thus too tender for cars, flat-bottomed air boats whiz across the short straits, and what an amazing ride that is.

The **Madeline Island Ferry** (715/747-2051, www.madferry.com) departs from Bayfield and is a landmark of the region. Ferries run from Bayfield to the island 6:30 A.M.–11 P.M. daily Memorial Day weekend–Labor Day weekend, with trips going every half hour 9:30 A.M.–6 P.M. and a midnight trip Friday and Saturday. Fewer trips run in the off-season. Round-trip rates are $24 auto; passengers $11.50. There are no reservations.

Getting Around

The **Madeline Island Bus Tour** (1:30 P.M. Tues.–Sat. mid-late June–mid-August, $12 adults), operated by the ferry line, departs a half block to the right of the ferry dock. Tours take in the whole island and include some hiking.

Chequamegon-Nicolet National Forest: Chequamegon Side

First the name. That's "shuh-WAH-muh-gun." It used to be "shee-KWAM-uh-gun," and, for tourists, any approximation is OK. The name—Ojibwa for "land of shallow waters"—appears often across the northern tier of the state. A staggered series of four rough parallelograms stretching from the Bayfield Peninsula south 120 miles, the Chequamegon is Wisconsin's—and one of the Midwest's—largest national forest at just under 850,000 acres, larger than Rhode Island. It's essentially the entire northern "cap" of Wisconsin.

Natural History

It comprises one-third of Wisconsin's north-south latitude; more, the geology of the central patches includes some of the oldest formations in the United States, forming an 80-mile ridgeline—the Great Divide, which continues into Michigan—that separates basins draining north and south. The range, at one time higher than the Alps, held one of the United States' greatest concentrations of iron ore. (Subterranean chasms still hold what is believed to be the planet's most comprehensive reserves of untouched taconite ore—3.7 billion tons.)

Unfortunately, early rapacious forest practices have, by most biologists' standards, affected the eco-diversity of the forest. Vast tracts of mixed forest have been replaced by fast-growing trees such as aspen, and cutover land is left open for bird hunting. Somehow, there are still stands of old-growth trees—some more than 200 years old—in the forest.

Flora and Fauna

Two hundred twenty-nine species of birds inhabit the national forest as planted breeders, migrants, or permanent residents; you'll incessantly hear the forest called the "Ruffed Grouse/Muskellenge/etc. Capital of the World." Hundreds of mammal species also live within the forest's confines. The black bear population, particularly around Glidden, is the highest in the state. Even once-doomed species such as martens and fishers are rebounding. There are wildlife-viewing areas dotted throughout.

Human History

Ancient powwow sites or burial grounds sit adjacent to abandoned European homesteads decaying in the weeds, while gracefully rusting logging machinery lies nearby.

Archaeological evidence dates human occupation of the northern swath of the forest, near Chequamegon Bay, back as far as 1000 B.C.—the early Woodland period Indians. It was a strategic Indian trail stretching south from Chequamegon Bay to the Chippewa River headwaters. Radisson and De Grossilliers established the first aboriginal contact in 1659 near Hayward, just west of the forest.

The seemingly triple-thick forest canopy brought Wisconsin's largest share of timber

COMEBACK KIDS OF THE CHEQUAMEGON

In the 1990s, the state began efforts to bring back the **timber wolf,** which had been all but exterminated by the 1940s because of misinformation, fear, and rapacious bounty-hunting. Now (2010) up to an estimated 725(!) wolves in more than 185 packs roam throughout virtually all of northern Wisconsin, with other packs in the west-central area of the state; one wolf was even spotted just 30 miles north of Madison, and two more were spotted in two southeastern counties. This is great news for a species down to just 15 survivors in 1985.

But things may not be so rosy for the majestic animal. The state Department of Natural Resources in 2009 announced that the wolf was no longer to be listed as "threatened," much less "endangered." (The feds revoked then reinstated it as protected later in 2009.) The state also wants to allow hunting, including using traps and dog packs. Environmentalists are naturally, well, howling.

In 1995, the state launched a project to reintroduce **elk,** importing 25 from Michigan into the Chequamegon National Forest. Things have gone so well (they number around 164 at present) that the state has been reintroducing elk as far south as the Black River State Forest in west-central Wisconsin. Now, this is great, but in 2010 the state was relocating some due to wolf depredation; moreover, some northern highways must at times close, since heavy traffic was spooking the elk away from their needed birthing areas. Check out elk information pulloffs and information centers between Clam Lake and Glidden.

opportunists, with full-scale logging beginning in the 1820s, upward of 100 million board feet of lumber per year by the 1880s. Dams, reservoirs, mills, and CCC camps all still stand. The Chequamegon National Forest took shape in the 1930s.

Recreation

Note that the national forest has a $5 daily ($20 annual) fee for *some* places (beaches, boat launches, etc.) inside the forest, but not all. Basically, if you can park there, you need to pay the fee. Camping does not cost extra.

TRAILS

The forest boasts two National Scenic Hiking Trails: the **North Country** and the **Ice Age.** Other trails total more than 200 miles, all doubling as cross-country ski trails in winter; 50 miles of that total is tracked weekly.

The Chequamegon is a point of pilgrimage for mountain bikers. Most flock to the Cable and Hayward areas for the magnificent, 200-mile **Chequamegon Area Mountain Bike Association (CAMBA)** trail system, most of which is not in the forest proper. More than 100 miles of trail "clusters" are maintained inside the forest, and there are hundreds of miles of service roads and logging roads that I've never been kicked off of.

WATER SPORTS

The forest has 800-plus lakes, 411 larger than 10 acres. Lakes under 10 acres all go without names because there are so damn many. Officially, there are 632 miles of navigable river and stream inside the forest, including the best options—the Flambeau (particularly the South Fork), Chippewa, and Namekagon Rivers. The latter is a federally recognized National Wild and Scenic River with Class II and III rapids. The former two are being considered for National Scenic Riverway status for their splendid wildlife habitats.

It's no wonder that landing a lunker is the number one recreational activity in these parts. It's beyond the scope—or ability—of this guide to suss out the whys and wherefores of fishing in the forest. According to statistics, the Clam Lake area offers the forest's highest concentration of lakes, containing the most consistent fish populations.

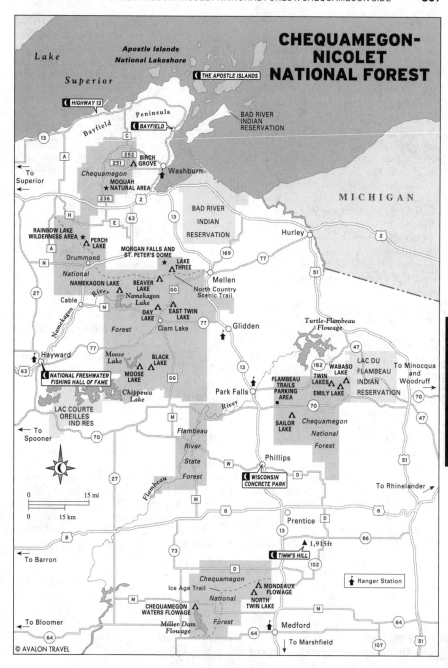

CHEQUAMEGON-NICOLET NATIONAL FOREST

Lake Superior

Apostle Islands National Lakeshore

THE APOSTLE ISLANDS

HIGHWAY 13

Peninsula

Bayfield

BAYFIELD

BAD RIVER INDIAN RESERVATION

To Superior

13

A

C

252 251 BIRCH GROVE

Chequamegon MOQUAH NATURAL AREA

236

Washburn

H

E

63

2

13

MICHIGAN

RAINBOW LAKE WILDERNESS AREA

PERCH LAKE

A

N

Drummond

MORGAN FALLS AND ST. PETER'S DOME

BAD RIVER INDIAN RESERVATION

Hurley

2

National

27

NAMEKAGON LAKE

BEAVER LAKE

Namekagon Lake

LAKE THREE

169

77

51

Mellen

North Country Scenic Trail

GG

Cable

M

River

DAY LAKE

EAST TWIN LAKE

Forest

Clam Lake

77

Glidden

13

Turtle-Flambeau Flowage

47

To Minocqua and Woodruff

Hayward

77

63

NATIONAL FRESHWATER FISHING HALL OF FAME

Moose Lake

BLACK LAKE

MOOSE LAKE

GG

Chippewa Lake

Park Falls

FLAMBEAU TRAILS PARKING AREA

182 WABASO LAKE

TWIN LAKES

EMILY LAKE

LAC DU FLAMBEAU INDIAN RESERVATION

70

LAC COURTE OREILLES IND RES

River

M

SAILOR LAKE

70

47

51

To Spooner

70

27

Flambeau

River

State

Forest

W

Phillips

D

WISCONSIN CONCRETE PARK

Chequamegon

National

Forest

To Rhinelander

0   15 mi
0   15 km

M

8

Prentice

13

D

8

86

To Barron

8

73

1,915ft

TIMM'S HILL

102

To Bloomer

D

Chequamegon

Ice Age Trail

National

CHEQUAMEGON WATERS FLOWAGE

Miller Dam Flowage

Forest

MONDEAUX FLOWAGE

NORTH TWIN LAKE

M

Ranger Station

M

64

Medford

64

107

51

To Marshfield

© AVALON TRAVEL

CAMPING

The Chequamegon side of the forest supports nearly 30 **campgrounds** of varying size and seclusion; all but two are on lakes, and those two are on fishing rivers. Rates range from free to $20 (averaging $12), and reservations can be made at some campgrounds by calling 877/444-6777 or on the Internet at www.recreation.gov. Outside of Memorial Day, the Fourth of July, and Labor Day weekends, you're likely to find something open, and even during those times sites are sometimes available.

Backcountry camping is free and permitted anywhere within the forest, as long as the site is at least 50 feet from any trail or water source. *Note that 14 percent of the lands within the forest boundaries are privately owned.* Campgrounds are maintained May–mid-October, but you have every right to camp there at other times though you'll need to lug your stuff in and get your own water.

"Without a trace" is, it shouldn't need to be said, emphasized here.

Scenic Drive

WI 77 spans the 29 miles between Glidden and Lost Lake. Recognized federally as the Great Divide Scenic Byway, its stretches reveal systematic reforestation and an engaging mixture of natural history and immigrant settlement. Along the corridor, the highway crosses the Great Divide, creating drainage basins to the north and south. Stop in Clam Lake for a great **wood carvers museum.** Clam Lake is also the best place to spot **elk**—you can't miss the "Elk Crossing" signs (and even pulloffs for viewing) along WI 77 and other roads.

Accommodations

About a zillion resorts line the shores of Chequamegon lakes. You'll find the usual gamut, from 1920s-era musty mom-and-pop operations to slick resorts. Thankfully, not many of those treacly Vail-style condo operations have infiltrated the forest yet.

Information

The **Chequamegon Forest Supervisor office** (1170 4th Ave. S, Park Falls, 715/762-2461, 8 A.M.–4 P.M. Mon.–Fri.) has basic information and numerous options for maps on sale. Contacting individual district ranger stations is a better way to get information on the specifics.

PARK FALLS DISTRICT

The Park Falls District of the National Forest graces the western edge of the Lac du Flambeau Indian Reservation and just a few miles to the east of the town of Park Falls. To the south is the Flambeau River State Forest.

Sights

East of Fifield are three wildlife-viewing areas, including Popple Creek, at which nests one of the only colonies of yellow-headed blackbirds in northern Wisconsin. Then there's the **Round Lake Logging Dam,** built in the 1880s on the South Fork of the Flambeau River to facilitate floating logs downstream.

At the Smith Rapids Campground, the **Smith Rapids Covered Bridge** is the only covered bridge built in the state in a century. It's a Town Lattice Truss bridge with a modern twist—its use of glue-laminated lumber, allowing continuous chords on the top and bottom of the trusses. Better, it's on an established state Rustic Road—#105 to be precise.

Recreation

The **Flambeau Trail System** offers 69 miles of multiuse trails. Smith Rapids bridge is found along one route, as well as ridgeline rides, a couple of impoundment flowages, and even an old log-driving dam. The Round Lake area here is a nonmotorized area and has an old logging dam. Primitive campsites lie along the lake.

Camping

Of the half dozen campgrounds near Park Falls, **Sailor Lake** is the closest—seven miles east of Fifield on WI 70. Farther east on WI 70 and then north on Forest Road 148 is **Smith Rapids,** good for canoeists, as it's on the South Fork of the Flambeau River. Still farther east is the primitive, isolated **Wabasso Lake,** so secluded that it's a walk-in-only campground (and free).

BETWEEN THE DISTRICTS: PRICE COUNTY
Park Falls

Park Falls caters to shotgun-toting hunters looking for the *Bonasa umbellus* (ruffed grouse), as the USFS maintains more than 5,000 acres of habitat near Park Falls. A gateway community, Park Falls is not only the headquarters of the Chequamegon, but also of the wild Turtle-Flambeau Flowage.

Park Falls has **camping** at Hines Memorial Park downtown, right on the Flambeau River. Motel rates in Park Falls can dip below $30 in the off-season at some places. Nothin' in town like the **Northway Motor Lodge** (S. WI 13, 715/762-2406 or 800/844-7144, $50), offering a sauna, recreation center and—you read this right—a bowling alley.

Four miles south of town is **Hick's Landing** (N12888 Hicks Rd. in Fifield, 715/762-5008, dinner Tues.–Sun.), overlooking the national forest Sailor Creek Flowage. Serving classic Wisconsin rustic supper club fare since the early 1950s, the Landing's got steaks and lobster. It's one of the few places that still has traditional relish trays before the meal. Northeast of Park Falls in Butternut are the largest porterhouse steaks you'll ever see at the **Butternut Resort** (11633 Hwy. B, 715/769-3333, from 3 P.M. Wed.–Mon.).

Lots and lots of local resorts offer canoe shuttling and rentals, and a few rent mountain bikes. The **Tuscobia State Trail** runs along an abandoned railroad grade for 76 miles to Rice Lake. Linked with the Flambeau River Forest trails, its western end also comprises a segment of the Ice Age National Scenic Trail.

Contact the **Park Falls Chamber of Commerce** (400 S. 4th Ave., 715/762-2703 or 800/762-2709, www.parkfalls.com) for information.

◖ Wisconsin Concrete Park

The town of **Phillips**'s main claim to Badger fame is the fabled Wisconsin Concrete Park. Local logger, jack-of-all-trades, and folk artist-

---

A BADGER BIGFOOT?

There are those who believe, passionately, that the dense forests in these parts are home to a Sasquatch, or family thereof. A hunter reported the first one in 2002 and sightings continued right up to the time of writing; in fact, a Bigfoot research organization (www.bfro.com) struck out on not one, but two expeditions (2006 and 2007) and one researcher claimed to have heard otherworldly howls not of any canine throat from deep within the forest (I'm hoping to hear tapes on the website at some point). The little A-frame information kiosk in Phillips (summer only) is getting kinda used to jokesters inquiring about it.

---

gone-overboard, Fred Smith began in his old age to assemble images wrought from wire, concrete, glass, mirrors, shells, beer bottles, and assorted other stuff. Painstakingly creating humanoid and animal forms, he had singlehandedly created the world's largest collection—200 cowpokes, bulls, bears, farmers, beer wagons, and more—of concrete art by the time he died in 1976. The park is sort of an atheist's retreat from all those fervid stone religious grottoes spread across the Midwest. After Smith's death, decay and storm damage set in before the National Endowment for the Arts stepped in and began restoration. It's an eerie, personal place.

Phillips also annually fetes its ethnicity with a **Czech festival** (http://czech-slovak.tripod.com) in late June.

Flambeau River State Forest

This managed, multiuse 87,000-acre forest dates to a 1930 state attempt to preserve dwindling northern forests. Riparian stretches are the key to the forest—50 miles along the north and south forks of the Flambeau River. Canoeing is the primary activity besides fishing, and the south fork has some of the most perfect white water in Wisconsin. The timber's not bad either—one stretch along Highway M is the largest virgin white pine stand in the state.

The north fork's upper section is generally the tamest stretch of the river; parts of the southern section can be killer.

A half dozen larger lakes in the forest—a couple are designated wilderness lakes—are muskie rich. Besides fishing, a park highlight is **Big White Pine,** more than 130 feet tall and 300 years old, off Highway M.

Family camping is found at Connors Lake and Lake of Pines, both off Highway W, and there are a dozen or so primitive canoe campsites (free, permit needed). Eight or nine resorts and lodges are found along the riverway. The **Oxbo Resort** (6275 N Oxbo Dr., 715/762-4786, www.oxboresort.com, $75–150) offers cabins and a whole slew of canoe and ski rentals, along with a shuttle service.

Two primary trails wend through the forest. The **Oxbo** begins east of Oxbo on WI 70 and is eight miles long. Larger **Flambeau Hills** trail is nearby and stretches for 13 miles. Trails also connect with country trails and the Tuscobia State Trail.

The forest headquarters is at the Highway W crossing of the Flambeau River.

◖ Timm's Hill

For most of its early statehood, Wisconsin's highest spot was believed to be Rib Mountain, near Wausau. Eventually, someone got around to the nitty-gritty surveying work and discovered that Timm's Hill, 25 miles south of Phillips, was actually higher. Along WI 13 and WI 86 and then down lovely rustic Highway RR and surrounded by a county park, the hill sports a 45-foot observation tower and, after the wobbly climb, about the only truly vertiginous heights in the state. Not Rocky Mountain majesty, but your spine will feel shivers. Just under 2,000 feet above sea level, the platform at the top at times attracts enough day-trippers to warrant a numbering system. Hiking and ski trails wend around the base of the hill. Camping is not allowed.

Rib Lake

Due south of Timm's Hill is a smattering of lakes, the nucleus of which is Rib Lake, a very northern European busy-as-a-beaver place.

In the village itself you'll find a **campground** at Lakeview Park.

North of Rib Lake, between WI 102 and Highway D, is Wisconsin's first established **Rustic Road.** This gravel ribbon stretches five miles past a handful of lakes (and one beach), resorts, and a scenic overlook.

The community-maintained **Jaycee Trail** is a system of interconnected hiking and ski trails to the north and east. The Jaycee links with one of the better stretches of the **Ice Age National Scenic Trail.** Along the Ice Age Trail to the west, you'll pass glacial eskers, a county forest (with a homesteader's cabin), and the **Deutsches Wiedervereinigkeits Brucke** (German Reunification Bridge), built by Ice Age Trail volunteers to commemorate the German Volksmarch tradition, which reportedly inspired the Ice Age Trail movement. Two glacially formed "mountains" are strewn with glacial boulders (erratics) and offer nice views from the top. If you're up for it, a hike to the western end of Rib Lake's Ice Age Trail segment brings you to a great blue heron rookery. Beyond there lies East Lake, a glacial pothole lake almost totally undeveloped and open for wilderness camping.

East on the Ice Age Trail you'll find parking for access to the local trails, north-south watershed-line markers, a trailside shelter, an enormous erratic boulder about 20 feet across, and a marker pointing out an old logging "sleigh road" linked to the Ice Age Trail. The Jaycee Trail branches here, continuing with the Ice Age, but if you stay on the Jaycee you'll pass an almost perfectly preserved logging camp, including a well, bunkhouse, cook shanty, and root cellar. The trail along here is an old "tote road," a supply route between logging villages. Eventually, the Jaycee Trail links back with the Ice Age Trail, passing scores of logging camps, bridges, farmsteads, gravel pits, and tanning bark camps. The Ice Age/Jaycee Trail then connects with the Timm's Hill National Trail leading directly to Timm's Hill.

WHOSE FOREST IS IT, ANYWAY?

The age-old battle of who controls national forests and for what purpose is being fought stridently here. The combatants are the usual players: hunters, environmentalists, the United States Forest Service, loggers and, of course, you and I.

Environmentalists bemoan the Forest Service's Ecosystem Management practice of replacing original woods with faster-growing-stands of evergreen (easier to recover from logging; in fact, only 15 percent of the state's public lands are reforested with original species) and its catering solely to hunting and timber interests at the expense of the forest's dwindling diversity. A University of Wisconsin study rated forests by a Biosphere Wilderness Suitability Index: 0–5, with 5 being pure wilderness. Only 6 percent of Wisconsin's forests rated a 5.

Why? The Chequamegon-Nicolet National Forest is the country's most heavily logged – 100 million board feet per year. The USFS shoots back that not only do bylaws of national forests insist the forest be maintained for multiuse purposes, but that the economy of northern Wisconsin demands it. Indeed, the timber industry points out that this national forest is in far better shape than it was 50 years ago and the state's crucial timber industry – 15,100 jobs and nearly $500 million in revenues – could perish. Nobody, naturally, interviewed the fauna.

Environmentalists were elated when the Clinton administration imposed a freeze on road building in 33 million acres of federal forests (69,000 acres here). A Chequamegon-Nicolet National Forest spokesperson said only 312 miles of roads had been built 1986–1996, but the forest had reclaimed nearly 600 miles in the same time. Thus the state's federal lands were already becoming more "wild." The Bush Administration took it to court (still pending), but the Obama administration re-upped the mandate in 2010.

Consider: The insatiable need for a piece of the pie puts us all under the microscope. It is *your* land, after all; the Forest Service (http://fs.fed.us) is perfectly willing to hear your side, so why not participate in the discussion?

Ladysmith

Though Ladysmith is well west of any of the national forest along U.S. 8, it does sit along the banks of the Flambeau River. Environmentalists abhorred the area because of the **Ladysmith Mine,** the state's last—and largest—copper mine. During its production life, almost two million tons of ore were extracted. The company says its reclamation efforts were phenomenally successful—the DNR seems ready to agree—but some locals are still wary of groundwater contamination.

MEDFORD DISTRICT
Sights

The Medford District is in the far southern area of the national forest, separated from the rest of the forest by the Flambeau River State Forest and an entire county. The chief draws for most travelers are the Ice Age National Scenic Trail and the **Mondeaux Flowage and Recreation Area.** The local concessionaire building has a few exhibits detailing the Corps' work with the WPA during the Great Depression. The area has been called one of the most perfect examples of New Deal works in the Midwest.

Recreation

Mondeaux Flowage and the recreation area has small boats for row fishing; four campgrounds and three boat landings line the northern half of the flowage. The **Ice Age Trail** from the east loops north around the flowage before heading west, totaling about 40 miles through the district; numerous trailheads branching off offer primitive camping.

Another impoundment—more than 2,700 acres along the Yellow River—is known for wildlife habitat in the Beaver and Bear Creek Waterfowl Management Areas. Of the waterfowl, tundra swans, sandhill cranes, and double-crested cormorants make up the most interesting snag dwellers. This place is also quite popular with canoeists.

The Jump River is one of the forest's primary canoeing rivers. While not a section amateurs want to challenge, the Big Falls are worth a stop. Just north of the district boundary along Highway N, south of Kennan, **Big Falls County Park** is one of the prettier stretches of river in this district.

Out of the town of Medford and running 25 or so miles to the north is the **Pine Line,** an aptly named wilderness recreation trail.

Camping

Medford District campgrounds are quite munificent—there's free firewood at most in the district, and all but Kathryn Lake are reservable. The only warm showers in the Chequamegon National Forest are found at the **Chippewa Campground,** on the 2,174-acre Chequamegon Waters Flowage in the southwestern part of the district.

Other campgrounds are packed close together in the northeastern section, along the Mondeaux Flowage, roughly between Highways D and E. They all are on or near the flowage and offer access to the Ice Age Trail, and a couple are wheelchair-accessible.

Information

The **Medford Ranger District Office** (850 N. 8th St., 715/748-4875) in Medford can offer advice.

Medford

Medford is one endpoint to the 26-mile-long **Pine Line Recreation Trail;** the other is in Prentice. The northern tier of the trail runs through the terminal moraine of the last glacial period, through hardwood forests, cedar swamps, and rich bog land.

Simple fare predominates, but you won't get friendlier proprietors than the namesakes of **Phil and Eleanor's Steakhouse** (N2319 WI 13, 715/748-0700)—a true-blue North Woods–style eatery. The kinda place where Phil might sit down and chat with you while you eat, if you're traveling/eating alone.

GLIDDEN (GREAT DIVIDE) DISTRICT
Sights and Recreation

The **Penokee Overlook,** four miles west of Mellen along Highway GG, is an easy stroll up a few stairs for a top-notch view of billion-year-old hummocks. Speculators began trickling into the region—technically part of the Penokee-Gogebic Iron Range—in the 1880s to sniff about for profit possibilities. Before the bottom fell out before the Great Depression, 300 million tons of ore were shipped from the Wisconsin-Michigan range. You can also get to the **Penokee Trail System** here.

Standing 1,710 feet above sea level, **St. Peter's Dome** is the aptly named second-highest point in the state. On a clear day, three states are visible from the crown. **Morgan Falls** drops a frothy but tame 80 feet over onyx-colored granite. A trailhead leaves the parking area at Penokee Overlook and then forks in opposite directions to the falls and the dome. Stream crossings and rough stretches mark the way to St. Peter's Dome, so be forewarned.

Most popular with families, the **Day Lake Recreation Area** is now a 640-acre lake, but once was marshland along the Chippewa River. A campground and short **nature trail** are found here.

Northeast of Mellen a few miles, check out more grand northwest Wisconsin waterfalls at **Copper Falls State Park**—great hiking as well.

Southwest of Mellen via Highway GG is a lovely backwoods drive. It wisps along the Penokee Range past oodles of wildlife, including a chance to see Wisconsin's only **elk herd.** Do meander around this road, WI 77, and any forest road for a chance to espy them, especially in September and October. Local businesses even have maps.

Camping

The largest campground in the Glidden District is **Day Lake.** This campground (accessible and with reservable sites) sits on a 600-acre muskie-laden lake. Nearby off Highway GG is **East**

Twin. East of Clam Lake off Highway M, you'll find pack-out-only **Stockfarm Bridge,** with seven very secluded sites (no reservations) in a copse of red pine along the Chippewa River.

The remainder of the campgrounds in the district are west of Mellen via Forest Roads 187 and 198. The most popular is **Lake Three,** with its hardwood setting on the North Country National Scenic Trail; the Penokee Overlook isn't far away. The North Country Trail is also connected to the **Beaver Lake** campground, on Forest Road 198.

Information

Information on the Glidden District is available from the **Glidden District Ranger Station** (North WI 13, 715/264-2511).

HAYWARD (GREAT DIVIDE) DISTRICT
Sights and Recreation

At the **Lynch Creek Habitat,** west of Clam Lake via WI 77, four species of nesting duck are a highlight.

The Hayward District has by far the most of the forest's 550 historic sights. Many of the best preserved are the skeletal remnants of Swedish farmsteads in the forest meadows. The highlight of the Hayward District, the **North Country Scenic Trail (NCST),** passes quite a few of them, mostly in the Marengo River Valley.

Another fave highlight? The **Porcupine Wilderness** is 4,450 acres of rolling uplands, wetland, lake, and swamp, and is totally motor-free. Porcupine Lake covers 75 acres and is rife with trout. Four established campgrounds are found along the trail, along with one primitive site on Tower Lake. Adirondack shelters can be used just west of Mellen near the Penokee Range Ski Trails.

Around **Black Lake** and leading from the campground, an interpretive trail details the lake's pine and hemlock "eras," starting around 1880 and lasting until the Great Depression.

The very much praised **Rock Lake Trail Cluster** is a system of six interconnecting loops for hikers, skiers, and mountain bikers.

COAST TO COAST: NORTH COUNTRY SCENIC TRAIL

The highlight of the Hayward District is the **North Country Scenic Trail (NCST).** Entering the forest a couple of miles west of Mellen, the NCST stretches for 60 miles through the forest and exits five miles southwest of Iron River. Some 150 miles of Wisconsin's projected 225 miles are done. When completed, it will be the longest unbroken walking path in the United States at 3,200 miles, stretching from Crown Point, New York, to Lake Sakakawea, North Dakota, where it will link with the Lewis and Clark and then Pacific Crest Trail to total out at 4,600 miles! Check www.northcountrytrail.org.

The Chequamegon National Forest walking trail, in fact, inspired the whole trail and lent its name.

Camping

The Hayward District has what may be the most primitive camping experience in the park: **Black Lake,** 26 miles east of Hayward.

Not far from Black Lake, **Moose Lake** is accessible off WI 77 east of Hayward. The fishing is not bad.

Seventeen miles east of Cable on Highway M and then north on Highway D and west on Forest Road 209, is **Namekagon,** offering 33 campsites (full of RVs). Easily accessible from here are biking trails and the North Country Scenic Trail.

Information

The **Hayward District Ranger Station** (715/634-4821) is north off U.S. 63.

WASHBURN DISTRICT
Sights and Recreation

The stands of Norway and red pine in this district of the forest were among the purest and densest ever found during the last century. The **Drummond Rust-Owen Mill Reservoir** is the last residual of a sawmill dating from 1883.

Built from fieldstone and displaying a unique conical silo, it was used to power the mills in Drummond—one of the largest 50-odd lumber towns that sprouted in northern Wisconsin. Though the roof has fallen and weeds are encroaching, the walls for the most part are structurally sound. It's just west of town adjacent to Forest Road 223, north of U.S. 63.

The enormous 6,600-acre **Rainbow Lake Wilderness Area** lies southwest of Delta along Forest Road 228. Off-limits to motorized anything, it's prime backwoods land for hikers and canoeists. The North Country Trail cuts through for six miles; Tower Lake, one of the forest's most isolated, is linked to the trail by an access route. Reynard and Wishbone Lakes are good for canoers and birders.

The **Valkyrie** multiuse trail is accessible west of Washburn off Highway C. One of the most respected trail systems in the forest, it departs near the Mt. Valhalla Winter Sports Area (an old ski jump hill).

The **Drummond Trail** is east of Drummond along Forest Road 213. The North Country Scenic Trail intersects a Chequamegon Area Mountain Bike trail network northwest of town.

Camping

The closest campground to Washburn and definitely the most popular in the district is **Birch Grove,** 12 miles west of Washburn. There are some decently secluded sites here on a long lake, and, man, are loons loud around here. The Valhalla Trail is accessible from here for hikers and mountain biking.

East of Iron River along U.S. 2 is troutfilled **Wanoka Lake,** popular with bikers traveling the Tri-County Corridor stretching from Ashland to Superior.

Six miles north of Drummond on Forest Road 35 is the **Perch Lake** campground (no reservations), on a 75-acre bass lake; it's near the Rainbow Lake Wilderness. The **Two Lakes** campground (reservations) is five miles southeast of Drummond and among the largest campgrounds in the Chequamegon. Porcupine Lake Wilderness Area is nearby.

Food

You gotta check out the (**Delta Diner** (14385 Hwy. H, 715/372-6666, www.deltadiner.com, 8 A.M.–4 P.M. Sun.–Mon. and Wed.–Thurs. summers, Fri.–Sat. only otherwise, from $5). A retro diner in the backwoods, it's got Wisconsin-centric fare—wild rice casserole, for example—and an utterly cheery, friendly atmosphere.

Information

The **Washburn District Ranger Station** (715/373-2667) is right along WI 13.

Hayward-Cable

The Hayward-Cable region is probably the most visited area in the northwestern lakes region. Seventeen miles may lie between Hayward and Cable, but they're in the same breath locally. Surrounded by county and federal forest, and bisected by the Namekagon (the north fork of the St. Croix National Scenic Riverway), the area's got lakes and chains of lakes in every direction and a decided recreational bent.

History

Human occupation on present-day Lac Courte Oreilles Indian Reservation dates to 5000 B.C.

The Namekagon River was a strategic waterway for the Ojibwa, French, and early settlers.

Hayward at one time was a planetary timber big shot, its boom status starting when a lumberman—named Hayward—established the first lumber mills. (Cable, an afterthought as a community today, actually arose first, as a railroad center and headquarters.) Hayward's ribaldry and raucousness when timber laborers came roaring into town to spend their pay was unrivaled (and fully detailed by national media). Timber still plays a role in the local economy, but the area has fully embraced

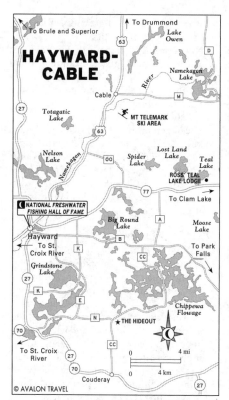

HAYWARD-CABLE

© AVALON TRAVEL

whose innards are also a museum (you *will* snap a photo!). The real museum is serious business, a four-building repository of freshwater fishing history and records: 5,000 lures, thousands of antique rods and reels, outboard motors, and 400 mounted fish, including more than one world record. Etcetera!

Scheer's Lumberjack Shows

Scheer's Lumberjack Shows (Hwy. B, 715/634-6923, www.scheerslumberjackshow.com, $10) are a hoot and a real-deal look at timber skills. Speed climbing, team sawing, ax throwing, and canoe jousting are a perfect example of familial delight. Arrive early and get a camphouse lumberjack meal of barbecue, home-smoked meats, and German apple pancakes. Shows go down at 7:30 P.M. Wednesday and Friday mid-June through late August, with Tuesday, Thursday, and Saturday matinees. Scheer's shows are held in the "Bowl," an 1890s holding area for logs being floated south to mills. Now it's the site of a logrolling school—that's how big timber still is around here.

Wilderness Walk

South on WI 27 is the family-specialty Wilderness Walk (WI 27, 715/634-2893, 10 A.M.–4:30 P.M. daily mid-May–Labor Day, $11 adults), a 35-acre wildlife menagerie and petting zoo.

The Hideout

Long a Hayward Lakes area fave, The Hideout, 17 miles southeast of Hayward, was the lair of "Scarface" Al Capone. Shockingly, at the time of research, it had been auctioned to a local bank, and its immediate history is up in the air.

Hopefully, it'll return as a tourist attraction (and restaurant). The northern lakes of Wisconsin were rife with Windy City wiseguys in the 1920s and 1930s, and this is likely the best extant example of their sanctuaries. Situated within 400 acres of pines, the fieldstone buildings and their interiors were incredible works of art. The main lodge features a hand-hewn, 100-ton stone fireplace.

tourism. The first resort went up on Spider Lake in 1885, and the little town today absolutely swells in summertime. Even governors have maintained a "Northern Office" in Hayward.

SIGHTS
◖ National Freshwater Fishing Hall of Fame

Shameless kitsch or North Woods work of art? Judge for yourself the 143.5-foot-tall muskie and other assorted behemoths in the fiberglass menagerie outside the National Freshwater Fishing Hall of Fame (Hwy. B, 715/634-4440, www.freshwater-fishing.org, 10 A.M.–6 P.M. daily June–Aug., less often the rest of the year, $7 adults). Kids will make a beeline to climb the planet's only 4.5-story climbable muskie,

A wooden spiral staircase was crafted in Chicago and transported here. The dining room and bar were built in what was likely the most ornate garage ever constructed in the lakes region of the state. Also still intact are the machine-gun turret manned by thug bodyguards, a bunkhouse, and an eerie "jail." There's even a doghouse built for Capone's German shepherds.

Cable Natural History Museum

Cable has a natural history museum (43570 Kavanaugh St., 715/798-3999, www. cablemuseum.org, 10 A.M.–4 P.M. Tues.–Sat., free), a couple of blocks east of U.S. 63, with mostly wildlife exhibits and some summer lectures. Of special interest is a permanent exhibit on the eastern timber wolf.

ENTERTAINMENT AND EVENTS

Hayward isn't the hedonistic, piano-pounding saloon town it once was, but there are always a couple of joints around that have sporadic live music in summer. I adore the **Moccasin Bar** (15820 U.S. 63, 715/634-4211) at the corner of WI 27 and U.S. 63, where even an outsider can chew the fat with local jokesters and see the world-record muskie, a five-foot, 67-pounder; all the beers on tap are made in Wisky, too. It'll pay $100,000 for a world-record muskie! (So locals say, though it's got to be a joke!)

Hayward also bills itself as a rival for Boulder Junction's claim of "Muskie Capital of the World." (A world record was caught here, which facilitates bragging rights.) The muskie is celebrated the third week of June in the **Musky Festival** (www. haywardareachamber.com). The largest parade in northern Wisconsin also files through Hayward's downtown.

The third weekend of July Hayward hosts the **Lumberjack World Championships** (www.lumberjackworldchampionships.com); no joke, the competition is televised on ESPN. The pro competition features chopping, sawing, tree climbing, and the perennial crowd pleaser, logrolling—all great fun. I love the hands-on chopping booths.

Northeast of Cable is little Grand View, which hosts late August's **Firehouse Fifty** (www.firehouse50.org), the oldest and largest on-road bike race and tour in the Midwest. Spectators will find unbeatable scenery along the forest roads.

The largest off-road bike race in the United States goes down near the Telemark Lodge the second weekend after Labor Day, the **Chequamegon Fat Tire Festival** (www. cheqfattire.com). Umpteen thousand riders will gear up, ride, and party hard for this one, a 40-miler through the forest.

RECREATION
CAMBA Trails

Hands down the most comprehensive trail system for off-road bike riders in the Midwest is CAMBA (Chequamegon Area Mountain Bike Association, 800/533-7454, www.cambatrails. org). More than 200 total miles use old logging roads, ice-sled byways, and whatever ridgelines the glaciers left behind (and add to that about a lifetime's worth of forest roads not technically part of the system). Expect varying conditions: from perfect to carpets of leaves, boggy and sandy muck, rutted dirt, and the occasional frightening python-sized tree root hidden beneath topcover. The **Namekagon** trails might be the most popular, with both the easiest and most difficult trails in the forest (Patsy Lake and Rock Lake, respectively), as well as access to the semiprimitive Rock Lake Area and the remoter regions of the forest. The longest cluster, the **Delta,** has some killer trails and arguably the best views—along the White River Valley—also offering access to the North Country National Scenic Trail. Dozens of operations in the area have biking supplies and rentals. One, **New Moon** (800/754-8685), is along U.S. 63 North in Hayward.

Chippewa Flowage

Abutting the Chequamegon National Forest and the Lac Courte Oreilles Indian

THE BIRKIE

In the depths of winter in 1973, 53 local ski aficionados headed northeast out of Hayward and skied their tails off 52 kilometers to Cable. They were attempting, for whatever reason, to re-create the famous Norwegian **Birkebeiner** race, an annual celebration of the desperation skiing of a duo of Norwegian militiamen trying to save the life of the country's infant king.

If they had known...Within two decades the Birkie, as it's affectionately known, has become the Super Bowl, if you will, of Nordic skiing. Annually in late February, around 7,500 skiers from around the world – especially Norway – turn up. The DYNO American Birkebeiner – its official name – is now the largest and most prestigious ski event in North America. They do it for the spirit, but certainly don't do it for the dough – a relatively paltry $7,500 for the winner, but still an improvement, since no money at all was offered until 1996. And it's now a three-day blowout, featuring the main Birkie, a 25-kilometer *kortelopet*, or half-race, and a delightful children's race, the Barnebirkie (1500 kids!). Events kick off with a 10-kilometer torch-lit race Thursday evening after the afternoon sprint races down Hayward's Main Street. Snowshoe races are part of the fun on Friday.

Reservation is Wisconsin's third-largest lake (and largest wilderness lake), the 15,300-acre Chippewa Flowage (lovingly, the "Big Chip"). This labyrinthine waterway is surrounded by 233 miles of variegated, heavily-wooded shoreline, an endless array of points, bays, stagnums, sloughs, and seemingly hundreds of isolated islands. Primitive camping is permitted on the islands, but the 18 sites are first-come, first-served. There is no dispersed camping, but you will find a couple of private operations on the shoreline. Nearly every species of bird and mammal indigenous to northern Wisconsin is found within the acreage. The flowage is

also a nationally known muskie lake and no slouch for walleye. The world-record muskie was caught right here in 1957.

Canoeing

The 98-mile-long Namekagon River is the northern tributary of the federally established St. Croix National Scenic Riverway System, and it flows smack through the Hayward-Cable area, its headwaters at the Namekagon Lake dam northeast of Cable. The river is no white-knuckler, though some high-water periods create medium to high hazards. For the most part, it's an exaggerated trout stream running a wide river valley and dammed into four flowages.

Visitors centers and the USFS ranger office in Hayward have information on water levels, rentals and more.

Fishing

To cover all the area's fishing options would be a book in itself. Musky and walleye are found here, first and foremost.

Camping

The Hayward vicinity offers 17 private campgrounds alone; factor in the half dozen communities of the Cable area, and there are easily 30 resorts or camping-only operations where you can pitch a tent. But why on earth would you want to stay there? You've got more than a million square acres of county, state, and federal forest around you.

ACCOMMODATIONS

This author stopped counting after reaching 150 resorts, hotels/motels, B&Bs (and shotgun shacks, private homes, etc.) in the area. One thing the area noticeably lacks is a preponderance of those ersatz condo ghettoes sprouting up to make the local area look like a silly copy of Vail.

If you show up unannounced during summer, you can likely nail down some accommodation, but you can't be picky. During festivals, especially the Birkebeiner ski race (in late Feb.), plan way ahead.

$50-100

The reliable **Riverside Motel** (Lake Hayward, 715/634-2661, $60–95) has a variety of rooms—standard to upgraded knotty pine and some waterfront studios (with masseur baths that give your body a reason to live), not to mention a few German-style cabins.

Dun Rovin Lodge (Hwy. B, 715/462-3834, www.dunrovinlodge.com, from $665 weekly rentals) is on the Chippewa Flowage. There's a taxidermy display, including the flowage's world-record 70-pound muskie, and the flowage's aquatic life is displayed in 6,000-gallon tanks. Around 20 remodeled cabins are available, and there is a restaurant.

Over $100

"Resorts" in the Hayward-Cable area run the range of dusty old cottages that look as if they were built in the 1930s by the CCC to sybaritic digs that look suspiciously like modified condos. Surprisingly, some places around these parts do not have a high-season ban on one-night rentals, though on weekends that may change suddenly.

The Chippewa Flowage southeast of Hayward has the most lodging options in the area, simply because it's so damn big. Organized and with-it **Treeland Resorts** (9630 Treeland Rd., 715/462-3874, www.treelandresorts.com, $95–360 daily, $750–2,300 weekly) dates from 1928 and today offers luxurious digs. A couple of dozen posh cedar-lined vacation homes and newer motel suites make up the lodging options.

In the Chequamegon National Forest is **Lost Land Lake Lodge** (9436 W. Brandt Rd., 715/462-3218, www.lostlandlakelodge.com, $750–1,300 weekly), another old-timer (from 1922) offering one- to three-bedroom well-kept cabins on spacious, isolated grounds. The restaurant here is quite good also.

In the same conglomeration of lakes you'll find the excellent (though pricey) ❰ **Ross' Teal Lake Lodge** (WI 77, 715/462-3631, www.tealwing.com, $240–680 nightly, also weekly rentals), an old-style lodge from the mid-1920s that started as little more than a fishing camp.

(The family's been in the business so long they once housed Abe Lincoln.) Two dozen one- to four-bedroom cottages are available, all with a cool screened porch. The lodge has become fairly well known for its new golf packages (the course is highly rated by golf media), though family-oriented media still gush about the mix of rustic with contemporary comfy.

Then again, Hayward's not *all* lolling at a lazy resort. Those aficionados of historic inns have an outstanding choice right in Hayward. The ❰ **McCormick House Inn** (15844 E. 4th St., 715/934-3339, www.mccormickhouseinn.com, $135–195) was well known before it was even finished. A regional newspaper back in 1887 said this: "When completed, it will be the finest house in town and one of the best on the line." Well, after a complete renovation using period photos in the 1990s, it was later purchased by a transplanted Londoner, who's done another extraordinary job of design—in short, a fabulous mix of modern chic with history, all with an English flair.

FOOD
Resorts

Some resort dining rooms could be mistaken for standard family-fare eateries, a couple offer "lumberjack"-style dining, and there is of course the classic Wisconsin from-way-back-when supper club, still allowing resort guests to pour their own brandy Manhattans on the honor system.

All accommodations listed (save for the first) have well-regarded restaurants.

Supper Clubs

A fave stop for this roadie is fish of any sort (especially walleye...mmmm) at **Karibalis** (S. Main St., 715/634-2462), a longtime local standby.

The **Fireside** (Hwy. K, 715/634-2710, dinner daily)—locals may still refer to "Tony's Fireside" in honor of the longtime owner—is, gasp, approaching fine dining levels. Yes, in the Great North Woods. You need fried avocado appetizers or herb risotto, this is your place. Go eight miles south on WI 27, then east on Highway K.

Since 1934, folks have streamed to **Turk's Inn** (N. U.S. 63, 715/634-2597, dinner nightly, $11–22) for the hand-cut and aged (and huge) steaks, and sublime knick-knacky, many-photo'd walls. Turk's also makes good shish kebob and cheese *burek*.

Brewpub
Excellent beer (oatmeal stout!) and bistro pub grub at **Angry Minnow** (10440 Florida Ave., 715/934-3055), a restaurant and brewery that seriously has some wonderful food. Better, one might actually get cheery and prompt service even when the place is packed (worth a trip right there).

Wine Bar
A group of chi chi shops and a wine cave are tucked inside the fun **Pavilion Wine Bar** (10551 Main St., 715/634-6035 or 715/634-3923), with a tapas menu, wine—natch—and live entertainment from a precarious ledge (no joke) high above the action. One of the co-owners is a long-time Wisconsin musician. It's great fun!

INFORMATION
The **Hayward Visitors Information Center** (U.S. 63/WI 27 junction, 715/634-8662 or 800/724-2992, www.haywardlakes.com) is well stocked.

GETTING THERE
Denizens of the Mini-Apple can get to Hayward, but no one else can, as there's no longer any intercity bus service. **Northern Wisconsin Travel** (715/634-5307, www.nwtexpress.com) operates bus shuttles to and from Minneapolis's airport, serving Spooner and Rice Lake en route.

LAC COURTE OREILLES INDIAN RESERVATION
Southeast of Hayward and sandwiched between two lakes and the Chippewa Flowage, the Lac Courte Oreilles ("Lake of the Short Ears"—and it's "lah-koo-duh-RAY") Indian Reservation (tribal office 715/634-8934, www.lco-nsn.gov) is a 31,000-acre federal trust reservation, home to the Lac Courte Oreilles Band of Lake Superior Chippewa, who arrived at these lakes sometime in the mid-18th century. But the area's human occupation dates back much further—more than 7,000 years. The North West Fur Trading Company established a trading post on a nearby lake in 1800; treaties with the federal government were finally signed in 1825, 1837, and 1842, which permanently placed the band here. With a tribal membership of 5,000, the population on the reservation itself is around 3,000. The reservation's location adjacent to the Chequamegon National Forest, the expansive Chippewa Flowage, and within the hundreds of lakes and lake chains also give it a strategic importance for outdoors lovers. The reservation's radio station, WOJB (FM 89), is about the only thing worth listening to in the region.

Sights and Activities
The tribe holds an annual **Honor the Earth Traditional Powwow** the third week of July, the largest in North America; other powwows are scheduled for Veterans Day and Thanksgiving.

North of the powwow grounds along Trepania Road/Indian Route 17 is the **Ojibwa Cultural Village.** Wigwams sit in a forested setting, and visitors are guided through a group of educational displays on Ojibwa heritage, from wild-rice fanning to blanket weaving. Some of the activities are hands-on.

Also on the reservation, along Highway E, the **St. Francis Solanus Indian Mission** is a site dating from the mid-19th century. The buildings include a rectory, a convent, and school. Inside you'll find assorted Native American artifacts. It's open daily.

GREAT RIVER ROAD

Forsake the mad swells of traffic on the interstates and major highways and give yourself at least a glimpse of one of the most precious, wonderfully undeveloped areas of the state—the Great River Road.

This famed road stretches from the source of the Mississippi River in Lake Itasca, Minnesota, and parallels the Ol' Miss all the way to New Orleans. Wisconsin's mileage is serious road-tripper eye candy—the Big Ol' Man River and nary a whiff of chichi overgentrification. This includes the best known stretch, the 85 miles north from La Crosse; the southern half seems at times to be absolutely untouched.

Along the way the road bypasses anachronistic ferries, big-time barge traffic, loads of archaeologically and historically significant sites, superb scenery, a gazillion eagles, and fun stuff like religious grottoes, colossal flea markets, cozy eateries, turtle jerky, and barge fishing. But the towns are the thing, tidy north-to-south platted hamlets that basically have the river as a main drag, some but certainly not all prettied up for river road traffic. Near Prairie du Chien be wowed at the crucial conjoining of the Wisconsin and Mississippi Rivers; at the northern end of the road stand atop a bluff and espy the mighty confluence of the Ol' Miss with the St. Croix River, itself a grand river valley.

There's an astonishing absence of tourist traffic on this road—never been able to figure that out—but no matter where you are, freight trains roar by with an alarming regularity, the

© THOMAS HUHTI

HIGHLIGHTS

LOOK FOR  TO FIND RECOMMENDED SIGHTS, ACTIVITIES, DINING, AND LODGING.

■ **Alma:** This, a perfect somnolent river community – long, straight, and quiet, save for the odd freight train (page 326).

■ **Trempealeau:** River rats may also rightly argue this is the winner of Most Unpretentious River Road town (page 329).

■ **Granddad's Bluff:** No doubt where the best Ol' Miss vistas are – here in La Crosse. Wow (page 331)!

■ **Villa Louis:** You'll find riverine island scenery and authentic fur trade-era history to boot in Prairie du Chien (page 343).

■ **Wyalusing State Park:** The Old Man River conjoins with the hardworking Wisconsin River south of Prairie du Chien here (page 344).

■ **Cassville:** Surrounded by nature preserves supporting one of the Upper Mississippi's most thriving eagle populations, chug across the Mississippi River aboard one of the last remaining river ferries (page 344).

south clashing with the barges chugging along the river.

Start with the best website (www. wigreatriverroad.org) you'll find. Then one from the Mississippi Valley Partners (www. mississippi-river.org), which includes some, but not all, communities in Wisconsin and Minnesota.

PLANNING YOUR TIME

The Great River Road is the *perfect* weekend getaway, going in either direction. You can't beat it, what with lovely **La Crosse** at the halfway point, which gives you loads of time to meander about. Don't forget that La Crosse's Granddad's Bluff is a must-see!

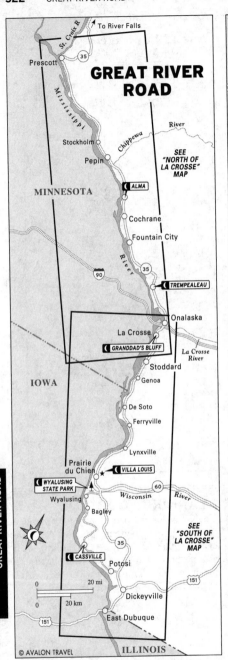

Prescott to La Crosse

PRESCOTT

At Prescott, the westernmost community in the state, the disparately colored Mississippi and St. Croix Rivers merge into one mighty waterway. Heading north, the river roads roll on—this time tracing the St. Croix National Scenic Riverway, the top half of Wisconsin's "West Coast."

The best point to view the confluence is **Mercord Park,** right downtown, which also has an original 1923 bridge gear. The steely blue hues of the St. Croix, seen in the right light, seem impossibly different from the silty Mississippi; on joining, the Miss's waters dominate. **Freedom Park** is high above the southern end of town with a lovely riverwalk, bike trail access, and a Great River Road learning center.

North of town via Highway F is the superb 1,150 delta acres of the St. Croix and Kinnickinnic River confluence at **Kinnickinnic State Park** (715/425-1129). Likely the most unusual camping option in the area is found here—all sites are designed along sandy spits and are accessible only via the water. Canoeing should be limited to the Kinnickinnic as well; leviathan barges give narrow berth to tiny craft in their way.

The **Welcome and Heritage Center** (233 Broad St. N, 715/262-3284 or 800/474-3723, www.prescottwi.com) has travel information as well as displays of local history.

TO LAKE PEPIN
Diamond Bluff, Hager City, and Bay City

The road gets serious outside of Prescott, rolling and bending, swooping and descending. Later, it gets even more ambitious, a downright roller coaster toward Diamond Bluff. Up and up and up and then a stomach-churning descent with spectacular scenery the whole way. The road, in fact, is bending around prominent Dry Run Coulee.

Beyond this, WI 35 forsakes the river altogether, whipping eastward in a grand curl before cutting south toward Diamond Bluff. This flyspeck town was the site of the state's largest river disaster in the 19th century (a plaque tells the story); today you keep an eye out for clamming boats. Better, heading west onto Highway E will take you along hills and small roads to grand vistas.

Once again, the river bends sharply away from straight-as-a-preacher WI 35; Hager City comes and goes—oops, missed it. That's OK, as south of town you can jump off onto U.S. 63 south and scout around for pulloffs. This is among the first areas to thaw in spring and thus is one of Wisconsin's best places to view migrant water birds. Eagle-eyed travelers can also spot the pullout area for a bow-and-arrow-shaped outline in the bluffs on the way to the next town.

That town? Bay City. Take Highway EE east—lovely birding along Isabelle Creek. Sitting at the head of Lake Pepin, Bay City was a key transit point for shipping fish to Chicago. Later, it had a dubious honor as the location of the county's first murder. Today it's got an 1850s Irish immigrant elm **log house and history center** (open one weekend per month June–Aug.; for more information call the county historical association at 715/273-6611) and decent camping.

West of Bay City in the main channel of the Mississippi River lies Trenton Island, regularly swallowed by Mississippi River mud floods. Still, none of the 100 residents will leave—a cogent reminder of the river's irresistible nature and the unvanquishable attitude of residents descended from pioneers hardy enough to hack a home out of a wilderness. In the early 1990s, state and county officials began—imperiously, say locals—to "prod" the residents into relocation and government buyouts, i.e., no disaster-relief money. Good luck.

Maiden Rock

On the way out of Bay City, keep those eyes to the left—bluffs, coulees, green gumdrops everywhere. The Miss gets so wide it is, actually, a lake—Lake Pepin. Between Bay City and Maiden Rock, taking Highway A east and then south to a bridge over the Rush River before heading back to WI 35 via 385th Street is a lovely scenic route—and one of the Midwest's top birding stretches, mile for mile. The appellation of the next village, Maiden Rock, gets a visual aid. A Native American "maiden" preferred a plunge off the crown of the hill to an arranged marriage. Maiden Rock is another artistic enclave on Lake Pepin. North of town is a wayside with unsurpassed lake vistas and the Rush River, a stream splashing with trout.

Part winery, part pumpkin farm, part al fresco Italian eatery, **Vino in the Valley** (W3826 450th Ave., 715/639-6677, Thurs. and Sat. evenings and Sun. afternoons only) is easy to dismiss as something of a gimmick. But there's really nothing like eating a grand plate of pasta and salad of local ingredients in a lovely rural setting. It's tough to find: from Maiden Rock it's Highway S, west on WI 10, then follow signs.

South of Maiden Rock the road grips the river's edge; it's not quite type-T thrilling, but do keep those hands at 10 and 2 o'clock! A mile south for a brief side trip, take Highway AA east on another of Wisconsin's Rustic Roads; you could whip out the gazetteer and cobble together roads to the Laura Ingalls Wilder wayside in Pepin.

STOCKHOLM

The name of this place belies its actual size, in the top five for dearth of population in Wisconsin. But what an unbelievable amount of stuff this town of fewer than 100 people has to offer—artists and galleries (even Mississippi pearls, extinct since dredging reduced the numbers in the 1930s, appear in shops), upscale eateries, and great lodging.

The name was no accident. Scandinavian settler Eric Peterson showed up in 1851 and stuck around; others from his hometown of Kalskoga arrived soon after, making it one of the oldest Swedish settlements in the state. The toponymy is a loopy mishmash of river jargon and "-son" appellations.

Well, there's nothing to do here, really, other than to snoop around the tomes of history and a few Swedish artifacts at the **Swedish Institute** (www.stockholmwisconsin.com) under the old post office. Shopping is the real lifeblood of the town. Artisan galleries and shops galore line the few streets. The **Maiden Rock Winery & Cidery** (W12266 King Ln., 715/448-3502, www.maidenrockwinerycidery. com) has tours ($3) by appointment. An annual July art fair, organized back in the 1970s by artisans attracted to the gorgeous river scenery, has become a huge event.

A mile south of town is a **historic overlook** at the site of a 1686 fort built by Nicholas Perrot. From here the French laid claim to all of the Mississippi's drainage—"no matter how remote"—for King Louis XIV.

The **Stockholm Village Park** has a boat ramp, swimming area, and **camping** for $10. Not to mention a few grand B&Bs. Oh, they're all so good I couldn't decide, so check out the village website (www.stockholmwisconsin. com) and have a gander at the options!

You will probably eat at least once at the **Bogus Creek Café** (715/442-5017, 9 A.M.–5 P.M. daily), a wonderful place—soups, salads, fresh specialty-bread sandwiches, and lovely garden seating. They do have barbecue nights Friday and Saturday.

One of the coolest experiences: if you're here on a Tuesday night, head east of town on Highway J and follow the cars along Anker Lane to **A to Z Produce** (715/448-4802), a pizza farm—that's what everyone calls it— where you can indulge in a massive pizza with all ingredients made on the farm in a friendly picnic atmosphere.

Thursday nights **Smith Gardens Community Farms** (608/626-2122) fires up an oven and creates magical pizza with ingredients from local farms! Go east on Highway O, then north on 88 to Yaeger Valley Road.

PEPIN

The road still sits astride the river, and one can race the Burlington and Northern freight trains rolling parallel to the road. (Pass by my favorite bluff on the whole route—Bogus Bluff; always wondered about that nomenclature.) It's little wonder some have dubbed the stretch in and around Pepin the most perfectly realized stretch of the Great River Road. When the U.S. government made the heavy decision to dam the Mississippi, it had already been second-guessed by geology. Glacial retreat and its "wash" had deposited silt at the mouth of the Chippewa River, eventually backing up enough water to form a 22-mile-long by 2.5-mile-wide winding gem of a lake, **Lake Pepin.** William Cullen Bryant wrote that Lake Pepin "ought to be visited in the summer by every poet and painter in the land." Father Hennepin later dubbed it, somewhat cryptically, the "Lake of Tears." Lake Pepin is so unique geologically that for years in the early 20th century Wisconsin and Minnesota authorities quibbled as to where, exactly, the river channel—and thus the state boundary—lay.

Pepin is also lousy with "Little House" affixations. Laura Ingalls Wilder, the author of the *Little House* books, was born on a homestead nearby in 1867, and the villagers are not about to let you forget it.

Sights

Seven miles northwest of Pepin via Highway CC (or Sand Ridge or Short Cut Road) is the **Laura Ingalls Wilder Little House,** the birth cabin and wayside picnic grounds spread out over a handful of acres. More Little House amusement? In town there is a **Pepin Historical Museum,** better known as the **Laura Ingalls Wilder museum** (WI 35, 715/442-2142, 10 A.M.–5 P.M., free). It's full of displays and memorabilia pertaining to the woman in the famed line of books.

Practicalities

Pepin's got a romantic feel to it, and three historic B&Bs are found here, including the **Summer Place** (106 Main St., 715/442-2132, $115), with a great arbor deck overlooking Lake Pepin.

Near the marina is one of the state's best-known eateries, the 〖 **Harbor View**

© THOMAS HUHTI

Laura Ingalls Wilder Little House, near Pepin

Cafe (314 1st St., 715/442-3893, lunch and dinner Thurs.–Sun., May–late Nov., $10–20). Somewhat upscale continental and creative international cuisine is the ticket here, and this is definitely the place to go for something other than eggs or a hot beef special. You'll have an hour wait ahead of you—it's worth it!

But on a Friday I'd head for the fish at **Ralph's Bar & Mary's Kitchen** (206 Lake St., 715/442-3451)!

PEPIN TO ALMA
Tiffany Bottoms Wildlife Area

At the confluence of the Chippewa and Mississippi Rivers spreads a magnificent marsh—an island-dotted wetland over 12,500 acres from Mississippi and up the Chippewa River Valley. WI 25 passes two noticeable coulees. Paved roads did not pentrate these capacious tracts of water-pocked bottomlands until WPA and CCC projects in the 1930s. An undeveloped network of "trails"—mostly those old logging roads—branches out all over the place (outstanding for berry picking and inward contemplation). Amateur shutterbugs should have a field day with the ambient sunset beams playing havoc with the oddball topography's colors.

Nelson

An additional few miles down the road is Nelson, crowded along a bluff line so high that hang gliding and soaring above town is becoming something of a draw. About the only other draw is the family-owned **Nelson Cheese Factory** (south of town on WI 35, 715/673-4725, 9 A.M.–7 P.M. daily), dispensing awesome squeaky cheese curds since the 1850s. It offers tours. South of town you'll find excellent cabins at the four-acre **Cedar Ridge Resort** (south of town on WI 35, 608/685-4998, www.cedarridgeresort.com, $75); one enormous "loft" building is gorgeous and sleeps 11. Have grand pizza at the **Stone Barn** (Hwy. KK, 715/673-4478, dinner Fri.–Sun.) in a real-deal old barn on a real-deal farm. Go north on WI 35, east on Highway D, then north on Highway KK. Munch with the chickens!

Buffalo Slough

Then, the road rolls into geology mashed with history. Skirting the wetlands doused by seepage from Buffalo Slough, the roadway is hacked out of a bluff face or supported by concrete pylons atop mucky soil where "burrow pits" were dug out of the land.

At the mouth of the Buffalo River is what's known as Buffalo Slough; the site is historically the most significant from lumber's heyday. A staggering amount of timber was floated down the Chippewa, St. Croix, and Eau Claire Rivers and stored in enclosed ponds here. For a spell, the powers that be in the "Buffalo" virtually controlled the northern timber industry, inciting Wisconsin's version of a range war between the mills of the upper Chippewa River and the Buffalo Slough mills. One river, the Chippewa, drained one-third of northern Wisconsin and led directly to Buffalo Slough.

◀ ALMA

Alma forms so gradually that it's really tough to gauge exactly where the city starts. Tough, that is, until you get a gander at weathered Twelve Mile Bluff standing guard. Mississippi river pilots at one time used the bluff as a landmark and navigational aid. Founded in the 1850s by Swiss immigrants who set up a supply depot for riverboats, this tranquil little town of understated houses makes for a low-key overnight between La Crosse and Prescott. Ever so long, aerobically inclined wanderers have had a ready-made workout, huffing up the steps etched into the bluffs. And for scenic drives, the "dugways," what locals call roads that wind through the bluff country backing east off the river, can't be beat.

The result? Shh, this place (www.almawisconsin.com) is your author's personal "secret" getaway.

Sights

Lock and Dam 4 sits across the street from the busiest part of the "center" of town. It's got the requisite observation platform and the largest fishing float on the river. Right above the town off Highway E is likely the best public park along the road: **Buena Vista Park,** a vantage point for thousands of migrating **tundra swans,** which lay up in the sloughs north of town. Alternatively, **Rieck's Lake Park** north of town has a wildlife-observation deck atop the water. Your humble scribe's fave is the **Mossy Hollow Trail** (Cemetery Road between Countryside and Buffalo Electric, ask locally for specifics).

Of late, Alma has seen a trickle of artists arriving, usually in summer. The old hotels and theaters in town now support a somewhat thriving theater culture.

Accommodations

The steal of the whole trip are the sub-$50 rooms (I slept for $14 once, on the honor system) at the Italianate **Laue House B&B** (1111 S. Main St., 608/685-4923), on the south edge of town. Originally built by a German immigrant whose sawmill essentially gave life to the city, it has been updated, but definitely not over-renovated, from a tiny one-person alcove to a huge room for four overlooking the river. **Felice Patra Inn** (609 N. Main St., 715/579-4483, www.felicepatra.com) is extraordinarily welcoming (well, Connie, the owner, is) and very cheap. It gets absolute mad raves.

Historic lodging is at **Hotel De Ville** (612/423-3653, www.hoteldevillealma.com, $95–180), a lovely renovated set of clapboard buildings with Italianate gardens.

The Alma Marina (608/685-3333) also has **houseboats** for rent.

Food

◖ **Pier 4 Café & Smokehouse** (600 N. Main St., 608/685-4923, 6 A.M.–2 P.M. Wed.–Mon., $3–7) features straight-up simple café fare—creative enough to avoid eggs monotony—on a screened-in porch, with river-lock views and lumbering freight trains whizzing by just a few feet away. It's a personal favorite spot for unique atmosphere in the state. Try the potato pancakes!

TO FOUNTAIN CITY
Buffalo City

Just off the road, Buffalo City was for a long time the smallest incorporated city in the

United States (now pop. 915). There's not much to do other than spend time in a host of **city parks,** one of which contains the original 1861 jail, or wander riverside nature trails in a 10-acre wooded park.

The restaurant of choice is the **Paradise Bay** (8th and WI 35, 608/248-2464), an 1891 saloon and dance hall converted into a fish house and later restaurant.

Cochrane

Along the way from Buffalo City and onto Prairie Moon Road is another folk-art oddity. The **Prairie Moon Museum and Sculpture Garden** (Prairie Moon Rd., 608/687-9511, afternoon Sun. May–Oct., free), a hodgepodge of human (or animal) concrete figurines and a kind of folk-art stone wall, all created by a local artist. It was recently recognized as a significant state cultural site by the philanthropic Kohler Foundation.

The local **high school** (608/687-4391) has a taxidermy display of local fauna, including eagles and a rare albino deer from the surrounding hills.

Merrick State Park

North of Fountain City, the Mississippi River widens to almost two miles because of damming. Right along the **Whitman Dam State Wildlife Area** is one of the smaller—320 acres—state parks in the northwestern part of the state. Merrick nonetheless has prime waterfront property, and blue herons frolic on the marshy backwater islands. There is only one short (1.4 mile) hiking trail; boating is king, with boat moorings right at the campsites.

You'll find perfect water's edge campsites here.

FOUNTAIN CITY

Fountain City's **Eagle Bluff** commands the highest point on the Upper Mississippi River at 550 feet. (Another bluff nearby is claimed by locals to resemble an Indian chief's head.) And the city (nay, village) seems carved right out of the steep-walled cliffs, descending into the postcard-quality town. The squat bungalows and their lawns, the tiniest pea patches of verdance imaginable, back into the windward side of the big bluff as it curves along the river. Smacking a bit of the European feel of New Glarus or Mount Horeb in southwestern Wisconsin, Fountain City has more of a Mediterranean island fishing village atmosphere, though there are more than a few pockets of Bern-style Swiss architecture. The town was named for rivulets of spring water cascading out of the "hard heads," or sandstone bluffs. The waters at one time ran off the bluffs and through the streets—no longer, however, as the springs were capped and turned into fountains—but you can still have a drink!

Most just go on to **Lock and Dam 5A,** which forms another pool north of town. A viewing platform available to the public nearby has the honor of being the only floating bar on the Mississippi, the **Dam Saloon** (WI 35, 608/687-8286).

Handfuls of crafts, antiques, and "used" detritus can be found in Fountain City. Of particular note is the studio of **Leo Smith** (121 S. Main St., 608/687-6698), a folk art wood carver of national repute. The shop is open daily by chance, late morning to whenever.

The most unusual tourist attraction in Fountain City, the **house with a rock in it** (hours vary Mar.–Nov., $1), is north along WI 35. In 1995, a 50-ton boulder fell off the majestic bluff line and smashed into a house at the base. A shrewd investor turned it into a bizarre tourist attraction. Another unique sight is **Elmer's Auto and Toy Museum** (Hwy. G, 608/687-7221, www.elmersautoandtoymuseum.com, 9 A.M.–5 P.M. weekends early May–late Oct., $7), purportedly one of the largest collections of pedal cars in the world.

Practicalities

The tiny **Fountain Motel** (810 S. Main St., 608/687-3111, $50) has perhaps the best location of any motel on the road.

Enjoy rubbing elbows with the locals? You can't go wrong in Fountain City. The **Monarch** tavern (19 N. Main St., 608/687-4231, 11 A.M.–close Fri.–Tues., 4 P.M.–close Wed.–Thurs.) downtown is a classic Wisconsin tavern with original dark wood interiors and, seemingly, the original bottles that went with it; it's also got the most popular lunch and dinner restaurant in these parts.

Out of town via WI 95 and Highway M you can get dinner at the **Hill Top Bar and Ballroom** (Hwy. M, 608/687-8731), but I'd go every first and third Thursday (5–8 P.M.) for sure for the copious chicken feed or the occasional polka dancing!

Trempealeau National Wildlife Refuge

The super 6,200-acre Trempealeau National Wildlife Refuge is a major link in the Mississippi River migratory flyway. Besides marshland, the preserve also has site-specific tracts of sand prairie and bottomland hardwood forest—lovely stands of river birch, silver maple, and swamp white oak. A five-mile auto tour offers access to two shorter nature trails open to hikers. Get off the beaten path by hiking along the spiderweb of old dikes and service roads dating from the 1930s. Be careful, though; lots of the heath now shrouds old ditches, and mantrap-size holes have snared more than a few. Bikers are not allowed off-road within the refuge, but it is linked to local bike trails along the river.

Side Trip

From WI 35 take WI 93/54 east to trim and busy **Galesville,** parked in a crook of bluffs overlooking Lake Marinuka. See the lake from lovely **High Cliff Park** and an anachronistic wobbly footbridge and path along a bluff, leading to a spring.

Otherwise, Galesville is chockablock with gingerbread Victorian and Queen Anne mansions; the Town Square and assorted streets are on the National Register of Historic Places. The **AA Arnold Farm** (19408 Silver Creek Rd., www.eastsidefarm.org, 2–4 P.M. Sun. in summer, free) is a magnificent Italianate edifice; more so is the farm's indoor silo. For something completely different, check out the **Phoneco Antique Phone Museum** (19813 E. Mill Rd., 608/583-2230, free), actually a dealer in collectible phones—a treasure trove of early Americana!

Return via Highway K.

◖ TREMPEALEAU

From a distance, it's impossible to miss the imposing bluffs along the Mississippi floodplain above tiny Trempealeau. So eye-catching were they that the Native Americans, French, displaced Acadians, and the odd Kentuckian referred to the "bump" at the northern end of the bluff line—now, of course, Trempealeau Mountain—either as "Soak Mountain" or "Mountain in the Water."

Even William Cullen Bryant was an early admirer of the local landscape. Early settlers were no less enamored; a local minister spent feverish years honestly trying to prove that Trempealeau was the site of the Garden of Eden.

Dunno 'bout that, but the lovely backbone of historic structures of Trempealeau is officially recognized by the National Register of Historic Places.

Lock and Dam 6 in Trempealeau is one of the best sites to get an operations-level gander at a dam. From the tower right over the water, you could damn near hop aboard a passing boat. The lock and dam, including an earth dam extending all the way to the Minnesota shore, completed in 1936, cost an astonishing $5 million.

South of Trempealeau you'll find a chain of seven spring-fed lakes, two in yet another fish and wildlife refuge. This is the area for canoeing, and assorted private cabins on stilts over the marshy waters are available; most are decidedly low-key.

Practicalities

The reason everyone should take a spin to Trempealeau is the flaxen-yellow ◖ **Trempealeau Hotel** (150 Main St.,

© THOMAS HUHTI

GREAT RIVER ROAD

everyone's favorite pit stop, the Trempealeau Hotel

608/534-6898), one of Wisconsin's most endearing, grande dame anachronisms. The proprietors thankfully resisted the generally addictive impulse to transmogrify a cool old haunt into a syrupy B&B with prices hiked way up. The eight, tight upstairs rooms share a bath, not unlike a European-style hotel, and get this, they run from $45! (With private bath a room is $70.) A quaint one-bedroom cottage with private sundeck is available riverside for around $300; newer luxury suites have whirlpool baths, fireplaces, and great views for $130 per night on weekends.

Wall to wall with locals and itinerant tourists, the hotel's equally famed restaurant (11 A.M.–9 or 10 P.M. daily May–Oct., closed Mon.–Tues. Apr. and Nov.–Dec.) offers traditional fare—try the Walnut Burger—plus vegetarian-friendly entrées. A regular schedule of live entertainment is offered in the outside beer garden. The hotel rents bikes and canoes and can help arrange local river and refuge tours.

TO ONALASKA
Perrot State Park
During the winter of 1685–1686, fur trader Nicholas Perrot wintered at the confluence of the Trempealeau and Mississippi Rivers; Hopewell burial mounds here beat him by five millennia. Known as the Trempealeau Bluffs, the crown of the ridge swells to 500 feet above the bottomland of the Mississippi River.

Brady's Bluff is the crown jewel of the four primary bluffs, a towering 520-foot terrace rising steeply above the floodplain. Climbing up Brady's Bluff is essentially a sweaty Geology 101; you'll pass 600 million years of geological stratification. Trempealeau Mountain though, that landmark beckoning to Native and settler alike, is even more intriguing. A fragmented part of the bluff line, it is now a 384-foot-high island sitting in the Trempealeau River bay.

The Great River State Trail tangentially scrapes the northern park boundary.

Canoeists can even launch from the campground and follow an established canoe trail through Trempealeau Bay. Whatever you do, do not leave the bay and head out into the river, unless you've got superhuman strength.

A few lucky campers get riverside sites.

More Wildlife Areas and Midway
You can explore along the southern tier of marshy Black and Mississippi River bottomland (a salient "terrace") in the Van Loon Wildlife Area. The Mississippi River bottomland on either side of road is part of the protected Brice and Amsterdam Prairies. Exploring all the alphabet-soup highways of Z, ZB, ZH, ad nauseam, could take most of a day—note that these dead-end, so you'll have to backtrack to WI 35. And at some point you'll likely end up in Midway.

For a short side trip, take WI 53/35 out of Midway to Old 93 Road, which leads to Amsterdam Prairie Road. The ride twists through gorgeous homestead farmland and along bluff lines before reaching McGilvray Road, at this point just a foot path. Also known as Seven Bridges Road, the official state Rustic Road features historic bowstring arch-truss bridges.

Getting from the GRR to Onalaska and La Crosse can be a bit of a hassle, not to mention a bit saddening, what with the increase in vehicular traffic. Under the curl of the bluff line, follow WI 35 around the edge of Lake Onalaska, an enormous pool formed above Lock and Dam 7. Acre for acre the lake is one of the most active fishing spots on the Mississippi River.

ONALASKA
Onalaska lies north of La Crosse at the hook in the Mississippi that forms the eponymous Onalaska Lake and Spillway—much loved by anglers, who take a huge number of sunfish from the waters. The oddball name, inspired by a late-18th-century poem (spelled "Oonalaska" in that usage), is one of three in the United States. The other two are in Texas and Washington, but Wisconsin's "Oonalaska" was the first.

Sights

Onalaska is technically the southern terminus of the **Great River State Trail,** a 24-mile multipurpose rail-to-trail paralleling the Mississippi River. Dozens of great partially forged iron bridges (under careful restoration by the DNR and private contractors) are scattered along the route, and the trail also passes through lovely Trempealeau. One frightening highlight is the still-active Burlington Northern railroad line directly next to the trail. Another highlight is the Midway Prairie, a small swath of extant virgin prairie north of the trail, now maintained by the U.S. Fish and Wildlife Service.

For information, check out www.discoveronalaska.com.

Accommodations and Food

Mostly chain lodgings are apparent around here. The **Lumber Baron Inn** (421 2nd Ave. N, 608/781-8938, $89–129) is a mammoth 1888 B&B dream home replete with carriage house, landscaped grounds, and nice detailings.

Intriguing is **Lakeview** (N5135 WI 35, 608/781-0150, 5:30 A.M.–2 P.M. daily, 5–9 P.M. Tues.–Fri., $5–11), a family-style eatery with a specialty of bison. Some Wisconsin-oriented dishes are occasionally prepared as well.

Some have called **Traditions** (201 Main St., 608/783-0200, 5:30–10 P.M. Tues.–Sat., $25–30) one of the best restaurants in the state. Housed in an old bank building—the intimate private rooms are in the vault!—it offers consistently excellent creative cuisine.

La Crosse

The castellated and craggy circumference of one of Wisconsin's prettiest cities, spread along the Mississippi River, is often voted number one by Midwestern travel mavens as far as aesthetics goes. Even Mark Twain, after a visit, referred to it as "a choice town." Buffalo Bill Cody found the town so much to his liking that he brought his Wild West Show back again and again, and he eventually bought part of Barrons Island.

Situated where the mini-mighty La Crosse and Black Rivers flow into the Mississippi, La Crosse is situated below one of the Mississippi's major bights, allowing heavy commercial traffic. Here, the prairie, and thus all paths on it, literally march to the river's edge. The initial name—"Prairie La Crosse"—came when voyageurs saw the Winnebago playing the fast-paced game of lattice-head sticks, permanently infusing the original name with cruciform symbolism. The equally apropos nickname "Gateway City" is a more mundane take on city history.

SIGHTS
Granddad's Bluff

This famed rock upthrust, towering (for Wisconsin, anyway) more than 550 feet above the back haunches of La Crosse is without question the number one scenic spot in western Wisconsin. Overlooking three states (Wisconsin, Minnesota, and even Iowa—a viewing radius of some 40 miles) and the Mississippi Valley, the bluff is a perfect representation of the 15-million-year-old geology of the Mississippi Valley. On a clear day, when the muggy August weather doesn't vaporize the whole thing into a translucent haze, the view can be superlative. To get there, follow Main Street east until it becomes Bliss Road; a hiking trail also leads there from Riverside Park.

Museums and Historic Structures

Chief among the jaw-droppers is the **Hixon House** (429 N. 7th St., 608/782-1980, 10 A.M.–5 P.M. daily summer, $8.50 adults), an opulent, flaxen-colored Italianate mansion. With nary a reproduction within, the place is beloved by Victorian buffs, especially for the "Turkish Nook"—inspired by a late-1890s predilection for everything oriental—a room worthy of a sultan. Woodworkers will appreciate the variegated native Wisconsin woods.

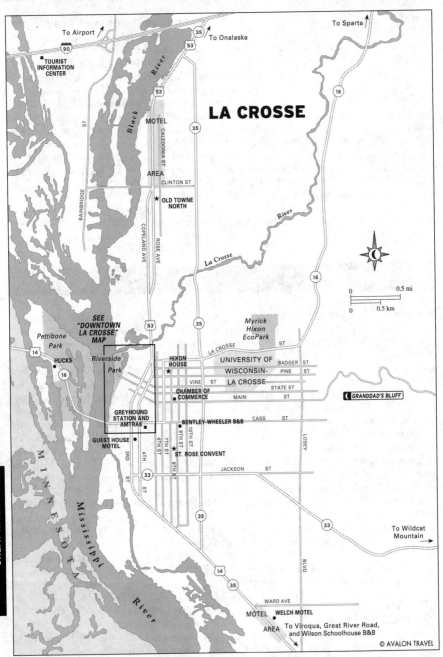

To Airport

90 TOURIST INFORMATION CENTER

35
53 To Onalaska

To Sparta

16

LA CROSSE

Black River

BAINBRIDGE ST

53

MOTEL

CALEDONIA ST

35

AREA

CLINTON ST

ROSE AVE

COPELAND AVE

★ OLD TOWNE NORTH

River

La Crosse

16

0   0.5 mi
0   0.5 km

SEE "DOWNTOWN LA CROSSE" MAP

53

35

Myrick Hixon EcoPark

Pettibone Park

14

HUCKS

16

Riverside Park

Mississippi River

MINNESOTA

HIXON HOUSE ★

LA CROSSE

UNIVERSITY OF WISCONSIN– LA CROSSE

BADGER ST

PINE ST

STATE ST

MAIN ST

CASS ST

VINE ST

CHAMBER OF COMMERCE

BENTLEY-WHEELER B&B

GREYHOUND STATION AND AMTRAK

GUEST HOUSE MOTEL

3RD ST

4TH ST

6TH ST

7TH ST

8TH ST

9TH ST

10TH ST

★ ST. ROSE CONVENT

JACKSON ST

33

35

33

LOSEY

BLVD

C GRANDDAD'S BLUFF

To Wildcat Mountain

14

35

WARD AVE

MOTEL   ● WELCH MOTEL

AREA   To Viroqua, Great River Road, and Wilson Schoolhouse B&B

© AVALON TRAVEL

© THOMAS HUHTI

view from Granddad's Bluff, one of the best along the Great River Road

La Crosse has *plenty* of museums. The University of Wisconsin-La Crosse has an **archaeological museum and lab** (near 17th and State Sts., 608/785-8454, call ahead for times, free). You can watch scientists at work processing artifacts from the region.

On the grounds at Riverside Park is the **Riverside Museum** (608/782-2366, 10 A.M.–5 P.M. daily in summer, free), a local historical repository for La Crosse and Mississippi River history. Expect a bent for riverboats.

Scenic Drives

Start with the **Mindoro Cut.** The southern terminus is northeast of La Crosse in West Salem, and then it stretches up to Mindoro. A massive project when undertaken around the turn of the 20th century, the road was literally shorn into a ridge between the La Crosse and Black River Valleys. The cut was considered one of the most ambitious hand-carved roads in the United States when it was finished in 1906. Even with modern, leviathan earth-movers and assorted belching technology, it's a marvel.

In Mindoro, you must head for **Top Dawgs** (608/857-3077), home of—count 'em—108 hamburger choices!

Three other routes, established as state Rustic Roads—and three outstanding ones at that—are definitely among the best in the state. Highway MM begins at the junction of U.S. 14 and U.S. 61 east of La Crosse and stretches along Morman Coulee Creek Valley. The trip features eye-catching vistas of the Mississippi Valley and passes the wildlife refuge at Goose Island and the first area mill site, dating from 1854. Note that local temperature inversions can produce dense fogs and an opaque sort of atmosphere.

Rustic Road 31 starts in West Salem at the exit off I-90, running through city streets and outskirt roads and passing the Hamlin Garland Homestead, a few parks, and the local octagon house. While in West Salem, check out the Neshonoc Dam, Mill, and Powerhouse, all examples of 19th-century residual architecture.

GREAT RIVER ROAD

THE MIGHTY MISSISSIPPI

The Mississippi River takes the bronze medal at 2,350 miles, though some say the Missouri River headwaters would jack that number up to 3,890 miles. It's impressive anyway, its wildly tornado-shaped drainage basin spreading across 30 U.S. states and creeping into two Canadian provinces, draining 41 percent of the United States' water.

The Wisconsin-Minnesota Mississippi trench runs for more than 200 miles from Prescott, Wisconsin, to East Dubuque, Iowa, with average widths ranging 1–6 miles and bluff lines rising to nearly 600 feet above the floodplain. The Upper Mississippi's bluffs are the most salient features and distinguish the Mississippi from other major rivers with their lack of a vertiginous backdrop. The Wisconsin bluffs, facing west and thus drier, are grassier and rockier, and the surrounding prairie can resemble regions of the West.

EUROPEAN DISCOVERY

The Ojibwa called it Messipi – appropriately, "Big River." Lookout Point in Wyalusing State Park overlooking the confluence of the Wisconsin and Mississippi Rivers was purportedly the first vantage point over the Ol' Miss for Father Marquette and Louis Joliet, who wrote on July 17, 1673, of their "joy that cannot be expressed" at finally espying the rumored Great River. After exploring as far south as Arkansas, the pair realized they had found the link-up with the Gulf of Mexico and thus proved a waterway existed between Acadia and the Gulf. Nicholas Perrot laid claim to all lands drained by the Mississippi for France in 1686 with the establishment of a fur-trade outpost/fort near Pepin.

The first permanent settlement came near Prairie du Chien. Larger boats displaced Native canoes for transporting beaver and iron goods. The Chippewa, Buffalo, St. Croix, and tributaries drain most of northern Wisconsin via the Mississippi, and, for a time, Wisconsin sawmills and log transportation villages con-

trolled the vast industry. Between 1837 and 1901, more than 40 million board feet were floated down the Mississippi from Wisconsin.

MODERN MISSISSIPPI

Mark Twain would hardly recognize the river of his mind's eye, barefooted boys mucking about in mudflats. During the Civil War, the river, in particular La Crosse, Wisconsin, was invaluable to Union transportation networks (up to 1,000 boats per day to/from La Crosse!). Thereafter, river traffic for commercial purposes soared.

Thus, natural history changed big-time in 1930, with the first locks and dams built by U.S. Army Corps of Engineers. Ten locks and dams form the western boundary of Wisconsin between Prescott and Dubuque, Iowa. Instead of a free-flowing body of water with a mind of its own, an ersatz mocha-colored chain of lakes, each 15–30 miles long, was formed above dam lines, with sloughs and tidepools below. The sludgy backwater regions are amazing, swamplike groupings of lake and pond, up to 200 in a given 20-square-mile area.

ENVIRONMENTAL ISSUES

As the waters were corralled, and ebbed into sluggish lakes and pools, sediment dropped and gradually squeezed out the riparian aquatic life. Factories and sewer lines discharged effluents directly into tributaries and agricultural pesticides and fertilizer seeped in.

Now, biologists fret that the five-decades-old "lakes" are gradually exhausting their livability and becoming inhospitable to aquatic life. Sedimentation – mostly due to agricultural runoff – remains a vexing part of the problem. More worrisome is flooding. The dams may ensure commercial traffic year-round, but that's only for the dry season. They do nothing to control flooding, and as the massive Midwestern floods of the mid-1990s proved, dikes and levees have severe limitations. American Rivers has put the Mississippi on its "endangered rivers" list. Environmentalists have heard it before; the Corps of Engineers is one of the densest layers of bureaucracy and is often criticized. River lovers say the Wisconsin stretch of the Mississippi, already the most dammed section of the whole river, should be allowed to return to its presettlement natural state by just ripping the locks out and shipping by rail (which would be cheaper by most estimates). Some backwater areas would be allowed to dry out, preserving the ecosystem for the following floods.

RECREATION

Today, most of Wisconsin's segment of the Mississippi is protected as part of the Upper Mississippi National Wildlife Refuge. The refuge, stretching 261 miles south of the mouth of Wisconsin's Chippewa River, is the longest refuge

in the United States. Some say this happened just in time, as Wisconsin had lost 32 percent of its wetlands by its establishment. This refuge is a crucial link in a migratory flyway, including points south to the Gulf of Mexico or to the Atlantic seaboard.

And while recreation brings in more than $1 billion a year to regional coffers, some claim the darting personal watercraft and wake-inducing pleasure craft are abrading the shoreline and causing untold damage to the aquatic ecosystem.

For anglers, walleye and sauger are most common, but still, the waters are rife with catfish, and a catfish fish fry is a Great River Road classic. The area of Genoa has one of the best walleye runs on the Mississippi. Oddball creatures include the paddlefish and the infrequent snapping turtle.

© THOMAS HUHTI

chugging on the Ol' Man River

My favorite scenic drive starts northwest of Holmen on Amsterdam Prairie Road and Old 93, adjacent to the Van Loon Wildlife Area, which sits between the east and west channels of the Black River. The trip features plenty of charming river-valley views but also allows for a short walk—along McGilvray Road, also known as "Seven Bridges Road." The bowstring arch construction of the bridges has placed it on the National Register of Historic Places.

Riverside Park

La Crosse seems to have a park for every resident of the city, including funky river island parks. Chief among them is Riverside Park, home to a museum and the La Crosse Convention and Visitors Bureau office. Park legends say that the 25-foot, 25-ton sculpture of Hiawatha here acts as a talisman against natural calamity. The park is also a departure point for riverboat cruises.

Myrick Hixon EcoPark

Along La Crosse Street (WI 16) in the northern section of town is a park and nature center (789 Myrick Park Dr., 608/784-0303, www.myrickecopark.com, 9 A.M.–4 P.M. Mon.–Sat., noon–4 P.M. Sun., free).

From there, it's just a hop over to the Hixon Forest nature trails, the nucleus of an intricate network of hiking and cross-country ski trails throughout the city. The Hixon Forest surrounding the center has hundreds of acres and outstanding trails to explore.

Pretty much all the trails pass by "goat" prairie—that is, sad residuals of once-proud oak savannas, left only because they were too steep for agricultural plows.

Riverboat Tours

Boat tours depart from Riverside Park.

Mississippi Explorer (877/647-7397, www.mississippiexplorer.com) has riverboat tours all along the Big Miss. Tours vary widely, but they generally run Wednesday–Sunday at 10 A.M. and cost $15 adults. Friday and Saturday sunset cruises are offered too.

The **La Crosse Queen** (608/784-8523, www.lacrossequeen.com) is, engineering-wise, true to the past. Its propulsion is generated wholly from its split stern-wheeled design. (Most contemporary takes on the old ships have "free" paddle wheels, which look nice, but the ship has modern screws underneath for real power.) Fares and schedules are fairly complex: call or check online.

City Tours

Downtown La Crosse comprises one of the largest historic districts in the state of Wisconsin. Well-done walking (and driving) tour information can be found at the visitors bureau in Riverside Park.

Or, just hop aboard the local **trolley tour,** which runs Tuesday–Sunday afternoons through the downtown area, the riverfront, and other districts.

Mary of the Angels Chapel at St. Rose Convent

Since August 1, 1878, two or more Franciscan sisters from this convent (715 S. 9th St., guided tours 9 A.M. and 1 P.M. Mon.–Sat., 1 P.M. Sun.) have kept a continuous prayer vigil, dedicated to the community and the world. Known as the "Perpetual Adoration," the vigil has been well documented in international media. The Mother House itself is quite impressive—a grand mash of Corinthian and Romanesque styles, with intricate bronze pieces and mosaics handmade by international artists.

The St. Rose Grotto and its Virgin Mary have fallen on hard times, but a better one is the **Grotto of the Holy Family** (grounds open for viewing 9–11 A.M. Mon.–Sat., 1–3 P.M. Sun.) 10 miles east on WI 33 in St. Joseph, at the Franciscan Sisters of St. Joseph's Ridge (believe me, you can't miss the semiotics of the beckoning). Saints and Mary, Mary and the saints; wearied and either tacky or reverent. Still, it's one of the largest in western Wisconsin.

ENTERTAINMENT

Enjoy freebie concerts from the **La Crosse Concert Band** on Sundays during summer in

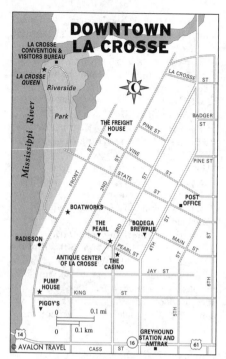

DOWNTOWN LA CROSSE

school here, you're never far from a watering hole or an entertaining bar-time parade of inebriated students.

Pearl Street and environs generally offers something, whether a pub or a nightclub. Highly recommended by those who know is the jazz aficionado's dream joint, **The Casino** (304 Pearl St., 608/782-1910), with a great long bar and good jazz collection, and it's easily spotted by the sign "Good Drinks, Bad Service" out front.

A number of pubs downtown offer live music on a changing schedule, including **Bodega Brew Pub** (122 S. 4th St., 608/782-0677), the longest-running. It's outstanding.

EVENTS

In addition to Oktoberfest, La Crosse celebrates its heritage with Riverfest, a July gathering mostly of music performances.

Oktoberfest

It's not surprising to discover that the largest German-heritage festival in the Midwest is held in Wisconsin. La Crosse's legendary blowout (608/782-2366 or 800/658-9424, http://oktoberfestusa.com), held the last week in September and first week in October, features a 7:30 A.M.–midnight slate of beer, polka, beer, varied music, beer, and a host of family events—sports to carnivals to parades. Almost half a million people attend this one, including a number of German musical acts.

SHOPPING

There's a huge conglomeration of chichi antiques and crafts shops in Old Towne North along Caledonia Street; also, the **Antique Center of La Crosse** (110 S. 3rd St., 608/782-6533) has about 75 boutiques of anachronisms—the largest collection in western Wisconsin.

RECREATION
Trails

The city of La Crosse has a notable network of trails following the La Crosse River through marsh and bottomland. Canoe trails also snake

Riverside Park, or at the summertime Sunset Jazz Series.

Pump House

The local clearinghouse **Pump House Regional Center for the Arts** (119 King St., 608/785-1434, www.thepumphouse.org) is a stately 19th-century Romanesque revival structure, La Crosse's first water-pumping station. Art galleries within feature revolving multimedia exhibits and live music throughout the year—folk, mostly.

Bars and Live Entertainment

La Crosse for a time had somewhat of a reputation for carousing—in fact, the downtown 3rd Street district was once a statistic right out of the *Guinness Book* for most bars per capita. Later on, a debauched annual festival turned violent and was canceled. A stronger arm of the law has curtailed this a bit, but with a UW

through these sloughs down toward Ol' Miss. Easiest is to depart Riverside Park. Most keep on the main trail to Myrick Hixon EcoPark and Granddad's Bluff.

The **La Crosse River State Trail** is a 22-miler on the packed limestone screenings spanning the abandoned grade of the Chicago and Northwestern Railroad. The western trailhead isn't in La Crosse technically, but in Medary, northeast of La Crosse along WI 16. The eastern terminus is the Bicycle Capital of the United States, Sparta. Keep your eyes peeled for osprey nests or Neshonoc geese. Hard-core cyclists can hook up with both the Elroy-Sparta and Great River Trails.

Camping

La Crosse County takes its camping seriously. Better than 90 percent of state campgrounds, the huge **Goose Island Campground** (608/788-7018) is three miles south along WI 35. More than 400 sites—rustic to drive-through—are available here, with a nice sandy beach and the cleanest bathrooms you will likely ever see. Its location can't be beat—on the backwaters of the Mississippi River bordering a wildlife refuge full of egrets and eagles.

ACCOMMODATIONS
Downtown

Most inexpensive lodging downtown is the **Guest House Motel** (810 S. 4th St., 608/784-8840 or 800/274-6873, www. guesthousemotel.com, from $60). A coffee shop and outdoor pool are on-site. Some swear by it; others have opined it's overrated. I've never had issues.

Also downtown is the full-service **Radisson** (200 Harborview Plaza, 608/784-6680 or 800/333-3333, $139–149 s/d), with superb river views (ask for one), a pool, sauna, exercise room, and decent dining. Decor is a bit generic but it's well-taken care of.

Outskirts

Numerous hotels and motels are on the north side of town along Rose Street (WI 53).

But the best of all hotels is actually on the south side, the **Welch Motel** (3643 Mormon Coulee Rd., WI 35, 608/788-1300, www. welchmotel.com, $55), with no frills at all, but always clean, reliable, and the owners are very friendly.

Bed-and-Breakfasts

The ornate dwellings of **(Bentley-Wheeler B&B** (410 Cass St., 608/784-9360 or 877/889-8585, www.bentley-wheeler.com, $135–175) took six years to build. And it shows. Stay in a ballroom—I'm not kidding—or in a luxurious guesthouse. Wherever you stay, the attention to detail and service are unparalleled here.

There's something charming about the restored 1917 **Wilson Schoolhouse** (W5718 U.S. 14/61, 608/787-1982, www. wilsonschoolhouseinn.com, $155). Yup, it's a real-deal school, a lovely red brick edifice on 10 acres overlooking a valley. Better, as it can welcome up to six people, it's quite economical.

Houseboats

A unique local vacation is to rent a houseboat and take to the waters of any of the triumvirate of rivers. Some are bare bones, some are absolutely posh. You can't beat plowing the waters of the Mississippi in your own hotel room. Generally, these are all-inclusive—you might need to bring nothing. **Huck's** (699 Park Plaza Dr., 608/625-3142, www.hucks. com) has immaculate—nay, sybaritic—boats starting at around $1,500 for a three-day rental during high season. (You can also just keep it parked and stay if the idea of chugging along the Ol' Miss freaks you out.)

FOOD
Fine Dining

Renowned eatery **(The Freight House** (107 Vine St., 608/784-6211, 5:30–10 P.M. daily, $7–30) is a 120-year-old edifice with the original old swooping beams that line the high walls, now set off by lovely blond wainscoting. This erstwhile brick storage structure for the Chicago, Milwaukee, and St. Paul Railroad is on the National Register of Historic Places. Famed for its naturally aged and hand-cut steaks, it also offers a tremendous selection of seafood entrées (it brags of its Alaskan king crab), and a respectable wine list is available. All this amid a slew of railroad mementos, including an antique railroad car parked in front in which Buffalo Bill Cody once rode. If nothing else, perch at the bar and watch the barkeeps climb the ladder up the immense back wall.

The ineffable **(** **Piggy's** (501 Front St., 608/784-4877, www.piggys.com, from 5 P.M. Mon.–Fri., from 4 P.M. Sat.–Sun., $14–27). Once specifically contrived for the engorgement of the carnivore—the restaurant does up hickory-smoked barbecue ribs as well as anybody—after a massive relocation into a stunning 1871 foundry building (the suspension of the second floor is extraordinary), the restaurant has added some creativity. Not to mention there's a ballroom with blues and jazz acts, a cigar room, and more. It's a fabulous place.

Brewpubs

Did you know La Crosse once had the world's largest six-pack? The Old Style sixer of the Heileman Brewing Co. towers no more (it actually does, but not as Old Style—it's La Crosse Lager of the City Brewery), but La Crosse's microbreweries and brewpubs are picking up the slack. A good one is **Bodega Brew Pub** (122 S. 4th St., 608/782-0677). The Bodega's bar is particularly nice, right aside the brass kettles, with a nice vintage bottle collection. It is also a prime spot for live music.

Dessert

A treat for anyone is **The Pearl** (Pearl St., 608/782-6655, 8 A.M.–9 P.M. Sun.–Thurs., 8 A.M.–10 P.M. Fri.–Sat.), a 1930s-style soda fountain and confectionery along Pearl Street downtown. Besides homemade ice cream in the shakes, malts, and phosphates, there's a respectable selection of candies.

Updating that by about two decades is **Rudy's** (10th St. and La Crosse St., 608/782-2200, 10 A.M.–10 P.M. daily Mar.–Oct., $3–5), a 1950s-era drive-in with Super Burgers, assorted chicken sandwiches, hot dogs, and the requisite roller-skating car hops. Best of all is the root beer brewed daily.

INFORMATION AND SERVICES

The **La Crosse Convention and Visitors Bureau** (608/782-2366 or 800/658-9424, www.explorelacrosse.com) is in Riverside Park.

Additionally, the state of Wisconsin maintains a Wisconsin Travel Information Center a mile east of the Minnesota border.

GETTING THERE
By Bus and Train

There's an **Amtrak** depot (601 Andrew St., 608/782-6462) in town. **Greyhound** (800/231-2222, www.greyhound.com) also stops here.

By Air

The **La Crosse Municipal Airport** (2850 Airport Dr., 608/789-7464), northwest out of town near Onalaska, is served by Delta and American with 10 flights daily.

Vicinity of La Crosse

EAST OF LA CROSSE
Norskedalen

The 400-acre "Norwegian Valley" is a hodgepodge nature and heritage center in Coon Valley, approximately 16 miles southeast of La Crosse. Beginning as an outdoor arboretum laboratory, it grew to include many surrounding Norwegian and Bohemian homesteader lands. Also on-site you'll find the Skumsrud Heritage Farm. Sankt Hans Dag, an ancient Scandinavian summer solstice festival, jamborees, and classes in ecology and Norwegian language are great. Most popular are the nature trails (608/452-3424, www.norskedalen.org, grounds open daily May 1–Nov. 1, less often otherwise, $6).

Hamlin Garland Homestead

Six miles east of La Crosse is **West Salem,** known for no other reason than as the boyhood home (357 Garland St., 608/786-1399, tours: 1–4:30 P.M. daily Memorial Day weekend–Labor Day, $1) of Wisconsin native and Pulitzer Prize–winner Hamlin Garland. Born in 1860, Garland was among the first—if not the first—writers to use Midwest farm life as a central focal point, in particular creating strong female characters. Writing mostly as a social realist, he later turned to a style that pulled no punches in its grim land—and human—scapes of the Midwest; he undoubtedly had a profound effect on August Derleth. Virtually unread in his lifetime until being awarded the Pulitzer Prize in 1922, he is now remembered mostly for *A Son of the Middle Border,* a bittersweet fictionalization of growing up on a coulee country farm.

TO PRAIRIE DU CHIEN
Stoddard

Before the construction of Genoa's lock and dam, Stoddard wasn't even close to the Mississippi, but upon completion of the dam almost 20,000 acres of bottomland was covered, and suddenly Stoddard could call itself a riverboat town. There's great ornithology along the Coon Creek bottoms in federal refuge land.

Stoddard has one of the best county parks in the state—**Goose Island,** with more than 1,000 acres, six miles of trails, and more than enough camping.

Better: you've gotta have yourself a burger at **Thirsty Turtle** (608/457-9115); man, they're good.

To the south, the river views turn splendid, and pulloffs are pocked into the roadside—you can espy three states! Midway between Genoa and Stoddard is an outstanding drive off the road to the east, to the Old Settlers Overlook, about 500 feet above the river.

SOUTH OF LA CROSSE

© AVALON TRAVEL

Genoa

Here opens the mouth of the Bad Axe River proper, near Genoa, an untouched classic river town. The town grew with a decided Italian flavor as many early settlers were Italian fishermen who started out as lead miners in Galena, Illinois, before migrating here for the fishing. The Dairyland Power Cooperative began the first rural electric (here, hydroelectric) project in western Wisconsin. The state's first nuclear power plant was also located here, built in 1967 and taken offline in 1987. Fishing is key, with one of the upper Mississippi's best walleye runs; there's even **Clement's Barge,** since 1937 anchored below the lock for fishing—the oldest operation on the Mississippi. Much of the fish is stocked by the **Genoa Fish Hatchery** (608/689-2605, Mon.–Fri.) actually closer to Victory. Another of the "largest anywhere" variety of fish hatcheries the state seems to specialize in, this one is the most diverse, raising cold- and warm-water fish. Otherwise, Genoa's **Lock and Dam 8** is one of the river's best for viewing "lock throughs" as the ships pass.

Accommodations and catfish-cheek dinners are found at **Big River Inn** (500 Main St., 608/689-2652, rooms from $44). Five-buck (or less) emergency camping is available at local businesses!

For grub, there's a decent burger pub, but I'd grab some smoked catfish from **Beck's** north of town and then head for the **Old Settlers Overlook** nearby for a picnic.

De Soto

Miles of birds hovering over waters lead to De Soto, named for you-know-who, the European commonly held as the first to espy the Mississippi River (and who eventually wound up in its watery clutches—his soldiers depositing his body there to protect it from the "desecration of savages") back in 1541.

De Soto served as the western endpoint to one of the state's least proud moments, the pursuit of Chief Black Sparrow Hawk (immortalized erroneously as Black Hawk) and his Sauk and Fox Indians across the state, culminating in the Battle of Bad Axe at the mouth of the river of the same name, two miles north. The battle had two effects: It ended serious Indian resistance, and, when Black Hawk became a nationally prominent figure, a flood of settlers poured into the state. Today, the U.S. Army Corps of Engineers has established a somewhat somber **park** at the battle site with riverfront camping, a sandy beach, and a slew of historical sites. Ironically, two miles to the north, Victory was named in honor of Black Hawk's defeat. (At which, oddly, is the **Red Lion,** a British-style pub with imported beers and even curries!)

Ferryville

Ferryville has a fairly long main street itself—it is in point of fact recognized as the longest in any town or village with only one street. (Apocryphal or not, the more colorful stories tell it that local laws allowed for the dispensation of liquor only every mile; saloonkeepers dutifully measured exactly one mile between each.) They should have kept the original name—Humble Bush—because that's sure what it is today. Ferryville's got your best cheese pickings at **Ferryville Cheese** (WI 35, 608/734-3121, 5 A.M.–10 P.M. Mon.–Sat., 8 A.M.–9 P.M. Sun.), with more than 100 varieties to pick from. It's also a good spot to pick up Amish or country-style quilts, and stop by the **Swing Inn** (106 Main St., 608/734-9916) to get a peek at the four-foot-plus rattlesnake skin, taken from surrounding hills, which are rumored to be rife with rattlers. The village allows free camping in the town park, or there is the **Mississippi Humble Bush B&B** (148 Main St., 608/734-3022, $65), which has four rooms and a large loft for dorm-style group lodging.

(One note: Lovely little Ferryville has been noted by certain obsessive websites that fret about such things as having quite a few, er, driving citations for its size.)

After this, it's nine more miles of railroad accompaniment. WI 35 runs through a historical recreation area and more old river towns, or you can jump onto county roads east to loop through rolling hills for some S-curve road routes to classic southwestern Wisconsin river villages. This is the area to pull out the county road maps and snoop around atop the bluff lines; lots of grand river vistas are apparent north of Lynxville.

Side Trip

Not quite halfway to Lynxville, head east 13 miles along WI 171 through Mt. Sterling into the topography of green gumdrops that the region is known for. Mount Sterling has little other than a cheese factory specializing in award-winning goat cheese. Another unknown Wisconsin writer—Ben Logan—grew up in the surrounding coulees and wrote a touching memoir, *The Land Remembers*. Eventually, you'll come to **Gays Mills,** legendary for its apple orchards. Just after the turn of the 20th century, the state of Wisconsin scoured the southern tier of the state for promising orchards in which to plant experimental apple trees. The coulee valleys between the Wisconsin and Mississippi Rivers turned out to be perfect for the hardy fruit. Come spring and fall, photo road-trippers flock to the blossoms or the harvesting. Along WI 131 (which you'll need for the next stop) is **Log Cabin Village,** a grouping of original structures from the region.

North from Gays Mills along WI 131 takes you directly to the cutting edge community of **Soldier's Grove,** notable as the only solar-powered community you'll probably ever see. Lying in a dangerous floodplain in a cleft along the Kickapoo River, Soldier's Grove was incessantly lapped at by floodwaters before a new dike was built in the 1960s. Naturally, in 1978, the town was devastated by a flood. Picking up the pieces and moving to higher ground, the town had the commendable foresight to plan its current eco-friendliness—all of the buildings of **Solar Town Center** are heated at least 50 percent by the sun. The martial moniker inspired the park south of town, designed as a war memorial to local and regional veterans.

From here, WI 61 leads to **Viroqua,** one of the prettiest towns in southwestern Wisconsin; its Main Street has undergone a careful restoration. Along Main Street, the **Sherry-Butt House** was constructed southern-style in 1870. Tours are also available for an old country church and one-room school along Broadway. Call 608/637-7396 for information. Otherwise, there's not a damn thing to do in Viroqua other than wander around, go to the last county fair of the season in the state (September), or watch an occasional yet outstanding demolition derby.

Out of Viroqua, WI 56 cuts back to the Great River Road, or you can head up to Westby, another of the "New Norways" in southwestern Wisconsin, for a malt or cappuccino at the indescribably wonderful **Westby Pharmacy** (608/634-2222). Otherwise, the town has one of the largest Syttende Mai Norwegian independence festivals in May (quilting by local Amish!) and a great ski-jump festival in late January. Then head out of town to see some of the county's 15-odd **round barns;** you'll definitely need help from locals (www.westbywi. com) with directions.

Somehow or other, from here, you'll want to head back to Lynxville via WI 27 and Highway E.

Lynxville

Lynxville was described by an old tour guide as "another faded village on a river bluff." Soporific still, the shells of old standing structures seem proud, if a bit bored. The largest log raft ever on the Mississippi River was put together and floated from the quay here in 1896, a monstrous beast at 250 feet wide, 1,550 feet long, and comprising 2.3 million board feet (rivaling the barges of today). All in all, the town back then was probably eight times as large as it is today, with many residents living on then-extant islets dotting the river before locks and dams flooded them out. The village today sits at the southern cusp of a 17-mile-long lake created by engineers. Lynxville offers a dearth of practicalities—a tavern, a gas station, an antiques shop, and very basic sustenance dining—but there's some decent river scenery along **Lock and Dam 9.** Don't be shocked to see eateries labeled as "fishing float and diner" around here! When you arrive at Gordon's Bay boat landing, just raise the flag and the float boat will come down on the hour to get you.

PRAIRIE DU CHIEN

To secure the strategic viability of the Fox and Wisconsin River corridors, the U.S. military started hacking a road and stringing forts through the wilderness to put a damper on the pesky Indians—and the British and French interlopers. Prairie du Chien, chronologically the second-oldest settlement after Green Bay, would become the westernmost point of that chain of forts.

Native Americans originally inhabited the islands in the Mississippi River channels—up to several thousand on this site. Nicholas Perrot showed up not long after Marquette and Joliet and may or may not have erected a fort on one of the islands, by now a main node on the fur-trade network. The name comes not from a ubiquity of prairie rodents, but from a respected Indian chief, honored by French settlers. It was at one time a major "clamming" center—clams were all the rage as buttons, and the oysters could command thousands in eastern markets.

◖ Villa Louis

One of the state's most respected historical sites is Villa Louis, in its time likely the most ostentatious and opulent home in all the Upper Midwest. Fort Shelby was originally constructed on this island site immediately after the War of 1812 to protect the lucrative trade routes from the British. (Native Americans had used the island for numerous burial mounds, and the structures were built right atop some of them.) In 1840, Hercules Dousman, a phenomenally wealthy (he's known as Wisconsin's first millionaire) fur trader, originally built a home here—the House on the Mound, in a nice slap to the face of Native Americans. His son, H. Louis Dousman, for whatever impels otherwise rational folks to do such things, decided to raise the most palatial estate of them all. Like all great acts of such caliber, this one went belly up. In 1995 the estate underwent

extensive (and expensive at $2 million) restoration work, begun in an attempt to correct earlier historical renovations; the friendly invasion force even used the original designs and implements, some in vaults in London. Even better, curators have managed to relocate original artwork and furniture. Its collections are now unparalleled in the country. The museum (521 N. Villa Louis Rd., 608/326-2721, 9:30 A.M.–5 P.M. daily mid-May–late Oct., $9) conducts tours on the hour 10 A.M.–4 P.M. The grounds are always open, and nearby on the same island is a Victorian historical education walk.

Other Sights

Somewhat lesser known is the **Prairie du Chien Museum at Fort Crawford** (717 S. Beaumont Rd., 608/326-6960, 9 A.M.–4 P.M. daily May–Oct., $5 adults), the remainder of the fort where Black Hawk surrendered. On the site of the second Fort Crawford, both Zachary Taylor and Jefferson Davis spent military service time. The more intriguing segment of the museum, "Medical Progress," features Dr. William Beaumont's experiments on the human digestive system (on an Acadian fur trader with an untreatable belly wound) in the 1830s, in which he tied bits of food to surgical string to time the digestive process of the willing patient—200 times. Among the results: the first recorded temperature of the human stomach. Fascinating is the look at Mississippi clamming.

The **Old Rock School,** on the edge of downtown, is considered the oldest surviving school structure in Wisconsin.

Events

Prairie du Chien, over Father's Day weekend, hosts one of the Midwest's largest **Rendezvous,** when buckskin-clad and beaverhat-adorned trapper, trader, and soldier wannabes congregate. The biggest of them all, the **Villa Louis Carriage Classic,** comes up in September.

Recreation

La Riviere Park on the south end of town offers primitive camping and nature trails through some native prairie swaths where you might spot a rare poppy wallow flower, once thought wiped out by agriculture.

Accommodations

South Marquette Road (WI 60) has the greatest share of accommodations, most of them chains. Oddly enough, it's hard to get value for the buck here. Extremely cheap **Holiday Motel** (1010 S. Marquette Rd., 608/326-2448, $55–100) has rooms decorated in historical themes.

An enormous step up in price but also quality is the **AmericInn** (130 S. Main St., 608/326-7878, from $130), with a whole array of services, but quite honestly some of the most solicitous service ever on the road.

Food

You'll note the amazing number of places dishing up or selling the local specialty—Mississippi catfish, smoked or fresh—or even the odd purveyor of turtle meat.

A Sunday institution of sorts in the tri-states area is a leisurely drive to Prairie du Chien to sample the slider-burgers at **❮ Pete's** (118 S. Blackhawk, 11 A.M.–8 P.M. Fri.–Sun.), a dainty burger-only joint built out of a caboose right downtown. A couple of bucks will fill you up.

The venerable **Kaber's** (225 W. Blackhawk, 608/326-6216, dinner daily, $6–12) has been around since the 1930s and still serves standard supper club fare. One reader has insisted that the *very* unassuming **Spring Lake** (608/326-6907) north of town 10 miles is the place to go for a surprisingly good meat-based meal.

This author would just pick up some cheese and fish (if not turtle jerky) at **Valley Fish** (304 S. Prairie St., 608/326-4719, 9 A.M.–5 P.M. Mon.–Thurs., 9 A.M.–6 P.M. Sat., 10 A.M.–5 P.M. Sun. Mar.–Dec.) and set off on a picnic! (It also does Friday outdoor fish fries in season.)

Information and Services

At the bridge along WI 18 is the the Wisconsin Travel Information Center. The **Prairie du Chien Chamber** (211 S. Main St., 608/326-8555, www.prairieduchien.org) also has information.

❮ WYALUSING STATE PARK

Here, high above the confluence of the Wisconsin and Mississippi Rivers was where Father Jacques Marquette and Louis Joliet discovered the upper Mississippi in 1673. The most popular spot in the park is Point Lookout, 300 feet above the rich blue waters of the two rivers. Sixteen impeccable miles of trails branch and twist through variegated topography. **Sentinel Ridge Trail** passes amazingly well-preserved effigy mounds—and wild turkeys. Along the Wisconsin River a trail follows segments of a real-life immigrant path; another wagon trail loops back to the main trails and goes past a settler's semipermanent "pit stop" point. Canoeists have marked routes totaling 20 miles along the backwater sloughs of the Mississippi; fishing is excellent. Winter camping is permitted.

Also find superlative hiking but none-too-special camping—large sites but not very secluded (at least they're reservable).

Oh, and another thing: Local legend has it that there's gold treasure buried somewhere in the bluffs. . . .

Highways X, A, and then VV lead to Cassville through deep, winding valleys—a pretty drive via Wyalusing village and Bagley. The former features some of the best river views along the route while the latter offers a sandy swimming beach; neither is very large. Wyalusing, once a rousing 600 people, now counts a dozen permanent residents. In comparison Bagley looks absolutely worldly, and in fact there is a bar in Bagley that has a large world map full of push-pins left by international visitors.

❮ CASSVILLE

Eagles. The majestic birds and their migratory journeys up and down the Mississippi River draw most folks here—one of the top spots in the region to witness them.

With a solitary general store after its founding in 1831, locals nonetheless championed the village for capital status. The California gold rush and silting on the Grant River doomed once-booming Potosi; Cassville took over the crucial river traffic control and soon eclipsed its neighbor.

EAGLE-WATCHING

One of the primary U.S. eagle habitats is the Lower Wisconsin State Riverway, starting in Sauk City in south-central Wisconsin and stretching to the confluence of the Mississippi River. South of here to the state line, the Upper Mississippi Wildlife Refuge is another, and the Cassville area is one of the best areas to view eagles within that region. Having rebounded from perilously low levels, Wisconsin now has more than 1,100 eagle nesting sites, an eightfold increase since 1972 and a federal endangered listing. Though eagles are still getting pushed out by development, poached by knuckleheads, electrocuted by power lines, and poisoned by toxic fish, the future isn't quite so grim. (In fact, the Wisconsin DNR even transplanted four eagle chicks into New York City parks.)

Bald eagles really aren't bald; that false-cognate word came from the Middle English ball(e)d – "white spot." The much more impressive scientific name, Haliaetus leucocephalus, roughly translates as "white-headed sea bird." (The white head doesn't fully appear until the bird is 4-5 years old.)

Some incidental data: Eagles travel 30-40 mph in flight but in dives can eclipse 100 mph and their vision is six times more acute than a human's!

Eagles generally live 30-50 years, though in the wild that number has slowly dropped. Generally, nesting pairs mate for life; and both birds incubate the eggs. One nest weighed in at two tons!

HABITAT AND VIEWING

Situated near Lock and Dam 10 along the Mississippi River, and with two riverside power plants, Cassville has open water year-round. Furthermore, the craggy variations in southwestern Wisconsin's topography allow nests maximum isolation. Fish are attracted to the warm waters of the power plant discharge.

In the winter, Cassville can have as many as 200 eagles in one location; as many as 10 will stay in the region for the summer, with the rest moving back to northern Wisconsin or Michigan's Upper Peninsula. They do not migrate per se; they simply move south in winter for food and stop when they find it. Best sites around town to view the eagles are the Wisconsin Power and Light Company generating station along Highway VV northwest of Cassville (look for the road marked "Boat Landing"), and the bluffs of Nelson Dewey State Park, also accessible from Highway VV. The other power plant is on the south side of town, via WI 133.

One obscure spot is six miles north of Nelson Dewey State Park along Highway VV and then west on Duncan Road. The Eagle Valley Nature Habitat-Glen Haven is a grouping point for up to 1,000 birds in winter. Don't expect a sparkling visitors center; it's nothing but tranquil Mississippi River banks and lots of eagles on 1,500 acres.

River transportation began with a ferry as far back as 1836, and today the **Cassville Car Ferry** (608/725-5855, 9 A.M.–9 P.M. daily Memorial Day weekend–Labor Day, Fri.–Sun. May and Sept.–Oct., $13 per car) still plows across the Mississippi into Iowa. This is one of the few remaining river ferries in the United States (another is in Merrimac, Wisconsin); the paddle wheel and horse-and-treadmill versions have finally been retired, but it's still a tri-states area tradition. (In fact, in 2011 a new one is scheduled to be operational.)

The big draws for Cassville are the **Stonefield** agricultural heritage and village life museum (12195 Hwy. VV, 10 A.M.–5 P.M. daily late May–early Oct., shorter hours July and Aug., $8 adults), and across the road Nelson Dewey State Park, both a mile north of town. Docents lead tours of a contiguous 1900 farmstead and the "innovations" (antique equipment and designs) of the time. Farther along across Dewey Creek (through a covered bridge) are the 30 reconstructed buildings done up as an explicatory showcase of turn-of-the-20th-century Midwest village life. Proudly overlooking all is the homesite of

Lancaster's distinctive dome

© THOMAS HUHTI

Wisconsin's first governor, Nelson Dewey. It's a particularly rare architectural specimen—southern plantation amid pastoral dairyland, fitting the mold of rural Gothic, a leading design of the time, though not in Wisconsin. Dewey meticulously planned his rustic vision of a gentleman's retreat down to the stone fences snaking through the fields, also done to give local masons jobs. For more information about Stonefield, contact the State Historical Society at 866/944-7483.

Nelson Dewey State Park is a 750-acre plot hewn from the original 2,000 acres of the Dewey family spread along Dewey Creek, one of the only large plantations in the Upper Midwest. Most visitors head up to the majestic belvedere bluffs for miles-long vistas of the Mississippi River valley. Along the bluffs you'll see groupings of prehistoric **Indian mounds,** the two most prominent at the cliff top (no effigy mounds, such as those found up the road in Wyalusing State Park). A seven-acre bluff facing southwest above the river encompasses the Dewey Heights Prairie,

a dry, limy prairie set aside by the state as a scientific reserve.

The always-helpful chamber of commerce has brochures for a **historical walking tour** of Cassville, taking in historic structures. Most are in use for purposes other than their original designs, including the Denniston Building, once a proud and opulent hotel built by Nelson Dewey.

One place most don't know anything about is the sublime **Cassville Bluffs-Roe Unit,** southeast along WI 133 2.5 miles to a right onto Sand Lake Lane. This State Natural Area has rare flora such as goat prairie, Kentucky coffee tree (a true Wisky unknown), and honey locust. Trails bypass an eagle effigy mound. Even if you know zilch about trees, go for the great views!

One of the largest assemblages of bald eagles along this stretch of the Mississippi River (one link in a massive national wildlife refuge) is on display in January during **Bald Eagle Days.**

In July, national attention focuses on Cassville's **Twin-O-Rama,** feting multiple births from across the country since 1929. It's a photo-op from heaven for three days—a town populated wholly by twins and triplets. However, it has had to be canceled in the past due to organizational difficulties, so keep in touch with the Cassville Tourism office (www. cassville.org).

LANCASTER

You may as well take a side trip on your way from Cassville, since you won't see the river anyway. Lancaster, known as the "City of the Dome," is a 15-mile jump up the road. Once you espy the glass-and-copper-topped dome of the courthouse, modeled after St. Peter's Basilica, you'll know why. Check out the murals of regional history inside the courthouse (done by Franz Rohrback, who also did huge murals in the State Capitol rotunda). Or get a gander at the Civil War Monument and GAR (Grand Army of the Republic) display on the grounds, the first such memorial in the United States. Public areas have innumerable historical monuments, including not one but two of the state's first governor, Nelson Dewey, who's buried in a nearby cemetery. A block east of the courthouse is the **Cunningham Museum** (129 E. Maple St, 608/723-2287, by appointment only), the local take on a historical society museum, loaded with martial history and an interesting exhibit on the state's earliest African American settlement.

From Lancaster, take the scenic country route along Highways N and U to Potosi.

POTOSI

The state's self-proclaimed "Catfish Capital," the town proudly boasts the longest main street in the world without an intersection—that's three miles without a stop, or even a glance sideways at a cross street. Potosi was the earliest in the state to open a mine, and the last to close one; the town name even means "mineral wealth." "Badger huts," the hastily constructed sleeping quarters that lead miners burrowed into hillsides and inspired the state's nickname, can still be seen in the bluffs above the town. The largest port on the upper Mississippi (predating statehood) and the lead

mines supplying Union forces (and, some say, the Confederates) solidified the local economy to the extent that Potosi real estate was the most valuable in the state by 1850. The **Dutch Hollow Stone House,** built in 1847, is the Wisconsin turn on the George Washington-slept-here approach—only here it was John Wilkes Booth (and it's a private home now).

Real, grimy history can be found at the **St. John Lead Mine** (Main St., 608/763-2121, 9 A.M.–5 P.M. Thurs.–Tues., $6 adults), purportedly the oldest lead mine—and thus permanent commercial enterprise—in the state and visited by Nicholas Perrot before the turn of the 18th century. Tours take in the entire mine and offices (get a gander at the shingles). Take a jacket!

Potosi even has the **National Brewery Museum** (209 S. Main St., 608/763-4002). Yeah—go figure, little Potosi beat out St. Louis and Milwaukee for this baby. It's actually within the old complex of the Potosi Brewing Co., which itself has a free transportation museum. If that weren't enough, also on-site is a Great River Road interpretive center and a restaurant/pub! All of this is open 10 A.M.–9 P.M. daily; entrance to the brewery museum is $7.

South of Potosi along WI 133 is the **Grant River Recreation Area** (608/763-2140), a U.S. Army Corps of Engineers–maintained riverside campground. The managers can give good advice on **canoeing** in the area.

North of Potosi a mile and then east on Hippy Hollow Road brings you to the **British Hollow Smelter,** the last of its kind in this region. With a 200-foot underground chimney thrust deep into the hillside, the smelter was once one of the largest around.

Restaurants abound in the Potosi area, but wherever you eat, sample the Mississippi catfish (as if they'd let you avoid it). The main street features a bunch of supper clubs, and you'll find more places to eat in Tennyson.

Triangular brown and yellow signs, marking an **auto tour** that takes in all regional points of historical significance, line the roads around Potosi and Tennyson.

TRI-STATES AREA

South of Potosi you have no choice but to link up with a—sigh—U.S. highway (U.S. 63) and little to see till you whip over the Platte River. The road runs away from the Mississippi as the river rolls toward it. One more must-see before you hit the corner of three states—Dickeyville.

The over-the-top marriage of jingoism and religious reverence, the **Dickeyville Grotto** (305 W. Main St., grounds open all the time; tours 9 A.M.–5 P.M. daily June–Aug. and weekends May, Sept., and Oct., free) is one of innumerable Midwest grottoes constructed around the turn of the 20th century, when a papal blessing allowed many religiosos to go off the deep end and build what became serious tourist attractions. Constructed around an Italian-carved statue of the Virgin Mary cradling Jesus, the Dickeyville Grotto was the 10-year devotional labor of Reverend Father Mathias Wernerus. Like other grottoes, it is an odd, aesthetically challenging assemblage of broken glass, tile, stone, gravel, petrified wood, shells, and even gems, affixed to virtually every nook and cranny of the place. Linings are even done in onyx.

Then there's the patriotic wall displaying Abe Lincoln and George Washington next to Christopher Columbus, not to mention the Stars and Stripes joined with the Vatican's standard. The rear is buttressed by a wall of saints. Flower beds explode in color come spring. And this just begins to describe the visual business.

Dickeyville Grotto

Some view religious grottoes as an embarrassment to the devout, others will road-trip through two states to pick up a tacky souvenir, and still others find them truly inspirational. Whatever the case, this one is one of the best.

Beyond here, not a darn thing to see till the Wisconsin Information Center near the Illinois and Iowa borders. One intriguing idea is to head east on WI 11 and link up with southwestern Wisconsin's Lead Zone.

THE DRIFTLESS REGION: SOUTHWESTERN WISCONSIN

Ten thousand years ago, as the icy bulldozers of the ultimate glacial epoch gouged their way across the hemisphere, two adjacent thrusting lobes were rerouted by the declensions of natural valleys (and immovable quartzite). The forks twisted around the natural borders of southwestern Wisconsin but never encroached on the interior—as had none of the previous mantles of glaciers. The inspiring result is Wisconsin's Driftless Region, encompassing nearly one-quarter of the state's geography—four times the square mileage of Connecticut—and the world's only pocket of land completely surrounded by glacial drift.

Early geologists to the state remarked on the region's similarities to the Cumberland plateau in the Appalachians. An oddball topographical hodgepodge, the swooping "coulees" in the upper quarter are the uplands' most salient feature, marked by ambitious valleys so imposing and eye-catching that early Wisconsinites could find no English-language equivalent. In the north, northern and southern biotic regions intermingle. Farms predominate today where mines once took ore. The rolling, variegated terrain, splattered with red barns and roads slowed by chugging tractors, is likely the most quintessentially rural in America's Dairyland.

© THOMAS HUHTI

SOUTHWESTERN WISCONSIN

HIGHLIGHTS

LOOK FOR ◖ TO FIND RECOMMENDED SIGHTS, ACTIVITIES, DINING, AND LODGING.

◖ **The Lower Wisconsin State Riverway:** Nothing's lovelier than a drive (or canoe) along this beauty (page 352).

◖ **Spring Green:** Artists live in a bucolic town synonymous with Frank Lloyd Wright and his inspiring Taliesin (page 355).

◖ **The House on the Rock:** Sensory overload equal parts kitsch and pack rat's dream comes from one man with a singular vision (page 358).

◖ **Mineral Point:** You could be in the 1850s in the place that gave us the name "Badger" (page 364).

◖ **New Glarus:** Find a little slice of Switzerland in America (page 371).

◖ **Elroy-Sparta State Recreational Trail:** This is the granddaddy of all U.S. rail-to-trail efforts with grand tunnels and gregarious small towns (page 378).

◖ **Kickapoo Valley Reserve:** Enjoy lazy canoeing past gumdrop topography along America's "crookedest" river (page 382).

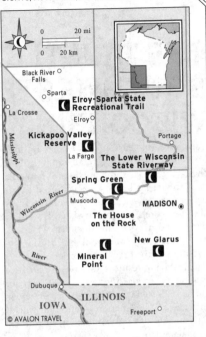

PLANNING YOUR TIME

Let this author request that you spend more time than you'd have planned here—you'll regret it not a whit. Virtually every small town in southwestern Wisconsin is a readymade weekend trip, each with a distinct flavor—ethnic heritage, recreation, or other draw. The choices: the **Kickapoo Valley Reserve** and **Black River State Forest** (splendid isolation and canoeing); **Spring Green** and the **Lower Wisconsin State Riverway** (Frank Lloyd Wright and recreation); **Monroe** and **New Glarus** (Swiss and cheese—yes, two words); **Mineral Point** (arts and crafts and figgyhobbin); or the **Lead Zone** (mining heritage).

You could do it all in a mad-drive week.

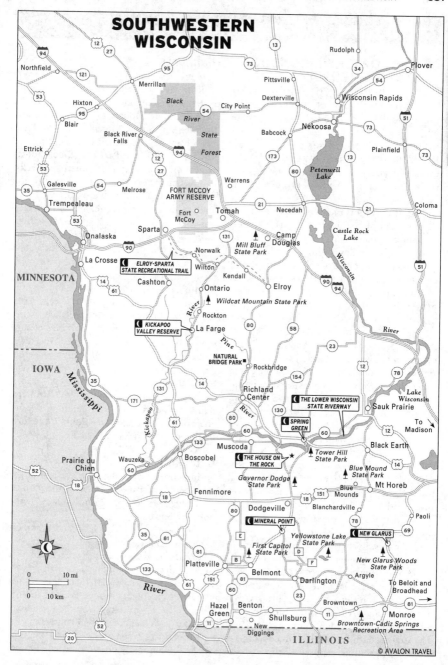

SOUTHWESTERN WISCONSIN

MINNESOTA

IOWA

ELROY-SPARTA STATE RECREATIONAL TRAIL

KICKAPOO VALLEY RESERVE

NATURAL BRIDGE PARK

THE LOWER WISCONSIN STATE RIVERWAY

SPRING GREEN

THE HOUSE ON THE ROCK

MINERAL POINT

NEW GLARUS

Northfield, Merrillan, Black River, City Point, Dexterville, Rudolph, Plover, Pittsville, Wisconsin Rapids, Hixton, Blair, Black River Falls, State, Babcock, Nekoosa, Plainfield, Coloma, Ettrick, Forest, Petenwell Lake, Galesville, Melrose, Warrens, Trempealeau, Fort McCoy Army Reserve, Tomah, Necedah, Castle Rock Lake, Onalaska, Sparta, Fort McCoy, Camp Douglas, Mill Bluff State Park, La Crosse, Norwalk, Wilton, Kendall, Cashton, Ontario, Elroy, Wildcat Mountain State Park, Rockton, La Farge, Rockbridge, Richland Center, Sauk Prairie, To Madison, Prairie du Chien, Wauzeka, Boscobel, Muscoda, Tower Hill State Park, Black Earth, Blue Mound State Park, Mt Horeb, Fennimore, Governor Dodge State Park, Blue Mounds, Paoli, Dodgeville, Blanchardville, First Capitol State Park, Yellowstone Lake State Park, New Glarus Woods State Park, Platteville, Belmont, Darlington, Argyle, To Beloit and Broadhead, Hazel Green, Benton, Browntown, Monroe, Shullsburg, New Diggings, Browntown-Cadiz Springs Recreation Area

ILLINOIS

0   10 mi
0   10 km

© AVALON TRAVEL

Along the Wisconsin River

◖ THE LOWER WISCONSIN STATE RIVERWAY

From Sauk Prairie, in south-central Wisconsin just north of Madison, to its confluence with the Mississippi River, these 92.5 miles of officially sanctioned casual wilderness definitely make up an "Old Man River," shuffling instead of rushing, lolling instead of cascading. It's also the longest remaining never-dammed stretch of river in Wisconsin.

A grand achievement of civic middleground cooperation—well, after seven strenuous years of hard fighting and horse-trading—these miles couldn't have been better chosen: Precious little development had ever taken place. Ultimately the state hopes to own up to 80,000 acres of riverfront property; slightly more than half that is now under state control.

The riverway subsumes 19 official Natural Areas as diverse as Bakken's Pond near Spring Green, to the haunting battlefield park of the Battle of Wisconsin Heights. It has been called one of the most amazing conglomerations of natural history, ecology, state and Native American history, recreation, flora and fauna, and topography in the Midwest. Shoreline incursion is barred, keeping the bluffs and greenery intact, and any off-bank timber extraction has to first pass muster with a tough advisory-board review. About 350 species of flora and fauna are found inside the riverway's parameters. Sixty or more threatened or endangered species live within its boundaries, as do 35 flora species specific to the unglaciated Driftless Region.

The riverway is also very much a work in progress. Development of new campgrounds, rustic or otherwise, are ever planned, as are a scattering of new boat landings. Most are to be concentrated on the Sauk City–Spring Green upper third and gradually diminish as the river rolls southwest toward Wyalusing State Park. The stretch south and west of Boscobel is earmarked for primitive status.

Highlights

Four miles south of Sauk City is the ever-inspiring **Ferry Bluff,** just off WI 60. From the bluff, the Baraboo Range is visible to the east, as is Blue Mound to the south. Many disembark in Spring Green for an extended stay. Near the Lone Rock Boat landing is a protruding cliff called **Devil's Elbow** for its hazardous navigation and numerous wrecks. The **Avoca Prairie,** seven miles west of the WI 133 Lone Rock bridge, is almost 1,000 acres of wet-mezic prairie, the largest tall-grass-prairie remnant east of the Mississippi River. (Turn north off WI 133 onto Hay Lane Road, past Marsh Creek to the parking area; be very aware of wet conditions or you will get stuck.) You'll pass two of the last extant hand-operated draw-span bridges built by the railroads before reaching Bear Creek. After passing Richland City, **Bogus Bluff** comes into view, rich with apocryphal tales of subterranean riches, as well as splendid views. **Muscoda** is the only town of any size before Boscobel, and to the west is the **Blue River Sand Barrens,** a genuine desert—cacti, snakes, and a species of lizard all live here. (On the other side of the river, along WI 60, you can hop into legendary **Eagle Cave** for a small fee; look for Eagle Cave Road.)

Canoeing

Spring Green marks the southern end of the most populated canoe segment of the 92-mile riverway; Sauk Prairie, 25 miles away, is the northern terminus.

The whole of the thing can be canoed, as there is nary a dam, cascade, rapids, or portage—among the longest unimpeded stretches of river in the Midwest. Many Spring Green–area travelers pitch a tent at Tower Hill State Park. Other popular access points include Peck's Landing, beneath the WI 23 bridge, and the Lone Rock Landing, just east of the WI 130 bridge.

A number of canoe operations offering trips on the Wisconsin can be found in Sauk Prairie.

© THOMAS HUHTI

looking for a Wisconsin River swimming hole

Hiking

Hiking is grand, with trail networks along the Black Hawk Unit between Mazomanie and Sauk City, and more between Muscoda and Blue River. Better—these 40 grand acres have the wonderful challenge of no established trails. *Know where you are, as private land does exist.*

Swimming

No matter what you see the locals doing, respect this river. Monthly drownings are not uncommon. The sandbars make for enticing beach-the-canoe-and-frolic spots, but the current is misleadingly slow; the layered currents can drag you under. Worse, river fluctuations create deep sinkholes, which can be neither seen nor predicted by observing the current—step in one and say bye-bye.

Fishing

Gamefish are present in the Wisconsin River's main channel, but panfish predominate on poles and are especially pervasive in the sloughs and bayous off the river channel. For serious anglers, it might be worth a 17-mile drive east along U.S. 14 to Black Earth Creek, one of the top 100 trout streams in the country, with more than 1,500 brownies per mile.

Camping

Free dispersed camping is allowed on all state-owned lands, whether inner-stream islands or banks. Trouble is, it isn't always easy to know what land is in state hands—*check locally before setting up camp.* In certain areas, only sandbars are not privately owned, and thus, those are what you've got. They're grand, Huck Finnish ways to experience the river, but then again, this is a river and water levels fluctuate and sandbars disappear, so keep aware. *No glass containers whatsoever are allowed.*

Information

The first place anyone should start is with the **Lower Wisconsin State Riverway Commission** (800/221-3792, http://lwr.state. wi.us).

SAUK PRAIRIE

Sauk Prairie is actually both Sauk City and Prairie du Sac. In the 1840s, Upper and Lower Sauk were founded by Hungarian immigrant and dandy Agoston Haraszthy, before he lit out for California to become the "Father of the California Wine Industry." Sauk City managed to one-up Prairie du Sac by incorporating first (becoming Wisconsin's oldest incorporated village). It also gained fame throughout Europe as one of the country's last bastions of Freethinkers.

The cities were inspiration for native son August Derleth, the verbose wordsmith who championed the common Wisconsinite (his "Sac Prairie" stories were modeled on the area).

The ice-free and calm, free-flowing waters of the lower Wisconsin River (thanks, oddly, to power plants) and notched sandstone bluffs for roosts have also given rise to a phoenixlike reappearance of endangered bald eagles. Of the state's nearly 1,150 nesting pairs of eagles, up to 10 percent are concentrated in the Sauk Prairie stretch of river.

Sights and Recreation

January eagle-peering comes in Prairie du Sac, which has an information kiosk and viewing scopes; Veterans Park, which has in-car-only viewing; a mile north of Prairie du Sac and then onto Dam Road to the hydroelectric plant; and, if you're feeling ambitious, head out Highway PF, where you might get a gander at eagles feeding on farmland flotsam.

Wollersheim Winery (WI 188, 608/643-6515, www.wollersheim.com, 10 A.M.–5 P.M. daily) has been producing wines since before the Civil War and now accounts for over half of the wine produced in Wisconsin. The antebellum buildings, limestone aging caverns, and vineyards are an official National Historic Site. Popular and fun volunteer grape harvesting and stomping weekends are held in autumn. The winery offers tours ($3.50 adults) hourly 10:15 A.M.–4:15 P.M.

Northwest of Sauk Prairie approximately 10 miles is a day-use and seasonal state park focused on the only natural bridge in Wisconsin,

Natural Bridge State Park. Crags and battlement outcroppings such as this are found throughout the state's Driftless Area. This wind-eroded hole in a sandstone promontory measures 25 by 35 feet and is one of the oldest sandstone natural features on the planet. Stratigraphic dating has also revealed Paleo-Indian encampments as far back as 12,000 years—among the oldest sites in the Upper Midwest. A couple of trails lead to a natural area. North of the park you'll find **Orchard Drive** (and parts of Schara and Ruff Roads), one of Wisconsin's official Rustic Roads. This six-miler serpentines through grand glacial topography and plenty of wildflowers. This is as off-the-beaten path as it gets.

Approximately eight miles northwest of town via U.S. 12 and Highway C is the amazing **Baxter's Hollow,** a 4,950-acre parcel of the extraordinary Baraboo Hills, itself a vast tract of 144,000 acres and one of the last vestiges of contiguous upland hardwood forest in the United States. So rich with flora and fauna are these regions that Baxter's Hollow has been listed by The Nature Conservancy as one of the 75 Last Great Places in the Western Hemisphere. Better—it has been cited as the state's second official Important Birding Area.

The most humbling site in central Wisconsin is the **Black Hawk Unit** of the Lower Wisconsin State Riverway. The unit is of archaeological note for the rare and somewhat mysterious linear-type effigy mounds from the Late Woodland period (A.D. 600–1300), found only in the quad states region including southwestern Wisconsin. Unfortunately, that splendid and cryptic history is overshadowed by the massacre that occurred along the park's northern perimeter—the **Battle of Wisconsin Heights**—between Fox-Sauk warriors and a militia that had pursued them across the state. To get there, take U.S. 12 south to Highway Y and west to WI 78 and then go south.

Sauk Prairie is among the most popular spots to indulge in a favorite pastime on the lower Wisconsin—**canoeing.** The float from around WI 60 and back to town is easiest; you could theoretically go all the way to Spring Green.

© THOMAS HUHTI

Natural Bridge State Park

Figure $35–40 for a canoe rental and shuttle service on a 2.5-hour trip; multi-night trips are also possible. Among the half-dozen outfitters is **Wisconsin River Outings** (608/643-6589, www.spcanoerentals.com).

Sauk Prairie is also the proud parent of the annual **Wisconsin State Cow Chip Throw** (www.wiscowchip.com), held Labor Day weekend. At the **Riverview Ballroom,** a 1942 beaut, plans are in the wind to establish a Lower Wisconsin State Riverway museum (and perhaps add a brewpub to pay some bills). We'll see if it flies.

Practicalities

The **Skyview Inn** (U.S. 12 and Hwy. PF, 608/643-4344 or 888/643-4344, $55 s or d) offers a spacious, grassy setting (with a view of the Baraboo Bluffs over yonder) and one suite with a whirlpool bath.

The dense German food at the 【 **Dorf Haus** (Hwy. Y in diminutive Roxbury, 608/643-3980, 5–9 P.M. Wed.–Sat., 11:30 A.M.–8:30 P.M. Sun., $8–22) includes real-deal Teutonic specialties— even *leberkaese* (pork and beef loaf)—one of

the few spots in the state you'll see it. Special Bavarian smorgasbords are offered the first Monday of every month year-round and the first and third Mondays in summer. And polka predominates!

【 SPRING GREEN

Famed Wisconsin curmudgeon Frank Lloyd Wright found the area's lush beauty, nestled into the crook on the north side of a Wisconsin River bight, to fit his architectural visions so well he founded a groundbreaking design school here and lived here for five decades.

That prime, luck-of-the-draw geographical plunk-down on the edge of the Wyoming Valley has given Spring Green the edge on any tourist town around. From an afterthought hog and cattle shipping point, Spring Green has become a serious tourist town. Mingling are river rats, artisans, and a lot of Wright devotees trooping around to view The Master's works. Yet there's still a large sense of pastoral simplicity. Farmers still roll tractors down the roads and through town. Expansion of village roadwork coincided with equal-size projects to build ponds, wetlands, and a wildlife area, a green tension line of sorts. In fact, Spring Green didn't get a stoplight along busy U.S. 14 until 1995!

Sights

Throw a dart blindfolded in the Spring Green area and it'll hit the word "Wright." In 1911, three miles south of Spring Green's village center in the Jones Valley, Frank Lloyd Wright began work on **Taliesin** (Welsh for "Shining Brow") on the homestead of his Welsh ancestors. He had already made quite a name and reputation for himself in Wisconsin and in architectural circles, both good and bad. An unabashed, monumental egoist, Wright in his lifetime had a profound artistic and architectural influence upon the Badger State. He also enraged proper society with his audacity and uncanny ability to *épater les bourgeois,* that is, to stroke his own famed who-gives-a-damn-what-they-think predilections. When he wasn't dashing off preternaturally radical designs, he was alternately a deadbeat dad,

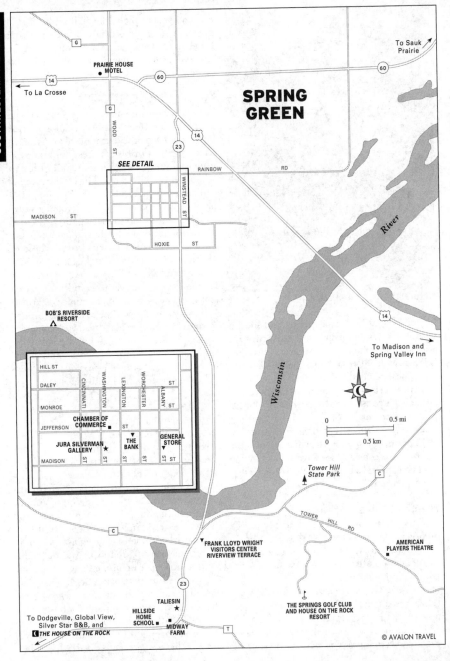

G

PRAIRIE HOUSE
MOTEL

60

To Sauk
Prairie

14

To La Crosse

60

SPRING
GREEN

G

WOOD ST

14

23

WINSTEAD ST

SEE DETAIL

RAINBOW   RD

River

MADISON   ST

HOXIE   ST

BOB'S RIVERSIDE
RESORT

14

To Madison and
Spring Valley Inn

HILL ST

DALEY

CINCINNATI

WASHINGTON

LEXINGTON

WORCHESTER

ST

ALBANY

ST

MONROE

ST

CHAMBER OF
COMMERCE

JEFFERSON

ST

Wisconsin

0   0.5 mi

JURA SILVERMAN
GALLERY

THE
BANK

GENERAL
STORE

0   0.5 km

MADISON

ST

ST

ST

Tower Hill
State Park

C

TOWER   HILL   RD

C

FRANK LLOYD WRIGHT
VISITORS CENTER
RIVERVIEW TERRACE

AMERICAN
PLAYERS THEATRE

23

TALIESIN

To Dodgeville, Global View,
Silver Star B&B, and
THE HOUSE ON THE ROCK

HILLSIDE
HOME SCHOOL

MIDWAY
FARM

T

THE SPRINGS GOLF CLUB
AND HOUSE ON THE ROCK
RESORT

© AVALON TRAVEL

a browbeater, and—one dare say—a megalomaniac. And one who cut a figure with his ever-present cape and porkpie hat. As he said, "I had to choose between hypocritical humility and hated arrogance." His most famous exchange occurred over a client's phoning Wright to inform him that rainwater was dripping on his table in his new Wright home. To which the master purportedly replied, "Move your table."

Wright stressed the "organic" in everything, and his devotion to the natural world predated environmental consciousness by generations (though the Japanese had it figured out millennia before Wright visited Tokyo and apparently had an epiphany). Taliesin is a perfect example—gradually pulling itself along the crown of a hill, not dominating the peak.

As it's the preeminent architectural design school, today thousands of acolytes (not really an exaggeration) study under the Taliesin Fellowship. The 600-acre grounds consist of his residence, Taliesin; Hillside Home School, a boardinghouse for a school run by an aunt; a home built for his sister (Yan-Y-Deri, Welsh for "under the oaks"); a windmill (his first commissioned project); and Midway Farm, all built between 1902 and 1930 while Wright and his associates operated his studio and workshop from the main building. Locally quarried sandstone is the predominant rock, and everywhere, those unmistakable Frank Lloyd Wright roofs. Wright would shudder to see how time has begun to ravage his estate—herculean efforts are under way to restore aging and nature-damaged structures.

The visitors center (877/588-7900, www.taliesinpreservation.org or www.wrightinwisconsin.org), more like a huge gift shop, is open 9 A.M.–5 P.M. daily May 1–October 31, shorter hours April and November–mid-December.

Myriad tours are available May 1–October 31. The basic Hillside Tour ($17 adults) is an hour long; the biggie is the Estate Tour ($80), a four-hour sweaty traipse around the entire grounds. There are lots of options between these.

Then the wonderful alternative to everything-must-be-Wright: **American Players Theatre** (608/588-2361, www.playinthewoods.org). APT has created a cult following of sorts for its broad palette of offerings and for its accessible direction. Carved into a hillside, it's a personal fave: a steamy evening with nighthawks swooping and actors literally crashing through the underbrush. (Although they do have a new indoor theater just in case!) Performances generally rotate Thursday–Sunday, with matinees weekends. The season runs mid-June–early October. Tickets average $50.

In the mid-1800s, what is today **Tower Hill State Park** was the site of a major lead-shot-production operation as cannonballs started to fly across the Mason-Dixon line, but it went belly up in competition with farther-flung and cheaper facilities, all made possible by the railroad. The old shot tower and smelter have been refurbished, and it's a cool (literally and figuratively) traipse down into the cooling tank, where the lead pellets fell 180 feet to the bottom, rounding and cooling as they went.

Shopping

The Wisconsin Artists Showcase at the **Jura Silverman Gallery** (143 S. Washington St., 608/588-7049, 11 A.M.–5 P.M. Wed.–Sun. June–Dec., less often otherwise) has art furniture, slumped glass, handmade-paper art, photography, prints, paintings, and a whole lot more by Wisconsin artists, showcased in a 1900 cheese warehouse.

From the other side of the planet, the wares at **Global View** (608/583-5311), off Highway C along Clyde Road in a reconverted barn, are not your usual import-export, they-don't-know-any-better, Asian "crafts." Global View maintains a reference library and location photographs of the source of each item, if not of the artists themselves, and tours to meet the artists are also organized here.

The whole of the Wisconsin River Valley can be thought of as one big farmers market. Summertime vegetable stands crop up every half mile, or turn up in autumn for pumpkins as big as a kid.

Accommodations

Don't bet on finding too much budget lodging in Spring Green, at least not between Memorial Day and Labor Day.

Not designed by Wright, but by an "associate," **Prairie House Motel** (U.S. 14, 608/588-2088 or 800/588-2088, $75 s or d) provides a countryside setting, comfortable rooms, a cozy atrium with a gently sloping wood-wainscoted ceiling, a whirlpool, sauna, and exercise room.

Appealing for Wright aficionados is the **Spring Valley Inn** (U.S. 14 and Hwy. C, 608/588-7828, www.springvalleyinn.com, $98–110), designed by Taliesin Associates. You can't miss its steepled upthrust, and its location is secluded but still prime. There are large rooms, with an indoor pool, whirlpool, sauna, rec room, and 28 kilometers of cross-country ski trails for guests. The restaurant features alfresco dining by a huge stone fireplace.

The most all-encompassing resort around is **The Springs Golf Club and House on the Rock Resort** (400 Springs Dr., 608/588-7000 or 800/822-7774, www.houseontherock.com, $140–225), a spread with a Robert Trent Jones Jr. championship course out your window as well as hiking/biking and tennis. A new inn has more family-style rooms, and lots of package deals are offered. It's a bit dated, but very clean and comfortable.

Cozy B&Bs and historic inns are ubiquitous. You'll find an artistic air at the oversize log building (**Silver Star** (3852 Limmex Hill Rd., 608/935-7297, www.silverstarinn. com, $117–154), displaying professional regional photographers' works within its chic café/coffeehouse and in all the rooms—minor museums of historical photographic figures. It's all spread out over 300 aces of farmland; sticklers for tradition are happy to find a cozy main room with large fieldstone fireplace.

For the best **camping** head to Tower Hill State Park. For tenters in Spring Green is **Bob's Riverside Resort** (S13220 Shifflet Rd., 608/588-2826), offering canoe rentals.

Food

Classic road-food-quality eats, greasy eggs diners, hard-core Midwest supper clubs, and wannabe chichi restaurants: Check!

A real "I went there" meal is at the (**Frank Lloyd Wright Visitors Center Riverview Terrace** (lunch daily, dinner Tues.–Sat. May–Oct., $4–11). Heretofore the planet's only Frank Lloyd Wright–designed restaurant, it was constructed out of a popular 1940s local diner and a WWII aircraft carrier! Expect grand river views.

A friendly-family-run natural foods café and grocery in an old cheese warehouse, the inimitable (**General Store** (137 S. Albany St., 608/588-7070, 9 A.M.–6 P.M. Mon.–Fri., 8 A.M.–6 P.M. Sat., 8 A.M.–4 P.M. Sun., $4–9) serves healthful yet creative lighter fare—absolutely everything from scratch—keeping vegetarians squarely in mind. They have the best espresso too and are always on my itinerary.

At **The Bank** (134 E. Jefferson St., 608/588-7600, www.thebankrestaurantandwinebar .com, $12–25) the menu changes weekly (they'll cook what locals produce/grow/raise), all in the cozy confines of the erstwhile local neoclassical-style bank. It's a wondrous addition to town, and the wine list is astounding.

Information and Services

Contact the **Spring Green Chamber of Commerce** (608/588-2042 or 800/588-2042, www.springgreen.com) for all your needs.

(THE HOUSE ON THE ROCK

The House on the Rock (south of Spring Green along WI 23, 608/935-3639, www.the-houseontherock.com,) absolutely defies lexical trickery in nailing it down. Novella-length magazine articles have gushed about the, well, left-handed grandeur and spectacle of its true-blue Americana, anything-can-happen overkill. Cynical scribes come and near-religious epiphanies ensue over this Shangri-La—contrived solely to club tourists over the head aesthetically. This is the grandest shakedown of them all in Dairyland, mere miles from the amok-dom of the Wisconsin Dells. Best of all, it all goes down less than 10 miles from that enclave to natural architecture—that altar to an ego, that House that Wright Built—Taliesin, in Spring Green.

Come to Wisconsin and you absolutely cannot miss this eighth-dimension tourist trap's ad barrage—Wisconsin's version of a two-drink minimum. Way back in the 1940s, otherwise-sane Alex Jordan literally stumbled over a 60-foot candlelike outcropping in the Wyoming Valley. Intending to construct a weekend retreat and artists' haven, Jordan somehow or other wrestled the original structure into completion atop the chimney. Bit by bit, this architectural gem began to transmogrify into what it is today—the original house atop the rock, plus several other mind-blowing rooms and add-ons, all stuffed with the detritus that Jordan accumulated through a lifetime, much of it museum-worthy in quality or scope.

The catalog: Mill House, Streets of Yesterday, Heritage of the Sea, Pizza Atrium, Transportation Building, Music of Yesterday, World's Largest Carousel (20,000 lights and 275 handcrafted wooden animals, not one of which is a horse), Organ Room (three of the world's greatest right here), and so on ad nauseam.

The best? Try the loopy Infinity Room, a glassed-in room that spikes 218 feet over the valley floor.

But a list doesn't do it justice—it isn't just a selection of junk; it's a wild, shotgun-spattered Attic of the Damned. Is it art? Is it a giant Rorschach test of the mental wilds of an inspired eccentric? Well, equal parts all, perhaps, but an indescribable feeling of visionary honesty pervades the place—never a feeling that it's all a sham or simple stupid overindulgence. The method to the madness is there.

Many visitors overlook what a remarkable artistic and design achievement it was. Jordan never failed to think of how the visitor would see it all, from the 30-mile-panorama observation decks to the floral displays. Those devoted to tackiness have found their Mecca; best of all, even jaded tourist hacks have to shake their heads and grin.

You can experience all of this March 15 through the last weekend in October. High season hours are 9 A.M.–dusk June–September, shorter hours for the rest of season. There are also special holiday seasons. Three tours are offered: You can fork over $12 each or take a package of $28.50 for the whole slew.

WEST TO THE MISSISSIPPI
Muscoda

The story goes that the Fox and Sauk who lived in encampments on this site lent the descriptive moniker *mash-ko-deng,* or "meadow of prairie" to their home; or Henry Wadsworth Longfellow's "Hiawatha," which includes the line, "Muscoday, the meadow." Longfellow at least got the pronunciation to fit the spelling; most massacre it into "mus-KOH-duh." It's "MUS-cuh-day."

Sleepy little Muscoda gets its kicks as the "Morel Mushroom Capital of the World." The tasty mushroom, tough to find but worth the woods-scouring, is feted annually with a festival in May. You might also stop by relic-quality **Tanner Drug Store** (N. Wisconsin Ave., 608/739-3218), a working drugstore with original oak and pine counters and some antiques. Right on the river at **Victoria Park** outside of town sits the Muscoda Prairie, a lovingly restored stretch of prairie. (Here in June? The Sand Barrens section has cactus!) A **campground** is here, the only one on the Lower Wisconsin State Riverway. Northwest of town is a **bison ranch** (33502 Sand Ln., 608/739-3360) operated by the Ho Chunk Nation and seasonally available for tours, and effigy mounds are on the property.

An optional jaunt between Muscoda and Boscobel is to cross the river to WI 60. Six miles west at Eagle Cave Road is the state's largest onyx cave, **Eagle Cave,** discovered in the 1840s by a puzzled bear hunter who couldn't figure out where his quarry had gotten to.

Boscobel

Back on the south side of the river, charming little Boscobel's location was pegged as *bosquet belle*, or "beautiful woods," by Marquette and Joliet, who passed through in 1673. There's great turkey hunting and canoeing, but another claim to perpetuity is the Christian Commercial Travelers Association. That'd be the Gideons to you and me, founded in downtown's stone Hotel Boscobel in 1899. The story goes that two devout Christian salesmen were forced to double up in the hotel and got to discussing how tough it was to be a God-fearing traveling man, especially in hellhole river towns, and hatched the idea of an interdenominational fraternity for travelers. By 1914, almost a quarter million Bibles had been placed from sea to shining sea. The old stone hotel still stands today. Bought in the early 1990s and de-mothballed, it has had reincarnations as restaurants.

Various other structures are under restorative saws and blades, including the railroad depot, which is also a mini museum and the offices of the chamber of commerce. An old **Grand Army of the Republic** building—the only surviving Wisconsin GAR building—on Mary Street houses a Civil War museum, open by appointment.

In one of the oldest buildings in town, the aptly named **(Unique Cafe** (1100 Wisconsin Ave., 608/375-4465, 5 A.M.–8 P.M. daily, $3–6) features killer pies, from-scratch café food, and an amazing assortment of "memorabilia"

gathered by the proprietor. It's a genuinely interesting place to sit and eat and gander about.

Fennimore, 10 miles south of Boscobel, was once a major player in the lead trade. People generally stop by to see the **Fennimore Doll and Toy Museum** (1135 6th St., 608/822-4100, 10 A.M.–4 P.M. daily May–Oct., $3). The displays of tractors, trucks, cars and more from various museums is ever-increasing.

Then there's the **Fennimore Railroad Museum** (610 Lincoln Ave., 608/822-6319, 10 A.M.–4 P.M. daily Memorial Day weekend–Labor Day, free) down the street. Smaller steam engines ride on a 15-inch track, and children can ride. The claim to fame here is the "Dinky," significant as one part of the most extensive operations in the state—16 total miles throughout the Green River Valley, and famed for its horseshoe curve, necessitated by the grade of the valley.

Backtrack through Boscobel and across the river and then head west along WI 60 toward the Mississippi. At the midpoint is flyspeck Wauzeka, site of the **Kickapoo Indian Caverns** (WI 60, 608/875-7723, $5) tourist trap. Geologically significant for their size—larger than better-known caverns throughout southwestern Wisconsin—and historically significant for sheltering the eponymous Indian tribe, the onyx caverns weren't discovered until the 19th century. The caverns pretty much can't be missed with the ubiquitous signs.

From Wauzeka, it's only about 10 miles west to Prairie du Chien and the Mississippi River.

The Old Military Road

Essentially a cobbling together with lots of ancient Indian trails south of the Wisconsin River, the historic Old Military Road, the first overland link east to west in the state, constructed in 1835–1836 by soldier labor, used to stretch as far as Prairie du Chien. Today, you're as likely to see bicyclists along the route as you are cud-chewing bovines on the Fitchburg-Dodgeville Military Ridge State Trail.

MOUNT HOREB

The "Trollway," as the main drag in predominantly Norwegian Mount Horeb is known, is reminiscent of a northern European mountain village. Predating statehood, Norwegian and Swiss (and a few Irish) farmers staked out the rolling ridges and valleys around these parts, and the whole area boasts a thoroughly northern European brick-and-frame

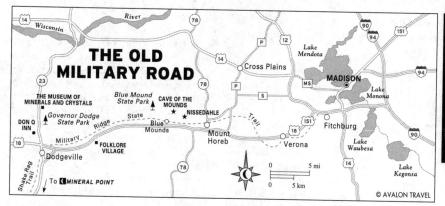

architecture and not a few log structures and octagonal barns.

Mount Horeb is a fine place to set up base camp for state parks, the Military Ridge Trail, and other regional attractions.

Otherwise, the **Mount Horeb Area Historical Museum** (Main and 2nd, 608/437-6486, noon–5 P.M. Fri.–Sun., Memorial Day weekend–Labor Day, free) is housed in the old municipal building. This 1918 home features a dozen rooms—more than 4,000 square feet!—that regularly change themes.

Bust-the-wallet-wise, there are more Scandinavian gift huts than trolls in this town.

All the information you need is at trollway.com.

Practicalities

The **Karakahl Inn** (1405 U.S. 18/151, 608/437-5545, www.karakahl.com, $60) was designed as a retreat for patients of famed chiropractor Clarence Gonstead. Shaped like a fierce Viking ship, it supposedly follows the dictums of Frank Lloyd Wright. It's seen better days for sure, but the staff is nice and it's inexpensive.

Housed in an old cheese factory, the **Grumpy Troll Brewpub** (105 S. 2nd St., 608/437-2739, $6–14) is pretty much the perfect spot to unwind after you've just ridden 25 miles on a bike!

Yet for something special, drive north to Mazomanie (via Hwy. F and U.S. 14) to the

Old Feed Mill (114 Cramer St., 608/795-4909, lunch and dinner Tues.–Sat., brunch and dinner Sun., $11–25). The eclectic heartland fare is luscious, true enough, but the exquisitely well-renovated 1857 mill and period detailing are equally fine—garnering nods from the state's historical society.

BLUE MOUNDS AREA

Three short miles west of Mount Horeb, the town, centered between three highlights on the Old Military Road, began as a tiny mining encampment and an ungodly amount of lead was extracted from its grounds.

Nissedahle

Transliterated, roughly, as "Valley of the Elves" (but better known as "Little Norway") and tucked into the rain-shadow edge of big Blue Mound next to a bubbly spring, this outdoor living museum (608/437-8211, www.littlenorway.com, 9 A.M.–7 P.M. daily July–Aug., 9 A.M.–5 P.M. daily May–June and Sept.–Oct., $12 adults) features more than a dozen log buildings from a Norwegian homestead. The massive Norway Building, a replica of a 12th-century Norway *stavkirke*, or stave church, is replete with Cathay-esque steeples and dragon heads. The interiors of the buildings house what is arguably the most exhaustive display of Norwegian-American culture in the United States, including the original manuscript of an Edvard Grieg musical composition and, of course, intricate rosemaling.

Blue Mound State Park

Penning notes of his Wisconsin River explorations in 1776, Jonathan Carver detailed extensively the "mountains" due south of the river. The highest point in southern Wisconsin at 1,719 feet above sea level, the salient upthrust—which can indeed seem a steely blue—doesn't exactly spur migratory peregrinations, but it's rumored to hold Native treasure.

Note the singular Blue Mound park and the plural Blue Mounds town; no historical mistake, there are in fact two mounds—the shorter eastern twin is now Brigham County Park in Dane County. Both are multilayered candy drops of geology.

One of the extras at this park is a real swimming pool. For the more ambitious, a number of trails wind throughout the area. Mountain bikers actually have a trail just for themselves, unsurprising as this is in close proximity to the Military Ridge State Trail.

Cave of the Mounds

Cave of the Mounds (608/437-3038, 9 A.M.–6 P.M. daily summer, shorter hours mid-Mar.–mid-Nov. outside summer, $15) is yet another residual of the eons-old limestone cementation process; another cave, Lost River Cave, exists near Blue Mound State Park.

Oddly, though the area above the subterranean caverns was settled, mined, plowed, and grazed starting as far back as 1828 (making the homestead the oldest in the county), these caves weren't discovered until 1939. It took until the 1980s for geologists of the U.S. Department of the Interior to declare it a National Natural Landmark. It's better known as the "jewel box" of large caverns, neither as large nor as famous as others, but, as the Chicago Academy of Sciences called it, "the significant cave of the upper Midwest."

The farm grounds up top, with a few assorted gardens, also make for great walking and picnicking!

Cheese

A few miles south of Blue Mounds, **Bleu Mont Dairy** (3840 Hwy. F, 608/767-2875) has become one of the best-known of the back-to-the-land cheesemakers. Solar-and-all-else-sustainable-powered, and of course only organic, the operation is absolutely artisanal and the quality shows it. (One has to love how the owner, master Willi, only deals with one farmer's cows at a time to maximize consistency!) It's open by appointment only, generally Saturday mornings, and if you can't make it, you can get some at the Dane County Farmer's Market in Madison on Saturday mornings.

DODGEVILLE

The name "Dodge" is big in these parts—all thanks to one seemingly omnipresent man, Henry Dodge. A miner, Dodge became a leading figure in the Black Hawk War, which thrust him into regional prominence. Capitalizing on his fame, he was elected Wisconsin's first territorial governor. Dodgeville today is a bit somnolent but not forlorn—the downtown district has been touted for its careful balance of historic preservation.

Sights

You may know the city as the headquarters of Land's End clothiers. But the second-largest state park in Wisconsin and definitely worth any sweat-or-scenery buff's time, massive 5,000-acre **Governor Dodge State Park** has just about everything a visitor could want, including some noticeable examples of Driftless Area terrain (read, awesome bluffs). Naturalist-led hikes are scheduled during summers. Otherwise, 35 miles of multipurpose trails wind throughout the woodlands, open meadows, and around the two lakes.

Two trails, totaling 10 miles, are also open to mountain biking. The shorter, three-mile **Mill Creek Trail** is more popular, mostly owing to the fact that it hooks up with the popular **Military Ridge State Trail.** Thirty-nine miles total from Dodgeville east to Fitchburg (which in turn has lovely trails into Madison), the trail skirts the watershed between the Wisconsin

River to the north and the Pecatonica and Rock Rivers to the south. The trail is wide and easy, passing primarily through bucolic moo-cow ranges. But there're plenty of woods, prairies, wetlands, and the Sugar River Valley—and almost 50 bridges. One problem: there's little camping along the way.

Governor Dodge State Park has about a million campsites. Six backpack sites are also available.

The Museum of Minerals and Crystals (N. WI 23, 608/935-5205, 9 A.M.–5 P.M. daily May–Oct., $5 adults) has about 3,500 striking geologic specimens, including Smithsonian-quality fluorites, Mexican geodes, and calcite from the legendary Sweetwater Mine in Missouri.

Take a free gander at the residue of Dodgeville's lead-mining days; the **first slag furnace** sits along East Spring Street, next to the lumber yard. Extra lead was extracted from molten waste rock, and according to period reports the glow could be seen for miles.

The Greek revival limestone courthouse, the oldest in the state, is open to self-guided walking tours during business hours.

Folklore Village (3210 Hwy. BB, six miles east off U.S. 18/151, 608/924-4000, www.folklorevillage.org) is a farmland experience of fiddle, accordion, and the rural life. The farm features a huge activities center, an 1893 school, a one-room church, old Danish and Swedish bunkhouses, and a farmhouse. Myriad workshops or events in dance, music, material arts, and foods are offered—including a great weekly community potluck dinner. Reservations are essential.

Accommodations and Food

It would be nearly impossible to miss the regionally famous **Don Q Inn** (WI 23 N, 608/935-2321 or 800/666-7848, www.fantasuites.com, $80–225), one of Wisconsin's most "distinctive" lodging options. You can't miss the landmark C-97 Boeing Stratocruiser parked out front. How about the trademarked "FantaSuites"? Jungle Safari and Sherwood Forest are good examples. Some rooms are the real thing—the original, the Steeple, is an 1872 church steeple; the erstwhile Dodgeville Station of the Chicago and Northwestern Railway now also houses several rooms. Kitsch-worthy? Definitely. That said, there has been a growing rumbling that it's seen better days; others still love it.

For **camping,** head immediately to Governor Dodge State Park, and if it's full, drive north to Spring Green and Tower Hill.

For dessert, try the only old-fashioned **soda fountain** (206 N. Iowa St., 608/935-3661) in the county, at the Corner Drug Store.

The Lead Zone

And there's gold in them thar hills. Well, not precisely "Au," but wealth of a sort. The hills around these parts were the first reason—the *real* reason—any white interloper who wasn't seasonal or a soldier stayed for long. Natives had forever scavenged lead deposits in the area—so rife that lead littered the topsoil. The earliest European to cash in on the ready-made ore, Nicholas Perrot, started bartering with the Natives around 1690. A century later perceptive homesteaders quickly turned mining opportunists and wound up as the first "Badgers." Mines were hewn into the sides of hills every which way one looked. Accidentally forming the first cohesive region in the state, these early pioneers solidified an economy of sorts and in many respects got the state on its feet.

The results were staggering—the region poured forth a half million pounds of lead. Only 200 intrepid miners populated the region when the federal government began to stick it to the Fox, Sauk, and Miami Indians. By 1830 that number had grown to almost 10,000. It's no surprise, then, that the resident Native Americans suddenly felt they had been cheated and no longer agreed to cooperate. The resulting Black Hawk Wars flared on and off until the U.S. Army slaughtered Black

Hawk's band at the Battle of Bad Axe near Prairie du Chien.

Settlers then poured in and made the region the United States' largest lead producer, yet by the mid-1840s railroads had stretched far enough to transport cheaper lead from other areas, and the mining petered out. The Swiss and Germans, along with Irish and Yankee settlers, helped the area bounce back with the dairy industry.

◖ MINERAL POINT

Only 2,500 friendly souls, yet what a huge place Mineral Point really is, in many ways the heart and soul of the state's heritage. So important was—and still is—it that the National Trust for Historic Preservation called it one of America's Dozen Distinctive Destinations.

The name was no fluke—ore fever coursed through the region when a prospector discovered huge deposits under Mineral Point Hill. Hordes of Cornish immigrants took right to the hills. Tirelessly scratching into the hillsides, they even scraped gouges into the bluff sides where they could rest and escape the elements. Many thus believe Mineral Point to be the origin of the nickname "badger," as these ubiquitous holes and the miners in them were dubbed.

Soon the heart of the region, it was in Mineral Point that the Territory of Wisconsin was established on July 4, 1836. The railroads rolled through, and Mineral Point soon had the largest zinc operation in the United States; it persisted (more or less) through 1979, when the last mine closed down after 150 years.

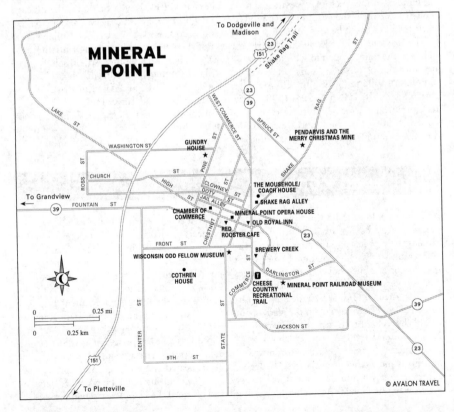

© THOMAS HUHTI

downtown Mineral Point

More than 500 structures in this small town still stand on 1837 plattings. Most buildings contain locally quarried limestone and feature Cornish designs, and all date from the century after 1830. The town's gemlike status has impelled artisans to move to Mineral Point and set up studios, shops, and galleries. "Art" or "gallery" or "antiques" is affixed to absolutely everything; don't be surprised to see "bar-antiques."

And the pervasiveness of "shake rag" this and "shake rag" that stems from a Cornish tradition. At noontime, wives summoned their husbands home from the mines by waving dishcloths. The name stuck.

Sights

Pendarvis and the Merry Christmas Mine
(114 Shake Rag St., 608/987-2122, www.wisconsinhistory.org, 10 A.M.–5 P.M. daily May–Nov., $9 adults) is judged by many as the most thorough and best preserved view of the region's mining heritage. While the rest of this historic district was being demolished in the 1930s for scavenged building blocks, a foresighted local bought rundown Cornish cottages and set to renovating. For a while, it was a Cornish restaurant before the state historical society took over. Quite small actually, the complex has a long three-unit rowhouse, the oft-photographed Polperro House, and stone-and-log cottages (six structures in all), linked together by narrow stone paths through gardens.

Even better might be the stroll up, over, and through Mineral Point Hill and the Merry Christmas Mine on a set of trails snaking up from the back of the parking lot. Miners took 80 years to get around to this side of the hill, firing up the lanterns about 1906 and mining for seven years in the largest zinc operation in the area. Assorted hulks of rusting equipment and more than 100 abandoned crevice shafts dot the 43 acres. Native prairie restoration is ongoing, and big bluestem is already blooming again.

Guided tours led by garbed docents depart regularly (schedule varies); last tickets sales are at 4 P.M.

Up Shake Rag Street from Pendarvis you can espy other stone and stone-and-log dwellings originally put up in the 1830s by Cornish potters, weavers, and other artisans (even Wisconsin's first pottery). This is yer **Shake Rag Alley** (www.shakeragalley.com). Nine historic structures, including one of the oldest log cabins in the state, are surrounded by tailored gardens. Find artisan galleries/workhops, inns, a café, and other worthy sights. Just gandering at the classic structures is worth a few minutes.

North of the chamber of commerce is the **Gundry House** (234 Madison St., 608/987-3670, 1–5 P.M. Fri.–Sat., 11 A.M.–2 P.M. Sun., June–late Sept., free), a cut sandstone and limestone Victorian built in 1867 by a prominent local merchant, Joseph Gundry, notable because his business featured the local-legend *Pointer Dog* statue. Otherwise, it's an impressive home with period furnishings, offering tours.

Not many get around to the 1838 **Wisconsin Odd Fellow Museum** (Front St. and State St., 608/987-3093, 9 A.M.–3 P.M. daily June–Sept., free), the first Odd Fellow Hall west of the Allegheny Mountains. Built and dedicated by Thomas Wildey, founder of the order, it's the only hall dedicated by him and still standing.

Mineral Point's classic railroad depot—once called one of the 10 most endangered historic rail structures in the country (it is the oldest in Wisconsin)—has been restored into the **Mineral Point Railroad Museum** (10 A.M.–4 P.M. Thurs.–Sat., noon–4 P.M. Sun., summer, less often spring and fall, $3 adults) and has collections of southwest Wisconsin rail artifacts. The Wisconsin Trust for Historic Preservation called it the best interpretive site in Wisconsin.

If you're up for a road trip, 13 miles east of town is Hollandale, a mile west of which along WI 39 is **Grandview,** the erstwhile home of folk artist Nick Engelbert. Engelbert, an immigrant dairy farmer turned self-taught artist, in the 1930s began to transform his artistic visions into concrete, glass, and stone and scattered them throughout the gardens around his farm. It's a great minitrip and a splendid look at rural folk art.

Nobody's ever really come here to actually exercise before, but the locals are trying to change that. They've recently completed a dandy **hike/bike trail** to Dodgeville, linking with the Military Ridge State Trail.

Tours

The chamber of commerce (237 High St., 608/987-3201, www.mineralpoint.com) has detailed maps ($3) of **historic walking/driving tours.**

Entertainment

The **Mineral Point Opera House** (139 High St., 608/987-2642) has undergone a long, painstaking but loving renovation into its erstwhile grandeur, reopening in 2010. It features a slate of live performances during its May–October season. Once a major stop on the Midwest theater tour, it now also shows movies—daily in summer!—as well as occasional theatrical presentations by the local Shake Rag Players and some traveling shows.

Shopping

Get ready to unshackle the calf hide. Ever since some pioneering artisans discovered the tasteful architecture and low-key small-town tranquility in the 1940s, Mineral Point has been a hotbed for Wisconsin artisans. More than 40 galleries and studios populate the town, and more seem to spring open annually. One weekend each October southern Wisconsin artisans open their studio doors for back-room views of the artistic process; Spring Green and Baraboo participate, but Mineral Point is the place to start any tour. The three-day festival is a great combination of art and halcyon autumn. They also do this the first Saturday of April, June, August and December.

Accommodations

This is the town that time forgot, so take your pick from lodging in a baker's dozen—or more—absolutely authentic historic structures.

Laying your head on Mineral Point's Shake Rag Street, just a skip from Pendarvis, would be the way to go. Choose between **The Mousehole,** an 1839 cottage, and rooms/suites in the **Coach House,** an 1840s structure. It doesn't get much more historic than these—and for rates starting at $99, for not much moolah. For information, call 608/987-3292, or log on to www.shakeragalley.com.

Stay at the ◖ **Cothren House** (320 Tower St., 608/987-1522, www.cothrenhouse.com, $139–159) and you'd swear you were back in the old country, such is the architecture and landscaping—it in fact was modeled on Redruth, Cornwall. Choose from a stone cottage or rustic log cabin (both with two bedrooms) and relax in the secluded gardens. The cabin, a pioneer dwelling from 1835, might be the most perfectly realized historic lodging experience in southwestern Wisconsin.

A caveat is perhaps in order. Mineral Point's historic dwellings are legendary for having, er, let's say paranormal guests. Just so you know. . . .

The closest public **campground** is at Governor Dodge State Park in Dodgeville. East and south along Highways D and F is **Yellowstone Lake State Park,** a modest state park with 128 campsites, showers, a good fishing lake, and eight miles of hiking trails. A wildlife reserve is also part of this 2,600-acre park.

Food

Better get used to hearing *figgyhobbin* (or *figgihobbin*), because you'll see the word incessantly. Yes, it is of course a Cornish dish, and no, it isn't the roast beast the name connotes. It's actually a pastry of raisins and walnuts, and it's quite rich. Other Cornish food might include saffron cakes, Mawgan meatballs, and pasty.

Once a county bank, the ◖ **Red Rooster Cafe** (158 High St., 608/987-9936, 5 A.M.–5 P.M. daily, $2–7) is a one-of-a-kind road-food-quality eatery where diners sit at a horseshoe-shaped counter on old red vinyl and chrome swivel chairs underneath a coffered

ceiling. The café serves pasty and figgyhobbin in a diner atmosphere—classic.

For now, lovely old-mashed-with-new ambience, with century-old limestone walls from its previous incarnation as a brewery storehouse, comes at **Brewery Creek** (23 Commerce St., 608/987-4747, 11:30 A.M.–8 P.M. daily, $7–15). Today it's a B&B and restaurant. The fare is upper-end pub grub and homebrewed beer, and while you wait, notice the meticulous woodworking and imported tables. The B&B also has historic (from the 1830s!) cottages for rent.

Great fish fry (and martinis) at the erstwhile 19th-century hotel **Old Royal Inn** (43 High St., 608/987-4530) at the corner of High and Vine.

Information and Services

Friendly are those at **Mineral Point Chamber of Commerce** (237 High St., 608/987-3201, www.mineralpoint.com).

PLATTEVILLE

The name doesn't exactly flow like honey, does it? Yet it is as pleasant as any hilly, agrarian town you'll find.

It began as Platte River Diggings—not much better, eh? The progenitor proper of the town, Major John Rountree, bought a load of lead in 1827 and had the hilly patterns of the new town configured after his home, Yorkshire. The christening name—Platteville—was inspired by the long, gray, end-result "bowls" of the lead-smelting process practiced by the Native Americans. While the lead lasted it turned Platteville into "the present metropolis of the lead industry," as the old guidebooks referred to it. As the nucleus for the tri-state mining industry, it became home to the country's first mining college—immortalized by the world's largest "M" east of town atop Platteville Mound.

Sights

An exhaustive examination of the lead industry is at the **Bevans Lead and Mining Museum** (385 E. Main St., 608/348-3301). The Bevans mine was the regional golden goose, as it were, pushing out two million pounds per year.

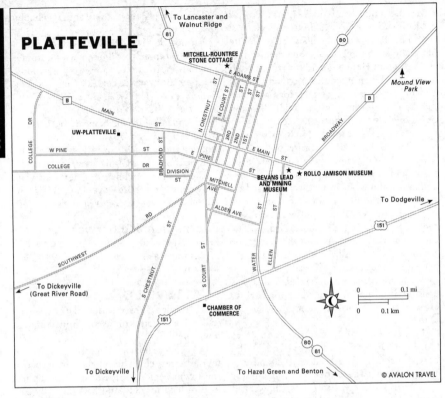

To Lancaster and Walnut Ridge

PLATTEVILLE

MITCHELL-ROUNTREE
STONE COTTAGE ★

E ADAMS ST

Mound View Park

UW-PLATTEVILLE ■

MAIN

W PINE ST

COLLEGE DR

DIVISION ST

BEVANS LEAD
AND MINING
MUSEUM

★ ROLLO JAMISON MUSEUM

To Dodgeville →

MITCHELL AVE

ALDEN AVE

To Dickeyville
(Great River Road)

SOUTHWEST

To Dickeyville ↓

■ CHAMBER OF
COMMERCE

0   0.1 mi
0   0.1 km

To Hazel Green and Benton ↘

© AVALON TRAVEL

Guided tours include clammy shaft walks replete with simulated mining. Top it all off with a hop aboard a genuine 1931 mine locomotive for a chug around the grounds, perhaps to the contiguous **Rollo Jamison Museum,** best described as a world-class junk collection with a keen eye on history. Keep in mind that the detailed exhibits of carriages and tools, and the general store, kitchen, and parlor mock-ups are the work of a single pack rat. These museums are open 9 A.M.–5 P.M. daily May–October, less often the rest of the year. Admission is $9 adults and includes entrance to both museums. The changing exhibit galleries are open at no cost.

Mitchell-Rountree Stone Cottage (corner of Lancaster and Ann Sts., 608/348-2287, guided tours weekends Memorial Day–Labor Day, free) is the oldest surviving homestead in Platteville, and one of the oldest in the state. Built in 1837 by a local veteran of the Revolutionary War, it's distinctively constructed after the Tidewater Virginia style.

Accommodations

A true and significant slice of history is found at Platteville's 【 **Walnut Ridge** (2238 Hwy. A, 608/348-9359, www.walnutridgewi.com, $155). These three meticulously restored buildings date from the very beginnings of the lead era, including an 1839 miners' bunkhouse relocated from British Hollow, now a bungalow, and an immigrant family's house-barn for a kitchen. Not the usual motley arrangement of mismatched antiques—here you'll sleep in real, believe it or not, rope beds, and bathe in tin bathtubs.

PLATTEVILLE VICINITY
Belmont
Don't blink or you'll whiz right past what is likely Wisconsin's smallest state park— **First Capitol Historic Park** (608/987-2122, 10 A.M.–4 P.M. daily in summer, free), seven miles east of Platteville at Highways B and G. The glad-handing politics of pork were alive and well in Wisconsin long before it was even a state. The powers that be finagled microscopic Belmont into accepting territorial-capital status, though it was a lame duck from the start. The hogs, chickens, and cows that stunk up the overhead gallery in the original building are long gone now (legislators would stir up the piggies below with long poles when things weren't going their way), as is the edifice. Two buildings do remain and are now restored and feature small exhibits on early-19th-century Wisconsin and a diorama of the first Capitol. Though it's open daily in summer, getting in requires advance notice.

Up the road a half mile is the **Belmont Mound State Park,** a day-use park with some trails leading to the mound itself. The mound was used by the first legislators as a landmark while traversing the prairies to find Belmont, no doubt wondering the entire way what in the hell they were doing there in the first place.

Shullsburg
This Tinytown with the inspirational street names of Charity, Friendship, Justice, Mercy, Hope, and Judgment (and the inexplicable Cyclops) was founded by a trader and platted by a priest. The city still has a 19th-century feel, with four dozen or so museum piece—mostly Vernacular—buildings along its Water Street Commercial Historic District, built mostly between 1840 and the turn of the 20th century. There are no despoiling tactless gentrification and clapboard fakeries yet.

A walk-through museum of mining life known as the **Badger Mine** (279 W. Estey St., 608/965-4860, noon–4 P.M. Wed.–Thurs., 11 A.M.–4 P.M. Fri.–Sun. summers, $5 adults) showcases the erstwhile Badger Lot Diggings,

dating from the 1820s. Tours descend the same 51 steps the miners took into the ore shafts, extending about a quarter mile into the hillsides. Other lead mines exist and are open to the public, but none this extensive. Among aging artifacts, keep an eye open for Jefferson Davis's John Hancock on the old Brewster Hotel register book.

Outside of town to the south is **Gravity Hill,** a supernaturally charged hill where cars drift backward up a hill, or so it appears. Ask for directions in town.

A number of historic inns line downtown Water Street, including the most economical (and historic) **Water Street Place** (202 W. Water St., 608/482-1438, www.waterstreetplace.com, from $75), originally a bank but pretty much every incarnation since the 19th century as well.

The Brewster Cafe (208 W. Water St., 608/965-4485, $3 and up), in a renovated 1880s creamery, is a gem and also has a sister-operation cheese store. Pasties supplement the café fare.

Brewster Cafe in downtown Shullsburg

Benton

In this former mining hub once named Cottonwood Hill, all that's left are the tailing piles. Benton is the final resting spot of Friar Samuel Mazzuchelli, the intrepid priest and architectural maven who designed two dozen of the regional buildings and communities (and gave Shullsburg its sweet street names), who's buried in St. Patrick Church cemetery. The church itself was the first stone structure in the area, and Mazzuchelli's restored home is on the church grounds; ask at the new rectory for tour details. Mazzuchelli's 1844 masterpiece, the church of St. Augustine, is in New Diggings, about five miles southeast, the priest's last still-intact wood structure, though a half-million-dollar restoration has given it a new sheen. Only one Mass a year is held here, at 2:30 P.M. on the last Sunday of September. Otherwise, it's open 1–4 P.M. Sunday late May–late September. If religious peregrination doesn't compel you, local taverns offer other entertainment.

Learn about the ugly shenanigans that went along with the mining at the truthfully named **Swindler's Ridge Museum,** named after a nearby bluff notorious for thievery. Father Mazzuchelli's original rectory, once here, was recently moved down the street.

Hazel Green

They should have called this place "Point of Beginning," since that's exactly what it was. In 1831, a U.S. land commissioner sank a post along the 4th Meridian. Every single piece of surveyed land in the state of Wisconsin is referenced from this point. It's marked along WI 80, south of town. (Actually, it's more of a sweaty, half-hour trudge to find the damn thing.) Wisconsin's only disputed nonnatural border was the segment near Hazel Green separating Illinois from what was then Michigan Territory.

About the only thing to do in Hazel Green is head down to the **Opera House and Old Town Hall** (2130 N. Main St.). Stroll through the auditorium, which was the original stage and has a new hand-painted curtain. Believe it or not, it's now a fully-realized puppetry house with amazing classes, demonstrations, and performances.

Equally historic is the wonderfully original 1846 B&B ◖ **Wisconsin House Stage Coach Inn** (2105 Main St., 608/854-2233, www.wisconsinhouse.com, $65–125), a multilevel abode framed in native oak with clapboard siding and six over six windows. The Wisconsin House Inn, lore has it, was the only thing left standing after an 1876 tornado leveled everything else in the village.

West of Hazel Green along WI 11 and Highway Z, Mazzuchelli also founded a men's college, now home to **Motherhouse of Sinsinawa Dominica** (608/748-4411), high upon Sinsinawa Mound (a sheer rise of Niagara dolomite), with awesome vistas. Some buildings date from the 1840s; the complex also has an exhibit on Father Mazzuchelli, a sustainable agricultural farm, and, best of all, a great bakery!

Darlington

This impeccably preserved anachronism along the Pecatonica River features wide streets and a host of extant preserved architecture. The **Lafayette County Courthouse** (627 Washington St.) is the only courthouse in the United States built using the funds of a solitary individual; note the lovely rotunda with Tiffany glass. And, foot for foot, there is arguably more mural space in this courthouse than any other in the state. Alexander Hamilton's son staked a claim in Darlington in 1828; later, Fort Hamilton became one of the oldest permanent settlements in the state (a marker on WI 78 shows where).

Nine miles north of Darlington is the **Prairie Springs Hotel,** one of the earliest buildings in the region. It's one of the most unusual, well built in the southern vernacular style by an early miner turned soldier and local leader.

Swiss Valley

Green County might as well be called "Little Switzerland." The Swiss culture shows itself most prominently in New Glarus, an amazing alpine-esque village. In Monroe, farther south, world-famous swiss cheese comes thanks to a substrata of limestone soil, allowing a certain digestive process by which cows produce creamy gold.

In the 1930s, Monroe cheesemaking had grown so prodigious that a postmaster in Iowa grew weary of the waftings of ripe Monroe limburger passing through his tiny post office. The Depression-era WPA guide captured the moment:

Cheese was stoutly defended when Monroe's postmaster engaged in a sniffing duel with a postmaster in Iowa to determine whether or not the odor of Limburger in transit was a fragrance or a stench. Well publicized by the press of the Nation, the duel ended when a decision was reached which held that Limburger merely exercised its constitutional right to hold its own against all comers.

PAOLI

Before reaching Green County, you pass through some ready-made Sunday drive country and charming towns, including the quaintest of them all, Paoli. Known mostly for its somnolent waterside small-town appeal, and now, due to its renovated, grand 1864 **Paoli Mill,** it's full of shops, galleries, and chi-chi but relaxed cafés. Next door the Artisan Gallery (6858 Paoli Rd., 608/845-6600, www.artisangal.com) is an outstanding gallery of 125 Midwest artisans working in virtually every medium.

◖ NEW GLARUS

In 1845, a group of 190 Swiss left the Canton of Glarus during an economically devastating period. Scouts dispatched earlier had quite literally stumbled into southwestern Wisconsin and

marveled at its similarities to Switzerland—nestled in the crook of a short but steep valley. Only 100 made it this far. After toughing out a rough winter, the Swiss farmers attempted to grow wheat, but they were unaccustomed to growing the grain and, returning to dairy, they soon began to pique interest in the east for their trademark cheeses.

New Glarus is full of white-and-brown architecture, umlauts, and scrolled Swiss-German sayings, gift shops every 10 feet, a Swiss festival that seems biweekly, and Swiss music piped throughout the village—sounds dangerously close to tacky tourist trap. Fear not—it's done with class.

So classy, in fact, that in 2002, the Swiss ambassador dropped by to drop off a $4 million check for the establishment in New Glarus of a North American Swiss Heritage Center (www.theswisscenter.org).

Sights

One word can fully encapsulate this town: Festivals. Celebratory shindigs feting the Swiss heritage are held continually. The big draw is the **Wilhelm Tell Pageant,** held on Labor Day since 1938. Virtually the whole town puts on the lederhosen—half of the town in the grandiloquent play of Swiss independence that nobody in the other half can understand but enjoys nonetheless. The real Independence Day, or **Volksfest,** is celebrated with another festival, this one on the first Sunday in August. Swiss consular officials and other dignitaries often make happy appearances. June features a first-week **Polkafest,** a real hoot; and another popular drama during the **Heidi Festival,** on the last full weekend of the month. And, of course, an obligatory **Oktoberfest** goes down in early October. Most of the festivals feature oddities such as Swiss flag throwing (don't ask), yodeling (of course), *thalerschwingen* (let the locals tell you), or any combination of the above.

SOUTHWESTERN WISCONSIN

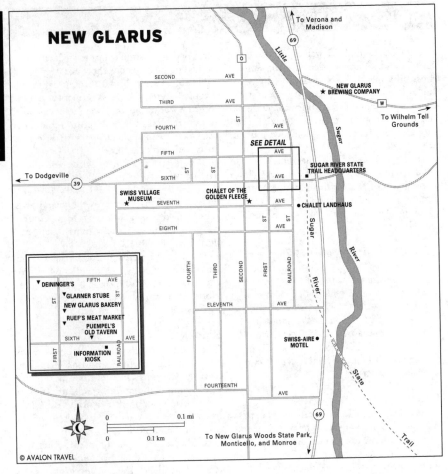

© AVALON TRAVEL

Up the hillsides you'll find 13 buildings comprising the **Swiss Village Museum** (612 7th Ave., 608/527-2317, 10 A.M.–4 P.M. daily May–mid–Oct., $9 adults), centered around flower gardens and an educational exhibit detailing the Swiss immigrant movement to New Glarus; all have period demonstrations. Local schoolchildren sometimes attend class in the old schoolhouse. A display on the Glarner industries of Sap Sago cheese, slate, and fabrics was donated from Glarus, Switzerland.

The **Chalet of the Golden Fleece** (618 2nd St., 608/527-6838) is a Bernese mountain-style chalet built in 1938 by the founder of the village's Wilhelm Tell tradition. Three creakingly full floors have a huge assortment of immigrant everything-but-the-kitchen-sink—artifacts such as Gregorian chants written on parchment from the 15th century, Etruscan earrings, and a host of folk art. Problem is, it's open only for group tours.

New Glarus has, in this, my humble opinion, the best of the state's small-town breweries, the eponymous **New Glarus Brewing Company** (Hwy. W at WI 69, 608/527-5850, www.newglarusbrewing.com, tours and tastings

10 A.M.–4 P.M. daily). The *braumeister,* trained in Europe, reaps accolades and ribbons at every World Beer Championship. Do stop by the brewery's Hilltop site south of town (the original is north of town) for its tasting room and views of the brewery process; self-guided tours (free, but $3.50 for the tasting room) leave daily.

Once a dense wood impeding travel to and from Milwaukee, **New Glarus Woods State Park** (608/527-2335) has arguably the best state park campsites (some bike-in!) in this part of Wisconsin. The 11 hiking miles are excellent, through dense woods or deep valleys. This is the western endpoint of the **Sugar River State Trail,** a 23-mile path from New Glarus to Brodhead along the Sugar River ravine. (In Monticello it will link up to the Badger State Trail.) The whole shooting match is part of the Ice Age National Scenic Trail. In Brodhead, lots of secondary trails branch off, including one to the popular "Half-Way Tree"—a spot used as a landmark by the Winnebago, who knew this point was equidistant between the Mississippi River and Lake Michigan. Bicycles are available for rent at the refurbished New Glarus depot, the trail headquarters.

Off Highway H on the way to Blanchardville is a gorgeous official state Rustic Road, great for a Saturday drive.

Should you wish to get some non-Swiss history, continue to Blanchardville, once a Mormon settlement called Zaramhemba or "City of God." (The Latter-day Saints had fled Illinois after the killing of Joseph Smith.) The only things left are the gravestones in the cemetery at the Highway F and WI 78 junction.

Accommodations

The cheapest lodging in New Glarus is the **Swiss-Aire Motel** (WI 69 S, 608/527-2138 or 800/798-4391, www.swissaire.com, from $69), a basic but clean motel right on the Sugar River Trail.

The **Chalet Landhaus** (801 WI 69, 608/527-5234 or 800/944-1716, www.chaletlandhaus. com, $110) is built in rustic, traditional Swiss style. The main room features a bent staircase, Swiss detailing, and a fireplace. Rooms have

balconies strewn with geraniums, and there are a few suites available with whirlpools.

You'll find loads of quaint farmhouse B&Bs and cottages in the surrounding countryside; the village's website has 'em all, with pictures.

Food

The eateries listed offer any number of Swiss cuisine items. One unique drink is *rivela,* a malted, milky, alcohol-free, sweet sports drink of sorts popular in Switzerland.

Ruef's Meat Market (538 1st St., 608/527-2554, www.ruefsmeatmarket.com, 9 A.M.–4 P.M. Mon.–Wed., to 4:30 P.M. Thurs.–Fri., 10 A.M.–5 P.M. Sat.) offers real-deal Swiss food. Ruef's smokes its own meats and makes *kalberwurst* and *landjaegers.* The best for cheese variety might be **Prima Kase** (W6117 Hwy. C, Monticello, 608/938-4227), a cheesemaker just 10 minutes away in Monticello and the United States' only maker of wheel and sweet swiss cheese.

For delectable Swiss-style baked goods, the **◖ New Glarus Bakery** (534 1st St., 608/527-2916, 7 A.M.–5 P.M. Tues.–Sat., 9 A.M.–4 P.M. Sun., $2–6) is the only stop necessary. The Swiss-trained bakers turn out the house specialty, "Alpenbread," but you might also find stollen, a dense, *two-pound* bread concoction of raisins, spices, marzipan, and almonds, often served at the end of meals or as the centerpiece at brunches.

Along the main drag, **Glarner Stube** (518 1st St., 608/527-2216, lunch and dinner Tues.–Sun., $13–22), on a restaurant site dating from 1901, specializes in fondue (cheese cooked in wine), and *Genschnitzelettes* (tender veal sautéed in white wine sauce). This place is immensely popular and no reservations are taken—so get there early, especially since they close at 8 P.M. Tuesday–Thursday!

◖ Deininger's (119 5th Ave., 608/527-2012, 11:30 A.M.–2 P.M. Sat.–Mon., 4:30–9 P.M. Thurs.–Mon., shorter hours in winter, $10–22) was opened by an Alsace-trained chef and his German wife, both groomed in Chicago eateries. An outstanding restaurant with continental-Swiss-German heavy fare, it's standing-room only on weekends.

The requisite watering hole in New Glarus

is a classic 1893 tavern, **Puempel's Old Tavern** (608/527-2045, www.puempels.com). This is the real thing, with the original back bar, dark woods, high ceilings, and the real draw—patriotic folk-art murals painted in 1913 by Andrea Hofer.

Information and Services

The exceedingly tiny New Glarus **information kiosk** is open and run by the New Glarus chamber of commerce (608/527-2095 or 800/527-6838, www.swisstown.com).

MONROE

Swiss settlers in these parts took cheesemaking from a home industry to a little gold mine just before the crack in the state's wheat industry. Fabulous timing: By the 1880s, about 75 area cheese factories were producing swiss, limburger, gruyere, and other of the more odoriferous varieties of cheese.

How serious is cheese in Monroe? Besides "Swiss Cheese Capital of America" everywhere, the biannual Cheese Days draws in more than 100,000 people for equal parts revelry, education, and respect. Monroe has one of the country's only limburger cheese factories, and the only swiss and gruyere cheese factory still using traditional copper vats is in Monroe. Appropriately, the local high school nickname is the "Cheesemakers"—how's a Monroe Cheesemakers sweatshirt for an ineffably kitschy souvenir?

Beyond this, an official from the National Trust for Historic Preservations once said it best: "If you put up a fence around Monroe, you could charge admission to get in."

Note: Listen to the **Swiss Program,** still heard on local radio station WEKZ 1260 AM, around 1 P.M. Monday–Saturday.

Sights

The nucleus of town is the stately, almost baroque **Green County Courthouse,** with a quad-faced clock on the Yankee-style square. The architecture of Monroe displays an intriguing blend of subtle Swiss, common worker bungalow, and gingerbread Victorian, plus the odd octagon house or two.

The countryside no longer reeks of cheese,

but close. No maker receives more attention than **Alp and Dell** (657 2nd St., 608/328-3355 or 800/257-3335). Carpeted walkways with large viewing windows overlook the famed copper vats, this being the only remaining cheese factory still using traditional copper. It's open during business hours, but it recommends arriving between 9 A.M. and 1 P.M. for optimal cheese-viewing. An aside: Diminutive operation **Franklin Cheese** (7256 Franklin Rd., 608/325-3725, Mon.–Sat., tours by appointment) is one of the few remaining cooperatives in the United States and still offers tours if you ring 'em up first.

Indescribably pleased was this author upon hearing that tours were finally being offered (damn those insurance companies) at the brewery of the college student's staple beer—eminently rich and tasty yet respectfully undervalued Huber. **Minhas Brewing** (1208 14th Ave., 608/325-3191, www.huberbrewery.com, 8 A.M.–5 P.M. Mon.–Fri., 1–5 P.M. Sat.–Sun., closed Sun. in winter, museum free, $10 tour) is the oldest continually operating brewery in Wisconsin (and second-longest in the United States). Tours are daily in summer but complicated, so ring 'em first.

Starting in Monroe, the **Cheese Country Recreational Trail** rides 47 miles of railroadbed. The multipurpose trail parallels the Pecatonica River and touches the edge of Cadiz Springs State Park and its two lakes. A historic 440-foot skeletal bridge is just west of Browntown; the remainder of the trail, passing through Browntown, South Wayne, Gratiot, Darlington, and Calamine, and finishing in Mineral Point, has an additional 55 or so overpasses. Darlington has refurbished its depot into a historic museum. Gorgeous sections of this trail pass through native grass prairie and magnificent stands of oak. In Calamine, the trail links up with the **Pecatonica River State Trail,** which itself runs across the Bonner Branch Valley fork of the Pecatonica and leads to an additional 200 miles of trails. A hefty $6 trail fee is assessed.

See rare (today) Old World alpine Swiss cabinetry and folk painting at the studio of **Gottlieb Brandli** (508 17th Ave., 608/325-6681, 8 A.M.–6 P.M. Mon.–Fri., Sat. by appointment). Gottlieb, a former *Bauernmalerei,*

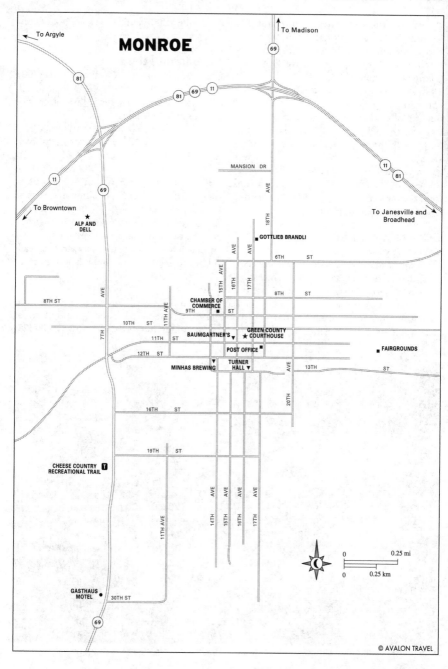

MONROE

To Argyle

To Madison

81

69

81 69 11

11

69

MANSION DR

AVE

18TH AVE

To Browntown

★ ALP AND DELL

11 81

To Janesville and Broadhead

■ GOTTLIEB BRANDLI

6TH ST

AVE

AVE

15TH AVE

16TH AVE

17TH AVE

8TH ST

8TH ST

AVE

CHAMBER OF COMMERCE ■
9TH ST

10TH ST

11TH AVE

7TH AVE

11TH ST

BAUMGARTNER'S ★

GREEN COUNTY COURTHOUSE ★

POST OFFICE ■

■ FAIRGROUNDS

12TH ST

MINHAS BREWING ▼

TURNER HALL ▼

AVE

20TH

13TH ST

16TH ST

19TH ST

CHEESE COUNTRY RECREATIONAL TRAIL 🚂

11TH AVE

14TH AVE

15TH AVE

16TH AVE

17TH AVE

0   0.25 mi

0   0.25 km

GASTHAUS MOTEL ●

30TH ST

69

© AVALON TRAVEL

or Swiss-German folk artist immigrant, has lectured on the stylistics of Alpine design at the Smithsonian. Their custom design work can be viewed at the shop, or drive up to New Glarus to see more of it.

West of Monroe, **Argyle** is a lovely little community on the Pecatonica River. Check out the old gristmill on the river and then head for the old Partridge Hall/Star Theatre and gaze at the lovely trim work (it's a restaurant, so perhaps have a bite to eat). Argyle was the boyhood home of Fightin' Bob La Follette, a legendary Badger progressive politico, and local communities are pitching in to preserve and restore his family's home.

Entertainment and Events
Cheese Days (www.cheesedays.com), held the third weekend of September *of even-numbered years,* has feted "Cheese Country" since 1914 with celebratory fairs, Swiss musicians, fun runs, a street dance, a carnival, exhibitions, an absolutely enormous cheese-flavored parade, and tons and tons of swiss and limburger (including a 200-pound wheel produced on the square over the weekend).

Accommodations
Cheap and good is the **Gasthaus Motel** (685 WI 69 S, 608/328-8395, www.gasthausmotel. com, $50–85), a well-spruced little place with a bonus of bike rentals.

West of town, **(Inn Serendipity** (7843 Hwy. P, 608/329-7056, www.innserendipity. com, $105–125) is in a heavenly, bucolic location, but it's so much more. The innkeepers—corporate refugees from Chicago—show us all what could be done. It's an admirable exercise in purely sustainable living—100 percent powered by renewable sources, organic gardens (their greenhouse even has papayas year-round!), and on and on (it's won virtually every accolade available for their efforts). It's simply a pure escape.

Food
A prerequisite while in Monroe is the local delicacy, the swiss cheese sandwich, at **(Baumgartner's** (1023 16th Ave., 608/325-

A limburger and onion sandwich at Baumgartner's is a classic choice.

6157, from just over $1), a southwestern Wisconsin institution since 1931. It's a cheese shop and locally favorite tavern, though you'd hardly know the supersized cheese operation when waltzing in the front door. Through the swinging saloon doors you'll enter a six-decade-old Shangri-La of small-town life—a long polished bar, wooden-flat ceiling, horn racks, and mural-maps of Wisconsin. Be daring and go native—try limburger and braunschweiger, just like the locals.

Local flavor equally precious is at the wonderful ◖ **Turner Hall** (1217 17th Ave., 608/325-3461, lunch from noon Tues.–Sat.,

dinner Tues.–Sun., $3–7), which serves lunch and dinner and offers a Friday night fish fry. There's great basic Midwestern fare, along with some creative Swiss-style food. There's even a great bowling alley. Show up for polka dances Sunday.

Information and Services
The **Monroe Depot** (2108 7th Ave., 608/325-7648, www.greencounty.org) is a county tourist information center as well as the trail headquarters of the Cheese Country Recreational Trail and a museum and heritage center to cheesemaking.

Cranberry Country

The word "Cranberry" in southwestern Wisconsin essentially means Monroe County and its primary community, Tomah, though 20 counties in the state participate as well. The county is one of the top producers of cranberries in the nation—4.3 million barrels in 2009 (57 percent of the nation's total!).

TOMAH
Forty percent of the state's cranberries are produced within a 15-mile radius. Cranberry heritage is best viewed 12 or so miles to the north (Hwy. E) in Warrens at the **Cranberry Discovery Center** (608/378-4878, www.discovercranberries.com, 9 A.M.–5 P.M. daily Apr.–Oct., shorter hours otherwise, $5 adults). A hands-on museum devoted to the cranberry, this is a fun place with a business-like approach to a vital, local industry. The old-time harvesting equipment is worth the price. Cranberry ice cream can be sampled in the gift shop.

Warrens's September **Cranberry Festival** (www.cranfest.com) is one of the most popular in the state. A red explosion with cranberry products as far as the eye can see, it's a good time to take a bog tour. Organized tours on bike are offered over Memorial Day; 20- to 30-mile tours roll through cranberry marshes,

sphagnum moss drying beds, great blue heron nesting sites, and old European (and one Mormon) homesteading enclaves.

Back in Tomah proper, head to Milwaukee Street and Superior Avenue—better known as "Gasoline Alley," after local boy-done-good Frank King's comic strip, which used Superior Avenue as its inspiration. At the far end of Superior Avenue is Gillett Park, which houses the **Little Red Schoolhouse,** a Civil War–era one-room schoolhouse of which locals are particularly proud.

SPARTA
Bike trail capital—it's on the La Crosse River and Elroy-Sparta State Recreational Trail—Sparta is great for a cyclist's trail-end cooldown. Canoeing is also good along the La Crosse River all the way to the Mississippi. Sparta also has the **Deke Slayton Memorial Space and Bike Museum** (208 Main St., 608/269-0033, www.dekeslayton.com, 10 A.M.–4:30 P.M. Mon.–Sat., 1–4 P.M. Sun. in summer, shorter hours in winter, $3), devoted to the local boy turned NASA astronaut…and bicycling, since it is one hub of Wisconsin biking. More eye-catching is amazing **F.A.S.T Corporation,** northeast of Sparta in Angelo, along WI 21—that's "Fiberglass, Animals,

Shapes, and Trademarks" to you and me. Chances are you've spotted one of the 20-foot fiberglass sculptures of animals, logos, and so on at a business somewhere. The grounds are often liberally strewn with the product, which is why locals refer to it as the "Sparta Zoo."

Even farther north along WI 27/71 is another roadside-kitsch attraction—the **Paul and Matilda Wegner Grotto** (608/269-8680, dawn–dusk daily in summer, free), two miles south of Cataract, a half mile west of the 71/27 split, another in southwestern Wisconsin's lengthy list of folk-art mini masterpieces—concrete sculptures with broken glass and crockery facades, imbued with equal parts patriotism and religious fervor. The philanthropic Kohler Foundation rehabilitated the site and donated it to the county.

Even the town library is worth a look, built to resemble a Roman temple with an open palladian portico and short Ionic support columns.

Practicalities

Perhaps that perfect synthesis of bucolic relaxation and recreation is at the super **(Justin Trails** (7452 Kathryn Ave., 608/269-4522, www.justintrails.com, $135–325), a combination country B&B, Nordic ski area, and even pro disc golf course.

The name says it all at **(Caboose Cabins** (1102 Water St., 608/269-0444, www.caboose-cabins.com, $145)—it warrants a top pick as they really are cabooses and you'll never have more fun sleeping in them!

FORT MCCOY

The only U.S. Army installation in Wisconsin sprawls around the community of Fort McCoy for about 60,000 acres. While this isn't particularly impressive to many travelers, the two recreation areas within the confines are. **Whitetail Ridge Recreation Area** has ski areas and **Pine View Recreation Area** has a beach, boat rentals, mini golf, and a large campground. A rather comprehensive **historical center and equipment park** is also on the base. The historical center is open sporadically; contact the public affairs office (608/388-2407, http://

mccoy.army.mil) for information and to request a great driving tour guide of the base.

For more military history, head east along I-90/94, to Camp Douglas and the **Volk Field Air National Guard Training Site Museum** (608/427-1280, call for hours), an 1890s-era log cabin housing a full history of the National Guard, from the Civil War to the present. The camp also offers tours of the facilities—you can even watch bombing runs. The Hardwood Air-to-Ground bombing range's schedule changes; for more information, call 608/427-1509 for a recording.

Mill Bluff State Park

Along U.S. 12/WI 16 near Camp Douglas and Volk Field is the underappreciated Mill Bluff State Park. A geologist's palette, Mill Bluff is one of the region's only true mesas; most others are a hodgepodge of buttes, or the rarer pinnacle (such as Mill Bluff's Devil's Needle). Inspiring Mill Bluff was so high that when glacial Lake Wisconsin covered all of the central part of the state, this mesa and the assorted buttes around it were rocky islands. The geology is so diverse in this park that it was chosen as one of the nine units of the Ice Age National Scenic Trail. Petroglyphs have been found on bluff faces.

(ELROY-SPARTA STATE RECREATIONAL TRAIL

In a state that popularized the "rails-to-trails" system, the big daddy, the one that pioneered them all—finished in 1967—is the nationally regarded Elroy-Sparta State Recreational Trail. The 32-plus miles, virtually surrounded by wildlife refuge lands, roughly parallel WI 71 and dance with the headwaters of the Kickapoo River, along with the Baraboo River and numerous trout-laden creeks.

There are three otherworldly railroad tunnels, hand-carved into massive limestone rises for the railroad. Two tunnels are a mere quarter mile, but the other—the terrifying Norwalk Tunnel—is a full three-quarters of a mile of drippy, spelunkers'-delight darkness. There are no lights, so bring a flashlight—and a jacket.

© THOMAS HUHTI

buttes near Mill Bluff State Park

It's an ineffable experience—the light at the end of the tunnel disappears and all you can hear in Tunnel 3 is the overhead natural springs cascading through the faults worn in the cement through the passage of time. The tunnels took 2–3 laborious years each to bore out in the 19th century, and at present it can feel as if it takes that long to get through. Tunnel 3 still has the old "keeper's shack" in which a solitary—I daresay lonely—watchman kept vigil on the thunderous doors, clapped shut between trains during winter to protect the tunnels from heaving and cracking from winter cold.

Yet this author's fave part is one mile from Sparta, where the path crosses over I-90; take a break and wave at the truckers to honk!

Trail Passes and Services

Trail passes, available in Kendall, are required; hiking is and always will be free. Rentals and repairs are available at all communities along the route. Of note is Kendall, offering an electric vehicle for people with disabilities and a drop service for a nominal fee.

One-Horse Towns

Kendall's historic railroad depot is now the headquarters for the state trail; it serves as a repository for trail information, as well as being a small museum. Camping is available at the village park, and Kendall, the most "cosmopolitan" along the route, also has a B&B, a motel, and a restaurant, not to mention a great horse- and pony-pull festival on Memorial Day weekend.

Wilton serves a copious, farmhand-size pancake breakfast every Sunday morning Memorial Day–Labor Day; the village park also offers a public campground. (Another campground is directly on the trail—the Tunnel Campground.) Wilton offers bike rentals and has, a mile south, a habitat for rare wood turtles.

In addition to the epic tunnel, **Norwalk** also offers easy access to Tunnel 2 (that is to say, for lazybones just looking for photos). North of town, a flood-control dam has created an additional recreation area. Right on the trail you'll find the Norwalk Cheese Factory.

Elroy

Elroy is the hub of two additional trails—the **400 State Trail** (not 400 miles), stretching to Reedsburg, and the **Omaha Trail,** a 12.5-mile seal-coated trail to Camp Douglas. The coolest accommodations along the trail are the domed units at Union Center's **Garden City Motel** (326 Bridge St., Wonewoc, 608/462-8253). Wonewoc also has an interpretive nature trail as well as a camp hall of the **Modern Woodmen of America** (Hwys. EE and G, 608/983-2352, open Sat. afternoon in summer, generally). The century-old landscape murals covering the entire interior were restored by the Kohler Foundation. It's *quite* a trip, visually. La Valle's **Hemlock Park,** west of town, has great sandstone bluffs for hiking, as well as lakes on either side. The Omaha Trail features another monster tunnel, about 875 creepy feet long. Both trails require trail passes.

The lovely common area of central Elroy links all three trails and features an old depot chock-full of rentals and information for bikers, along with public restrooms. Call (608/462-2453) for information. Saturday nights during summer, the live entertainment is a real hoot.

For practicalities, the **Elroy City Park,** on WI 80/82 on the edge of town, offers a swimming pool and is a good place for a shower. **Waarvik's Century Farm** (N4621 Hwy. H, 608/462-8595, $125) is a fourth-generation family B&B with a separate house and a log cabin, offering a bike shuttle service.

Coulee Range

Best representing what southwestern Wisconsin is all about is a part of Monroe and all of Vernon and Richland Counties. Well within the topography of the challenging coulee country, the area also features excellent state parks, interesting architecture, glimpses of Amish life, and even classic pastoral grazing land.

Scenic Drives

Pick any country road and it will roll, dip, turn back on itself and then seemingly forget itself in gravel and dissipate into something else—but always run along (or over) a creek or past a dilapidated homesteader's cabin, a rusted wreck, an Amish home-bakery, bent-stick furniture maker, or black horse buggy, and through fields of trillium.

The Ontario–La Farge stretches (north of Richland Center), around Wildcat Mountain State Park, are a perfect encapsulation of everything the region offers. Two state-designated Rustic Roads also run within these parameters. The shorter **Tunnelville Road** begins along WI 131 south of La Farge and twists for almost three miles to Highway SS. Spectacular countryside wildflowers line Tunnelville, and there are few people. More popular is the nine-mile trail including Lower Ridge, Sand Hill, and Dutch Hollow Roads, all off WI 131. Dutch Hollow Road is right at the southern tip of Ontario-Amish country. Fantastic old-style architecture—a couple of Vernon County's 15 round barns!—can be seen all along this road, as well as some contour farming. Highway D, east of Cashton, has the **Old Country Cheese** factory (S510 Hwy. D, 608/654-5411, www.oldcountrycheese.com)—a cooperative of hundreds of Amish farmers.

KICKAPOO RIVER WATERSHED

WI 131 runs the course of the Kickapoo River watershed south from Tomah through Wilton, past the river's headwaters north of Ontario and Wildcat Mountain State Park, and into undiscovered federal "wild" lands before hitting its southern half around Soldiers Grove, a total of 65 miles. The Kickapoo River, which doesn't stretch even as far north as Tomah when total the serpentine bights and watery switchbacks, tops out at 120 miles. Thus it has become known as "the crookedest river in the nation," as one soon discovers when canoeing.

AMISH COUNTRYSIDE

In the mid-1960s, "pioneer" Amish began escaping stratospheric land prices, urban encroachment on their pastoral way of life, and droves of camera-toting tourists.

With a verdant landscape resembling the eastern Appalachians, southwestern Wisconsin – Vernon, Trempealeau, and Taylor Counties, along with some in Monroe County – was initially welcoming at first. The region was in an economic depression, and the injection of hard work and cash was much appreciated. But welcome soon turned to uneasiness when the Amish started to "pester" (as locals said) folks incessantly for rides or to use the phone, and when it was discovered that these ardent homeschoolers might be costing the townships state educational aid.

LIFE AND ETHIC

There are approximately 100,000 Amish spread across North America today, and many more Mennonites, who are often mistaken for Amish. The crux of Amish life is a strong community, based on two central tenets: separation and obedience. Separation (from the outer community) is necessary as the "outside" is inherently distracting. The Amish live by an ethereal concept called *gelassenheit*, very roughly translated as "yielding" or "submission to an authority." This is part of the *Ordnung* ("Order"), the unwritten collection of social mores to which each member must subscribe.

There are many kinds of Amish. Old Order Amish are more conservative, but bit by bit more progressive communities are taking hold. For example, some will ride in automobiles, although they still won't drive them; some will use electricity, if it isn't theirs; some own property, and so on. All Amish still cultivate the ethic of hard work, thrift, and community support.

Though most people recognize the Amish by their black horse-drawn carriages, more widely discussed are the dictums regarding electricity. Most, but not all, electricity is banned in Wisconsin Amish communities. Electricity plays a significant role in Wisconsin Amish history for one big reason: milk. America's Dairyland understandably has rather stringent rules pertaining to milk storage and transport. The Amish, if they wanted to conduct commercial operations, had to be up to code, impossible without electricity. After years of negotiations, agreements were reached.

WISCONSIN AMISH TODAY

Population estimates are tough to fix precisely, but it's close to 8,000 statewide. Most are still concentrated in Vernon County – La Farge and Ontario are the largest centers for Amish agriculture in the state.

The Amish are particularly well known for their Old World artisanry. Bent-hickory furniture is a staple of regional shops, as are the meticulously handcrafted quilts. Home-based bakeries and other cottage industries are found along every country road.

© THOMAS HUHTI

Amish life in southwestern Wisconsin

RURAL WISCONSIN AFRICAN AMERICAN HERITAGE

Today the majority of Wisconsin's African American population is concentrated in southeastern counties, particularly Milwaukee, Racine, and Kenosha.

Few realize that the state's African American history goes back to the initial presettlement voyageur exploration, and fewer still realize that the state once had thriving African American rural communities. Of these, perhaps best known was/is Pleasant Ridge in rural Grant County in southwestern Wisconsin.

Pleasant Ridge started in 1850 with the arrival of an ex-slave owner, who relocated to the rolling hills of southwestern Wisconsin from Virginia, along with two of his erstwhile slaves and some of their family members. Whites and blacks settled in the agriculturally fecund (and cheap) region together; settlement grew with a hodgepodge of freed and escaped slaves and other migrants drawn to the "virgin" territory. Within a half decade, there were more than 100 African Americans farming in the county.

This was certainly not utopia – there were two racially motivated murders – but the community achieved remarkable results in cross-racial tolerance, given the time. Blacks and whites intermarried, attended schools together (blacks also went on to college), and farmed land side by side. However, the growth of urban economies shrank the town; by the 1920s Pleasant Ridge was nearly gone.

Another interesting African American community of note was found in the Cheyenne Valley area near Hillsboro in Vernon County. Founders followed a trail similar to that of the early settlers of Pleasant Ridge, making their way from North Carolina and Virginia. By 1880 more than 150 African American residents had settled the area. Their legacy remains in both the population and in the new Cheyenne Settlers' Heritage Park in Hillsboro, the starting point of a regional heritage driving tour detailing the lives of Wisconsin's early African American settlers (for information and a downloadable map, check www.hillsborowi.com).

The original inhabitants of most stretches were the Algonquian Kikapu. The word *kika-pu* translates roughly as "one who travels there, then here," describing quite well both the rolling river as well as the peripatetic Native American tribe (which wound up in the Texas-Mexico region).

Note that the area has seen "road improvements" along WI 131. Safer, yes, but, well, it ain't what it used to be for road-trip fun driving.

◖ Kickapoo Valley Reserve

Many hydrophiles would finger the Kickapoo as numero uno in the state for paddlers. The water is always low, challenging canoeists only during springtime meltoffs or summer deluges, and the scenery is superb—craggy, striated bluffs with pockets of goat prairie, oak savanna, and pine. The Ocooch Mountains along the west fork are legendarily gorgeous.

Escape the madding crowd and head for the depths of the Kickapoo River Impoundment area at Rockton. Or head south to La Farge and beyond to almost 9,000 acres of the Kickapoo Valley Reserve. For two decades, the feds had hemmed and hawed and vacillated over whether to dam the Kickapoo near La Farge, hoping to put a damper on spring floods and create a lake and recreation area. Opposed by some environmentalists, the project never got far off the ground; 1,100 acres were returned to the Ho Chunk Nation and the rest back to nature. Remember: Pockets of private land do exist everywhere, so prudence dictates checking first if you're hoping to leave the river.

The west fork draws lots of serious anglers, and the main fork is almost perfect for lolling rolls. If you do want to start in Ontario (easiest for novices, as the outfitters are all right there), figure 12 hours (more if you like to take your time) to get to La Farge; most operations take you halfway, to Rockton.

The reserve has 50 miles of hiking/biking/ horse trails, along with 21 primitive campsites, most not reachable by car. You must have a permit to use the reserve; costs are $4 daily, $10 more for camping. Information is found at the reserve office (S3661 WI 131 N, La Farge, 608/625-2960, http://kvr.state.wi.us). Another great source of information is the links section of the Kickapoo Valley Association's website (www.driftlesswisconsin.com).

Practicalities

I love both the **Driftwood Inn** (608/337-4660, $55) in Ontario and even more, the **Hotel Hillsboro** (608/489-3000, $60), both for basic but clean and very friendly budget lodging.

La Farge is small, but the countryside, the largest Amish farming area in the state, does have the wonderful **◖ Trillium** (E10596 Salem Ridge Rd., 608/625-4492, www.trilliumcottage.com, $65–105), a private cottage B&B with nook-size rooms and zillions of cushiony pillows. Appropriately named as well, the farm sits on 85 acres of trillium-strewn meadow, forest, and an organic garden.

A lovely drive to the northeast near Hillsboro you'll find the equally admirable **Inn Serendipity Woods** (S 3580 St. Patrick's Rd., 608/329-7056, www.innserendipity. com, $395/795 weekend/week), an A-frame retreat cabin by a pond surrounded by a 30-acre wildlife conservation area. It's run by the same earth-conscious folks who run the top-pick Inn Serendipity in Monroe in southwestern Wisconsin.

If the primitive Kickapoo Reserve sites are full, most campers go to Wildcat Mountain State Park. La Farge's Village Park has primitive sites and does charge a few bucks.

Some fine burgers (never had the steaks but others recommend them) come in Cashton at the **Badger Crossing Restaurant** (909 Front St., 608/654-6706); it's in a cool old 19th-century general store and all meat is made by a local butcher.

WILDCAT MOUNTAIN STATE PARK

This is the best "secret" state park in Wisconsin. It ain't for nothing that the Wisconsin Department of Natural Resources has called this little park one of its "undiscovered gems." It isn't exactly empty, but it's amazing how often it's not full.

The topography is splendid. Canoe the languid Kickapoo a stone's throw from Amish enclaves and some of the southern state's most unusual ecosystems. This is even the only state park that caters to equestrians.

Much of the park's interior is established as a wildlife refuge. Along the line of demarcation separating biotic zones, the natural areas include plant and tree life from northern and southern Wisconsin, some of them rare stands.

Canoeing

The Kickapoo grazes the far northwestern perimeter of the state park and then bends away and doubles back into the park's interior.

Trails

The shortest of three exceedingly short hikes is the **Ice Cave Trail,** south off WI 33 onto Highway F. You could broad-jump to the end of this trail. The **Hemlock Nature Trail** leads into the Mt. Pisgah Hemlock Hardwoods Natural Landmark Area and ascends the mini mighty mountain to the modest pinnacle at 1,220 feet, offering the best views in the park. Look for wild ginseng and trillium, as well as shaggy mane and puffball fungi (not found in too many other places). The longest trail, **Old Settler's,** incorporates pathways foot-hewn by homesteaders.

Camping

The main campground offers 30 sites, but it isn't much to ballyhoo. Not far beyond the park's canoe landing, and east of WI 131, is a primitive campsite.

RICHLAND CENTER

Frank Lloyd Wright was born here in 1869, and several of the community's buildings were designed by the famed architect. Ada James, a

SUFFRAGETTE CITY

Richland Center, Frank Lloyd Wright's birthplace, was also arguably the birthplace of women's suffrage.

This was due to the many women recently successful in the Temperance movement, who then turned their sights onto the equally egregious American predisposition toward sexism. The town was one of the few to allow women to work in the newsrooms of the local papers. Richland Center fiercely debated the inclusion of a suffrage clause in its charter when the city finally incorporated in 1887; it didn't pass, but that galvanized the movement even more.

ADA JAMES

Ada James, a pioneer in U.S. women's suffrage, was born in Richland Center, the daughter of a founding member of one of the original Women's Clubs in the state. James was a po-litical progressive from the start, destined by a familial predilection for activism. In 1910, she founded the Political Equality Club and instituted an unheard-of notion for the time – grassroots campaigning.

James's father and uncle were the first politicians to introduce Wisconsin legislation for suffrage. Both failed, yet James was ultimately successful in dispatching her father to Washington to present Wisconsin's 19th Amendment ratification papers, giving women the right to vote. (Most assumed Wyoming would be the first state to force the issue – many believed Wisconsin's progressives talked the talk but rarely walked the walk.)

As a direct result, four decades later Dena Smith was elected state treasurer in 1960, the first woman elected to a statewide office in Wisconsin. (James herself never held elected office.)

pioneer in U.S. women's suffrage, was also born in Richland Center; she led a second wave of women's rights campaigners to its ultimate fruition with the passage of the 19th Amendment.

Sights

Designer Frank Lloyd Wright dubbed it his "Mayan House," and the red-brick **A. D. German Warehouse,** with its flat roof and concrete frieze, does show some temple overtones. Designed and built in 1915, during what many experts have called the zenith of his artistry, it is one of few surviving structures of this period.

Rockbridge is a well-named spot five miles north of town. Right off WI 80 is legendary **Natural Bridge Park,** right in the Pine River Valley. The site is of historic significance, as it was one of the shelters for Black Hawk and his band in their doomed flight from the U.S. Army in 1832.

In addition to the famed natural bridge, along Highway SR you'll find another oddity, **Steamboat Rock,** as they say around here, "dry-docked above the Pine River." A final rock whittled into the regional menagerie is **Elephant Rock,** viewed along WI 58.

CENTRAL WISCONSIN SANDS

I-39, the four-lane artery clogging the region's midsection, as soulless as any other interstate, generally engenders a lash-the-wheel-and-doze traveling philosophy.

Yet meander a mere mile off and you'll stumble upon a most variegated and challenging topography—multicolored striations in mammoth sandstone cliffs, wetlands, residual prairie and woodland, superb major riverways, and that famous (but underappreciated) gritty soil.

Gazing at a map, it's hard not to notice the Wisconsin River, the Sand Country's most salient feature, slicing through the heart of the region. This "Hardest Working River in the Nation" and its valley have given central-region residents sustenance and have sculpted an amazing topographical diversity. Within the region is Wisconsin's third-highest point (in

the north), flat lands (in the center), and a touch of chocolate-drop undulation (in the southwestern corner). Through it all, the terminal moraine line of glacial advancement meanders north to south from Sauk County to Marathon County near Wausau and then loops back to the south before cutting west out of Wood County.

Eons of primeval lakes and oceans washing in and out of the central region have produced a mishmash of predominantly bog and marshland interspersed with spinneys of forest, bits of grassland, and plenty of agricultural spreads. It also gave the central region its aesthetic highlight—pockets of sandblow, soil-poor but geologically profound. A mile off the otherwise uninspiring interstate, you can find yourself among dunes—real sand dunes,

CENTRAL WISCONSIN SANDS

HIGHLIGHTS

LOOK FOR 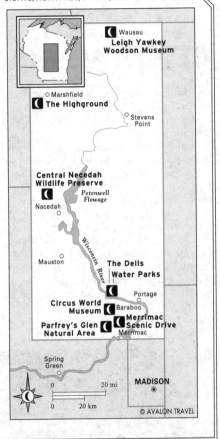 TO FIND RECOMMENDED SIGHTS, ACTIVITIES, DINING, AND LODGING.

The Dells: Absolutely do not miss a river cruise through the otherworldly Upper and Lower Dells of the Wisconsin River (page 390).

Water Parks: Then again, let's be frank. Most come to the Dells for these: the biggest parks, the most slides, the wildest rides, and so on ad nauseam. (page 391).

Circus World Museum: Let everyone scream for joy at the jugglers and clowns at Baraboo's fave spot for kids of all ages (page 398)!

Merrimac Scenic Drive: Roll through glacial terrain to the Merrimac Ferry – among the last free river ferries in the country (page 400).

Parfrey's Glen Natural Area: Devil's Lake State Park features bluff trails and obsidian waters. Yet how can so many miss the real highlight (page 403)?

Central Necedah Wildlife Preserve: Here, find a splendid locale for spotting cranes (page 408).

The Highground: The drive here runs through charming communities and stops at the inspiring Highground Memorial, a beckoning for world peace (page 416).

Leigh Yawkey Woodson Museum: Wausau's wowser of a museum draws visitors for its amazing ornithological art collections (page 417).

in the landlocked Midwest. If it weren't for the hardy evergreens in lieu of cacti, you'd swear you were in the Sonoran desert.

HISTORY

According to stratigraphic dating, a spot in the southwestern tip of this region (Natural Bridge State Park) is one of the oldest inhabited sites in the Upper Midwest. Early settlement of this point was logical, since the glacial lobes had stopped dead at just about this point. As

the glaciers retreated, the Paleo-Indians forged north with them.

European expansion into south-central Wisconsin was second only to that in the Fox River Valley. From the famed portage between the Fox and Wisconsin Rivers arose the town of the same name, and from there, intrepid fur traders plying the Wisconsin were followed by hardy settlers, who found the sandy or marshy soils often unsuited for agriculture. Timber opportunists found the northern stretches of

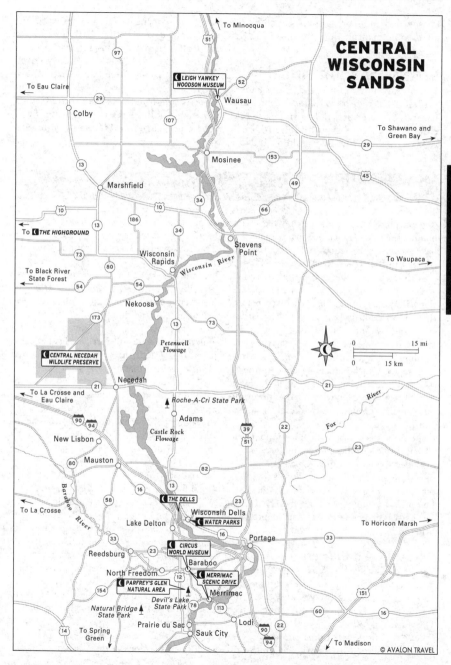

CENTRAL
WISCONSIN
SANDS

To Minocqua

To Eau Claire

Colby

LEIGH YAWKEY
WOODSON MUSEUM

Wausau

To Shawano and
Green Bay

Mosinee

Marshfield

To THE HIGHGROUND

Wisconsin
Rapids

Stevens
Point

To Waupaca

To Black River
State Forest

Nekoosa

Petenwell
Flowage

CENTRAL NECEDAH
WILDLIFE PRESERVE

To La Crosse and
Eau Claire

Necedah

Roche-A-Cri State Park

Fox River

Adams

Castle Rock
Flowage

New Lisbon

Mauston

Baraboo River

To La Crosse

THE DELLS

Wisconsin Dells

WATER PARKS

Lake Delton

To Horicon Marsh

Portage

Reedsburg

CIRCUS
WORLD MUSEUM

Baraboo

North Freedom

PARFREY'S GLEN
NATURAL AREA

MERRIMAC
SCENIC DRIVE

Merrimac

Natural Bridge
State Park

Devil's Lake
State Park

Prairie du Sac

Sauk City

Lodi

To Spring
Green

To Madison

0   15 mi

0   15 km

© AVALON TRAVEL

dense woodland more hospitable, and by the 1820s, a permanent white presence had been hacked out of the forests.

PLANNING YOUR TIME

You simply must come and experience a summertime trip to Wisconsin Dells and its orgy of water parks. That'll be a weekend, but then you've got hiking in Devil's Lake, circus clowns in Baraboo, and the whole Wisconsin River to explore! So let's call it four days. The first day and a half in the **Dells,** then a day (or so) in **Baraboo/Devil's Lake State Park** (definitely do the Merrimac Scenic Drive), and keep following the Wisconsin River north via **Portage** (the historic canal), **Necedah** (the Central Necedah Wildlife Preserve), **Stevens Point** (awesome nature), to **Wausau** (whitewater and a gorgeous museum).

Wisconsin Dells

Once nothing more than a sleepy backwater bend in the river—albeit one that happened to have the most spectacular stretches of riverside geology in the state—the Wisconsin Dells is now the state's number one tourist attraction, with a capital "T." Door County (not to mention Milwaukee) might squawk a bit at that statistic, but thanks in part to a public-relations campaign rivaling a presidential election, the Dells has become for some the free-associative symbol of Wisconsin. Three *million* people visit the Dells each year. They come for the inspiring 15-mile stretch of the upper and lower dells of the Wisconsin River, a serpentine, tranquil journey through breathtakingly beautiful 150-foot sandstone bluffs.

This popularity has not come without controversy. Spirit-killing crass commercialism has exploded in all directions. (One national tour operator association tagged it with the dubious honor of the "tackiest place in America.") So much development has gone on that Dells businesses, desperate for workers, contract to bring in foreign college students.

Serpents and Glaciers

The media kit on the Wisconsin Dells does a great PR two-step on the region's history by juxtaposing images and text from a Ho Chunk Nation tribal member and a University of Wisconsin geology professor. The Ho Chunk attributes the geology to an age-old serpent that slithered southward along the Wisconsin River fleeing the frigid beginnings of the ice ages. Upon reaching a large rock wall, it plowed through, scattering smaller snakes ahead of it. Voila!—a riverway and smaller canyons. The professor dryly explains that the Dells came about from the ineluctable advance of billions of tons of ice, primeval seas, and more—long before the ice ages. Take your pick. Somehow, the lower region of the Wisconsin River managed to carve magnificent dells through intensely colored sandstone escarpments.

Several state natural areas have been established in the canyons. The sandstone facings are home to unique plant species, including the state's only native rhododendron (endangered) and cliff cudweed, an aster found only in Wisconsin.

Human History

Indians of the Ho Chunk (formerly Winnebago) Nation were the first inhabitants in the region. Little European settlement took place until Newport sprouted up five miles south of present-day Wisconsin Dells, at a site where Indian trails and wagon-train routes had always naturally come together. A rival community, Kilbourn—expediently named itself after a railroad magnate—got the trains to stop there, and Newport shriveled up and effectively blew away.

Stopover rail passengers soon discovered the multihued striations of the sandstone, and by

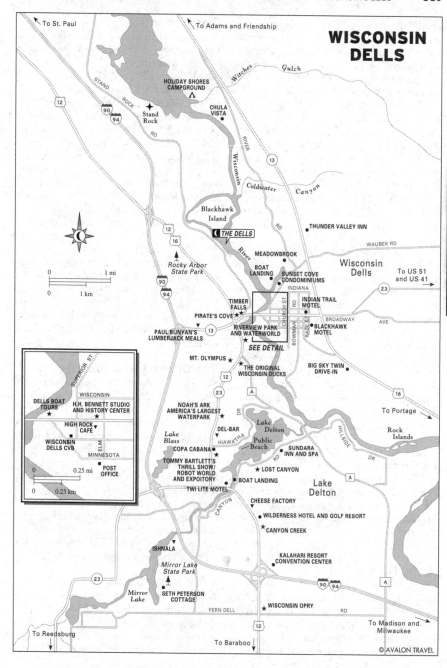

WISCONSIN DELLS

To St. Paul

To Adams and Friendship

Witches Gulch

HOLIDAY SHORES CAMPGROUND

CHULA VISTA

STAND ROCK RD

Stand Rock

STAND ROCK RD

Wisconsin River

Coldwater Canyon

Blackhawk Island

THE DELLS

THUNDER VALLEY INN

WAUBEK RD

Wisconsin Dells

To US 51 and US 41

Rocky Arbor State Park

River

MEADOWBROOK

BOAT LANDING

SUNSET COVE CONDOMINIUMS

INDIANA

TIMBER FALLS

PIRATE'S COVE

INDIAN TRAIL MOTEL

BROADWAY

PAUL BUNYAN'S LUMBERJACK MEALS

RIVERVIEW PARK AND WATERWORLD

SEE DETAIL

BLACKHAWK MOTEL

AVE

MT. OLYMPUS

THE ORIGINAL WISCONSIN DUCKS

BIG SKY TWIN DRIVE-IN

NOAH'S ARK AMERICA'S LARGEST WATERPARK

DEL-BAR

Lake Delton

To Portage

Rock Islands

Lake Blass

Public Beach

SUNDARA INN AND SPA

COPA CABANA

TOMMY BARTLETT'S THRILL SHOW/ ROBOT WORLD AND EXPOSITORY

LOST CANYON

BOAT LANDING

Lake Delton

TWI LITE MOTEL

CHEESE FACTORY

WILDERNESS HOTEL AND GOLF RESORT

CANYON CREEK

ISHNALA

Mirror Lake State Park

KALAHARI RESORT CONVENTION CENTER

Mirror Lake

SETH PETERSON COTTAGE

FERN DELL

WISCONSIN OPRY

RD

To Madison and Milwaukee

To Reedsburg

To Baraboo

© AVALON TRAVEL

0   1 mi
0   1 km

Detail

SUPERIOR ST

WISCONSIN

DELLS BOAT TOURS

H.H. BENNETT STUDIO AND HISTORY CENTER

HIGH ROCK CAFÉ

WISCONSIN DELLS CVB

ELM

MINNESOTA

POST OFFICE

0   0.25 mi
0   0.25 km

the 1850s, individual rowboats were carrying well-to-do passengers up and down the river between train stops. In the 1870s, George Crandall started the first riverboats and steamships up and down the waters. By the 1880s, encroaching development threatened the shoreline.

Crandall may have started the whole touristic expansionism of the Dells, but he is also credited with applying the first preservation pressure to protect this stretch of magical beauty. He used the tourism money he'd amassed and began making wholesale riverfront purchases, letting the land revert to its natural state and planting trees where settlers had clear-cut. He also established a conservation trust to see that others didn't muck it up later.

Crandall more than likely saved the day, although he was aided by the fact that newspapers nationwide were publishing photos of the area by Henry Hamilton Bennett, the inventor of the stop-action shutter. The pictures included the legendary first freeze-frame photograph—of Bennett's son jumping the crevasse at Stand Rock.

By 1931, tourism was firmly entrenched as the region's number one economic base. Town fathers, in another expedient move, later renamed the town the more mellifluous Wisconsin Dells.

It hasn't much ebbed yet. Hotels and motels knock out end walls every September to expand yet again. Every week another ride, attraction, feature, or museum is added. Still, for all its garish kitschiness and frustrating inanity, the town has managed to protect the beauty of the dells themselves. Once you're on the river, just a few miles from the strip, you get the feeling old George Crandall isn't spinning in his grave after all.

A Big Note

Do your homework. The Dells don't come cheap. It's not so much Big Apple pricing as the preponderance of stuff to see and do. Remember: This place caters slavishly to the traveler, so literally zillions of coupons, package deals, partnerships, and more are out there.

Orientation

Wisconsin Dells is effectively a sister city to **Lake Delton;** you can hardly tell the two strips of highway apart.

◖ THE DELLS

So what exactly is all the fuss about? Well, there are freaks of nature with oddball names such as Devil's Elbow, Fat Man's Misery, Witches Gulch, Cold Water Canyon, and others along 15 miles of upper and lower dells, and everywhere you see craggy palisades and soft-hued sandstone. The trademark of the Wisconsin Dells is **Stand Rock,** a mushroom-shaped sandstone protuberance made famous in 19th-century, first-of-its-kind, stop-action photography. Stand Rock is accessible via Highway A and Stand Rock Road to the north of town.

Rental operations can set you up for personal scenery-snooping; a public boat launch is right off the strip. **Lake Delton Water Sports** (U.S. 12 bridge, 608/254-8702, www.dells-watersports.com) has paddleboats, kayaks, canoes, pontoon boats, ski boats, and even parasail rides.

The Original Wisconsin Ducks

Some absolutely swear by the Ducks. The Ducks (608/254-8751, www.wisconsin-ducktours.com, tours 8 A.M.–7 P.M. daily Apr.–Oct., shorter hours the rest of the season, $24.50 adults) are green-and-white, 14,000-pound behemoth amphibious World War II (the real thing) landing craft. These roar (quite literally, albeit slowly) along the main drag of the Dells, picking up passengers for a one-hour, eight-mile-plus trip that includes jaunts through restored prairie lands and access to wilderness trails. You won't have any trouble finding a Ducks info kiosk. Tours depart whenever enough passengers show up.

Dells Army Ducks

Not to be confused with the Original Wisconsin Ducks, this operation (608/254-6080, www.dellsducks.com, tours 9 A.M.–6 P.M. daily in summer, 10 A.M.–4 P.M. daily May and Sept., $24 adults) also tours the Lower Dells Islands.

© WISCONSIN DELLS VISITOR & CONVENTION BUREAU

a WWII vintage Duck – the only way to travel in the Dells

Tours depart the main dock along U.S. 12 every 15–20 minutes. The company also runs the **Mark Twain Yacht Tour,** taking in 15 sites along the river.

Dells Boat Tours

This operation (608/254-8555, www.dells-boats.com) uses modern cabin cruisers and offers separate Upper Dells tours (two hours), the only boat tour that offers a stop at Stand Rock, another Dells trademark. The Lower Dells tour takes half as long. Tours operate about every 20–30 minutes, 8:30 A.M.–6 P.M. daily in high season, less frequently in lower spring and fall seasons mid-April–October. Upper Dells tours cost $23, $10 for children 6–12; the Lower Dells trip is $18 adults. A combination ticket for both tours costs $31 adults. How about tours on 700-hp jet boats? Right—nothing like the tranquility of the Dells at 40 mph.

◖ WATER PARKS

Mere minutes in the Dells and your eyeballs begin to prune from just looking at all the water.

Yup, right here are more big-draw water parks than in any other U.S. tourist trap. Consider this thumbnail sketch of the highlights a mere appetizer for your inner hydrophile!

The granddaddy is the Brobdingnagian-in-scope **Noah's Ark, America's Largest Waterpark** (S. U.S. 12/WI 23, 608/254-6351, www.noahsarkwaterpark.com, 9 A.M.–8 P.M. daily Memorial Day weekend–Labor Day, $36 adults). This place is housed on *70 acres* with more than 60 separate activities. The nuts and bolts: On-site are three dozen waterslides, two wave pools, a kiddie pool, mini golf, bumper boats, kids' world, go-carts, a surf pool, a white-water raft adventure, and oh, so much more. Its legendary Big Kahuna is one of the largest wave pools in the country—big enough to offer surfing. The Incredible Adventure is a water ride with the effects of a roller coaster (a 10-story, five-second drop). And there's the Time Warp, on which you race down at 30 miles per hour into the nation's largest "family bowl." There's also the Scorpion's Tail, a 10-story drop (50 feet per second), with a nearly vertical loop. All told, nearly five million gallons of water gush through the place.

Mt. Olympus (S. U.S. 12, 608/254-2490, www.mtolympuspark.com, $39 adults) is another original city-state-size park à la Noah's Ark—1.3 million square feet (indoor and out), which makes it the world's largest water resort. (Technically, it's more than a half dozen parks and properties combined that have transmogrified into a megalopolis of fun.) More than three dozen waterslides are the highlight, but on its crown jewel, Poseidon's Rage, two million gallons of water create a nine-foot wave. This author must vouch for its go-carts—again, on the largest course in the world—including racing underwater *and* through the colossal wooden Trojan Horse that has become a landmark in town.

Riverview Park and Waterworld (S. U.S. 12, 608/254-2608, www.riverviewpark.com) is another big'un, totaling 75 attractions and specializing in kids (four children's activities pools alone) with 30 hydrocentered attractions all along The Beach. And it has the best go-carts—mini Grand Prix driving! Even one of the United States' largest Ferris wheels is here. Ticket packages vary wildly but you can get an online pass for ten bucks!

OTHER SIGHTS
Tommy Bartlett's Thrill Show

Just count the "Tommy Bartlett" bumper stickers on Wisconsin roads. For more than 45 years, this man and his show have defined the Dells (though it's run by others now). It runs three times daily, rain or shine, through Labor Day. It's a two-hour grand mélange of vaudeville, three-ring circus, laser light show, and sheer daredevil gonzo on the stunt boats, or, perhaps contortionists and frenetic juggling acts. One of the best acts is the Sky Flyers Aerial Helicopter Trapeze. Tickets to the water-ski show (560 Wisconsin Dells Pkwy., 608/254-2525, www.tommybartlett.com) are $16, $23 reserved seating.

Adjacent to the ski show is **Tommy Bartlett's Robot World and Exploratory** (8 A.M.–10 P.M. daily Memorial Day weekend–Labor Day, 10 A.M.–4 P.M. the rest of the year, $12 adults), a surreal mix of high-tech and kitsch set aboard an intergalactic cruiser and house of the future. Hundreds of hands- and feet-on activities explore gravity, energy, light, and motion. Robots actually guide the tours. The original MIR space station is here too!

Broadway: Museums, Freaks, and Kitsch

The Dells' main drag is Broadway, the netherworld of Americana, commercialism, and bad T-shirts. Duck into a couple haunted houses or have your picture taken Wild West style, or perhaps engage in laser tag or some sort of wizard quest. Top it all off with a sarsaparilla at an old timey saloon!

H. H. Bennett Studio and History Center

This museum (215 Broadway, 608/253-3523, hhbennettstudio.wisconsinhistory.org, 10 A.M.–5 P.M. daily May–Oct., weekends only spring and fall, $7 adults), the *yin* cultural spirit to Broadway's *yang* weirdness, is the historic former studio of renowned photographer H. H. Bennett, the man who literally put the Dells on the map a century ago with his glass negative prints of the sandstone escarpments (developed in the oldest darkroom and photographic studio in the United States). There are interactive exhibits, with the overall theme of the evolution of the Dells region from prehistory to the 21st century, and, obviously, lots of photography is featured—vintage prints adorn the walls. The Ho Chunk Nation isn't overlooked.

Steam Train

A real 15-inch narrow-gauge railway (albeit on a one-quarter scale) journey begins at Hyde Park Station, a mile north of the Dells on Stand Rock Road. The **Riverside and Great Northern Railway** (608/254-6367, trains depart throughout the day, $12 adults) takes you three miles through the countryside and takes in all the great Dells sights.

Mini Golf

Duffer-delight holes abound in the Dells; the architectural ambition of some of the courses is mind-boggling. Top of the line is the lushly astroturfed **Pirate's Cove** (U.S. 12 and WI 13/16/23, 608/254-8336), overlooking the sandstone sentinel rises. Pirate's Cove also has the longest average holes in the Dells. For $13 you get 18 holes and admission to their new family fun center.

Timber Falls (Wisconsin River Bridge and Stand Rock Rd., 608/254-8414) allows one to whack a ball within sight of the river (and the courses have shade!). It also has its famous Timber Mountain Log Flume Ride, a soaking-wet quarter-mile ride, partly through total darkness and then up and around a 40-foot mountain before the plummet. Enjoy—this baby cost more than $2 million and is one of only five in the country. A $20 pass lets you play 90 holes of golf and ride the log flume among almost every other ride.

Horse and Wagon Rides

One tradition in the Dells is taking a jaunt through the narrow back canyons via **Lost Canyon** (608/254-8757, 8:30 A.M.–dusk daily

DOIN' THE DELLS

The first road signs – huge and color-splashed and screamingly designed – crop up somewhere around Madison if you're coming in from the south. With each mile clicked, the traveler becomes more fully informed as to the delights that the distant oasis offers. It's a numbing – nay, insulting – onslaught of countryside visual pollution.

There are those (this author included) who believe – stridently – that the Wisconsin "experience" necessitates, without dissent, a descent into the kitschy, cacophonic purgatory of the Strip in the Dells and Lake Delton, that multi-mile Middle America meander clogged (by 10 A.M.) with belching RVs and minivans disgorging sunburned consumers like Marines wading ashore in Normandy. It's a giant corny shakedown.

Obscenity or pure Americana? Well, both. It's got the classic symptoms of a Niagara Falls: magnificent aesthetics and geological history mashed with the dizzying clatter of a tourist trap run amok. There are miles and seemingly endless miles of water parks and water parks and water parks and braying, tape-looped freak-shows, embarrassingly stupid knickknacks and curio shops, miniature golf courses, a Statue of Liberty–size Trojan horse, go-carts, bungee jumping, helicopter rides, an odd casino or two, otherwise rational people with arrows sticking out of their heads, and – oh, yes – a ticket tout on every corner. The entire design of this Wisconsin city is aimed at the sheer, unadulterated, hedonistic delight of the child, real and inner. Parents have to choke on the exhaust, pray for parking, and get in line to start shelling out the cash.

And it's wonderful – every damn frightening, wearying second of it. Sure, the jaded, the agoraphobic, the old, and anyone who opposes sprawling economic explosion should hunker down and barrel on through this area without stopping. But for those who appreciate an absolutely indescribable, surreal slice of Americana at its most over the top, it's a trip.

in high season, $9.50 adults). The simple half-hour trips on wagons accommodate up to 15 people and leave every 15 minutes from the south shore of Lake Delton. The operation also has a separate stable for individual horseback riding, **Canyon Creek** (608/253-6942), south on U.S. 12; basic rates start at $20 per hour with a coupon. Children also get a pony ring.

ENTERTAINMENT
Big Sky Twin Drive-In
Catch it while you can, this nearly dead American tradition. Two huge screens show four shows nightly—all first-run Hollywood stuff. The snack bar is huge. Big Sky (608/254-8025) is one mile south via U.S. 16E.

Wisconsin Opry
Though Nashville's Grand Ole Opry stars do make appearances here (U.S. 12 at I-90/94, 608/254-7951 or 800/453-2593, $15 show, $31 show and dinner for adults), usually it's regional or local acts performing in the state's only real country music performance venue. Shows are at 8 P.M. Monday–Saturday late May–late September. Tuesday matinees are also offered. A country-style dinner package with show is available. A weekend flea market is ongoing on the grounds, and hayrides are a popular new attraction. The Opry is really a slick, professional operation, according to many.

EVENTS
The biggest festival of the year in the Dells is January's **Flake Out Festival** (www.flakeout-festival.com), with a host of winter activities, including snowmobile radar running, music, and the state's only sanctioned snow-sculpting competition.

The newest festival, May's **Automotion,** is a showcase of nearly 1,000 cars—antiques, street machines, and classics—that includes swap meets, a car corral, cruises, and motorcycle classes.

Fall is feted with not one but two blow-outs: the **Wo-Zha-Wa** autumn welcome in mid-September, followed by **Autumn Harvest Fest** in mid-October, with lots of scarecrow stuffing, pumpkin carving, food, and very scenic boat, train, and Duck tours.

ACCOMMODATIONS

It's hard to believe that with room numbers totaling nearly 7,000, at times finding a place to stay in peak season without a reservation can be a chore. Still, odds aren't too bad that there's going to be something out there—excluding major holidays. And what a bizarre and entertaining range of accommodations there is.

The area has nearly two dozen "official" water-park resorts (that is, those of 5,000 square feet or more), but everyplace has somewhere to splash—indeed, consultants intone sagely that any lodging option without an indoor water park is not economically feasible for the long haul.

Unless otherwise stated, all options are open year-round; plenty of others are seasonal. Single-night stays on weekends in summer are not allowed at many places.

During the high summer months, you'll pay no less than $50 a night for one person, and as much as $200 in a swankier place. Weekly rentals cost less, and securing a multiperson cabin and splitting the cost is a great way to save funds.

Consider: Basic motels are losing out seriously to water-themed resorts and in recent years several were offering doubles for as low as $40, even during Memorial and Labor Day weekends! These motels, desperate for business, also often have connections for discounted tickets to water parks.

The usual rule: If you can stay Monday through Thursday, you save a bundle on lodging. Off-season, rates can dip as low as $30 for a single. All prices listed are the lowest high-season rates.

Under $50

Good luck. Not to be flip, but June–August, be glad you find anything near $50. That said,

show up Monday–Thursday and the Dells do have some $50-ish options, including the **Twi Lite Motel** (111 Wisconsin Dells Pkwy. S, 608/253-1911, $49–60). Absolutely no frills but it's a decent place with a pool and some room fridges. This is incredible pricing for this area.

Camping is always an option. Public options are **Mirror Lake and Rocky Arbor State Parks.** Mirror Lake is just south of Lake Delton along U.S. 12 and is the better known—and, thus, more populated—of the two. Considering it's a large-capacity campground (145 sites), privacy is fairly decent. Rocky Arbor is closer to the Dells and not as well-known.

Eighteen private campgrounds are in and around the Dells. Come summertime, they will be chock-full and boisterous—not an isolated, bucolic experience. A large popular operation is the **Holiday Shores Campground** (3900 River Rd., 608/254-2717, www.holiday-shores.com, $26–36), a resort operation along the Wisconsin River with camping available in a separate tenting area, along with a whole catalog of extras.

$50-100

The **Indian Trail Motel** (1013 Broadway, 608/253-2641, www.indiantrailmotel.com, $69) is always a good budget option. A motel on 15 acres, it remains within walking distance to downtown—for that it created nature trails! All rooms have fridges and microwaves; amenities include a whirlpool and sauna, laundry, and restaurant.

No rooms? Excellent too is the **Blackhawk Motel** (720 Race St., 608/254-7770, www.blackhawkmotel.com, $75), which many, many folks have written to me about. It's clean and reasonable, and the owners are friendly.

One of the best B&Bs in the Midwest is the isolated Scandinavian-style 130-year-old farm-hus, the ◖ **Thunder Valley Inn** (W15344 Waubeek Rd., 608/254-4145, www.thunder-valleyinn.com, $69–145), also a sublime eatery. Original farm rooms have Franklin stoves; some feature balconies overlooking the woods.

Even little cabins tucked into trees are available. Entertainment includes fiddling hoedowns and some weekend chautauquas (outdoor cultural education assemblies) and threshing suppers.

$100-150

A secluded option for families is the cottage colony on 12 acres, **Meadowbrook** (1533 River Rd., 608/253-3201, www.meadowbrookresort.com, $99–300), featuring a log motel, log lodge, and rustic cabins. Amenities include a huge pool, playground, large expanse of grounds, barbecue grills, and picnic tables. Some find it kitschy or not-so-delightfully retro; others (and this author) find it just fine, kind of like the old days.

Budget friendly is the smaller resort **Copa Cabana** (611 Wisconsin Dells Pkwy., 800/364-2672, www.copacabanaresort.com, from $130), with perfectly lovely rooms and indoor/outdoor water parks.

Over $150

The only resort along the Upper Dells is

Sunset Cove Condominiums (Upper Dells, 608/254-6551, www.sandcounty.com, $150–255). There's a gorgeous view of Crandall Bay, all units are spacious and have patios, and it's just a hop to downtown. There are plenty of extras, including a private marina.

Best-known along River Road is undoubtedly **Chula Vista** (4031 N. River Rd., 608/254-8366, www.chulavistaresort. com, $199–300), a full-service resort on seriously attractive grounds. The resort is redecorated in a Southern California "desert oasis" theme. It isn't tacky, as it may sound. A centerpiece is the 150,000-square-foot outdoor water park and 110,000-square-foot indoor water-park areas (plural necessary), not to mention grounds large enough for nature trails and hiking trails. Myriad rooms and suites are available; the themed fantasy suites are popular.

The 🄲 **Kalahari Resort Convention Center** (1305 Kalahari Dr., 608/254-5466, www.kalahariresort.com, $219–429) is a whopping *125,000 square feet* (and, naturally,

the Swahili Swirl, Kalahari Resort

growing) of fun, once again—*the largest indoor water park in the United States* (number three in the world, but give it time). Highlights include: a 920-foot-long indoor "river" (kids walk, parents do the "current walk"), numerous two- to four-person raft/tube rides, the country's only uphill water slide, water walks, body flume rides, and even a zoo. Still not interested? How about the world's largest indoor wave pool? All of this is in a funky African-themed style. Parents will love the new spa. Rooms have satellite TV, hair dryer, fridge, microwave, hot tub, and fireplace.

Another massive operation with endless additions is the **(Wilderness Hotel and Golf Resort** (511 E. Adams St., 800/867-9453, www.wildernessresort.com, $200–400). All 135,000 square feet of outdoor (65,000 square feet indoor) water fun are exclusively for guests. The absolute draw here is the spanking new $150 million high-tech foil dome that lets in sunlight. Yup, January tanning in Wisconsin! Otherwise, there's a championship golf course and the well-regarded Field's at the Wilderness restaurant. Luxury condo rooms and cabins in the woods are also available.

Inside tranquil Mirror Lake State Park in Lake Delton is the **(Seth Peterson Cottage** (608/254-6551, www.sethpeterson. org, $275), a Frank Lloyd Wright–designed cottage available for overnighting (the only one, actually). It's been described as having "more architecture per square foot than any other building Wright designed." The one-room cottage with a splendid view is fully furnished with a complete kitchen, enormous stone fireplace, flagstone terrace, floor-to-ceiling French doors and windows, and complete seclusion. Reservations are necessary very far in advance. Tours ($2) are also available 1–4 P.M. the second Sunday of every month.

The most sybaritic choice in the Dells is without question **(Sundara Inn and Spa** (920 Canyon Rd., 888/735-8181, www.sundaraspa. com, $320–700), the only free-standing spa devoted exclusively to luxury pampering. It's won oodles of major awards in the industry—for its devotion from luxury to eco-mindedness—and been absolutely gushed over by media. It offers simply otherworldly comfort and serenity, especially in the amazing villas. The organic cuisine is heaven-sent, too.

FOOD

Many, but by no means all, of these restaurants are open seasonally. These usually bolt shut for the winter sometime between late October and December, reopening in May.

Family-Style Dining

Paul Bunyan's Lumberjack Meals (near I-90/94 and WI 13 junction, 608/254-8717, 7 A.M.–9 P.M. daily, $10) is every kid's favorite place to eat. All-you-can-cram-in meals are served, specializing in breakfast and chicken-and-rib feeds.

New American

Broadway's strip is generally a fried-food or raucous bar hell. But how wonderful then is **High-Rock Café** (232 Broadway, 608/254-5677, lunch and dinner daily, $7–13)? It has creative but not trendy cuisine; it's cool but not chic. And it's healthy. They have tapas till 2 A.M. as well, bless 'em.

Supper Clubs

The **(Del-Bar** (800 Wisconsin Dells Pkwy. S, 608/253-1861, 4:30–9:30 P.M. daily, $17–39) is a six-decade-old institution in the Dells. Bistro-cum-supper club, it has the most exquisite custom dry-aged Angus steaks and prime rib as well as some excellent seafood. Even better is the ambience—the building was designed by a protégé of Frank Lloyd Wright, and the dining rooms feature fireplaces.

Ishnala (Ishnala Rd., 608/253-1171, 5–10 P.M. daily, $12–30) offers superlative vistas on a 100-acre spread of meadow overlooking Mirror Lake, as well as 40 years of steaks, prime rib (it serves literally tons of this during the year), seafood, ribs, and a house special roast duck and baby-back pork ribs. Before-dinner cruises are available. Check out the Norway pines growing right through the roof.

Vegetarian

In the prime rib heartland of Americana, the **C** **Cheese Factory** (521 Wisconsin Dells Pkwy., 608/253-6065, www.cookingvegetarian.com, 9 A.M.–9 P.M. daily in high season, Thurs.–Sun. thereafter, $5–13) features— believe it or not—world-class international vegetarian cuisine. Carnivores should belay their skepticism and indulge—you'll go away wowed. (The cookbook produced by this restaurant is one of the Internet's best sellers.) The interior of the multilevel 1940s-theme eatery retains the original knotty pine and oak. Live entertainment is offered on weekends. An espresso and specialty coffee bar sits next to a great ice-cream soda fountain.

Farm Restaurant

Take a wondrous step back in time. Just north of town stands a pocket of old country dwellings, the **C** **Thunder Valley Inn** (W15344 Waubeek Rd., 608/254-4145, www.thundervalleyinn.com, hours vary). It's a working farm with goats and chickens dashing about; chores are optional. The food is in the grand Old World style, from German potato salad to roast chicken, and the inn does a superb fish fry. Many ingredients are grown on-site; the restaurant even grinds its own wheat and rye berries. This is *the* spot for breakfast; the family-style breakfast is worth much more than the price, considering the work that goes into it, and each bite is a bit of Wisconsin culinary heritage (such as unbeatable Norwegian pancakes with lingonberries). Hours vary a lot, depending on shows, so call ahead. You'll need a reservation for the dinner shows and/or chautauquas. The restaurant is open seasonally, the inn year-round.

INFORMATION AND SERVICES

The **Wisconsin Dells Visitors and Convention Bureau** (701 Superior St., 608/254-4636 or 800/223-3557, www.wisdells.com) is a gem of professionalism and helpfulness. June–August it's open basically dawn to dark (no exaggeration), shorter hours thereafter.

GETTING THERE
By Bus

Wisconsin Dells has no central bus station. **Greyhound** (800/231-2222, www.greyhound.com) buses arrive and depart from the Travelmart station (611 Frontage Rd., 608/254-5077).

By Train

Amtrak (www.amtrak.com) stops at the junction of Superior and Lacrosse Streets north of downtown; this stop has no quick ticket machine, so you'll have to use the Web or a travel agent.

Vicinity of the Dells

BARABOO

If you had to draw up quaint little communities for tourist brochures, this could be the model, a Tinytown, USA, where life still revolves around the courthouse square. Baraboo consistently earns top-10 finishes in its category in media rankings of livability quotients of U.S. cities.

And then there's the circus. Though Baraboo has always been an important regional cog in dairy distribution, the local circus museum is what really draws folks. In 1882, a family of enterprising local German farmboys named Ringling, much enamored of a traveling troupe's performance in Iowa, organized the Ringling Brothers' Classic and Comic Concert Company. Thus began that "greatest show." Wisconsin would become the "Mother of Circuses"—more than 100 circuses have had their origins and based their operations here.

Baraboo was home to the Greatest Show on Earth until 1918, and the Ringlings' legacy remains its biggest draw.

◖ Circus World Museum

The site of the Circus World Museum (426 Water St., Baraboo, 608/356-0800, www.circusworldmuseum.com, 9 A.M.–6 P.M. daily May–Labor Day, 10 A.M.–4 P.M. Mon.–Sat. and 11 A.M.–4 P.M. Sun. the rest of the year, $15 adults) was the original headquarters of the Ringling Brothers circus, in an attractive setting along the Baraboo River. Summertime (May–Sept.) is the best time to visit, when the capacious 51-acre grounds are open and the three-ring circus and sideshows reappear. Under the big top is a dazzling, frenetic, fun-as-heck mélange of jugglers, aerialists, clowns, bands, magic, circus nuts-and-bolts, steam-driven calliope concerts, and animal shows. Another hall has memorabilia and displays from the past century of all circuses: rare circus miscellany

from long-gone U.S. circuses, an exhaustive historical rundown of the Ringlings, and, in the video theater, ongoing films. Also in the hall is the world's most complete collection of circus vehicles (214 and counting) and circus posters (8,000 and counting). Maybe ride a pachyderm or a pony if you prefer. Great family entertainment includes kids' clown shows, in which ecstatic urchins can slap on the face paint and go wild, and circus music demonstrations, which feature hands-on access to rare circus musical instruments. A $2.5 million expansion has added a state-of-the-art facility for restoring circus wagons.

International Crane Foundation

The most inspiring attraction is the respected ornithological preservation ongoing northeast of Baraboo at the International Crane Foundation (E11376 Shady Lane Rd., 608/356-9462, www.savingcranes.com, 9 A.M.–5 P.M. daily mid-April–late Oct., $9.50 adults). This

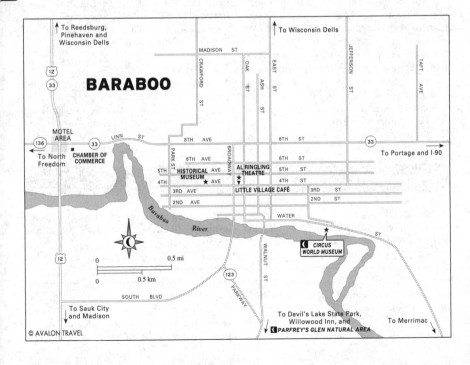

© THOMAS HUHTI

Circus World Museum, the coolest place in Baraboo

world-renowned institution is dedicated to saving the world's largest flying birds, all 15 species of which are endangered or threatened; this is the only place in the world that houses all species. The whooping crane population, from a nadir of 15 birds in 1940, has amazingly rebounded to more than 200 birds. So respected is this place that the crown princess of Japan came as a researcher and Indira Gandhi later founded the Keoladeo Ghana National Park to protect the Siberian crane after a visit. Guided tours are given at 10 A.M. and 1 and 3 P.M. daily (weekends only in spring and early fall); self-guided tours to view adult birds, restored Wisconsin prairie, and marshland are always available.

The center sponsors a spring sandhill crane volunteer count, the largest such endeavor in the country. Wisconsin, a Mississippi Flyway hot spot, holds almost 13,500 sandhill cranes, with more than 1,000 in Marquette County alone. Quite a change from six decades ago, when sport and commercial hunters and predatory agricultural expansion had pared sandhill numbers to two digits.

Other Baraboo Sights and Recreation

Modeled on European opera houses, in particular the Great Opera Hall at the Palace of Versailles, the **Al Ringling Theatre** (136 4th Ave., 608/356-8844) is a local fetching gem of architecture. Tours ($4) are given in summer or just show up for one of the movies or live music events held regularly. A multimillion-dollar renovation really brought back the resplendence.

In nearby North Freedom is another favorite—the chugging iron roosters at **Mid-Continent Railway and Museum** (608/522-4261, museum 9:30 A.M.–5 P.M. mid-May–Labor Day and weekends through Oct., free), west of Baraboo on WI 136 and Highway PF. The last operating steam engine of the Chicago and North Western Railroad is the granddaddy here. All of these trains are refurbished originals; many serviced the area's quartzite mines. Most visitors come, however, for the nine-mile train ride through the Baraboo River Valley. Special seasonal trips

the Mid-Continent Railway, a blast from the past

also depart. Trains depart daily at 11 A.M. and 2 and 3 P.M. on days the museum is open. Tickets are $15–32 adults.

Totally cool is a one-of-a-kind sculpture collection just south of town via U.S. 12. Dr. Evermor, better known as Tom Every, has placed a what-exactly-is-it? assemblage of sculptures created from what could best be described as the detritus of the Cold War and its belching factories; it is in fact directly opposite the hulking remains of the dormant Badger Munitions Depot. This menagerie of machines has the **Forevertron** as its nucleus; it is a 400-ton monstrosity—the largest in the world, apparently (so says the *Guinness Book of World Records*). This author was amazed that it contained the decontamination chamber from the Apollo 11 moon landing. The creator would like to use the erstwhile armaments factory as a sculpture garden dedicated to the munitions industry of the United States throughout history.

Baraboo has also become intriguing for paddlers. With the removal of the Glenville Dam

in 2002, the Baraboo River became the United States' longest restored free-flowing river, 115 miles from Elroy to the confluence of the Wisconsin River near Portage.

◖ Merrimac Scenic Drive

A great side trip out of Baraboo is a spin through Devil's Lake State Park and then a trip across the Wisconsin River via the *Colsac III,* one of the last free ferries in the country, operated by the state Department of Transportation. This site has had one form of ferry or another since 1844. Every year beginning in mid-April (until sometime in late fall), the only way to get from the town of Merrimac to Okee is on this chugger. It goes half a mile in 10 minutes or so, all day and all night. If you see flashing lights on the highway approaches, however, drive on; it means the ferry's down.

Plenty of folks in the area would love to ditch the ferry in favor of building a highway bridge nearby. Incessant state and community meetings try to hash out one of five options; three involve keeping the ferry, two involve a bridge only. For now it's a superb memento of bygone days. On summer weekends, you might wait up to an hour or two to cross.

From there, you can head in to the scenic Lake Wisconsin resort area, which stretches 53 miles from Farmer's Bay, south of Portage, to Prairie du Sac. Every species of fish native to Wisconsin is found in the lake, so, needless to say, anglers flock here. Blue highways stretch the length of the river, offering splendid river vistas and access to trim Wisconsin towns. Little **Lodi** is the sleeper of southern Wisconsin, a picturesque off-river town of winding streets, cheery old buildings, and not much tourist traffic. From there, head northwest out of town to **Gibraltar Rock Park** (via, get this, Highway J, then Highway JV, then Highway V, then, somehow, Highway VA—got all that?) and get a bird's-eye view of the Wisconsin River Valley. It's slightly less inspiring than Devil's Lake but has about a tenth of the crowd, if any. Lodi also contains an over-three-mile segment of the **Ice Age National Scenic Trail,** which passes through bluff-view topography (you can see Devil's Lake), a grand overlook, and oak savannas.

Man Mound Park Scenic Drive

Another side trip you don't hear about often is a hop east to a countryside park holding what is believed to be the only **man mound** in the world. From Baraboo, take WI 33 to T and Man Mound Road. The park's humanoid effigy mound is 215 feet long and 48 feet wide at the shoulders. Unfortunately, road engineers shaved off parts of the lower extremities around the turn of the 20th century. You can combine this with a trip to the *Colsac III* Merrimac ferry; leaving the park, take Rocky Point Road south for some inspiring scenery in the bluffs of the Baraboo Range. East on WI 33 brings you to Bluff Road, another scenic trip through the South Range of the Baraboo Range leading directly to Merrimac.

Accommodations and Food

Everyday lodgings are found at the junction of WI 33 and U.S. 12. A good bet is the mom-and-pop style (friendly, cheap, clean) **Willowood Inn** (S. WI 123, 888/356-5474, www.willowoodinn.com, $65), in an excellent location; it also has a cottage for six.

An interesting B&B is **Pinehaven** (E13083 WI 33, 608/356-3489, $99–145), an enormous dwelling out of town atop a rise and near a spring-fed lake. There's also a private guest cottage. Four rooms are available.

Every corner seems to have a classic, small-town eatery with pressed-tin ceilings reminiscent of the pages of *Roadfood*.

But then, just a few steps from the Al Ringling Theatre, the hip Southwestern (and Caribbean, and Latin American) flavors of the **❰ Little Village Cafe** (146 4th Ave., 608/356-2800, 11 A.M.–8 or 9 P.M. Tues.–Sat., $5–12) are a lovely find. Vegetarians are generally able to find something great here.

Information

The **Baraboo Chamber of Commerce** (660 W. Chestnut St., 608/356-8333 or 800/227-2266, www.baraboo.com) is near the U.S. 12 and WI 33 junction.

DEVIL'S LAKE STATE PARK

The diamond-hard, billion-and-a-half-year-old quartzite bluffs of the Baraboo Range tower above a primevally icy lake of abysmal depth. The lake reflects the earthy rainbow colors of the rises—puce to steel to blood red—and mixes them with its own obsidian for dramatic results, to say the least. It's Wisconsin's number one state park, in constant battle with Door County's Peninsula State Park. Devil's Lake is larger, at more than 8,000 acres, and it draws more visitors annually than Yellowstone National Park.

Devil's Lake State Park lies at the junction of three imposing ranges of impenetrable geology constituting the magnificent—*no* exaggeration—Baraboo Range.

Glaciers starred in the final act, gouging out the eastern half of the range of hills, but stopping just short of the western edge, where a terminal moraine lies today. The Wisconsin Glacier rerouted glacial rivers and gapped the endpoints of the north and south ranges, forming a lakebed, now fed by subterranean springs.

view from the rugged trails of Devil's Lake State Park

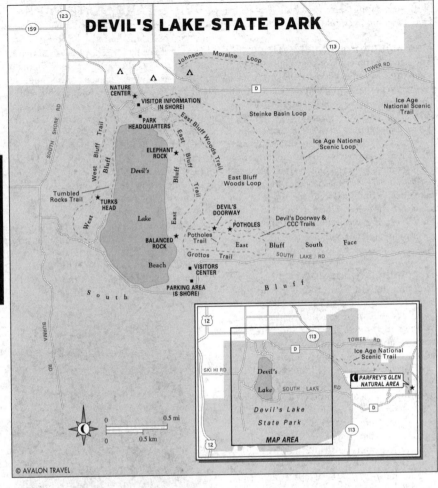

DEVIL'S LAKE STATE PARK

© AVALON TRAVEL

The result is one of the most topographically diverse areas of Wisconsin—challenging bluffs adjacent to pastoral dairyland, both next to a tranquil river valley. The natural areas of Devil's Lake are among the most scrutinized by scientists in the state.

Or maybe, as the Winnebago story of the area's formation has it, giant thunderbirds warred with the spirits in the depths of the lake, hurling thunderbolts and dodging the water gods' boulders and water spouts. The battle raged for eons, until the thunderbirds flew away victorious, leaving the rocks and bluffs scarred from battle and the spirits in the depths licking their wounds and waiting.

Human History

The Winnebago Indians were the first known inhabitants of the area, fishing the lake and hunting nearby lowlands; several burial and effigy mounds are still within the park. Steam trains opened the Devil's Lake region, but development was slow since the recalcitrant Baraboo Range made access difficult. After hacking and blasting through, a minor golden age of hotel building began after the Civil War. While not as extensive as in the Lake Geneva resort area of southeastern Wisconsin, it was no less posh. Four grand hotels were raised but, because of inefficient train service and unmanageable vagaries of early summer weather, by 1910 resort owners gave up, leaving the lodging business to the more mundane mom-and-pop cottages and minor resorts. In 1911, the land was taken over and made into a state park.

Badger Ammo

In a major coup for environmentalists and locals, in 2007 the enormous, 7,500-acre-plus plot once home to the defunct Badger Munitions plant was officially handed off to be shared by the Wisconsin DNR and the Ho Chunk Nation (and a couple of federal agencies)—thus a new fallow area destined for a return to a natural state, rather than be made into yet another "business park." As it abuts the south end of Devil's Lake and links to the Wisconsin River, it's a huge deal to an already important park. Scientists are highly interested in the chance to watch how, exactly, nefarious industrial practices through decades might affect an attempt to "reclaim" the land.

Climate

One revealing aspect of Devil's Lake is how the ranges affect the temperature. It's more than 500 feet from the top of the bluff to the lake; the quartzite traps the air and inverts it—warmer air up and cooler air down. Even the flora is affected—more climatically hardened plantlife flourishes at the base of the rises, while easygoing oak and hickory are scattered across the top reaches.

Hiking

The hiking cannot be beat. Nearly 30 miles encompass both the east and west bluffs. The west has only two trails and is a bit easier in grade.

On the east bluff, the best trails are the **Grottos Trail,** an easy one-mile skirt of the

bottom of the south end of the bluffs; from here, you can connect to the heart-stopping, knee-bending, straight-uphill **Potholes Trail,** one-third of it torture (not for the faint of heart). Two more trails follow the woodland topography off the bluff (you can combine these). Another good idea is to connect them and then take a leg of the **Ice Age National Scenic Trail** loop, which you come across; this in turn runs into the **Parfrey's Glen Ice Age Trail.**

Many of these trails are used in winter for cross-country skiing, and eight miles are also available for mountain biking (so be sure you know if you're on a bike-friendly trail). The **Naturalist Program** leads lots of hikes to the rock highlights as well as Elephant Rock and Cave.

Other Recreation

The hard quartzite bluffs of the park are ready-made for excellent rock climbing. It is, in fact, the only state park permitting rock climbing in Wisconsin. At one time, it maintained rock-climbing routes, but numerous falls from neophyte climbers shut it down. Thus: Climb at your own risk.

The name Devil's Lake was applied since no one ever really knew just how deep the foreboding icy lake was. And no one really wanted to find out. If you're interested in plumbing those depths, **3 Little Devils** (S5780 WI 123, 608/356-5866, www.3littledevils.com) is a full-service scuba operation with equipment, training, repair, rental, and air fills.

Ice Age Reserve

Devil's Lake is one of nine official reserve segments of the **Ice Age National Scenic Trail.** The nature center has exhibits on the geology of the surrounding area and on the trail itself, a moderately difficult four-miler, wooded and grassy, between Parfrey's Glen and the park's 16 miles of trails.

◀ Parfrey's Glen Natural Area

It's astonishing how many people come through Devil's Lake and completely miss this place, not far from the Devil's Lake campgrounds.

Parfrey's Glen near Devil's Lake State Park

Thick, moss-covered ridge walls; hushed, damp silence; a creaking boardwalk; gurgling waters—it's all in the state's oldest natural area, four short miles from the perimeter of the park. A quarter-mile trek through a minor canyon, cool and dripping, is all that's required. The area is meticulously studied by research scientists for its dramatic microclimates and oddball geology. Hundred-foot canyon walls are studded with enormous quartzite boulders (amazingly having ridden four miles on glacial wash); the flora consists of hardy northern-clime plants and ferns not found elsewhere in the state.

Camping

Wisconsin's granddaddy state park has three campgrounds with 425 sites total, but they're little more than open-air sites spread over large expanses of grass—little seclusion and a lot of popularity. Seventy sites stay open in winter. Most are reservable and, given the popularity of the place, reservations well in advance are advised for weekends.

Information

The **park office** (608/356-8301) is open 8 A.M.–11 P.M. in summer, shorter hours the rest of the year. Wisconsin park admission stickers are required.

Note that though under the auspices of the Wisconsin DNR, the park is also a part of the Ice Age National Scientific Reserve; thus, federal Golden Eagle, Golden Age, and Golden Access passports are honored.

REEDSBURG

Slightly off the beaten track 15 or so miles southwest of the Dells stands Reedsburg.

Reedsburg is the southern terminus of the grand 22-mile **400 State Trail,** a multipurpose resurfaced railroad-bed trail spanning from here along the Baraboo River to Elroy, where you can hook up with the Elroy-Sparta Trail for more than 100 miles of superlative Wisconsin countryside.

For a great side trip, northwest of town via WI 33 and Woolever Road in tiny Valton is **The Painted Forest,** a venerable old 1890s camp hall. The name comes from the lovely folk art murals painted from 1897 to 1899 by an itinerant landscape painter, Ernst Hupeden.

PORTAGE

The name says it all. In June of 1673, intrepid Jesuit Father Jacques Marquette, along with Louis Joliet, happened upon the half-mile gap between the Fox River and the Wisconsin River, which empties into the Mississippi in southwestern Wisconsin. The Winnebago had been well aware of the site for centuries, calling it Wa-U-Na, "Carry-on-Shoulder." When trappers and traders began filtering through the new territory, *le portage* became a crucial point in the land-and-water trade routes. Jefferson Davis even found himself here, fresh from West Point, in 1829, hacking logs to help raise Fort Winnebago, upon which much of the region depended.

Sights

A quarter mile or so east of town and a tight turn off WI 33 onto what must be the state's

LINK-UP: THE PORTAGE CANAL

In the early 1800s, travel by water from Green Bay to the Mississippi River was still impossible; goods were hauled by ox team along a rickety plank road. A canal was proposed at *le portage*, the half-mile gap between the Fox and Wisconsin Rivers. Ha!

Machinations were under way by 1829. And, as with other opportunistic ventures of the period, canal-waiters suffered through now-you-see-them canal companies, joint-venture land grants, and general frontier avarice and ineptitude. Finally, in 1848, the state legislature got involved and, with federal help, rammed through enough of the project's particulars to get a makeshift canal dug.

Yet by this point, the project was nearly out of money – perfect timing for a financial scandal. The state, mired in debt and fearful of not completing the canal, handed the project to a private investor, whose mysterious golden touch with federal regulators and legislators aroused suspicions. Somehow, by 1851, the canal was nearly finished, though most river traffic still couldn't get through until major – and costly – riverside adjustments were made.

During Wisconsin's financial panic of 1857 the project once again ran out of money. A canal was there, but still no river traffic. Another consortium of interests wrested control of the project but couldn't finish the Herculean task on the Wisconsin River side. Enter – again – the federal government, whose engineers this time frittered away three years and all of the project capital while not one commercial boat passed through the canal.

This comedy persisted until the late 1870s, when enough rough work was done on the Wisconsin side to allow for large transport barges and ferries. Unfortunately, and naturally, the railroad had already arrived. Large pleasure boats mostly used the canal for 75 years, until the locks were filled in to create an earthen dam.

---

shortest Rustic Road (less than a mile), and along the way, you'll espy sandhill cranes, blue herons, and even a link to the Ice Age National Scenic Trail.

Also along the road stands the **Old Indian Agency House** (off WI 33, 608/742-6362, 10 A.M.–4 P.M. Mon.–Sat., 11 A.M.–4 P.M. Sun., mid-May–mid-Oct., $5 adults), opposite the site of Fort Winnebago. The house was built in 1832 (extraordinarily plush for the period) for John Kinzie, the federal government's Indian agent with the Winnebago tribe. An enigmatic man, Kinzie spoke virtually every Indian dialect used in the Indiana Territory. Juliette Kinzie later wrote a book of modest fame titled *Wau-Bun,* recounting their tenure in the state.

Two miles farther east along WI 33 is the **Surgeon's Quarters** (608/742-2949, 10 A.M.–4 P.M. Mon.–Sat., 11 A.M.–4 P.M. Sun., mid-May–mid-Oct., $4 adults), built during the 1820s and the only extant building from Fort Winnebago. It once housed the medical officers of the garrison. Noteworthy among the rooms of artifacts and antiques are the original plans for the fort and some papers of Jefferson Davis.

Downtown is **Zona Gale's home** (506 W. Edgewater, 608/742-7744), built by Gale for her parents after her first novel was a success in 1906; she did most of her writing here until she won the Pulitzer Prize, in 1928. There are a few antiques and pieces of Gale memorabilia. It's open by appointment only and charges a nominal fee.

Getting There

The **Amtrak** (www.amtrak.com) Empire Builder train, on its Chicago–Seattle run, makes a stop in Portage (401 Oneida St.).

Mackenzie Environmental Center

In Poynette, 12 miles southeast of Portage, is this environmental education center (along

Hwy. CS/Q, 608/635-4498, 8 A.M.–4 P.M. daily May–mid-Oct., 8 A.M.–4 P.M. Mon.–Fri. the rest of year, free) and state of Wisconsin game farm (specializing in pheasant reintroduction). A museum dedicated to the oft-overlooked world of conservation game wardens is a wonderful and intriguing highlight. Yeah, you probably never give these folks a second thought, but they are on the front line of ecological conservation—the under-fire deputies of the environment. The collection, held in an extant 19th-century barn, is huge and fascinating. Trail highlights are bison, wolves, and eagles.

Wisconsin Rapids

The nucleus of the nation's top cranberry-producing region, Wisconsin Rapids is also a leading reason for Wisconsin's status as the nation's number one paper-producing state. Show up in autumn for glorious color photo opportunities in the surrounding cranberry bogs.

History

The first sawmills went up more than half a century before the town appeared, as early as 1831. During June 1880, forest fires raged through the area. No sooner had the beleaguered citizenry gone to bed after extinguishing one threatening fire than the Wisconsin River's charming rapids turned ugly, rising 100 feet after midnight and sweeping away much of the downtown area. The hardened residents rebuilt, incorporated as Grand Rapids, and later changed the name to avoid confusion with towns in both Michigan and Minnesota.

SIGHTS

The chamber of commerce (2507 8th St. S, 715/423-1830 or 800/554-4484, www.visitwisrapids.com) has an excellent fold-out map highlighting three local **historical walking tours.**

Paper

The major industrial force in Wisconsin Rapids is shown (albeit briefly) at the **Wisconsin River Papermaking Museum** (730 First Ave. S., 715/424-3037, 1–4 P.M. Tues. and Thurs., free), which shows not just local history of paper but the whole world (the Japanese exhibits are amazing).

Cranberries

You can tour the post-harvest processing at **Glacial Lake Cranberries** (2480 Hwy. D, 715/887-4161, www.cranberrylink.com, tours: seasonal hours).

Wisconsin Rapids' chamber of commerce can provide a map for the lovely **Cranberry Highway Tour,** a 60-mile route for bikes and cars taking in sights and farms crucial to the local agricultural linchpin product. September and October basically comprise a nonstop cranberry festival. (You'll probably see trumpeter swans along here as well.)

Alexander House

The Alexander House (1131 Wisconsin River Dr., 715/887-3442, 1–4 P.M. Sun., Tues., and Thurs., free) is the former residence of a Nekoosa Edwards Paper Company executive. Now refurbished with original furnishings, it houses a ground-floor exhibit area displaying work of local, regional, and national artists to buttress local history holdings.

Side Trips

Eight miles north of Wisconsin Rapids along WI 34 is the **Rudolph Grotto Gardens and Wonder Cave** (WI 34, 715/435-3120). Inspired by the grotto at Lourdes, the founder, Father Philip Wagner, vowed to construct one if he recovered from an illness. Evidently, Our Lady responded; Father Wagner worked diligently for 40 years—until his death—to create his dream. The gardens are a hodgepodge of flora and assorted rocks, including a boulder the size of a barn the priest moved

WISCONSIN RAPIDS

here somehow; the Wonder Cave is a representational collection of kitschy shrines and statues. The attractive gardens are free and open to the public; the Wonder Cave is open 10 A.M.–5 P.M. daily in summer and costs $2.50 adults.

Also on WI 34 near here is **Dairy State Cheese Company** (715/435-3144, open daily but irregular hours), where you can watch from an observation area.

Eight miles south of Wisconsin Rapids is **Nekoosa,** the site of the original settlement (1831) along the rapids. The town has attractive flower gardens, some nature trails, and a summertime Pioneer Festival. **Historic Point Basse,** on the east bank of the Wisconsin River just south of Nekoosa, is an old cabin and is thought to date from 1837, probably the oldest building in the county.

To the west near Babcock, believe it or not, is the National Guard's **Hardwood Bombing Range** (608/427-1509) and the locals really do pack a picnic lunch to watch the planes practice their runs; call for the schedule.

ACCOMMODATIONS
During cranberry season, some decent packages are available. Lots of chain options exist, all what you'd expect.

Undoubtedly the tops in town—though with some mixed reviews—is **Hotel Mead** (451 Grand Ave., 715/423-1500 or 800/843-6323, www.hotelmead.com, $89–204), in the heart of downtown along the river. Full-service amenities include a health club, lounge, indoor pool, sauna, and whirlpool.

Camping
Public camping is available on the south side of the lake at **South Wood County Park,** five miles southeast along Highway W.

FOOD
Baker Street Grill (1716 Baker St., 715/421-5858, 11 A.M.–9 P.M. Mon.–Fri., 4–9 P.M. Sat., $10–30) has creative food (pepper crusted duck a recent special) and a casual atmosphere. It's probably the most dependable restaurant in town.

The **Hotel Mead** (451 Grand Ave., 715/423-1500 or 800/843-6323, www.hotelmead.com) and its restaurants are consistently well worth a visit—in part because of an excellent downtown location along the river. Good steaks, seafood, prime rib, and diverse (often Wisconsin-centric) daily specials.

INFORMATION AND SERVICES
The **Wisconsin Rapids Chamber of Commerce** (2507 8th St. S, 715/423-1830 or 800/554-4484, www.visitwisrapids.com) has tourist information.

VICINITY OF WISCONSIN RAPIDS
Castle Rock-Petenwell Flowages
The Castle Rock and Petenwell Dams are consummate examples of why the upper Wisconsin River has been called the "Hardest Working River in the Nation." These two dams—east and southeast of Necedah—created the fourth- and second-largest bodies of water in the state, respectively 23,300 and 32,300 acres.

Surrounding the two lakes are numerous county parks, most of which have great tent-pitching options. Camping—few sites, so it's quiet—is also available at the nearby Roche-A-Cri State Park, west 10 miles on WI 21. You can't miss this park; it's dominated by a towering, 300-foot-tall crag jutting from a hill at the base, resulting in a height of more than 1,200 feet. A trail leads to the top of the spire, where outstanding views of the surrounding countryside unfold.

Parts of the Castle Rock dike system are being used as a trout fishery, and the local power company has constructed osprey nesting stands. Petenwell Dam sloughs are a great place to spot bald eagles. East of the Petenwell Dam is the **Van Kuren Trail,** a short multipurpose trail with excellent vistas; to the southwest is the **Petenwell Wildlife Area Hiking Trail,** skirting the shallow southern rim of Petenwell Lake through Strongs Prairie. These and other county parks are accessible along WI 21 and Highway Z.

Also check out **Petenwell Rock** on the west bank of the river, the largest rock formation in the region. Apocryphal tales tell of a man who showed up and fell in love with an already betrothed maiden. They both leaped to their deaths rather than lose each other, and the maiden, Clinging Vine, had her spirit returned to this rock, which was named after her lover.

◀ Central Necedah Wildlife Preserve
Sprawling north and west of Necedah and bordered by WI 80 and WI 21 is the stark, moving Central Necedah Wildlife Preserve, almost 44,000 acres that allow up-close glimpses at isolated wildlife and awesome scenery. Once in the confines, you'll understand soon why Native Americans dubbed the area Necedah, "Land of Yellow Waters."

The preserve makes national news annually

for its ambitious whooping crane recovery program—ultralight planes launched here guided the birds all the way to Florida. Thus, the first whooping crane migrations since 1878 took place.

The preserve is essentially what remains of an enormous peat bog—residual glacial Lake Wisconsin—eons ago called the Great Central Wisconsin Swamp. It's now one-quarter wetlands, home to 20,000 ducks and Canada and snow geese, all introduced beginning in the 1950s.

A total of 35 miles of hiking and skiing trails wind throughout the Necedah refuge. The 11-mile auto tours outlined in maps obtained from the nature center at the south end of the refuge are good. There's even great berry picking. Be careful while hiking, though; the state reintroduced the eastern massasauga rattlesnake in 2000. The nature center office is open 7:30 A.M.–4 P.M. daily.

Contiguous to the refuge are three national wildlife areas: To the west is **Meadow Valley Wildlife Area,** bisected by WI 173; north is the **Wood County Wildlife Area;** and farther north along Highway X and bordered to its north by WI 54 is the **Sandhill Wildlife Demonstration Area,** which houses a fenced-in bison herd, tons of eagles, a 12-mile loop trail, and a 20-mile hiking trail. Native prairie oak savanna restoration is ongoing. The Sandhill WDA has an outdoor skills center devoted to instruction in game-tracking skills using firearms, bow, or camera. Both the Sandhill and Necedah confines are home to more than 700 majestic sandhill and trumpeter swans, the latter transplanted from Alaskan nesting pairs.

Free, very primitive **camping** is allowed two miles west of Sandhill Headquarters in the Wood County Wildlife Area September–December. It is also allowed at the Wood County and Meadow Valley Wildlife Areas during the same times. Summer camping is not permitted. Campers can self-register; you'll need to stop at the nature center first.

Buckhorn State Park

This diverse 2,500-acre promontory southeast of Necedah juts into the Castle Rock–Petenwell Flowages. A short boardwalk trail leads to what could be the dunes and sandblow of the Sonoran Desert—if it weren't for the evergreens present. A wide array of ecosystems native to the state are protected here, from oak forests to restored grasslands. Rare species of turtle can be found along a wonderful interpretive canoe trail in the backwaters; the canoeing is very isolated and a good gaze into what the land looked like 100 years ago.

The **camping** is even better because there isn't much. Forty-two primitive sites and a mere eight "family"—i.e., drive-in—sites means good bets for solitude. Bless you, state—keep it this way!

New Lisbon

Due south of the Central Necedah Wildlife Refuge is this pleasant town of 1,491 folks. One of the Upper Midwest's largest groups of **effigy mounds** is south of town off WI 12/16. Even rarer are the **Twin Bluff petroglyphs,** done by early Woodland tribes, west along Highway A; hardy hikers can make it up Twin Bluff and to the caverns to check out the Thunderbird etchings. West of town five miles you can pick up the Omaha multiuse recreational trail as it passes through Hustler. Much of the area's history is on display at both the **New Lisbon Library** (608/562-3213) and **Raabe's Pharmacy** (608/562-3302), together representing the state's largest private prehistoric Native American artifact collection.

Stevens Point

At approximately the halfway point north-south in Wisconsin, Stevens Point is a picturesque city spread out along the Wisconsin and Plover Rivers, smack within the fecund "Golden Sands" region. Travelers note an inordinate amount of green space and parkland—perhaps one reason why the University of Wisconsin-Stevens Point is so renowned for its environmental science disciplines.

Gateway to the Pineries

City settlement happened almost accidentally. Starting in 1830, enterprising lumber speculators had been pushing northward from the forts of the lower Fox and Wisconsin Rivers. Lumberman George Stevens temporarily deposited supplies at this spot, later called "the Point," and unwittingly founded the town.

The city wasn't close enough to the timber tracts to experience overnight or sustained boomtown status. By 1850, three years after the first platting of the town, there were only 200 citizens.

Later, sawmills became paper mills, and, blessed with prime agricultural fields surrounding, the local economy drew more settlers—mainly Polish immigrants.

SIGHTS
Farmers Market

The oldest continuously operated farmers' fair in Wisconsin is held spring through fall in the public square downtown.

Point Brewery

The third-oldest continuously-operated (from 1857) brewery in the U.S., Point Brewery concocts the beers of choice for many a North Woods resident and college student (this author once had a friend lug a six-pack to Taiwan). A personal fave is the Spring Bock and their excellent root beer. One Chicago newspaper

the lands that inspired naturalist Aldo Leopold – the Sands

© THOMAS HUHTI

called Point the best beer in America; it won a gold medal for its Horizon Wheat beer at the 2010 World Beer Cup. The brewery (2617 Water St., 715/344-9310, www.pointbeer. com, $3) gives hourly tours 11 A.M.–2 P.M. Monday–Saturday June–August, fewer hours off-season.

UW-Stevens Point
WISCONSIN FORESTRY HALL OF FAME AND AVIARY

One of Wisconsin's best environmental resources programs is housed at the UWSP—fitting, since these are the lands immortalized

by naturalist Aldo Leopold. Leopold himself is immortalized in a corner of the hall of fame. In addition to the shrine to Leopold, there are exhibits on mammals, fish, turtles, and more. It's in the east lobby of the first floor of the Natural Resources building (715/346-4617).

SCHMEEKLE RESERVE

On the northern edge of the university campus, this diminutive 200-acre tract could be the city's crown jewel, an amalgam of pristine ecology with a quarter-mile interpretive trail and other walking trails through the interspersed wetland, prairie, and woodland

CENTRAL WISCONSIN SANDS

SAND COUNTY SAGE

There are some who can live without wild things, and some who cannot.... Like winds and sunsets, wild things were taken for granted until progress began to do away with them.

– Aldo Leopold, from the foreword to
A Sand County Almanac and Sketches Here and There

Leading experts on environmentalism were once asked to name the most influential work in raising ecological consciousness. The hands-down winner was Aldo Leopold's *A Sand County Almanac and Sketches Here and There.*

Aldo Leopold was a seminal naturalist, a pioneering figure in ecology and especially conservation. He introduced the idea of setting aside protected forest land and later devised the concept of wildlife management. Not a native Badger, Leopold nonetheless lived the better part of his life not far from where John Muir grew up. Above all, he was a polished writer, with a lucid, engaging, eloquent style celebrating life and its connection to the land.

EARLY YEARS

After attending Yale – its graduate forestry program was ultra-progressive, controversial, and the first of its kind – in 1909 Leopold went to work for the United States Forest Service (USFS). In Arizona, when he looked into the dying eyes of a wolf that had been shot – eradication was the norm – his passion for educating people on the need to coexist may have germinated right there.

He accepted a fortuitous transfer to a new USFS lab in Madison in 1924 and within a few years had revolutionized how we view the natural world. His belief in a cause-and-effect relationship with the land led him to a two-year survey of game in North America and his founding of game-management theory.

By 1933, he was named the chair of UW's new game-management department. Part of his job was to examine and basically repair central Wisconsin, which had been laid waste during previous generations of misinformed agricultural exploitation. Leopold's tenure oversaw reforestation, wetland restoration, establishment of state and county forests, game preserves, parks, and more.

A SAND COUNTY ALMANAC

While covering the central region for his work, Leopold found the perfect retreat. He spent most of the rest of his life in examination of this land. The result is his evenhanded and scientifically pragmatic masterpiece for which he is justly famous, setting down what is now referred to as land ethic, the origin of modern-day land-use management.

A Sand County Almanac was in essence a florid, cheerful way of describing the symbiotic nature of humans and the land. What we today couch in multisyllabic jargon (biodiversity or ecoawareness), Leopold recognized intuitively.

One fantastic way to get a glimpse of the lands he so adored is to travel **Rustic Road 49,** Levee Road – 10 miles stretching along the Wisconsin River between WI 33 and Highway T and passing through the Aldo Leopold Reserve. You can also take self-guided or guided tours of the original **shack** and the wondrous new **Aldo Leopold Legacy Center** a mile away via a trail. Check www.aldoleopold.org.

topography (the latter features an imposing stand of tall pines). The visitors center houses the Wisconsin Conservation Hall of Fame—UWSP initiated the country's first natural resources degree program. The reserve is open daily dawn–dusk; the visitors center is open 8 A.M.–5 P.M. daily.

OTHER ATTRACTIONS

The **Museum of Natural History** (715/346-2858) contains a nationally recognized collection of ornithology. The **planetarium** (4th Ave. and Reserve St.) holds regular free programs at 2 P.M. every Sunday October–May; ditto with Night Sky programs at

8 p.m. Monday. For general campus information, call 715/346-4242 or view the university website at www.uwsp.edu. When strolling around campus, check out the side of the Natural Resources building, which showcases the world's largest (25 tons of tile) computer-designed mosaic.

George W. Meade Wildlife Area

Fourteen miles west of town via WI 10, in Milladore, is this prime wildlife-viewing area (free), with 28,000 acres of wildlife, marsh, and farmland. There are nesting eagles in parts of the preserve, a plethora of mammals, and a few prairie chickens. Rough and not-so-rough trails constantly are being expanded.

Historic and Scenic Tours

The downtown **Main Street Historic District** contains more than 60 buildings in the Mathias Mitchell Public Square. A printed guide is available at many locations throughout town for a small fee.

ENTERTAINMENT AND EVENTS
Culture

The best place for cultural events is the UWSP (715/346-0123), or the **Sentry Theater** (2100 Main St.), which draws some national and international acts. For schedules and ticket information at the Sentry, call the box office (715/346-4100).

The **Rising Star Mill** (715/344-6383) is an 1860s mill in Nelsonville along WI 161 operated by the Portage County Historical Society with occasional poetry readings, concerts, and an annual art show coinciding with a huge car show.

Events

On a decidedly weirder note is UWSP's **Trivia Weekend,** held each April. The largest of its kind in the world, this event is a 54-hour, excruciating brain-tease hosted by the university radio station (WWSP 90 FM) and broadcast throughout central Wisconsin. It's great fun—and hard as hell.

RECREATION
SentryWorld

The SentryWorld Sports Center (601 N. Michigan Ave., 715/345-1600) is highly rated. The golf course is rated by a variety of duffer media as one of the best in the country and certainly in Wisconsin; the trademark hole is the 16th, the "flower hole," adorned with more than 90,000 individual plants.

Green Trail

The Green Trail is a fantastic 24-mile multipurpose loop trail that skirts the Wisconsin and Plover Rivers. There's lots of wildlife- and bird-watching. Ten parking areas are interspersed along the trail's length; the easiest to reach is downtown along Main and 1st Streets.

Camping

The nearest public parks for camping are **Lake DuBay** (715/346-1433), northwest off WI 10 onto Highway E, and **Jordan Park** (715/345-0520), six miles northeast on WI 66. Both have sites for $10–12.

ACCOMMODATIONS

The cheapest lodging close to downtown is the **Point Motel** (209 Division St., 715/344-8312 or 800/344-3093, www.pointmotel.com, $37–44), with clean if aging rooms and free coffee if not doughnuts. Note that we've had a couple of complaints about this place, but others have found it just fine.

A step up in amenities and price is the **Comfort Suites** (300 Division St. N., 715/341-6000 or 800/228-5150, $73 s or d), with exceptional decor, rooms varying in size, an indoor pool, exercise room, and more.

Still higher in price is the nearby **Holiday Inn** (1501 N. Point Dr., 715/341-1340, $99 s, $109 d), one of the Midwest's largest facilities and sporting a new water park, great for the littl'uns.

FOOD
Cafés

Very cozy and aesthetically pleasing is the **Wooden Chair** (1059 Main St., 715/341-1133,

7 A.M.–2 P.M. daily, $3–9), a warm and spacious eatery with hardwood-floor areas, bookshelves, brick walls, fireplaces, and wide tables with elbow room. The specials change monthly, and the eggs selection is as diverse as it gets. There are good healthy options, too.

Fish Fries
A great fish fry is off U.S. 51 at the **Hilltop Pub** (4901 WI 10 E., 715/341-3037, lunch and dinner daily, $5–15), with outdoor seating in the summer and great burgers to boot. This old pub—now a microbrewery—is chock-full of Point memorabilia, including photos and an antique bottle collection. Diners eat in a comfy screened porch.

Supper Club and American Food
An excellent creative eatery with a wide range of regional dishes is the local institution **(Silver Coach** (38 Park Ridge Dr., 715/341-6588, 5–10 P.M. Mon.–Sat., $7–19), serving from a turn-of-the-20th-century rail car since World War II. The ribs are killer here, as are the blackened steaks and the seafood. Wisconsin-themed artwork is displayed on the wall.

German and Continental
(Bernard's (701 2nd St. N., 715/344-3365, 4–9 P.M. Tues.–Sun., $9–19), the restaurant illuminated by small white lights, has fare varying from American supper club (steaks and fish) to southern German dishes such as veal schnitzel (five schnitzels in all) to a few French specialties. You can even get its famed "German" pizza with smoked sausage and sauerkraut (on a delicious homemade rye crust).

Be not at all surprised to find venison or bison on the menu.

Fine Dining
The place to go in Point for a splurge night is **(@1800** (1800 N. Point Dr., 715/346-1800, 11 A.M.–2 P.M. Mon.–Fri., 5–9 P.M. Mon.–Sat., $18–32), the eatery in the labyrinth of the SentryWorld Insurance complex. It is consistently rated as one of the top restaurants in Wisconsin. Bacon-wrapped elk impeccably done in a sophisticated atmosphere? It's here and not in a major metropolitan area. It's got incredibly beautiful views, with expansive windows overlooking the oh-so-wide terraced concentric courtyards and a garden; you may even get a gander at wildlife through the windows.

INFORMATION AND SERVICES
The **Stevens Point Area Convention and Visitors Bureau** (340 Division St., 715/344-2556 or 800/236-4636, www.stevenspointarea.com) is next to the Holiday Inn.

GETTING THERE
By Air
The **Central Wisconsin Airport** (715/693-2147, www.fly-cwa.org) is in nearby Mosinee and is served by several regional airlines.

By Bus
Lamers bus line (800/261-6600, www.lamers.com) runs between Wausau and Milwaukee, with stops here at the Olympic Family Restaurant (200 Division St.) and in New London, Appleton, Oshkosh, and Fond du Lac.

Marshfield

The Depression-era WPA guide summed up Marshfield with the line, "The city is sprinkled out on a flat green prairie . . . patterned rigidly as a chessboard, and industries are as diverse as pawns, knights, bishops, queens, and kings." As far as overnight stops go, one could do far worse than this attractive city. State residents associate the city mainly with its cutting-edge Marshfield Clinic, a major medical group practice of some national repute. But Marshfield's livability quotient is also always tops in the state and among the top five in the Midwest.

The city is now one of the state's leading dairy research areas and hosts a dairy festival and regional fair. (At the fairgrounds, check out the world's largest round barn—a lovely 1916 edifice still used to house purebred animals.)

SIGHTS
Marshfield Clinic and New Visions Gallery

Not a tour spot per se, this clinic does sport some impressive credentials. One of the leading private group practice medical facilities in the United States, with 21 regional Wisconsin satellites (and 5,000 employees), the Marshfield Clinic began in 1916 as a dedicated group of six physicians trying to give the rural communities a higher standard of medical care. It now comprises three massive facilities—Marshfield Clinic, Saint Joseph's Hospital (19,000 patients per year), and the Marshfield Medical Research Foundation, a consortium of more than 100 research projects.

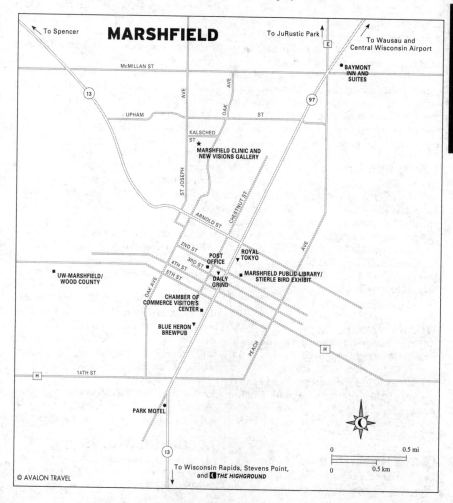

© AVALON TRAVEL

Adjacent to the clinic, in a space it donated, New Visions Gallery (1000 N. Oak Ave., 715/387-5562, 9 A.M.–5:30 P.M. Mon.–Fri., free) is an educational gallery; permanent holdings include Marc Chagall prints, West African sculpture and masks, Australian aboriginal arts, Haitian painting, and world folk arts. Temporary exhibits change every few weeks. St. Joseph's Hospital also has a corridor of Wisconsin artists—about 50 are displayed.

JuRustic Park

Cheeky and fun is JuRustic Park (715/387-1653, www.jurustic.com, grounds open till 5 P.M., free), north of town a handful of miles via Highway E, a collection of "dinosaur" sculptures that, rumor has it, once inhabited this marsh! In all seriousness, the 250 metal sculptures, ranging from less-than-a-foot spiders to massive, 45-foot-long beasts, are fantastic pieces of art from a local couple. Local bike trails are being built out this way, so it'd be a lovely ride.

Stierle Bird Exhibit

The subdued Stierle Exhibit (211 E. 2nd St., 715/387-8495, free), in the Marshfield Public Library, is one of the country's most complete and diverse collections of bird eggs (110 species and 1,900 or so eggs). It also features 140 species of birds (380 birds total), all collected by a local taxidermist and photographer. The library is open 9 A.M.–9 P.M. weekdays (shorter hours weekends) Labor Day–Memorial Day, fewer hours during summer.

Wildlife-Viewing

Adjacent to Marshfield in the north/northwest is the **McMillan Marsh Wildlife Area,** with trails for bikes, hikes, and canoes. South of town via WI 13 and then north on Highway X leads to the 9,500-acre **Sandhill Wildlife Area,** a marshland dedicated to the restoration of sandhill cranes; there are also even a few bison herds.

◖ The Highground

Eerie silence pervades the Highground, Wisconsin's Veterans' Memorial Park on 100 acres surrounded by one of the largest glacial moraines in the state. A most somber memorial, dominating a central rise, is the Vietnam Veterans' Memorial statue, while a nearby grove of trees forms a five-star pattern, dedicated to sacrifices of families in wartime. Most compelling is the Effigy Mound, an enormous dove-shaped earthen mound for POWs and MIAs and all those "prisoners of their own experience." (A similar mound is gradually being constructed in Vietnam by Vietnamese veterans, with the cooperation of Wisconsin vets.) An admirable mixture of flora and sculpture, the park is designed for the sound of wind chimes (many constructed from military hardware) to pervade the entire expanse. Lighted at night, the park is open 24 hours a day, seven days a week. Memorials also honor Native Americans and vets of the Persian Gulf War and the Korean War. Some picnic tables are available, and walking trails are constantly being developed. The whole experience is quite moving, particularly at night. Various festivals, including emotional powwows, take place throughout the year. It's 37 miles south and west of Marshfield, via U.S. 10; follow WI 13 south out of town to reach U.S. 10. Just west of Highground is a lovely Wisconsin **Rustic Road** drive through a decaying settlers' village.

Near Highground is charming little **Neillsville,** which is famed for a huge statue of Annabelle the cow on the east side of town. In town itself is an 1897 reconstructed jail listed on the National Register of Historic Places. U.S. 10 west of town brings you first to a lovely arboretum adjacent to the Black River and then, after five miles, to the fetching Silver Dome Ballroom, a Great Depression WPA project with original decorations and fixtures.

North of Neillsville, just east of Withee, is another fantastic **Rustic Road** through classic Amish country; this one also rolls across an old wooden bridge to herds of bison and elk.

ACCOMMODATIONS

Marshfield's most centrally located lodging is the **Park Motel** (1806 Roddis Ave., 715/387-1741, $35–50).

The best option is probably the **Baymont Inn and Suites** (2107 N. Central Ave., 715/384-5240, $75–135), with an indoor pool, fitness center, and continental breakfast.

FOOD

This is another city of cafés. You'll find the best java in two counties at the **Daily Grind** (236 S. Central Ave., 715/387-6607) downtown. There are handcrafted beers and above average pub grub at **Blue Heron Brewpub** (108 W. 9th St., 715/389-1868, 11 A.M.–late daily, $5–15).

For something completely different, Marshfield's old train depot has been achingly well restored and now houses **Royal Tokyo** (112 E. 1st St., 715/486-8868, 11:30 A.M.–2:30 P.M. and 4:30–9 P.M. daily, $7–23). The sushi is enhanced by the slice-and-dice teppanyaki chefs preparing food before your eyes.

INFORMATION

The **Marshfield Chamber of Commerce** (700 S. Central Ave., 715/384-3454 or 800/422-4541, www.marshfieldchamber.com) is friendly.

Wausau

Wausau is the last city of any real size all the way to Superior in the northwest. Underrated and unseen by many, it features the mighty Wisconsin waterway and hourglass-shaped Lake Wausau. Just south of town, Rib Mountain—for centuries erroneously assumed to be Wisconsin's pinnacle—dominates the topography.

The heart of Marathon County, Wausau has become legendary since the late 1980s for something decidedly unexpected from north-central Wisconsin: ginseng. The county is now the nation's number one producer of high-quality ginseng, second worldwide only to Korea in exports. Dairying hasn't completely been replaced, however; Marathon County is still number one in milk and cheese output (colby cheese got its name from a town in this county).

History

There's already a Wisconsin Rapids to the south, but the name might be more appropriate for Wausau—four communities stretched along a segment of roaring Wisconsin River cascades so incessantly punishing they were dubbed by early voyageurs Gros Taureau— "Big Bull Falls."

New plank roads allowed the exploitation of the area's staggering wood supply. Within a decade, there was one sawmill for every 100 residents of the city, which was soon refitted

with the Native American name Wausau— "Far Away Place."

SIGHTS
◖ Leigh Yawkey Woodson Museum

Ornithological mavens rub elbows with puzzled ginseng buyers during the internationally regarded early autumn **Birds in Art** exhibition at the Leigh Yawkey Woodson Museum (700 N. 12th St., 715/845-7010, www.lywam.org, 9 A.M.–4 P.M. Tues.–Fri., noon–5 P.M. Sat.–Sun., free), when the museum rolls out its exquisite and astonishing menagerie of birds in all media. The little museum in a grand Cotswold-style mansion has holdings that draw artists and birders worldwide. The 8–12 exhibitions each year, plus a steadily growing permanent collection, include rare Royal Worcester porcelain, Victorian glass baskets, and complete multimedia artist collections with birds as the focus.

Rib Mountain

Dominating the terrain—if not the local psyche—is Rib Mountain, for most of the state's history presumed by most to be the highest point in the state. Technically not a mountain, Rib is a 70-billion-year-old quartzite monadnock rising 1,940 feet above

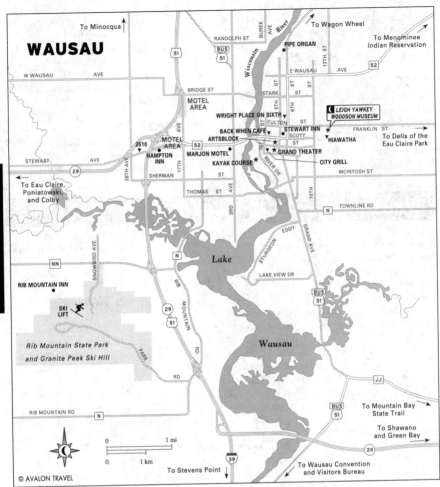

WAUSAU

To Minocqua

RANDOLPH ST

BUREK AVE

To Wagon Wheel

PIPE ORGAN

To Menominee
Indian Reservation

W WAUSAU   AVE

E WAUSAU   AVE

52

BRIDGE ST

MOTEL
AREA

STARK   ST

WRIGHT PLACE ON SIXTH

FULTON

LEIGH YAWKEY
WOODSON MUSEUM

BACK WHEN CAFE

STEWART INN

FRANKLIN   ST

ARTSBLOCK

SCOTT

HIAWATHA

To Dells of the
Eau Claire Park

MOTEL
AREA

2510

52

MARJON MOTEL

GRAND THEATER

HAMPTON
INN

KAYAK COURSE

CITY GRILL

To Eau Claire,
Poniatowski,
and Colby

29

STEWART   AVE

MCINTOSH ST

SHERMAN   ST

THOMAS   ST

TOWNLINE RD

N

NN

RIB MOUNTAIN INN

Lake

STURGEON EDDY

GRAND AVE

SKI
LIFT

LAKE VIEW DR

BUS
51

Rib Mountain State Park
and Granite Peak Ski Hill

Wausau

RD

JJ

RIB MOUNTAIN RD

N

BUS
51

To Mountain Bay
State Trail

To Shawano
and Green Bay

0   1 mi

0   1 km

39

29

© AVALON TRAVEL

To Stevens Point

To Wausau Convention
and Visitors Bureau

sea level and 800 feet above the surrounding peneplain. Though not exactly imposing in height, its slopes are steep—there's a 1,200-foot rise per mile.

The Depot

For years national exposure to Wausau came from TV ads poking fun at the linguistic dexterity necessary to say the town's name (it ain't "Warsaw") and from a legendary train depot used in Wausau Insurance TV ads.

The railroad depot isn't exactly mythical, but some marketing sleight of hand was involved. Ads take a depot and superimpose it over the Wausau skyline as seen from a different depot. Through nonstop tourist badgering and civic pride, Wausau Insurance—one of the largest insurers in the nation—bought the depot in the commercial in 1977, constructed a replica at corporate headquarters, and then donated the building to charity. It still stands at 720 Grant Street. Another depot, with the skyline, is along Washington Street and houses businesses. (And to be utterly technical, there was yet another way back when.)

ArtsBlock

Wausau is to be commended for its devotion to cultural affairs. The block bordered by Scott, Fourth, Jefferson, and 5th Streets now comprises an arts district unrivaled in Wisconsin. The cornerstone 1927 Greek revival **Grand Theater** (427 4th St., 715/842-0988, www. grandtheater.org) was recently given a multimillion-dollar facelift to bring back its original shine and allow space for national and international acts. Studios and galleries of **Center for the Visual Arts** (427 4th St., 715/842-4545, www.cvawausau.com, 10 A.M.–3 P.M. Mon.–Sat., free) and performances by the **Performing Arts Foundation** are also right there.

Historic District

The lumber wealth of the area went to some superlative use. More than 60 structures of many architectural styles are showcased in a well-planned **walking tour** through part of downtown. The maps are available at the information center.

The Center

Take WI 29 west to Poniatowski (follow the signs) and at some point you might start feeling some odd twinges inside. It could be you're approaching 45 degrees longitude and 90 degrees latitude—the exact center of the northwestern hemisphere and the midpoint of Greenwich, England, the international date line, the north pole, and the equator. It's well marked with a little park.

Pipe Organ

Decidedly offbeat is the pipe organ, designed after a 17th-century Bach favorite, at the Salem Lutheran Church (2822 6th St., 715/845-2822). The pipes are German, the intricate oak woodwork from the United States. Contact the church ahead of time and someone will arrange for demonstrations.

Ginseng

This trim, solidly Wisconsin city turns into an ersatz Asian nation come autumn, when buyers from Hong Kong, Taiwan, Korea, China, and all the American Chinese communities converge en masse to begin the cryptic ritual of sorting through the ginseng harvest.

If you're serious about ginseng, contact the **Ginseng Board of Wisconsin** (7575 Bombardier Ct., 715/845-7300, www.ginsengboard.com) for details on regional growers and crops. Some offer tours (sometimes for a fee) of operations.

Dells of the Eau Claire County Park

A gem by any standard is this Marathon County Park. Officially a state Scientific Area, it's a freak of geology, with striated rock outcroppings and, as the name hints, recessed water valleys with bluffs up to 70 feet high. In parts, the surrealistic rocky surfaces look like hardened cottage cheese. The park has superlative scenery and a segment of the Ice Age National Scenic Trail to supplement the grand hiking. To get there, head out to Highway Y, 15 miles east off WI 29.

Side Trip

Head out of town west along WI 29 about 30 miles and you'll come to little **Colby,** the birthplace of the eponymous cheese. Also of interest here is the **Rural Arts Museum** (715/223-2264, open Sun. Memorial Day–Labor Day), a country museum with an old box factory, a depot, cabins, and more.

ENTERTAINMENT AND EVENTS
Cultural Events

This author's favorite cultural pastime is to grab a sandwich and head to the popular **Concerts on the Square,** held 6–8 P.M. Wednesdays across from the Great Hall of the ArtsBlock.

Kayaking Events

The city hosts its own Whitewater Weekend in mid-June, followed by two national kayaking competitions, one each in July and August

GINSENG: WISCONSIN'S GOLDEN ROOT

Wisconsin may be America's Dairyland, but in the Wausau area, the revered root ginseng is an – if not *the* – economic mainstay. Between 90 percent and 95 percent of the United States' ginseng crop comes directly from the somewhat secretive farmers of Marathon County, now the world's fourth-largest ginseng producer at a half-million pounds (up to 1.5 million!) annually. It's among the top (often number one) agricultural cash crop exports for the state.

THE IMAGE OF MAN

Jin chen, ren shen . . . whatever transliteration method you use, "ginseng" means the "root in the image of man." Ginseng's the cure-all for any (I mean *any*) ailment.

In essence, ginseng preserves the crucial balance of yin (cool, dark, feminine) and yang (warm, light, masculine). In Asia, you don't simply slam a glass of ginseng daily. It's part of a whole package of life. (And certain personality types – especially "hot" ones – shouldn't drink it at all.)

Ginseng is most highly revered in China and Korea. Legends tell of "mountain ginseng" as being a gift from the gods, caught in a mountain stream through lightning. Koreans say that if a fortunate event occurs in your dreams, you'll find wild ginseng – and maybe save someone's life. The Chinese will pay a month's wages for prime ginseng.

Western scientists remain divided on any of its efficacy. This mostly stems from lack of research – despite the boom in the popularity of supplements such as ginseng, testing lags behind in this country. A stimulantlike effect has been observed on the central nervous and endocrine systems, and it has also been shown to affect hormones and decrease blood sugar.

THE PLANT

All ginseng is not the same. All are members of the Aralinceae family, relatives of celery and carrots. Ginseng has always grown wild across the eastern half of the United States from as far south as Mississippi. Daniel Boone traded it, and John Jacob Astor got his legendary fur company started by dealing it to the Chinese.

It's tremendously difficult to cultivate. Cash- and labor-intensive, the root is extraordinarily sensitive to temperatures and susceptible to rot and basically every known pest and blight. One acre can yield a good 2,000 pounds. Unfortunately, however, it takes four seasons to reach maturity – and, once an acre has grown ginseng, it's "dead" for at least another century.

WISCONSIN SHANG

Known locally as "shang" or "sang," Wisconsin's ginseng (*Panax quinquefolim*) is among the most valuable – economically and pharmacologically – in the world. First cultivated by German farmers, it was first commercially raised by a pair of Marathon County brothers around the turn of the 20th century.

Some big thorns have arisen. Local overproduction, newer competition from British Columbia, and – worst of all – piracy (putting the Wisconsin seal on cheap Chinese shang in Chinatowns) has caused prices to plummet from highs of $80 a pound to a recent $22 a pound (and the state now has a mere 200 farmers, down from 1600 in the 1990s). The state has organized a Ginseng Board to coordinate efforts and smooth out problems.

(for more information, check out www.wausau whitewater.org). Super fun!

RECREATION
Skiing

The highest ski hill in the state, Rib Mountain's **Granite Peak** (715/845-2846, www.skigranitepeak.com) has the second-longest vertical drop in the Midwest at just under 700 feet. There are 74—yep!—runs (bunnies, steep chutes, and even forest glades) plus an enormous original chalet. It does a great job on kidcentric activities, too. Prices vary wildly according to season and day/night periods.

For **cross-country skiing,** a personal favorite is the hidden, classical-style **Ringle Trail,** a three-plus-mile trail for beginners in isolated hardwood stands east along WI 29 and then north on Highway Q, and east on Poplar Lane.

Kayaking

Lumber boomtowns in the Fox and Wisconsin riverways notwithstanding, Wausau lays claim to the most persistent set of rapids. No longer powering the mills, the water now attracts thousands of white-water aficionados and pro kayakers to make use of its downtown, dam-controlled white-water course in national and international competitions. Not many other cities can brag about a course right through the city, complete with bankside seating. The city's program garnered kudos from the U.S. Canoe and Kayak Team, which has made Wausau its top training site. The Wisconsin River and Lake Wausau are part of a popular water trail; portaging is required.

Biking

Wausau's segment of the **Mountain-Bay Trail** is an 83-miler constructed along the former Chicago and Northwestern Railroad railbed and stretching from Weston to Green Bay. The trailhead begins by the Weston Community Center, 5500 Schofield Avenue. A daily pass ($4) is required and can be obtained at the trailhead.

Outside of Wausau a few miles to the southwest, the county maintains 27 miles of off-road trails at **Nine Mile Recreation Area;** the paths double as cross-country trails in winter.

The city convention and visitors bureau (exit 185 of I-39/U.S. 51, 888/948-4748, www.wausaucvb.org) has excellent maps.

Snowshoeing

Rib Mountain State Park is one of the few in Wisconsin to offer trails specifically designed for snowshoeing—five miles total. The sport is so popular in the Wausau area you shouldn't have any trouble finding rentals at downtown sporting-goods stores.

Camping

At 1,940 feet, the campground at **Rib Mountain State Park** is unquestionably the highest camping opportunity in Wisconsin. The grounds have a mere 40-odd sites and, truth be told, privacy here isn't the greatest. But the view you get after hiking up the seven miles of trails past eons-old quartzite geology sure is killer.

It's worth a drive to **Council Grounds State Park,** 15 miles to the north. There are 55 isolated sites in a heavily wooded park along the Wisconsin River. Not much else is here, but at least the camping's private in some fairly impressive stands of proud pines.

Both state parks offer reservable sites.

Otherwise, Wausau has a fantastic county park system; all others pale in comparison to Dells of the Eau Claire Park, along Highway Y, 15 miles east of town, with a swimming beach, hiking trails, and some of the most isolated county park grandeur in the state. It's definitely worth it.

ACCOMMODATIONS
Under $50

The junction of Stewart and 17th Avenues on the west side of town, essentially the interchange of U.S. 51/WI 29 and Highway 52, has the largest grouping of accommodations. Here you'll find most rooms over $50, but just to the east from here, the closest motel to downtown is one for *very* budget-conscious travelers, the **Marjon Motel** (512 S. 3rd Ave., 715/845-3125 or 800/286-7503, $45 and up). Some rooms have kitchenettes.

$50-100

Mid-range, the best hotel close to downtown is the **Hampton Inn** (615 S. 24th Ave., 715/848-9700, hamptoninn.hilton.com, from $89), a chain that—gasp—doesn't feel generic.

The Rib Mountain area, south and west of Wausau, has the top-notch **Rib Mountain Inn** (2900 N. Rib Mountain Way, 715/848-2802, www.ribmtninn.com, $75–298). There are two villas and 25 rooms here, many with balcony views of the mountain; fireplace studios to two- and three-bedroom town homes are available. Naturally, some ski packages are possible, and golfing isn't far away, either. There is a sauna and picnic facilities. Some rooms have patios and refrigerators.

Over $100

The **Stewart Inn** (521 Grant St., 715/849-5858, www.stewartinn.com, $170–215), hmm, well, let's just say you'd be nuts to stay in another hotel for the same price, so smashing is the cool modernity meshed with historicity here. And proprietors are wonderful as well. This is absolutely a top pick in northern Wisconsin.

FOOD
Quick and Casual

"Upscale family-style" best describes **2510** (2510 Stewart Ave., 715/845-2510, $5–20), farther west on Stewart Avenue. The place also has its own bakery and deli and a great fish fry.

Right near the ArtsBlock district, the **Back When Cafe** (606 N. 3rd St., 715/848-5668, lunch and dinner Tues.–Sat., $5 and up) has healthful sandwiches on homemade breads and slightly more gourmet options in the evening, and is the best local option for vegetarians. Jazz is here Fridays.

Fish Fry

The fish fry at the **Hiawatha** (713 Grant St., 715/848-5166, lunch and dinner daily, $6–15) is where locals will tell you to go. It's also got sandwiches, steaks, salads, and pastas, and nice outdoor dining.

Supper Clubs and Fine Dining

Downtown in the Jefferson Street Inn the **City Grill** (203 Jefferson St., 715/848-2900, 6:30 A.M.–10 P.M. Mon.–Thurs., 7 A.M.–11 P.M. Fri.–Sat., 7 A.M.–9 P.M. Sun., $7–20) and its casual contemporary American fare has been raved about by more than one reader (and citizens of Wausau in the local papers). It has a comfortably chic atmosphere.

North of here along 6th Street is the even more upscale **Wright Place on Sixth** (901 N. 6th St., 715/848-2345, dinner Mon.–Sat., $8–20). The restaurant offers contemporary American with dashes of French. It's housed in an 1881 mansion.

Ah, the **Wagon Wheel** (3901 N. 6th St., 715/675-2263, 5–9 P.M. Mon.–Sat., $12–50)—it's a seven-decades-old local rustic eatery famed for dry-aged steaks, barbecue ribs, and a dripping butterball tenderloin (more than three inches thick); there are also bison and New Zealand venison. *Wine Spectator* has favorably acknowledged its wine cellar. Expect homemade everything and a funky, *very* unpretentious vibe.

INFORMATION AND SERVICES

The **Wausau Convention and Visitors Bureau** (888/948-4748, www.wausaucvb.org) is a huge place at exit 185 of I-39/U.S. 51.

The local daily is the decent *Wausau Daily Herald; City Pages* is a thin but intelligently written free weekly with great local info.

GETTING THERE
By Air

The Wausau area is served by the **Central Wisconsin Airport** (715/693-2147, www.fly-cwa.org) in nearby Mosinee.

By Bus

Lamers bus line (800/261-6600, www.lamers.com) runs between Wausau (depot: 2514 Trailwood Ln.) and Milwaukee, with stops in Stevens Point, New London, Appleton, Oshkosh, and Fond du Lac.

BACKGROUND

The Land

Topographically, Wisconsin may lack the jaw-dropping majesty of other states' vaulting crags or shimmering desert palettes. But it possesses an equable slice of physicality, with fascinating geographical and geological highlights—many of them found nowhere in the country—or world—outside of Wisconsin.

Yet never with any drama. This author holds that the Midwestern aw-shucks, taciturn stereotype—not always untrue—stems from an innate sense of the land itself.

Where in the World . . . ?

Where is the state? Sticklers say "eastern north-central United States." In a guidebook (*another* guidebook), one outlander classified it simply as "north," which makes sense only if you look at a map. Wisconsinites themselves most often consider their state a part of the Midwest—more specifically, the Upper Midwest. And some even prefer you call it a Great Lakes State.

The Basics

Extend your left hand, palm outward. There—pretty much—is Wisconsin (albeit with a large pinky knuckle and superfluous index finger).

One-third of the U.S. population lives within a day's drive of the state. Its surface area of 56,514 square miles ranks it 26th largest in the nation.

WISCONSIN GLACIATION

Continental Ice Sheet

EXTENT OF GLACIATED AREA

Superior Lobe

Chippewa Lobe

Wisconsin Valley Lobe

Terminal Moraine

Chippewa Moraine

Green Bay Lobe

Two Creeks Forest

Northern Kettle Moraine

Campbellsport Drumlins

Horicon Marsh

Terminal

Lake Michigan Lobe

Moraine

0   40 mi
0   40 km

© AVALON TRAVEL

Shield, which includes about two-thirds of eastern Canada along with Wisconsin, Minnesota, Michigan, and New York. A half billion years ago, a glacial lake flooded the Wisconsin range—the northern section of present-day Wisconsin.

Glaciation during the two million years of the four glacial periods—geologically, a blink of an eye—is responsible for Wisconsin's one-of-a-kind topography. (The final advance, occurring 70,000–10,000 years ago, was even named the Wisconsin period.) Wisconsin endured five glacial "lobes" penetrating the state, reducing the state's previous ambitious heights to knobs and slate-flat lands and establishing riverways and streambeds. Only the southwestern lower third of the state escaped the glaciers' penetration, resulting in the world's largest area surrounded completely by glacial drift.

Wisconsin is by no means high, yet this is a state of rolling topography, chock-full of hills and glacial undulation. The highest point is Timm's Hill in north-central Wisconsin; at 1,953 feet it's nothing to sneeze at for the Midwest.

Hydrophiles love it here. Even excluding all the access to the Great Lakes, approximately 4 percent of the state's surface is water—including more than 16,000 ancient glacial lakes (40 percent of which have yet even to be named).

Most of Wisconsin's perimeter sidesteps surveyors' plotting. The grandest borders—Lakes Michigan and Superior—are unique to Wisconsin and only one other state (Michigan). Superior occupies the far-north cap of the state, ensconcing the Bayfield County promontory and its Apostle Islands. More subdued Lake Michigan runs for an enormous stretch down the state, interrupted only by the magnificent Door County Peninsula.

GEOGRAPHY

Wisconsin was once at the earth's equatorial belt buckle. Plate shifting created the Canadian

Northern Highland

Covering 15,000 square miles, the Canadian Shield is the most salient physiogeographical feature of northern Wisconsin. Underlain by crystalline rock on a peneplain, the bedrock and glacial soils are particularly suited to growing timber.

More: Its high concentration of lakes is what separates the region from the rest of the Midwest—and, in fact, distinguishes it in the world, since only the remotest parts of Quebec and Finland have more lakes per square mile.

Lake Superior Lowlands

Wisconsin's northern cap along Lake Superior displays a geological oddity, unique in the Great Lakes—a fallen trench of Lake Superior, flanked by palisades. Before the glaciers arrived to finish carving, shifting lowered this 10- to 20-mile-wide belt (now a half mile lower than the surrounding land). This wedge-shaped red-clay plain consists mainly of copper-hued outcroppings and numerous streams and rivers (and waterfalls).

Eastern Ridges and Lowlands

Bordered by Lake Michigan on the east and north, this 14,000-square-mile region was much richer in glacial deposits, and the fecund soils attracted the first immigrant farmers. The impeded waterways were ideal conduits for floating timber to mills.

The Kettle Moraine region southeast of Lake Winnebago is a physical textbook of glacial geology.

Central (Sand) Plain

Bisected by the mighty Wisconsin River, the crescent-shaped Central Plain region spreads for 13,000 square miles. Once the bottom of enormous glacial Lake Wisconsin, the region is most noted for its oddball topography of sand dune-esque stretches mingled with peat bog, cranberry marsh, buttes and outliers (younger

hoodoo-shaped oddities) and jack pine and scrub oak—all made famous by Aldo Leopold's *A Sand County Almanac*. The central section of this region is relatively flat, but the lower third contains buttes and outliers (younger rock formations). All this at the Wisconsin Dells!

Western Uplands

The Western Uplands region subsumes the radical Driftless Area. Geologically the roughest and wildest sector of Wisconsin, it contains rises up to 400 feet higher than the contiguous Central Plain. The unglaciated plateau experienced much stream erosion, and the result is an amazing chocolate-drop topography of rolling hillock and valley—with the odd plateau and ridges not unlike West Virginia—capped by hard rock and sluiced by the lower Wisconsin and Mississippi Rivers.

CLIMATE

Contrary to what you may have heard, Wisconsin weather ain't all that bad. Sure, temperatures varying from 105°F to -30°F degrees spice things up a bit and, come late February, most people are psychotically ready for the snow to go, but overall it isn't terrible.

Wisconsin is near the path of the jet stream, and it lacks any declivity large enough to impede precipitation or climatic patterns. Its northerly latitude produces seasonal shifts in the zenith angle, which result in drastic temperature fluctuations. It's not unusual for farmers near Lake Geneva to be plowing while ice fishers near the Apostle Islands are still drilling holes in the ice.

Temperatures and Precipitation

The state's mean temperature is 43°F, though this is not a terribly useful statistic. You'll find 100°F in the shade come

PHYSIOGRAPHIC REGIONS

Lake Superior

Lake Superior Lowlands

MICHIGAN

Northern

Highland

Central

Western

Plain

Uplands

Eastern Ridges And Lowlands

MINNESOTA

IOWA

Lake Michigan

ILLINOIS

0   40 mi
0   40 km

© AVALON TRAVEL

AVERAGE TEMPERATURES

All temperatures are listed in degrees Fahrenheit.

LOCATION	JULY high/low	JANUARY high/low
Superior	78/52	20/0
Ashland	79/54	22/0
St. Croix Falls	82/58	20/-1
Eau Claire	81/58	20/0
Eagle River	78/52	19/1
Wausau	80/57	20/1
Stevens Point	81/58	23/4
Green Bay	80/58	23/6
Sturgeon Bay	76/56	26/11
La Crosse	83/62	23/5
Wisconsin Dells	82/59	25/6
Prairie du Chien	85/62	27/8
Madison	81/57	27/9
Milwaukee	81/59	28/12
Kenosha	81/60	29/13

August, 40°F or more below with wind chill in winter, and everything in between.

The average precipitation amount is 38.6 inches annually. Northern counties experience more snowfall than southern ones, and anyplace near the Great Lakes can see some sort of precipitation when the rest of the state is dry. Snow cover ranges from 140 days per annum in the north to 85 days in the south. Snowfall ranges from 30 inches in the extreme south to 120 inches or more in Bayfield County and the Lake Superior cap.

"But Cooler Near the Lake"

Wisconsin has two contiguous sea-size bodies of water, which give rise to their own littoral microclimates. Get used to hearing "cooler near the lake" in summer and "warmer near the lake" in winter. This moderating influence is particularly helpful for the orchards and gardens in Door County on Lake Michigan and Bayfield County on Lake Superior. On the other hand, it also means more precipitation: One freaky day in 2009, Milwaukee's south side had 14.8

inches of snow, while 30 miles to the west it was sunny all day!

Tornadoes

Generally, not much here in Wisconsin can kill you—no hurricanes, freeway snipers, or grizzlies. But the state does endure the eye-popping experience of tornadoes, generally averaging six *serious* twisters and many more near-misses or unsubstantiated touchdowns each year.

Tornado season begins in March and peaks during late May, June—especially—and July. A secondary spike occurs during September and extends occasionally into mid-October. Many of the midsummer tornadoes are smaller and less intense than the ones in April–June or in September.

A **tornado watch** means conditions are favorable for the development of a tornado. A **tornado warning** means one has been sighted in the vicinity. In either case, emergency sirens are active almost everywhere in Wisconsin. *Get yourself an emergency weather radio and keep it with you.*

Seek shelter in a basement and get in the southwest corner (they often, but not always, move from the southwest), under a table if possible. Avoid windows at all costs. If there is no basement, find an interior room, such as a bathroom, with no windows. Avoid rooms with outside walls on the south or west side of a building. If you are driving, position yourself at right angles to the tornado's apparent path. If overtaken, you've got a dilemma: experts howlingly disagree about whether to stay in the car with your seatbelt on or get out and lie flat in a ditch.

Thunderstorms and Lightning

Lightning still kills about 200–300 people per year nationwide, more than tornadoes and hurricanes combined. Wisconsin averages two serious thunderstorms per year, with a midsummer average of two relatively modest ones each week. Don't let this lull you into complacency in autumn, however; this author scribbled edition number one of this guide during ferocious thunderstorms on Halloween, replete with marble-size hail, flash floods, and tornadic activity.

Thunderstorms are often deadlier than tornadoes, particularly when you're driving or when isolated in open areas. Lightning is serious stuff—remember, if you're close enough to hear thunder, you're close enough to get fried. The cardinal rule when lightning is present: Do the opposite of what gut instincts tell you. Avoid anything outside—especially trees. If you cannot get indoors, squat on the balls of your feet, hugging your knees in a balled position, reducing your contact with the ground and your apparent size. If indoors, stay away from anything that has a channel to the outside: telephones, TVs, radios, even plumbing.

Snowstorms

Technically, four inches of snow per 24-hour period qualifies as heavy snowfall (but to that paltry amount a Wisconsinite would just sniff in derision).

Six inches in 8–12 hours will cause serious transportation disruptions and definitely close airports for a while. Snow generally begins to stick in mid- to late October in northern Wisconsin, and early December in southern Wisconsin, though snow has fallen as early as September and as late as May on rare occasions.

Odds are, if you're in Wisconsin in the winter you're going to be driving in the stuff. Still, even the hardiest winter drivers need to practice prudence. If you're a novice at winter driving, don't learn it on the road, especially on a crowded highway at dawn or dusk.

Rule One: It's important to *slow down*. Be cautious on bridges, even when the rest of the pavement is OK; bridges are always slippery. In controlled skids on ice and snow, take your foot off the accelerator and steer *into* the direction of the skid. Follow all owner's manual advice if your car is equipped with an Anti-Lock Braking System (ABS). Most cars come equipped with all-season radials, so snow tires aren't usually necessary. *Tire chains are illegal in Wisconsin.*

During nighttime snowstorms, keep your lights on low beam. If you get stuck, check your owner's manual for the advisability of "rocking" the car; be sure to keep the front wheels cleared *and pointed straight ahead.* Do not race the engine; you'll just spin your wheels into icy ruts. Winterize your vehicle. Most important, carry an emergency kit including anything you may need to spend the night in a snowbank (I can't tell you how many people have learned this the hard way in a blizzard that's trapped them on an interstate for ten hours.)

And please, if you see someone hung up in a snowbank, stop and help push him or her out.

The Department of Transportation's website (dot.state.wi.us) updates winter driving conditions from November to late March four times daily. You can also call the state's toll-free roads hotline at 511 on your mobile phone (Iowa and Minnesota also participate in the program, Illinois and Michigan hopefully soon)—it's a brilliant service.

Wind Chill and Frostbite

The most dangerous part of winter in Wisconsin is the wind-chill factor—the biting effect of wind, which makes cold colder and more lethal. For example, when the temperature is 30°F, with a wind of 40 mph the temperature is actually -6°F; if the temperature were 0°F, 40 mph winds would make it -54°F—the point at which it's no longer a joke how cold a Wisconsin winter is.

When the wind chill takes temperatures low enough, exposed skin is in immediate danger. Lots of Badgers still remember one serious case of frostbite (probably frostnip) that they swear they can still feel today when the weather changes. The most serious cases of frostbite—you've seen photos of mountain climbers with black ears and digits—can require amputation.

Worse, without proper clothing, you're at risk for **hypothermia.**

ENVIRONMENTAL ISSUES

A state that produced both John Muir and Aldo Leopold must have a fairly good track record of being "green." If you discount the first century of statehood, during which the state—like most states at the time—pillaged the natural world full-bore, Wisconsin has in fact been ahead of its time environmentally. The state government initiated exceptionally far-sighted environmental laws beginning in the 1950s, when tourism loomed as a major industry. The state was the first to meet the 1972 Clean Water Act; it had put similar legislation on its own books a half decade earlier. Former Wisconsin governor and U.S. senator Gaylord Nelson founded Earth Day in 1970.

Superfund Sites and Dirty Water

Still, as always, things could be better. Wisconsin retains more than three dozen EPA Superfund sites (areas so contaminated that the EPA allots large amounts of money to clean them up). The Wisconsin Department of Natural Resources has found that about 900 miles of rivers in the state flunked environmental standards since the mid-1990s, and another 50 or so lakes were "questionable" or worse. Twenty-two percent of rivers and streams fail, one way or another, to meet the state's clean-water goals. Fish-consumption advisories have been in effect since 2000 for well over 300 lakes and rivers. Though the figures may constitute less than 5 percent of riverways and an even lower percentage of lakes, it portends worse things to come.

Though the state has some of the strictest groundwater laws and is pointed to by the EPA as one of three exemplary states, not enough local water sources pass muster. Land use, particularly agriculture, forestry, and construction, often creates eroded soils and runoff polluted with fertilizers and toxins. But agriculture cannot hold all the blame; urban runoff potentially causes up to 50 times as much soil erosion and dumps whatever is on the street into the water (like your oil leak).

Contaminated sedimentation from decades of abuse remains a secondary problem. Pulp and paper mills discharged almost 300 million gallons of wastewater, most of it untreated, into surface water. The EPA was asked to declare

39 miles of the Fox River—the heart of papermaking—a Superfund site because *40 tons* (of an original 125 tons) of toxic PCBs (polychlorinated biphenyl) remained from factory waste discharge.

As a result of other pollution, the Wisconsin DNR issues almost 200 "boil water" notices annually (one Wisconsin county found half of its 376 wells to be seriously contaminated by pollutants such as atrazine and nitrates). More than 90 percent of state lakes have been affected one way or another, including sedimentation, contamination, and (the most common and difficult to handle) eutrophication—when increased nutrients in the water lead to algae blooms and nuisance weeds, which eventually kill off aquatic life (visit Madison, the city on four lakes, in July and you'll know what I mean).

Mercury and Other Toxins

Some say toxic environmental pollutants are among the most pernicious, silent crises in health of the North Woods today. No big deal? Government statistics estimate that annually 1,200 Wisconsin children are exposed to elevated levels of mercury. The CDC in Atlanta says 1 woman in 10 in the United States already has dangerous levels of mercury in her blood.

Now, mercury isn't a problem in Lakes Superior and Michigan; however, fish consumption advisories exist there as well because of a cousin toxin—PCBs, different but equally awful. (It can cause cancer.) Mercury warnings for U.S. waters increased more than 100 percent since 1993. Scientists announced a somewhat shocking discovery—that dioxins were the likely culprit of swooning lake trout stocks, not invasive species or overfishing.

Whether you agree or not on the dangers, here are official government statistics. In bottom feeders such as carp and Mississippi River channel catfish, the ppm contamination levels are at 0.11 and 0.09, respectively. Contrast this with predators such as bass and walleye, both with much higher levels, with the latter at a somewhat whopping 0.52 ppm. Northwestern Wisconsin, oddly enough, despite all those lush tracts of trees, has a rather high level of mercury contamination when compared to the rest of the state, mostly because of airborne contaminants.

This is in part why recommended daily intake of fish for women of childbearing years, nursing mothers, and children under 15 is one meal per week of bluegill, sunfish, yellow perch, and bullheads (among panfish), and one meal per month of walleye, northern pike, bass, channel catfish, and flathead catfish (among predators and bottom feeders). Note: Do not eat walleye longer than 20 inches, northern pike longer than 30 inches, or muskellenge.

For men and women beyond childbearing years, the former group (panfish) isn't limited, while the latter group (predators and bottom feeders) is recommended at one meal per week. If you eat fish only during vacation or sporadically otherwise, you can double these amounts. To increase your chances of eating a healthy fish, eat smaller fish, eat panfish (sunfish, crappies, etc.) rather than predators (walleye, northern pike, etc.), and trim skin and fat.

Sprawl Mall Hell

With 90.1 people per square mile, Wisconsin ranks in the middle of American states for population density. However, two-thirds of the people dwell in the dozen southeastern counties, creating a serious land-use and urban-sprawl issue. In southeastern Wisconsin, agricultural land is being converted to urban use at a rate of 10 square miles per year. All of southern Wisconsin may be in danger—Scenic America declared three sites (Vernon County's Kickapoo River Valley, Washington County around Erin, and Mississippi River bluffs) as some of the worst examples of rural landscape degradation; then again, we're not as bad as Colorado (the entire state made the list).

Northern forests are being encroached upon as flight from burgeoning urban areas continues. This sprawl results in diminished air quality (from excess use of commuters' automobiles), loss of farmland and wildlife habitat, more toxic runoff, and continued erosion.

Air Quality

At one point in the 1970s, fully half of Wisconsin counties failed standards for ozone, total suspended particulates, and sulfur dioxide. All have gotten better, save for ground-level ozone—the main ingredient of smog—still found in 11 southeastern counties. The problem is so severe that southeast Wisconsin was forced by federal law to begin using expensive reformulated gas in the mid-1990s. (Wisconsinites naturally blamed Chicago for the pollution!)

Once a grave crisis for northern lakes and forests, acid deposition, known as acid rain when it falls from the sky, has been slowed, largely through strict national legislation enacted in the mid-1980s. It's still a problem, however; 90 percent of the pollutants in Lake Superior come from the air.

Give 'Em Hell

Pick an issue and Wisconsinites will passionately—but politely—be involved, pro or con. The longstanding tradition of grassroots activism in the state is alive and well, especially in environmental issues. But here's the good part: It often ain't your stereotype granolas versus timber cutters. In fact, in many environmental issues, hunters, fishers, and snowmobilers work for common ground with heretofore "enemies"— the tree-huggers of Madison. No coincidence that the Progressive Party of Fightin' Bob La Follette was founded here.

Visually Busy

In this author's opinion, another piece of the pollution puzzle—not lethal but certainly important—needs scrutiny: Wisconsin's lovely countryside is absolutely scarred by the visual pollution of "litter on a stick," or billboard advertising. States and communities across the nation have awakened to the fact that not only is it disgustingly ugly, but it can also distract drivers. The state has nearly 15,000 ugly popsicles gracelessly attesting to our state's, well, if not greed then certainly bad taste; only three states have more billboard advertising than Wisconsin.

FLORA AND FAUNA

Flora

The Eastern Transition and Great Lakes Forest Zones cover most of Wisconsin. Both are primarily mixed meadow and woodland, a far cry from presettlement periods when 85 percent of the state was covered by forest and the rest by tall grass. By the mid-19th century, those numbers had dipped to 63 percent forest, 28 percent savanna, and 9 percent grassland. Today, the state's forest cover is 37 percent, and precious little of that is original. Of the two million acres of prairie that once covered the state, only 2,000 scattered acres survive. In all, Wisconsin has more than 2,100 species of plants, approximately a tenth of which are classified as rare, and some of them are threatened.

Four major vegetation types cover Wisconsin: **boreal forest,** a subarctic coniferous spread near Lake Superior; **deciduous forest** makes up the second-largest swath of Wisconsin woodlands; **mixed forest,** consisting of species of both, is found throughout the

Door County cherries

white-tailed deer

state; and **nonforest/grasslands,** are found throughout the southern third of the state and up into west-central Wisconsin along the Mississippi River.

In settlement periods, Wisconsin had a huge expanse of wetlands, including more than 10,000 acres along Green Bay alone. Today, that amount has dwindled by more than half but still constitutes the largest amount remaining on the Great Lakes—a pathetic indication of rapacious development and overuse.

Fauna

Wisconsin lies within three well-defined "life zones" conducive to species diversity: the Canadian, the transition, and the upper austral (or Carolinian). The Canadian, not surprisingly the coldest, features small mammals such as the snowshoe hare but also the state's primary large mammals, the deer and the black bear. The warmest zone, the Carolinian, falls in the southern tier of the state and lacks big game mammals. In total, Wisconsin has 73 species of mammals, 339 native bird species,

and more than 200 species of amphibians, reptiles, frogs, bats, butterflies, and insects.

Of Wisconsin's two large mammals, the ubiquitous **white-tailed deer** is a traffic (and garden) nightmare. The other resident big mammal, the **black bear,** is still relatively common in the North Woods and has also been seen in central and—gasp—southern counties.

Wisconsin lies smack in the middle of several migratory waterfowl flyways, so birding is a big activity in the state. **Tundra swans, sandhill cranes,** and **Canada geese** are three of the most conspicuous species. The latter are so predominant at the Horicon Marsh National Wildlife Refuge that ornithologists make pilgrimages there each spring and especially fall.

Threatened, Endangered, Exterminated

The last plains buffalo was shot five years before the state became a territory. The next to become extinct within the state of Wisconsin were the Richardson's caribou, the American elk, the cougar, the Carolina paroquet, the passenger pigeon (the world's last was shot in Wisconsin), the peregrine falcon, the pine marten, the trumpeter swan, the whooping crane, the wild turkey, the moose, the fisher, and, in 1922, the common wolverine.

Jump forward to today. First, the bad news: Wisconsin has more than 200 species of flora or fauna listed as either endangered or threatened by state or federal agencies. The state ranks in the middle for species diversity and at-risk status—0 percent of mammals are at risk, but 6.2 percent of fish are at serious risk (the rest are in the middle).

Yet all is not lost. Wisconsin instituted preservation measures long before the federal government did and is consistently recognized by environmental groups for at least trying (one reason so many green groups are here). The fisher, falcon, pine marten, trumpeter swan, and wild turkey have been reintroduced to varying degrees of success.

Perhaps befitting a state in which the International Crane Foundation is headquartered, cranes are making a comeback. The regal, French horn–sounding trumpeter swans, once nearly extinct, are well on the way to the target of 51 breeding pairs by 2020 (they now total about 300 birds in 14 counties). A great big by-the-way: The International Crane Foundation (E11376 Shady Lane Rd., 608/356-9462, www.savingcranes.com) has information on wonderful volunteer opportunities to tramp through central Wisconsin counting the birds—great fun!

In 2000 the state also established nesting sites for whooping cranes over 100,000 acres in central Wisconsin; eventually nests will be found at the Sandhill State Wildlife Area, Necedah National Wildlife Refuge, and two other sites. In 2002, before national media, the first eight whooping cranes made their migration to Florida behind an ultralight plane (most returned). By 2020 hopes are to have 125 of the majestic birds in the state. Most amazing was the return of a nesting pair of **piping plovers** to the shores of the Apostle Islands National Lakeshore in 1999. In the entire Great Lakes only 30 nesting pairs exist, all in Michigan. As a result, the U.S. Fish and Wildlife Service has proposed setting aside nearly 200 miles of shoreline—20 in Wisconsin—for critical habitats, and possibly to establish a colony.

One of the most visually amazing birds—the white pelican—has also made a recent comeback. Thank the universe if you spot one in the Horicon Marsh National Wildlife Refuge.

Though never extinct, the bald eagle, once perilously close to vanishing, may have had the most successful recovery of all. The state now harbors about 850 pairs of breeding eagles, and the birds are so prevalent along the Wisconsin and Mississippi Rivers that certain communities make much of their tourist income because of them. The state is also gobbling up riverine land near Prairie du Sac to continue the comeback.

Wisconsin does take forceful steps to preserve wildlife through its Department of Natural Resources. It was the first state in the United States to designate Natural Areas throughout the state. These vigilantly protected areas harbor fragile geology, archaeology, or plant and animal life; some are even being nudged toward a return to their presettlement ecology.

Absolutely the most intriguing question now is if **cougars** are preying the woods. Since 1994, more than 300 sightings have been reported and many of these confirmed (the last one supposedly perished in 1908); they're most likely migrating from the Black Hills of South Dakota.

If there is one endangered fish all Badgers worry about, it's the **perch,** especially the yellow perch. In a state that treats fish fries as quasi-religious experiences (there is no better fish than perch for a fish fry), plummeting lake perch populations in the early 1990s absolutely freaked out the fish-loving population. But since the turn of the new millennium, sufficient numbers were being seen for the DNR to be "cautiously optimistic." Trout lovers rejoice—blue-ribbon status streams have increased 1,000 percent in 20 years!

Still, the picture could be much better. Even

as many species are rebounding, annually other native species are added to the threatened and endangered lists. Just under 3 percent of native plants are now threatened or endangered. And one-quarter of the state's species are nonnative, or invasive.

Birder Heaven

Avian species have always found the state's flyways crucial to survival. With the reintroduction of so many—along with wetlands restoration and protection—the state has fantastic birding opportunities. The statewide **Oak Leaf Birding Trail** (www.dnr.state.wi.us) has 35 prime birding spots; the terminus is Whitnall Park in Milwaukee. Even better is the newer **Great Wisconsin Birding and Nature Trail,** which covers the whole state; check wisconsin-birds.org for more information.

One place few people visit is the outstanding **Baraboo Hills** region in central Wisconsin, a major node on a transcontinental birding flyway.

The **Great River Birding Trail** (www.audubon.org) along the Mississippi River possibly equals it; head to the La Crosse/Onalaska area for mid-May's grand **Mississippi Flyway Birding Festival.** (Actually, the Mississippi River region has year-round birding festivals!)

Zebra Mussel

One culprit for the decline in Lake Michigan's yellow perch population could be this pesky little mollusk, the species that best represents what can happen when a nonnative species is introduced into an environment. Transplanted most likely from a visiting freighter from the Caspian Sea in the mid-1980s, the zebra mollusk is a ferocious, tough little Eurasian mollusk that found it loved the warmer waters and phytoplankton of the Great Lakes. Problem is, it loves to breed near warm areas—such as at discharge pipes around power plants. They breed so rapidly they create unbelievably dense barnacle-like crusts that do serious damage. Worse, they're being blamed for the decline if not decimation of native species as they literally suck all the nutrients out of an area. Great Lakes states are frantically fighting a war to keep them from spreading into inland lakes and streams.

Asian Carp

This tough-nut alien species is poised to, quite literally, invade Lake Michigan via Illinois, which is doing everything save for poisoning rivers to keep it out. If it gets into Lake Michigan, it could mean doom for species present there.

History

EARLY ARRIVALS

The Siberia-to-Alaska Beringia theory, which posits that the progenitors of North America's Native Americans arrived over a land bridge that rose and submerged in the Bering Strait beginning as many as 20,000 years ago, was dealt serious blows in the late 1990s. Provocative new anthropological discoveries in North and Latin America have forced a radical reconsideration of this theory (a Wisconsin archaeologist was one of the first to bring up the topic—Kenosha County in southeastern Wisconsin has revealed key new finds). The last of the glacial interludes of the Pleistocene era, the Two Rivers, probably saw the first movement into the state of early Paleo-Indians about 11,500 years ago. The time is based on examinations of fluted points as well as a rare mastodon kill site, the Boaz Mastodon, which established Paleo-Indian hunting techniques of the Plains Indians in Wisconsin.

Glacial retreat helps explain why the Paleo-Indian groups entered the state from the south and southwest rather than the more logical north. Nomadic clans followed the mastodon and other large mammals northward as the glaciers shrank.

Later Stages

Solid archaeological evidence establishes definite stages in Wisconsin's earliest settlers. The **Archaic** period lasted, approximately, from 8000 B.C. to 750 B.C. The tribes were still transient, pursuing smaller game and the fish in the newly formed lakes. Around 2000 B.C., these Indians became the first in the New World to fashion copper.

The later **Woodland** Indians, with semi-permanent abodes, are generally regarded as the first Natives in Wisconsin to make use of ceramics, elaborate mound burials (especially in southern Wisconsin) and, to a lesser extent, domesticated plants such as squash, corn, pumpkins, beans, and tobacco. Lasting from around 750 B.C. until European exploration, the Woodland period was a minor golden age of dramatic change for the Native cultures. Around 100 B.C., the Middle Woodland experienced cultural and technological proliferations, simultaneous with the period of Ohio's and Illinois's Hopewell societies, when villages formed and expanded greatly along waterways.

The people living during the tail end of the Woodland period have been classified into two additional groups: the **Mississippian** and the **Oneota.** The former's impressive sites can be found from New Orleans all the way north into Wisconsin and parts of Minnesota. Mississippian culture showed high levels of civic planning and complex social hierarchies, and it lasted at least until the Spanish arrived (Spanish records reported contact).

EUROPEAN CONTACT

Spanish, Portuguese, and English were all blazing a trail westward. The main directive was to circumvent the Arabs, reach the courts of the Great Khan, and establish channels to appropriate the riches of new lands. Along the way, the natives, if any, were to be "pacified" under papal hegemony. After England came to naval power under the Tudor monarchies and began taking swipes at the French, the New World became the proving ground for the European powers.

New France: Black Robes and the Fur Trade

The French, relative latecomers to maritime and thus expansionist endeavors, were, thanks to the Reformation, conveniently freed of papal dicta for divvying up the new continent and its inherent wealth. With the Spanish in the Caribbean and Gulf Coast and the up-and-coming English having a foothold in the mid-Atlantic colonies, France was effectively forced to attempt to penetrate the new land via the northern frontier.

Jacques Cartier first opened the door to the Great Lakes region with his "discovery" of the Gulf of the St. Lawrence River, in 1534. The insular French monarchy, though, left the scattered outposts to simmer for another 40 years—except for several fur traders, who, it turns out, were on to something.

The French did establish sparse settlements in the early 16th century, though they were dismayed by the lack of ready riches, the roughness of the land, and the bitter weather. However, the original traders possessed one superlative talent: forging relationships with the Natives, who became enamored of French metal implements—firearms in particular. Eventually, the French found their coveted mother lode: beavers.

Paris hatmakers discovered that beaver pelts—especially those softened for a year around the waists of Indians—made a superior grade of felt for hats, and these soon became the rage in Paris and other parts of Europe, becoming the lifeblood of the colonies, sustaining the region through the mismanagement and general vagaries of both British and French rule.

Facilitating both the fur trade and French control over the colonies were the missionaries of the Society of Jesus—the Jesuits. These "Black Robes" (so-called by the Huron and Ottawa) first arrived during a time of atavistic religious fervor in France. The Franciscans had originally set down here but found the task of conversion too daunting for their small order. The Jesuits became the very foundation upon which New France operated. The traders needed them to foster harmony with Native American traders. More important, the often complicated French systems of operation required that all day-to-day affairs be carried out at the local level. By 1632, all missionary work in French Canada was under the auspices of the Jesuits.

The Jesuits also accompanied voyageurs (explorers) as New France attempted to widen its sphere of influence westward. Eventually, the Black Robes themselves, along with renegade fur traders, were responsible for the initial exploration and settlement of present-day Wisconsin.

THE FRENCH IN WISCONSIN

Samuel de Champlain, who first arrived in Quebec in 1603, was the province's most famous and effective leader, despite an obsession with the legendary route to the Great Khan. After arriving and hearing of the "People of the Stinking Waters" (the Winnebago), which he surmised to mean an ocean-dwelling people, he dispatched the first Europeans from Acadia to explore the wild western frontier.

Though there is speculative evidence that Étienne Brulé, Champlain's first explorer, may have poked around Wisconsin as early as 1620—the same year many assume the pilgrims founded the new colonies—most historians credit Jean Nicolet with being the first European to turn up in Green Bay, landing at Red Banks in 1634. Garbed in Chinese damask and using thunderstick histrionics to impress the natives (the Potawatomi he met immediately dubbed him Thunder Beaver), Nicolet efficiently and diplomatically forged immediate ties with the Indians, who guided him throughout the region to meet other tribes.

As before, Nicolet couldn't rouse the wilted interest of the French royalty—all it wanted to see was bags of Chinese silk—and the country once again let the matter drop. Legitimate French fur traders were scooped by Pierre Esprit Radisson and Médard Chouart des Groseilliers, two pesky *coureurs-de-bois* (renegade trappers) who couldn't be bothered to get licensed by the crown. They delved farther into Wisconsin than any had before but had nowhere to trade their furs after being blacklisted by the ruling powers in New France. This led them to England, which gave them a charter to establish the Hudson's Bay Company north of New France—one reason for the later conflict between France and Britain. In 1666, these two were followed by Nicholas Perrot, who extended Nicolet's explorations and consequently opened the French fur trade with natives in Wisconsin.

The seasoned Father Claude Allouez simultaneously founded the first mission at La Pointe in the Apostle Islands and founded St. Francois Xavier, Wisconsin's first permanent European settlement, at De Pere, south of Green Bay.

The most famous Jesuit explorer was Father Jacques Marquette, who, along with Louis Jolliet, was sent by La Salle in 1673 to discern whether the Mississippi emptied into the Gulf of Mexico. The first Europeans to cross Wisconsin, they made it to the Mississippi on June 17, 1673, and went as far south as Arkansas, where they saw Indians with European goods, confirming both a route to the Gulf and the presence of the Spanish. The French hesitated in buttressing their western frontier—and it wound up costing them dearly.

Conflict with the British and British Rule

The fate of New France and, thus, Wisconsin was determined not in the New World but on the European continent, as Louis XIV, who had reigned during a zenith of French power, frittered away French influence bit by bit in frivolous, distracting battles.

The French never fully used the western edges of the Great Lakes and James II's rise to the throne in England marked the end of France's never-exactly-halcyon days in the Great Lakes. James forced Louis into wild strategies to protect French interests in the New World—strategies that did lead to further exploration of the hinterlands but also drove France to overextend itself and, eventually, collapse in the region.

At the behest of the Jesuits, who hoped to corral some recalcitrant Indian tribes, Louis closed trade completely in the Great Lakes interiors, thus cutting off possible ties to the English or the Spanish. Louis correctly reckoned that whoever the Indians sided with would end up controlling the new lands. This naturally drained royal coffers and he decided instead to keep the Indians, the English, and the Spanish in check by exploring as far inland as possible and trying to establish a line of garrisons from Montreal all the way to New Orleans.

Louis succeeded in this second plan but in the process alienated the uneasy Indians who *had* sworn loyalty to France and, worse, aroused the ire of France's bitterest enemies—the Iroquois and the Fox Indians. Wars with the Fox, which raged 1701–1738, sapped the determination of the French temporarily, but they had enough pluck—and military might—to string forts along the Mississippi to look for inroads into territories already held by the British in the Ohio River Valley. By 1750, British colonists in the western Great Lakes outnumbered French 20 to 1, and many Indians, discovering that the English made higher-quality goods more cheaply, switched to the British side.

The French and Indian War (1755–1763) was a thorough thrashing of the French by the British and greatly determined European spheres of influence in North America.

Under the British, little changed in daily life. (The English never even had an official presence in present-day Wisconsin.) One Englishman of note, however, was Jonathan Carver, a roguish explorer who roamed the state 1766–1768 and returned to England to publish fanciful, lively, and mostly untrue accounts of the new lands west of the inland seas.

The French had been content simply to trade and had never made overtures for the land itself. But the British who did come—many barely able to conceal their scorn for the less-than-noble savages—began parceling up property and immediately incited unrest. Pontiac, an Ottawa chieftain, led a revolt against the British at Muscoda.

Additionally, the British monarchy's finances were in disarray from the lengthy conflicts with the French in North America and with other enemies in European theaters. And then the monarchy decreed that the colonies could foot their own bill for these new lands and instituted the Stamp Act.

THE AMERICAN REVOLUTION

British settlers in Wisconsin who remained after the area was made part of British Quebec Province under the Quebec Act of 1774 stood resolutely loyal to the British crown but remained out of the American Revolution other than scattered attempts by both sides to enlist the Indians.

The 1781 surrender of Cornwallis at Yorktown cost Britain a great part of its holdings, including the Northwest Territory, which included Wisconsin, yet practical British influence remained in the state until after the War of 1812.

British commercial interests had little desire to abandon the still-lucrative beaver trade, and the Indians had grown, if not loyal to, then at least tolerant of, the British. When hostilities broke out in 1812, the British, aiming to create a buffer zone of Indian alliances in Indiana and Illinois, quickly befriended the Indians—an easy venture, as the Natives were already inflamed over the first of many U.S. government snake-oil land treaties.

The Northwest, including Wisconsin, played a much larger role in this new bellicosity than it had in the Revolution; British loyalists and American frontiersman fought for control of the Natives as well as of the water-route forts of the French and British. British forts, now occupied (and undermanned) by U.S. troops, were easily overwhelmed by English and Indian confederates. However, Commodore Perry's victory on Lake Erie in 1813 swung the momentum to the American side. Treaties signed upon reaching a stalemate in 1814 allowed the United States to regain preexisting national boundaries. Almost immediately, John Jacob Astor's American Fur Company set up operations in Wisconsin, but by this time the golden age of beaver trade in the area was over.

Though not yet even a territory and despite both the intractability of the Indians and the large populations of British and French, Wisconsin was fully part of the United States by 1815. In 1822, the first wave of immigration began, with thousands of Cornish and other miners burrowing into the hillsides of southwestern Wisconsin to search for lead (the origin of the Badger State moniker). As miners poured into Wisconsin to scavenge lead, speculators multiplied, land offices sprang up, and the first banks opened; everyone was eager to make money off the new immigrants. Before the area achieved territorial status, in 1836, more than 10,000 settlers had inundated the southern part of the state.

NATIVE AMERICAN RELATIONS

Unfortunately, none of the foreign settlers consulted the indigenous residents before carving up the land. The United States practiced a heavy-handed patriarchal policy toward the Native Americans, insisting that they be relocated west—away from white settlers on the eastern seaboard—for the betterment of both sides. Simultaneously, the new government instituted a loony system designed to reprogram the Natives to become happy Christian farmers. Land cessions, begun around the turn of the 19th century, continued regularly until the first general concourse of most western Indian tribes took place, in 1825, at Prairie du Chien, Wisconsin, at which time the first of the more draconian treaties was drawn up. The first New York Indians—the Oneida, Stockbridge, Munsee, and Brothertown—were moved to Wisconsin beginning in 1823. The cocktail of misguided U.S. patronization and helplessly naive Native negotiations turned lethal when many tribes came to realize what had been done to them.

The first skirmish, the so-called Winnebago War of 1827, was nothing more than a frustrated attempt at vengeance by a Winnebago chieftain, Red Bird, who killed two settlers before being convinced to surrender to avert war. The second was more serious—and more legendary.

The Black Hawk War

In 1804, William Henry Harrison, a ruthless longtime foe of Indians in the west, rammed through a treaty with Native Americans in St. Louis that effectively extinguished the tribes' title to most of their land. Part of this land was in southwestern Wisconsin, newly dubbed the "lead region."

Mining operations—wildcatters, mostly—proliferated but ebbed when the miners began to fear the Natives more and more. The ire and paranoia of the federal government, which had assumed carte blanche in the region, was piqued in 1832, when a militant band of Fox-Sauk Indians refused to recognize treaties, including the one that had forcibly moved them out of the southern part of Wisconsin.

Their leader was Black Sparrow Hawk, better known as Black Hawk, a warrior not so much pro-British as fiercely anti-American. With blind faith in the British, obdurate pride, and urging from other Indian tribes (who would later double-cross him), Black Hawk initiated a quixotic stand against the United States, which culminated in tragic battles staged in Wisconsin.

Black Hawk and his group of about 1,000 recalcitrant natives, dubbed "the British Band," balked at U.S. demands that the tribe relocate across the Mississippi. Insisting that they were exempt because Black Hawk had been blacklisted from treaty negotiations, in April 1832 the band began moving up the Rock River to what they deemed their rightful lands. Other tribes had promised support along the way, in both provisions and firepower. Instead, Black Hawk found his erstwhile exhorters—the Potawatomi, Sioux, and Winnebago—turning on him. Worse, news of Black Hawk's actions was sweeping the region with grotesque frontier embellishment, and the U.S. military, private militias, and frontiersmen under their control were all itching for a fight.

His people lacking provisions (one reason

for the band's initial decampment was a lack of corn in the area after the settlers squeezed in) and soon tiring, Black Hawk wisely realized his folly and in May sent a truce contingent. Jumpy soldiers under Major Isaiah Stillman instead overreacted and attacked. Black Hawk naturally counterattacked and, although seriously outnumbered, his warriors chased the whites away—an event that became known as Stillman's Run. Nevertheless, the fuse was lit.

The band then crossed into Wisconsin near Lake Koshkonong and began a slow, difficult journey west, back toward the Mississippi River. Two commanders led their forces in pursuit of the hapless Indians, engaging in a war of attrition along the way. They cornered Black Hawk and fought the quick but furious Battle of Wisconsin Heights along the Wisconsin River. The tribe escaped in the darkness, with the soldiers pursuing hungrily. One large group of mostly women, children, and old men tried to float down the Wisconsin toward the Mississippi but were intercepted by soldiers and Indians; most were drowned or killed.

What followed is perhaps the most tragic chapter in Wisconsin history, the Battle of Bad Axe, an episode that garnered shocked national attention and made Black Hawk as well known as the president. On August 1, 1832, Black Hawk made it to the Mississippi River. Hastily throwing together rafts, the band tried to cross but was intercepted by a U.S. gunboat. The U.S. forces opened fire mercilessly for two hours, despite a white flag from the Indians. Black Hawk and a group of 50 escaped, assuming the other group—300 women, children, and elderly—would be left alone. Instead, this group was butchered by General Henry Atkinson's men and their Sioux cohorts when they reached the opposite shore.

Black Hawk and the 50 warriors were pursued by legions of soldiers and Indian accomplices. Black Hawk was eventually brought in alive to St. Louis (guarded by Jefferson Davis) and later imprisoned on the East Coast, where he found himself in the media spotlight. He later wrote a compelling autobiography, one of the first documents offering a glimpse of

the baffled, frustrated Native American point of view. Black Hawk was eventually sent back to Wisconsin.

In truth, Black Hawk was likely never half as belligerent as he's been characterized. By the 1830s he was well into his 60s and weary of protracted and unbalanced negotiations and battles with the whites. The Black Hawk War marked a watershed of Native presence in Wisconsin: By 1833, the few cessions the United States had gained to Native lands below the Fox-Wisconsin Rivers had been extracted. However, in 1837 the northern Wisconsin tribes signed away for a pittance more than half of the land area north of the Fox River, giving free reign to the rapacious lumbermen. Perhaps directly because of Black Hawk's sad grasp for legitimacy, the U.S. government began playing hardball with the Native Americans.

THE WISCONSIN TERRITORY

The Northwest Ordinance of 1787 established many of the borders of present-day Wisconsin; Thomas Jefferson had initially envisioned dividing the region into 10 states. Later, before the War of 1812, Wisconsin became part of first the Indiana Territory and then the Illinois as the Northwest was chiseled down. In 1818, the Illinois Territory was further hacked to create the Michigan Territory. Finally, in 1836, the Wisconsin Territory was established, taking in all of modern Wisconsin, the Upper Peninsula of Michigan, Iowa, Minnesota, and parts of North and South Dakota.

Despite the loss, the Black Hawk fiasco had another effect contrary to the Sauk leader's intentions: The well-publicized battles put Wisconsin on the map. This, combined with the wild mining operations in the southwestern part of the state, burgeoning lumber operations along the Great Lake coast, and discovery of the fecund soils outside of Milwaukee, ensured Wisconsin's status as the Next Big Thing. The new Erie Canal provided immigrants a direct route to this new land. By 1835, 60,000 eager settlers were pushing through the Erie Canal each year, and most were aiming for what the following year became the Wisconsin Territory.

Two years later, in 1838, when the chunk of Wisconsin Territory west of the Mississippi was lopped off, more than half of the 225,000 settlers were in Wisconsin proper. With the enforcement of Indian land cessions after Black Hawk's defeat, up to three *billion* acres became available for government surveyors; the first land title sales started in 1834. Wisconsin had fully arrived—and it still wasn't even a state.

STATEHOOD: GROWING PAINS

Wisconsin's entrance into the Union as the flag's 30th star was a bit anticlimactic; there wasn't even a skirmish with Canada over it. In fact, the populace voted on the issue of statehood in 1841, and every year for nearly the entire decade, but distinctly disinterested voters rejected the idea until 1848, when stratospheric levels of immigration impelled the legislature to more animated attempts, and the first measures passed.

Incessant immigration continued after statehood. Most newcomers arrived from New England or Europe—Ireland, England, Germany, and Scandinavia. The influx of Poles was still decades away. Milwaukee, a diminutive village of 1,500 at the time of territorial status, burgeoned into a rollicking town of 46,000 by the start of the Civil War, by which time the population of the state as a whole was up to 706,000 people.

During the period leading up to the Civil War, Wisconsin was dominated by political (and some social) wrangling over what, exactly, the state was to be. With the influence of Yankee immigrants and the Erie Canal access, much of Wisconsin's cultural, political, and social makeup finally resembled New England. In fact, New York legislation was the model for many early Wisconsin laws. The first university was incorporated almost immediately after statehood, and school codes for primary and secondary education soon followed—a bit ahead of the Union as a whole.

Abolition was a hot issue in Wisconsin's early years. It reached top-level status after the annexation of Texas and the Mexican-American War; as a result of this and many other contentious issues, Ripon, Wisconsin, became the founding spot of the Republican Party, which soon took hold of the legislature and held fast until the Civil War.

During the Civil War, despite being among the first states to near enlistment quotas, Wisconsin suffered some of the fiercest draft rioting in the nation. Many new immigrants had decamped from their European homelands for precisely the reasons for which the government was now pursuing them. Eventually, 96,000 Wisconsinites would serve.

Post-Civil War: Immigrants, Dairy, and Industry

After the Civil War and through the turn of the 20th century, Wisconsin began getting its economic bearings while politicians wrestled over issues as disparate as temperance, railroads, and immigrants' rights. The latter hot potato galvanized enormous enclaves of German Americans into action; they mobilized against anti-immigration laws sweeping through the legislature. Despite the mandates (banning the German language in schools, for one), successive waves of immigrants poured into the state.

The first sawmills had gone up in Wisconsin at the turn of the 19th century. Yankee and British settlers put them up to use the timber they were felling in clearing farmland. One area of the Chippewa River possessed one-sixth of all the pine west of the Adirondacks—and Wisconsin pine was larger and harder than that in surrounding states. Easily floated down streams and rivers, pine became an enormous commodity on the expanding plains. In Wisconsin, even the roads were fashioned from pine and hardwood planks. By 1870, more than one billion board feet of lumber was being churned out through the state's 1,000-plus mills each year, easily making Wisconsin the country's largest timber producer (it was one-fourth of all state wages). In time, more than 20 billion board feet were taken from the shores of Green Bay alone; one year, 425 million board feet were shipped through Superior.

Wisconsin wood was used in other parts of the expanding country to make homes, wagons, fences, barns, and plank roads. As a result, by the turn of the 20th century, more than 50 million acres of Wisconsin (and Minnesota) forest had been ravaged—most of it unrecoverable. By 1920, most of the state was a cutover wasteland.

Land eroded, tracts of forest disappeared and weren't replaced, and riparian areas were destroyed to dam for "float flooding." Worst, the average pine tree size was shrinking rapidly, and the lumber barons expressed little interest in preparing for the ultimate eradication of the forests. The small settlement of Peshtigo and more than 1,000 of its people perished in a furious conflagration made worse by logging cutover in 1871, and in the 1890s vast fires swept other central and northern counties.

Badgers began diversify. A handful of years after the Civil War, the state kicked its wheat habit (by 1860, Wisconsin was producing more wheat than any other state in the United States) and began looking for economic diversity. Wheat was sapping the soil fertility in southern Wisconsin, forcing many early settlers to pick up stakes once again and shift to the enormous golden tracts of the western plains states. Later, when railroads and their seemingly arbitrary pricing systems began affecting potential income from wheat, farmers in Wisconsin began seriously reviewing their options. Farmers diversified into corn, cranberries, sorghum, and hops, among others. Sheep and some hogs constituted the spectrum of livestock, but within two decades, the milk cow would surpass everything else on four hooves.

Myriad factors influenced the early trend toward dairy. Most of the European immigrant farmers, many of them dairy farmers in the old country, found the topography and climate in Wisconsin similar to those of their homelands. Transplanted Yankees had seen it before in New York and Vermont and knew a dairy revolution was coming. Led by foresighted dairying advocate William Hoard and his germinal journal, *Hoard's Dairyman,* and by the new Wisconsin Dairymen's Association, farmers began adding dairy cattle to their other crops and livestock until, by 1899, 90 percent of Wisconsin's farmers were keeping cows predominantly.

Butter production initially led the new industry, since it was easier to keep than milk. But technology and industrialization, thanks in large part to the University of Wisconsin Scientific Agriculture Institute, propelled Wisconsin into milk, cheese, and other dairy-product prominence. The institute was responsible for extending the dairy season, introducing several highly productive new methods, and the groundbreaking 1890 Babcock butterfat test, a simple test of chemically separating and centrifuging milk samples to determine its quality, thereby ensuring farmers were paid based on the quality and not just the weight of the milk.

By 1880, despite less-fecund land and a shorter growing season than other agricultural states, Wisconsin ranked fourth in dairy production, thanks to university efficiency, progressive quality control, Herculean effort in the fields, and the later organization of powerful trade exchanges. The southern half of the state, with its minerals in the southwest and rich loamy soils in the southeast, attracted European agrarian and dairy farming immigrants and speculators. "America's Dairyland" made it onto state license plates in the 1930s.

THE PROGRESSIVE ERA

Wisconsinites have a rather fickle political history. Democrats held sway in the territorial days; then, in 1854, the newly formed Republican Party took the reins. The two monoliths—challenged only occasionally by upstarts such as the Grangers, the Socialists (Milwaukee consistently voted for Socialist representatives), Populists, and the Temperance movement—jockeyed for power until the end of the century.

The Progressive Party movement, formed of equal parts reformed Democrats and Republicans, was the original third-party ticket, molted from the frustrated moderates of the Wisconsin Republican Party keen on challenging the status quo. As progressivism gained steam and was led on by native sons, the citizenry of Wisconsin—tireless and shrewd salt-of-the-earth workers—eventually embraced the movement with open arms, even if the rest of the country didn't always. The Progressive movement was the first serious challenge to the United States' political machine.

Fightin' Bob: Legacy of Progressivism

If there is one piece to the Wisconsin political mosaic that warrants kudos, it's the inveterate inability to follow categorization. Whether politically prescient or simply lacking patience, the state has always ridden the cutting edge. These qualities are best represented physically by the original Progressive: Robert La Follette, a.k.a. "Menace to the Machine." One political writer in the early 20th century said of La Follette: "The story of Wisconsin is the story of Gov. La Follette. He's the head of the state. Not many Governors are that." The seminal force in Wisconsin, La Follette eschewed the pork-barrel status quo to form the Progressive Party. In Wisconsin, the La Follette family dominated the state scene for two generations, fighting for social rights most people had never heard of.

Robert M. La Follette was born on a Dane County farm in 1855, where the typically hardscrabble life prepared him for the rigors of the University of Wisconsin, which he entered in 1875. He discovered a passion and talent for oratory but, too short for theater, gravitated to politics—a subject befitting the ambitious young man. He was elected Dane County district attorney in 1880. Well liked by the hoi polloi, he gave them resonance with his hand-pumping and his off-the-cuff speeches on hard work and personal responsibility in government. An entrenched Republican, he was more or less ignored by the party brass, so in 1884 he brashly ran for U.S. Congress on his own—and won. He was the youngest state representative in U.S. history.

Initially, La Follette toed the party line fairly well, though he did use his position to crow elegantly against the well-oiled political infrastructure. After the Republicans were voted out en masse in 1890, La Follette returned to Wisconsin and formed the Progressive Party. He ran for governor and, after two tries, landed the nomination. A tireless circuit and chautauqua lecturer, he relied on a salt-of-the-earth theme and left audiences mesmerized. This marked the birth of the "Fightin' Bob" image, which persists to this day. He was elected governor three times, returned to the Senate for a tempestuous career, and made serious runs at the presidency.

La Follette's critics found him as self-righteous and passionately tactless as he was brilliant, forthcoming, gregarious, and every other superlative by which he remains known today. This driven man of the people was no more enigmatically contradictory than many other public figures, but historians have noted that even his most vehement opponents respected his ethics. Under him, Wisconsin instituted the nation's first direct primary and watershed civil-service systems, passed anticorruption legislation and railroad monopoly reforms, and, most important, formed the Wisconsin Idea.

Progressivism and the Wisconsin Idea

Progressivism represented a careful balance of honest-to-goodness idealism and what may today be termed Libertarian tenets. La Follette saw it as an attempt to overcome, on a grassroots level, the dehumanizing aspect of corporate greed and political corruption. *The Progressive,* the Madison-based periodical he founded, remains the country's leading medium for social justice.

Fightin' Bob's most radical creation was the Wisconsin Idea. Officially a system whereby the state used careful research and empirical evidence in governing, in reality it meant that La Follette kept a close-knit core of advisers as de facto aides. His was the first government—state or federal—to maintain expert panels and commissions, a controversial plan at the time. Some criticized it as elitist, but he argued that it was necessary to combat well-funded industry cronyism.

THE OTHER LA FOLLETTE

While Robert La Follette Sr. dominated Wisconsin politics for most of three decades, he by no means did it alone. He and his wife, Belle, were an inseparable team, both passionate crusaders for social justice.

Belle La Follette (1859–1931) was behind Bob in every way and in many cases, it could be said, *was* Bob. Her grandmother inculcated in her a fierce determination to obtain the education she herself had been denied. It was at the University of Wisconsin that this very independent woman caught the eye of her soulmate, Bob La Follette. The two rewrote many of society's constricting traditions. They were the first couple in Wisconsin to delete "obey" from their marriage vows. Belle later became the first woman to graduate from the University of Wisconsin law school.

Her postcollegiate life was an amazing blend of supporting Bob and maintaining her own

crusading career as a journalist, editor, and suffrage leader. She marched in the state's first major suffrage parade and became a leading researcher and writer on practices of segregation, welfare, and other social issues. In addition to all that, she lectured, acted as her husband's attorney, and raised the La Follette brood.

She knew Bob would need an enlightened insider, so she chose to study law. She immersed herself in the issues and became his most trusted adviser. When Bob La Follette died, she refused public life; instead, she devoted herself to the *Progressive* magazine, which Bob had founded. Her own activism may be best remembered in her moving, eloquent 1913 speech to a transfixed U.S. Senate Committee on Woman's Suffrage, during which she quoted Abraham Lincoln in asking, "Are women not people?"

EARLY 20TH CENTURY

Robert La Follette's most (in)famous personal crusade was his strident opposition to U.S. participation in World War I due equally to Wisconsin's heavy German population and La Follette's vehement pacifism. He suffered tremendous regional and national scorn and was booted to the lower echelons of politics. Interestingly, when the United States officially entered the war, Wisconsin was the first state to meet enlistment requirements. Eventually, La Follette enjoyed something of a vindication with a triumphant return to the Senate in 1924, followed by a final real presidential run.

Also a political activist, Bob's wife, Belle La Follette, mounted a long-standing crusade for women's suffrage that helped the 19th Amendment get ratified; Wisconsin was the first state to ratify it. In other political trends starting around the turn of the 20th century, Milwaukee began electing Socialist administrations. Buoyed by nascent labor organizations in the huge factory towns along Lake Michigan, the movement was infused with an

immigrant European populace not averse to social radicalism. Milwaukee was the country's most heavily unionized city, and it voted Socialist—at least in part—right through the 1960s. The Progressive banner was picked up by La Follette's sons, Phil and Robert Jr., and the Wisconsin Progressive Party was formed in 1934. Robert Jr. took over for his father in the U.S. Senate, and Phil dominated Wisconsin politics during the 1930s. Despite these efforts, the movement waned. Anemic and ineffective from internal splits and World War II, it melded with the Republican Party in 1946.

Dairying became Wisconsin's economic leader by 1920 and gained national prominence as well. The industry brought in nearly $210 million to the state, wholly eclipsing timber and lumber. This turned out to be a savior for the state's fortunes during the Depression; dairy products were less threatened by economic collapse than either forest appropriation or manufacturing, though farmers' management and methodology costs skyrocketed. Papermaking, in which Wisconsin is still a world leader, ameliorated the blow in the jobless cutover north- and east-central parts of the state. Concentrated fully in southeastern Wisconsin, heavy industry—leather, meatpacking, foundries, fabrication, and machine shops—suffered more acutely during the Depression. Sales receipts plummeted by two-thirds and the number of jobs fell by nearly half in five years. Brewing was as yet nonexistent, save for root beer and some backroom swill.

POST-WORLD WAR II TO THE PRESENT

Wisconsin's heavy manufacturing cities drew waves of economic migrants to its factories after World War II, and agribusiness rose in income despite a steady reduction in the number of farms. The state's economic fortunes were generally positive right through the mid-1980s, when the state endured its greatest recession since the catastrophic days of the Depression. Wisconsin companies lost control to or were bought out by competitors in other states. In the early 1990s, agribusiness, still one of the top three Wisconsin industries, became vulnerable for the first time when California challenged the state in production of whole milk.

The one industry that blossomed like no other after the war was tourism. Forethinking Wisconsin politicians enacted the first sweeping environmental legislation, and North Woods resort owners instituted effective public relations campaigns. By the late 1950s, Wisconsin had become a full-fledged, four-season vacation destination, and by the early 1990s tourism had become a $6 billion industry in Wisconsin, which established a cabinet-level Department of Tourism and opened regional travel centers in other states.

Government and Economy

GOVERNMENT

Wisconsin entered the Union as the 30th state with the final signing, by President James K. Polk, on May 29, 1848.

Wisconsin has a bicameral legislative system, with a 99-member Assembly elected every two years and a 33-member Senate elected every four years. The governor wields veto power and also has a powerful weapon: the line-item veto.

Wisconsin has always relished its penchant for progressive, and occasionally even radical, politics.

ECONOMY

Wisconsin may be "America's Dairyland," but it isn't *only* America's Dairyland. The economic triumvirate of the state is agriculture, manufacturing, and tourism. Wisconsin is an international exporter, tallying $6 billion in receipts in 15–20 foreign markets. Leading exports include computers, industrial machinery, and transportation equipment (crops come fifth).

© THOMAS HUHTI

Wisconsin's grand capitol in Madison

THE BUTTER BATTLE

You doubt Wisconsin's a dairy state? Consider the Butter Battle, or Oleo Wars. Oleomargarine was developed in 1895. It would take until 1967 – that's right – that selling or buying the creamy concoction wasn't a *crime*.

Farmers initially feared that the golden-colored spread would ruin them; later they would march and protest for a ban on anything resembling butter. Of course, margarine smuggling started up (kinda lacks the romanticism of moonshine running, doesn't it?), and those consumers watching their diets would cross the Illinois line to the "margarine villages"

that sprouted alongside border service stations. Butter's most partisan supporter was Gordon Roseleip, a Republican senator from Darlington, whose rantings against oleo could occasionally overshadow Joseph McCarthy's anti-Communist spewings. But the good senator doomed the butter industry in 1965 when he agreed to take a blind taste test between butter and oleo. And lost. His family later admitted that he had been unknowingly consuming oleo for years; he weighed 275 pounds and his family had switched, hoping to control his weight.

Since 1990, the state has had one of the country's fastest-growing per capita income levels, topping $18,000. It's been one of the top 10 nationally for fastest-growing economies. This is tempered somewhat by the state's high income tax.

The state is tops in the United States for percentage of the workforce in manufacturing (16 percent); manufacturing accounts for up to 30 percent of Wisconsin's income—$37.1 billion. Wisconsin leads the nation in the fabrication of small engines, metals, paper products, printing, food processing, mineral extraction equipment, electrical machinery, and transportation equipment. The paper product industry is particularly strong, number one in the nation since 1953, accounting for 12 percent of the national total, to the tune of $12.4 billion. One of every 11 jobs in the state is tied to paper.

The new kid on the block, economically speaking, is tourism, which really got its start after World War II. The state now rakes in more than $12 billion annually.

Agriculture is the linchpin: 41 percent of the state remains devoted to agricultural products. The industry is worth more than $80 billion, with 25 percent of that from dairying. Wisconsin ranks first to third in the United States for dairy and a lengthy list of vegetables. Interestingly, it's the fastest-growing state in organic farming (a 91 percent increase 1997–2010): first in organic dairy farms and second in organic farms (that's total, not per capita!).

People and Culture

THE PEOPLE

Wisconsin inches up from the six million mark. With 90.1 people per square mile, the state ranks 24th nationally in population density. (It rarely feels that crowded.) General population growth in the state is 3.9 percent annually, unusual because the upper Great Lakes area as a whole shows steadily declining numbers,

though this decline is slowing. At the turn of the 20th century, it was the most ethnically diverse state in the Union, with most of us having family ties to Germany.

And while still predominantly European-American, the state has a fast-growing non-white population—12-plus percent and growing fast.

Native American tribal dance in Minocqua

Native Americans

Wisconsin has one of the most diverse Native American populations of any state, taking into account the number of cultures, settlement history, linguistic stock, and affiliations. The state is home to six sovereign Native American nations on 11 reservations, not all of which are demarcated by boundaries. In addition to the six nations, Wisconsin historically has been the home of the Illinois, Fox, Sauk, Miami, Kickapoo, Satee, Ottaway, and Mascouten Indians. The total Native American population is around 40,000, or 1 percent of the population.

The largest native group is the **Ojibwa.** (Formerly rendered as "Chippewa," the Euro-transliteration of what trappers thought they heard, it has returned to the more appropriate approximations of Ojibway, Ojibwe, and Ojibwa. Ethnologists, historians, linguists, and even tribal members disagree on the spelling. *Ojib* means "to pucker up" and *ub-way* "to roast," and the words together denote the tribe's unique moccasin stitching. In any event, all are

really Anish'nabe anyway.) Wisconsin has five Ojibwa tribes. The Ojibwa inhabited the northern woodlands of the upper Great Lakes, especially along Lakes Huron and Superior. They were allied with the Ottawa and Potawatomi, but branched off in the 16th century and moved to Michigan's Mackinac Island. The Ojibwa said that their migration westward was to fulfill the prophecy to find "food that grows on water"—wild rice. The **Bad River** group today lives on a 123,000-acre reservation along Lake Superior in Ashland County. It's the largest reservation in the state and is famed for its wild rice beds on the Kakogan Sloughs. The **Red Cliff** band, the nucleus of the Ojibwa nation, has been organized along the Bayfield Peninsula's shore since 1854. The **St. Croix** band—"homeless" tribes scattered over four counties with no boundaries—lives in northwest Wisconsin. The **Lac du Flambeau** band is the most visited and recognizable because of its proximity to Minocqua and state and federal forests and for exercising its tribal spearfishing rights. **Lac Courte Oreilles** is originally of the *Betonukeengainubejib* Ojibwa division. The **Sokaogan** (Mole Lake) band of Lake Superior Ojibwa is known as the "Lost Tribe" because its original legal treaty title was lost in an 1854 shipwreck. Originally from Canada, the band moved along to Madeline Island before defeating the Sioux near Mole Lake in 1806.

The Algonquian **Menominee** have been in Wisconsin longer than any other tribe. The Menominee once held sway south to Illinois, north into Michigan, and west to the Mississippi River, with a total of 10 million acres. Known as the "Wild Rice People"—the early French explorers called them "Lords of Trade"—Menominee were divided into sky and earth groups and then subdivided into clans. Though the hegemony of the Menominee lasted up to 10,000 years in Wisconsin, they were almost exterminated by eastern Canadian Indians fleeing Iroquois persecution and by pestilence imported by the Europeans. Today the population has rebounded to around 3,500, and the Menominee reservation constitutes an entire Wisconsin county.

WISCONSIN LINGUISTIC PRIMER

The source of the majority of Wisconsin's names is illiterate (and occasionally innumerate) trappers and traders struggling to filter non-Indo European words and speech through Romance and Germanic language sensibilities. Toponymy generally falls into several categories – bastardized Native American lexical items (the peskiest to suss out), practical monikers pertaining to local landforms or natural wonders, and memorials to European American "founding" fathers.

Even "Wisconsin" is etymologically slippery; a historical linguist has called Wisconsin's name the most cryptic of all 27 states with Native American names. As early as 1673, Father Marquette named the river from which some say the state's name derived Meskousing ("red stones"), perhaps because of a red tinge of the banks. "Ouisconsin" appeared on a Jesuit map in 1688. But most widely accepted is the Ojibwa word for the state, "Wees-kon-san" – "gathering place of waters."

WISCONSINISMS

Perhaps the most famous example of a Wisconsinism is "bubbler," for drinking fountain. The *Dictionary of American Regional English* (out of UW-Madison) says that the other truly Wisconsin word is "golden birthday," the birthday year that matches the date of the month (for example, if you were born on January 13, your 13th birthday is your golden birthday). Those in common Midwestern (or national usage) but started in Wisconsin include "flowage" (water backed up behind a dam), "hot dish" (casserole), and this author's favorite, "ishy" ("icky").

Milwaukee colloquialisms – though some vociferously deny it – include "bumbershoot," for umbrella, and "ainah hey?" for "isn't that so?" (In Wisconsin outside of Milwaukee, folks – especially this author's mom and aunt! – say, "inso?") You'll also hear "down by" – everything is "down by" something. Or, even "Grease yourself a piece of bread and I'll put you on a hamburger" – a Milwaukeeism if ever there was one. Wisconsinites also seem somewhat averse to liquid sounds; it's "M'waukee" as often as not.

The Forest County **Potawatomi,** also Algonquian, are the legacy of the tribe that made the most successful move into Wisconsin, beginning in the 1640s. Originally inhabitants of the shores of Lake Huron, the Potawatomi later moved to Michigan, Indiana, and places along the St. Joseph's River. The name means "People of the Fire" or, better, "Keeper of the Fire," after their confederacy with the Ojibwa and Ottawa. The Potawatomi tribe stretched from Chicago to Wisconsin's Door County and was one of the tribes to greet Jean Nicolet when he arrived in 1634. Wisconsin's band of Potawatomi was one of the few to withstand relocation to Oklahoma in 1838.

Wisconsin's only Mohicans, the **Stockbridge-Munsee,** live on a reservation bordering the Menominee. The Stockbridge (also called Mahican—"Wolf") originally occupied the Hudson River and Massachusetts all the way to Lake Champlain. The Munsee are a branch of the Delaware and lived near the headwaters of the Delaware River in New York, New Jersey, and Pennsylvania.

The **Oneida** belonged to the Iroquois Five Nations Confederacy consisting of the Mohawk, Oneida, Onondaga, Cayuga, and Seneca. The Oneida, originally from New York, supported the colonists in the American Revolution but were forced out by Mohawks and land-grabbing settlers along the Erie Canal after the war. Beginning in the 1820s, the Iroquois-speaking Oneida merged with the Mahican, Mohegan, Pequot, Narragansett, Montauk, and other tribes in Wisconsin.

The erstwhile **Winnebago Nation** has reverted to its original name, **Ho Chunk,** or, more appropriately, **Ho Cak** ("Big Voice" or "Mother Voice"), in an attempt to restore the

HOWZAT AGAIN?

The phonology of Wisconsin English contains only one dramatic sound: the "ah," seriously emphasized and strongly run though the nasal cavity, as in wis-KHAN-sin. (And please, never, ever say WES-khan-sin.)

Required reading/listening: www.misspronouncer.com, a site to learn the pronunciation of the state's towns!

- **Algoma** – al-GO-muh

- **Chequamegon National Forest** – shuh-WAHM-uh-gun

- **Fond du Lac** – FAHN-duh-lack

- **Green Bay** – green-BAY, *not* GREEN-bay

- **Kenosha** – kuh-NO-shuh

- **Lac Court Oreilles** – la COO-der-ray

- **Manitowoc** – MAN-ih/uh-tuh-wock

- **Menominee/Menomonie** – muh-NAH-muh-nee

- **Minocqua** – min-AHK-wah

- **Muscoda** – MUSS-kuh-day

- **New Berlin/Berlin** – new BER-lin

- **Nicolet National Forest** – nick-oh-LAY (but don't be too surprised to hear "nick-ul-ETT")

- **Oconomowoc** – oh-KAHN-uh-muh-wahk (the first syllable is sometimes pronounced "uh")

- **Oshkosh** – AHSH-kahsh

- **Prairie du Chien** – prairie du SHEEN

- **Racine** – ruh-SEEN

- **Ripon** – RIP-pin

- **Shawano** – SHAW-no (though SHAH-no is possible)

- **Sheboygan** – shuh-BOY-gun

- **Trempealeau** – TREM-puh-low

- **Waupun** – wau-PAHN

rightful cultural and linguistic heritage to the nation. Also known as Otchangara, the group is related to the Chiwere-Siouxan Iowa, Oto, and Missouri Indians, though their precise origin is unknown. Extremely powerful militarily, they were nonetheless relatively peaceful with the Menominee and Potawatomi, with whom they witnessed Jean Nicolet's 1634 arrival. French scourges and encroaching tribes fleeing Iroquois hostilities in New York devastated Ho Chunk numbers; later, forced relocation nearly killed off the rest. The tribe pulled up stakes in Oklahoma and walked back to Wisconsin, following its chief, Yellow Thunder, who bought the tribe a tract of land, deftly circumventing relocation and leaving the federal government no way to force it out of Wisconsin.

An excellent resource is the website of the Great Lakes Intertribal Council (www.glitc.org).

European Americans

At statehood, only 10 nationalities were represented in Wisconsin; by 1950, more than 50 could be counted. The vast majority of these were European, and Wisconsin is still 88 percent Caucasian.

A decidedly **German** state, Wisconsin boasts more residents claiming Teutonic roots (54 percent) than anywhere else in the country. So thick is the German milieu of Milwaukee (34 percent) that German chancellors visit the city when they're in the United States for presidential summits. Wisconsin has more than 50,000 native speakers of German—quite remarkable for a century-old ethnic group. Germans came in three waves. The first arrived 1820–1835 from both Pennsylvania and southwestern Germany. The second wave, 1840–1860, came mostly from northwest Germany and included the legendary "48ers"—enlightened intellectuals fleeing political persecution. During this wave, as many as 215,000 Germans moved to Wisconsin each year; by 1855, fully one-third of Wisconsin's Germans had arrived. The third wave occurred after 1880 and drew emigrants mainly from Germany's northeastern region to southeastern Wisconsin, where they worked in the burgeoning factories.

The state's **French** roots can be traced back to the voyageurs, trappers, and Jesuit priests. They started the first settlements, along the Fox and Wisconsin River Valleys. Though Wisconsin shows no strong French presence in anything other than place-names, the Two Rivers area still manifests an Acadian influence.

As the **British** and the French haggled and warred over all of the Wisconsin territory, many crown-friendly British Yankees did move here, populating virtually every community. The **Irish** began arriving in the late 19th century in numbers second only to the Germans. Irish influence is found in every community, especially Milwaukee's Bay View, Erin in Washington County, Ozaukee County, Adell and Parnell in Sheboygan County, and Manitowoc County.

Pockets of **Welsh** and **Cornish** are found throughout the state, the latter especially in the southwestern lead-mining region of the state. A distinct **Belgian** influence exists in Kewaunee County, where Walloon can still be heard in local taverns.

Poles represent the primary Eastern European ethnic group. The largest contingent is in Milwaukee, where kielbasa is as common a dietary mainstay as bratwurst. Most Poles arrived 1870–1910. At that time, Poland was not recognized as a country, so Ellis Island officials erroneously categorized many of the immigrants as Prussian, Austrian, or Russian. While 90 percent of Wisconsin's Polish immigrants moved into the cities, about three-tenths of those who arrived farmed, mostly in Portage and Trempealeau Counties; the latter is the oldest Polish settlement in the United States. **Czechs,** another large Eastern European group, live mostly in north and east-central Wisconsin, especially Kewaunee and Manitowoc Counties.

Many **Norwegians** also emigrated to the Upper Midwest, primarily Minnesota and Wisconsin. Most were economic emigrants trying to escape Norway's chronic overpopulation. Most Norwegians in Wisconsin wound up in Dane and Rock Counties. **Finnish** immigrants to the United States totaled 300,000 between 1864 and 1920, and many of these settled in the Upper Peninsula of Michigan and northern Wisconsin. **Swedes** made up the smallest Scandinavian contingent, the original settlement made up of a dozen families near Waukesha.

By the turn of the 20th century, Wisconsin was home to almost 10 percent of all the **Danes** in the United States—the second-largest national contingent. Most originally settled in the northeast (the city of Denmark lies just southeast of Green Bay), but later immigrants wound up farther south. To this day, Racine is nicknamed "Kringleville," for its flaky Danish pastry.

The **Dutch** settled primarily in Milwaukee and Florence Counties beginning in the 1840s, when potato crops failed and protests flared over the Reformed Church. These southeastern counties today sport towns such as Oostburg, New Amsterdam, and Holland.

In 1846, a large contingent of **Swiss** from the Glarus canton sent emissaries to the New World to search out a suitable immigration site. Eventually, the two scouts stumbled upon the gorgeous, lush valleys of southwestern Wisconsin. A great deal of Swiss heritage remains in Green County.

Italians began arriving in the 1830s—many Genoese migrated north from Illinois lead camps to fish and scavenge lead along the Mississippi River—but didn't arrive in substantial numbers until the early 1900s. Most settled in the southeast, specifically Milwaukee, Racine, and especially Kenosha.

Perhaps unique to Wisconsin is the large population of **Icelandic** immigrants, who settled on far-flung Washington Island, northeast of Door Peninsula. It was the largest single

Icelandic settlement in the United States when they arrived in 1870 to work as fishers.

African Americans

Some theories hold African Americans first arrived in Wisconsin in 1835, in the entourage of Solomon Juneau, the founder of Milwaukee. But records from the early part of the 18th century detail black trappers, guides, and explorers. In 1791 and 1792, in fact, black fur traders established an encampment estimated to be near present-day Marinette. Though the Michigan Territory was ostensibly free, slavery was not uncommon. Henry Dodge, Wisconsin's first territorial governor, had slaves but freed them two years after leaving office. Other slave owners were transplanted Southerners living in the new lead-mining district of the southwest. Other early African Americans were demi-French African immigrants, who settled near Prairie du Chien in the early 19th century. Wisconsin's first African American settlement was Pleasant Spring, outside Lancaster in southwest Wisconsin; the State Historical Society's Old World Wisconsin in Eagle has an exhibit on it.

After passage of the Fugitive Slave Act, which allowed slave catchers to cross state lines in pursuit, many freed and escaped slaves flocked to the outer fringes of the country. Wisconsin's opposition to the act was strident. One celebrated case involved Joshua Glover, an escaped slave who had been living free and working in Racine for years. He was caught and imprisoned by his erstwhile master but later broken out by mobs from Ripon, Milwaukee, and southeastern Wisconsin. The state Supreme Court ruled the act unconstitutional.

After the Civil War, the African American population increased, and most chose to live in rural, agricultural settings. Large-scale African American migration to Milwaukee, Racine, and Kenosha took place after World War II, as northern factories revved up for the Korean War and, later, the Cold War. Today, the vast majority of Wisconsin's nearly 300,000, or 80 percent of, African Americans (around 6 percent of the state total) live in these urbanized

southeastern counties. The black population is one of the fastest growing, increasing by 25 percent per decade.

Hispanics

Wisconsin's Hispanic population has doubled in the last two censuses. **Puerto Ricans** began arriving in Milwaukee after World War II as blue-collar laborers. **Mexicans** represent one of the more recent immigration waves, many of them having arrived in the mid-1960s, though Mexican immigrants have been in the state since as far back as 1850. Mexicans today live mostly in southeastern Wisconsin— Milwaukee, Madison, and, especially, Racine.

Asians

Wisconsin has upward of 77,000 residents of Asian descent, about 2 percent of the population. One of the fastest-growing elements, **Laotian Hmong,** began arriving during the Vietnam War and settled mostly in Appleton, Green Bay, the Fox River Valley, Manitowoc, Eau Claire, La Crosse, and pockets in southeastern Wisconsin. The state also has substantial **Chinese** and **Korean** populations.

CULTURE
Art Museums and Galleries

The smashing addition to the **Milwaukee Art Museum** by Santiago Calatrava has drawn media from around the world, yet don't overlook its phenomenal holdings. Milwaukee otherwise is rated in the top 5 percent for cultural attractions per population in the United States!

Madison has so many museums that one nickname for downtown is "Museum Mile," of which the **Madison Museum of Contemporary Art** and UW's **Chazen Art Museum** will be superb art aficionado bookends.

One would be amazed by how much art is outside the two population centers. Essential art attractions are the **Leigh Yawkey Woodson Museum** in Wausau, with astonishing ornithological art; the country's best folk art collection at the new **Racine Art Museum;** and Sheboygan's **John Michael Kohler Arts**

© THOMAS HUHTI

the Milwaukee Art Museum's Calatrava addition

Center, respectable for its community-focused efforts. The entire Door County must be noted, home to more galleries and artisan retreats than one would think possible in such a small place—even home to some of the country's oldest theatrical troupes. Ditto on the galleries for the diminutive communities of Mineral Point and Spring Green in lovely Southwestern Wisconsin.

Handicrafts

There are dozens of types of handicrafts in Wisconsin. Every community has artisans specializing in various ethnic styles: Norwegian rosemaling, for example, is a flowery, colorful, painted trim artwork. Unique are the creations of the Amish and the Hmong. A large contingent of Amish families, famed for their quilting, crafts, bent-hickory furniture, and outstanding bakeries, live in the southwestern and west-central sections of Wisconsin.

Hmong crafts include storycloths, which recount narratives visually, and exquisite decorative *paj ntaub,* a 2,000-year-old hybrid of needlework and applique, usually featuring geometric designs and, often, animals. These quilts and wall hangings require more than 100 hours of work. Some Amish and Hmong young women are synthesizing their quilt styles into wonderful bicultural mélanges. Hmong artisans are often found at craft fairs and farmers markets. Amish wares are found both in home shops throughout southwestern Wisconsin and in a few stores.

Food

Midwestern cuisine. An oxymoron? Hardly. Banish those visions of tuna casserole dancing in your head. Midwestern cuisine—real, original fare handed down generationally—is more eclectic and more representative of "American" heritage than better-known, better-marketed cooking styles.

If you search out the latent Americana in Wisconsin cooking, you'll be amazed. Wisconsin's best cooking is a thoughtful mélange of ethnicities, stemming from the diverse populace and prairie-cooking fare that reflects a heritage of living off the land. Midwest regional cuisine is a blend of originally wild food such as cranberries, wild rice, pumpkins, blueberries, whitefish livers, catfish cheeks, and morel mushrooms incorporated into standard old country recipes. Added to the mix are game animals, such as deer, pheasant, and goose. Many Midwesterners simply shoot their own, rather than raising them or buying them from a grocery wholesaler. It's a home-based culinary style, perfected from house to house through generations of adaptation.

And while the state features a panorama of European fare, the rest of the culinary spectrum is also represented. Milwaukee's got real-deal soul food and a fantastic array of Puerto Rican and Mexican restaurants, and in Madison you'll find Asian eateries rivaling any city's. In short, despite the preponderance of hot beef and meat loaf, it's quite possible to find good imaginative food in Wisconsin.

Wisconsin is well represented foodwise on the Web. Surprised? **SavorWisconsin. com** is a wonderful compendium (run by the state government) of information on local agricultural producers, food events, and more. Others of note: WisconsinCooks.org, chew.wisconsincooks.org, WisconsinMade. com, and even SlowFoodWisconsin.org. My grandmother could have written the recipes at bratwurstpages.com!

CHEESE

Wisconsin produces more than a third of the nation's cheese (leading in cheddar, colby, brick, muenster, limburger, and many Italian varieties). More than 500 varieties of cheese come out of Wisconsin. And, yes, we really do eat a great deal of it. The loyal dairy consumption shouldn't come as a surprise—laws prohibiting the use of margarine remained on the books until 1967.

The most common cheese in Wisconsin is the ever-versatile **cheddar.** For something different, eat it with fruit (apples are best) or melt it on hot apple pie.

Colby cheese was invented in the northern Wisconsin town of the same name. The cheese

has a very mild, mellow flavor and a firm, open texture. It's most often eaten breaded and deep fried, but try cubing it in fruit or vegetable salads. Firmer, with a smooth body, **colby jack** cheese is marbled white and yellow—a mixture of the mellow colby cheese along with the distinctive broad taste of **monterey jack,** a semisoft, creamy white cheese.

Wisconsin effectively brought **swiss** cheese to prominence in the United States more than a century ago. Swiss cheese fans should head immediately for the town of Monroe in southwestern Wisconsin; there you'll find the greatest swiss you've ever tasted, as well as a milder **baby swiss.** While there, slip into a tavern or sandwich shop and really experience Wisconsin culture by sampling a **limburger** sandwich— the pungent, oft-misunderstood swiss on pumpernickel, with onions and radishes. Wisconsin may be the last place on earth where it's couth to munch limburger in polite company; it *is* the last place in the world making the cheese.

Another Wisconsin original is **brick cheese,** a semisoft cheese with a waxy, open texture. Creamy white, young brick has a mild flavor; when aged, it becomes sharp. It's perfect for grilled cheese sandwiches or with mustard on pumpernickel bread.

Two transplants the state produces to near perfection are **gouda** and **edam** cheeses, imported by Western Europeans. They're semisoft to firm and creamy in texture, with small holes and mild, slightly nutty flavor.

Finally, for the most authentic cheese-eating cultural experience, go to a bar and order **cheese curds,** commonly breaded and deep fried. When bought at a dairy or a farmers market, cheese curds leave a distinctive squeaky feeling on the teeth and are a perfect snack food. Another unique cheese dish, especially in Green Bay, is beer cheese soup.

The Wisconsin Milk Marketing Board (www.wisdairy.com) is a wonderful place to peruse the "Joy of Cheese" and to request a copy of the fantastic *Taster's Guide to Wisconsin,* a scenic agricultural tour of the Dairy State, highlighting each cheese factory (and dairy, winery, brewery, etc.) that offers tours. And

MAJOR EVENTS AND FESTIVALS

In mid- to late January, in Eagle River's wild **World Championship Snowmobiling Derby,** the world's best snowmobile drivers compete on a half-mile, iced oval track, followed by February's awesome **Klondike Days** with a frontier winter rendezvous, lumberjack demonstrations, chainsaw carving, sled dog rides, and more.

In late February, the largest cross-country ski race in North America, the **Birkebeiner,** is held in Hayward and Cable. Six thousand competitors from around the world race on the grueling 55-kilometer course. The four-day event features tons of smaller races.

Late, late April to mid-May heralds the beginning of the festival season, which runs through autumn. An amazing way to start it is with Door County's monthlong **Festival of Blossoms,** a riot of color rivaled perhaps only by Holland's tulips!

One apt nickname for Milwaukee is the "City of Festivals." Milwaukee's **Polish Fest** is one of the larger ethnic festivals in the country, but the city really gets into high gear the last week of June when it hosts the mammoth **Sum-merfest,** billed as the largest music festival in the United States. In the 11-day extravaganza, more than 2,500 national acts perform everything from big band to heavy metal.

Wausau hosts the **National Kayak Racing Competition** to coincide with its **Logjam Festival** late in June.

July brings cars and parades. The largest automotive festival in the Midwest, the **Iola Old Car Show and Swap Meet,** takes place in the southeastern town of Iola. Milwaukee's major ethnic festival of July is **German Fest.**

Wisconsin's Lac Courte Oreilles Indians honor the Earth in late July with a **powwow and homecoming celebration** of ceremonial dancing, drumming, food, games, workshops, and speakers.

The most prestigious event outside of Summerfest is likely Oshkosh's **EAA International Fly-In Convention** in July, the world's most significant aviation event. Fifteen thousand experimental and historic aircraft – including NASA-designed craft – descend on the city and surrounding area for a week.

check out their Cheese Cupid (cheesecupid) section; it'll pair up whatever you're drinking with the appropriate cheese!

SUPPER CLUBS

What, exactly, is a supper club? What the *zócalo* is to Latin Americans, the sidewalk café to Parisians, the *biergarten* to Bavarians, so is the supper club to Wisconsinites. It sometimes seems as if the state charter requires every Badger State community to have one. It's the social and culinary underpinning of Wisconsin. Indeed, though supper clubs exist in many Midwestern states, Wisconsin's density is difficult to fathom.

Equal parts homey, casual meat-and-potatoes restaurant and local kaffeeklatsch (better make that "brandyklatsch"), supper clubs traditionally have a triumvirate of obligatory specialties: prime rib, always on Saturday, although some serve it every day; homestyle chicken; and invariably a Friday-night fish fry. No fish fry, no business. Most menus feature steaks in one column, seafood in the other. Regional variations buttress these basics with anything from Teutonic carnivore fare to Turkish food. This being Wisconsin, venison occasionally makes an appearance. One side dish will always be a choice of potato. If it's a true supper club, a relish tray comes out with the dinner rolls. On it, you'll find everything from sliced vegetable sticks to pickles to coleslaw—and sometimes an indescribably weird "salad" concoction such as green Jell-O with shaved carrots inside.

No two supper clubs look alike (the only prerequisites are an attached bar and perhaps faux wood paneling somewhere), but all can be partially covered by clichés such as "rustic," "cozy," and "like someone's dining room." Nicer supper clubs will have crackling fireplaces; low-end joints feel more like run-down family restaurants, in both decor and menu. The coolest

In August, Milwaukee hosts the **Wisconsin State Fair,** the state's largest annual event, with more than a million visitors over 11 days. In late August, Milwaukee features **Irish Fest,** the world's largest Irish cultural event outside of the Emerald Isle.

New Glarus shows itself as North America's most Swiss village during its **Wilhelm Tell Pageant** in early September. The famous Tell drama is presented in both English and Swiss German. And, of course, there's plenty of yodeling, log throwing, and the like.

Next, the nation's largest Native American festival is Milwaukee's **Indian Summer.** Mid-September also brings the nation's premier off-road bike race, the **Chequamegon Fat Tire Festival** in Hayward and Cable – three days of off-road racing, orienteering, 16- and 40-mile events, and criterium lap racing.

Believe it or not, up to 80,000 people crowd west-central Wisconsin, near Warrens, for late September's **Cranberry Festival,** which celebrates the tart little fruit.

Nature's autumn majesty is a big deal in Wisconsin, drawing thousands of tourists annually. Local news reports even feature nightly **leaf color watches.** The state Department of Tourism maintains 24/7 color updates via phone and website!

One of October's major festivals is **Oktoberfest** in La Crosse, fashioned after Munich's celebrations. There is a Maple Leaf Parade, music, rides, and a lot of beer.

Being America's Dairyland, it seems appropriate for Wisconsin to hold the world's largest dairying trade show, the **World Dairy Expo.** More than 50 countries participate in the event, held yearly in Madison.

Bayfield closes out the season of warm-weather festivals with its early October **Apple Fest,** featuring food booths, parades, arts and crafts, carnivals, and music. It's worth going just to see the Apostle Islands.

In mid-November, more than 50 ethnic groups participate in the Milwaukee **Holiday Folk Fair.** The largest annual multiethnic festival in the country, it's a great place to shop for folk art, and the ethnic dancing is quite popular.

---

ones have animal heads dangling above the diners; the tackiest ones feature overdone nautical decor. Dress is completely up to you. Wear a suit and you'll be conspicuous. Jeans are perfectly acceptable. In many places—especially Madison—Badger red is de rigueur on football Saturdays. Beware impostors: In recent years, the words "supper club" have been adopted by fancy restaurants on both coasts, but a co-opted supper club is not the real thing. If you ever see a dress code posted, you're not at a real supper club.

A Drinking Life

While living in Korea, I had an expat friend once say, "Good Lord Korean men drink like mad, don't they?" To which I could only think, "Well, not really." For you see, I'm from Wisconsin.

Yes, Badgers drink a lot. Alcohol is the social lubricant of the state, and many out-of-staters are a bit wide-eyed when they move here. We rank fourth nationally in per capita consumption; that's the only place we don't finish first. Just over 69 percent of the drinking-age population report participation in legal imbibing: first in the nation. Madison and surrounding Dane County have one of the highest percentages of binge drinkers in the United States, but Milwaukee actually took the crown away in 2009. (The state is of course first in binge drinking overall.) We're also number one—sadly—in driving under the influence. At last count, the state had more than 13,000 taverns, by far the most per capita in the country, in fact per person *three times* as many. One town of 69,000 in Wisconsin, it was reported, had more bars than in all of Memphis!

BEER

To disabuse: Wisconsinites do not drink more beer (per capita, anyway) than residents of any other state in the country—Nevada does (though that number is admittedly tourist heavy). Alas, the days of quaffing a brew with breakfast and finding a *biergarten* on every street corner are long gone.

Wisconsin beer drinking began with the hordes of European immigrants. The earliest brewery has been traced back to an 1835 operation in Mineral Point, but there may have been one a few years before that, though what most early southwestern Wisconsin brewers were making was actually top-fermented malt liquor (which to some aficionados is akin to cutting a porter with antifreeze). Surprisingly, Germans did not initiate Milwaukee's legendary beermaking industry; it was instead a couple of upstarts from the British Isles. But massive German settlement did set the state's beer standard, which no other state could hope to match. By 1850, Milwaukee alone had almost 200 breweries, elevating beermaking to the city's number one industry. Throughout the state, every town, once it had been platted and while waiting for incorporation, would build three things—a church, a town hall, and a brewery, not necessarily in that order.

The exact number of breweries in the state in the 19th century isn't known, but it is easily in the thousands; up to 50 years ago, local brew was still common. At that time, beermaking went through a decline; industry giants effectively killed off the regional breweries. But by the 1970s, a backlash against the swill water the big brewers passed off as beer sent profits plummeting. In stepped microbreweries and brewpubs. The nation is going through a renaissance of beer crafting, and Wisconsin is no different; Madison and Milwaukee have numerous brewpubs and a few microbreweries. In other parts of the state, anachronistic old breweries are coming back to the fore, usually with the addition of a restaurant and lots of young professional patrons. Time will tell if this trend marks a permanent national shift toward traditional brews (made according to four-century-old purity laws), or if it's simply a fad.

Some local standards still exist. **Leinenkugel's** (or Leinie's) is the preferred choice of North Woods denizens, closely rivaled by Point, which is brewed in Stevens Point. In the southern part of the state, Monroe's Joseph Huber Brewing Company puts out the college-student-standard (cheap but tasty) **Huber**—the Bock is worth the wait. In Middleton, west of Madison, the **Capital Brewery** has been restored to its early-century standards.

BRANDY

What traditionally has made a Badger a Badger, drinkwise? Brandy, of any kind. (The author's father still gets stares from *auslander* wait staff with the very Wisconsin drink request of "brandy old-fashioned with mushrooms, not fruit"—they're surprised by the brandy, not the mushrooms, and they usually get it wrong.) When the Wisconsin Badgers play a football game on the road, the 30,000-plus Cheeseheads who follow generally get newspaper articles written about their bratwurst, postgame polka dancing, and prodigious brandy drinking. In 1993, when the rowdy Badger faithful descended on the Rose Bowl in a friendly invasion, Los Angeles hotels essentially ran dry of brandy; by the time the Badgers returned in 1999 (and again in 2000), local hoteliers had figured it out!

Truth be told, the state has—egads!— slipped to second place behind Washington, DC (of all places), in per capita consumption, but Korbel still sells just under half its brandy in the state!

Wisconsinites are decidedly *not* connoisseurs of brandy; you'll never hear discussions of "smoky" versus "plump" varieties, or vintages. Try to chat somebody up about cognac versus brandy in a bar and you'll probably just be met with an empty stare. (For the record, cognac is a spirit distilled from the white wine grapes of Cognac in France; brandy is a more general term for a spirit distilled from wine.)

Here's how to make Wisconsin's fave drink: Put ice cubes in a glass. Add two ounces of brandy (any kind you wish), one lump of sugar, and one dash of cocktail bitters. Fill remaining glass with water or white soda. Top off with fruit or mushrooms.

ESSENTIALS

Getting There

BY AIR

The major U.S. airlines have some direct domestic flights into Wisconsin, but you often have to stop first in Chicago, Minneapolis, or another major hub. Ticket prices vary wildly depending on when you travel and, more important, when you buy the ticket. The best way to find out about deals is through a travel agent or, yes, mucking about on the Internet.

Milwaukee's **Mitchell International Airport** (www.mitchellairport.com) is the only international airport in the state and the airport offering the most direct flights across the country (Madison has a few as well).

Madison, Green Bay, Stevens Point/ Wausau, La Crosse, Oshkosh, Eau Claire, Marinette, Rhinelander, Appleton, and a few other minor locations are served by interstate and intrastate flights, often branches of the major carriers. During Memorial Day–Labor Day in Eagle River and Minocqua/Woodruff (occasionally to Sturgeon Bay but not at present), **Trans-North Aviation** operates a once-daily shuttle to and from Chicago's Palwaukee Airport.

BY BUS

Greyhound (800/231-2222, www.greyhound.com) operates in major Wisconsin cities, but only along major interstate routes.

© DOOR COUNTY CHAMBER OF COMMERCE

Van Galder (800/747-0994, www.vangalder-bus.com) operates between Chicago (O'Hare airport and downtown) and Madison, making stops at Wisconsin communities along the way. You can also hop aboard Wisconsin Coach Lines' **Airport Express,** which goes from Milwaukee to Chicago via Racine and Kenosha.

One shuttle van does operate between the Twin Cities Airport and Hayward in Northwestern Wisconsin.

BY TRAIN
Amtrak (800/872-7245) operates trains through Wisconsin. The long-distance **Empire Builder** originates in Chicago and runs through Milwaukee, Columbus, Portage, Wisconsin Dells, Sturtevant, Tomah, and La Crosse on its way to Seattle/Portland.

Metra (312/322-6777, www.metrarail.com) offers train service between Kenosha and Chicago's Madison Street Station.

Many Midwestern states are beginning discussions about creating a Midwest rail network, with Chicago as the hub and Milwaukee/Madison as one of many branches. Express light rail between Madison and Milwaukee will probably be debated until the end of time.

BY WATER
The **SS *Badger*** (www.ssbadger.com), the only active passenger/car steamship left on the Great Lakes, runs daily in season between Manitowoc, Wisconsin, and Ludington, Michigan. A new **ferry** to Michigan from Algoma, WI, could be up and running in the life of this edition.

Milwaukee has the high-speed **Lake Express** ferry (866/914-1010, www.lake-express.com) to Muskegon, Michigan, a blessing for those not wanting to suffer the white-knuckle tour of outer Chicago's interstate arteries.

On a much smaller scale, one of the few remaining interstate ferries left in America, the **Cassville Car Ferry,** operates seasonally in southwestern Wisconsin. It shuttles passengers across the Mississippi River between Wisconsin and Iowa.

Getting Around

HIGHWAYS
In *Midwest Living* magazine reader surveys, Wisconsin's roadways rank the best in most categories—best roads overall, best maintained, and others. Despite a few problem areas, the state's 110,300 miles of roads are all in pretty good shape. Best of all—no toll roads yet!

Then again, the stretch of I-94 running through Milwaukee is one of the nation's 10 most congested highways. The next-worst roads you'll experience are Madison's Beltline Highway and I-90 interchange, both of which, along with Milwaukee's interstates, are inhospitable during rush hours. The state Department of Transportation is now operating under a 20-year plan to improve existing multilane highways and expand certain two-lane highways. These two-lane roads are crucial, as they constitute only 4 percent of the state's highways but carry 42 percent of the traffic.

County roads are designated by letters. You can determine in advance the general condition of the road by the letters designating it. The road deteriorates in direct proportion to the number of letters. Thus, Highway RR will be narrower than Highway R—and possibly decaying. County roads are generally paved, but don't be surprised if they're not.

Regulations and Etiquette
Wisconsin permits radar detectors in cars. There is a mandatory motorcycle helmet law for people under 18 years old. All vehicle passengers are required by law to wear seatbelts. Child restraints are mandatory for children under four.

The speed limit on Wisconsin interstates

ROADKILL

Driving in Wisconsin you *will* experience the insanely high numbers of deer (and carcasses roadside); we are second in the United States for number of collisions. The modern rite of passage for "my first deer" no longer necessarily implies one downed with a weapon.

DEER DISPLACEMENT

The fecund croplands and suburban gardens that replaced the state's original meadows and forests have also lured huge numbers of deer back, to the point that some suburban areas ringed with rural lands have higher deer concentrations than public parklands. Some wildlife biologists now worry that the social carrying capacity of the land, or the number of deer that humans can tolerate, has been maxed out in the south, while in the sparsely populated north, the reverse is true – the biological carrying capacity is bulging at the seams. The primary cause is once again a lethal modern combination of an abundance of crops available for the deer to eat and refusal to allow hunting on private land, which results in no thinning of the herd. And it's not the same old divisions in this debate – some environmentalists are pro-deer hunting, as enormous deer populations destroy fragile and rare flora in winter feeding.

THE NUMBERS

The Department of Natural Resources estimates the deer herd at anywhere between 1.4 and 1.9 million (estimates vary wildly). Annu-ally, more than 20,500 car-deer crashes are reported (causing a dozen deaths and 700 injuries); since these are only the investigated ones, you can probably safely double that number. Statewide, deer account for more than 10 percent of crashes as of 2010 (up from 5.1 percent in 1978); then again, it's 33 percent lower than 2005. A conservative estimate puts the damage total, including cars and agricultural losses, at around $100 million per year. Thankfully, less than 2 percent of car-deer crashes result in human fatality.

PREVENTIVE MAINTENANCE

If you're driving in Wisconsin, face the fact that at some point you're going to meet a deer on a highway. October and November are the worst months statistically, but May and June are pretty bad, too. April-August, crashes happen mostly after 8 P.M.; the rest of the year, they typically occur 5-7 P.M. Deer, like any wildlife, are most active around dawn and dusk, but they are active day and night. Most crashes occur on dry roads on mostly clear days. And the old adage about their freezing in the headlights is absolutely true. The best thing you can do is pay close attention, don't speed, and keep an intelligent stopping distance between you and the next car. Use your peripheral vision, and if you see one deer, expect more. If one appears, *do not swerve or slam on the brakes*, even if this, sadly, means running through the deer. All experts agree this only causes much more danger to you and other motorists.

---

is 65 mph, reduced to 55 mph in metropolitan areas. Milwaukee's fringes are well monitored, so be forewarned. You can travel 65 mph on some four-lane highways in the northern part of the state, to the relief of many travelers.

Drivers in the state are very courteous. In fact, many acquaintances of this author have grumbled about the, er, *methodical* pace of Wisconsin traffic. The interstate arteries surrounding larger cities, especially Milwaukee, are the only places conducive to speeding.

Road Conditions

The state Department of Transportation maintains a **road condition hotline** (800/762-3947, dot.wisconsin.gov/travel) detailing the conditions of all major roads across the state; it also lists construction delays. Hit 511 on your mobile phone to get it.

It's important to winterize your vehicle while driving in Wisconsin. Always keep your antifreeze level prepared for temperatures of -35°F (half water, half fluid usually suffices). Most important: Keep a full tank of gas—it helps prevent freeze-ups in the line and lets you run your car if you're stuck in a ditch.

BY BUS

You can always hop aboard **Greyhound,** but only as long as you're traveling to communities along very main highways. **Lamers** is a bus service traveling to and from central Wisconsin to Milwaukee through the Fox River Valley.

The communities of Janesville, Beloit, Racine, Kenosha, Milwaukee, and Bayfield Peninsula have bus systems linking nearby communities. Madison and Milwaukee are linked by the oft-running **Badger Bus** (608/255-6771, www.badgerbus.com).

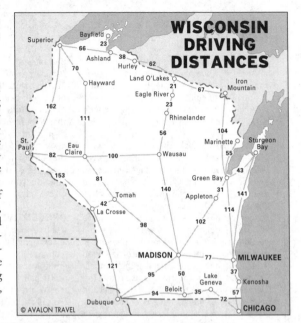

Outdoor Recreation

"Work hard, play hard" is the ethic in Wisconsin. There's always a trail, a lake, or an activity within shouting distance. Wisconsin contains a fairly remarkable 95 state parks, forests, and trails, varying in size from Green Bay's 50-acre living museum **Heritage Hill** to the 225,000-acre **Northern Highland American Legion State Forest** near Woodruff and Minocqua. A state park lies within an hour of every Wisconsin resident, a deliberate feature of the state park system; they've been dubbed the most diverse in the Midwest. A few of them—**Devil's Lake State Park, Peninsula State Park,** and the **Kettle Moraine State Forest,** for example—rival other major state parks in the nation. Since 2000, Wisconsin's state park system has been a finalist in the national Gold Medal Parks award for the best in the country.

Wisconsin alone has the **Ice Age National Scientific Reserve,** highlighting crucial zones

of the state's 1,200-mile-long Ice Age National Scenic Trail.

The state also boasts a mammoth national forest: the **Chequamegon-Nicolet,** totaling 1.5 million acres and inspiring two national scenic trails. And the final jewel is a rare national lakeshore—**Apostle Islands National Lakeshore.**

State parks and forests require a park sticker, which you can buy daily ($7 resident, $10 nonresident) or annually ($25 resident, $35 nonresident). Camping fees in state parks are also $10–15 (electricity and prime sites cost more), depending on location and campsite (some primitive camping is free)—nonresidents pay $2 more. Reservations in state parks are a good idea—a must for holiday weekends in summer—and be prepared to reserve 11 months ahead of time for the most popular parks. The Wisconsin Department of Natural Resources

sailing on Lake Michigan

(DNR, 608/266-2181, www.wiparks.net) is an invaluable source of information on state lands and environmental issues. A separate entity, ReserveAmerica (888/947-2757, www.reserveamerica.com) handles reservations for a $10 fee (fees for canceling or changing).

Wisconsin's mammoth multiuse trail system is also under the Department of Natural Resources, and a trail pass (residents $4 daily, $15 annually) is needed; note that some trails are not *state* trails but county trails and you'll need a different pass—them's the rules! Also note that hikers do *not* need to pay; only those using bikes, horses, skis, or ATVs do.

National forests now charge a $3–5 daily user fee for things such as picnic areas and beaches, and camping runs $8–18 (though things vary). Reservations (www.recreation.gov) are available at some campgrounds.

BIKING

Bicycling magazine rates Wisconsin one of the top three states for cyclists. Madison is second only to Seattle in the list of the nation's most bike-friendly cities. The Elroy-Sparta State Recreational Trail was the country's first rail-to-trail system and is regarded as the grand-daddy of all multipurpose state recreational trails, and the Chequamegon Area Mountain Bike Trail (CAMBA) system is among the most respected outside Colorado and Utah. All this, combined with the immense concatenate labyrinth of rural farm-to-market roads, makes it obvious why Wisconsinites leave bike racks on their cars year-round. In total, the state maintains more than 10,000 miles of established, mapped, and recommended bike routes.

Since the completion of the Elroy-Sparta State Recreational Trail, the state has added 41 other rail beds, logging roads, and state park trails to its State Trail System for a total of nearly 1,700 miles. It's impossible to keep up with how many more miles are added annually since cities and counties are establishing their own networks to link with state trails.

The state of Wisconsin tourist information centers dispense excellent free cycling maps and booklets. Two good organizations are the **Bicycling Federation of Wisconsin** (www.bfw.org) and the **Wisconsin Off-Road Bicycling Association** (www.worba.org).

Trail passes ($4 daily, $15 annually) are *not* required for hikers, but are necessary for all others 16 and over.

HIKING

With more than two million acres of state and federal land open for public consumption, along with 34 state recreation trails, hiking opportunities are endless. Two trails of interest to serious backpackers are the **Ice Age National Scenic Trail** and the **North Country National Scenic Trail.** The ultimate goal is to link Wisconsin's 42 rails-to-trails trails via city-county-state plans. This would double the state's trail mileage.

FISHING

Given that Wisconsin has more than 16,000 lakes, 27,000 miles of fishable river and stream, and more than 1,000 miles of Lake Superior, Lake Michigan, and Mississippi River coastline, and that most of the state's 135 native

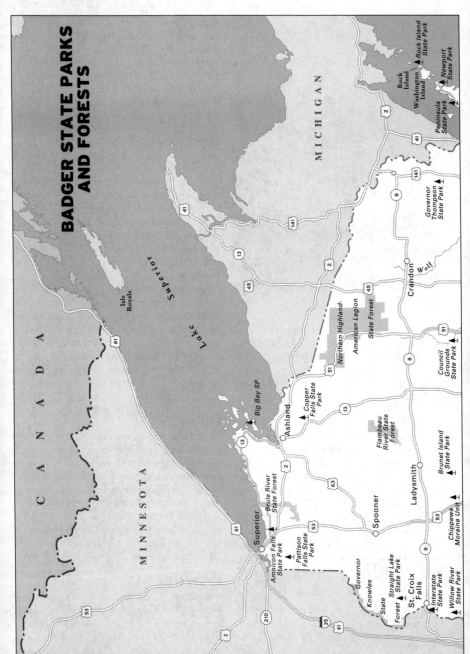

BADGER STATE PARKS AND FORESTS

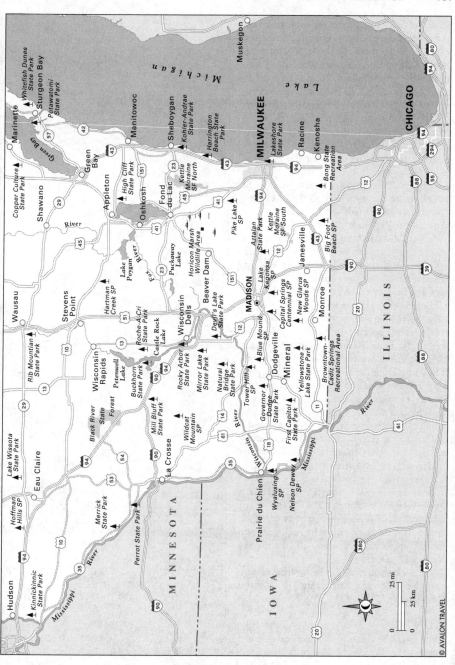

© AVALON TRAVEL

species of fish are fair game, it's no surprise that the number one activity is angling. Wisconsin ranks in the top five states nationwide for number of fishing licenses dispensed and is first in number of nonresident licenses sold annually. Most of the North Woods resorts cater to muskie anglers and tagalong families. Boulder Junction and Hayward both claim to be the Muskie Capital of the World. Though the **muskellunge** is revered as king of the waters, in sheer numbers the most popular sportfish is the **walleye.**

Wisconsin's only native stream trout is the **brook trout,** closely related to the lake trout. Good news—hundreds of blue-ribbon streams are chock-full of these suckers.

Great Lakes fishing has grown to become an enormous industry, with entire fleets devoted to working the well-stocked waters. Not all the fish in the Great Lakes are native species, but nobody seems to mind. Much of the restocking took place in response to early-century overfishing and the decline of fish stocks due to exotic species. In terms of fish taken per angler hour, Kenosha, Racine, and the Kewaunee/Algoma stretch rate extremely high. The entire Door Peninsula is also hugely popular. In all, the state Department of Natural Resources stocks more than 2.1 million coho and chinook salmon, 1 million lake trout, and 2 million brook, brown, and steelhead trout.

Driving the truck out on a frozen lake to a village of shanties erected over drilled holes, sitting on an overturned five-gallon pail, stamping your feet quite a bit, and drinking a lot of schnapps is a time-honored tradition in the Great White North. **Ice fishing** is serious business in Wisconsin: Up to two million angler-days are spent on the ice each year, and ice fishing accounts for up to one-fifth of the state's annual catch.

For all information, it's imperative to contact the Wisconsin Department of Natural Resources (877/945-4236, dnr.state.wi.us).

HUNTING

Hunting, like fishing, is a well-established business in Wisconsin, though far less so on

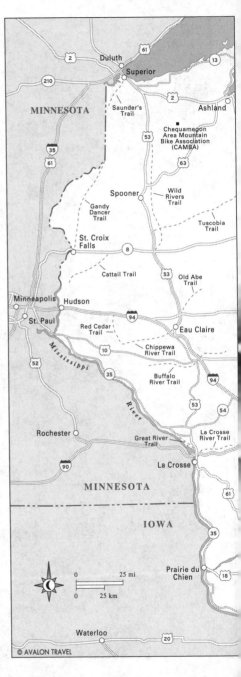

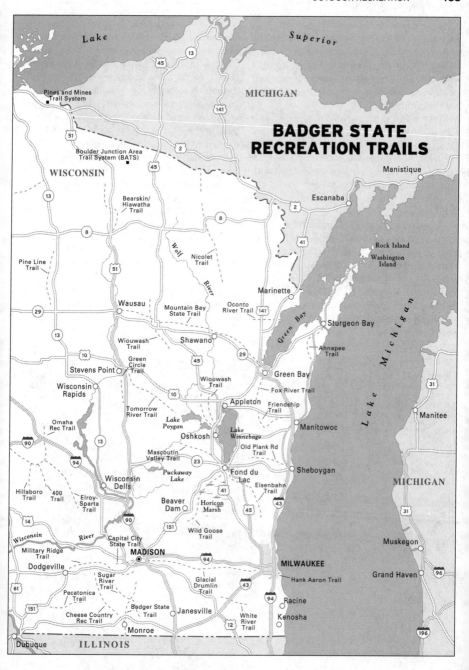

BADGER STATE RECREATION TRAILS

a tourist level. The nine-day gun deer season alone generates $250 million for the state. Fortunately, hunters are often more conservation-oriented than their civilian brethren. Many animal species owe their continued existence to hunting and conservation groups.

Deer hunting is essentially a rite of passage in Wisconsin's North Woods even today. Entire school districts in the area shut down for the November white-tailed deer season. Other popular hunts include **goose, duck, pheasant,** and especially **ruffed grouse.**

SKIING

Wisconsin mountains will never be mistaken for the Rockies or the Grand Tetons, but the state's heights give it a fairly decent concentration of downhill ski facilities. Cross-country ski buffs can indulge themselves in an orgy of skiing statewide. It's such a big deal in Wisconsin that the nation's largest cross-country ski race, the Birkebeiner, is held here every year in February, in Hayward.

SNOWMOBILING

Snowmobiling is a big deal here. In some communities, snowmobiling accounts for more business than even fishing. In fact, with more than 175,000 registered riders spending $40 million, it accounts for more money in some parts of the state than angling, hunting, and skiing combined. In *Snowgoer* magazine, reader polls have ranked northeastern Wisconsin and Minocqua best overall, eclipsing better-known, better-financed Rocky Mountain operators. Antigo passed ordinances giving snowmobiles rights similar to those of cars on city streets. Restaurants and nightspots often list their addresses according to the snowmobile route you'll find them on.

In total, the state maintains 25,000 miles of interconnected trails, so well linked that you can travel on them continuously from Kenosha in southeastern Wisconsin all the way to Lake Superior in the northwest. Nearly half of the 42 state recreation trails permit snowmobiling; so do 15 state parks and forests; and the national forests are wide open.

snowmobiling in northeastern Wisconsin

© WISCONSIN DEPT. OF TOURISM

CANOEING AND KAYAKING

Wisconsin features unbeatable canoeing and kayaking. Nationally regarded or federally designated Wild Rivers include the **Wolf River,** a federal Outstanding Water Resource coursing through the Menominee Indian Reservation; the **Flambeau River** system, one of the wildest in the Midwest; the **Bois Brule River,** famed for its trout; the **Montreal River,** home of the Junior World Kayak Championships; the unknown but exquisite **Turtle River,** leading into Wisconsin's Turtle-Flambeau Flowage in the most unspoiled section of the state; the **Pine** and **Popple Rivers** in the Nicolet National Forest; the wild **Peshtigo River;** the lazy, classic **Lower Wisconsin State Riverway;** the **La Crosse River;** the **Kickapoo River** (the "crookedest in the world"); the **Yahara River,** one reason *Canoeist* magazine calls Madison a canoeing mecca; and perhaps the most popular, the **Manitowish River,** in the Northern Highland American Legion State Forest in one of the planet's densest concentrations of lakes.

The **Namekagon-St. Croix National Scenic Riverway** stretches west from northeast of Cable, joins the St. Croix River and its smashing geology, and eventually flows to the confluence with the Mississippi River.

Kayakers enjoy the superb **Apostle Islands National Lakeshore** along Lake Superior—an experience impossible to overstate—and, to a lesser extent, the magnificence of Door County on the Lake Michigan side.

GOLF

Believe it or not, forlorn, wintry Wisconsin has one of the nation's highest concentrations of golf courses per capita. Go figure. Nearly 430 courses are listed in the state's *Wisconsin Golf Guide.* Among the courses most often pursued are **Blackwolf Run** in Kohler, **Lawsonia** in Green Lake, **Sentryworld** in Stevens Point, **University Ridge** in Madison, and **Brown Deer Golf Course** near Milwaukee.

Information and Services

INFORMATION

For information on anything and everything in the state, contact the **Wisconsin Department of Tourism** (800/432-8747, www.travelwisconsin.com), which has a decent website and offers fantastic printed guides.

Regarding the Internet, precious few sites are really all that worthy. First stop for culture, arts, and history should be portalwisconsin.org, a superb site; cheekier but filled with tidbits is classicwisconsin.com, good for information on fish fries. An idiosyncratic site—is it travel or geography or what?—is www.wisconline.com. You can thereafter peruse all you want, but this author has never found an otherwise worthy website on pan-Wisconsin travel.

Media

The only publication that covers Wisconsin on a macro scale is the monthly magazine *Wisconsin Trails* (www.wistrails.com). It's a slick periodical with a nice balance of road warrior personality and nostalgia. It dispenses with the political and social and just focuses on where and when to go, providing lots of good cultural bits and stunning photography. *Midwest Living* magazine, another monthly, features Wisconsin regularly. More for the conservation-minded, *Wisconsin Natural Resources* (www.wnrmag.com) is published by the state Department of Natural Resources. The well-put-together periodical features detailed natural history and is so well written and photographed that it might let you truly understand and appreciate science for the first time.

The *Journal Sentinel,* the largest and best of Wisconsin's newspapers, is a daily morning paper out of Milwaukee. This leaves Madison as the only major Wisconsin city

TRAVEL GREEN WISCONSIN

In 2007, in a U.S. first, Wisconsin launched its *Travel Green* program, designed to highlight businesses, lodging, attractions, and so on for their efforts to reduce the environmental impact of tourism. (And, naturally, to highlight the existence of the fact that this can, in fact, be done.) Kind of a no-brainer, eh? Wanna rent a hybrid car? Wanna eat in a restaurant that follows a protocol of sustainability? Then check out www. travelgreenwisconsin.com and find out what it's all about!

with three papers—the morning *Wisconsin State Journal,* the biweekly *Capital Times,* and *Isthmus.* In general, folks consider the former more conservative, the latter two more liberal.

LGBT Resources
Madison has been ranked third-best (after San Francisco and Bloomington, Indiana) by LGBT media for quality of life, and the gay community is organized and active there. In fact, Madison is actually the place to go for LGBT information. One great website covering everything (clubs to health to accommodations) everywhere is madisongaypride.com. Milwaukee's LGBT Community Center (www.mkelgbt.org) can also help.

MAPS
You can get a decent Department of Transportation state road map free by calling the state Department of Tourism hotline (800/432-8747). The *best* maps for snooping around the state are those contained in the *Wisconsin Atlas and Gazetteer,* available from any outdoors store or direct from the DeLorme Publishing Company (207/865-4171, www.delorme.com). On a somewhat smaller scale than topo maps, the maps in this 100-page, large-

format book are absolutely indispensable for exploring the back roads.

Topographic, planimetric, and 7.5-minute quadrangle maps can be obtained from the Wisconsin Geological and Natural History Survey (3817 Mineral Point Rd., Madison, WI 53705, 608/263-7389). The 7.5- or 15-minute maps cost $3.50 each. County topographical maps (1:1,000,000 scale) are available for $4 each.

MONEY
Wisconsinites are taxed to high heaven, but in general travelers don't have to share the burden; the state doesn't even have toll roads. Prices in general are lower in Wisconsin than in the rest of the country, and gasoline is usually cheaper than anywhere else in the Midwest except maybe Iowa. Once you get out into the rural areas, prices for goods and services are absolutely dirt cheap. Wisconsin's sales tax is 5 percent. Some counties or cities tack on an additional half percent. There may also be additional room taxes.

Travelers checks are accepted in most hotels and motels; those that don't take them are few and far between, usually the low-end places. Some restaurants will accept them, others won't—inquire ahead of time. Credit cards are widely accepted—*though not universally.* (Some resorts in the north woods region will still not accept them!)

Exchanging foreign currency can be a bit more problematic. If you arrive with foreign currency, it may be difficult to exchange it for U.S. dollars. Banks in Madison and Milwaukee will often have just one branch that deals with money-changing. In smaller cities, such as Green Bay, La Crosse, and Appleton, it isn't advisable to arrive with foreign currency.

COMMUNICATIONS
Telephone
Wisconsin has five area codes and it may soon have six. Milwaukee, along with most of southeastern Wisconsin, is in the 414 area code; areas immediately outside of Milwaukee are 262 area code; Madison and the southwestern and south-central regions fall in the 608 area code; and the

rest—most of the northwest—lies in the 715 area code. All else is area code 920.

Internet Access

If you need to log on and don't have your laptop, you generally have the public library. Sure, coffee shops exist in spades in Madison and, to a lesser extent, Milwaukee, but they come and go a lot—and are mostly wireless equipped, so if you're sans laptop, you're out of luck. Otherwise, the most popular destinations in this guide have wireless-equipped coffee shops and accommodations, but don't absolutely count on it.

WEIGHTS AND MEASURES
Voltage

Electrical outlets in the United States run on a 110V or 120V AC. Most plugs are either two flat prongs or two flat and one round. Transformers and adapters for 220V appliances are available in hardware or electronics stores.

The Metric System

Let's just say it doesn't come up a whole lot in Wisconsin. Foreign visitors can reference the U.S.-Metric Conversion Table in the back of this guide for help with distance and temperature conversions.

Time Zones

All of Wisconsin falls on central standard time (CST), which is six hours earlier than Greenwich mean time. However, if you plan a trip north of the border into Michigan's Upper Peninsula, you'll enter eastern standard time, which is one hour ahead of CST.

RESOURCES

Suggested Reading

If you're in Madison, head directly to the State Historical Society Museum, whose gift shop bookstore has better holdings than the library.

DESCRIPTION AND TRAVEL

Lyons, John J., ed. *Wisconsin. A Guide to the Badger State.* American Guide Series, Works Projects Administration, 1941. From the mother of all guidebook series, the Wisconsin edition, nearly seven decades old, is still the standard for anyone interested in the history, natural history, and culture of the state.

Ostergren, Robert C., and Vale, Thomas R., ed. *Wisconsin Land and Life.* Madison: University of Wisconsin Press, 1997. This amazing (heavy but eminently readable) book may be the most perfect synthesis of natural history and cultural geography.

OUTDOORS AND ENVIRONMENT

Leopold, Aldo. *A Sand County Almanac.* New York: Oxford University Press, 1949. An absolute must-read for anyone who considers himself or herself to be at all attuned to the land. Also an education for those superficial enough to think central Wisconsin is a vast nothingland.

Olson, Sigurd. *Collected Works of Sigurd Olson.* Stillwater, MN: 1990. Wisconsin's seminal ecologist besides Aldo Leopold, Olson had as much influence as his more famous contemporary. This is an excellent overview of his life's work, writings that show an incredible depth of ecological awareness but are very approachable for a layperson.

HISTORY

McAnn, D. *The Wisconsin Story: 150 Years, 150 Stories.* Milwaukee: *Milwaukee Journal Sentinel,* 1998. Most articles are about historical minutiae most folks have never heard about but are fascinating highlights to the general history books. It's engaging and probably your best bet for an easy vacation read.

Nesbit, Robert. *Wisconsin: A History.* Madison: University of Wisconsin Press, 1989. This is standard reading.

FOLKLORE

Leary, J. *Wisconsin Folklore.* Madison: University of Wisconsin Press, 1998. Linguistics, storytelling, music, song, dance, folk crafts, and material traditions. The chapter on Milwaukeeisms is worth the price of the book. Even the Smithsonian has recognized the uniqueness of the book.

NATURAL HISTORY

Martin, Lawrence. *The Physical Geography of Wisconsin.* Madison: University of Wisconsin Press, 1965. This is the granddaddy of all Wisconsin geography books, first published in 1916 and updated in subsequent editions.

Reuss, Henry S. *On the Trail of the Ice Age.* Sheboygan, WI: Ice Age Park and Trail Foundation, 1990. This is a good compendium of the oddball geology of the state and the effort to establish the Ice Age National Scenic Trail.

PEOPLE

The state historical society has produced brief booklets profiling every immigrant group in Wisconsin. They're available from the State Historical Society Museum in Madison.

Bieder, Robert E. *Native American Communities in Wisconsin, 1600–1960*. Madison: University of Wisconsin Press, 1995. The first and, really, only comprehensive, in-depth look at Native Americans in the state.

Maxwell, R. S. *La Follette and the Rise of the Progressives in Wisconsin*. Madison: State Historical Society, 1956. This is a fine account of Robert La Follette, the much-beloved Progressive Party politician of the late 1800s and early 1900s.

McBride, G. *On Wisconsin Women*. Madison: University of Wisconsin Press, 1993. An excellent newer book, this is one of few sources of information about many of the important women in the state's history.

Meine, C. *Aldo Leopold: His Life and Work*. Madison: University of Wisconsin Press, 1988. The best book on ecologist Aldo Leopold.

LITERATURE

Boudreau, Richard, ed. *The Literary Heritage of Wisconsin: An Anthology of Wisconsin Literature from Beginnings to 1925*. La Crosse, WI: Juniper Press, 1986. This is a condensed version of the state's literary canon.

Perry, Michael. *Population: 485* (Harper Perennial, 2002), *Truck: A Love Story* (Harper Perennial, 2006), and *Coop* (HarperCollins, 2009). Wisconsin has had a few luminaries of literature (Jane Hamilton, Kelly Cherry, Lorrie Moore, et al.), but I think he's the oughta-be-read author scribbling in the state (my poet laureate). To experience small-town

Wisconsin in a wonderfully low-key, hilarious way, read these books.

Stephens, Jim, ed. *The Journey Home: The Literature of Wisconsin Through Four Centuries*. Madison: North Country Press, 1989. A remarkable multivolume set of Wisconsin literature, tracing back as far as the trickster cycles of Native Americans.

CUISINE

More and more cookbooks detail Midwestern cuisine. Any bookstore worth its salt will have great selections on regional cooking.

Allen, T. and Hachten, Harva. *The Flavor of Wisconsin*. Madison: State Historical Society of Wisconsin, 2009. A dense volume cataloging all—and this means all—the ethnic groups of the state and their contributions to the cuisine. Terese Allen is one of Wisconsin's most noted food writers, so look for her name; she updated Harva Hachten's legendary book.

Apps, Jerry. *Breweries of Wisconsin*. Madison: University of Wisconsin Press, 2004. This amazing book came out and surprised everyone—a thorough examination of the culture of beer in Wisconsin as had never been done before. It's not just a guidebook, but a cultural journey. Jerry Apps, too, has written other great Wisconsin books.

Boyer, D. *Great Wisconsin Taverns*. Black Earth, WI: Trails Book Guides, 2002. The name pretty much says it all. It sounds hokey, but the author is a professional folklorist and storyteller and it shows.

Revolinski, Kevin. *Wisconsin's Best Beer Guide*. Holt, MI: Thunder Bay Press, 2010. It's informative but also fun, from the kind of guy you'd like to have in the shotgun seat on a long trip.

Stuttgen, Joanne Raetz. *Café Wisconsin*. Madison: Terrace Books, 2004. A folklorist covers the coffeklatsch culture; this is a personal favorite.

Internet Resources

Sconnie Nation
www.sconnie.com
Wisconsinites will likely appreciate Sconnie Nation. Started by a couple of genius UW undergrads, the online company sells all sorts of apparel with "Sconnie" written on it (I can't stop wearing my camo hat). But they have a hilarious section on what it means to be "Sconnie." You'll spend hours just perusing the videos submitted by proud Badgers (gotta love the tractor square dance . . .).

TRAVEL
Travel Wisconsin
www.travelwisconsin.com
From the state's Department of Tourism, it's *loads* more useful than some other states' websites. Seriously, give it a look.

Wisconsin Association of Convention and Visitors Bureaus (WACVB)
www.escapetowisconsin.com
This is a good starting point to local information sources.

Wisconsin Online
www.wisconline.com
It doesn't have everything in the state, but it has lots!

STATE PARKS
Wisconsin Department of Natural Resources
www.wiparks.net
This is a good resource from the Department of Natural Resources. It also covers state trails.

RECREATION
Wisconsin Bicycling Federation
www.bfw.org
They're an educational and advocacy group working strenuously for bikers' rights (and more trails and bike lanes in cities). They have awesome maps for sale.

Wisconsin Off-Road Bicycling Association
www.worba.org
Check it out for its expanding list of downloadable trail maps.

ARTS AND CULTURE
Portal Wisconsin
www.portalwisconsin.org
This is a fantastic resource for all visual and performance arts in the state.

Wisconsin Arts Board
www.arts.state.wi.us
The website of the Wisconsin Arts Board has great sections on art fairs, galleries, and art museums.

HISTORY
State Historical Society of Wisconsin
www.wisconsinhistory.org
This is the best starting place for state history.

ACCOMMODATIONS
Wisconsin Bed & Breakfast Association
www.wbba.org
This site is from the Wisconsin Bed & Breakfast Association.

Wisconsin Lodging
www.wisconsinlodging.org
Visit this site to view photos and information of lodging options around the state.

FOOD
Classic Wisconsin
www.classicwisconsin.com
I like it for its rundown of fish fries statewide!

Culinary History Enthusiasts of Wisconsin
www.chew.wisconsincooks.org
This is a fabulous site for anything food-worthy in the state.

Wisconsin Agricultural Marketing Board
www.wisdairy.com
This is a great place to find resources on seeing/tasting/buying cheese or dairy products.

Wisconsin Cooks
www.wisconsincooks.org
A fun guide run by Wisconsin foodies, it has a good list of food-centric events and some recipes.

Wisconsin Department of Agriculture
www.savorwisconsin.com
From the Department of Agriculture, it's got a mammoth list of where to find stuff grown/made here.

TRANSPORTATION AND ROAD TRIPS
Wisconsin Department of Transportation
www.dot.wisconsin.gov
The state's Department of Transportation website has all necessary information on construction, road conditions, etc. Do check out its "Rustic Roads" section for fantastic country drives.

Index

List of Maps

Acknowledgments

This book is dedicated to my family, for absolutely everything, even more than you all know.

Thanks and endless positive mental energy to my family and friends for sofa space, meals, advice, and tolerance of a vagabond's announced (and not) visits. A nod as always to the people I meet on the road—you keep the cliché of warm and friendly Midwesterners alive and well.

I must give a special shout out to the wonderful CVB/chambers of commerce staffers—without whom books such as this could never, ever be written.

Once again—thank, thank, thank you to WESLI-ites, for help, support, encouragement when the mental tanks run low…and always letting me get away with the Life.

Readers: I appreciate your letting me accompany you on the road. More—bless everyone who took the time to write or email to point out new things, tweak details, berate me, or simply say hi. *All* feedback is welcome and much appreciated—we do want this to be a participatory endeavor! Let me know!

For strengthening the mojo during tedious crunch times or when the miles begin to pile up, I thank Bob Uecker and the Brewers Radio Network, NPR in all its manifestations, and the inventor of MP3 technology.

Special thanks to Meredith, Samaria, Gabby, and Leo—for friendship and community, without which this wanderer could never keep it all going.

Most of all—to Yuki and the Monkey, for always being there, even when not.

www.moon.com

DESTINATIONS | ACTIVITIES | BLOGS | MAPS | BOOKS

MOON.COM is ready to help plan your next trip! Filled with fresh trip ideas and strategies, author interviews, informative travel blogs, a detailed map library, and descriptions of all the Moon guidebooks, Moon.com is all you need to get out and explore the world—or even places in your own backyard. While at Moon.com, sign up for our monthly e-newsletter for updates on new releases, travel tips, and expert advice from our on-the-go Moon authors. As always, when you travel with Moon, expect an experience that is uncommon and truly unique.

MAP SYMBOLS

▦	Expressway	🄲	Highlight	✈	Airfield	⚓	Golf Course
	Primary Road	○	City/Town	✈	Airport	🄿	Parking Area
	Secondary Road	◉	State Capital	▲	Mountain	⬟	Archaeological Site
▪▪▪▪	Unpaved Road	⊛	National Capital	✛	Unique Natural Feature	⛪	Church
- - - -	Trail	★	Point of Interest			⛽	Gas Station
....	Ferry	•	Accommodation	⟅	Waterfall		
▬▬▬	Railroad	▼	Restaurant/Bar	▲	Park	〰	Glacier
▦	Pedestrian Walkway	■	Other Location				Mangrove
▦	Stairs	Λ	Campground	⬟	Trailhead		Reef
				⛷	Skiing Area		Swamp

CONVERSION TABLES

$°C = (°F - 32) / 1.8$
$°F = (°C \times 1.8) + 32$
1 inch = 2.54 centimeters (cm)
1 foot = 0.304 meters (m)
1 yard = 0.914 meters
1 mile = 1.6093 kilometers (km)
1 km = 0.6214 miles
1 fathom = 1.8288 m
1 chain = 20.1168 m
1 furlong = 201.168 m
1 acre = 0.4047 hectares
1 sq km = 100 hectares
1 sq mile = 2.59 square km
1 ounce = 28.35 grams
1 pound = 0.4536 kilograms
1 short ton = 0.90718 metric ton
1 short ton = 2,000 pounds
1 long ton = 1.016 metric tons
1 long ton = 2,240 pounds
1 metric ton = 1,000 kilograms
1 quart = 0.94635 liters
1 US gallon = 3.7854 liters
1 Imperial gallon = 4.5459 liters
1 nautical mile = 1.852 km

°FAHRENHEIT / °CELSIUS thermometer:
230 / 110
220 / 100 WATER BOILS
210 / 100
200 / 90
190
180 / 80
170
160 / 70
150
140 / 60
130
120 / 50
110
100 / 40
90 / 30
80
70 / 20
60
50 / 10
40
30 / 0 WATER FREEZES
20 / -10
10
0 / -20
-10
-20 / -30
-30
-40 / -40

INCH ruler: 0 1 2 3 4

CM ruler: 0 1 2 3 4 5 6 7 8 9 10

MOON WISCONSIN

Avalon Travel
a member of the
1700 Fourth St
Berkeley, CA 9
www.moon.com

917.75 HUH
Huhti, Thomas
Wisconsin /

Series Manage
Copy Editor: N
Graphics Coordinator: Kathryn Osgood
Production Coordinators: Sean Bellows and
  Domini Dragoone
Cover Designer: Domini Dragoone
Map Editor: Brice Ticen
Cartographer: Kat Bennett
Indexer: Greg Jewett

ISBN: 978-1-59880-745-5
ISSN: 1092-3322

Printing History
1st Edition – 1997
5th Edition – April 2011
5 4 3 2

Text © 2011 by Thomas Huhti.
Maps © 2011 by Avalon Travel.
All rights reserved.

Front cover photo: Apostle Islands National
  Lakeshore, © Getty Images/Stone/Tom Bean
Title page photo: rapids near Devil's Lake State Park,
  © Jason Ross/123rf.com

Interior color photos: pg. 4–5 (center), 7 (top
, 19 (both) © Door
:e; pg. 5 (left) ©
ight), 10, & 22 ©
Henryk Sadura/123rf.
om left), 14, & 15 © RJ &
(top), 11 (bottom), & 12
onvention Bureau; pg.
Abrams; pg. 9 (bottom)
© Karl Soehnlein/123rf.com; pg. 16 (bottom) © Dean
Pennala/Dreamstime.com; pg. 18 © Gary Knowles;
pg. 20 © David Lushewitz/Dreamstime.com; pg. 21
(top) © John Dankwardt; pg. 21 (bottom) © Scott
Nesvold/123rf.com; pg. 23 © Princely Nesadurai; pg.
24 © Clay Shannon/Dreamstime.com.

Printed in Canada by Friesens

KEEPING CURRENT

If you have a favorite gem you'd like to see included in the next edition, or see anything
that needs updating, clarification, or correction, please drop us a line. Send your
comments via email to feedback@moon.com, or use the address above.

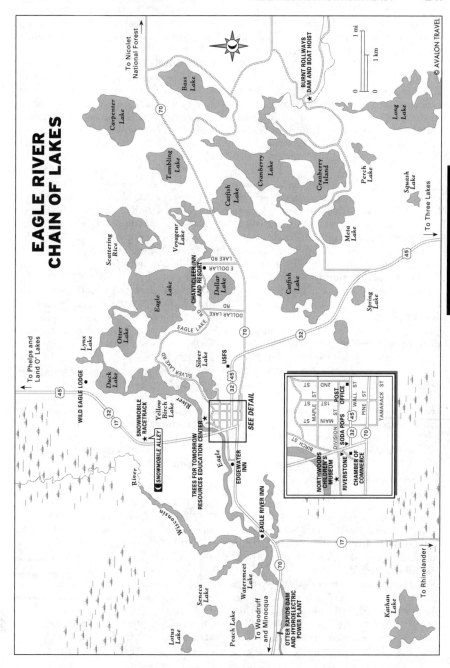

NORTHEASTERN WISCONSIN

shorter hours for tours) is in an old railroad depot. Tours and tastings are free, and there are some fantastic local cranberry wines.

Events

A follow-up event to the snowmobile world championships is the **Klondike Days** festival, generally held at the end of February. Everyone comes to see the World Championship Oval Sled Dog Sprints—billed as "the fastest sled dog racing in the world"—on the same track as those monster machines. This is not some tongue-in-cheek laugh-fest; teams compete over two days in three classes for more than $20,000 in purse money—no small potatoes. Otherwise, it's as if the whole town were transported back a century ago. Very cool.

Anglers own the summer, and their own crown jewel is August's **National Championship Muskie Open**—the largest amateur muskie tournament anywhere.

Recreation

Fishing first. Muskie, walleye, and bass predominate. (Hint: The Lac du Flambeau chain of lakes has world-class muskie fishing.) Your best bet is to contact **Eagle River Area Guides** (715/479-8804, www.eagleriverguides.com).

If you're heading out on your own, boat rentals are available from **Heckel's** (437 W. Division St., 715/479-4471, www.heckels.com).

Pick up a copy of *Fishing Hot Spots,* an angling guide series published in the area.

The excellent **Razorback Ridge** ski trails (12 miles) are a short drive west of Sayner along Highway N. These double as mountain-bike trails.

If you're not up for paddling the 28 lakes yourself, **Hawk's Nest** (715/479-7944, www.hawksnestcanoe.com) offers tranquil runs down the Wisconsin River and does outfitted tours throughout Wisconsin.

It is beyond the scope of this guide to detail the massive networks of snowmobile trails to the east and west (and through) Eagle River. **Decker Sno-Venture Tours** (715/479-2764, www.sno-venture.com) is rated number one almost annually by *Snowgoer* magazine, beating

out weighty competitors such as Yellowstone Tour and Travel and Togwotee's Sno World.

Accommodations

Resorts, resorts everywhere, though in town there are a few basic motels, some right on the Eagle River, many with boat docks and to-the-door sled access. Many of the motels are friendly and not too pricey, considering, including **Edgewater Inn** (5054 U.S. 70 W, 715/479-4011, www.edgewater-inn-cottages.com, $85 rooms, $125 cottages), with charming rustic rooms and cottages overlooking the water.

Also west along WI 70, the **Eagle River Inn** (5260 WI 70 W, 715/479-2000, www.eagleriver-inn.com, $119–249) has basic rooms, "bunk bed rooms" great for families, condos, and some kitchenette units available—they can handle 2–6 (or more) folks. Full recreation amenities are here.

Chanticleer Inn and Resort (1458 Dollar Lake Rd., 715/479-4486, www.chanticleerinn.com, $129, more for cottages and houses) offers motels, cottages, and town houses right on the chain of lakes. The dining room is exceedingly popular.

North of downtown on Duck Lake ◖ **Wild Eagle Lodge** (4443 Chain O' Lakes Rd., 715/479-3151 or 877/945-3965, www.wildeaglelodge.com, from $200) is just about the most smashingly rustic yet sybaritic place in the region. There are raves about this place, its one- to three-bedroom lodge homes, and its friendliness.

Food

The ◖ **Riverstone** (219 N. Railroad St., 715/479-8467, dinner daily, brunch Sun., $6 and up) takes you back to logrolling days with its 1880s oak back bar and vintage ceilings and floors. Then it lurches you forward into the present with a state-of-the-art exhibition kitchen and awards for its wine cellar and cuisine, which it precisely describes as from comfort to creative.

Jump back in time but in a much more lighthearted way at the fab ◖ **Soda Pop's** (125 S. Railroad St., 715/479-9424, lunch and dinner